# THE ENGLISH SERMON 1550-1650

*General editors*
C. H. Sisson
Val Warner
Michael Schmidt

# THE ENGLISH SERMON
volume I: 1550~1650

an anthology

MARTIN SEYMOUR-SMITH

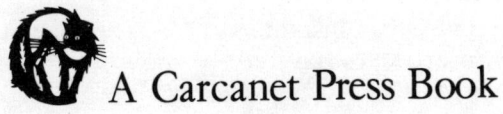
A Carcanet Press Book

SBN 85635 093 1

Copyright © Martin Seymour-Smith 1976

*All Rights Reserved*

First published in 1976
by Carcanet Press Limited
266 Councillor Lane
Cheadle Hulme, Cheadle
Cheshire SK8 5PN

Printed in Great Britain
by Unwin Brothers Limited
The Gresham Press, Old Woking, Surrey.

CONTENTS

GENERAL PREFACE vii
CALENDAR ix
INTRODUCTION 1

ROGER EDGEWORTH
(?-1560)     Of Idols and Images     5

THOMAS CRANMER
(1489-1556)     An Homily of the Salvation of Mankind, by Only Christ Our Saviour, from Sin and Death Everlasting     22
A Short Declaration of the True, Lively, and Christian Faith     32
An Homily or Sermon of Good Works Annexed unto Faith     42

HUGH LATIMER
(c. 1485-1555)     The Sermon of the Plough     56

EDWIN SANDYS
(c. 1516-88)     [A Sermon Preached at Paul's Cross]     75

BERNARD GILPIN
(1517-83)     A Godly Sermon Preached in the Court at Greenwich on the First Sunday after Epiphany, 1552     92

RICHARD BANCROFT
(1544-1610)     A Warning against Puritans     123

THOMAS DRANT
(?-1578)     O Men, O Lilies     129

ROBERT ROLLOCK
(c. 1555-99)     [Out of the deep places...]     135

HENRY SMITH
(1550-91)     The Poor Man's Tears     149

RICHARD HOOKER
(1554-1600)     A Remedy against Sorrow and Fear     168
Mr Hooker's Answer to the Supplication that Mr Travers made to the Council     178

ROBERT SANDERSON
(1587-1663)

THOMAS ADAMS
(c. 1612-53)

LANCELOT ANDREWES
(1555-1626)

JOHN DONNE
(1572-1631)

JOHN HALES
(1584-1656)

WILLIAM LAUD
(1573-1645)

THOMAS HOOKER
(c. 1586-1647)

MARK FRANK
(1613-64)

HUGH PETERS
(1598-1660)

HENRY FERNE
(1602-62)

JOHN COSIN
(1594-1672)

[In St Paul's Church, London—
   *Ad Populum*]   202

The White Devil: or, The Hypocrite Uncased   247

Sermon of the Passion, Good Friday, 1604   299
Sermon of the Nativity, Christmas, 1622   318

A Sermon of Valediction at My Going into Germany   338
A Lent Sermon Preached to the King, at Whitehall   354
Death's Duel, or, A Consolation to the Soul, against the Dying Life, and Living Death of the Body   370

Of Dealing with Erring Christians   393

[Preached at Whitehall]   428

The Danger of Desertion   449

[The First Sermon on Christmas Day]   455

[The Storming of Basing House]   468

Comfort in Adversity   472

[If Thou be the Son of God...]   482

GENERAL PREFACE

ONE DOES not have to be a Christian to be interested in sermons, nor a non-Christian to be bored by most of them. For the three hundred years covered by the three volumes of this anthology, preaching was one of the main vehicles for current reflections about the way of the world. It was so because, at any rate until the latter part of the period, the Christian religion was generally regarded—as it still regards itself—not as a matter of private whim or opinion but as something which has to be understood, to the limit of each one's capacity, by anyone trying to understand the nature of man and the universe into which men are born. Many now think differently, but only those who are sure that their ancestors were bigger fools than they are themselves will think that they can discard the explorations which went on for centuries—and still go on, if less prominently—in the language of Christian theology. Moreover, anyone who wants to understand the literature in which Donne, Swift and Johnson are prominent figures must make some attempt to understand the notions of religion in which they and indeed all but a few very recent contributors to our literature were, to a greater or lesser degree, educated and which are intertwined in the texture of their thought. These considerations apart, the volumes of sermons now left so largely unread—or read only in short extracts for particularly colourful passages—contain what is, in its own right, an important branch of our literature. Much of the finest English prose is there, an indispensable study for anyone who is interested in the development and decay of the medium.

The pretensions of these three volumes are modest. There can be no question, in this space, of more than an introduction to the subject. With a few exceptions in the first volume, only complete sermons have been included, so that the construction and development of the genre can be fully appreciated. Not more than three sermons of any one author have been selected, and some forty-eight preachers are represented, including all the most famous and a number of those whose names are less familiar. Most of the material here reprinted is not now readily accessible, so that the volumes will enable many readers to acquaint themselves with the work of men who have hitherto existed for them only as figures in a history-book or as allusions in the writings of Coleridge or Eliot. The sermons have been chosen for their intrinsic interest and for their qualities as representing important streams of thought and literature. There has been no attempt at a consistent theological orientation. Among the editorial names appearing on the title pages, there are three who pretend to no religious faith, and two Anglicans. That the sermons themselves are predominantly—overwhelmingly—from Anglican sources owes something to the prejudices of one of the editors, but more to the fact that this literature is primarily the voice of the main stream of English Christianity, muddied by all our English affairs.

The authors are arranged in a rough chronological order, with a short biographical introduction for each author. Each sermon has a further introductory note, giving something of the context of the sermon and of the issues discussed in it, or drawing attention to other points of interest. Each volume has a short general introduction to the century it covers. The whole production is therefore at once a guide to the principal authors and to some of their work. It is hoped that the books will be of value to students of English literature as well as to those whose interest is primarily in the history and literature of the Church.

C. H. SISSON

CALENDAR

| | |
|---|---|
| 1550 | England returns Boulogne to France |
| | John Marbeck: *The Booke of Common Praier noted*, first musical setting of English liturgy |
| 1551 | First licensing of alehouses and taverns in England and Wales |
| | Second session of Council of Trent |
| | Jesuits found Collegio Romano |
| 1552 | Second Uniformity Act authorises more radical Second Prayer Book of Edward VI |
| | Christ's Hospital and some thirty-five grammar schools founded in the name of Edward VI |
| | Birth of Spenser |
| 1553 | Accession of Queen Mary |
| | Latimer sent to Tower |
| | Protestant emigrations to Geneva and Zurich begin |
| | Gavin Douglas: translation of the *Aeneid*, first classical translation published in Britain |
| | Roman Catholic bishops restored in England |
| | Act of Uniformity repealed (restored 1559) |
| | Death of Rabelais |
| 1554 | Cranmer, Ridley and others in public disputation at Oxford on the doctrines of the mass |
| | Parliament re-establishes Roman Catholicism |
| | John Knox flees; meets Calvin in Geneva |
| | Calvin defends execution of Servetus; others publish tract in favour of religious toleration |
| | Birth of Sidney |
| 1555 | Trial of Cranmer, Ridley and Latimer |
| 1556 | Cranmer dies |
| | Loyola dies |
| 1557 | First Covenant signed in Scotland |
| | Continual burning of Protestants at Smithfield |
| 1558 | French capture Calais from England |
| | Accession of Elizabeth I |
| | 'Gresham's Law' |
| | Knox: *The first blast of the trumpet against the monstrous regiment of women* |
| 1559 | Papal bull advocates deposition of sovereigns supporting heresy |
| | 'Apology for the Church of England' controversy |

| | |
|---|---|
| 1560 | 'Breeches Bible'—first 'family' Bible—published<br>Scottish Parliament adopts Calvinist Confession, abolishes Papal jurisdiction |
| 1561 | Birth of Bacon |
| 1562 | Third session of Council of Trent<br>Thirty-Nine Articles |
| 1563 | 20,000 die of plague in London<br>*Foxe's Book of Martyrs*<br>Birth of Dowland |
| 1564 | First use in England of term 'Puritan'<br>Birth of Shakespeare<br>Birth of Galileo<br>Death of Michelangelo<br>Death of Calvin |
| 1568 | English College founded at Douai to train Jesuits for work in England |
| 1569 | Mercator's Map |
| 1570 | Papal excommunication of Elizabeth I, absolving her subjects from their allegiance |
| 1571 | Latimer: *Frutefull Sermons* |
| 1572 | Death of Knox |
| 1573 | Birth of Laud |
| 1574 | First auto-da-fé (in Mexico) |
| 1575 | Byrd and Tallis: *Cantiones Sacrae* |
| 1576 | Puritan failure in Parliament to reform Church of England |
| 1581 | Severe legislation framed against Roman Catholics<br>Execution of Campion<br>Galileo discovers principle of pendulum |
| 1582 | *The New Testament* (Rheims and Douay Bible) |
| 1585 | Act outlawing Jesuits and Seminarists from Britain |
| 1587 | Execution of Mary Queen of Scots |
| 1588 | Defeat of Spanish Armada<br>William Morgan's translation of the Bible into Welsh<br>*Martin Marprelate Tracts*, Presbyterian tracts issued from secret press |
| 1590 | Spenser: *The Faerie Queen,* books 1-3 |
| 1593 | Henry Barrow (Puritan) executed for slandering Elizabeth<br>Birth of Herbert |
| 1594 | Huguenots granted freedom of worship in France<br>Shakespeare: *Titus Andronicus* published |

| | |
|---|---|
| 1595 | Robert Southwell (a Jesuit) hanged at Tyburn |
| 1596 | Birth of Descartes |
| 1597 | Bacon: *Essays: Civil and Moral* |
| | Shakespeare: *Richard II, Romeo and Juliet, Richard III* |
| 1598 | Huguenots given equal political rights in France |
| | Chapman: translation of the *Illiad* |
| | Bodleian Library refounded |
| | Shakespeare: *Henry IV (i), Love's Labours Lost* |
| 1599 | Death of Spenser |
| | Birth of Cromwell |
| 1600 | English East India Company founded |
| | Shakespeare: *As You Like It, The Merchant of Venice, A Midsummer-Night's Dream* |
| 1601 | Essex's unsuccessful revolt against Elizabeth I |
| | Shakespeare: *Twelfth Night* |
| 1603 | Accession of James I and VI |
| | Shakespeare: *Hamlet* ('bad' quarto) |
| 1604 | King James and Archbishop Whitgift support a new translation of the Bible |
| 1605 | Gunpowder Plot |
| | Bacon: *The Advancement of Learning* |
| | Shakespeare: *Macbeth* |
| 1606 | Parliament outlaws Catholics from public office |
| | Birth of Rembrandt |
| 1607 | First English settlement on American mainland at Jamestown, Virginia |
| | Jonson: *Volpone* |
| | Tourneur: *The Revenger's Tragedy* |
| 1608 | Galileo invents telescope |
| | Shakespeare: *King Lear* |
| | Birth of Milton |
| 1609 | Shakespeare: *Sonnets* (original quarto) |
| 1610 | Jonson: *The Alchemist* |
| | Shakespeare: *The Tempest* |
| 1611 | King James institutes baronetage |
| | The Authorized Version of the Holy Bible |
| 1612 | Bartholomew Legate and Edward Wightman are the last persons to be burnt for their religious opinions in England |
| | Webster: *The White Devil* |
| 1614 | Chapman: translation of *Odyssey*, books 1-12 |
| 1616 | Death of Shakespeare |

| | |
|---|---|
| 1619 | Harvey discovers circulation of the blood |
| 1620 | *Mayflower* sails for America |
| 1621 | Burton: *Anatomy of Melancholy* |
| | Birth of Marvell |
| | Webster: *Duchess of Malfi* |
| 1623 | Death of Byrd |
| 1625 | Inigo Jones: Covent Garden Church and Square |
| 1626 | Donne: *Five Sermons* |
| | Death of Dowland |
| | Death of Bacon |
| 1628 | Charles I under pressure accepts Petition of Right |
| | Laud appointed Bishop of London |
| | Descartes: *Règles pour la direction de l'esprit* |
| 1630 | Middleton: *A Chaste Mayd in Cheapside* |
| 1631 | Death of Donne |
| 1633 | Laud elected Archbishop of Canterbury |
| | Trial of the Lancashire witches |
| | Donne: *Poems* (posthumous) |
| | Herbert: *The Temple; or Sacred Poems* (posthumous) |
| | Birth of Pepys |
| 1636 | Roger Williams founds Providence, R. I., a colony with complete religious freedom |
| 1637 | Trial of William Prynne for criticism of Laud: sentenced with two others to mutilation |
| | Descartes: *Discours sur la méthode* |
| | Death of Jonson |
| 1639 | Episcopacy abolished in Scotland by the Assembly |
| 1640 | Long Parliament |
| | Laud impeached |
| 1641 | Further outbreaks of Irish Catholic rebellion; Ulster Protestants massacred |
| | Abolition of Star Chamber |
| | Evelyn begins *Diary* |
| 1642 | Charles and family flee London |
| | Parliament forms Committee of Public Safety to conduct impending war |
| | Theatres in England closed by order |
| | Death of Galileo |
| | Birth of Newton |
| 1643 | The Assembly of Westminster, summoned by Long Parliament, inaugurates a Presbyterian establishment for England and Wales |

| | |
|---|---|
| 1644 | Battle of Marston Moor (Royalist defeat) |
| | Milton: *Areopagitica* (a plea for uncensored printing) |
| 1645 | Laud beheaded |
| | Cromwell defeats Royalists at Naseby |
| | Lilburne founds Leveller movement |
| 1646 | Surrender of Oxford to Roundheads |
| | Charles surrenders to Scots at Newark |
| 1647 | Scots sell Charles I to Parliament for £400,000 |
| | Beaumont and Fletcher: *Comedies and Tragedies* |
| 1648 | Peace of Westphalia ends Thirty Years War |
| | George Fox starts Society of Friends |
| 1649 | Charles I beheaded |
| | Parliament abolishes House of Lords and the monarchy |
| | England declared a Commonwealth |
| | English becomes language of all legal documents in place of Latin |
| 1650 | The term 'Quaker' first used of Fox and his followers |
| | Death of Descartes |

# INTRODUCTION

THIS VOLUME begins with the establishment of the Church of England as we now know it. There had been a church in this island before England was invented; bishops from Britain attended the Council of Arles in 325. Augustine was sent from Rome in 597. The Norman Conquest meant not only Norman domination but the strengthening of the Roman administration. The sixteenth century was the classic period of Reformation and Counter-Reformation all over Europe, and a number of currents which had shown some turbulence in preceding centuries finally broke their banks. What emerged in England was a compromise in which all the virtues and vices of our insular temper had their part. Viewed non-theologically—and perhaps even theologically, though that depends a little on the kind of theology you favour—churches like other societies of men and women have their political aspects and their administrative habits. The Reformation of the sixteenth century was, in this country, a time at once of a new influx of ideas from the Continent and a new national impulse to deal with them in our own way. There have been endless arguments, most of them tendentious, about the parts played respectively by politics and theology in the events of the sixteenth century in England, as well as about the theological merits and demerits of the solutions adopted. There were, anyhow, new ecclesiastical arrangements and at the centre of these changes was the figure of the reluctant Archbishop of Canterbury, Thomas Cranmer, whose character, for better or worse, as you view the matter, was imprinted on the formularies of the new Church of England. Cranmer started his work under a king who was certainly an ugly customer to have at one's elbow; he pursued it among the uncertainties of Edward VI's reign, and met his end on a bonfire in Oxford, when the Roman administration was temporarily reinstated under Mary and burning people became a fashionable way of enforcing opinion. Cranmer has often been spoken of with great condescension by people who neither faced his difficulties nor perhaps would have shown the courage he did had they faced his dangers. G. M. Trevelyan, from the comfort of the upper middle classes of the early twentieth century, and an Oxford where no one ever said 'Boo!' to a don, was one of them. By his time the characteristic resilience of our political traditions, which operated under terrible stresses in Cranmer's day, had declined to a cosy mushiness which was liberal only because it was so protected. The section on Cranmer in this volume (p. 12) should be read as part of this introduction, and in a sense is the main part. Without an understanding of Cranmer what follows—in this and indeed in the succeeding volumes—is hardly to be understood.

Much of the theological controversy of the Reformation centres around the doctrine of the Eucharist. In 'the Supper of the Lord and the Holy Communion, commonly called the Mass', as Cranmer called it in the Prayer Book of 1549, the priest takes bread and wine, and consecrates them in prayers which include what are called the Words of Institution—words which recall what happened at the Last Supper. Christ,

> in the same night that he was betrayed, took bread, and when he had given thanks, he brake it, and gave it to his disciples, saying, Take, eat, This is my body which is given for you; do this in remembrance of me. Likewise after supper he took the cup; and when he had given thanks, he gave it unto them, saying, Drink ye all of this, for this is my blood of the new Testament, which is shed for you and for many for the remission of sins: do this as oft as ye shall drink it in remembrance of me.

The priest then partakes of the consecrated elements and distributes them to the communicants. Put crudely, the question over which Reformation and Counter-Reformation spilt so much bitterness was: In what sense, if any, are the bread and wine changed in the course of the Communion Service, and at what point? Is it literally the Body and Blood of Christ which is eaten and drunk, or does everything depend on the faith of the recipient? The implications of these questions are neither more nor less wide than the implications of the entire Christian religion—whatever you take those to be. In controversial practice the subject has been confused—one might say, bedevilled—by all kinds of limitations and misunderstandings, like any other subject people disagree about. It is the distinction of the Anglican formularies—to which Cranmer contributed so much—that these questions are not resolved in them, and that it is possible to follow the Prayer Book without concluding the question one way or the other. The old Elizabethan rhyme sums the matter up:

> It was the Word who spake it;
> He took the bread and brake it

> And what his word doth make it
> That I believe, and take it.

That may be regarded as a wise or a cynical conclusion; it is in any case peaceable.

In spite of the attempt at comprehensiveness, which was pursued under Elizabeth and in the history of which Hooker (see p. 164) is a key figure, the establishment was in ruins before the end of the hundred years covered by this volume. In 1644 there was 'an Ordinance of Parliament for the taking away of the Book of Common Prayer' and establishing instead a *Directory for the Public Worship of God* which was a Puritan production—pure of those echoes of fifteen hundred years of the Church's history which fill the Prayer Book, pure of Cranmer's eirenic spirit as of his sense of prose style. Before this ruin came, and the Church of England was cast in what must seem, to those who think only of what the nineteenth and the early twentieth century made of her, the improbable role of a resistance movement, there was the brilliant period which threw into prominence such men as Andrewes and Donne and produced some of the greatest literature of the English Church, including the Authorized Version of the Bible, to which Andrewes himself made important contributions. The selection in this volume ends with a sermon by John Cosin, who lived to become Bishop of Durham after the Restoration in 1660. There is one great and unassuming figure of the early seventeenth-century Church, specimens of whose sermons one would wish to have included in this volume, had any been extant. This is George Herbert, who served the little church of Bemerton near Salisbury and remains a pattern of Anglicanism, however little followed. His first sermon he delivered, according to his biographer Walton, 'after a florid manner, both with great learning and eloquence; but at the close' he told his parishioners, 'That should not be his constant way of preaching; ... his language and his expressions should be more plain and practical in his future sermons', for 'Almighty God does not intend to lead men to heaven by hard questions.'

NOTE ON THE TEXT

The spelling of the sermons has been modernized throughout.

## Roger Edgeworth

LITTLE IS known about Edgeworth, except that he died in 1560, and was educated at Oriel College, Oxford, and then became, successively, Prebendary at Bristol (1542) and Canon of Wells and Salisbury (1554). His sermons were published in the year before Elizabeth ascended the throne.

## Of Idols and Images

THIS SERMON was preached about 1540. It is an example of the conservative view of the Reformation. Obviously Edgeworth was worried and disturbed at the developments; as obviously, he played safe. He survived both Marian Catholicism and the first three years of Elizabeth's reign. Here he is cautiously reminding his congregation that an *image* is not an *idol*: he is as conservative as he dares to be. At the close he even warns against 'newfangled' heresies.

DOMINE VERBA vitae eternae habes. O Lord God, thou hast the words of everlasting life. The words be good because they be the words of God, although I do not understand them. Thus ordering yourselves in the study of holy scripture you do like good men, and like God's servants, and God will be good Lord unto you. *Et non dabit ineternum fluctuationem iusto.* And will not suffer you finally for ever to fleet and waver inconstantly, running from one opinion to an other, from one illusion to an other, thou shalt stay thy self by the anchor of faith, and that shall keep thee from the rocks, that be perilous heretics. For if thou fleet and waver till thou fall on one of them, thou shalt have such a crash of false doctrine and lewd understanding that thou shalt not avoid shipwreck, thou shalt not come to the port of safe knowledge, nor to the port of ease, quietness, and calmness everlasting in heaven, if thou be made by such false doctrine to err in the essential and necessary points of thy belief.

Therefore in your learning see that you use charity with humility and lowliness of heart, and then you shall show your self that your learning is the true science given of the holy ghost, of which we now entreat. And by the same gift you shall as well know what you shall believe, as to judge and discern the things that you shall believe, from the things that you shall not believe, And also you may ascend to so high knowledge, that you shall be able to declare the articles of your faith, and to induce and persuade other men to believe, and also to convince and overcome countersayers, and such as would impugn the faith, Although it be not given to all men to ascend unto so high a degree of science. And because I spoke even now of Images and Idols, I would you should not ignorantly confound and abuse those terms, taking an Image for an Idol, and an Idol for an Image, as I have heard many do in this city, as well of the fathers and mothers (that should be wise) as of their babies and children that have learned foolishness of their parents. Now at the dissolution of Monasteries and of friars' houses many Images have been carried abroad, and given to children to play withal. And when the children have them in their hands, dancing them after their childish manner, cometh the father or the mother and saith: What nasse, what hast thou there? the child answereth (as she is taught) I have here mine idol, the father laugheth and maketh a gay game at it. So saith the mother to another, Iugge, or Tommy, where hadst thou that pretty Idol. John our parish clerk gave it to me, saith the child and for that the clerk must have thanks, and shall lack no good cheer. But if this folly were only in the insolent youth, and in the fond unlearned fathers and mothers, it might soon be redressed. But your preachers that you so obstinately follow, more leaning to the vulgar noise and common error of the people, than to profound learning they babble in the pulpits that they heareth people rejoice in.

And so of the people they learn their sermons, and by their sermons they indurate [harden] their audience and make the people stubborn and hard to be persuaded to science, contrary to their blind ignorance, as well in this point of Images and Idols, as in many other like. They would have that this latin word *Imago* signifieth an Idol, and so these new translations of the english bibles hath it in all places, where the translators would bring men to believe that to set up Images, or to have Images is idolatry, And therefore where the scriptures abhorreth idols, they make it Images, as though to have imagery, were idolatry, that God so greatly abhorreth. But you must understand and know that an Image is a thing carved, or painted, or cast in a mould, that representeth and signifieth a thing that is in deed, or that hath be or that be in deed. And so speaketh our Saviour Christ of an Image, when the Pharisees send their disciples with Herod's servants, to ask him this question: whether it were lawful for the Jews to pay tribute to the Emperor or not: He called them Hypocrites, and bade them show him the coin or money that was usually paid for the tribute. They brought him a denarius, we call it a penny. He asked them: *Cuius est Imago hec et superscriptio Mat. xxii.* Whose is this Image and the scripture about? They answered: the emperor's. Note here (good friends) that Christ ask not *cuius est idolum hoc?* Whose is this idol? for he knew it was none, but that it was an image, as is the Image of our sovereign Lord the king upon his money coined in London, in Bristol, or in other places, which no man that hath wit would call an Idol. For Saint Paul saith, *i Cor. viii. Scimus quia nihil est Idolum in mundo, & quod nullus est deus nisi unus.* We know that an idol is nothing in the world, and that there is no God but one. Where the blessed Apostle refereth much unto science in this matter of idols, and of meat offered unto them, and spoke to them that were learned, and should have cunning to discern in this matter: saying in the beginning of that. viii. Chapter. *Scimus quoniam omnes scientiam habemus.* We know, for all we have science and cunning to judge of these meats that be offered to Idols, what know we? *Scimus quia nihil est Idolum in mundo*

*& quod nullus est deus nisi unus.* We have this science, and this we know, that an Idol is nothing in the world, and that there is no God but one. An image is a similitude of a natural thing, that hath been, is, or may be. An idol is a similitude representing a thing that never was nor may be. Therefore the image of the crucifix is no idol, for it representeth and signifieth Christ crucified, as he was in deed. And the Image of Saint Paul with the sword in his hand, as the sign of his martyrdom is no Idol, for the thing signified by it, was a thing in deed, for he was beheaded with a sword in deed: but an Idol is an image that signifieth a monster that is not possible to be, as to signify a false God which is no God in deed. For as S. Paul said, *There is no God but one*: As the Image of Jupiter set up to signify the god Jupiter, is a false signifier, and signifieth a thing of nothing for there is no God Jupiter. And the Image of *Venus* to signify the goddess *Venus* is nothing, for what is signified by it, is nothing, for there is no she goddess *Venus*: As in a like speaking we say *Chimera* is nothing, because the voice is sometimes put to signify a monster, having a head like a Lion, with fire flaming out of his mouth, and the body of a goat, and the hinder part like a serpent or a dragon, there is no such thing, although the poets feign such a monster, therefore the voice *Chimera* is a false signifier, and what is false is nothing, therefore we say *Chimera* is nothing but *Chimera* signifying a certain mountain in the country of *Lycia*, flaming fire out of the top of it, breeding and having Lions nigh about the higher part or top of the same hill, and downward about the middle part, having pastures where breedeth goats or such other beasts, and at the foot of it marshes or moist ground breeding serpents: such an hill there is in the said country, and of the diverse disposition of the parts of the said hill, the fiction of the foresaid monster is imagined, which is nothing, and therefore so we say that *Chimera* is nothing, but the same vocable put to signify the hill in *Lycia* aforesaid is somewhat, and a true signifier, for it signifieth a thing that is in deed as appeareth by *Pomponius Mela, lib. i.* and *Soline Cap. lii.* with their expositors, and even so it is true that Paul saith that an Idol is nothing, for there is none such thing as is signified by it, there is no God *Saturn*, there is no God *Jupiter*, there is no Goddess *Venus*, but I say more, that if a man could carve or paint an Image of *Jupiter's* soul burning in the fire of hell, or likewise an Image of *Venus'* soul there burning; If Saint Paul had seen such a picture or image, he would never have called it an idol, or a thing of nothing, for

it should signify a thing that is in deed, for *Jupiter's* soul is in hell in deed, and so is *Venus'* soul, and other like taken for Goddess made of mortal men. After this manner good friends, you must by science and cunning, learnedly speak of Images and Idols, and not to confound the words, or the things signified by them, taking one for an other. And by this you may perceive, that when you will arrogantly of a proud heart meddle of matters above your capacity, the holy ghost withdraweth his gift of science from you, and that maketh you to speak you can not tell what, for the holy ghost will not inspire his gifts but upon them that be humble and lowly in heart. And because I said heretofore, that this gift of science as it is here taken, extendeth to mechanical science, and handicrafts. This appeareth by the text. *Exo. xxxi.* when the holy tabernacle should be made in desert, almighty God provided an artificer and workman for the same nonce called *Beseleel* son of *Huri*, son of *Hur*, of the tribe of *Juda*. I have filled him (saith God) with the spirit of God *Sapientia, intelligentia, & scientia in omni opere*. I have given him sapience, by which he might well discern and judge of the things that god would have made, in so much that he was able to teach others the things that he knew by god's revelation and instruction. And this properly pertaineth to the gift of *Sapience*, as I have said afore. I have filled him with the spirit of *intelligence* or wittiness, and fine and clear perceiving and understanding, by which he may more perfectly pierce and enter with his wit into the things that be taught him, than he should have done if he had lacked the said gift of *intelligence*. I have also (saith God) fulfilled *Beseleel* with the gift of science. Of which speaketh Christ oft in a sermon of the holy ghost after this manner. When *Moses* made the tabernacle in wilderness, he had need then not only of doctrine and learning, but also of the gift of a master craftsman, to know how he should sew together fine clothes and silks of precious colours, and how to weave them, plait them, and shape them together, And how he should cast gold and other metals necessary for the ceremonies there to be used, and how to polish precious stones, and also to frame the timber for the same tabernacle. For there and such other purposes almighty God gave him and to his workman *Beseleel*, the spirit of science, that they might frame all such things accordingly. And even so in your occupations and handicrafts, when you exercise your selves diligently and truly without sloth, without deceit, guile, or subtlety in all your exercise, ordering your selves to your neighbour, as you would be ordered yourself, so long your occupation, exercise, and labour is annexed and joined with charity, and seemeth plainly to come of the holy ghost: for without charity this gift of science coming of the holy ghost will not be, no more than other virtues infused. And contrary, like as every good thing hath an enemy, or at the least wise an ape or a counterfeiter, as fortitude or manliness hath foolish hardiness or rash boldness, which seemeth manliness and is not so, so hath science or cunning, guile or subtlety, which counterfeiteth cunning, and is no true cunning, in as much as it is without Charity, and also without justice. *Cicero ex platone. i. offic. Sciencia que est remota a iusticia calliditas potius quam cientia est appelanda.* Science removed from justice is rather to be called wiliness than science. And to this purpose, it is necessary that you servants do your duty to your masters obediently with fear and quaking, in simplicity and plainness of heart, as unto Christ, not serving to the eye, as to please man, but like the servants of Christ, doing the will of God with heart and all. *Eph. vi.* not deceiving your masters by your idleness, or else being occupied about your own business, when your master thinketh that you be in his labours. And likewise you masters do you to your servants, instructing them in their occupations, for which they came to your service, according to the truth that their parents and friends hath put you in, that they may get them living and yours with truth and just dealing and honesty, and meddle not too much with other men's occupations that you cannot skill on, lest while ye be so curious in other men's matters not pertaining to your learning, you decay as well in your own occupation, as in the other, so falling to penury, extreme poverty, and very beggary. For when a tailor forsaking his own occupation will be a merchant vintner, or a shoemaker to become a grocer, God send him well to prove. I have known many in this town, that studying divinity, hath killed a merchant and some of other occupations by their busy labours in the scriptures, hath shut up the shop windows, fain to take Sanctuary, or else for mercery and grocery, hath be fain to sell godderds [drinking-cups], steans [clay vessels], and pitchers, and such other trumpery. For this I shall assure you, that although divinity be a science very profitable for the soul health, yet small gains to the purse, or to the world ariseth by it. Not that I intend to reprove the study of scriptures, for I extoll it and praise it above all other study, so that it be used as I have said afore, with modesty and charity, with longanimity [patience] and easy sufferance, till God send them a true instructor, not infected with wilful and newfangled heresies: From which I pray God to defend you all, and send you teachers indued with such science as may instruct you in the truth, by which you may attain to joys everlasting. Amen.

# Thomas Cranmer

CRANMER IS the most important figure in the history of the Church of England: he saw the institution into existence, and his influence upon it remains inestimable. Anglicanism as we now know it was the creation of Queen Elizabeth I and her clergy; but they built upon ('recaptured') Cranmer's foundations. Though his brilliance as a writer of religious prose is undisputed (the Prayer Book, the Litany, the Homilies given below, and much else), Cranmer is, naturally, a man who has given rise to controversy, some of it bitter. Was he an ambitious opportunist who helped to destroy the spiritual authority of the Church by mixing it inextricably with politics? Was he the founder-hero of the Church of England? Was he a mixture of deviousness and integrity? The lucid sincerity of his prose, best seen in the revision and translation of the Book of Common Prayer over which he presided, gives the lie to the first judgement: many English non-Christians still respect the Church of England above all others because of this inspired and stately prose. As to the rest: he was, as they say, 'human', and the famous theological elasticity of the Church of England reflects this humanity, in its human frailty, its strengths and its certainties.

Cranmer, born in Nottinghamshire in 1489, attended and then became a Fellow of Jesus College, Cambridge. Erasmus was at Cambridge from 1511, and his reforming ideas may well have been a decisive influence. Cranmer was ordained in 1523. He lost his fellowship (1510) because of marriage (his first, to 'black Joan of the Dolphin tavern', of short duration, for she died within a few months), but was re-elected. In 1529, when Henry VIII's divorce proceedings against Catherine of Aragon first seemed in danger, he privately suggested that the (reforming) universities of Europe might be consulted. This came to Henry's notice, and from thence onwards the course of Cranmer's career was determined. He became first a private counsellor to the King in his marriage problems, and then (1533) Archbishop of Canterbury. From Henry's point of view Cranmer, like all his other servants, was to become an instrument of his will. From Cranmer's point of view a new Church, of England, could now be fostered into being. He annulled the offending marriage, and in 1536 the succeeding one; he authorized and annulled the ill-fated marriage to Anne of Cleves; he conveyed to the King the news of Catherine Howard's pre- and post-marital infidelity.

But until the death of Henry Cranmer was to a large extent hamstrung: Henry was by temperament a religious conservative. That under him English religion was 'Catholicism without the Pope' is a myth; but he usually inclined towards Catholic theological interpretations, and was not on the whole interested in taking his own church beyond the limits of the external Erasmian reforms. He was quick-minded and intelligent—but too proud of these qualities to be able to give a consistent lead. His interest was sporadic, cleverly pedantic, anti-clerical, heterodox, somewhat confused and Pelagian (a man of his very bad character needed to be); and, of course, he was inevitably influenced by diplomatic and other factors. Although he had tolerated certain Protestant practices, all the time with the aim of preserving his own popularity and testing public opinion, the Six Articles (1539) made further doctrinal advance virtually impossible during Henry's reign: he was never really in sympathy with Cranmer's own aim, which was to bring England into some measure of agreement with the newly reformed European churches—though, being moody, he could occasionally incline in that direction. Cranmer had had a hand in the Ten Articles (1536), superseded by the Bishop's Book of 1537; but, to the extent that he safely could, he opposed the Six Articles—which enjoined celibacy on the clergy, and obliged him to banish his own second wife, a niece of the Lutheran Andreas Osiander, whom he had secretly married (and kept in seclusion) in 1532—he recalled her from Germany nine years later. Cranmer, moreover, was himself in some danger at the end of the decade: if he was to preserve any of his work, he had to tread with great care. Norfolk, Bishop Gardiner and others eventually succeeded in their plot to destroy Thomas Cromwell, who was in sympathy with Cranmer. It was not until almost a year after Cromwell's execution that Henry realized by what means he had been deprived of his most able servant.

Cranmer was, however, able to pursue his cherished purpose of making an English version of the Bible freely available (one of the more curious tenets of Roman Catholicism being that the Holy Book was dangerous to the minds of those who knew no Latin). Copies of Tyndale's English New Testament (1526) had been coming into England, but only illegally. In 1534, at the direct instigation of Cranmer, Convocation petitioned Henry that the whole Bible might be done into English. The King, though he had described Tyndale's version as marred by 'pestilent glosses', tried to ignore the request; but he did not forbid it. In 1535 Coverdale's complete Bible was issued, dedicated to Henry. This was revised two years later, and was now actually authorized by the King. The 'Great Bible' of 1539 was reissued in the following year with Cranmer's own preface. In 1538 this version, then being printed by Richard Grafton in Paris, was ordered, by Royal Injunction, to be set up in all churches. Cranmer was responsible for this vitally important innovation; he had, all the time, to contend with the powerful opposition of the time-serving Stephen Gardiner (c. 1490-1555), Bishop of Winchester from 1531, who found it in his conscience to work for Henry and then for Mary Tudor; by a stroke of irony it was he who had in 1529 informed the King of Cranmer's suggestion that the European universities might be consulted. In 1546 Gardiner and the other conservative bishops were able to get the injunction of 1538 reversed in favour of the (comparatively corrupt) Vulgate. Not until Edward VI succeeded his father could Cranmer make the English Bible legally available.

Under Edward he was able to push forward his reforms, virtually creating the Church of England (which Mary, Gardiner and Bonner, the more consistent Bishop of London—who died in 1569 in prison—were unable to destroy). He was responsible for the 1549 Book of Common Prayer—revised in 1552—and for the Forty-Two Articles (1553); the latter were not enforced, but they are the firm basis of the Thirty-Nine Articles (1563), the most masterly and tolerant (because often ambiguous) summary of tenets of faith of any church in the world. Despite the threat to his massive achievement, Cranmer was scrupulous in the matter of the unfortunate Lady Jane Grey's succession: he argued with Northumberland—as ruthless as Cranmer was gentle—against it, and it was only with the utmost reluctance, and under pressure from the dying King himself, that he voted (1553) in Lady Jane's favour. For this, when Mary—daughter of the King's first marriage —succeeded, he was tried and sentenced for high treason; but the Queen spared him. He was sent to Oxford so that he might argue in justification of his 'heresies'. Here he showed great courage (Gardiner, in the Tower for most of Edward's reign, had crowned the Queen, and was now Lord Chancellor—he who had in 1535 signed his renunciation of obedience to the Pope, and who had in that same year maintained the supremacy of secular princes over the Church), for he persisted in justifying his Church. He was of course adjudged to be in the wrong, and in 1555 was cited to appear (he was still Archbishop) before the Pope. He refused, thus sealing his fate. Reginald Pole, who had just missed the Papacy in 1549, was in 1556 made Archbishop of Canterbury; Cranmer, still defiant, refused to recognize the Pope's authority. He saw Latimer and Ridley die from the window of his prison in Oxford, and, as he later said, 'for fear of his life', signed six humiliating recantations. But he was condemned to be burned (despite the discreet efforts of Gardiner to save him), and when told to read out his final recantation, refused to do so, and instead smilingly thrust the hand which had signed the documents into the flames. Within a short time the wretched Queen was herself an enemy of the Pope (a notable reviver of the Inquisition) because of the war between him and her husband, Philip II of Spain.

Cranmer was more consistent than has been supposed. Of course some of his actions were discreditable: he lived in a difficult time, and (incidentally) his doctrine especially excluded all possibilities of human perfection. But he was not, by the standards of the time, an opportunist, as has been charged; and opinion hostile towards him has tended to judge him outside his historical context.

His chief misdeeds date from the period of the reign of the sickly boy, Edward VI, when first Somerset and then Northumberland were protectors of the realm. The Duke of Somerset (Edward Seymour) was, for the sixteenth century, a man of serious and liberal aims, and perhaps the greatest politician of his century; he lost some of his popularity as a result of the religious reforms he allowed Cranmer to institute (notably the 1549 Act of Uniformity). When, after being deposed (1550), Somerset was arrested on a trumped-up charge and executed, it was Cranmer who signed, in defiance of the canon law, his death-warrant. However, he had never played a part in the discreditable aspect of the dissolution of the monasteries, and he had objected to Somerset's continuation of Henry's grasping policies in this respect. Somerset, though in some respects arrogant, and a rash idealist, was a tolerant man who believed in tolerance, and Cranmer acquiesced in few executions for heresy. The evidence of his part in the burning of Frith (1533) is not clear; but it was into Thomas More's hands that Frith's private book, denying transubstantiation and purgatory as necessary dogmas, fell: it was a cruel age, and not long afterwards Cranmer interceded in vain for Fisher and for More himself, as he was to do for Thomas

Cromwell in 1540. What else could Cranmer do, one must ask, except desert Somerset? His unscrupulous successor had in any case chosen to pursue the Protestant way.

He is frequently made out to have been of 'timid nature': in G. M. Trevelyan's words, a 'man of perpetual moral hesitations and mental revisions . . . with occasional bursts of courage . . . like [that] of a timid woman turning to bay in defence of her children'. The first part of this judgement is surely a compliment: are not moral hesitation and mental revision two of the qualities especially distinguishing the Church of England? The second part is simply untrue. Henry, as unpleasant if not unintelligent a monarch as England has ever possessed, was a masterful and ruthless man who retained his own ill-earned popularity by sacrificing, at intervals, the instruments of his policies. To serve Henry was—and there is no other way of looking at it—to be, to some extent, a cat's-paw. Cranmer remained his trusted friend, could handle him as perhaps no other of his servants could: as he lay dying he said that if he should need anyone then it would be Cranmer, and his last conscious act was to 'wring his [Cranmer's] hand in his as hard as he could'.

Cranmer had not wanted the office of Archbishop of Canterbury fourteen years earlier. He had been no more than a humble archdeacon. But to refuse Henry would have been impossible. Besides, had he not, since at least the days of 1521 when he gathered for conversations with such as Coverdale, Latimer and Tyndale in 'Germany'—the White Horse tavern in Cambridge—been, in effect, a convinced Protestant? When one thinks of the nature, function and history of the Church of England, one may be forgiven for wondering whether—as Henry's extraordinary instruction (for such in reality it was) that he be appointed Archbishop of Canterbury came to his ears—he may not have been stirred by a certain sense of mission.

Timid he was not. He fought Henry fiercely and, as a recent historian has put it, on occasions tartly, over the Ten Articles, the Bishop's Book, the Six Articles and over the so-called 'King's Book' (*A Necessary Doctrine and Erudition for any Christian Man*) of 1543, whose general reorientation towards Catholicism and a Catholic definition of transubstantiation must have dismayed him. Cranmer stood up to Henry more firmly than anyone else who did not actually choose, as More did, to die; but Henry was not a ruler with whom anyone ever had his way. Cranmer thus achieved much. The legend of Cranmer's timidity arises, perhaps, from his comparative humaneness and scrupulosity. A careful study of his *Works* (1833) and, more particularly, of *Miscellaneous Writings* (1846) reveals him as firm, courageous and even exasperated in his dealings with Henry over theological matters. When, for example, Henry ingeniously wrecked one of his passages—on the meaning of faith—in the Bishop's Book by adding two words he wrote: 'These two words may not be put in this place in anywise.'

There is a remarkable consistency in this man. He early turned from the virtual ecumenicity of Erasmus towards Lutheran reform. But he was always English in his attitude: he worked towards a Church of *England*—not so much towards a compromise as towards a specifically English Protestant formula. In matters of theological interpretation the influence of Erasmus—who, though he opposed the Reformation, was, ironically, one of the chief destroyers of his own Church—is always greater over Cranmer than that of the Protestants Luther, Calvin, Zwingli or even Bucer: Erasmus was as, or more, relentless a spiritualizer of the Mass as any of these.

Cranmer's difficulties of conscience during his ordeal under Bloody Mary, and much of his earlier behaviour, may be explained by his convinced Erastianism. Thomas Erastus (real name Luber, Lieber or Liebler), a Swiss, did not write his *Explicatio Gravissimae Questionis* until after Cranmer's death, but the term Erastianism has come to stand for the (anti-Papist) view that the Church is not infallible, and that the civil authorities in a state should exercise all jurisdiction, ecclesiastical as well as civil. And so Cranmer has been called an Erastian. The term is somewhat misleading, for Erastus does not consider the question of what the relationship between State and Church should be; and in any case his attitude had long before been anticipated by Marsilius (Marsiglio) of Padua (*c.* 1275-1342), a lawyer and a layman, whose tract *Defensor Pacis* (1324) maintained that the Church derives its authority from the people: the Church must own no property, but only borrow it from the State; it is human and not a divine institution. This was a great early blow at the foundations of Roman Catholic absolutism. The English Wycliffe—one of Cranmer's spiritual forebears, as were all the Lollards, an order of poor priests Wycliffe instituted—had some half century later developed these ideas about property further: *dominium*, the ownership of property, he asserted, is in God's province; man may only use it (*usus*). Now this is a convenient doctrine from the point of view of a ruler (for example, the regent John of Gaunt in Wycliffe's time; or Henry, and then Somerset, in Cranmer's) who wants to sequester Church property; so it is notable that Cranmer, the convinced Erastian, should have taken no significant part in the suppression of the monasteries—which had in any case for the past two centuries been, in general, mediocre. It was doubtless under Cranmer's influence that Henry ordered the translation into English and publication of Marsilius' tract. But Cranmer's Erastianism was never opportunistic: it arose from his non-Roman Catholic theology, his tolerance, his desire to establish a true Church that could stand assaults from both extremes. For Cranmer no man, let alone a Pope, ought to take upon himself the inscrutability of God. Although the King actually encouraged Cranmer in his great work on the Book of Common Prayer, even though this did not come to fruition until 1549, he never accepted, and perhaps never even fully understood, Cranmer's view of man as totally dependent on God's grace. Cranmer shared Luther's view that no humanly administered Church could possibly regard itself, or be regarded, as infallible. Truth resides in Christ and in the Scriptures. Yet it was heretical (though the infallibility of the Pope himself was not pronounced until the nineteenth century) to deny that what the Roman Catholic Church actually did was not divine. . . . Faith was by grace, and by grace alone.

So when Cranmer admitted only cowardice as his motive in signing the recantations, he was not doing himself justice. For he was in an agonizing position. Mary was Queen, and he was an Erastian. . . . We hear at least his voice in the Book of Common Prayer, sense the power and subtlety of his mind in the Thirty-Nine Articles. Those who wish to pronounce adverse judgement on his lapse under threat of burning must be fully confident of their own ability not to lapse: be assured of their own grace, rather than that of the God to whose grace Cranmer submitted.

An Homily of the Salvation of Mankind, by Only Christ Our Saviour, from Sin and Death Everlasting

A Short Declaration of the True, Lively, and Christian Faith

An Homily or Sermon of Good Works Annexed unto Faith

THE FIRST Book of Homilies, containing twelve homilies, was prepared in 1542, but Henry VIII probably would not authorize it, since it is hardly in accord with his own capricious theology. It was therefore not issued until 1547. A second book appeared in 1571; this contained thirty-three homilies.

During the sixteenth century many of the clergy were unlearned or confused by the doctrinal toings and froings of the time. They were not competent to produce their own sermons. The Book of Homilies was issued for their use. Of the original twelve homilies, four, probably five, are by Cranmer; he in any case presided over the compilation. Both books are regarded as valuable repositories of Anglican doctrine, and they still retain authority: they are listed in the Thirty-Fifth Article, and Cranmer's *Of the Salvation of All Mankind*, mentioned in the Eleventh Article, remains central to Anglicanism. (The two homilies of Cranmer not printed here are the first, *A fruitful Exhortation to the Reading of Scriptures*, and the ninth, against the fear of death—probably his. The text of only one other sermon by Cranmer survives: *Sermon Concerning the Time of Rebellion*. This is less interesting and less instructive than his three homilies here given; it shows him eloquently reacting to a situation as a good Erastian Archbishop should.)

In the homilies printed here we see Cranmer as a writer of great English prose; moreover, we are in the presence of the true spirit of Anglicanism. Cranmer here made his position on all but one of the fundamentals of theology clear. Though the position of the Church itself was not wholly established until after the death of Bloody Mary and the country's final emancipation from Papal interference (the attempts of James II to force Catholicism on the kingdom soon led to his expulsion), most will, in reading Cranmer, detect a confident substance that his Protestant successors under Elizabeth lacked. Though a man of acute intelligence (this is often woodenly called 'deviousness'), Cranmer has a kind of directness, a lack of *politesse*, of compromise for its own sake (as distinct from deliberate ambiguity), that we shall not often meet again. The homilies, of course, needed to be simple and lucid, since they were intended for unsophisticated audiences. They are so much the better for this.

One point, however, Cranmer leaves untouched: the matter of the Eucharist. (The attitude of the Church of England to this has been discussed in the introduction.) Cranmer did write on it elsewhere (against transubstantiation), but it is fairly clear that while he himself thought deeply on this, at the time fiercely debated, matter, he would have preferred to leave the question as open as possible to individual conscience. Cranmer himself certainly utterly rejected the Aristotelian metaphysical trickery of transubstantiation (the bread and wine are 'accidents'). He seems himself to have leant towards the Zwinglian, and Bucerian, rather than the Lutheran notions: whereas Luther asserted consubstantiation (co-existence of bread and wine and Body and Blood), Zwingli held that the rite was purely memorial, purely symbolic. The anti-mystical attitude taken up by Cranmer is indicative of his temperament. Here again, he may have been influenced by the attitude of Erasmus.

These homilies are cheering documents in the context of Roman Catholic threats of damnation; but they are not so in any disingenuous manner. The beginning of the Salvation homily is thoroughly Lutheran in spirit. *Justification* (p. 22), it should be explained, is here used in the (Lutheran) sense: it is the act of God by which, because of Christ's sacrifice, he spares men from the deserts they have earned by their sins because of their faith. Faith, for Cranmer as for the Church of England, involves *trust*. As he writes: 'only a true and lively faith, which nevertheless is the gift of God, and not man's only work without God' (p. 24) can lead to our justification. Following this is an important point: true faith, which brings with it justification, does not preclude good works (which we are 'most bounden' to do, to 'serve God'—p. 24); but we cannot earn our salvation simply by good works, and we must not try to do so. Luther himself, a more melancholy and tormented man than Cranmer, might have written: 'So that Christ is now the righteousness of them that truly do believe in him' (p.24).

Cranmer now continues, in the Protestant manner of the times, to find support from within the Scriptures (the notion that these are the concatenation from which anything might be 'proved' had not then been formed; it did not begin to dominate theology until the nineteenth century). It will also be noted that he appeals, in the true Erasmian spirit, only to the Fathers of the first six centuries, and particularly to St Augustine (in one sense the real founder of the Protestant way). After this Cranmer shows his awareness of the danger of giving the impression that we need 'do no good works at all' (p.26). That is why one of the homilies is about good works. What he is anxious to establish here, though, is the 'arrogancy and presumption' (p.27) of the idea that salvation can come about *simply* by good works. As he clearly shows, good works must inevitably flow from a 'quick and lively' faith. He praises Henry VIII (p.51), but does not mention Luther. In general, his homilies (they are really a single homily divided into three parts) are so lucid that they require no further commentary. The main point to grasp is that, while thoroughly Protestant and Erastian (for example, his marginal gloss 'Man's laws must be observed and kept, but not as God's laws', and the relevant paragraph—p.47), Cranmer is as 'open' as he can possibly be. For Luther there were some who were elected and some who were damned; but the elect were only known to an inscrutable God. For Zwingli the elect could be identified by their public adherence to the faith (a somewhat curious doctrine). Even for Calvin there were three (fairly) certain tests. But the proto-Protestant Roman Catholic Erasmus clearly could not believe in a God who would choose some for election and some for damnation: such a God would be a tyrant. He thus, like St Augustine, put emphasis—which Luther refused to acknowledge—on free will, on man's capacity to cooperate with God to ensure his salvation. Cranmer does not want to confuse his largely unsophisticated audience with theological subtleties, but his very openness suggests that his Lutheranism is strongly tempered by Erasmianism. Indeed, one of the fundamental differences between the Church of England and Lutheranism lies in this point, and we may infer it from Cranmer's general attitude as here presented. Since God is inscrutable, it is safer, in any case, to leave the entire question of the existence or non-existence of an elect open.

# An Homily of the Salvation of Mankind, by Only Christ Our Saviour, from Sin and Death Everlasting

BECAUSE ALL men be sinners and offenders against God, and breakers of his law and commandments, therefore can no man by his own acts, works, and deeds (seem they never so good) be justified and made righteous before God: but every man of necessity is constrained to seek for another righteousness or justification, to be received at God's own hands, that is to say, the remission, pardon, and forgiveness of his sins and trespasses in such things as he hath offended. And this justification or righteousness, which we so receive by God's mercy and Christ's merits, embraced by faith, is taken, accepted, and allowed of God, for our perfect and full justification. For the more full understanding hereof, it is our parts and duty ever to remember the great mercy of God, how that (all the world being wrapped in sin by breaking of the law) God sent his only son our saviour Christ into this world, to fulfil the law for us, and by shedding of his most precious blood to make a sacrifice and satisfaction, or (as it may be called) amends to his Father for our sins, to assuage his wrath and indignation conceived against us for the same.

*The efficacy of Christ's passion & oblation.* Insomuch that infants being baptized, and dying in their infancy, are by this sacrifice washed from their sins, brought to God's favour, and made his children, and inheritors of his kingdom of heaven. And they which actually do sin after their baptism, when they convert and turn again to God unfeignedly, they are likewise washed by this sacrifice from their sins, in such sort, that there remaineth not any spot of sin that shall be imputed to their damnation. This is that justification or righteousness which St. Paul speaketh of, when he saith: *No man is justified by the works of the law, but freely by faith in Jesus Christ* (Rom. iii). And again he saith: *We believe in Christ Jesu, that we be justified freely by the faith of Christ, and not by the works of the law, because that no man shall be justified by the works of the law* (Gal. ii).

And although this justification be free unto us, yet it cometh not so freely to us, that there is no ransom paid therefore at all. But here may man's reason be astonied, reasoning after this fashion: *An objection.* If a ransom be paid for our redemption, then it is not given us freely. For a prisoner that payeth his ransom is not let go freely; for if he go freely, then he goeth without ransom: for what is it else to go freely, than to be set at liberty without payment of ransom? This reason is satis- *An answer* fied by the great wisdom of God in this mystery of our redemption, who hath so tempered his justice and mercy together, that he would neither by his justice condemn us unto the perpetual captivity of the Devil and his prison of hell remediless for ever without mercy; nor by his mercy deliver us clearly, without justice, or payment of a just ransom: but with his endless mercy he joined his most upright and equal justice. His great mercy he showed unto us in delivering us from our former captivity, without requiring of any ransom to be paid, or amends to be made upon our parts, which thing by us had been impossible to be done. And whereas it lay not in us that to do, he provided a ransom for us, that was the most precious body and blood of his own most dear and best beloved son Jesu Christ, who, besides his ransom, fulfilled the law for us perfectly. And so the justice of God and his mercy did embrace together, and fulfilled the mystery of our redemption. And of this justice and mercy of God knit together, speaketh St. Paul in the third chapter to the Romans: *All have offended, and have need of the glory of God; justified freely by his grace, by redemption which is in Jesu Christ, whom God hath set forth to us for a reconciler and peacemaker, through faith in his blood, to shew his righteousness.* And in the tenth chapter: *Christ is the end of the law, unto righteousness, to every man that believeth.* And in the eighth chapter: *That which was impossible by the law, inasmuch as it was weak by the flesh, God sending his own son in the similitude of sinful flesh, by sin damned sin in the flesh, that the righteousness of the law might be fulfilled in us, which walk not after the flesh, but after the Spirit.*

In these foresaid places, the Apostle toucheth special- *Three* ly three things, which must concur and go together in *things* our justification. Upon God's part, his great mercy and *must be* grace; upon Christ's part, justice, that is, the satisfaction *in our jus-* of God's justice, or price of our redemption, by the of- *tification.* fering of his body and shedding of his blood, with fulfilling of the law perfectly and thoroughly; and upon our part, true and lively faith in the merits of Jesu Christ, which yet is not ours, but by God's working in us. So that in our justification, is not only God's mercy and grace, but also his justice, which the apostle calleth the justice of God; and it consisteth in paying

23

our ransom, and fulfilling of the law: and so the grace of God doth not exclude the justice of God in our justification, but only excludeth the justice of man, that is to say, the justice of our works, as to be merits of deserving our justification. And therefore St. Paul declareth here nothing upon the behalf of man concerning his justification, but only a true and lively faith, which nevertheless is the gift of God, and not man's only work without God.

<small>How is it to be understand that faith justifieth without works.</small> And yet that faith doth not exclude repentance, hope, love, dread, and the fear of God, to be joined with faith in every man that is justified; but it excludeth them from the office of justifying. So that although they be all present together in him that is justified, yet they justify not altogether. Nor that faith also doth not exclude the justice of our good works, necessarily to be done afterward of duty towards God; (for we are most bounden to serve God, in doing good deeds commanded by him in his holy scripture, all the days of our life;) but it excludeth them, so that we may not do them to this intent, to be made good by doing of them. For all the good works that we can do be unperfect, and therefore not able to deserve our justification: but our justification doth come freely by the mere mercy of God, and of so great and free mercy, that whereas all the world was not able of theirselves to pay any part towards their ransom, it pleased our heavenly Father of his infinite mercy, without any our desert or deserving, to prepare for us the most precious jewels of Christ's body and blood, whereby our ransom might be fully paid, the law fulfilled, and his justice fully satisfied. So that Christ is now the righteousness of all them that truly do believe in him. He for them paid their ransom by his death. He for them fulfilled the law in his life. So that now in him, and by him, every true Christian man may be called a fulfiller of the law; forasmuch as that which their infirmity lacketh, Christ's justice hath supplied.

Before was declared at large, that no man can be justified by his own good works, that no man fulfilleth the law, according to the full request of the law. And St. Paul in his Epistle to the Galatians proveth the same, saying thus: *If there had been any law given, which could have justified, verily righteousness should have been by the law* (Gal. iii). And again he saith: *If righteousness be by the law, then Christ died in vain* (Gal. ii). And again he saith: *You that are justified in the law are fallen away from grace* (Gal. v). And furthermore he writeth to the Ephesians on this wise: *By grace are ye saved through faith, and that not of yourselves, for it is the gift of God, and not of works, lest any man should glory* (Ephes. ii). And, to be short, the sum of all Paul's disputation is this; that if justice come of works, then it cometh not of grace; and if it come of grace, then it cometh not of works. And to this end tendeth all the prophets, as St. Peter saith in the tenth of the Acts: *Of Christ all the prophets*, saith St. Peter, *do witness, that through his name, all they that believe in him shall receive the remission of sins.*

And after this wise to be justified only by this true and lively faith in Christ, speaketh all the old and ancient authors, both Greeks and Latins; of whom I will specially rehearse three, Hilary, Basil, and Ambrose. St. Hilary saith these words plainly in the ninth canon upon Matthew; 'Faith only justifieth.' And St. Basil, a Greek author, writeth thus; 'This is a perfect and an whole glorying in God, when a man doth not boast himself for his own justice, but knoweth himself certainly to be unworthy of true justice, but to be justified by only faith in Christ. This is a perfect and a whole rejoicing in God, when a man advanceth not himself for his own righteousness, but knowledgeth himself to lack true justice and righteousness, and to be justified by the only faith in Christ.' 'And Paul,' saith he, 'doth glory in the contempt of his own righteousness, and that he looketh for his righteousness of God by faith' (Philip. iii). <sub>Faith only justifieth is the doctrine of old doctors.</sub>

These be the very words of St. Basil; and St. Ambrose, a Latin author, saith these words; 'This is the ordinance of God, that he which believeth in Christ should be saved without works, by faith only, freely receiving remission of his sins.' Consider diligently these words, 'without works,' 'by faith only,' 'freely we receive remission of our sins.' What can be spoken more plainly, than to say, that freely without works, by faith only, we obtain remission of our sins? These and other like sentences, that we be justified by faith only, freely, and without works, we do read ofttimes in the most best and ancient writers: as, beside Hilary, Basil, and St. Ambrose, before rehearsed, we read the same in Origen, St. Chrisostome, St. Cypriane, St. Augustine, Prosper, Oecomenius, Photius, Barnardus, Anselme, and many other authors, Greek and Latin.

Nevertheless, this sentence, that we be justified by faith only, is not so meant of them, that the said justifying faith is alone in man, without true repentance, <sub>Faith alone, how is it to be</sub>

hope, charity, dread, and the fear of God, at any time or season. Nor when they say, that we be justified freely, they mean not that we should or might afterward be idle, and that nothing should be required on our parts afterward. Neither they mean not so to be justified without good works, that we should do no good works at all, like as shall be more expressed at large hereafter. But this proposition, that we be justified by faith only, freely, and without works, is spoken for to take away clearly all merit of our works, as being insufficient to deserve our justification at God's hands, and thereby most plainly to express the weakness of man, and the goodness of God; the great infirmity of ourselves, and the might and power of God; the imperfectness of our own works, and the most abundant grace of our saviour Christ; and therefore wholly for to ascribe the merit and deserving of our justification unto Christ only, and his most precious blood-shedding. This faith the holy scripture teacheth; this is the strong rock and foundation of Christian religion; this doctrine all old and ancient authors of Christ's church do approve; this doctrine advanceth and setteth forth the true glory of Christ, and suppresseth the vain-glory of man; this whosoever denieth, is not to be reputed for a true Christian man, nor for a setter-forth of Christ's glory; but for an adversary of Christ and his gospel, and for a setter-forth of men's vain-glory.

*understand.*

*The profit of the doctrine of faith only justifieth.*

*What they be that impugn the doctrine of faith only justifieth.*

And although this doctrine be never so true, (as it is most true indeed,) that we be justified freely, without all merit of our own good works, (as St. Paul doth express it,) and freely, by this lively and perfect faith in Christ only, (as the ancient authors use to speak it,) yet this true doctrine must be also truly understand, and most plainly declared, lest carnal men should take unjustly occasion thereby to live carnally after the appetite and will of the world, the flesh, and the devil. And because no man should err by mistaking of this true doctrine, I shall plainly and shortly so declare the right understanding of the same, that no man shall justly think that he may thereby take any occasion of carnal liberty to follow the desires of the flesh, or that thereby any kind of sin shall be committed, or any ungodly living the more used.

*A declaration of this doctrine, faith without works justifieth.*

First, you shall understand, that in our justification by Christ it is not all one thing, the office of God unto man, and the office of man unto God. Justification is not the office of man, but of

God; for man cannot justify himself by his own works, neither in part, nor in the whole; for that were the greatest arrogancy and presumption of man that Antichrist could erect against God, to affirm that a man might by his own works take away and purge his own sins, and so justify himself. But justifica- *Justification is the office of God only* tion is the office of God only, and is not a thing which we render unto him, but which we receive of him; not which we give to him, but which we take of him, by his free mercy, and by the only merits of his most dearly beloved son, our only redeemer, saviour, and justifier, Jesus Christ. So that the true understanding of this doctrine, we be justified freely by faith without works, or that we be justified by faith in Christ only, is not, that this our own act to believe in Christ, or this our faith in Christ, which is within us, doth justify us, and merit our justification unto us; (for that were to count ourselves to be justified by some act or virtue that is within ourselves;) but the true understanding and meaning thereof is, that although we hear God's word, and believe it; although we have faith, hope, charity, repentance, dread, and fear of God within us, and do never so many good works thereunto; yet we must renounce the merit of all our said virtues, of faith, hope, charity, and all our other virtues and good deeds, which we either have done, shall do, or can do, as things that be far too weak and insufficient and unperfect, to deserve remission of our sins, and our justification; and therefore we must trust only in God's mercy, and in that sacrifice which our high-priest and saviour Christ Jesus, the son of God, once offered for us upon the cross, to obtain thereby God's grace and remission, as well of our original sin in baptism, as of all actual sin committed by us after our baptism, if we truly repent, and convert unfeignedly to him again. So that, as St. John Baptist, although he were never so virtuous and godly a man, yet in this matter of forgiving of sin, he did put the people from him, and appointed them unto Christ, saying thus unto them, *Behold, yonder is the lamb of God, which taketh away the sins of the world* (John i); even so, as great and as godly a virtue as the lively faith is, yet it putteth us from itself, and remitteth or appointeth us unto Christ, for to have only by him remission of our sins, or justification. So that our faith in Christ (as it were) saith unto us thus: It is not I that take away your sins, but it is Christ only; and to him only I send you for that purpose, renouncing therein all your good virtues, words, thoughts, and works, and only putting your trust in Christ.

Thus you do see that the very true sense of this proposition, We be justified by faith in Christ only (according to the meaning of the old ancient authors) is this: We put our faith in Christ, that we be justified by him only, that we be justified by God's free mercy, and the merits of our Saviour Christ only, and by no virtue or good work of our own that is in us, or that we can be able to have or to do, for to deserve the same; Christ himself only being the cause meritorious thereof.

Here you perceive many words to be used to avoid contention in words with them that delighteth to brawl about words, and also to shew the true meaning to avoid evil taking and misunderstanding; and yet peradventure all will not serve with them that be contentious; but contenders will ever forge matter of contention, even when they have none occasion thereto. Notwithstanding, such be the less to be passed upon, so that the rest may profit, which will be more desirous to know the truth, than (when it is plain enough) to contend about it, and with contentious and captious cavillations to obscure and darken it.

Truth it is, that our own works doth not justify us, to speak properly of our justification; that is to say, our works do not merit or deserve remission of our sins, and make us, of unjust, just before God: but God of his mere mercy, through the only merits or deserving of his son Jesus Christ, doth justify us. Nevertheless, because faith doth directly send us to Christ for remission of our sins, and that by faith given us of God we embrace the promise of God's mercy and of the remission of our sins, (which thing none other of our virtues or works properly doth,) therefore the Scripture useth to say, that faith without works doth justify. And forasmuch that it is all one sentence in effect, to say, faith without works, and only faith, doth justify us; therefore the old ancient fathers of the church from time to time have uttered our justification with this speech; Only faith justifieth us: meaning none other thing than St. Paul meant, when he said, Faith without works justifieth us. And because all this is brought to pass through the only merits and deservings of our saviour Christ, and not through our merits, or through the merit of any virtue that we have within us, or of any work that cometh from us; therefore, in that respect of merit and deserving, we renounce, as it were, altogether again, faith, works, and all other virtues. For our own imperfection is so great, through the corruption of original sin, that all is imperfect that is within us, faith, charity, hope, dread, thoughts, words, and works, and therefore not apt to merit and deserve any part of our justification for us. And this form of speaking we use, in the humbling of ourselves to God, and to give all the glory to our saviour Christ, which is best worthy to have it.

Here you have heard the office of God in our justification, and how we receive it of him freely, by his mercy, without our deserts, through true and lively faith. Now you shall hear the office and duty of a Christian man unto God, what we ought on our part to render unto God again for his great mercy and goodness. Our office is, not to pass the time of this present life unfruitfully and idly, after that we are baptized or justified, not caring how few good works we do, to the glory of God, and profit of our neighbours: much less it is our office, after that we be once made Christ's members, to live contrary to the same; making ourselves members of the Devil, walking after his enticements, and after the suggestions of the world and the flesh, whereby we know that we do serve the world and the Devil, and not God. For that faith which bringeth forth (without repentance) either evil works, or no good works, is not a right, pure, and lively faith, but a dead, devilish, counterfeit, and feigned faith, as St. Paul and St. James call it. For even the devils know and believe that Christ was born of a virgin; that he fasted forty days and forty nights without meat and drink; that he wrought all kind of miracles, declaring himself very God: they believe also, that Christ for our sakes suffered most painful death, to redeem us from eternal death, and that he rose again from death the third day: they believe that he ascended into heaven, and that he sitteth on the right hand of the Father, and at the last end of this world shall come again, and judge both the quick and the dead. These articles of our faith the devils believe, and so they believe all things that be written in the New and Old Testament to be true: and yet for all this faith they be but devils, remaining still in their damnable estate, lacking the very true Christian faith.

*They that preach faith only justifieth, do not teach carnal liberty, or that we should do no good works.*

*The devils have faith, but not the true faith.*

For the right and true Christian faith is, not only to believe that holy Scripture, and all the foresaid articles of our faith are true; but also to have a sure trust and confidence in God's merciful promises, to be saved from everlasting damnation by Christ: whereof doth follow a loving heart to obey his commandments. And this is true Christian faith neither any devil hath, nor yet any man, which in the outward

*What is the true and justifying faith.*

profession of his mouth, and in his outward receiving of the sacraments, in coming to the church, and in all other outward appearances, seemeth to be a Christian man, and yet in his living and deeds showeth the contrary. For how can a man have this true faith, this sure trust and confidence in God, that by the merits of Christ his sins be remitted, and he reconciled to the favour of God, and to be partaker of the kingdom of heaven by Christ, when he liveth ungodly, and denieth Christ in his deeds? Surely no such ungodly man can have this faith and trust in God. For as they know Christ to be the only saviour of the world; so they know also that wicked men shall not possess the kingdom of God. They know that God *hateth unrighteousness*; that he will *destroy all those that speak untruly* (Psal. v); that those that have done good works (which cannot be done without a lively faith in Christ) *shall come forth into the resurrection of life, and those that have done evil shall come unto resurrection of judgment* (John v). And very well they know also, that *to them that be contentious, and to them that will not be obedient unto the truth, but will obey unrighteousness, shall come indignation, wrath, and affliction,* &c. (Rom. ii).

<small>They that continue in evil living have not true faith.</small>

Therefore, to conclude, considering the infinite benefits of God, showed and exhibited unto us mercifully without our deserts, who hath not only created us of nothing, and from a piece of vile clay of his infinite goodness hath exalted us, as touching our soul, unto his own similitude and likeness; but also, whereas we were condemned to hell and death eternal, hath given his own natural son, being God eternal, immortal, and equal unto himself in power and glory, to be incarnated, and to take our mortal nature upon him, with the infirmities of the same, and in the same nature to suffer most shameful and painful death for our offences, to the intent to justify us, and to restore us to life everlasting: so making us also his dear beloved children, brethren unto his only son our saviour Christ, and inheritors for ever with him of his eternal kingdom of heaven: These great and merciful benefits of God, if they be well considered, do neither minister unto us occasion to be idle, and to live without doing any good works, neither yet stirreth us by any means to do evil things; but contrariwise, if we be not desperate persons, and our hearts harder than stones, they move us to render ourselves unto God wholly, with all our will, hearts, might, and power, to serve him in all good deeds, obeying his commandments during our lives, to seek in all things his glory and honour, not our sensual pleasures and vain-glory; evermore dreading willingly to offend such a merciful God, and loving Redeemer, in word, thought, or deed. And the said benefits of God, deeply considered, do move us for his sake also to be ever ready to give ourselves to our neighbours, and, as much as lieth in us, to study with all our endeavour to do good to every man. These be the fruits of the true faith, to do good as much as lieth in us to every man, and, above all things, and in all things, to advance the glory of God, of whom only we have our sanctification, justification, salvation, and redemption: to whom be ever glory, praise, and honour, world without end. Amen.

# A Short Declaration of the True, Lively, and Christian Faith

THE FIRST entry unto God, good Christian people, is through faith, whereby (as it is declared in the last sermon) we be justified before God. And lest any man should be deceived for lack of right understanding hereof, it is diligently to be noted, that faith is taken in the Scripture two manner of ways. There is one faith, which in Scripture is called a dead faith, which bringeth forth no good works, but is idle, barren, and unfruitful. And this faith, by the holy apostle St. James, is compared to the faith of devils, which believe God to be true and just, and tremble for fear; yet they do nothing well, but all evil (James ii). And such a manner of faith have the wicked and naughty Christian people, *which confess God*, as St. Paul saith, *in their mouth*, but *deny him in their deeds, being abominable, and without the right faith, and in all good works reprovable* (Titus i). And this faith is a persuasion and belief in man's heart, whereby he knoweth that there is a God, and assenteth unto all truth of God's most holy word, contained in holy Scripture. So that it consisteth only in believing of the word of God, that it is true. And this is not properly called faith. But as he that readeth Caesar's Commentaries, believing the same to be true, hath thereby a knowledge of Caesar's life and noble acts, because he believeth the history of Caesar: yet it is not properly said, that he believeth in Caesar, of whom he looketh for no help nor benefit. Even so, he that believeth that all that is spoken of God in the Bible is true, and yet liveth so ungodly, that he cannot look to enjoy the promises and benefits of God; although it may be said, that such a man hath a faith and belief to the words of God; yet it is not properly said that he believeth in God, or hath such a faith and trust in God, whereby he may surely look for grace, mercy, and eternal life at God's hand, but rather for indignation and punishment, according to the merits of his wicked life. For as it is written in a book, intituled to be of Didymus Alexandrinus, 'Forasmuch as faith without works is dead, it is not now faith, as a dead man is not a man.' This dead faith therefore is not that sure and substantial faith which saveth sinners.

Another faith there is in scripture, which is not, as the foresaid faith, idle, unfruitful, and dead, but *worketh by charity*, (as St. Paul declareth, Gal. v) which as the other vain faith is called a dead faith, so may this be called a quick or

*Faith*
*A dead faith.*
*A lively faith.*

lively faith. And this is not only the common belief of the articles of our faith, but it is also a sure trust and confidence of the mercy of God through our lord Jesus Christ, and a steadfast hope of all good things to be received at God's hand: and that although we, through infirmity, or temptation of our ghostly enemy, do fall from him by sin; yet if we return again unto him by true repentance, that he will forgive and forget our offences for his son's sake, our saviour Jesus Christ, and will make us inheritors with him of his everlasting kingdom; and that in the mean time, until that kingdom come, he will be our protector and defender in all perils and dangers, whatsoever do chance: and that though sometime he do send us sharp adversity, yet that evermore he will be a loving father unto us, correcting us for our sin, but not withdrawing his mercy finally from us, if we trust in him, and commit ourselves wholly to him, hang only upon him, and call upon him, ready to obey and serve him. This is the true, lively, and unfeigned Christian faith, and is not in the mouth and outward profession only, but it liveth, and stirreth inwardly in the heart. And this faith is not without hope and trust in God, nor without the love of God and of our neighbours, nor without the fear of God, nor without the desire to hear God's word, and to follow the same in eschewing evil, and doing gladly all good works.

This faith, as St. Paul describeth it, is the *sure ground and foundation of the benefits which we ought to look for, and trust to receive of God, a certificate and sure expectation of them, although they yet sensibly appear not unto us* (Heb. xi). And after he saith, He that cometh to God, must believe, both that he is, and that he is a merciful rewarder of well-doers (Heb. xi). And nothing commendeth good men unto God so much as this assured faith and trust in him. Of this faith three things are specially to be noted.

First, that this faith doth not lie dead in the heart, but is lively and fruitful in bringing forth good works. Second, that without it can no good works be done, that shall be acceptable and pleasant to God. Third, what manner of good works they be that this faith doth bring forth. Three things are to be noted of faith.

For the first, as the light cannot be hid, but will shew forth itself at one place or other; so a true faith cannot be kept secret; but when occasion is offered, it will break out, and shew itself by good works. And as the living body Faith is full of good works.

of a man ever exerciseth such things as belongeth to a natural and living body, for nourishment and preservation of the same, as it hath need, opportunity, and occasion; even so the soul that hath a lively faith in it will be doing alway some good work, which shall declare that it is living, and will not be unoccupied. Therefore, when men hear in the Scriptures so high commendations of faith, that it maketh us to please God, to live with God, and to be the children of God; if then they phantasy that they be set at liberty from doing all good works, and may live as they list, they trifle with God, and deceive themselves. And it is a manifest token that they be far from having the true and lively faith, and also far from knowledge what true faith meaneth. For the very sure and lively Christian faith is, not only to believe all things of God which are contained in holy Scripture, but also is an earnest trust and confidence in God, that he doth regard us, and hath cure of us, as the father of the child whom he doth love, and that he will be merciful unto us for his only son's sake, and that we have our saviour Christ our perpetual advocate and priest, in whose only merits, oblation, and suffering, we do trust that our offences be continually washed and purged, whensoever we, repenting truly, do return to him with our whole heart, steadfastly determining with ourselves, through his grace, to obey and serve him in keeping his commandments, and never to turn back again to sin. Such is the true faith that the Scripture doth so much commend, the which, when it seeth and considereth what God hath done for us, is also moved, through continual assistance of the Spirit of God, to serve and please him, to keep his favour, to fear his displeasure, to continue his obedient children, showing thankfulness again by observing his commandments, and that freely, for true love chiefly, and not for dread of punishment, or love of temporal reward, considering how clearly, without our deservings, we have received his mercy and pardon freely.

This true faith will shew forth itself, and cannot long be idle: for as it is written, *The just man doth live by his faith* (Habak. ii). He neither sleepeth, nor is idle, when he should wake and be well occupied. And God by his prophet Jeremy saith, that *he is a happy and blessed man, which hath faith and confidence in God. For he is like a tree set by the water-side, that spreadeth his roots abroad toward the moisture, and feareth not heat when it cometh; his leaf will be green, and will not cease to bring forth his fruit* (Jer. xvii): even so, faithful men, putting away all fear of adversity, will shew forth the fruit of their good works, as occasion is offered to do them.

The wise man saith, *He that believeth in God will hearken unto his commandments* (Ecclus. xxxii). For if we do not shew ourselves faithful in our conversation, the faith which we pretend to have is but a feigned faith: because the true Christian faith is manifestly showed by good living, and not by words only, as St. Augustin saith, 'Good living cannot be separated from true faith, which worketh by love.' And St. Chrysostom saith, 'Faith of itself is full of good works: as soon as a man doth believe, he shall be garnished with them.'

How plentiful this faith is of good works, and how it maketh the work of one man more acceptable to God than of another, St. Paul teacheth at large in the eleventh chapter to the Hebrews, saying, that faith made the oblation of Abel better than the oblation of Cain (Gen. iv). This made Noe to build the ark (Gen. vi). This made Abraham to forsake his country, and all his friends, and to go into a far country, there to dwell among strangers (Ecclus. xliv). So did also Isaac and Jacob, depending only of the help and trust that they had in God (Gen. xi). And when they came to the country which God promised them, they would build no cities, towns, nor houses; but lived like strangers in tents that might every day be removed. Their trust was so much in God, that they set but little by any worldly thing, for that God had prepared for them better dwelling-places in heaven, of his own foundation and building (Gen xxii). This faith made Abraham ready at God's commandment to offer his own son and heir Isaac, whom he loved so well, and by whom he was promised to have innumerable issue, among the which one should be born, in whom all nations should be blessed; trusting so much in God, that though he were slain, yet that God was able by his omnipotent power to raise him from death, and perform his promise (Ecclus. xliv). He mistrusted not the promise of God, although unto his reason every thing seemed contrary. He believed verily that God would not forsake him in dearth and famine that was in the country. And in all other dangers that he was brought unto, he trusted ever that God would be his God and his protector, whatsoever he saw to the contrary. This faith wrought so in the heart of Moses, that he refused to be taken for king Pharao his daughter's son, and to have great inheritance in Egypt, thinking it better with the people of God to have affliction and sorrow, than with naughty men in sin to live pleasantly for a time (Exod. ii). By faith he cared not for the threatening of king Pharao: for his trust was so in God, that he passed not of the felicity of this world, but looked for the reward to come in heaven; setting his heart upon the invisible God, as if he had seen him ever present before his eyes (Heb. xi). By faith the children of Israel passed through the red sea (Exod. xiv). By faith the walls of Jericho fell down without stroke, and many other wonderful miracles have been wrought (Josh. vi). In all good men that heretofore have been, faith hath brought forth their good works, and obtained the promises of God (Heb. xi). Faith hath stopped the lions' mouths (Dan. vi): faith hath quenched the force of fire (Dan. iii): faith hath escaped the sword's edges: faith hath given weak men strength, victory in battle, overthrown the armies of infidels, raised the dead to life: faith hath made good men to take adversity in good part; some have been mocked and whipped, bound and cast in prison; some have lost all their goods, and lived in great poverty; some have wandered in mountains, hills, and wilderness; some have been racked, some slain, some stoned, some sawn, some rent in pieces, some headed, some brent without mercy, and would not be delivered, because they looked to rise again to a better state (Heb. xi).

All these fathers, martyrs, and other holy men, whom St. Paul spake of, had their faith surely fixed in God, when all the world was against them. They did not only know God to be lord, maker, and governor of all men in the world; but also they had a special confidence and trust, that he was and would be their God, their comforter, aider, helper, maintainer, and defender. This is the Christian faith, which these holy men had, and we also ought to have. And although they were not named Christian men, yet was it a Christian faith that they had; for they looked for all benefits of God the father, through the merits of his son Jesu Christ, as we now do. This difference is between them and us, for they looked when Christ should come, and we be in the time when he is come. Therefore, saith St. Austen, 'The time is altered, but not the faith.' For we have both one faith in one Christ. The same Holy Ghost also that we have, had they, saith St. Paul (2 Cor. iv). For as the Holy Ghost doth teach us to trust in God, and to call upon him as our father, so did he teach them to say, as it is written: *Thou, Lord, art our father and redeemer; and thy name is without beginning, and everlasting* (Isa. lxiii). God gave them then grace to be his children, as he doth us now.

But now, by the coming of our saviour Christ we have received more abundantly the Spirit of God in our hearts, whereby we may conceive a greater faith, and a surer trust, than many of them had. But in effect they and we be all one: we have the same faith that they had in God, and they the same that we have. And St. Paul so much extolleth their faith, because we should no less, but rather more, give ourselves wholly unto Christ both in profession and living now when Christ is come, than the old fathers did before his coming. And by all the declaration of St. Paul it is evident, that the true, lively, and Christian faith is no dead, vain, or unfruitful thing, but a thing of perfect virtue, of wonderful operation and strength, bringing forth all good motions and good works.

All holy Scripture agreeably beareth witness, that a true lively faith in Christ doth bring forth good works; and therefore every man must examine himself diligently, to know whether he have the same true lively faith in his heart unfeignedly, or not; which he shall know by the fruits thereof. Many that professed the faith of Christ were in this error, that they thought they knew God and believed in him, when in their life they declared the contrary: which error St. John in his first Epistle confuting, writeth in this wise: *Hereby we are certified that we know God, if we observe his commandments. He that saith he knoweth God, and observeth not his commandments, is a liar, and the truth is not in him* (1 John ii). And again he saith: *Whosoever sinneth doth not see God, nor know him: Let no man deceive you, well-beloved children* (1 John iii). And moreover he saith: *Hereby we know that we be of the truth, and so we shall persuade our hearts before him. For if our own hearts reprove us, God is above our hearts, and knoweth all things. Well-beloved, if our hearts reprove us not, then have we confidence in God, and shall have of him whatsoever we ask, because we keep his commandments, and do those things that please him* (1 John iii). And yet further he saith: *Every man that believeth that Jesus is Christ, is born of God; and we know that whosoever is born of God doth not sin: But the generation of God purgeth him, and the devil doth not touch him* (1 John v). And finally he concludeth, and shewing the cause why he wrote this Epistle, saith: *For this cause have I thus written unto you, that you may know that you have everlasting life, which do believe in the son of God* (1 John v). And in his third Epistle he confirmeth the whole matter of faith and works in few words, saying: *He that doth well is of God, and he that doth evil knoweth not God* (3 John).

And as St. John saith, that the lively knowledge and faith of God bringeth forth good works; so saith he likewise of hope and charity, that they cannot stand with evil living. Of hope he writeth thus: *We know that when God shall appear, we shall be like unto him, for we shall see him even as he is: And whosoever hath this hope in him doth purify himself, like as God is pure* (1 John iii). And of charity he saith these words: *He that doth keep God's word or commandment, in him is truly the perfect love of God* (1 John ii). And again he saith: *This is the love of God, that we should keep his commandments* (1 John v). And St. John wrote not this as a subtle proposition devised of his own phantasy, but as a most certain and necessary truth, taught unto him by Christ himself, the eternal and infallible verity, who in many places doth most clearly affirm, that faith, hope, and charity, cannot consist without good and godly works. Of faith he saith: *He that believeth in the son hath everlasting life; but he that believeth not in the son shall not see that life, but the wrath of God remaineth upon him* (1 John v). And the same he confirmeth with a double oath, saying: *Forsooth and forsooth, I say unto you, he that believeth in me hath everlasting life* (John vi). Now forasmuch as he that believeth in Christ hath everlasting life, it must needs consequently follow, that he that hath this faith must have also good works, and be studious to observe God's commandments obediently. For to them that have evil works, and lead their life in disobedience and transgression of God's commandments without repentance, pertaineth not everlasting life, but everlasting death, as Christ himself saith: *They that do well shall go into life eternal; but they that do evil shall go into the eternal fire* (Matt. xxv). Again he saith: *I am the first letter and the last, the beginning and the ending: To him that is athirst, I will give of the well of the water of life freely: He that hath the victory shall have all things, and I will be his God, and he shall be my son: but they that be fearful, mistrusting God, and lacking faith, they that be cursed people, and murderers, and fornicators, and sorcerers, and idolators, and all liars, shall have their portion in the lake that burneth with fire and brimstone, which is the second death* (Apoc. xxi).

*Charity bringeth forth good works.* And as Christ undoubtedly affirmeth, that true faith bringeth forth good works, so doth he say likewise of charity: *Whosoever hath my commandments, and keepeth them, that is he that loveth me.* And after he saith: *He that loveth me, will keep my word, and he that loveth me not, keepeth not my words* (John xiv). And as the love of God is tried by good works, so is the fear of God also, as the wise man saith: *The dread of God putteth away sin* (Ecclus. i). And also he saith: *He that feareth God will do good works* (Ecclus. xv).

A man may soon deceive himself, and think in his own phantasy that he by faith knoweth God, loveth him, feareth him, and belongeth to him, when in very deed he doth nothing less. For the trial of all these things is a very godly and Christian life. He that feeleth his heart set to seek God's honour, and studieth to know the will and commandments of God, and to conform himself thereunto, and leadeth not his life after the desire of his own flesh to serve the devil by sin, but setteth his mind to serve God for God's own sake, and for his sake also to love all his neighbours, whether they be friends or adversaries, doing good to every man, as opportunity serveth, and willingly hurting no man: such a man may well rejoice in God, perceiving by the trade of his life, that he unfeignedly hath the right knowledge of God, a lively faith, a constant hope, a true and unfeigned love and fear of God. But he that casteth away the yoke of God's commandments from his neck, and giveth himself to live without true repentance, after his own sensual mind and pleasure, not regarding to know God's word, and much less to live according thereunto; such a man clearly deceiveth himself, and seeth not his own heart, if he thinketh that he either knoweth God, loveth him, feareth him, or trusteth in him. Some peradventure phantasy in themselves that they belong to God, although they live in sin, and so they come to the church, and shew themselves as God's dear children. But St. John saith plainly: *If we say that we have any company with God, and walk in darkness, we do lie* (1 John i). Other do vainly think that they know and love God, although they pass not of his commandments. But St. John saith clearly: *He that saith, I know God, and keepeth not his commandments, he is a liar* (1 John ii). Some falsely persuade themselves, that they love God, when they hate their neighbours. But St. John saith manifestly: *If any man say, I love God, and yet hateth his brother, he is a liar. He that saith that he is in the light, and hateth his brother, he is still in darkness. He that loveth his brother dwelleth in the light; but he that hateth his brother is in darkness, and walketh in darkness, and knoweth not whither he goeth: for darkness hath blinded his eyes* (1 John ii).

And moreover he saith: *Hereby we manifestly know the children of God from the children of the devil. He that doth not righteously is not the child of God, nor he that hateth his brother* (1 John iii).

Deceive not yourselves therefore, thinking that you have faith in God, or that you love God, or do trust in him, or do fear him, when you live in sin: for then your ungodly and sinful life declareth the contrary, whatsoever ye say or think. It pertaineth to a Christian man to have this true Christian faith, and to try himself whether he hath it or no, and to know what belongeth to it, and how it doth work in him. It is not the world that we can trust to; the world, and all that is therein, is but vanity. It is God that must be our defence and protection against all temptation of wickedness and sin, errors, superstition, idolatry, and all evil. If all the world were on our side, and God against us, what could the world avail us? Therefore let us set our whole faith and trust in God, and neither the world, the devil, nor all the power of them shall prevail against us. Let us therefore, good Christian people, try and examine our faith, what it is: let us not flatter ourselves, but look upon our works, and so judge of our faith what it is. Christ himself speaketh of this matter, and saith, *The tree is known by the fruit* (Luke vi). Therefore let us do good works, and thereby declare our faith to be the lively Christian faith. Let us, by such virtues as ought to spring out of faith, show our election to be sure and stable, as St. Peter teacheth, *Endeavour yourselves to make your calling and election certain by good works* (2 Pet. i). And also he saith, *Minister or declare in your faith virtue, in virtue knowledge, in knowledge temperance, in temperance patience, again in patience godliness, in godliness brotherly charity, in brotherly charity love* (2 Pet. i). So shall we shew indeed that we have the very lively Christian faith, and may so both certify our conscience the better that we be in the right faith, and also by these means confirm other men.

If these fruits do not follow, we do but mock with God, deceive ourselves, and also other men. Well may we bear the name of Christian men, but we do lack the true faith that doth belong thereunto: for true faith doth ever bring forth good works, as St. James saith: *Shew me thy faith by thy deeds* (James ii). Thy deeds and works must be an open testimonial of thy faith: otherwise thy faith, being without good works, is but the devil's faith, the faith of the wicked, a phantasy of faith, and not a true Christian faith. And like as the devils and evil people be nothing the better for their counterfeit faith, but it is unto them the more cause of damnation: so they that be christened, and have received knowledge of God, and of Christ's merits, and yet of a set purpose do live idly, without good works, thinking the name of a naked faith to be either sufficient for them, or else setting their minds upon vain pleasures of this world, do live in sin without repentance, not uttering the fruits that do belong to such an high profession; upon such presumptuous persons, and wilful sinners, must needs remain the great vengeance of God, and eternal punishment in hell, prepared for the devil and wicked livers.

Therefore as you profess the name of Christ, good Christian people, let no such phantasy and imagination of faith at any time beguile you; but be sure of your faith, try it by your living, look upon the fruits that cometh of it, mark the increase of love and charity by it toward God and your neighbour, and so shall you perceive it to be a true lively faith. If you feel and perceive such a faith in you, rejoice in it; and be diligent to maintain it, and keep it still in you; let it be daily increasing, and more and more be well working, and so shall you be sure that you shall please God by this faith; and at the length, as other faithful men have done before, so shall ye, when his will is, come to him, and receive *the end and final reward of your faith*, as St. Peter nameth it, *the salvation of your souls* (1 Pet. i): the which God grant us, that hath promised the same unto his faithful; to whom be all honour and glory, world without end. Amen.

# An Homily or Sermon of Good Works Annexed unto Faith

IN THE last sermon was declared unto you, what the lively and true faith of a Christian man is; that it causeth not a man to be idle, but to be occuppied in bringing forth good works, as occasion serveth.

<small>No good work can be done without faith.</small> Now, by God's grace, shall be declared the second thing that before was noted of faith; that without it can no good work be done, acceptable and pleasant unto God; *For as a branch cannot bear fruit of itself,* saith our saviour Christ, *except it abide in the vine; so cannot you, except you abide in me. I am the vine, and you be the branches: he that abideth in me, and I in him, he bringeth forth much fruit: for without me you can do nothing* (John xv). And St. Paul proveth, that Enoch had faith, because he pleased God: *For without faith,* saith he, *it is not possible to please God* (Heb. xi). And again, to the Romans he saith: *Whatsoever work is done without faith, it is sin* (Rom. xiv). Faith giveth life to the soul; and they be as much dead to God that lack faith, as they be to the world whose bodies lack souls. Without faith, all that is done of us is but dead before God, although the work seem never so gay and glorious before man. Even as a picture graven or painted is but a dead representation of the thing itself, and is without life, or any manner of moving; so be the works of all unfaithful persons before God: they do appear to be lively works, and indeed they be but dead, not availing to the eternal life: they be but shadows and shows of lively and good things, and not good and lively things indeed: for true faith doth give life to the work, and out of such faith come good works, that be very good works indeed; and without it no work is good before God.

As saith St. Augustin: 'We must set no good works before faith, nor think that before faith a man may do any good work; for such works, although they seem unto men to be praiseworthy, yet indeed they be but vain, and not allowed before God. They be as the course of a horse that runneth out of the way, which taketh great labour, but to no purpose. Let no man, therefore,' saith he, 'reckon upon his good works before his faith; whereas faith was not, good works were not. The intent,' saith he, 'maketh good works; but faith must guide and order the intent of man.' And Christ saith, *If thine eye be naught, thy whole body is full of darkness* (Matt. vi). 'The eye doth signify the intent,' saith St. Augustin, 'wherewith a man doth a thing: so that he which doth not his good works with a godly intent, and a true faith that worketh by love, the whole body beside, that is to say, all the whole number of his works, is dark, and there is no light in it.' For good deeds be not measured by the facts themselves, and so dissevered from vices; but by the ends and intents, for the which they be done. If a heathen man clothe the naked, feed the hungry, and do such other like works; yet, because he doth them not in faith for the honour and love of God, they be but dead, vain, and fruitless works to him. Faith it is that doth commend the work to God: 'for,' as St. Augustin saith, 'whether thou wilt or no, that work that cometh not of faith, is naught;' where the faith of Christ is not the foundation, there is no good work, what building soever we make. 'There is one work, in the which be all good works, that is, faith which worketh by charity:' if thou have it, thou hast the ground of all good works; for the virtues of strength, wisdom, temperance, and justice, be all referred unto this same faith. Without this faith we have not them, but only the names and shadows of them; as St. Augustin saith: 'All the life of them that lack the true faith is sin, and nothing is good without him that is the author of goodness: where he is not, there is but feigned virtue, although it be in the best works.' And St. Augustin, declaring this verse of the Psalm, *The turtle hath found a nest where she may keep her young birds*, saith, that Jews, heretics, and pagans do good works; they clothe the naked, feed the poor, and do other good works of mercy: but because they be not done in the true faith, therefore the birds be lost. But if they remain in faith, then faith is the nest and safeguard of their birds, that is to say, safeguard of their good works, that the reward of them be not utterly lost.

And this matter (which St. Augustin at large in many books disputeth) St. Ambrose concludeth in few words, saying, 'He that by nature would withstand vice, either by natural will or reason, he doth in vain garnish the time of this life, and attaineth not the very true virtues; for without the worshipping of the true God, that which seemeth to be virtue is vice.'

And yet most plainly to this purpose writeth St. John Chrisostome in this wise, 'You shall find many which have not the true faith, and be not of the flock of Christ, and yet, as it appeareth, they flourish in good works of mercy; you shall find them full of pity, compassion, and given to justice; and yet, for all that, they have no fruit of their works, because the chief work lacketh. For when the Jews asked of Christ, what they should do to work good works, he answered, *This is the work of God, to believe in him whom he sent* (John vi): so that he called faith the work of God. And as soon as a man hath faith, anon he shall flourish in good works; for faith of itself is full of good works, and nothing is good without faith.' And for a similitude, he saith, that 'they which glister and shine in good works without faith in God, be like dead men, which have goodly and precious tombs, and yet it availeth them nothing. Faith may not be naked without works, for then it is no true faith: and when it is adjoined to works, yet it is above the works. For as men, that be very men indeed, first have life, and after be nourished; so must our faith in Christ go before, and after be nourished with good works. And life may be without nourishment, but nourishment cannot be without life. A man must needs be nourished by good works, but first he must have faith. He that doth good deeds, yet without faith, he hath not life. I can show a man that by faith without works lived, and came to heaven: but without faith never man had life. The thief, that was hanged when Christ suffered, did believe only, and the most merciful God did justify him. And because no man shall object, that he lacked time to do good works, for else he would have done them: truth it is, and I will not contend therein; but this I will surely affirm, that faith only saved him. If he had lived, and not regarded faith and the works thereof, he should have lost his salvation again. But this is the effect that I say, that faith by itself saved him, but works by themselves never justified any man.' Here ye have heard the mind of St. Chrisostome, whereby you may perceive, that neither faith is without works, (having opportunity thereto,) nor works can avail to eternal life without faith.

<small>What works they are that spring of faith.</small> Now to proceed to the third part, which in the former sermon was noted of faith, that is to say, what manner of works they be which spring out of true faith, and lead faithful men unto eternal life: this cannot be known so well as by our saviour Christ himself, who was asked of a certain great man the same question: *What works shall I do*, said a prince, *to come to everlasting life?* To whom Jesus answered: *If thou wilt come to eternal life, keep the commandments.* But the prince, not satisfied herewith, asked farther: *Which commandments?* (Matt. xix). The scribes and Pharisees

had made so many of their own laws and traditions, to bring men to heaven, beside God's commandments, that this man was in doubt whether he should come to heaven by those laws and traditions, or by the laws of God; and therefore he asked Christ, which commandments he meant. Whereunto Christ made him a plain answer, rehearsing the commandments of God, saying: *Thou shalt not kill, Thou shalt not commit adultery, Thou shalt not steal, Thou shalt not bear false witness, Honour thy father and mother*, and, *Love thy neighbour as thyself* (Matt. xix). By which words Christ declared, that the laws of God be the very way that do lead to eternal life, and not the traditions and laws of men. So that this is to be taken for a most true lesson taught by Christ's own mouth, that the works of the moral commandments of God be the very true works of faith, which lead to the blessed life to come. *The works that lead to heaven be the works of God's commandments.*

But the blindness and malice of man, even from the beginning, hath ever been ready to fall from God's commandments: as Adam the first man, having but one commandment, that he should not eat of the fruit forbidden; notwithstanding God's commandment, he gave credit unto the woman seduced by the subtle persuasion of the serpent, and so followed his own will, and left God's commandment. And ever since that time, all his succession hath been so blinded through original sin, that they have been ever ready to decline from God and his law, and to invent a new way unto salvation by works of their own device; so much, that almost all the world, forsaking the true honour of the only eternal living God, wandered about in their own phantasies, worshipping some the sun, the moon, the stars; some Jupiter, Juno, Diana, Saturnus, Apollo, Neptunus, Ceres, Bacchus, and other dead men and women: some therewith not satisfied, worshipped divers kinds of beasts, birds, fish, fowl, and serpents; every region, town, and house in a manner being divided, and setting up images of such things as they liked, and worshipping the same. Such was the rudeness of the people after they fell to their own phantasies, and left the eternal living God and his commandments, that they devised innumerable images and gods. *Man from his first falling from God's commandments, hath ever been ready to do the like, and to devise works of his own phantasy to please God withal. The devices and idolatry of the Gentiles.*

In which error and blindness they did remain, until such time as Almighty God, pitying the blindness of man, sent his true prophet Moses into the world, to reprehend this extreme madness, and to teach the people to know the only living God, and his true honour and worship. But the corrupt inclination of man was so much given to follow his own phantasies, and, as you would say, to favour his own bird that he brought up himself, that all the admonitions, exhortations, benefits, and threatenings of God could not keep him from such his inventions. For notwithstanding all the benefits of God showed unto the people of Israel, yet when Moses went up into the mountain to speak with Almighty God, he had tarried there but a few days, when the people began to invent new gods: and, as it came into their heads, they made a calf of gold, and kneeled down and worshipped it. And after that they followed the Moabites, and worshipped Beelphegor, the Moabites' god. Read the book of Judges, the book of the Kings, and the Prophets; and there you shall find how inconstant the people were, how full of inventions, and more ready to run after their own phantasies, than God's most holy commandments. There shall you read of Baal, Moloch, Chamos, Mechom, Baalpeor, Astaroth, Bel the dragon, Priapus, the brazen serpent, the twelve signs, and many other, unto whose images the people with great devotion invented pilgrimages, preciously decking and censing them, kneeling down and offering to them, thinking that an high merit before God, and to be esteemed above the precepts and commandments of God. And where, at that time, God commanded no sacrifice to be made but in Jerusalem only, they did clean contrary, making altars and sacrifices every where, in hills, in woods, and in houses, not regarding God's commandments, but esteeming their own phantasies and devotion to be better than them. And the error hereof was so spread abroad, that not only the unlearned people, but also the priests and teachers of the people, partly by glory and avarice were corrupted, and partly by ignorance blindly seduced with the same abominations: so much, that king Achab having but only Helias a true teacher and minister of God, there were viii. hundred and fifty priests that persuaded him to honour Baal, and to do sacrifice in the woods or groves. And so continued that horrible error, until the three noble kings, as Josaphat, Ezechias, and Josias, God's elect ministers, destroyed the same clearly, and reduced the people from such their feigned inventions unto the very commandments of God: for the which thing their immortal reward and glory doth and shall remain with God for ever.

*The devices and idolatries of the Israelites*

And beside the foresaid inventions, the inclination of man to have his own holy devotions devised new sects and religions, called Pharisees, Sadducees, and scribes, with many holy and godly traditions and ordinances, as it seemed by the outward appearance and goodly glistering of the works, but in very deed all tending to idolatry, superstition, and hypocrisy; their hearts within being full of malice, pride, covetousness, and all iniquity. Against which sects and their pretensed holiness Christ cried out more vehemently than he did against any other persons, saying, and often repeating these words: *Woe be to you, scribes and Pharisees, ye hypocrites! for you make clean the vessel without, but within you be full of ravine and filthiness: Thou blind Pharisee and hypocrite! first make the inward part clean* (Matt. xxiii). For notwithstanding all the goodly traditions and outward shew of good works devised of their own imagination, whereby they appeared to the world most religious and holy of all men; yet Christ, who saw their hearts, knew that they were inwardly, in the sight of God, most unholy, most abominable, and farthest from God of all men. Therefore said he unto them, *Hypocrites, the prophet Esay spake full truly of you, when he said, This people honour me with their lips, but their heart is far from me. They worship me in vain that teach doctrines and commandments of men: for you leave the commandments of God to keep your own traditions* (Matt. xv; Isai. xix).

<small>Religions and sects among the Jews.</small>

And though Christ said, *They worshipped God in vain that teach doctrines and commandments of men*; yet he meant not thereby to overthrow all men's commandments; for he himself was ever obedient to the princes and their laws made for good order and governance of the people: but he reproved the laws and traditions made by the scribes and Pharisees, which were not made only for good order of the people, (as the civil laws were,) but they were so highly extolled, that they were made to be a right and sincere worshipping of God, as they had been equal with God's laws, or above them: for many of God's laws could not be kept, but were fain to give place unto them. This arrogancy God detested, that man should so advance his laws to make them equal with God's laws, wherein the true honouring and right worshipping of God standeth, and to make his laws for them to be omitted. God hath appointed his laws, whereby his pleasure is to be honoured. His pleasure is also, that all man's laws, being not

<small>Man's laws must be observed and kept, but not as God's laws.</small>

contrary to his laws, shall be obeyed and kept, as good and necessary for every commonweal, but not as things wherein principally his honour resteth: and all civil and man's laws either be, or should be made, to induce men the better to observe God's laws, that consequently God should be the better honoured by them.

Howbeit, the scribes and Pharisees were not content that their laws should be no higher esteemed than other positive and civil laws; nor would not have them called by the name of other temporal laws; but called them holy and godly traditions, and would have them esteemed, not only for a right and true worshipping of God, as God's laws be indeed, but also to be the most high honouring of God, to the which the commandments of God should give place. And for this cause did Christ so vehemently speak against them, saying, Your traditions, which men esteem so high, be abomination before God: for commonly of such traditions, followeth the transgression of God's commandments, and a more devotion in the observing of such things, and a greater conscience in breaking of them, than of the commandments of God (Luke xvi). As the scribes and Pharisees so superstitiously and scrupulously kept the sabbath, that they were offended with Christ because he healed sick men; and with his apostles, because they being sore hungry gathered the ears of corn to eat upon that day. And because his disciples washed not their hands so often as the traditions required, the scribes and Pharisees quarrelled with Christ, saying: *Why do thy disciples break the traditions of the seniors?* (Matt. xv.) But Christ objected against them, that they, for to observe their own traditions, did teach men to break the very commandments of God: for they taught the people such a devotion, that they offered their goods into the treasure-house of the temple, under the pretence of God's honour, leaving their fathers and mothers, to whom they were chiefly bound, unholpen; and so they brake the commandments of God, to keep their own traditions. They esteemed more an oath made by the gold or oblation in the temple, than an oath made in the name of God himself, or of the temple. They were more studious to pay their tithes of small things, than to do the greater things commanded of God, as works of mercy, or to do justice, or to deal sincerely, uprightly, and faithfully with God and man: *These*, saith Christ, *ought to be done, and the other not omitted* (Matt. xxiii). And, to be

[margin notes: Holy traditions were esteemed as God's laws. Holiness of man's device is commonly occasion that God is offended.]

short, they were of so blind judgment, that they stumbled at a straw, and leaped over a block; they would, as it were, *nicely take a fly out of their cup, and drink down a whole camel*; and therefore Christ called them *blind guides*, warning his disciples from time to time to eschew their doctrine. For although they seemed to the world to be most perfect men, both in living and teaching, yet was their life but hypocrisy, and their doctrine but sour leaven, mixt with superstition, idolatry, and preposterous judgment, setting up the traditions and ordinances of man, in the stead of God's commandments.

Thus have you heard how much the world, from the beginning until Christ's time, was ever ready to fall from the commandments of God, and to seek other means to honour and serve him, after a devotion imagined of their own heads; and how they extolled their own traditions as high or above God's commandments; which hath happened also in our times (the more it is to be lamented) no less than it did among the Jews, and that by the corruption, or at the least by the negligence of them that chiefly ought to have preferred God's commandments, and to have preserved the sincere and heavenly doctrine left by Christ. What man, having any judgment or learning, joined with a true zeal unto God, doth not see and lament to have entered into Christ's religion, such false doctrine, superstition, idolatry, hypocrisy, and other enormities and abuses, so as by little and little, through the sour leaven thereof, the sweet bread of God's holy word hath been much hindered and laid apart? Never had the Jews in their most blindness so many pilgrimages unto images, nor used so much kneeling, kissing, and censing of them, as hath been used in our time. Sects and feigned religions were neither the forty part so many among the Jews, nor more superstitiously and ungodly abused, than of late days they have been among us: which sects and religions had so many hypocritical works in their state of religion, as they arrogantly named it, that their lamps, as they said, ran always over, able to satisfy not only for their own sins, but also for all other their benefactors, brothers, and sisters of their religion, as most ungodly and craftily they had persuaded the multitude of ignorant people; keeping in divers places, as it were, marts or markets of merits, being full of their holy relics, images, shrines, and works of supererogation ready to be sold. And all things which they had were called holy, holy cowls, holy girdles, holy pardoned beads, holy shoes, holy rules, and all full of holiness. And what

*[margin: Sects and religions amongst Christian men.]*

thing can be more foolish, more superstitious, or ungodly, than that men, women, and children, should wear a friar's coat to deliver them from agues or pestilence? or when they die, or when they be buried, cause it to be cast upon them, in hope thereby to be saved? Which superstition, although (thanks be to God) it hath been little used in this realm, yet in divers other realms it hath been and yet is used among many, both learned and unlearned. But, to pass over the innumerable superstitiousness that hath been in strange apparel, in silence, in dormitory, in cloister, in chapter, in choice of meats and in drinks, and in such like things, let us consider what enormities and abuses have been in the three chief principal points, which they called the three essentials of religion, that is to say, obedience, chastity, and wilful poverty.

*The three chief vows of religion* First, under pretence of obedience to their father in religion, (which obedience they made themselves,) they were exempted, by their rules and canons, from the obedience of their natural father and mother, and from the obedience of emperor and king, and all temporal power, whom of very duty by God's laws they were bound to obey. And so the profession of their obedience not due was a renunciation of their due obedience. And how their profession of chastity was observed, it is more honesty to pass over in silence, and let the world judge of that which is well known, than with unchaste words, by expressing of their unchaste life, to offend chaste and godly ears. And as for their wilful poverty, it was such, that when in possessions, jewels, plate, and riches, they were equal or above merchants, gentlemen, barons, earls, and dukes; yet by this subtle sophistical term, *Proprium in communi*, they deluded the world, persuading, that notwithstanding all their possessions and riches, yet they observed their vow, and were in wilful poverty. But for all their riches, they might neither help father nor mother, nor other that were indeed very needy and poor, without the licence of their father abbot, prior, or warden; and yet they might take of every man, but they might not give aught to any man, no not to them whom the laws of God bound them to help: and so, through their traditions and rules, the laws of God could bear no rule with them: and therefore of them might be most truly said that which Christ spake unto the Pharisees: *You break the commandments of God by your traditions: you honour God with your lips, but your hearts be far from him.* And the longer prayers they used by day and by night, under pretence of such holiness, to get the favour of widows and other simple folks, that they might sing trentals and service for their husbands and friends, and admit them into their suffrages; the more truly is verified of them the saying of Christ: *Woe be to you, scribes and Pharisees, hypocrites! for you devour widows' houses under colour of long prayers; therefore your damnation shall be the greater. Woe be to you, scribes and Pharisees, hypocrites! for you go about by sea and by land to make mo novices, and new brethren; and when they be admitted of your sect, you make them the children of hell worse than yourselves be* (Matt. xxiii).

Honour be to God, who did put light in the heart of his faithful and true minister of most famous memory, King Henry the eight, and gave him the knowledge of his word, and an earnest affection to seek his glory, and to put away all such superstitious and pharisaical sects by Antichrist invented, and set up again the true word of God, and glory of his most blessed name, as he gave the like spirit unto the most noble and famous princes, Josaphat, Josias, and Ezechias. God grant all us the King's Highness faithful and true subjects, to feed of the sweet and savoury bread of God's own word, and (as Christ commanded) to eschew all our pharisaical and papistical leaven of man's feigned religion: which, although it were before God most abominable, and contrary to God's commandments and Christ's pure religion, yet it was extolled to be a most godly life, and highest state of perfection: as though a man might be more godly and more perfect, by keeping the rules, traditions, and professions of men, than by keeping the holy commandments of God.

And briefly to pass over the ungodly and counterfeit religions, let us rehearse some other kinds of papistical superstitions and abuses, as of beads, of lady psalters, and rosaries, of fifteen Oos, of St. Barnard's verses, of St. Agathe's letters; of purgatory, of masses satisfactory, of stations and jubilees, of feigned relics, of hallowed beads, bells, bread, water, palms, candles, fire, and such other; of superstitious fastings, of fraternities, of pardons, with such like merchandize, which were so esteemed and abused to the great prejudice of God's glory and commandments, that they were made most high and most holy things, whereby to attain to the eternal life, or remission of sin: yea also vain inventions, unfruitful ceremonies, and ungodly laws, decrees, and councils of Rome, were in such wise advanced, that nothing was thought comparable in authority, wisdom, learning, and godliness unto them; so Other devices and superstitions. Decrees and decretals.

that the laws of Rome, as they said, were to be received of all men as the four evangelists, to the which all laws of princes must give place: and the laws of God also partly were omitted and less esteemed, that the said laws, decrees, and councils, with their traditions and ceremonies, might be more duly observed, and had in greater reverence. Thus was the people through ignorance so blinded with the goodly shew and appearance of those things, that they thought the observing of them to be a more holiness, a more perfect service and honouring of God, and more pleasing to God, than the keeping of God's commandments. Such hath been the corrupt inclination of man ever, superstitiously given to make new honouring of God of his own head, and then to have more affection and devotion to observe that, than to search out God's holy commandments, and to keep them. And furthermore, to take God's commandments for men's commandments, and men's commandments for God's commandments, yea, and for the highest and most perfect and holy of all God's commandments. And so was all confused, that scant well learned men, and but a small number of them knew, or at the least would know, and durst affirm the truth, to separate God's commandments from the commandments of men. Whereupon did grow much error, superstition, idolatry, vain religion, preposterous judgment, great contention, with all ungodly living.

*An exhortation to the keeping of God's commandments.* Wherefore, as you have any zeal to the right and pure honouring of God, as you have any regard to your own souls, and to the life that is to come, which is both without pain and without end, apply yourselves chiefly above all thing to read and to hear God's word, mark diligently therein what his will is you shall do, and with all your endeavour apply yourselves to follow the same. First, you must *A brief rehearsal of God's commandments.* have an assured faith in God, and give yourselves wholly unto him, love him in prosperity and adversity, and dread to offend him evermore: then, for his sake, love all men, friends and foes, because they be his creation and image, and redeemed by Christ, as ye are. Cast in your minds, how you may do good unto all men unto your powers, and hurt no man. Obey all your superiors and governors; serve your masters faithfully and diligently, as well in their absence as in their presence, not for dread of punishment only, but for conscience sake, knowing that you are bound so to do by God's commandments. Disobey not your fathers and mothers, but honour them, help them, and please them to your power. Oppress not, kill not, beat not, neither slander nor hate any man; but love all men, speak well of all men, help and succour every man as you may, yea, even your enemies that hate you, that speak evil of you, and that do hurt you. Take no man's goods, nor covet your neighbour's goods wrongfully; but content yourselves with that which ye get truly; and also bestow your own goods charitably, as need and case requireth. Flee all idolatry, witchcraft, and perjury; commit no manner of adultery, fornication, nor other unchasteness, in will nor in deed, with any other man's wife, widow, maid, or otherwise. And travailing continually during your life thus in the observing the commandments of God, (wherein consisteth the pure, principal, and direct honour of God, and which God hath ordained to be the right trade and path-way unto heaven,) you shall not fail, as Christ hath promised, to come to that blessed and eternal life, where you shall live in glory and joy with God for ever: to whom be laud, honour, and impery, for ever and ever. Amen.

## Hugh Latimer

LATIMER, SECOND only in importance to Cranmer in the creation of the Church of England (and, eventually, theologically slightly to the 'left' of him), was born in about 1485. He was the son of a Leicestershire yeoman farmer. He went up to Clare College, Cambridge, in 1500, and in 1522 was made a university preacher. He had been ordained in 1514, as, in his words, 'obstinate a papist as any in England'. But by 1525 he had become a Protestant: probably converted by Thomas Bilney, who was burnt at Norwich in 1531 under circumstances that are not altogether clear. Latimer's views had been shifting in the decade following his ordination. But he underwent a crisis of conscience, for in 1524 he wrote a refutation of Melanchthon, one of the chief continental reformers. In 1525, though one of only twelve priests licensed by Cambridge to preach anywhere in England, he refused to refute Luther. He cleared himself, and continued to preach against abuses. The only time in his life that he submitted was in 1532, after he had been censured by Convocation for Protestant tendencies. He became Bishop of Worcester in 1535, but, although an adviser to the King, between then and the end of the reign was in more or less constant trouble. In 1539 he resigned his see, by the King's wish, after having bitterly opposed the Six Articles. He was in the Tower in that year and again in 1546. His main influence, like that of Cranmer, was exercised in the reign of Edward VI; but he refused reinstatement to his bishopric, preferring to devote himself to preaching. His real vocation was as a preacher. He preached his most famous and characteristic sermon, 'of the Plough', in 1548. This is given below. Until the end of Edward's reign he was a very popular figure; under Mary he was, of course, arrested (1553), excommunicated (1554) and finally—having steadfastly refused to recant—burnt at Oxford (1555). The manner in which he met his death, with Ridley (Bishop of Rochester), is famous and exemplary.

Latimer's private life is somewhat obscure. He was, in contemporary parlance, 'charismatic': he could move the hearts and minds of men. What he came to believe he believed with great intensity. He was not, perhaps, subtle; but he was not intellectually simple. His preaching seems to be rambling, homely, a 'matey chat' as one writer has put it: he seems to invite his listeners casually into the ramifications of his mind. But it is all planned and put together with great skill. He is vivid, witty and lucid, often sarcastic, and he understands the emotions of the common people as well as the simple-mindedness of most of them. Despite his gift for homeliness, his common touch—doubtless arising from his agricultural origins—he was not as gentle or as tolerant of others as Cranmer: he would preach at the execution of a heretic, and he would approve of the putting to death of the family of an absent Catholic (unfortunately that of Reginald Pole—including his mother the Duchess of Salisbury—who later became one of the instruments of his destruction). But these were immoderate days in matters of religion, and the humanity of Latimer's sermons is a unique quality: they can touch the hearts of learned and unlearned alike, and they reflect the desperate and often puzzled honesty that conflicted, within him, with his emotional intensity and consequent sense of commitment. They are at the beginning of the tradition of 'plain English'. As they demonstrate, he was most interested in the living hearts and souls of men; the subtleties of doctrine in themselves were less important to him than the notion of salvation by mere works; he was as vehemently anti-Papist as he was Protestant. Though Latimer was as obviously English as any of the original creators of the English Church, Luther's actual *doctrines* (for example, the Real Presence at Communion) would do more easily for him than for Cranmer, who was altogether more theologically inclined. But he rejected the notion of the priesthood of all believers, later to be revived by the Pietists.

## THE SERMON OF THE PLOUGH

(*A Notable Sermon of the Reverend Father Master Hugh Latimer*, Preached in the Shrouds at Paul's Church in London, on the 18th day of January, anno 1548)
Rom. 15:4.
*Quaecunque scripta sunt ad nostram doctrinam scripta sunt. [For whatsoever things were written aforetime were written for our learning.]*

THIS IS known as the 'Sermon of the Plough', though Latimer did not give it that title. It would have been preached on a wet or snowy day, since the Shrouds, or 'crowds', was a chapel under the choir of St Paul's Church which afforded shelter for the congregation. This would have been large, for Latimer was then at the height of his fame and influence. The 'first sermon', and the 'three sermons past' to which he refers at the beginning may be lost; but their substance is contained in the three extant sermons on the Sower and the Householder, which are to be found in his *Sermons and Remains* (1844-5).

It is witness to Latimer's lucidity that this sermon needs little commentary: its general intent, its vehement anti-Catholic individualism, its emphasis on reliance upon the Scriptures themselves, its definition of the priestly function, are perfectly clear. The reformers needed such a passionate but earthy voice, and they found it in Latimer. A farmer's son, the ploughman-prelate equation was for him a peculiarly appropriate one.

[Notes on asterisked passages in the text are at the end of the sermon.]

'ALL THINGS which are written, are written for our erudition and knowledge. All things that are written in God's book, in the Bible book, in the book of the holy scripture, are written to be our doctrine.' I told you in my first sermon, honourable audience, that I purposed to declare unto you two things, The one, what seed should be sown in God's field, in God's plough land. And the other, who should be the sowers.

That is to say, what doctrine is to be taught in Christ's church and congregation, and what men should be the teachers and preachers of it. The first part I have told you in the three sermons past, in which I have assayed to set forth my plough, to prove what I could do. And now I shall tell you who be the ploughers; for God's word is a seed to be sown in God's field, that is, the faithful congregation, and the preacher is the sower. And it is in the gospel; *Exivit qui seminat seminare semen suum*'; 'He that soweth, the husbandman, the ploughman, went forth to sow his seed.' So that a preacher is resembled to a ploughman, as it is in another place; *nemo admota aratro manu, et a tergo respiciens aptus est regno Dei.* 'No man that putteth his hand to the plough, and looketh back, is apt for the kingdom of God.' (Luke ix.) That is to say, let no preacher be negligent in doing his office. Albeit this is one of the places that hath been racked,* as I told you of racking scriptures. And I have been one of them myself that hath racked it, I cry God mercy for it; and have been one of them that have believed and expounded it against religious persons that would forsake their order which they had professed, and would go out of their cloister: whereas indeed it toucheth not monkery, nor maketh any thing at all for any such matter; but it is directly spoken of diligent preaching of the word of God.

For preaching of the gospel is one of God's plough-works, and the preacher is one of God's ploughmen. Ye may not be offended with my similitude, in that I compare preaching to the labour and work of ploughing, and the preacher to a ploughman: Ye may not be offended with this my similitude, for I have been slandered of some persons for such things. It hath been said of me, 'Oh, Latimer, nay, as for him, I will never believe him while I live, nor never trust him, for he likened our blessed lady to a saffron-bag:' where indeed I never used that similitude. But it was, as I have said unto you before now, according to that which Peter saw before in the spirit of prophecy, and said, that there should come afterward, 'men *per quos via veritatis maledictis afficeretur*, there should come fellows by whom the way of truth should be evil spoken of, and slandered.' But in case I had used this similitude, it had not been to be reproved, but might have been without reproach. For I might have said thus; as the saffron-bag that hath been full of saffron, or hath had saffron in it, doth ever after savour and smell of the sweet saffron that it contained; so our blessed lady, which conceived and bare Christ in her womb, did ever after resemble the manners and virtues of that precious babe that she bare. And what had our blessed lady been the worse for this? Or what dishonour was this to our blessed lady? But as preachers must be wary and circumspect,* that they give not any just occasion to be slandered and ill spoken of by the hearers, so must not the auditors be offended without cause. For heaven is in the gospel likened to a mustard-seed: it is compared also to a piece of leaven; and as Christ saith, that at the last day he will come like a thief; and what dishonour is this to God? Or what derogation is this to heaven? Ye may not then, I say, be offended with my similitude, for because I liken preaching to a ploughman's labour, and a prelate to a ploughman. But now you will ask me whom I call a prelate? A prelate is that man, whatsoever he be, that hath a flock to be taught of him; whosoever hath any spiritual charge in the faithful congregation, and whosoever he be that hath cure of souls. And well may the preacher and the ploughman be likened together: First, for their labour of all seasons of the year; for there is no time of the year in which the ploughman hath not some special work to do. As in my country in Leicestershire,* the ploughman hath a time to set forth, and to assay his plough, and other times for other necessary works to be done. And then they also may be likened together for the diversity of works, and variety of offices that they have to do. For as the ploughman first setteth forth his plough, and then tilleth his land, and breaketh it in furrows, and sometime ridgeth it up again; and at another time harroweth it and clotteth it, and sometime dungeth it and hedgeth it, diggeth it and weedeth it, purgeth and maketh it clean: So the prelate, the preacher, hath many diverse offices to do. He hath first a busy work to bring his parishioners to a right faith, as Paul calleth it; and not a swerving faith, but to a faith that embraceth Christ, and trusteth to his merits; a lively faith, a justifying faith;* a faith that maketh a man righteous, without respect of works: as ye have it very well declared and set forth in the Homily. He hath then a busy work, I say, to bring his flock to a right faith, and then to confirm them in the same faith. Now casting them down with the law, and with threatenings of God for sin; now ridging them up again with the gospel, and with the promises of God's favour. Now weeding them, by telling them their faults, and making them forsake sin; now clotting them, by breaking their stony hearts, and by making them supple-hearted, and making them to have hearts of flesh; that is, soft hearts, and apt for doctrine to enter in. Now teaching to know God rightly, and to know their duty to God and their neighbours. Now exhorting them when they know their duty, that they do it, and be diligent in it; so that they have a continual work to do. Great is their business, and therefore great should be their hire. They have great labours, and therefore they ought to have good livings, that they may commodiously feed their flock; for the preaching of the word of God unto the people, is called meat: scripture calleth it meat; not strawberries,* that come but once a year, and tarry not long, but are soon gone: but it is meat, it is no dainties. The people must have meat that must be familiar and continual, and daily given unto them to feed upon. Many make a strawberry of it, ministering it but once a year; but such do not the office of good prelates. For Christ saith, *Quis putas est servus prudens et fidelis? qui dat cibum in tempore.*—'Who think you is a wise and a faithful servant? He that giveth meat in due time.' So that he must at all times convenient preach diligently: therefore saith he, 'Who trow ye is a faithful servant?' He speaketh it as though it were a rare thing to find such a one, and as though he should say, there be but a few of them to find in the world. And how few of them there be throughout this realm that give meat to their flock as they should do, the visitors can best tell: Too few, too few, the more is the pity, and never so few as now.

By this then it appeareth that a prelate, or any that hath cure of soul, must diligently and substantially work and labour. Therefore saith Paul to Timothy, *Qui episcopatum desiderat, hic bonum opus desiderat,* 'He that desireth to have the office of a bishop, or a prelate, that man desireth a good work.' Then if it be a good work, it is work; ye can make but a work of it. It is God's work, God's plough, and that plough God would have still going. Such then as loiter and live idly, are not good prelates, or ministers. And of such as do not preach and teach, and do their duties, God saith by his prophet Jeremy, *Maledictus qui facit opus Dei fraudulenter,* 'Cursed be the man that doth the work of God fraudulently, guilefully or deceitfully; some books have it *negligenter,* negligently or slackly.' How many such prelates, how many such bishops, Lord, for thy mercy, are there now in England? And what shall we in this case do; shall we company with them? O Lord, for thy mercy! shall we not company with them? O Lord, whither shall we flee from them? But 'cursed be he that doth the work of God negligently or guilefully.' A sore word for them that are negligent in discharging their office, or have done it fraudulently; for that is the thing that maketh the people ill.*

But true it must be that Christ saith, *Multi sunt vocati, pauci vero electi.* 'Many are called, but few are chosen.' (Mat. xxii.) Here have I an occasion by the way somewhat to say unto you; yea, for the place that I alleged unto you before out of Jeremy, the forty-eighth chapter. And it was spoken of a spiritual work of God, a work that was commanded to be done, and it was of shedding blood, and of destroying the cities of Moab. For, saith he, 'Cursed be he that keepeth back his sword from shedding of blood.' As Saul, when he kept back the sword from shedding of blood, at what time he was sent against Amaleck, was refused of God for being disobedient to God's commandment, in that he spared Agag the king. So that, that place of the prophet was spoken of them that went to the destruction of the cities of Moab, among the which there was one called Nebo, which was much reproved for idolatry, superstition, pride, avarice, cruelty, tyranny, and for hardness of heart; and for these sins was plagued of God and destroyed.

Now what shall we say of these rich citizens of London?* what shall I say of them? Shall I call them proud men of London, malicious men of London, merciless men of London? No, no, I may not say so; they will be offended with me then. Yet must I speak. For is there not reigning in London as much pride, as much covetousness, as much cruelty, as much oppression, and as much superstition, as was in Nebo? Yes, I think, and much more too. Therefore I say, repent, O London; repent, repent. Thou hearest thy faults told thee, amend them, amend them. I think, if Nebo had had the preaching that thou hast, they would have converted. And, you rulers and officers, be wise and circumspect, look to your charge, and see you do your duties; and rather be glad to amend your ill living than to be angry when you are warned or told of your fault. What ado was there made in London at a certain man, because he said, (and indeed at that time on a just cause,) 'Burgesses,' quoth he, 'nay, Butterflies.' Lord what ado there was for that word; and yet would God they were no worse than butterflies. Butterflies do but their nature; the butterfly is not covetous, is not greedy, of other men's goods; is not full of envy and hatred, is not malicious, is not cruel, is not merciless. The butterfly glorieth not in her own deeds, nor preferreth the traditions of men before God's word; it commiteth not idolatry, nor worshippeth false gods. But London cannot abide to be rebuked; such is the nature of man. If they be pricked, they will kick; if they be rubbed on the gall, they will wince; but yet they will not amend their faults, they will not be ill spoken of. But how shall I speak well of them? If you could be content to receive and follow the word of God, and favour good preachers, if you could bear to be told of your faults, if you could amend when you hear of them, if you would be glad to reform that is amiss: If I might see any such inclination in you, that you would leave to be merciless, and begin to be charitable, I would then hope well of you, I would then speak well of you. But London was never so ill as it is now. In times past, men were full of pity and compassion, but now there is no pity; for in London their brother shall die in the streets for cold, he shall lie sick at the door between stock and stock, I cannot tell what to call it, and perish there for hunger: Was there ever more unmercifulness in Nebo? I think not. In times past, when any rich man died in London, they were wont to help the poor scholars of the universities with exhibition. When any man died, they would bequeath great sums of money toward the relief of the poor. When I was a scholar in Cambridge myself, I heard very good report of London, and knew many that had relief of the rich men of London; but now I can hear no such good report, and yet I inquire of it, and hearken for it; but now charity is waxen cold, none helpeth the scholar nor yet the poor. And in those days, what did they when they helped the scholars? Marry they maintained and gave them livings that were very papists, and professed the pope's doctrine: and now that the knowledge of God's word is brought to light, and many earnestly study and labour to set it forth, now almost no man helpeth to maintain them.

 Oh London, London, repent, repent; for I think God is more displeased with London than ever he was with the city of Nebo. Repent therefore, repent, London, and remember that the same God liveth now that punished Nebo, even the same God, and none other; and he will punish sin as well now as he did then: and he will punish the iniquity of London, as well as he did them of Nebo. Amend therefore. And ye that be prelates, look well to your office; for right prelating is busy labouring, and not lording.

Therefore preach and teach, and let your plough be doing. Ye lords, I say, that live like loiterers, look well to your office, the plough is your office and charge. If you live idle and loiter, you do not your duty, you follow not your vocation; let your plough therefore be going, and not cease, that the ground may bring forth fruit.

But now me thinketh I hear one say unto me: Wot ye what you say? Is it a work? Is it a labour? How then hath it happened, that we have had so many hundred years so many unpreaching prelates, lording loiterers, and idle ministers? Ye would have me here to make answer, and to show the cause thereof. Nay, this land is not for me to plough, it is too stony, too thorny, too hard for me to plough. They have so many things that make for them, so many things to say for themselves, that it is not for my weak team to plough them. They have to say for themselves long customs, ceremonies and authority, placing in parliament, and many things more. And I fear me this land is not yet ripe to be ploughed: for, as the saying is, it lacketh weathering: this gear lacketh weathering, at least way it is not for me to plough. For what shall I look for among thorns, but pricking and scratching? What among stones, but stumbling? What, I had almost said among serpents, but stinging? But this much I dare say, that since lording and loitering hath come up, preaching hath come down contrary to the Apostles' times: for they preached and lorded not, and now they lord and preach not. For they that be lords will ill go to plough: it is no meet office for them; it is not seeming for their estate. Thus came up lording loiterers: thus crept in unpreaching prelates, and so have they long continued. For how many unlearned prelates have we now at this day? And no marvel; for if the ploughmen that now be were made lords, they would clean give over ploughing; they would leave off their labour, and fall to lording outright, and let the plough stand: and then both ploughs not walking, nothing should be in the commonweal but hunger. For ever since the prelates were made lords and nobles, the plough standeth, there is no work done, the people starve. They hawk, they hunt, they card, they dice, they pastime in their prelacies with gallant gentlemen, with their dancing minions, and with their fresh companions, so that ploughing is set aside. And by the lording and loitering, preaching and ploughing is clean gone. And thus if the ploughmen of the country were as negligent in their office as prelates be, we should not long live, for lack of sustenance. And as it is necessary for to have this ploughing for the sustentation of the body, so must we have also the other for the satisfaction of the soul, or else we cannot live long ghostly. For as the body wasteth and consumeth away for lack of bodily meat, so doth the soul pine away for default of ghostly meat. But there be two kinds of enclosing,* to let or hinder both these kinds of ploughing; the one is an enclosing to let or hinder the bodily ploughing, and the other to let or hinder the holiday ploughing, the church ploughing.

The bodily ploughing is taken in and enclosed through singular commodity. For what man will let go, or diminish his private commodity for a commonwealth? And who will sustain any damage for the respect of a public commodity? The other plough also no man is diligent to set forward, nor no man will hearken to it. But to hinder and let it all men's ears are open; yea, and a great many of this kind of ploughmen, which are very busy, and would seem to be very good workmen: I fear me, some be rather mock-gospellers, than faithful ploughmen. I know many myself that profess the gospel, and live nothing thereafter. I know them, and have been conversant with some of them. I know them, and I speak it with a heavy heart, there is as little charity and good living in them as in any other; according to that which Christ said in the gospel to the great number of people that followed him, as though they had had an earnest zeal to his doctrine, whereas indeed they had it not; *Non quia vidistis signa, sed quia comedistis de panibus.* 'Ye follow me, saith he, not because ye have seen the signs and miracles that I have done; but because ye have eaten the bread, and refreshed your bodies, therefore you follow me.' So that I think, many one now-a-days professeth the gospel for the living sake, not for the love they bear to God's word. But they that will be true ploughmen, must work faithfully for God's sake, for the edifying of their brethren. And as diligently as the husbandman plougheth for the sustentation of the body, so diligently must the prelates and ministers labour for the feeding of the soul; both the ploughs must still be doing, as most necessary for man. And wherefore are magistrates ordained, but that the tranquillity of the commonweal may be confirmed, limiting both ploughs?

But now for the fault of unpreaching prelates, methink I could guess what might be said for excusing of them: They are so troubled with lordly living, they be so placed in palaces, couched in courts, ruffling in their rents, dancing in their dominions, burdened with ambassages, pampering of their paunches, like a monk that maketh his jubilee; munching in their mangers, and moiling in their gay manors and mansions, and so troubled with loitering in their lordships, that they cannot attend it. They are otherwise occupied, some in the king's matters, some are ambassadors, some of the privy council, some to furnish the court, some are lords of the parliament, some are presidents, and some comptrollers of mints.

Well, well, is this their duty? Is this their office? Is this their calling? Should we have ministers of the church to be comptrollers of the mints? Is this a meet office for a priest that hath cure of souls? Is this his charge? I would here ask one question; I would fain know who controlleth the devil at home in his parish, while he controlleth the mint? If the apostles might not leave the office of preaching to the deacons, shall one leave it for minting? I cannot tell you; but the saying is, that since priests have been minters, money hath been worse than it was before. And they say that the evilness of money hath made all things dearer. And in this behalf I must speak to England. 'Hear, my country, England,' as Paul said in his first epistle to the Corinthians, the sixth chapter; for Paul was no sitting bishop, but a walking and a preaching bishop. But when he went from them, he left there behind him the plough going still; for he wrote unto them, and rebuked them for going to law, and pleading their causes before heathen judges: 'Is there,' saith he, 'utterly among you no wise man, to be an arbitrator in matters of judgment? What, not one of all that can judge between brother and brother; but one brother goeth to law with another, and that under heathen judges? *constitute contemptos qui sunt in ecclesia*, &c. Appoint them judges that are most abject and vile in the congregation.' Which he speaketh in rebuking them; 'For,' saith he, *ad erubescentiam vestram dico*. 'I speak it to your shame.' So, England, I speak it to thy shame; is there never a nobleman to be a lord president,* but it must be a prelate? Is there never a wise man in the realm to be a comptroller of the mint? I speak it to your shame. I speak it to your shame. If there be never a wise man, make a water-bearer, a tinker, a cobbler, a slave, a page, comptroller of the mint: make a mean gentleman, a groom, a yeoman, or a poor beggar, lord president.

Thus I speak, not that I would have it so; but to your shame, if there be never a gentleman meet nor able to be lord president. For why are not the noblemen and young gentlemen of England so brought up in knowledge of God, and in learning, that they may be able to execute offices in the commonweal? The king hath a great many of wards, and I trow there is a court of wards; why is there not a school for the wards, as well as there is a court for their lands? Why are they not set in schools where they may learn? Or why are they not sent to the universities, that they may be able to serve the king when they come to age? If the wards and young gentlemen were well brought up in learning, and in the knowledge of God, they would not when they come to age so much give themselves to other vanities. And if the nobility be well trained in godly learning, the people would follow the same train. For truly, such as the noblemen be, such will the people be. And now, the only cause why noblemen be not made lord presidents, is because they have not been brought up in learning.

Therefore for the love of God appoint teachers and schoolmasters, you that have charge of youth; and give the teachers stipends worthy their pains, that they may bring them up in grammar, in logic, in rhetoric, in philosophy, in the civil law and in that which I cannot leave unspoken of, the word of God. Thanks be unto God, the nobility otherwise is very well brought up in learning and godliness, to the great joy and comfort of England; so that there is now good hope in the youth, that we shall another day have a flourishing commonweal, considering their godly education. Yea, and there be already noblemen enough, though not so many as I would wish, able to be lord presidents, and wise men enough for the mint. And as unmeet a thing it is for bishops to be lord presidents, or priests to be minters, as it was for the Corinthians to plead matters of variance before heathen judges. It is also a slander to the noblemen, as though they lacked wisdom and learning to be able for such offices, or else were no men of conscience, or else were not meet to be trusted, and able for such offices. And a prelate hath a charge and cure otherwise; and therefore he cannot discharge his duty and be a lord president too. For a presidentship requireth a whole man; and a bishop cannot be two men. A bishop hath his office, a flock to teach, to look unto; and therefore he cannot meddle with another office, which alone requireth a whole man: He should therefore give it over to whom it is meet, and labour in his own business; as Paul writeth to the Thessalonians; 'Let every man do his business, and follow his calling.' Let the priest preach, and the nobleman handle the temporal matters. Moses was a marvellous man, a good man: Moses was a wonderful fellow, and did his duty, being a married man; we lack such as Moses was. Well, I would all men would look to their duty, as God hath called them, and then we should have a flourishing Christian commonweal.

And now I would ask a strange question; who is the most diligentest bishop and prelate in all England, that passeth all the rest in doing his office? I can tell, for I know him who it is; I know him well. But now I think I see you listening and hearkening that I should name him. There is one that passeth all the other, and is the most diligent prelate and preacher in all England. And will ye know who it is? I will tell you: it is the devil. He is the most diligent preacher of all other; he is never out of his diocess; he is never from his cure; ye shall never find him unoccupied; he is ever in his parish; he keepeth residence at all times; ye shall never find him out of the way, call for him when you will he is ever at home; the diligentest preacher in all the realm; he is ever at his plough; no lording nor loitering can hinder him; he is ever applying his business, ye shall never find him idle I warrant you. And his office is to hinder religion, to maintain superstition, to set up idolatry, to teach all kind of popery. He is ready as can be wished for to set forth his plough; to devise as many ways as can be to deface and obscure God's glory. Where the devil is resident, and hath his plough going, there away with books and up with candles; away with bibles and up with beads; away with the light of the gospel, and up with the light of candles, yea, at noon-days. Where the devil is resident, that he may prevail, up with all superstition and idolatry; censing, painting of images, candles, palms, ashes, holy water, and new service of men's inventing;* as though man could invent a better way to honour God with, than God himself hath appointed. Down with Christ's cross, up with purgatory pickpurse, up with him, the popish purgatory, I mean. Away with clothing the naked, the poor and impotent, up with decking of images, and gay garnishing of stocks and stones: up with man's traditions and his laws, down with God's traditions and his most holy word. Down with the old honour due to God, and up with the new god's honour. Let all things be done in Latin: there must be nothing but Latin, not so much as *Memento homo quid cinis es, et in cinerem reverteris*. 'Remember man that thou art ashes, and into ashes shalt thou return:' which be the words that the minister speaketh unto the ignorant people, when he giveth them ashes upon Ash-wednesday, but it must be spoken in Latin. God's word may in no wise be translated into English.

Oh that our prelates would be as diligent to sow the corn of good doctrine, as Satan is to sow cockle and darnel! And this is the devilish ploughing, the which worketh to have things in Latin, and letteth the fruitful edification. But here some man will say to me, what, Sir, are ye so privy of the devil's counsel that ye know all this to be true?—Truly I know him too well, and have obeyed him a little too much in condescending to some follies; and I know him as other men do, yea that he is ever occupied, and ever busy in following his plough. I know by St. Peter, which saith of him, *Sicut leo rugiens circuit quaerens quem devoret.* 'He goeth about like a roaring lion, seeking whom he may devour.' I would have this text well viewed and examined, every word of it: *'Circuit,'* he goeth about in every corner of his diocess; he goeth on visitation daily, he leaveth no place of his cure unvisited: he walketh round about from place to place, and ceaseth not. *'Sicut leo,'* as a lion, that is, strongly, boldly, and proudly; stately and fiercely with haughty looks, with his proud countenances, with his stately braggings. *'Rugiens,'* roaring; for he letteth not slip any occasion to speak or to roar out when he seeth his time. *'Quaerens,'* he goeth about *seeking*, and not sleeping, as our bishops do; but he seeketh diligently, he searcheth diligently all corners, whereas he may have his prey. He roveth abroad in every place of his diocess; he standeth not still, he is never at rest, but ever in hand with his plough, that it may go forward. But there was never such a preacher in England as he is. Who is able to tell his diligent preaching, which every day, and every hour, laboureth to sow cockle and darnel, that he may bring out of form, and out of estimation and renown, the institution of the Lord's supper and Christ's cross? For there he lost his right; for Christ said, *Nunc judicium est mundi, princeps seculi hujus ejicietur foras. Et sicut exaltavit Moses serpentem in deserto, ita exaltari oportet filium hominis. Et cum exaltatus fuero, a terra, omnia traham ad meipsum.* 'Now is the judgment of this world, and the prince of this world shall be cast out. And as Moses did lift up the serpent in the wilderness, so must the son of man be lift up. And when I shall be lift up from the earth, I will draw all things unto myself.'—(John iii.) For the devil was disappointed of his purpose; for he thought all to be his own: and when he had once brought Christ to the cross, he thought all cocksure.

But there lost he all reigning: for Christ said, *Omnia traham ad meipsum.* 'I will draw all things to myself.' He meaneth, drawing of man's soul to salvation. And that he said he would do *per semetipsum* by his own self; not by any other body's sacrifice. He meant by his own sacrifice on the cross, where he offered himself for the redemption of mankind; and not the sacrifice of the mass to be offered by another.\* For who can offer him but himself? He was both the offerer and the offering. And this is the mark at the which the devil shooteth, to evacuate the cross of Christ, and to mingle the institution of the Lord's supper; the which although he cannot bring to pass, yet he goeth about by his sleights and subtil means to frustrate the same; and these fifteen hundred years he hath been a doer, only purposing to evacuate Christ's death, and to make it of small efficacy and virtue. For whereas Christ, 'according as the serpent was lifted up in the wilderness, so would he himself be exalted; that thereby as many as trusted in him should have salvation'; but the devil would none of that. They would have us saved by a daily oblation propitiatory; by a sacrifice expiatory, or remissory.

Now if I should preach in the country, among the unlearned, I would tell what propitiatory, expiatory, and remissory is; but here is a learned auditory: yet for them that be unlearned I will expound it. Propitiatory, expiatory, remissory, or satisfactory, for they signify all one thing in effect, and is nothing else but a thing whereby to obtain remission of sins, and to have salvation. And this way the devil used to evacuate the death of Christ, that we might have affiance in other things, as in the daily sacrifice of the priest; whereas Christ would have us to trust in his only sacrifice. So he was, *Agnus occisus ab origine mundi*. 'The lamb that hath been slain from the beginning of the world;' and therefore he is called, *juge sacrificium*, 'a continual sacrifice;' and not for the continuance of the mass, as the blanchers\* have blanched it, and wrested it; and as I myself did once mistake it. But Paul saith, *per semetipsum purgatio facta*. 'By himself, and by none other, Christ made purgation and satisfaction for the whole world.'

Would Christ this word, *by himself*, had been better weighed and looked upon, and *in sanctificationem*, to make them holy; for he is *juge sacrificium* a *continual* sacrifice, in effect, fruit and operation; that like as they, which seeing the serpent hang up in the desert, were put in remembrance of Christ's death, in whom as many as believed were saved; so all men that trusted in the death of Christ shall be saved, as well they that were before, as they that came after. For he was a continual sacrifice, as I said, in effect, fruit, operation, and virtue. As though he had from the beginning of the world, and continually should to the world's end, hang still on the cross; and he is as fresh hanging on the cross now, to them that believe and trust in him, as he was fifteen hundred years ago, when he was crucified.

Then let us trust upon his only death, and look for none other sacrifice propitiatory, than the same bloody sacrifice, the lively sacrifice; and not the dry sacrifice, but a bloody sacrifice. For Christ himself said, *consummatum est*. 'It is perfectly finished:' 'I have taken at my Father's hand the dispensation of redeeming mankind, I have wrought man's redemption, and have despatched the matter.' Why then mingle ye him? Why do ye divide him? Why make you of him more sacrifices than one? Paul saith, *Pascha nostrum immolatus est Christus*. 'Christ our passover is offered up;' so that the thing is done, and Christ hath done it, and he hath done it *semel, always*, once for all: and it was a bloody sacrifice, not a dry sacrifice.\*

Why then, it is not the mass that availeth and profiteth for the quick and the dead. Wo worth thee, O Devil, wo worth thee, that hast prevailed so far and so long; that hast made England to worship false gods, forsaking Christ their Lord. Wo worth thee devil, wo worth thee devil, and all thy angels. If Christ by his death draweth all things to himself, and draweth all men to salvation, and to heavenly bliss, that trust in him; then the priests at the mass, at the popish mass, I say, what can they draw, when Christ draweth all, but lands and goods from the right heirs? The priests draw goods and riches, benefices, and promotions to themselves; and such as believed in their sacrifices they draw to the devil. But Christ is he that draweth souls unto him by his bloody sacrifice. What have we to do then, but *epulari in Domino*, to eat in the Lord at his supper?

What other service have we to do to him, and what other sacrifice have we to offer, but the mortification of our flesh? What other oblation have we to make, but of obedience, of good living, of good works, and of helping our neighbours? But as for our redemption, it is done already, it cannot be better: Christ hath done that thing so well, that it cannot be amended. It cannot be devised how to make that any better than he hath done it. But the devil, by the help of that Italian bishop yonder, his chaplain, hath laboured by all means that he might, to frustrate the death of Christ and the merits of his passion. And they have devised for that purpose to make us believe in other vain things by his pardons; as to have remission of sins for praying on hallowed beads; for drinking of the bakehouse bowl; as a canon of Waltham Abbey once told me, that whensoever they put their loaves of bread into the oven, as many as drank of the pardon bowl should have pardon for drinking of it. A mad thing, to give pardon to a bowl. Then to Pope Alexander's holy water, to hallowed bells, palms, candles, ashes, and what not? And of these things, every one hath taken away some part of Christ's sanctification; every one hath robbed some part of Christ's passion and cross, and hath mingled Christ's death, and hath been made to be propitiatory and satisfactory, and to put away sin. Yea, and Alexander's holy water yet at this day remaineth in England, and is used for a remedy against spirits, and to chase away devils; yea, and I would this had been the worst. I would this were the worst. But wo worth thee, O devil, that hast prevailed to evacuate Christ's cross, and to mingle the Lord's supper. These be the Italian bishop's devices, and the devil hath pricked at this mark to frustrate the cross of Christ: he shot at this mark long before Christ came, he shot at it four thousand years before Christ hanged on the cross, or suffered his passion.

For the brazen serpent was set up in the wilderness, to put men in remembrance of Christ's coming; that like as they which beheld the brazen serpent were healed of their bodily diseases, so they that looked spiritually upon Christ that was to come, in him should be saved spiritually from the devil. The serpent was set up in memory of Christ to come, but the devil found means to steal away the memory of Christ's coming, and brought the people to worship the serpent itself, and to cense him, to honour him, and to offer to him, to worship him, and to make an idol of him. And this was done by the market-men that I told you of. And the clerk of the market did it for the lucre and advantage of his master, that thereby his honour might increase; for by Christ's death he could have but small worldly advantage. And so even now so hath he certain blanchers belonging to the market, to let and stop the light of the gospel, and to hinder the king's proceedings in setting forth the word and glory of God. And when the king's majesty, with the advice of his honourable council, goeth about to promote God's word, and to set an order in matters of religion, there shall not lack blanchers that will say; as for images, whereas they have used to be censed, and to have candles offered unto them, none be so foolish to do it to the stock or stone, or to the image itself; but it is done to God and his honour before the image. And though they should abuse it, these blanchers will be ready to whisper the king in the ear, and to tell him, that this abuse is but a small matter; and that the same, with all other like abuses in the church, may be reformed easily. 'It is but a little abuse, say they, and it may be easily amended. But it should not be taken in hand at the first, for fear of trouble or further inconveniencies. The people will not bear sudden alterations; an insurrection may be made after sudden mutation, which may be to the great harm and loss of the realm. Therefore all things shall be well, but not out of hand, for fear of further business.' These be the blanchers that hitherto have stopped the word of God, and hindered the true setting forth of the same. There be so many put-offs, so many put-byes, so many respects and considerations of worldly wisdom: And I doubt not but there were blanchers in the old time to whisper in the ear of good King Hezekiah, for the maintenance of idolatry done to the brazen serpent, as well as there hath been now of late, and be now, that can blanch the abuse of images, and other like things.

But good King Hezekiah would not be so blinded; he was like to Apollos, fervent in spirit. He would give no ear to the blanchers; he was not moved with the worldly respects, with these prudent considerations, with these policies: he feared not insurrections of the people: he feared not lest his people would not bear the glory of God, but he (without any of these respects, or policies, or considerations, like a good king, for God's sake and for conscience sake) by and by plucked down the brazen serpent, and destroyed it utterly, and beat it to powder. He out of hand did cast out all images, he destroyed all idolatry, and clearly did extirpate all superstition. He would not hear these blanchers and worldly wise men, but without delay followeth God's cause, and destroyeth all idolatry out of hand. Thus did good King Hezekiah; for he was like Apollos, fervent in spirit, and diligent to promote God's glory.

And good hope there is that it shall be likewise here in England; for the king's majesty is so brought up in knowledge, virtue, and godliness, that it is not to be mistrusted but that we shall have all things well, and that the glory of God shall be spread abroad throughout all parts of the realm, if the prelates will diligently apply their plough, and be preachers rather than lords. But our blanchers, which will be lords, and no labourers, when they are commanded to go and be resident upon their cures, and preach in their benefices, they would say, Why? I have set a deputy there; I have a deputy that looketh well to my flock, and the which shall discharge my duty. A deputy, quoth he, I looked for that word all this while. And what a deputy must he be trow ye? Ever one like himself; he must be a Canonist: that is to say, one that is brought up in the study of the pope's laws and decrees; one that will set forth papistry as well as himself will do; and one that will maintain all superstition and idolatry; and one that will nothing at all, or else very weakly, resist the devil's plough; yea, happy it is if he take no part with the devil: and where he should be an enemy to him, it is well if he take not the devil's part against Christ.

But in the mean time, the prelates take their pleasures. They are lords and no labourers; but the devil is diligent at his plough. He is no unpreaching prelate: He is no lordly loiterer from his cure; but a busy ploughman; so that among all the prelates, and among all the pack of them that have cure, the devil shall go for my money, for he still applieth his business. Therefore, ye unpreaching prelates, learn of the devil: to be diligent in doing of your office, learn of the devil: and if you will not learn of God, nor good men, for shame learn of the devil; *ad erubescentiam vestram dico*, 'I speak it for your shame:' If you will not learn of God, nor good men, to be diligent in your office, learn of the devil. Howbeit there is now very good hope that the king's majesty, being by the help of good governance of his most honourable counsellors, trained and brought up in learning, and knowledge of God's word, will shortly provide a remedy, and set an order herein; which thing that it may so be, let us pray for him. Pray for him, good people; pray for him. Ye have great cause and need to pray for him.

## NOTES

p. 57. *racked*: here used in the now obsolete sense of 'forced to a false interpretation'—by the scholasticism to which the Protestants objected. He here, with characteristic honesty, refers directly to his own previous Roman Catholicism.

p. 58. *wary and circumspect*: which Latimer, above all, refused to be. The ingenious justification of the saffron-bag simile parodies the manner of Catholic neo-scholastic disputation.

p. 58. *As in my country in Leicestershire*: this is typical of Latimer's personal, button-holing approach.

p. 58. *a lively faith, a justifying faith . . . very well declared and set forth in the Homily*: by Cranmer, and given in this book.   *strawberries*:

p. 59. *strawberries*: non-residents (also attacked by Bernard Gilpin in his 1552 sermon printed herein): Latimer's term became a proverbial one.

pp. 59-60. *By this it appeareth . . . people ill*: one of the many perfect answers to be found in Anglican teaching to the famous objection to Protestantism made by Keble, the nineteenth-century Anglo-Catholic, to the effect that it 'seems inseparable . . . from "Every man his own absolver" '.

p. 60. *Now what shall we say of these rich citizens of London? . . .*: this invective reveals Latimer's bewilderment at the social failure of the English Reformation: as he says, he cannot understand how Papists could have been more charitable than Protestants are today: cannot understand why the rejection of Catholicism has not lead to better 'works', why the spirit has not been regenerated.

p. 63. *But there be two kinds of enclosing . . .*: it is characteristic of Latimer to compare the practice of enclosure of common land, a serious social issue in Tudor times, with the hinderance of spiritual progress. The congregation would have immediately taken his point.

p. 64. *. . . is there never a nobleman to be a lord president . . .*: it was common practice for prelates to hold secular office. Latimer attacks it eloquently and convincingly.

p. 66. *. . . and new service of men's inventing . . .*: this is the heart of the objections of the reformers to Roman Catholicism: the Church must of necessity be human, and therefore reprobate; so although there must be a Church, it must of necessity rely only upon the Scriptures and the early interpretations of them, and not upon later scholastic and superstitious accretions.

p. 68. *He meant by his own sacrifice . . .*: for Protestants of Latimer's colour it was idolatrous for a priest, a human being, to *repeat* the atoning act of Christ himself. But those of Roman Catholic or conservative persuasion felt that they needed some *objective* reassurance. The conflict is resolved (i. e. left reasonably open to temperamental interpretation) in the Anglican Church if it is resolved anywhere.

p. 68. *blanchers*: here meaning those who turn away the truth.

p. 69. *. . . and it was a bloody sacrifice, not a dry sacrifice . . .*: the denial of the cup to the laity was one of the reformers' chief objections to Roman Catholic ritual. Latimer was content to regard Communion as involving no more than a 'true and faithful presence' of Christ.

# Edwin Sandys

EDWIN SANDYS was born in about 1516. He studied at St John's College, Cambridge, and in 1547 became Master of St Catherine's Hall. In 1553 he was appointed Vice-Chancellor of his university. Later in the same year he was imprisoned for his support of Lady Jane Grey's claim to the throne; but managed to escape to Europe. He was Bishop of Worcester (1559-70), Bishop of London (1570-5) and Archbishop of York from 1575 until his death in 1588. He worked on the Bishops' Bible of 1568, and on its revision in 1572. Both his son and grandson were distinguished: the first as a politician under James I and Charles I, the second as a minor poet best known for his rendering of Ovid's *Metamorphoses*. Sandys was one of the more prominent supporters of the English Reformation in the pre-Marian period; after the accession of Elizabeth I he became noted as one of the (theologically) Calvinistically inclined Church leaders, along with Parker, Grindal, Whitgift and, later, Abbot. But he was not a Puritan or even a proto-Puritan, even though his enforced sojourn in Europe strengthened his strongly anti-Catholic convictions.

[A Sermon Preached at Paul's Cross]
1 Peter 4.
7. *The end of all things is at hand. Be ye therefore sober and watching in prayer.*
8. *But above all things have fervent love among you; for love covereth the multitude of sins.*
9. *Be ye harbourous [hospitable] one towards another, without grudging.*
10. *Let every man, as he hath received the gift, minister the same one to another, as good disposers of the manifold graces of God.*

THIS SERMON was preached at St Paul's Cross when Sandys was Archbishop of York. It combines fierce anti-popery (too self-evident to draw attention to examples) with strong moral exhortation. Sanderson, in the 1621 sermon given here, expresses the same kind of moral exhortation; but in much more temperate language. However, in the 1580s, the time when the Church of England was seeking to establish itself on a secure and popular foundation in the face of opposition from both Puritanism and Catholicism, the problem of faith and works—as we have most clearly seen in Cranmer's work—was a serious one. The simultaneous exhortation to hate the Pope as anti-Christ and to behave with circumspection and charity therefore makes good sense. Sandys himself was a notable critic of abuses.

THE APOSTLE St. Peter, like a perfect workman and a skilful builder, first layeth a sure foundation, and then frameth and erecteth a good building thereupon. The foundation is Christ. 'Another foundation no man can lay' (1 Cor. iii). He is the rock, the foundation; and we as 'lively stones' (1 Pet. ii) must be framed thereupon, hewed and squared with the hammer and square of God's word, that we may grow to be 'a spiritual house, an holy priesthood, to offer up unto God through Jesus Christ spiritual and acceptable sacrifices' of piety, prayer, and thanksgiving. Through Christ we are brought from darkness unto light, that from henceforth we should walk as the children of that light wherein he hath placed us: of a perverse generation we are through him made an holy people, that we should be 'holy' as he is that called us: we are redeemed, 'not by gold and silver' (1 Pet. i), but by the innocent blood of the immaculate Lamb, to 'serve him that hath delivered us out of the hands of our enemies in holiness and righteousness all the days of our life' (Luke i): we are called to be the children of God, citizens of the heavenly Jerusalem, and to be fellow heirs with Christ of that his eternal kingdom; that we should be obedient and loving children, trusty and dutiful citizens, that we may be not only called, but chosen, accepted, and admitted to inherit with Christ, the first begotten of God. What building we be, whether 'gold or stubble,' what life we lead, it will one day appear. Our conversion will be called unto an hard account. In that day we must stand before the tribunal seat of God, and render a reckoning, yea, and receive as we have wrought in our bodies, good or bad. The judge is even at hand: *Veniens veniet*: 'He will come surely without fail, and without stay' (Habak. ii). 'He standeth before the door' (Rev. iii). This is the last hour: the trump is in a readiness to be blown to judgment.

2. For, saith Peter, 'the end of all things hangeth over us.' In which words the apostle doth both comfort us, and exhort us. Such as are the afflicted, oppressed with wrong, burthened with poverty, vexed with sickness, slandered, persecuted, or hated of the world, here they may receive comfort. Your misery shall be but momentary and short; your joy shall be great and endless. 'Lift up your heads, for your redemption draweth near' (Luke xxi). The end of your affliction, together with the end of all things, is at hand. Again, upon these words a most necessary exhortation is inferred. Christ is coming in the clouds: all flesh shall rise and reckon: he only that hath his lamp burning shall

enter in with the bridegroom: as we are found, so shall we be taken and judged. 'The end is at hand: be sober therefore, and watch unto prayer.'

3. Whereas the holy scriptures do make often mention of a double end: the one, wherein we are to yield up our mortal lives; the other, wherein Christ at his second coming shall finish the course of all this sinful world; the apostle treating in this place of the latter, I shall at this present follow his footsteps, and speak of Christ his second coming to put an end to all things. For they which say, 'Where is the promise of his coming?' (2 Pet. iii) deceive themselves. 'He hath set a day wherein he will judge the world in justice' (Acts xvii): 'he is appointed judge of quick and dead' (Acts x). The angel of God beareth witness of his coming. 'This Jesus, which is taken up into heaven, shall so come as ye have seen him go' (Acts i). And St. John, as if he beheld and saw him coming, saith, 'Behold, he cometh with clouds, and every eye shall see him' (Rev. i).

4. But as his coming is most certain, so the hour, day, month, year, or time, is most uncertain. 'It is not for you to know the seasons and precise points of time, which the Father hath appointed in his own power' (Acts i). 'Of that day and hour no man knoweth, no, not the very angels of heaven, but my Father only' (Matt. xxiv). 'The day of the Lord will come stealing upon us, as a thief in the night' (1 Thess. v).

5. Now, as we know not the day and time, so let us be assured that this coming of the Lord is near. He is not slack, as we do count slackness. That it is at hand, it may be probably gathered out of the scriptures in divers places. The signs mentioned by Christ in the gospel (Matt. xxiv), which should be the foreshewers of this terrible day, are almost already all fulfilled. The prophecies of Daniel of the four monarchies (Dan. vii), of the little horn, and of the times, weeks, and days, are manifestly come to pass (2 Thess. ii). The defections or fallings away, which are spoken of in holy scriptures, are also in great part accomplished. The provinces, the ten kingdoms, are fallen from the Roman empire, and that wicked one hath wrought the mystery of iniquity. Again, there hath been, in a manner, a general falling from the catholic faith, as the apostle long before foretold us; some unto Mahomet, some unto antichrist his brother. Even about one time Mahomet appeared, and the pope swerved from the true faith of Christ; the one renouncing him in name, the other in deed; the one quite blotting out the mention of Christ,

and denying at all to profess him in word, the other keeping his name, but robbing him of his office, and shutting him out of his right place; both falling from the faith. That defection also is come upon us, which St. Paul did prophesy of: 'In the latter times men shall fall from the faith, giving ear to deceiving spirits and doctrines of devils' (Tim. iv). And St. Peter: 'There shall come in the last days mockers, that walk after their own lusts, and say, Where is the promise of his coming?' (2. Pet. iii.) Thus heretics and atheists have fallen from Christ and christian faith. We that profess Christ and his gospel, are also charged with a defection, a schism, and a falling away. But in every apostasy two things must be considered, from whom and to whom this sliding is. We gladly grant that we are fallen away from the bishop of Rome, who long ago fell from Christ: we do utterly abandon his usurped and proud authority: we have happily forsaken that synagogue of Satan, that den of thieves, that polluted church, that simoniacal temple; and we joyfully confess that we have no society or fellowship with his darkness. In our sermons we preach Christ, and none else but him: we know nothing, we teach nothing, we believe nothing, but Christ and him crucified. In our sacraments we shew forth the Lord's death in no other sort, than he himself hath done and commanded us to do. In our lives we worship the Lord alone; and, in yielding up our souls, we fly for mercy only to the merits of Christ Jesus, our merciful Saviour. This is our apostasy. We have forsaken him that hath forsaken God, and whom God hath forsaken: we have left that man of sin, that rose-coloured harlot with whom the kings of the earth have committed fornication, that triple-crowned beast, that double-sworded tyrant, that thief and murderer, who hath robbed so many souls of salvation, and sucked so much innocent blood of christian martyrs, that adversary unto Christ, that pretensed vicar, who hath displaced the person, not only taking upon him Christ's room and office, but also boasting himself as if he were a god, and being content of his parasites so to be called. This wicked man of sin is at length revealed by the sincere preaching of the gospel. Daniel in his prophecies, Paul in his epistles, and John in his revelations, have most lively described and pointed him forth even as it were with the finger. Yea, through his pride and ambition, his usurping authority and worldly rule, his tyranny and persecuting of Christ in his members, he hath sufficiently revealed and detected himself, if none had done it for him.

6. This wicked man the Lord shall destroy with the breath of his mouth; and then shall be the end. The blast of God's trump hath made him already stagger: he hath caught such a cramp, that he beginneth now to halt: his long and far-reaching arm is marvellously shortened: his coffers are waxen leaner: his falsehood is espied: many princes refuse to taste any more of his poisoned cup: he is fallen from being the head, and come almost to be the tail: he was too cruel and too violent to continue. There is no counsel nor power against the Lord. And that, as all men, so especially he hath felt. It is too hard for him to kick against the spur, to fight against the Lord of hosts. Seeing therefore that this man of sin is not only revealed, but in a manner overthrown too, doubtless the Lord is coming, and the end of all things draweth near. 'Iniquity (saith our Saviour) shall abound, and charity shall wax cold: the gospel shall be preached in the whole world: and then an end' (Matt. xxiv). Iniquity doth abound: for, as the prophet saith, 'There is no truth, there is no pity, there is no knowledge of God in the earth. Slandering, lying, murdering, stealing, and whoring, have overflowed the world' (Hos. iv). Charity is frozen up, and become cold as ice. These latter days have bred and brought out swarms of such as love themselves, but neither God nor their neighbours. God's word never sounded more shrill, never was preached more sincerely, than at this day. It is not bound or shut up in straits: it hath free and large passage. Iniquity thus flowing, charity thus ebbing, and God's gospel thus sounding throughout the world, I may conclude with St. Peter, 'The end is near at hand.'

7. This coming of Christ will be a joyful day for God's children: they shall lift up their heads: but to antichrist, to the enemies of God's gospel, to the workers of iniquity, it will be a day of wrath, indignation, and all affliction. But they put far from them the remembrance thereof: they set it aloof, and go still forward, heaping up riches, though they know not how soon they shall depart from them; building, though they know not for what inhabitant; purchasing, though they know not who shall inherit; decking, feeding, pampering themselves, though they know not whether the next or this night, the next or this moment, their soul shall be taken from them. The world is towards an end. 'Love not the world therefore, neither the things that are in the world' (1 John ii); but 'be ye sober and watching in prayer, and above all things have fervent love amongst you.' This is St. Peter's exhortation in this place; wherein we learn

our duty towards God, and our duty towards our neighbour. Towards God: 'be sober, watch, and pray:' towards our neighbour: 'have fervent charity.'

8. There is an inward and an outward sobriety: 'inward sobriety,' as Origen defineth, 'is that whereby we keep our affections and desires within lists, that no man take more upon him than is meet, but every one according to the measure of his degree.' Which definition that father seemeth to have drawn out of the words of St. Paul: 'Let no man be more wise than behoveth him; but let every man be soberly minded' (Rom. xii). Angels, having too lofty a conceit of themselves, were not able to keep their first estate. Our first parents, for passing the limits of sobriety, lost the godly possession which God had given into their hands. Through an unsober desire of knowing all things, they knew too soon their own misery. This haughtiness of heart set Absolon so far besides himself, that neither force of nature, fear of God, nor shame of men and the world, could withhold him from traitorous attempting to tear the crown from his father's head. It is strange to see how Herod was swollen with the arrogant overweening and proud conceit of his own eloquence. His strange blasphemous pride had a strange and fearful punishment. Nabuchodonozor, through his affection being not content to be the highest amongst men, was made the vilest among beasts. Those are ugly patterns of monstrous minds, void of that sobriety which was in Paul, who, although God had exalted him to the third heaven, and there shewed him more than a man might conceive, thought nevertheless modestly and meekly of himself. 'I am the least of the apostles, not worthy to be called an apostle' (1 Cor. xv). The like affection was in St. Peter: it caused him to loathe himself at the sight of the majesty of the Son of God: 'Depart from me (saith he), I am a sinful man' (Luke v). It was in that centurion, which thought himself unworthy to open a door unto Christ Jesus. It was in the publican, that durst not cast so much as an eye up to heaven. Such again pass the bounds of this sobriety, as seek after needless things, neglecting necessary. The philosopher [Thales] that gazed upon the skies, heeding not the pit that was under his feet, was deservedly laughed to scorn by a girl. We are all tainted with this fault, whereby it cometh to pass, that we waste, saith Seneca, a great part of our life in doing nothing, a greater in doing evil, the greatest of all in meddling with those things which are not for us. They that in matters of religion will know more than

God hath revealed, think not soberly, but arrogantly of themselves. Wo be to them which are wise in their own eyes! they are foolish in the sight of God. The root of this vice is a false persuasion which we have taken, that we can stand of ourselves. Wherefore the apostle putteth us in mind of our danger, unless we be supported by other manner strength, than by our own feeble faith. 'I would not, brethren, that ye should be ignorant of this secret, lest you should be arrogant in yourselves' (Rom. xi). We bear not up ourselves: God doth bear up all; and each man is or should be a stay to bear up others. We are all members of one body; and we know we have need one of another. The hand cannot want [do without] the help of the toe, though the least and lowest member. Man alone were a miserable creature: he could neither clothe, nor feed, nor defend himself from violence. The wisest man oftentimes needeth counsel. Who was more wise than Moses? yet Moses knew he needed the advice of others, and therefore, occasion serving, disdained it not. Rebecca saw more than Isaac in things nearly concerning their children Esau and Jacob; Sarah more than Abraham in the mother of Ismael. Naaman followed the counsel even of his servants; and it did not repent him so to have done.

9. Now, as this inward sobriety of mind and judgment is required, so are we exhorted likewise to an outward sobriety, which consisteth in diet, in apparel, in gesture, and in speech. Be sober in diet. Nature is contented with a little: but, where sobriety wanteth, nothing is enough. The body must have sufficient, lest it faint in the midst of necessary duties: but beware of gluttony and drunkenness. And Christ saith, 'Take ye heed, overload not your hearts with these burthens of excess' (Luke xxi). Be not drunken with wine. These lessons are fit for England, where ancient sobriety hath given place to superfluity; where many such rich men are, as fare daintily day by day. God grant their end be not like his, who, riotously wasting here the creatures of God, wanted afterward a drop of water when he would gladly have had it! John Baptist was content with a simple diet, Christ with very slender fare; but there are of us, I fear me, whose god is their belly, and whose felicity is meat and drink. Our excess this way is intolerable and abominable: we strive to equal almost Vitellius, who had served unto him at one feast 2000 fishes, and 7000 birds; and Heliogabalus, that monster of the world, who at one supper was served with 600 ostriches. There is no bird that flieth, no fish that swimmeth, no beast that moveth, which is

not buried in our bellies. This excess is an enemy both to wealth and health: it hath cut off much housekeeping, and brought many men to extreme beggary; and as many great diseases are cured by abstinence, so fulness hath been the cause of sundry strange and unwonted sicknesses. Aurelian the emperor did never send for physician in time of his sickness, but cured himself only by thin diet. And as immoderate feeding doth much hurt to the body, so it is more noisome to the mind. For as the ground, if it receive too much rain, is not watered, but drowned, and turneth into mire, which is neither fit for tillage nor for yielding of fruit; so our flesh, over-watered with wine, is not fit to admit the spiritual plough, or to bring forth the celestial fruits of righteousness. The herbs that grow about it will be loathsome and stinking weeds; as brawling, chiding, blasphemy, slander, perjury, hatred, manslaughter, and such like bad works of drunkenness and darkness. Are not these unsavoury fruits enough to make us abhor the tree? A drunken body is not a man, but a swine, fit for devils to enter into. For these sins are against nature, which, being moderately refreshed, is satisfied; being stuffed, is hurt, violated, and deformed. God hath given us his creatures soberly to use, and not so shamefully to abuse: we should, if we did well, feed the body to serve and not to rule, to obey, and not to lead, the spirit. 'I chastise my body,' saith St. Paul, 'and bring it into servitude' (1 Cor. ix). Is it not perilous, trow you, to pamper and make strong our adversary? or have we a greater or stronger enemy than our rebellious flesh? Full-bellied drunkards are no better than traitors in this spiritual war. Gedeon, a figure of Christ, would no other soldiers to fight against the Madianites, but such as stood and took up water in their hand, and licked it out: of such there were but 300 in number: the rest, that were afraid, or lay down to drink their fill, he sent away: they were not for his purpose (Judges vii). Such filled bellies were not fit to serve God, nor able to fight against the Madianites, Satan, and sin, God's, and God's people's enemies. The Israelites lusted after quails, but to their own confusion. Esau, for his belly sake, sold his birth-right and inheritance. Beware their examples. Lucullus, a Roman, had a servant always at his elbow, to pull him by the sleeve at such times as he poured in too fast. But we have the blessed apostle of Christ, the servant of God, to put us in mind of sobriety in diet. Nor in diet only, but also in attire.

10. 'A man's apparel, laughter, and gait, doth shew his nature'

(Ecclus. xix). In apparel this is to be observed, that, avoiding vanity and pride therein, every man wear according to his calling. John Baptist ware a rough coat of camel's hair; but Solomon used rich and glorious apparel; and yet both used that which did become them. There is no more holiness in a friar's cowl, than in a shepherd's cloak: yet that is comely in one, which is not seemly in another. St. Paul is very earnest with women, and requireth them to go in sober apparel, decking themselves 'with shamefacedness and modesty, not with broidered hair, or with gold, or pearls, or sumptuous attire, but as becometh women that profess the fear of God' (1 Tim. ii). And St. Peter telleth them, that their godly mother Sarah went soberly apparelled. Sarah was a good woman, a rich woman, and a noble woman: such as follow her footsteps need not be ashamed. Yet do I not condemn all other apparel: yea, even such apparel as is costly and gorgeous may be fit for some states and personages. I do not doubt but that Hester and Judith did wear gold, and were gorgeously decked. But if Paul and Peter did live in our days, they would not spare the vanity of our women, much less of our men. The vain and monstrous apparel of all other countries and nations England hath scraped together, and in a bravery put it on; the estimation whereof is this: a light wavering mind, matched with a vain proud heart, desireth a light, vain, strange, proud, and monstrous apparel, to cover and clad it withal. But sobriety is content with that which is seemly. Be sober in your apparel.

11. Be ye sober also in your speech and gesture. Be slow to speak; and when you speak, let your words be so seasoned, that they may be wholesome, and not offensive to the hearer. Let no lewd speech proceed from your mouths. A man's speech and gesture will bewray his thoughts. The talk of a fool is unsavoury altogether, and his gesture uncomely; but a wise man's understanding is seen even in his looks. A fool exalteth his voice in laughter; but the man that is soberly minded will scarcely smile to himself. He that is guiltless hideth not his face; but the murderer's head is in his bosom. Our outward actions are lively tokens of our inward disposition from which they proceed. Wherefore it greatly behoveth all estates and conditions of men, both inwardly in mind, and outwardly in diet, attire, speech, and gesture, to be sober.

12. With sobriety St. Peter joineth watchfulness. 'Be sober and watching.' I will not here recite unto you the manifold

kinds of watching, whereof the scriptures make mention; but rather note a few unto you most necessary, and such as the apostle chiefly meaneth. Before we can watch, we must be wakened. Wherefore he saith, 'Awake, thou that sleepest, and stand up from the dead; and Christ shall give thee light' (Eph. v). He speaketh not of natural sleeping, but of a sleep which is in death. He that liveth in pleasures is dead being alive; and they that wake unto sin are asleep unto righteousness. All such as live in error, and lie in sin, are but dead men in the sight of God. Aristotle saith, that seven hours of sleep suffice naturally the body. Let it suffice the souls of men to have slept in the lap of antichrist 700 years, and to have been rocked so long in the cradle of that deadly error. It is now high time to awake, and arise from the dreams of popery; for they are not sickly, but deadly. At the length, let Christ shine unto thee: the light of his gospel, if thou embrace it, will drive away the dark clouds of error and ignorance. Awake, I say, at the sound of God's word, from thy former superstition; and at length embrace the truth, which will be as a lantern, nay, as a bright shining star to guide thee unto Christ. St. Paul speaketh to the elect of God, who doubtless will at length awake. As for the reprobate, they still shall sleep on in their errors and sins, unto their eternal death and confusion. But 'arise, Jerusalem, and be thou enlightened' (Isai. lx): arise, Jerusalem, from death to life, from error to truth, from darkness to light, from antichrist to Christ, who by his Holy Spirit will illuminate thee, that thou mayest know God the Father, and him whom he hath sent, Jesus Christ, and that is the only way to everlasting life. Pliny, reproving our drowsiness, saith, that sleep doth steal away the half of our life. But this sleep whereof we speak, stealeth away the whole life of the greatest part of men. David himself lay slumbering in the filthy sleep of whoredom a whole year at the least, and could not awake until Nathan blew in his ear and stirred him. But David's sleep was but a nap in comparison of such as are so hard and fast asleep, that they will never stir, until fire out of heaven flee about their ears to waken them. So were the Sodomites wakened and consumed. Awake therefore; and when ye are wakened, then watch.

13. Watch, that ye be not deceived by false prophets, who watch to deceive you, and teach otherwise than Christ hath taught. The devil is a subtile persuader of men: he is a lying spirit in the mouth of his prophets: his ministers and workmen are crafty companions, such as creep into houses and lead away the

simple as captives with them. A man of a watchful eye shall know these wolves by two properties. First, they are ravenous, cruel, bloody: they will persecute and kill: they will be as Cain, and not as Abel; as Ismael, and not as Isaac; as Esau, and not as Jacob; as Pharoah, and not as Moses; as Caiaphas, and not as Peter. The second note is that which Chrysostom mentioneth: 'Whoso in blasphemy yelleth and howleth with a foul and open mouth against the truth, he is a wolf.' Such they were of whom the prophet speaketh in the psalm, saying, 'They set their mouth against heaven' (Psal. lxxiii).

14. All must watch, that they be not themselves deceived by these deceitful wolves when they put on sheep's clothing. But God giveth charge to such as be the pastors of his people, to be watchful also over others; not only carefully to feed them, as his flock dearly redeemed, in good and wholesome pastures, but also to drive and chase away the wolves, lest God's sheep be devoured by them. And this pastoral office doth not only pertain unto priests and preachers, but also unto princes and temporal governors, whom God hath placed in authority to that end that they should promote his glory. For the which cause God calleth Cyrus the king, his shepherd. *Vigilate*: 'watch' the wolf to drive him away: watch the flock to feed it. (Isai. xliv.)

15. Let every one be watchful over his life, that his conversation be according to his profession. If we walk disorderly, we shall not walk alone: our example will draw others after it; and their sins we shall answer for. Lucifer fell not alone: he drew company from heaven with him. Jeroboam, being sinful, made Israel to sin. And he is burned in the hand with that mark of horror, for a warning to all succeeding ages: 'Jeroboam the son of Nebat, that made Israel to sin' (2 Kings xiii). Let us beware that we play not Simeon and Levi, and so make our father Jacob to be loathed of the Canaanites. We profess Christ and true Christianity: let us not through our lewd life be a slander to our Saviour, and a shame to his gospel. Watch therefore. But because, as St. Paul saith, neither planting nor watering will help, except God himself do give increase (1 Cor. iii); because our watching, as the prophet witnesseth, is in vain, neither can sobriety and heedfulness serve to keep a city, 'except the Lord himself do keep it' (Psal. cxxvii); let us crave help at God's merciful hands, and let us pray as well as watch. When St. Paul hath armed God's soldier, he biddeth him 'pray' (Eph. vi. 18). Man, be he never so well appointed for defence, never so strong and perfit, cannot

stand without God's strength. He that looketh but a little into the world, shall espy just cause to move us to prayer, if any men; now, if ever. The great devil in these our later days is let loose. Antichrist rageth and seeketh our confusion. The wicked glistering world marvellously deceiveth and bewitcheth. The flesh reigneth and beareth swine. The spirit is faint: sin overfloweth: Christ is coming in the clouds to call us unto judgment. Therefore 'be ye sober, watch, and pray.' Pray, I say, not in shew, but in deed; not in appearance, but from the heart; not for fashion, but in earnest. Babble not in words like hypocrites, but pour out thy heart before God, as did Hannah. And God grant, for his Christ our Jesus' sake, that in faith and love we may lift up pure hands, sincere affections, and hearty groans unto our Lord, that we may overcome our many and dreadful enemies, purchase pardon, and glorify God. Let us with David, with whom we have sinned, pray for mercy. Let us with the disciples of Christ, with whom we have wavered, pray for the increase of our faith, because the end of all things is now at hand.

16. It followeth, 'Have fervent charity amongst yourselves' (Rom. xiii). This concerneth our duty towards men, as the other did towards God. All our duty towards our neighbour consisteth in love. 'He that loveth another hath fulfilled the law.' John, the beloved disciple of Christ, was the preacher of love: it was ever in his mouth, as it is in his writings; insomuch that, lying upon his death-bed, his disciples requesting to have one lesson from him before his departure, he was able to devise no one thing more needful to be spoken of, than this which he had often said: 'Love one another, my little children.' Peter would have our love to be earnest and hot. Every one loveth himself very vehemently; but our love towards others is very cold and chill. Our love for the most part this way is in word and in phrase, but not in deed and in truth. This world is double-hearted: dissembling is made a trade to live by. There be many Labans, but few Jacobs; many that salute and say *ave* [hail], but their next word is *apprehendite* [lay hold on him] (Matt. xxvi). If Christ came now, he were like to find little faith, but less charity: yet without charity all that we do is vain: yea it is very sin. Let us therefore love as God hath loved us: he loved us not slenderly, when he took so bitter a death for us: a God for his enemies. See therefore that ye have vehement, sincere, and hearty love among yourselves; not contenting yourselves barely to have it in shew, unless ye shew it by these effects which St. Peter in this place

setteth down. Vehement love here spoken of is described by these properties. First, it 'covereth the multitude of sins:' secondly, it causeth us to be given to 'hospitality:' thirdly, it will not suffer men to hide those graces which they have received at God's hands, but is a cause of bestowing the same to the use and benefit of their brethren.

17. It is not our charity that can cover our sins from the sight of God. Christ is the propitiation for our sins. 'It is I that blot out your iniquities' (Isai. xliii), saith the Lord. But, as God's love to usward covereth our sins, so ours towards our brethren doth cover theirs. If God love us, his mercy is as a cloak that hideth all our shame: he seeth no blemish nor deformity in us. If we love our brethren, our charity is as a veil before our eyes: we behold not their faults. Although they be great, we do not weigh them; although many, we reckon them not. For 'charity covereth even the multitude of sins.' The eye of the charitable man is always viewing his own wounds: as for the scars of other men, he seeth them not. His hand is always occupied, not in picking out motes from other men's eyes, but in drawing out beams from his own. St. Augustine, to show the great dislike he had of such as uncharitably delighted to unfold other men's faults, wrote these verses over his table:

*Quisquis amat dictis absentum rodere vitam,*
  *Hanc mensam vetitam noverit esse sibi.*

Whoso loveth to gnaw upon men in their absence,
Let him know that this table doth not like his presence.

18. The next fruit of love is hospitality. 'Be harborous one toward another, without grudging.' St. Paul is of the same judgment; for having used this exhortation, 'Let brotherly love continue,' he immediately addeth: 'Be not forgetful to lodge strangers' (Heb. xiii). Hospitality hath respect unto all men, but chiefly to strangers, namely such as are of the household of faith, and are driven out of their country for the profession of Christ's gospel. Such are chiefly to be relieved. Of such especially it is written and provided for in the law: 'The stranger that dwelleth with you shall be as one of yourselves, and thou shalt love him as thyself; for ye were strangers in the land of Egypt: I am the Lord your God' (Lev. xix). God hath offered us at this time great occasion to show forth our charity. Many of God's good

children are strangers in England. Let us not omit this good occasion to do good. Abraham and Lot were liberal towards strangers; and, when they supposed to have received men, they received angels to their great benefit. But we no doubt, in receiving these strangers which wander from place to place, being cast out of their countries for confessing and professing Christ, receive not angels, but the Lord of angels. 'He that receiveth you receiveth me' (Matt. x). In doing good to strangers, we do good also to ourselves: for great shall be the benefit when Christ shall say, 'I was a stranger, and ye harboured me' (Matt. xxv): as great the curse to them to whom it shall be said, 'I was harbourless, and ye did not lodge me.' St. Peter would have us given to hospitality without murmuring, and with kindness entertain strangers. For in shewing of benevolence there are three special virtues, which if they be wanting, our benefits lose their grace and goodness. The first is willingness: 'God doth love a cheerful giver' (2 Cor. ix). The second is bountifulness: for 'he that soweth sparingly shall reap sparingly.' The third is singleness of heart: for if we give vain-gloriously to be seen of men, we lose our reward at God's hands, as by murmuring we deserve no thanks of men.

19. There be two grand enemies of hospitality. The one is covetousness, the other profuseness. Niggardliness would not suffer Nabal, that rich carl, to bestow a piece of bread to relieve the necessity of David a king. 'Shall I take my bread and my water and the flesh of my beasts that I have killed for my shearers, and give it to men whom I know not either who or whence they are?' (1 Sam. xxv.) Others, with the prodigal son, waste that unthriftily, wherewith they should relieve the poor and comfort strangers: some of them being eaten up, as they say, with three H. H. H., horses, hawks, and harlots; some with vain apparel, casting away as much upon a garment, as would almost ransom a king; some with building, some with banqueting; some by one mean, and some by another: whereby it is come to pass that hospitality itself is waxen a stranger, and needeth harbour: we have shut it quite and clean out of doors.

20. The last fruit of hearty love is the good bestowing of our graces and gifts to the benefit of others. 'Let every man, as he hath received a gift, minister the same one to another, as good disposers of the manifold graces of God.' The gifts that we have which be good, they be of God; for 'every good gift cometh down from the Father of lights' (James i). And these gifts we

receive to bestow upon others, as good stewards of the Lord. St. Peter doth seem chiefly as it were to point unto two sorts of high and principal stewards, at whose hands an especial reckoning of the graces of God will be required; the magistrate and the minister. For God 'leadeth his people like sheep by the hand of Moses and Aaron,' whose gifts are the sword and the word: whereof the one may not be borne in vain, but drawn to the punishment of evildoers, and to the advancement of them that do well; the other is to be preached in season and out of season, to the confirmation of the truth, the refutation of error, the exhortation to virtue, the dissuasion from vice, that the man of God may be perfectly enabled to every good work. Howbeit, as magistrates and ministers are principally meant in this exhortation, so are all sexes and sorts of people called upon. For we shall all give an account of our stewardship: we must all make a reckoning of the talents we have received; be they five, two, or one. No man is born nor brought up to himself, but to the benefit and behoof of another; and as stones in one building, or members in one body, so is every man interested and invested in the possession each one of another, to the end no man should seek his own things, but the things that make for the profiting of another. Which one lesson amongst many, if once we would hear to learn it, and learn to remember it, and remember to follow it, and follow to continue and persevere in it, we should not only declare ourselves to be good dispensers of the manifold gifts and graces of God, but hear also that blessed voice, *Euge, serve bone et fidelis*: 'Come, my good and faithful servant: I have set thee over a few small things, I will henceforth place thee over more and greater: come and enter into thy Master's joy' (Matt. xxv): whereunto he bring us, that so dearly bought it for us, even Jesus the price of our redemption: to whom, with the Father and the Holy Ghost, a Trinity in unity, be rendered all thanks, and all glory given from this time forth and for evermore. Amen.

# BERNARD GILPIN

THE 'Apostle of the North', Bernard Gilpin, was among the holiest of Church of England priests. Born in an age in which we, from our supposedly more civilized standards (and we are all prone to this error), find it easy to accuse even such gentle men as More or Cranmer of complicity in the cruel destruction of heretics, nothing can be found against Gilpin. The chief formative influence upon him was Erasmus, another man who distinguished himself by his dislike of all kinds of violence.

Gilpin was born in 1517 in Westmoreland. He was a great-nephew of the conservative and highly inconsistent Bishop of Durham, Cuthbert Tunstall. He was a wealthy man, but spent his money on others. At Queen's College, Oxford (M. A. 1542; B. D. 1549), he had a brilliant academic career, and he became a fellow of Christ Church. He accepted the English Reformation, but with, as one might put it, strong Erasmian reservations. His emphasis was usually on abuses rather than on doctrine, and he had serious misgivings about the dissolution of the monasteries.

He was wholly unambitious, and the fearless sermon given below has survived only because it made a stir; no other by him survives, for he regarded his preaching as simply a part of his pastoral duties, which he took with the utmost seriousness. During the period of Church reform under Edward VI Gilpin's sympathies lay with the conservative bishops, but unlike them he was horrified by the Marian persecutions, and from thenceforth became a more positive adherent of Anglicanism. The sermon below, however, belongs to the period when he was most apprehensive about the reforming movement.

He was the rector of Easington and the Archdeacon of Durham (1556). Twice he was denounced for heresy under Mary. In the first instance his great-uncle was able to protect him—and even to promote him to the benefice of Houghton-le-Spring, where he founded a grammar school. But he was called to London once again. Fortunately for him he broke his leg on the way: by the time he arrived in London the Queen was dead and Bonner, before whom he was to have appeared, was on the road to prison.

On Elizabeth's accession he was offered the bishopric of Carlisle and (1560) the provostship of Queen's. But he preferred to remain in his small parish near Durham, making long and difficult annual progresses in dangerous parts in order to give the inhabitants instruction and relief. His huge house was always full of poor and distressed people, whom he himself nursed and tended. These activities brought him the support of many Puritans, to whose doctrines he was profoundly opposed. He interceded for those who had taken part in the Catholic Northern Rebellion of 1569 (in mid-November they had restored the Mass in Durham Cathedral), but did not support them. He died in 1583.

A GODLY SERMON PREACHED IN THE COURT AT
GREENWICH ON THE FIRST SUNDAY AFTER EPIPHANY,
1552
Luke 2:41-50.
*Now his parents went to Jerusalem every year, at the feast of the passover. And when he was twelve years old, and they were come up to Jerusalem, after the custom of the feast, and had finished the days thereof; as they returned, the child Jesus remained in Jerusalem; and Joseph knew not of it, nor his mother. But they, supposing that he had been in the company, went a day's journey; and sought him amongst their kinsfolk and acquaintance. And when they found him not, they turned back to Jerusalem, and sought him. And it came to pass, three days after, that they found him in the temple, sitting in the midst of the doctors; both hearing them, and asking them questions. And all that heard him were astonished at his understanding and answers. So when they saw him, they were amazed: and his mother said unto him, Son, why hast thou thus dealt with us? Behold, thy father and I have sought thee with heavy hearts. Then said he unto them, How is it that ye sought me? Know ye not that I must go about my father's business? But they understood not the word that he spake unto them.*

THIS SERMON, preached before the King (it was published in 1581), could have caused serious trouble for Gilpin. He was forced to take Tunstall's advice and go abroad for a time; he also resigned his benefice. (It is clear from his behaviour in 1552, then, that had Gilpin's doubts about the Elizabethan settlement been so severe as to have included a return to Catholicism, he would actually have backed the Northern rebels in 1569.) But it is to be doubted if Cranmer, the Archbishop of Canterbury, would have been much offended: he had himself been conspicuously scrupulous on the matter of spoliation of church property, and had had virtually nothing to do with its administration. Latimer, Cranmer's chief spokesman, was as worried as Gilpin about the social results of the reforms in which he believed.

The style and presentation of this sermon, which Gilpin revised for the press, are admirably direct and concise. It shows considerable literary skill as well as courage: there was nowhere so dangerous to preach as at the Court itself, and at this time the dangerous, insincere and treacherous John Dudley, Earl of Warwick and then Duke of Northumberland, instead of the more tolerant Somerset, was in charge of affairs.

The second paragraph makes it clear that, although Gilpin had taken the conservative side in the famous dispute on the Eucharist of 1549 against the ultra-Protestant Hooper (a martyr under Mary), 'Peter Martyr' (Pietro Martire Vermigli) and other reformers, he was no Romanist: a Romanist would not have spoken of the 'elect and chosen'. The third paragraph is also anti-Romanist in its implications: we find Christ in the scriptures (our 'kinsfolk' might equally be the 'priests' which the Lutherans call all living Christians, or the specially appointed Council of Rome, which denounced all those who questioned its actions as heretics); 'mumbling things he understood not' is a clear hit at the Papists, who would not allow their congregations to hear the services except in a dead language (Erasmus, Gilpin's true mentor, was of course all for the vernacular). But this is a preamble to the main business of the sermon, which is a criticism of abuse. The reader will note that Gilpin steers a firm course between Lutheranism and Catholicism ('. . . the bishop of Rome, abusing always Peter's keys to fill Judas's satchels'), and that his main concern is to preserve the integrity of the priesthood against the rapacity of the *arrivistes,* to many of whom he was preaching. It is notable how Gilpin in the second section of the main part of the sermon gradually and skilfully works up to his main accusation: through a denunciation of Popery, he moves cleverly to a denunciation of other 'blasphemies'. Notable, too, is how straightforwardly he describes his listeners and their friends as common thieves, though they are 'gentlemen thieves', and finally, like the corrupt priests, as 'ravenous wolves'. In the first section he attacks corrupt and lazy clergy, who have failed to enter into the spirit of the reforms: he especially mentions pluralities and non-residence. The sermon is useful in identifying the abuses that still existed at mid-century. A glaring example is the farming out of benefices to 'gentlemen, laymen'.

[Notes on asterisked passages in the text are at the end of the sermon.]

FORSOMUCH AS the whole gospel is more full of matter, and plenteous in mysteries, than that it can well be discussed within the limits of one sermon; I have taken, for this time, to treat upon this one sentence spoken by Christ unto his parents, 'Know ye not that I must go about my father's business?' being content to omit the rest; taking only so much, as shall suffice to declare the occasion whereupon he spake these words, for the fuller understanding of the same.

Ye shall therefore understand, that when our Saviour was come to the age of twelve years, giving attendance upon his parents to Jerusalem, at the solemn feast of easter, whither they yearly did repair at that time of sincere devotion, and for the obedience of the law; after that Joseph and Mary had devoutly passed the days of the feast, and were returned home, it came to pass (not through blind fortune, but by God's providence, that his glory might appear) that the blessed Son Jesus tarried behind at Jerusalem; and while his parents, either not taking good heed of him, or else going apart in sundry companies, either of them trusting he had been with the other, they went one day's journey before they missed him: but after he was found wanting, they sought him diligently among their kinsfolk and acquaintance, but found him not; which was undoubtedly unto them a very cross of bitter affliction. So doth God many times exercise his elect and chosen with adversity, for their trial, and to keep them in humility. When they were returned to Jerusalem, and had long sought him with sorrowful hearts, after three days they found him in the temple.

Here then, by the way, methinks the holy Ghost teacheth us this spiritual doctrine: so long as we seek Christ in our own kinsfolk, that is, our own inventions and devices, we find him not; but to find Christ, we must accompany these godly persons, Joseph and Mary, unto the temple of his holy word: there Christ is found unto so many as seek him, with such humble spirits, and meek hearts, as Joseph and Mary did. They found him in the temple, not idly occupied as many are, not mumbling things he understood not, *sine mente sonum*, a confused sound without knowledge; but they found him occupied in his heavenly father's business, as all men should be in the temple, either in speaking to God by humble and hearty prayer, or hearing God speaking to them in his most blessed word. So was Christ occupied amongst learned men, and opposing them. Where he teacheth us, to be always as glad to learn as to teach. It is a probable conjecture that he opened to them the scriptures which spake of Messias; a matter then in controversy. But whatsoever their matter was, the evangelist saith, 'he made them all astonished at his understanding and answers.' So the glory of his Godhead even then began to shine. Where we may mark the wonderful power of the gospel: even the hard-hearted that will not receive it, the bright beams of the truth shining therein maketh astonished. It causeth also the godly to marvel, as Mary and Joseph; but their admiration always ended with joy.

Yet notwithstanding his heavenly majesty made all men to wonder, his mother thought she had some cause to expostulate with him for the great fear he had brought upon them, casting them into a dungeon of sorrows; and complaining, said, 'Son, why hast thou, &c.' She seemeth to charge him with the breach of the first precept of the second table, that he had not well intreated his parents. But Christ so shapeth his answer, that he taketh away all her complaint: teaching us, how the precepts of the second table may not be understood in any wise to be a hindrance to the first. 'Wist ye not that I must go about my father's business?' Where our duty and service to God cometh in place, all human service and obedience, which might be a hindrance thereto, to whomsoever it be, father or mother, king or Cesar, must stand back and give place. Besides this, he teacheth us here a most necessary lesson for all men to know and bear away, which is, that his whole life and death was nothing else but a perfect obedience to the will of his heavenly father, and that he was always most busily occupied therein: and teacheth us, that if we look by adoption to be brethren and coheirs with Christ of his father's kingdom, we must also with our master and lord yield up ourselves wholly to our heavenly father's will, and always be occupied in his business. 'I have given you an example, that ye should do even as I have done to you.' Which lesson being so necessary of all Christians to be kept, and the breach thereof the cause of all iniquity, I thought it good to pass over other places of ghostly instruction which this gospel might minister, and to tarry upon this one sentence, 'Know ye not that I must go about my father's business?' intending to shew in order, how all estates of men, the clergy, the nobility, and the commonalty, are under the band of this obligation, *oportet*, we must, and ought of necessity to be occupied in our heavenly father's business.—But first of all, mistrusting wholly mine own strength, I crave aid of you by your devout prayers.

*Know ye not that I must go about my father's business?*

After that our first parents through disobedience and sin had blotted and disfigured the lively image of God, whereunto they were created, and might have lived alway in a conformity to the will of God; man was never able to apply himself to God his father's business, nor yet so much as to know what appertained thereto. 'The natural man,' saith St. Paul, 'perceiveth not the things of the spirit of God,' till Christ, the very true image of God the father, did come down, and took man's nature upon him; which descent, as he declareth, was to fulfill for us the will of his father, that 'like as by disobedience of one man, many were made sinners; so by the obedience of one (Christ) many might be made righteous, what time as he became obedient unto death, even the death of the cross.' Which obedience, lest carnal men should challenge to suffice for them, howsoever their life be a continual rebellion against God and his holy will, (such as there be a great number, and have been in all ages) St. Paul wipeth them clean away, saying, 'Christ hath become salvation, not to all, but to all that obey him.' Let no man therefore flatter and deceive himself. If we will challenge the name of Christ's disciples, if we will worthily possess the glorious name of Christians, we must learn this lesson of our master, to be occupied in our heavenly father's business; which is, to fly our own will, which is a wicked and wanton will, and wholly to conform ourselves to his will, saying, as we are taught, 'thy will be done;' which, as St. Augustine saith, 'the fleshly man, the covetous, adulterous, ravenous, or deceitful man, can never say, but with his lips, because in his heart he preferreth his own cursed will, setting aside the will of God.'

Now forsomuch as the greatest part of the world hath at this day forsaken their father's business, applying their own, and are altogether drowned in sin; for 'the whole head is sick, and the whole heart is heavy: from the sole of the foot to the head, there is nothing whole therein,' and as St. Paul saith, 'all seek their own, and not that which is Jesus Christ's'; and as I am here ascended into the high hill of Sion, the highest hill in all this realm, I must needs, as it is given me in commission, 'cry aloud, and spare not; lift up my voice like a trumpet, and shew the people their transgressions.' I must cry unto all estates, as well of the ecclesiastical ministry, as of the civil governance, with the vulgar people.

But forasmuch as example of holy scriptures, with experience of Christ's church in all ages, hath taught us that the fall of priests is the fall of the people, and contrariwise the integrity of them is the preservation of the whole flock; and the ministers, as Christ saith, being 'the light of his mystical body, if the light be turned into darkness, there must needs follow great darkness in the whole body;' I think it fit to begin with them, who seem to have brought blindness into the whole body, making men to forget their heavenly father's business: they which should have kept the candle still burning, these will I chiefly examine in that business which Christ so earnestly committed to all pastors before his ascension, when he demanded thrice of Peter if he loved him; and every time upon Peter's confession, enjoined him straightly to feed his lambs and sheep: wherein we have the true trial of all ministers who love Christ, and apply his business.

But to consider how it hath been forgotten in the church many years, it might make a christian's heart to bleed. He that wrote the general chronicle of ages, when he cometh to the time of John VIII and Martin II bishops of Rome about 600 years ago, conferring the golden ages going before, with the iniquity of that time, when through ambition, avarice, and contention, the office of setting forth God's word was brought to an utter contempt, and trodden under foot, in token whereof the bible was made the bishop's footstool, he falleth to a sudden exclamation, and complaineth thus with the lamentable voice of the prophet Jeremy, 'O lord God, how is the gold become so dim? How is the goodly colour of it so changed? O most ungracious time, saith he, wherein the holy man faileth, or is not. All truths are diminished from the sons of men: there are no godly men left: the faithful are worn out among the children of men.' In that time, as it appeared both by this history and others, ambition and greedy avarice had taught ministers to seek and contend for livings, who might climb the highest by utter contempt of their office, and our heavenly father's business; and so to make Christ's flock a ready prey for the devil, 'who goeth about like a roaring lion, seeking whom he may devour.'

Then the bishop of Rome, abusing always Peter's keys to fill Judas's satchels, dispensed with all prelates that brought any money in obeying Christ's commission given to Peter, 'Feed, feed my lambs and my sheep;' and stretched it so largely, that instead of feeding Christ's lambs and sheep, he allowed them to feed hawks, hounds, and horses, I will not say harlots. Then, instead of fishers of men, he made them to become fishers of benefices and fat livings. He brought preaching into such a contempt, that it was accounted a great absurdity for a cardinal to preach, after he had once bestrid his mule.

But let us see after, how this evil increased. St. Bernard in his time, about 200 years after, lamented that when open persecution of tyrants and heretics was ceased in the church, then another persecution, far worse, and more noisome to Christ's gospel, did succeed; when the ministers, Christ's own friends by pretence, were turned into persecutors. 'My lovers and my kinsmen stand aside from my plague: and my kinsmen stand afar off.' The iniquity of the church, saith Bernard, began at the elders. 'Alas, alas, O lord God, they are the foremost in persecuting of thee, which are thought to love the chiefest place or preeminence in the church.' This complaint, with much more too long to be rehearsed, against the prelates of Rome, made St. Bernard in his time nothing afraid in the same place to call them antichrists; and for murdering of silly souls, redeemed with Christ's precious blood, he maketh them more cruel persecutors of Christ, than the Jews which shed his blood.

If the iniquity of Rome, 400 years ago, was so great, and since hath not a little increased, it was high time that God should open the eyes of some christian princes, to see the great abuses and enormities of Romish bishops, and to deliver Christ's gospel out of captivity, and to bring down his horns, whose pride, if he might have had success in his tyranny, began to ascend with Lucifer above the stars.

It is not many years ago, that a champion of theirs, named Pelagius,* writing against Marsilius Paduanus* in defence of Rome, hath not been ashamed to leave in writing, that the pope (*quodammodo*, after a fort) doth participate both natures, the godhead and manhood, with Christ; and that he may not be judged of the emperor, because he is not a mere man, but as a god upon earth; and God, saith he, may not be judged of man. What intolerable blasphemy is this? If I had not read it myself, I could scarcely believe any such blasphemy to proceed from him which professeth Christ. Do you not perceive plainly the hissing and poison of the old serpent, when he tempted our first parents, and promised they should become like gods? A vile wretched creature, worms' meat, forgetting his estate, must become a god upon earth.—Such gods shall follow Jupiter, Mars, and Venus, into the pit of damnation.

But some will say, What should we speak so much of the bishop of Rome? Is he not gone? His power taken away? If preachers would let him alone, the people would soon forget him. Truly, for my part, if I had that gift, strength, and calling, I had rather (though I were sure to smart therefore) speak against his enormities in Rome, than to speak of them here: and I think no man beareth, at least I am sure no man ought to bear, any malice or evil against his person, in speaking against his vice and iniquity: 'We fight not (saith St. Paul) against flesh and blood; but we fight against the prince of darkness, &c.' When any wicked man, adversary to God and his word, assaileth us; we must take him for no other, but as an instrument of the devil, and Satan himself to be our enemy, and none other: and even as when an enemy assaileth us on horseback, we wish to overthrow the enemy, and win the horse, which may be profitable to us; so if the devil could be cast out of such instruments as he hath in Rome, the men would become profitable members of Christ. But if the devil sit so fast in the saddle, that he cannot be turned out, we cannot amend it. Yet our duty is, to pray unto God for them; and to hate none of God's creatures, but rather that which Satan hath depraved, 'if peradventure God will turn their hearts.'

But notwithstanding,* their faults ought to be chiefly told them in their presence; yet not there only, but even here amongst us also. Although it come not to their ears, it is not a little expedient oftentimes to cry and thunder against their errors and vices; chiefly, that so oft as we hear it, we may give God thanks, as we are most bounden, for our deliverance from that captivity of Babylon, as St. Peter himself, by the mind of ancient writers, called it. Examples hereof we have in the scriptures: the song of the Israelites, after their deliverance out of Egypt; and afterwards, when they were delivered by Debora from the tyranny of Sisera; and after the deliverance from Holofernes by Judith. We must be thankful, lest for our unthankfulness God suffer us to fall into a worse bondage than ever we were in.—But most of all it is profitable, that we may from our hearts renounce with Babylon all the vices of Babylon. For what did profit the deliverance out of Egypt, to those that did still carry Egypt in their minds through the desert? What did it avail the deliverance out of Babylon to those, that did bring Babylon home to Jerusalem? —I fear me, yet in England a great many, like fleshly Israelites, are weary of the sweet manna of the gospel, and savour of the fleshly Egypt, desiring to live still under the bondage of Pharaoh.

But most of all it is expedient now for my purpose to speak of that sea, from whence, so far as ever I could learn, those intolerable abuses have overflown, and are come among us; which as yet are great enemies to Christ's gospel here in England, making his ministers to set aside his business: such abuses as cannot yet be driven away, nor sent home to Rome to their father: I mean, dispensations for pluralities, and totquots,* with dispensations for non-residents, which avarice and idleness transported hither from Rome. But for that they savour sweet for a time to carnal men, they have so many patrons, that they cannot be driven away with other abuses.

And because they are accounted to stand by law, they are used as cloaks for iniquity.* These may well be likened unto those fatlings which Saul, against God's commandment, did keep alive when he vanquished the Amalekites. And truly, till there be ordained some godly laws to banish these, with other abuses, God's wrath is kindled against us to destroy all such as are maintainers of them. So long as it shall be lawful for men to have so many livings as they can get, and discharge never a one; and so long as men may have livings to lie where they will in idleness, far from their cure, fatting themselves like the devil's porklings, and letting a thousand souls perish for lack of spiritual food, God's business shall never be well applied, nor his gospel have success in England.

It is pity that ever it should be needful to wish any laws to be made by man to bring ministers of God's word to do their duty, being so plainly expressed in God's law. If our hearts were not hardened more than Pharaoh's, our judgment more blinded with insensibleness of heavenly things than the Sodomites, we should tremble and quake more at one threatening of God's vengeance against negligent pastors that feed themselves, and set aside their heavenly father's business, whereof the scripture is full in every place, than we should fear all the powers upon earth, which, as Christ saith, having power only of the body, cannot hurt the soul.—O Lord, how dare men be so bold as to take on them the name of Christ's ministers, and utterly refuse the work of their ministry, by leaving their flock, God's word being so plain against them!

I marvel not so much at blind bayards,* which never take God's book in hand; ignorance hath blinded them; they know not the price of man's soul: but truly, I could never enough marvel at learned men, which read the scriptures, where their hearts and understanding should be, when they read almost in every leaf of scripture, besides all ancient writers, their own sharp sentence and judgment, which a whole day were too little to bring them in.—O merciful God, where be their eyes to see, their ears to hear! Do they think there is a God which is not master of his word? I will let pass how they are called of the holy Ghost by most odious names, thieves, robbers, hypocrites, idols, wolves, dumb dogs, with many such like, worthy their deserts. I will only declare, which methinks might suffice if there were no more, how the scripture maketh them most cruel murderers, and guilty of blood. In the thirty fourth of Ecclesiasticus it is written, 'The bread of the needful is the life of the poor; he that defraudeth them thereof is a man of blood.' If this sentence be true in them that defraud the needy of their corporal food, how much more are they which withhold the food of the soul, being the worthier part of man, guilty of blood? And therefore God, by his prophet Ezekiel telleth them, 'So many as perish by their negligence, their blood shall be required at their hands, as men guilty of blood.' Now let them consider, that if the blood of Abel, one man, cried up unto heaven for vengeance against *Cain*, what an horrible cry shall the blood of a thousand souls make before the throne of God, asking vengeance against that wicked pastor, which most cruelly hath hungered them to death, in withholding from them the food of life? The gold they lay up yearly, brought far off by farmers; their rings and jewels; their fine apparel; their beds they lie on; their meat and drink, being the spoil of the poor; cry all for vengeance: the stones in the wall, the timber over their heads, cry for vengeance.

Alas, how far are they from excusing themselves with St. Paul, saying to the people of Ephesus, 'I take you to record this day, I am pure from the blood of all men; for I have spared no labour, but have shewed all the counsel of God unto you.' But alas, these men may rather say, that they have kept counsel of God's counsel: and where St. Paul preached publicly, and by houses, these men keep silence, lest they should disquiet the devil in his fort; of whom Christ saith, 'When a strong man armed watcheth his house, the things that he possesseth are in peace.' They say with the evil servant, 'My master is long a coming; and so beats his fellow servants,' like cruel murderers and tyrants, whose judgment shall be straiter than any Pharaoh, Nero, or Domitian, that ever reigned. But alas, it helpeth nothing to call or cry upon them: 'They have hardened their hearts as an adamant stone.'

Lazarus hath lain so long buried and stinking in worldly lusts and sensualities, the preacher cannot call him out, nor yet remove the gravestone.—What shall I then do?—I must call unto you, most noble prince, and Christ's anointed.

I am come this day to preach to the king, and to those which be in authority under him. I am very sorry they should be absent, which ought to give example, and encourage others to the hearing of God's word: and I am the more sorry for that other preachers before me complain much of their absence. But you will say, they have weighty affairs in hand. Alas, hath God any greater business than this? If I could cry with the voice of Stentor, I would make them hear in their chambers; but in their absence I will speak to their seats, as if they were present.

I will call unto you, noble prince, as Christ's anointed. Christ's little flock here in England, which he hath committed to your charge, which wander by many thousands, as sheep having no pastors; they cry all unto you for succour, to send them home their shepherds, to the end that for things corporal, they may receive spiritual; and to let one pastor have one only competent living, which he may discharge. They call upon you to expel and drive away the great drones, which in idleness devour other men's labour; that after St. Paul's rule, 'He that will not labour, be not suffered to eat. The little ones have asked bread, &c.' Christ's little ones have hungered and called for the food of the gospel a long time, and none there was to give it them. Now they cry unto you, take heed you turn not your ears from them, lest their blood be required at your hands also, and lest God turn his ears from you. Samuel spake unto Saul fearful words, 'Because thou hast cast away the word of the Lord, the Lord hath therefore cast away thee from being king.' You are made of God a pastor, a pastor of pastors. When David was anointed king of Israel, God said, 'Thou shalt feed my people Israel.' You must feed, and that is, to see that all pastors do their duty. The eye of the master hath great strength. Your grace's eye to look through your realm, and see that watchmen sleep not, shall be worth a great number of preachers. They call unto you to awake not only negligent pastors, but also to take away other enormities, which have followed in heaps upon those evils, pluralities, and non-residents.

If I might have time, I think I should be able to prove, that the great swarm of evils which reign at this day, have flowed from those fountains, or rather puddles. But I will only speak of the great abuses which by spoil or robbery do hide the gospel, how they have ensued.

First of all, the dispensations of non-residents have brought forth farming of benefices to gentlemen, laymen, wherein they have found such sweetness and worldly wealth, that preachers cannot have them, they will be perpetual farmers; which hath opened a gap for the heathen, as David saith, or else for cloaked christians, much worse than the heathen, who have entered into Christ's inheritance, spoiled his holy temple, and robbed his gospel. Such seem to make composition with our great enemy satan: the idle pastor saying, Give to me riches, take the rest to thy share; whom satan answereth, If thou wilt betray to me the souls, take riches for thy part.

Another gap hath been opened, for that the learned have not done their duties, no more than the unlearned; hereby Christ's vineyard hath been utterly spoiled. Patrons see that none do their duty. They think as good to put in asses as men. The bishops were never so liberal in making of lewd priests; but they are as liberal in making lewd vicars. I dare say, if such a monster as Dervell Gatherel, the idol of Wales, burnt in Smithfield, should have set his hand to a bill to let the patron take the greatest part of the profits, he might have had a benefice. There is never any question how he can occupy himself in God's business. John Gerson,* a learned man in his time, witnesseth, that whosoever in that time was admitted to a benefice in France, must answer to this question, *Scis utrumque testamentum?* Knowest thou the old testament and the new? And the ignorant was put back. But with these men, it skilleth not if he never opened the bible, so much the meeter for their purpose, as he is not able to speak against their abuses, but will suffer them to sleep in their sin.—And will you see what preposterous judgment they use? For all worldly offices they search meet and convenient men; only christian souls, so dearly bought, are committed without respect, to men not worthy to keep sheep.

Your grace hath sent forth surveyors, as most needful it was, to see there should be no deceit in payment of pensions, and other offices abroad: would to God you would also send forth surveyors to see how benefices are bestowed and used; how Christ and his gospel are robbed and dishonoured, to the great decay of your realm and commonwealth: you should find a small number of patrons that bestow rightly their livings, seeking God's glory, and that his work and business may be rightly applied, without simony, or seeking their own profit.

For first, it is almost general, to reserve the farming to himself, or his friend; and to appoint the rent at his own pleasure.—But worse than this, a great number never farm them at all, but keep them as their own lands, and give some three halfpenny priest a curate's wages, nine or ten pounds. Even as Jeroboam made priests of his own for his hill altars, to sacrifice to his calves, that the people should not go up to Jerusalem. These Jeroboams will never let the people ascend to Jerusalem, to find Christ in the temple of his word. They began first with parsonages, and seemed to have some conscience towards vicarages; but now their hearts be so hardened, all is fish that cometh to the net. Gentlemen are parsons and vicars both, nothing can escape them. There be vicarages about London, having a thousand people, so spoiled; whereby it may appear what is done further off.—Your grace may find also, where gentlemen keep in their hands livings of forty or fifty pounds, and give one that never cometh there five or six pounds. Some change the ground of the benefice with their tenants, to the intent, if it be called for, the tenant shall lose it and not they. Is not this a godly patron?—It shall appear also, I could name the place, where a living of an hundred marks by the year, if I say not pounds, hath been sold for many years, I suppose an hundred save one, and so continueth still.—O good St. Ambrose, if thou hadst been bishop there, thou wouldst never have suffered such wolves to devour the flock. It may well be called a devouring; for this living in a godly learned pastor's hand might have refreshed five hundred in a year with ghostly food, and all the country about with God's word; which, as I perceive, in twenty miles compass hath scarce one man to preach; and yet no place in England more needful, for boys and girls of fourteen or fifteen years old cannot say the Lord's prayer. Shall such injury to Christ and his gospel be suffered in a christian realm? That one enormity crieth for vengeance till it be redressed.—What shall I speak? Your noblemen reward their servants with livings appointed for the gospel. Certainly I marvel that God holdeth his hand, that he destroyeth them not with Nadab and Abihu. Let them not abuse God's patience; for if they do not shortly repent, and bestow their livings better, both master and man shall burn in hell fire.

I am not able to rehearse, nor yet any man knoweth all the abuses which the simoniacs, ambitious and idle pastors, have brought unto your realm; by whose evil example ravenous wolves, painted christians, hypocrites, have entered and defiled the sanctuary, spoiled Christ and his gospel, to the destruction of his flock. How great enemies they be to Christ, by keeping away his gospel, it shall appear, if ye consider what gross superstition and blindness remaineth still among the people, only through lack of faithful preachers. I pass over much infidelity, idolatry, sorcery, charming, witchcrafts, conjuring, trusting in figures, with such other trumpery, which lurk in corners, and began of late to come abroad only for lack of preaching. Come to the ministration of the sacraments, set forth now by common authority after the first institution. They think baptism is not effectual,* because it wanteth man's tradition. They are not taught how the apostles baptized. A great number think it is a great offence to take the sacrament of Christ's body in their hands, that have no conscience to receive it with blasphemous mouths, with malicious hearts, full of all uncleanness. These come to it by threes of custom, without any spiritual hunger, and know not the end wherefore it was instituted. They come to the church to feed their eyes, and not their souls; they are not taught that no visible thing is to be worshipped; and for because they see not in the church the shining pomp and pleasant variety (as they thought it) of painted cloths, candlesticks, images, altars, lamps, and tapers, they say, as good to go into a barn; nothing esteeming Christ which speaketh to them in his holy word, neither his holy sacrament reduced to the first institution. To be short, the people are now, even as the Jews were at Christ's coming, altogether occupied in external holiness and culture, without any feeling of true holiness, or of the true worship of God in spirit and truth, without the which all other is mere hypocrisy. Many thousands know not what this meaneth; but seek Christ still among their kindred, in man's inventions, where they can never find him. As the Jews preferred man's traditions before God's commandments, even so it is now. Men think it a greater offence to break a fasting day, or work upon a saint's day, than to abstain from profitable labour, and turn it to Bacchus's feasts, exercising more ungodliness that day than all the week, despising or soon weary of God's word.—All this, with much more, cometh through lack of preaching, as experience trieth where godly pastors be.—It cannot much be marvelled, if the simple and ignorant people, by some wicked heads and firebrands of hell, be sometimes seduced to rebel against their prince and lawful magistrates, seeing they are never taught to know their obedience and duty to their king and sovereign, so straitly commanded in God's law.

But there hangeth over us a great evil, if your grace do not help it in time: the devil goeth about by these cormorants that devour these livings appointed for the gospel, to make a fortress and bulwark to keep learned pastors from the flock; that is, so to decay learning, that there shall be none learned to commit the flock unto. For by reason livings appointed for the ministry, for the most part are either robbed of the best part, or clean taken away; almost none have any zeal or devotion to put their children to school, but to learn to write, to make them apprentices, or else to have them lawyers. Look upon the two wells of this realm, Oxford and Cambridge; they are almost dried up. The cruel Philistines abroad, enemies to Christ's gospel, have stopped up the springs of faithful Abraham. The decay of students is so great, there are scarce left of every thousand an hundred. If they decay so fast in seven years more, there will be almost none at all; and then may the devil make a triumph. This matter requireth speedy redress. The miseries of your people cry upon you, noble prince, and Christ for his flock crieth to you his anointed, to defend his lambs from these ravenous wolves that rob and spoil his vineyard; by whose malicious endeavour, if your grace do not speedily resist, there is entering into England more blind ignorance, superstition, and infidelity, than ever was under the Romish bishop. Your Realm (which I am sorry to speak) shall become more barbarous than Scythia; which, lest God almighty lay to your grace's charge, for suffering the sword given to you for the maintenance of the gospel to lie rusting in the sheath, bestir now yourself in your heavenly father's business; withstanding these cormorants by godly laws, which rob Christ's gospel, and tread it down. 'They eat up God's people as it were bread.' Your grace shall have more true renown and glory before God by defending Christ's gospel against them, than by conquering all Africa. You shall do God more service by resisting this tyranny of the devil and his members, than by vanquishing the great Turk. Cut first away the occasions of all this mischief, dispensations for pluralities, and tot-quots for non-residents. Suffer no longer the tithes of the farthest parts of England to be paid at Paul's font. Cause every pastor, as his living will extend, to keep hospitality.—But many think themselves excused for a year or two, because their livings are taken away the first year; which undoubtedly doth not excuse them for their presence. I had rather beg or borrow of my friends, to help me to meat and clothes, than suffer the devil to have such liberty one year. It is no small number of souls that may perish by one year's absence. Moses was from the people but forty days, and they fell to idolatry.

Howbeit,* forasmuch as the scripture doth allow the minister a living the first year also ('He that serveth at the altar, let him live of the altar;' and again, 'Thou shalt not muzzle the ox that treadeth out the corn') I do not doubt, but after your grace, with the advice of your honourable council, have considered how much it may set forth God's glory, how many souls may be delivered from the devil by sending pastors to their livings the first month, and suffering them to have no cloak of absence, you will soon restore the first year's living, which in my conscience was wrongfully taken away at the first, as I suppose, by the bishop of Rome. But I doubt not, if all were well redressed to this, that this also should soon be amended. Wherefore, here I will desire God to assist your grace in the advancement of his gospel, which, like unto Josias, you have helped to bring to light where it lay hid.

But yet it is not heard of all your people. A thousand pulpits in England are covered with dust. Some have not had four sermons these fifteen or sixteen years, since friars left their limitations; and few of those were worthy the name of sermons. Now therefore, that your glory may be perfect, all men's expectation is, that whatsoever any flatterers, or enemies to God's word should labour to the contrary, for their own lucre; your grace will take away all such lets and abuses, as hinder the setting forth of God's most holy word, and withstand all such robbers, as spoil his sanctuary; travailing to send pastors home to their flocks, to feed Christ's lambs and sheep, that all may be occupied in their heavenly father's business. And for this your travail, as St. Peter saith, 'when the prince of all pastors shall appear, you shall receive an incorruptible crown of glory.'

And thus far concerning the ecclesiastical ministry.

But now to come to the civil governance,* the nobility, magistrates, and officers; all these must at all times remember, 'they must be occupied in their heavenly father's business.' They have received all their nobility, power, dominion, authority, and offices, of God; which are excellent and heroical gifts: and if they be occupied in God's business, it shall redound to his glory, and the wealth of his people; but if they fall from his business, and follow their own will, or rather the will of satan, the prince of darkness, and father of all the children of darkness, then shall all these glorious titles turn them to names of confusion. For falling unto ungodliness, and framing themselves to the shape and fashion of this world, nobility is turned into vile slavery and bondage of sin, power and dominion are turned into tyranny, authority is become a sword of mischief in a mad man's hand, all majesty and honour is turned into misery, shame, and confusion; and ever the higher men be, while they serve sin, the more notable is their vice, and more pestiferous to infect by evil examples; because all men's eyes are bent to behold their doings. 'Every fault of the mind is so much more evident, as the party is more notable who hath it,' saith Juvenal. For the worthier the person is which offendeth, the more his offence is noted of others; seeing that virtue in all whom God hath exalted is the maintainer of their dignity, without the which they fall from it. It shall be most needful for them to embrace virtue, and chiefly humility, which is the keeper of all virtues; which may put them ever in remembrance from whence power is given them, for what end, who is above them, a judge, an examiner of all their doings, who cannot be deceived. But as dignity goeth now a days, climb who may climb highest, every man exalteth himself, and tarrieth not the calling of God. Humility is taken for no keeper, but for an utter enemy to nobility. As I heard of a wicked climber and exalter of himself, who hearing the sentence of Christ in the gospel, 'He that humbleth himself shall be exalted,' he most blasphemously against God's holy word said, 'Sure it was not true; for if I, said he, had not put forth, nor advanced myself, but followed this rule, I had never come to this dignity;' for which blasphemy, the vengeance of God smote him with sudden death.

I fear me a great number are in England, which though in words they deny not this sentence of Christ's, yet inwardly they can scarce digest it; else certainly they would never seek so ambitiously to advance themselves, to climb by their own might, uncalled; never seeking the public weal, but rather the destruction thereof, for their private wealth and lucre; which causeth us to have so many evil magistrates. For all the while that men gather goods unjustly, by polling,* pilling,* usury, extortion, and simony, and therewith seek to climb with bribes and buying of offices, it is scarce possible for such to be wholesome magistrates.

They enter in at the window (which is used as well in civil government as ecclesiastical) and therefore may Christ's words well be verified, 'He that entereth not in at the door into the sheepfold, but climbeth up some other way, the same is a thief and a robber.' And Isaiah's complaint against Jerusalem taketh place among us, 'Thy princes are wicked, and companions of thieves; they love gifts altogether, and gape for rewards: as for the fatherless, they help not him in his right, neither will they let the widow's cause come before them.' They will not know their office to be ordained of God, for the wealth and defence of all innocents, for the aid of all that be in misery. The time is come that Solomon speaketh of, 'When the wicked man bears rule, the people shall mourn.' When had ever the people such cause to mourn as now, when the greatest number of all magistrates are occupied in their own business; seeking rather the misery of the people, than to take it away; rather to oppress them, than to defend them. Their hands be ready to receive their money, to rob and spoil them; but their ears are shut from hearing their complaints, they are blind to behold their calamities.

Look in all countries how lady Avarice hath set on work altogether mighty men, gentlemen, and rich men, to rob and spoil the poor; to turn them from their livings, and from their right; for ever the weakest go to the wall. And being thus tormented and put from their right at home, they come to London in great numbers, as to a place where justice should be had, and there they can have none. They are suitors to great men, and cannot come to their speech; their servants must have bribes, and that no small ones; 'all love bribes.' But such as be so dainty to hear the poor, let them take heed lest God make it as strange to them when they shall call: for as Solomon saith, 'Whoso stoppeth his ear at the crying of the poor, he shall cry and not be heard.' We find that poor men might come to complain of their wrongs to the king's own person. King Joram, although he was one of the sons of Ahab (no good king) yet heard the poor widow's cause, and caused her to have right: such was the use then.—I would to God that all noblemen would diligently note that chapter, and follow the example: it would not then be so hard for the poor to have access to them; nor coming to their presence, they should not be made so astonished and even speechless with terrible looks, but should mercifully and lovingly be heard, and succoured gladly for Christ's love, considering we are the members of his body; even as my hand would be glad to help my foot when it is annoyed.—O with what glad hearts and clear consciences might noblemen go to rest, when they had bestowed the whole day in hearing Christ himself complain in his members, and redressing his wrongs! But alas, for lack hereof, poor people are driven to seek their right among the lawyers; and there, as the prophet Joel saith, Look what the caterpillars had left in their robbery and oppression at home, all that doth the greedy locusts, the lawyers devour at London: they laugh with the money which maketh others to weep: and thus are the poor robbed on every side without redress, and that of such as seem to have authority thereto.

When Christ suffered his passion, there was one Barabbas, St. Matthew calleth him a notable thief, a gentleman thief, such as rob now a days in velvet coats; the other two were obscure thieves, and nothing famous. The rustical thieves were hanged, and Barabbas was delivered. Even so now a days the little thieves are hanged that steal of necessity, but the great Barabbases have free liberty to rob and to spoil without all measure, in the midst of the city. The poor pirate said to Alexander, We rob but a few in a ship, but thou robbest whole countries and kingdoms.—Alas, silly poor members of Christ, how you be shorn, oppressed, pulled, hauled to and fro on every side; who cannot but lament, if his heart be not of flint! There be a great number every term, and many continually, which lamentably complain for lack of justice, but all in vain. They spend that which they had left, and many times more; whose ill success here causeth thousands to tarry at home beggars, and lose their right—and so it were better, than here to sell their coats: for this we see, be the poor man's cause never so manifest a truth, the rich shall for money find six or seven counsellors that shall stand with subtleties and sophisms to cloak an evil matter, and hide a known truth.—A piteous case in a christian commonwealth! Alas, that ever manifest falsehood should be maintained, where the God of truth ought to be honoured!—But let them alone; they are occupied in their father's business, even the prince of darkness: 'you are of your father the devil.'

Yet I cannot so leave them; I must needs cry on God's behalf to his patrons of justice, to you, most redoubted prince, whom God hath made his minister for their defence, with all those whom God hath placed in authority under you. Look upon their misery, for this is our heavenly father's business to you, appointed by his holy word. When I come among the people, I call upon them, as my duty is, for service, duty, and obedience unto their prince, to all magistrates, to their lords, and to all that be put in authority over them; I let them hear their own faults: But in this place my duty is, and my conscience upon God's word bindeth me, seeing them so miserably, so wrongfully, so cruelly intreated on every side, in God's behalf to plead their cause; not by force of man's law, but by God's word, as an intercessor. For as they are debtors unto you, and other magistrates, for love, fear, service, and obedience under God; so are you again debtors unto them for love, protection, for justice and equity, mercy and pity. If you deny them these, they must suffer, but God shall revenge them. 'He standeth,' saith David, 'in the congregation of gods, and as a judge among gods.' Take heed all you that be counted as gods, God's ministers on earth; you have one God judge over you, who, as he saith in the same psalm, sharply rebuketh ungodly rulers for accepting of persons of the ungodly; so he telleth christian magistrates their true duties and business in plain words, 'Defend the poor and needy, see that such as be in necessity have right, deliver the outcast and poor, save them from the hands of the ungodly.' Here have all noblemen and christian magistrates most lively set forth to them their heavenly father's business, wherein he would have them continually occupied:—would to God the whole psalm were graven in their hearts!

Truly for lack that this business is not applied, but the poor despised in all places, it hath given such boldness to covetous cormorants abroad, that now their robberies, extortion, and open oppression, hath no end nor limits, no banks can keep in their violence. As for turning poor men out of their holds, they take it for no offence, but say, Their land is their own; and forget altogether, that 'the earth is the Lord's, and the fulness thereof.' They turn them out of their shrouds* as mice. Thousands in England, through such, beg now from door to door, which have kept honest houses. These cry daily to to God for vengeance, both against the great Nimrods, workers thereof, and their maintainers. There be so many mighty Nimrods in England, mighty hunters, that hunt for possessions and lordships, that poor men are daily hunted out of their livings; there is no covert nor den can keep them safe. These Nimrods have such quick smelling hounds, they can lie at London and turn men out of their farms and tenements, an hundred, some two hundred miles off.—O Lord, when wicked Ahab hunted after Naboth's vineyard, he could not, though he were a king, obtain that prey, till cursed Jezebel (as women oft-times have shrewd wits) took the matter in hand: so hard a thing it was then to wring a man from his father's inheritance, which now a mean man will take in hand. And now our valiant Nimrods can compass the matter without the help of Jezebels; yet hath England even now a great number of Jezebels, which to maintain their intolerable pride, their golden heads, will not stick to put to their wicked hands.—O Lord, what a number of such oppressors, worse than Ahab, are in England, which 'sell the poor for a pair of shoes!' of whom if God should serve but three or four, as he did Ahab, and make the dogs lap the blood of them, I think it would cause a great number to beware of extortion, to beware of oppression: and yet, escaping temporal punishments, they are certain by God's word, their blood is reserved for hell-hounds, which they nothing fear. A pitiful case, and great blindness, that, hearing God's word, man should more fear temporal punishment than everlasting.

Yet hath England had of late some terrible examples of God's wrath in sudden and strange deaths of such as join field to field, and house to house: great pity they were not chronicled to the terror of others, which fear neither God nor man; so hardened in sin, that they seek not to hide it, but rather are such as glory in their mischief. Which maketh me oftentimes to remember a writer in our time, Musculus, upon St. Matthew's gospel, which marvelled much at the subtle and manifold working of Satan; how he, after the expelling of superstition and hypocrisy, travelleth most busily to bring in open impiety: that whereas before, men feared men, though not God; now a great number fear neither God nor man: the most wicked are counted most manlike, and innocency holden beastliness.

Yet may we not say, hypocrisy is expelled: for as many of these Ahabs as signify they favour God's word by reading or hearing it, or with prayer, 'honouring him,' as Christ saith, 'with their lips, their hearts being far from him,' are as detestable hypocrites as ever were covered in cowl or cloister. I cannot liken them better than to the Jews, that said to Christ, 'Hail, king of the Jews.' What their painted friendship is, and how of Christ it is esteemed, St. Austin setteth forth by an apt similitude: 'Even as,' saith he, 'a man should come to embrace thee, to kiss and honour thee upward, and beneath, with a pair of shoes beaten full of nails, tread upon thy bare foot; the head shall despise the honour done unto it, and for the foot that smarteth, say, Why treadest thou upon me? So when feigned gospelers honour Christ our head sitting in heaven, and oppress his members on earth, the head shall speak for the feet that smart, and say, Why treadest thou on me?' Paul had a zeal towards God, but he did tread upon Christ's feet on earth, for whom the head cried forth of heaven, 'Saul, Saul, why persecutest thou me?' Although Christ sitteth at the right hand of his father, yet lieth he in earth, he suffereth all calamities here on earth, he is many times evil intreated here on earth.

Would to God we could bear away this brief and short lesson, that what we do to his members upon earth, we do to him; it would bring men from oppression to shew mercy, without which no man can obtain mercy. If they would remember how the rich glutton was damned in hell, not as we read for any violence, but for not shewing mercy, they might soon gather how sharp judgment remaineth for them, which are not only unmerciful, but also violently add thereunto oppression; who are so far from mercy, that their hearts will serve them to destroy whole towns; they would wish all the people destroyed, to have all the fields brought to a sheep pasture. O cruel mercy! It is like to the mercy of a bishop of Magunce in Germany, named Hatto, which, as the chronicles mention, five hundred years ago, in time of a great dearth, called all the poor people in all the whole country into a great barn, pretending to make a great dole; but having them sure, he fired the barn, and burnt them all up, saying, 'These be the mice which devour up the corn.' This was a policy to make bread more cheap, but for this unmerciful mercy, God made him an example for all unmerciful men to the world's end; for a multitude of rats came and devoured him in such terrible sort, that where his name was written in windows, walls, or hangings, they never ceased till it were razed out.—Some peradventure shrink to hear such cruelty: but doubtless there is almost daily as great cruelty practised among us by such blood-suckers, as being infected with the great dropsy of avarice, alway drinking, and ever athirst, by famishing poor people, drinking up their blood, and with long continuance therein, torment them more grievously than he that burnt them all in one hour.

Now seeing, as I said, this cruelty, robbery, and extortion, groweth daily to such intolerable excess, and overfloweth this realm, because it is not punished nor restrained; it is high time for all those magistrates that fear God, not only to abstain from this evil themselves, but to resist it also. It is God's business, he hath commanded it, and will straitly require it. Would to God all noblemen would beware by the example of Saul. He was commanded to apply God's business, 'Go and smite Amalek, and have no compassion on them, &c.' he left his business undone, spared Amalek, and the fairest of the beasts: but for this negligence he received of Samuel a sorrowful message from God; 'because thou hast cast away the word of the Lord, he hath cast thee off also from being king.' Even so in every christian commonwealth, God hath commanded rulers to destroy Amalek, all extortion, oppression, and robbery, to defend the needy and all innocents. If they look not to this business, but suffer Amalek to live, not only to live, but to grow in might; so truly as God liveth, he shall cast them off, they shall not be his magistrates.

But it let once be known, that not only our most noble king, whose godly example is a lantern to all other, but that also all his nobles about him have wholly bent themselves in his business, to withstand all violence, and to oppose all oppression, for defence of God's people; that the wicked Ahabs might know, that God had in England a great number of pastors, patrons, feeders and cherishers of his people: it should do that which the fear of God cannot do; that is, stop the great rage of violence, oppression, and extortion: which taken away, would pluck from many their vanity in superfluous and monstrous apparel, sumptuous building, such as seek to bring paradise into earth, being the greatest causes of all oppression and spoiling of poor people; which most unchristian vanities, and blind affections, never reigned so much in all estates in England as at this day. It was a notable saying of Charles V emperor of that name, to the duke of Venice, when he had seen his princely palace; when the duke looked that he should have praised it exceedingly, Charles gave it none other commendation but this, '*Haec sunt quae faciunt invitos mori*; These earlthly vanities,' said he, 'are what make us loth to die.' A truer sentence could not well be spoken by any man. I could wish we would look on all our buildings, when the beauty thereof so increaseth, that it would grieve us to depart from it, and to remember with all the holy patriarchs, and with St. Paul say, that 'we have not here a continuing city, but we seek one to come.'

But truly methinks now in England for our vain delight in curious buildings, God hath plagued us, as he did the builders of Babel, not with the confusion of tongues, but with the confusion of wits. Our fancies can never be pleased: pluck down and set up, and when it contenteth us not, down with it again. Our minds are never contented, nor ever shall be, while we seek felicity where it is not. Would God every one would consider what a hell it should be to all that vainly delight herein, when death shall with great violence pluck them from their earthly heaven. Moreover, extortion taken away shall soon abate the unmeasurable excess in costly fare. It would also abate the intolerable excess in apparel, which causeth us to have robbers in velvet coats, with St. Martin's chains.—But I must for lack of time pass over these enormities, which alone give matter enough for whole sermons: I leave them for others which shall follow, more able to paint out such monsters in their colours.

And here in conclusion, I desire all noblemen and godly magistrates, deeply to ponder and revolve in their memory, what acceptable service they may do, chiefly to God, and secondly to the king's majesty, and his whole realm, in employing their whole study how to resist all such as spoil Christ's people, whom he so tenderly loved that he shed his blood for them. Virtue joined with nobility, spreadeth her beams over a whole realm. And so your diligence in God's business shall soon inflame all other to follow your example, that all may occupy themselves in God's business.

But now that I have hitherto charged the ecclesiastical ministers,* and after, the civil governors, and all rich and mighty men with negligence in God's business; methinks I do hear the inferior members rejoice and flatter themselves, as if all were taken from them, and they left clear in God's sight: but if they consider their estate by God's word, they shall find small cause to advance themselves. For God's word plainly telleth us, both that evil and dumb pastors, and wicked rulers and magistrates, are sent of God, as a plague and punishment for the sins of the people; and therefore, both Isaiah and Hosea, after the most terrible threatenings of God's vengeance for sin, bring it in as a most grievous plague of all, that even the priests, which should call them from sin, shall become as evil as the people. Which plague St. Bernard said in his time was come with a vengeance, for because the priests were much worse than the people. And Amos, as a most grievous punishment of all other, threateneth hunger, not of bread, but of hearing God's word. And concerning the civil magistrates, it is plain in Job, that for the sins of the people God raiseth hypocrites to reign over them; that is to say, such as have the bare names of governors and protectors, and are indeed destroyers, oppressors of the people, subverters of the law and of all equity.

And seeing it is so, so many as feel the grief and smart of this plague, ought not to murmur against other; but patiently suffer, and be offended with their own sins, which have deserved this scourge, and much more; and study for amendment, that God may take it away. For if they continue as they do, to murmur against God and their rulers, as the Israelites did, to provoke daily his anger by multiplying sin in his sight, with envy, malice, deceit, backbiting, swearing, fornication, and with utter contempt of his word; he shall for their punishment so multiply the number of evil governors, unjust judges, justices, and officers, that as it was spoken by a jester in the emperor Claudius's time, the images of good magistrates may all be graven in one ring.

God hath cause greatly to be displeased with all estates. When every man should look upon his own faults to seek amendment, as it is a proverb lately sprung up, 'No man amendeth himself, but every man seeketh to amend other,' and all the while nothing is amended. Gentlemen say, the commonalty live too well at ease, they grow every day to be gentlemen, and know not themselves; their horns must be cut shorter, by raising their rents, by fines, and by plucking away their pastures.—The mean men, they murmur and grudge, and say, the gentlemen have all, and there were never so many gentlemen and so little gentleness: and by their natural logic you shall hear them reason, how improperly these two conjugata, these yoke-fellows, gentlemen and gentleness, are banished so far asunder; and they lay all the misery of this commonwealth upon the gentlemen's shoulders.— But alas, good christians, this is not the way of amendment: 'If ye bite and devour one another,' as St. Paul saith, 'take ye heed lest ye be consumed one of another.'

Histories make mention of a people called Anthropophagi, eaters of men, which all men's hearts abhor to hear of; and yet, alas, by St. Paul's rule, England is full of such man-eaters. Every man envieth another, every man biteth and gnaweth upon another with venomous adders' tongues, far more noisome than any teeth. And whereof cometh it? Covetousness is the root of all; every man scratcheth and pilleth from other; every man would suck the blood of other; every man encroacheth upon another. Covetousness hath cut away the large wings of charity, and plucketh all to herself; she is never satisfied; she hath chested all the old gold in England, and much of the new; she hath made that there was never more idolatry in England than at this day: but the idols are hid, they come not abroad.—Alas, noble prince, the images of your ancestors graven in gold, and yours also, contrary to your mind, are worshipped as gods; while the poor lively images of Christ perish in the streets through hunger and cold. This cometh when covetousness hath banished from amongst us christian charity; when like most unthankful children, we have forgotten Christ's last will, which he so often before his passion did inculcate, 'Love one another.'

And herein we shew ourselves worse than any carnal sons; be they never so unkind, yet always they remember the last words of their earthly parents. Nay rather I may say, we are much worse than the brute beasts; of whom, when we consider how wonderfully nature hath framed them to concord and unity, to preserve and help one another of their own kind, it may make us utterly to be ashamed. The harts, swimming, with much pain bear up their heads in the water; for the remedy whereof, every one layeth his head upon the hinder part of another: when the foremost, having no stay, is sore weary, he cometh behind, and thus every one in his course taketh pain for the whole herd.—If men, endued with reason, would learn of these unreasonable creatures this lesson, to help one another, as we are commanded by St. Paul, saying, 'Bear ye one another's burthen, and so you shall fulfill the law of Christ,' how soon then should charity, the bond of perfection, which seeketh not her own, but rather to profit others, be so spread among all degrees, that our commonwealth should flourish in all godliness? But alas! we see that all goeth contrary. For while all men, as St. Paul saith, 'seek the things that be their own, and not other men's, not things which appertain to Christ,' self-love, and love of private commodity, hath banished charity and love to the commonwealth.

And if we should seek the cause and ground of all these evils, why God's business is so neglected among all estates and degrees, I think it would appear to be ignorance of his will. For if Mary and Joseph, so godly and devout a couple, understood not for a time Christ's saying, 'Wist ye not that I must go about my father's business?' as St. Luke saith, 'they understood not that saying,' what marvel is it, if we, living so carnally, and drowned in worldly pleasures, and framed to the shape of this world, be ignorant in our heavenly father's business, and therefore cannot well apply it? But shall we think this to be very strange? Many apply not God's business nor his will, which yet would disdain to be counted ignorant therein. But undoubtedly, good christians, it is an infallible verity, that negligence in performing God's will cometh of ignorance. It is all one to know God and his will; and St. John saith plainly, 'He that loveth not, knoweth not God.' For if he do know God, he cannot but love him; and love is always occupied in God's business.

By this rule St. Augustine proveth, we cannot keep perfectly the first precept, to love God, so well as we ought to do while we are in this mortal life; for all our love cometh of knowledge, but in this life our knowledge is imperfect. And thus St. Augustine's rule, grounded upon St. John, is true, 'That so far as we do know God, so far we love him; and so they that love him nothing at all, they know him nothing at all, although they seem to have never so much windy knowledge, puffing up their stomachs with presumption,' as the apostle saith, 'Knowledge maketh a man swell:' so that if a man have studied the scripture all his life long, and learned the whole bible by heart, and yet have no love, he is ignorant of God's will. The poor man that never opened book, if the love of God be shed abroad in his heart by the holy Ghost, overcometh him in the knowledge of God's will. The godly Pembus, of whom we read in ecclesiastical history, when he was first taught the first verse of the thirty ninth psalm, 'I have said, I will take heed to my ways, that I offend not in my tongue,' refused a long time to take out a new lesson, judging his first lesson to be unlearned, till he could perfectly practise it by an holy conversation. So ought we always to make our account to have learned God's word, only when we have learned charity and obedience.

But this knowledge, though it lack in many learned, yet ordinarily it cometh by hearing God's word, 'Faith cometh of hearing, and hearing of the word of God.' Wherefore, as I said, their case is to be lamented, which would gladly hear God's word, and can have no preachers. Then may we say, God hath abundantly poured his grace among us, that have his gospel so clearly set forth unto us, and have such opportunity, that there wanteth nothing but ears to hear: we must have ears to let it sink into our hearts. But, O men, thrice unhappy, and children of greater damnation, if we harden our hearts, and receive such abundance of grace in vain. 'The earth,' saith St. Paul, 'which after the rain bringeth forth thorns and briars, is reproved, and is nigh unto cursing, whose end is to be burned.'

Would God all that be in the court, that will not vouchsafe (having so many godly sermons) to come forth out of the hall into the chapel to hear them, would remember what a heavy stroke of God's vengeance hangeth over all their heads that contemn his word; and over those in all places, which had rather be idle, and many times ungodly occupied in wanton and wicked pastimes, than come to the church; profaning the sabbath day, appointed for the service of God, and the hearing of his word, bestowing it more wickedly than many of the gentiles. Yet if they would come to the sermons, though their hearts were not well disposed, God's word might win them, as St. Augustine was won by the preaching of St. Ambrose, when he came only to hear his sweet voice and eloquence. O that they knew what dishonour they did to Christ, that esteem him so light, to prefer vain, nay, I say wicked things, to the hearing of his holy word. Are not these they, as St. Paul saith, 'which tread under foot the Son of God, count the blood of his testament, wherein they are sanctified, an unholy thing; and do despite to the Spirit of grace?' O Lord, how canst thou hold thy hands from punishing this unthankfulness? Certainly I think all other wickedness compared to this, is shadowed, and seemeth to be less.

I would to God we would remember many times the plagues and tokens of God's extreme wrath that came upon the Jews, when first unthankfully they rejected Christ, and after his word; when they were destroyed by Titus and Vespasian, such a plague as never came upon any other country. And look on their vices; there reigned avarice, ambition, pride, extortion, envy, adultery; but these reigned also in other countries about, where no such vengeance did light: but then did God thus exercise his wrath upon them to the terror of all other, for contempt of his holy word, and for their unthankfulness; which being called so many ways, by his prophets, by himself, by the apostles, still hardened their hearts: this exceeded all other wickedness in the world. Now if as great unthankfulness be found in many of us towards Christ and his gospel, set forth so plainly unto us; how can we, without speedy repentance, but look for the terrible stroke of vengeance. 'God,' saith Valerius Maximus, 'hath feet of wool; he cometh slowly to punish, but he hath hands of iron; when he cometh, he striketh sore.'

Philip, king of Macedonia, hearing of one in his kingdom which refused most unthankfully to receive a stranger, (of whom before he had been succoured in shipwreck) in extreme need; for a worthy punishment, caused to be printed in his forehead with an hot iron these two words, '*Ingratus hospes*, An unthankful guest.' O Lord, if we consider when we were strangers from God, in the shipwreck of sin, how mercifully Christ hath delivered us, and born our sins upon his body; if after all this, we most unthankfully refuse to receive him, by refusing his word, may we not think ourselves worthy many hot irons to print our unthankfulness to our shame? And undoubtedly, so many as continue thus unthankful, though it be not written in their foreheads to put them to worldly shame, yet shall it be graven in their conscience, to their everlasting confusion and damnation, when 'the books of every man's conscience shall be laid open,' as Daniel saith. Their judgment shall be more strait than that of Sodom and Gomorrah.—Let us all then, from the highest to the lowest, pray with one accord, that God may soften and prepare our hearts with meekness, and humility, and thankfulness, to embrace his gospel, and his holy word; which shall instruct us in his holy will, and teach us to know his business, every man in his vocation, 'that (as St. Paul saith) every man may give attendance to themselves, and to the flock, wherein the holy Ghost hath made them overseers, to feed the congregation of God which he hath purchased with his blood,' that all ravenous wolves may be turned to good shepherds. So that Christ's ministers may enjoy the portion assigned for the gospel; that all magistrates and governors may give their whole study to the public weal, and not to their private wealth; that they may be maintainers of justice, and punishers of wrong; and that all inferiors may live in due obedience, meekly contenting themselves every one in their vocation, without murmuring or grudging; that under Christ, and our noble prince, his minister here on earth, we all being knit together with christian charity, the bond of perfection, may so fasten our eyes upon God's word, that it may continually be a lantern to our feet, to guide our journey through the desert and dark wilderness of this world, that our eyes be never so blinded with shadows of worldly things, as to make us to embrace false, deceitful, and temporal felicity, for that which is true, steadfast, and everlasting; that this candle which shineth now, as St. Paul saith, 'as through a glass darkly,' when that which is imperfect shall be taken away, may present us to that clear light, which never is shadowed with any darkness; that we may behold that blessed sight of the glorious Trinity, the Father, the Son, and the Holy Ghost, to whom be all praise, all honour, and glory, world without end.

## NOTES

p. 98. *Pelagius*: not the early critic of original sin, but a (now quite obscure) Catholic bishop whose *De Planctu Ecclesiae* (1474) is an overstated argument in defence of papal supremacy.   *Marsilius Paduanus*: see p. 17. This paragraph affirms Gilpin's allegiance to the Church of England.

p. 99. *But notwithstanding* . . .: this is the transitional paragraph, in which Gilpin turns his attention from Romish to new English abuses; he cleverly (and surely sincerely) attributes them, of course, to 'Rome . . . their father'.

p. 100. *totquots*: Latin: as many as [there may be], i.e. unlimited pluralism.

p. 100. *And because they are accounted* . . .: this is thoroughly Erasmian in spirit, except that it is accusing the nobles who support the reform of not cutting themselves even further asunder from Rome! Tunstall, who accepted the Pope under Mary (though he declined to take part in the persecution of those who would not) and who refused to take the oath of supremacy under Elizabeth, must have been fond of his great-nephew, for he could hardly have agreed with the line of his argument.   *bayards*: a then current term meaning 'over-confident idiots'.

p. 103. *John Gerson*: Jean le Charlier de Gerson (1363-1429), French churchman and writer, and a precursor of Erasmus in his work for reform of the Church. He influenced Luther. He advocated a cutting down of papal power, but condemned the teachings of Huss.

p. 105. *They think baptism is not effectual* . . .: i. e. Anabaptists who reject infant baptism.

p. 107. *Howbeit, forasmuch as the scripture doth allow* . . .: Here begins a plea (unheeded) by Gilpin for the repeal of the Annates Act of 1534, by which the first year's revenue of a benefice was made payable to the crown and not to Rome. In 1703 by 'Queen Anne's Bounty' it was redistributed to poorer clergy.   *But now to come to the civil governance* . . . : Here begins the onslaught on the secular arm. It is interesting to read this in the light of, and as a development of, Cranmer's philosophy of the status of good works in his three homilies given in this book.

p. 108. *polling*: the word denoted despoliation, robbery and excessive taxation.   *pilling*: plundering, despoiling.

p. 111. *shrouds*: hovels, rough lodgings.

p. 115. *But now that I have hitherto charged* . . .: Gilpin ends his sermon with an exhortation to the oppressed people not to rebel, but to consider their own sins.

# Richard Bancroft

Bancroft was educated at Jesus College, Cambridge. His anti-Puritanism was evident from the first—the important sermon given below is an example of this—and Elizabeth saw in him an excellent weapon against the forces which were trying to abolish episcopacy and thus ultimately to undermine her personal authority. Being a Tudor, she liked to choose others to perform actions which might offend large sections of the populace—and she was very skilful at it, as indeed her father had been. Thus, in 1597 when Whitgift, the Archbishop of Canterbury (a staunch Church of England man, even though theologically Calvinist) became senile, she made Bancroft Bishop of London. This meant that in effect he held Whitgift's powers, though he was not actually made Archbishop of Canterbury until 1604, when Whitgift died. He did not, in fact, prove a tactful Archbishop, and some have attributed to him the failure of the Hampton Court Conference (but he was there dealing with men in whose vocabulary the very conception of tact did not exist). He worked hard to root Puritans out of the Church, and, not being theologically Calvinist, was better able than Whitgift to see their danger to it. He died in 1610 and was succeeded by George Abbot, who was markedly pro-Puritan in his sympathies.

# A Warning against Puritans

THIS SERMON was preached at Paul's Cross on 9 February 1589 (1588 old style). It is an eminently reasonable piece of preaching, done at a time when the situation might (possibly) have been saved. The spirit of the Church of England, as we have seen in the discussion of Cranmer, is contained in the masterly Thirty-Nine Articles. These have been seen as a disgraceful compromise; they have also been seen as a document of reasoned tolerance, leaving open to the individual conscience just those questions that must most vex the Christian believer. And although the Church was temporarily eclipsed after the defeat and execution of Charles I, the Commonwealth and Protectorate lasted for only twelve years. Since then the Church has resisted, if not uncontentiously, both extreme wings, seeking rather to accommodate them. So Bancroft's remark, 'It hath always been the manner of heretics, to bring their lives into hatred, whose Doctrine they cannot confute', has some significance in this matter of tolerance. His definition of the militant Puritan style is not altogether unfair: one must remember that if Sandys, Whitgift and Jewel and other such quasi-Calvinists could not not only stay in, but fight for, an established Church, then the compromise upon which that Church is based must mean something more than the word compromise is usually taken to mean today. This sermon, as might be expected, was highly offensive to the extreme Puritans.

THE DOCTRINE of the Church of *England*, is pure, and holy: the government thereof, both in respect of her Majesty, and of our Bishops is lawful, and godly: the Book of Common Prayer containeth nothing in it contrary to the Word of God.

All those points have been notably approved, and maintained not only against the Papists, but likewise against some other schismatics, and you your selves with great joy, and comfort have in time past embraced them accordingly. If any of you now, my brethren, be otherwise affected, the fault is in your selves: for they remain (as the nature of truth requireth) to be as they were before: but you through your rashness in following of every spirit, are grown to a wonderful newfangleness: and are in deed become mere changelings. *Quemadmodum eadem terra stat recte valentibus, quae vertigine correptis videtur moveri*: As the same Earth (saith *Greg. Naz.*) appeareth immovable to those that are in health, which to the giddy doth seem to turn about: so you, my brethren, by following the persuasions of false Prophets (who, as *Irenaeus* saith; *De iisdem non semper easdem sententias habent*: Of the self same things have not always the same opinions) are drawn to an unjust mislike of the Church; *Et amantes vel non amantes, haud eadem de eisdem judicatis*: And according to your love, or hate your judgments upon the self same things do vary, and alter.

See, I pray you, what dislike is able to work; and therefore take heed of those who shall endeavour, through lies, and slanders, to make the truth, and the preachers thereof odious, and hateful unto you. For as the Apostle writeth; *Aemulantur vos non bene, sed excludere vos volunt, ut, illos aemulemini: They are jealous over amiss*, even for their own purpose, and commodity: yea they would exclude you from the Doctrine you have received at our hands, and from the affection, and love, which you once bare unto us, that ye might altogether love them, and follow their devices.

And that is the end of their railings, and libelling. *Mos semper fuit haeretuorum, quorum doctrinam non possunt confutare, illorum vitam in odium adducere*: It hath always been the manner of heretics, to bring their lives into hatred, whose Doctrine they cannot confute. Knowing that by the contempt of the one, doth easily ensue the dislike of the other.

Howbeit, they will pretend that the zeal of God's glory doth move them unto such bitterness, against the present estate or Religion, and against the chief maintainers of it, and that for conscience sake, and for the glory of Sion they are driven to use such more than tragical outcries. But *Bernard* will not suffer them to hide their malice under these masks, who writing against certain schismatics in his time, saith, *Allii quidem nude atque irreverenter, uti in buccam venerit, virus evomant detractionis*: Some do plainly, and irreverently, even as it comes into their stomach, spew out the poison of their slanders. Many others there be, who cover their malice more cunningly, nay more hypocritically, as though all they said proceeded of mere love, and Christian charity, of whom it followeth, *Videas alta praemitti suspiria: sicque quadam cum gravitate et tarditate, vultu maesto, demissis superciliis et voce plangenti egredi maledictionem, et quidem tanto persuasibiliorem, quanto creditur ab his qui audiunt corde invito et magis condolentis affectu, quam malitiose proferri*. You shall see some, that after they have set diverse great sighs, and groans, will presently with great gravity, and drawing out of their words, with a heavy countenance, with casting down their heads, and with a pitiful voice, breathe out malediction, the which men do rather believe, because it seemeth by such their hypocritical dealing, rather to proceed of a sorrowful compassion, than of malice, and hatred. But dearly beloved, take heed of these spirits. Where you find these conditions, believe not, I pray you, any such protestations.

Furthermore, you shall have some that will come unto you with a long tale, protesting that they cannot refrain their tears; with the ancient men in *Ezra*, to see the foundation of our new Temple not to be answerable (as they say) to the beauty of the old. And herein they think they should be very acceptable unto you: whereas in truth the crying of these aged men, was a great discouragement to the builders, and one of the principal lets, why the work went no better forward: and the Prophet *Aggaeus* was sent from God to reprove them for it; allowing nay, preferring in some respects, the new building, which then they had in hand, before the other, which some so much affected.

So as, dearly beloved, when you hear the like cries, in any wise believe them not; but rather shout aloud for joy (as there it is likewise noted) in that you have lived to see your Temples purged from the leaven of Popery, and to flourish, as they do, with the sincerity, and truth of Christian Religion.

They will furthermore (the better to creep into your hearts) pretend great humility, and bitterly exclaim against the pride of Bishops as though they affected nothing else by their desired equality, but some great lowliness, and to prostrate themselves at your feet for your service: whereas in deed they shoot at greater superiority, and preeminence, than ever your Bishops did use of challenge unto them: and would no doubt tyrannize by their censures over both Prince, and people at their pleasure, in most intolerable, and popelike manner. As partly you may gather by the premises, and partly furthermore understand in that not only they do use the very same arguments for the sovereign authority of their presbyteries (against the Prince) in causes Ecclesiastical: that the Pope doth for his principality in the same (and none other so far as I can read, or I think can be shewed by any) but do likewise make to all our arguments for her Majesty's supremacy against them, the very same answers, (if not word for word, yet always in effect) that *Harding, Stapleton, Dorman,* and *Saunders\** have made to the same arguments, used by Bishop *Jewell*, Bishop *Horn*, Master Nowell, and others to the same purpose, and against the Pope. I cannot stand to enter into any particular examples of this matter, only I thought it necessary at this time to advertise you of it (take his advantage thereof who list) that you might the better beware of such kind of spirits.

You have heard them, I am sure, greatly exclaim against our Bishops' livings, as though they had too much, thereby to persuade you with what simple allowance they could content themselves: and yet (as you have heard) they reckon all the livings of the Church too little for themselves: condemning you of the laity, who either have or would have part with them, for cormorants, *Dionysians*, and for such wicked traitors against the Church, as *Judas* was against Christ.

They would gladly seem to be very godly, zealous, and religious: and yet notwithstanding, if you will rely upon Saint *James* his opinion, and judge of them by the usage of their tongues, in their immodest speeches, and libelling, you shall find their profession thereof to be full of so great vanity, as that particularly it may be verified almost of everyone of them: *Hujus vana est religio*.

If they set forth a book of Common Prayer, then caution is made that nothing be done contrary to any thing set down in the same. If they decree any thing in their synods (yea though it be in civil matters) against an act of Parliament, that treason is not treason, yet if you withstand them, you are forthwith accursed: or as touching Church causes, except it should so fall out, that they do err in their determinations, and that in some great matter of faith, all men must stand unto their orders, decrees, laws, and constitutions.

But on the other side, if the Church indeed, upon sufficient grounds shall either publish a book, or command any thing to be observed, though that which is commanded have been determined of, not only by provincial or national synods, but by all the general councils in effect, which were held before the tyranny of popery: yet (as Saint *Bernard* saith in the like case) *Haerent ad singula quae insunguntur, exigunt de quibusque rationem, male suspicantur de omni praecepto, nec unquam libenter acquiescunt, nisi cum audire contigerit quod forte libuerit*: they stick at all things which are enjoined, they require the reason of every thing, they suspect amiss of every precept, and will never willingly hold themselves contented but when they hear that, which peradventure doth please them—.

NOTE

p. 126. *Harding, Stapleton, Dorman and Saunders*: Catholics who went abroad in 1558 and from there issued polemics against Bishop Jewel.

## Thomas Drant

THOMAS DRANT, a Lincolnshire man, was educated at St John's College, Cambridge. He was one of Archbishop Grindal's chaplains; he became Archdeacon of Lewes in 1569, and died in 1578. He is best known for the literary influence he had on Edmund Spenser and Philip Sidney: he drew up 'rules' (known as 'Drant's Rules') by which, he claimed, English verse could be written in classical (i. e. quantitative) metres. The experiments of Sidney and his group are famous for their failure, though Spenser produced some interesting poems.

# O Men, O Lilies
*And to gather up Lilies.*

THIS WAS given at St Mary Spital on 'Tuesday in Easterweek, 1570'. It is included here as an example of euphuistic preaching: extravagant, rhetorical, ornate, literary in feeling and inspiration. The most famous of the euphuistic writers is Lyly. One can see the influence of the style in Andrewes.

OF GATHERING of Lilies, many things may be spoken many ways. And what Lilies do signify in this place, I am to say as before: that when the beloved goeth down into his spicery to be fed in the Orchards and to gather Lilies, is no more but that he goeth to be refreshed in the earth. Howbeit the fathers have made a further process in this matter, and some yield one sense, and some an other. But for my self I would not for anything rehearse opinions upon opinions, and notes upon opinions, and exhortations upon notes, for that would be now long and wearisome: only I will say something of one exposition which Rabbi Jarhi and S. Barnard do seem to embrace: that is, to gather up Lilies, is to gather up men: and yet even in this one exposition resteth to be handled that Christ is a gatherer, and men be flowers. If Christ be a gatherer, then he is no disperser. In deed it is meet that the shepherd should gather his sheep, and the hen her chickens, and the husbandman the grain into the barn. Even to the Prophet Ezekiel saith: That Christ should gather his sheep out of all lands, and gather them into their own land. So doth he himself say with an affection of most deep love: O Jerusalem, Jerusalem, how often would I have gathered thee together, as the hen gathereth her chickens under her wing, and thou wouldst not. And as Lilies grow dispersed here one, and there one: so good men grow rare and thin. And as Christ picketh Lilies from among thorns (for they grow among thorns): so picked he Abraham from the thorns of Chaldae, Job from the Hussites, Hiram from the Tirians, Naaman from the Syrians, the Ninivites from the Assyrians. Lilies grow rare, and good men grow rarer: Lilies amongst thorns, and good men amongst thorns. And as the gathering of Lilies and men be like: so men and Lilies be very like. I will speak a thing of marvellous troth: A man is but a Lily, the pride and glory of a man is but the pride and glory of a Lily. Solomon is a Lily, King Solomon is a Lily, King Solomon in his glory is a Lily, Sons of vanity to whom it is delightful to have feathers to dance in your tops as big as Ajax's shields, to have your heads turkish and your backs spanish, your waists italian, and your feet venetian, with such a world of hosen glory about your loins, Sons (I say) of vanity, ye are but Lilies, Solomon in all his glory is but a Lily. Solomon in his worst workaday apparel, is better than the best of you all. Solomon in his best holiday apparel, is not so brave as a Lily: ye therefore in the huff of your ruff are nothing comparable to a Lily, no not to a field Lily. Daughters of vanity, and dames of delicacy, ye think it fine and featous [handsome] to be called roses, primroses, and Lilies: and indeed it is true, in respects you are roses, primroses and Lilies. When ye have gotten all upon your heads and backs which English soil doth yield, and many a merchant hath fetched full far, when all your tailors have broken their brains about contriving of forms, and fashions, yet then are ye nothing so tricksy trim as the Lily. The best of ye all in all your best bravery, is not like to a field Lily, which haply tomorrow is plucked up, and flung into the furnace. Prick and prune your selves to the day of doom, ye will never be like to the field Lily. For the Lily of this our flesh is not so goodly gay, as the Lily of grass: otherwise and in many imperfections we are very perfect, and true Lilies. The Lily of grass shooteth up for a time, but then he layeth down his top, and is made even to the floor. The Lily of flesh flourisheth for a time, but then by honouring death he is taught to pour upon the ground, and to let down his top like a Lily. The wrath of winter doth conquer and kill the Lily of grass: there be more than many occasions to vanquish, and kill the Lily of flesh. Barnard saith that there is a worm that eateth up the root of the Lily of grass: Each Lily of flesh hath his worm and consumer. Julius Caesar, Hercules, and Mahomet have the falling sickness, Maecenas hath a three years' ague, Orestes hath the frenzy, Speusippus hath the palsy, Heraclitus and Aristarcus the dropsy, Marcus Crassus the stuffing in the head, Jeroboam the withered arm, Lazarus and Job, biles and botches, Aristotle an evil stomach, Euripides putrifaction of lungs, Corvinus the lethargy, Anacrion lack of sleep. Agesilaus and Ptolomeus the gout, Naaman and Mary the leprosy. But what do I say that every Lily of flesh hath his worm and consumer, sithens I may truly say that every part of every Lily of flesh hath his diverse worms and consumers. The head hath the Apoplexy, the Epilepsy, and the turnabout sickness, the eyes have the Opthalmy and the Migraine, the neck hath the palsy and the convulsion, the nose hath the Polyp, the palate hath the vulva, the gums have the canker, the teeth have the toothache, the throat hath the angina, the tongue hath blisters and swelling, the stomach hath the motive cause of the cardiacal passion, and murdering rheums (the student's sickness), the sides have colic's stitches, a prickling pleurisy, the reines [kidneys] have the stone, the legs have dropsies and cramps, the feet and hands have the knobbed gout. Besides that the Lily of flesh hath worms of mind and worms of conscience, many worms and sore worms.

The Lily of grass hath his own worm, and the Lily of flesh hath his thousand worms: the Lily of grass can not live from that one worm, but will be smitten of it nor the Lily of the flesh shall escape all these worms. Again, all the grass Lilies are dead and gone that have grown on the face of the earth and all flesh Lilies are dead that lived upon this earth, Abraham God's friend, and Noah that walked with God, Aaron full of dignity, and Moses full of authority, holy Melchisedec, and just Job, strong Sampson, and huge Ogge, vaunting Goliath and disdainful Senacharib, fair Absalom, and sweet lovely Jonathan, wise Solomon, rich Croesus, and wealthy Crassus, lucky Pompey, victorious Julius, royal Augustus, and triumphant Emilius, all these have had a time like a Lily, and died in time like a Lily. They have had the spring of their budding, and the summer of their blossoming, they have likewise come to the Autumn of their parching, and the winter of their perishing. O all ye, ye men that draw breath under the cope of the skies, ye spring up like Lilies, and go down like Lilies; ye flourish like Lilies and deflower like Lilies. Pindarus said thrice, Mammea, Mammea, Mammea. Jeremy cried thrice Earth, Earth, Earth; so I, Lilies, Lilies, Lilies; and then a second time, Lilies, Lilies, Lilies; and, for that I would have it remembered I cry again, Lilies, Lilies, Lilies; and then thus, O Men, O Lilies, O Men, O Lilies, O Men, O Lilies. O field of Grass, O Flowers of Decay; Yet came Christ among such Lilies to gather up such fleeting flowers of flesh, and to be conversant among his spicery.

# Robert Rollock

ROBERT ROLLOCK, whose name was sometimes spelt Rollok, was the son of David Rollock, Laird of Powis near Stirling. He and his brother Hercules, later to become Master of the High School, Edinburgh and a distinguished writer of Latin verses, were given a liberal education. Robert so impressed his teachers at St Salvator's College, St Andrews, that he was early elected professor; when the College that was to become Edinburgh University was founded (1583) he was the natural choice as its first principal. From 1587 he was Professor of Theology. He would have preferred a quiet existence as an academic, but, partly because of his moderation, his genius as a teacher—he was able to combine strict discipline with gentleness—and his much admired, eminently reasonable character, he was forced into public life. The strain imposed upon him probably led to his early death in 1599. There were extraneous reasons for this, the background to which must be briefly explained.

In 1561 the Roman Catholic Mary Queen of Scots returned to her own country, her French husband having died. But in the previous year the rabid Calvinist John Knox (1513 or 1514-72, a convert from Catholicism, *c*. 1545, who reached his Calvinist position before meeting the admired master himself) returned from exile in Geneva (which he called 'the most perfect school of Christ since the days of the apostles'), had prevailed upon the Scottish parliament (then, of course, entirely independent of England's) to accept Calvinism. One may sympathize with Mary's predicament in having Knox as her opponent, but she destroyed her cause and, eventually, herself, by double-dealing. When her well-intentioned, peace-loving but inept, weak, vain and ridiculous son James VI (later James I of England) took over control of government in 1578, his religious policy was for some time an apparently vacillating one. Its main direction, however, was evident: he wished to establish episcopacy and to defeat the Calvinistic Presbyterianism which Knox had enforced in 1560, and which was now forcefully upheld by his follower, Melville. In 1584 pro-Episcopalian laws were passed, but in 1592 Presbyterianism was again ratified. From 1598 James made his Episcopalian policy clear, and in 1612 this became the (official) Scottish religion. Clearly, however, between 1578 and the accession of James to the English throne, a power struggle was in progress. Catholicism ceased to be an important factor after the flight of

Mary (1568). The chief combatants were a divided nobility, an Episcopalian clergy generally supported by the King, and the 'Kirk' (Presbyterians) whom he came increasingly to hate.

In this confused situation the gentle Rollock, to whose nature contention was foreign, became a key figure. Elected Moderator of the Church Assembly, he tried to reconcile differences within the Church. In 1596 he was one of three ministers chosen to remonstrate with James for his 'hard dealings with the Kirk'. But before his death he had acquiesced in the King's policy. Scotland was torn asunder by religious dissension before England; but the character and practice of Rollock parallel those of other eminently reasonable, 'middle-of-the-road' but conscientious realists. He wrote many dissertations on the Scriptures and works on divinity. Many of his sermons, which were much admired, are unfortunately in a broad Scots which is unmodernizable. Some, however, exist in English texts, and one of these has been given here.

[OUT OF THE DEEP PLACES ...]
Psalm 130.
*1. Out of the deep places have I called unto thee, O Lord.*
*2. Lord hear my voice: let thine ears attend to the voice of my prayers.*
*3. If thou, O Lord, straitly markest iniquities, O Lord, who shall stand?*
*4. But mercy is with thee, that thou mayest be feared.*

IT IS not known when this sermon was preached, but it is likely to date from the last decade of his life. As I have indicated, Rollock was a moderate, a man who believed that controversy and extremism were harmful and should be avoided. This sermon is characteristic: it avoids allusion to the vexed question of Church organization (Presbyterianism as against Episcopalianism), instead concentrating mainly upon the question of God's mercy. As we should expect, Rollock is openly critical of Roman Catholicism: 'The vain Papist speaks little ... to the people of this mercy of God ...' But, as one should (once again) expect from one who was sent to remonstrate with his King for his harshness towards the Presbyterians, he does not explicitly refer to Calvinism. This sermon, however, contains strong anti-Presbyterian implications. Knox's *Treatise on Predestination* (1560) is rigorously Calvinistic, and his successor Andrew Melville was as rigid. The text upon which Rollock's sermon is preached is itself anti-Calvinist, and his interpretation of it is generous: for 'vain Papist' one might with equal justice read 'vain Presbyter'.

The context makes it clear enough when Rollock is using 'and', in the old Scottish manner, for 'if'. Otherwise this sermon presents few difficulties.

THE INSCRIPTION of this Psalm, brethren, declareth that it is a psalm most excellent; the excellency of it we remit to the matter contained therein. It hath been penned by some holy man and prophet of old, but by whom it is not certain: it is sufficient to us to know that the Spirit of God was the dyter of it.

To come to the matter and parts thereof, the prophet, whosoever he was, first setteth down the estate and disposition of his soul in trouble, to wit, that he ran to the Lord, and prayed to him for delivery: and this he doeth to the fifth verse. Next, finding in very deed the effects of the prayer he made, and finding mercy and delivery as he craved, he professeth before all the world, that as he had before awaited upon God, so he will await still upon him, and he will put his confidence in him. And this he doeth to the seventh verse. Lastly, from the seventh verse to the end, he recommendeth this duty to Israel, that is, to the Church of God, to wait upon the Lord, and, with the recommendation, he giveth in forcible reasons to move them. To come to the first part, first, he saith, that in his greatest danger he cried to the Lord Jehovah. Next, he setteth down the prayer. To come to the proposition, he saith, 'Out of the deep:' yet more, 'Out of the deep places have I called unto thee, O Jehovah.' By these deep places he understandeth great miseries, great dangers wherein his body was, great terror and fear in his conscience for his sin and offending of God: for the Scripture, as ye may see, (Psalm lxix, 1, 2) compareth great afflictions to deep waters, wherein a man is like to drown; and many a time, when the body is in danger, the soul will be like to drown in desperation. No doubt, the greatness of the danger, made him to utter to the Lord voices coming from the very depth of the heart. If we felt ourselves in great danger we would call from the depth of our hearts to God: he uttered not a voice only, but a loud voice, with a cry. This is the meaning of the words. We see here, first, that the children of God, whom God loveth most entirely, are many times subject to great and extreme dangers and troubles; and if ever thou thinkest to come to heaven, make thee [prepare yourself] in thine own course to suffer one trouble or other. Let no man, therefore, judge evil of a man because he suffereth. Next, we see the greater the danger be, the heavier the distress and the affliction wherewith the godly is exercised be, the more vehement, fervent and earnest, will their prayer be they have to God. And how cometh this to pass? Even in this manner, and by these degrees, oppression and affliction worketh in the hearts of the faithful a sense of the common misery of nature. When the hand of the Lord is upon a faithful man then he begins to feel his sin and corruption; and except the Lord exercise us in this life, either one way or other, the best of us all will fall into such a sound sleep, that we will neither remember what we have been, what we are, nor what we shall be, neither acknowledge ourselves to be sinners: so there is a necessity of afflictions, for affliction bringeth us to a feeling of our misery. Next, when through affliction the heart is prepared and brought to some sense of sin, then it is capable of grace, then it prayeth to God. (Look never to come to heaven if thou feelest not thy sin, yea, and that thou art a miserable sinner.) Then, if once thine heart be prepared with some sense of sin and misery, then cometh in that holy Spirit of Jesus Christ, which in the Scripture is called the Spirit of adoption, who, finding the heart dejected and made lowly, (the Spirit will never look in to a proud heart,) beginneth to work, and to touch the heart of the miserable sinner with a sweet sense of mercy through Jesus, he beginneth to shed abroad the love of Christ into the soul: and when once the heart hath tasted of the sweetness of mercy, and, as Peter saith, hath tasted how sweet and gracious the Lord is, and findeth this passing love of God in Jesus Christ, then it taketh a boldness, and beginneth with confidence and pertness [boldness] to present itself before God, and to put up prayers and requests; (Romans viii. 26). When once that Spirit hath given liberty, then we cry with an open mouth, for the heart is wide opened, Abba, Father, (Romans viii. 15) because we have gotten a sense of that fatherly love in Jesus Christ. The prayer of the faithful is most effectual when they are in greatest danger, and then the voice is loudest: for it is the Spirit of God who maketh intercession for us, with sighs which cannot be expressed; but God knoweth the meaning of his Spirit.

Now, Brethren, surely few of us have yet been in this deepness and extremity of misery. The Lord hath not yet so pressed us with his hand as he hath done many others; and, therefore, few there is amongst us who hath this feeling of sin and misery, and, consequently, few of us can pray so earnestly. How many are there amongst you that dare say, that ye feel sensible the common misery of nature? Go to your hearts and look if ye feel it not sleeping in sin; and so long as thou sleepest thus, and knowest not thy misery, how wilt thou be careful to feel the love of Christ? And how wilt thou earnestly pray to God? And certainly I take this coldness in prayer to be a forerunner of a judgment to overtake this land. No, it were better to be swimming in the waters of affliction, praying earnestly to God, than to be this way lying in prosperity without prayer.

Now I go forward. After he hath proposed, that out of the deepness he cried to Jehovah, then to let us see his cries, he setteth down the form of prayer that he used in his great miseries: First, he saith, 'O Lord hear my voice:' Next, in the other words he doubleth over the same petition, 'Attend to the voice of my prayers:' For he prayeth not coldly, but he crieth earnestly; certainly the doubling of the cry would be opened up from the ground. We should gripe [search] down to the heart from whence the prayers of the godly do flow, that when we hear them, or read them, we may get such a heart and disposition in prayer as they had. The doubling of the prayer, and the mouth wide opening, cometh of the doubling of the graces of the Spirit of God in the heart, and of a double opening of the heart; for, except the heart be opened in prayer, the mouth cannot be opened with pleasure, otherwise if thou speak any thing, I will not give one penny for it. So the opening of the mouth cometh from the opening of the heart. When the Holy Spirit so sweetly maketh manifest the love of God to the creature, then the tongue is loosed, and the second cry cometh of the second grace, and of the second opening of the heart; and so oft as thou criest, so oft is there a new grace and motion within the heart, wrought by the Holy Spirit, for it is he only, that openeth the mouth, piece and piece, to speak to God. For take this for certainty that Paul saith, 'there is none that can call Jesus Lord, without the Spirit come in,' (1 Cor. xii. 3). And again he saith, 'we know not what we should pray, or how we ought to pray, without that Spirit teach us,' (Romans 8. 26,) and if he teach not, no man or woman is able once to open the mouth with confidence and liberty to pray.

And so, Brethren, if ye would speak well, pray well, or do well, look ever to the disposition of the heart, and night and day pray for that Spirit, who may transchange thee, transform thee, and take thee out of nature, and plant thee in grace; for so long as thou remainest in nature, thou canst not think well, thou canst not speak well, thou canst do nothing well, yea, thou art worse than a very beast.

But because the words are very weighty, we will yet consider them better. What meaneth he when he saith, 'Lord let thine ear be attentive to my prayer?' Thought he that the Lord heard him not, and that the Lord played the part of a deaf man? No, he meaneth not this; look to the estate of the godly when the hand of the Lord is upon them, when the Lord afflicteth us any way, we think that he neither heareth nor seeth us, nor remembereth upon us: Indeed, I grant it is not so in effect, for God never altereth his affection towards his own; but the faithful oftentimes judge and apprehend so, and all the fault of this is in us. Ye see how David oftentimes complaineth to the Lord, that he had forsaken him, he had left him, and desireth that he should look upon him. I ask, is it so indeed, that when the faithful soul crieth, Lord hear, see, and remember, that he heareth not, he seeth not, he remembereth not? No question but he doth: 'For he that made the eye, seeth he not? He that made the ear, heareth he not? He that formed the heart of man, understandeth he not? Remembereth he not?' (Psalm xciv.) Yea, all things are patent to his Majesty, albeit, when he maketh it not manifest by some sensible effects and operation, we think he heareth not, he seeth not, he remembereth not, his favour and affection is never indeed altered nor changed from his own children: Then, when they cry for his presence, are they altogether destitute and deprived of his presence? No, they want it not: For who gave the heart to say, Lord hear me, Lord see and remember me? If that thou hadst not some presence of the Lord in thine heart, thou couldst never utter these voices to God. Then I say, if I have the presence of God when I cry unto him, why cry I, and pray I, as though I had not his presence? Are not such prayers in vain? No, for although we have the presence of God when we pray, yet for all that, our prayers to God are not in vain; for if we had him of before in any measure by our prayers, he will manifest himself more sensibly, piece and piece, more and more. And look how much more strongly thou criest, so much the more will the Lord be drawn to thy soul, and so much the more shalt thou find the increase and growth of grace in thy soul. It is impossible that the prayer of a faithful man, if it were but one word that proceedeth from the Spirit of adoption, can pass away without comfort: For the Lord giveth his Spirit to no man in vain, but because he knoweth the meaning of his own Spirit, therefore he will grant that thing for which he maketh request, there is nothing more certain; and therefore the Lord, (Mat. v. 6.) pronounceth them blessed, 'who hunger and thirst for righteousness, for' (saith he,) 'they shall be filled and satisfied:' And so

Christ speaketh to that woman of Samaria, (John iv. 13, 14,) 'If thou soughtest a drink, I should give thee a drink of the water of life: for the water that I shall give shall be, in a man (or woman) a well of water springing up into eternal life;' meaning, generally, that whosoever hath gotten the first fruits of the Spirit, and the beginnings of grace, desireth and seeketh for further progress and increase, that the Lord should ever furnish them with something to quench their thirst, and that because they should ever have a fountain within their belly, to furnish something to them when they thirsted; so that when as they should seek refreshment, they might get it in abundance. And if we felt this thirst and dryness of the soul, we should seek earnestly; for there was never such a dryness and such a heat in any man naturally, as there is in us through sin. Consider thine own experience, when thou hast felt sometimes the great burden of sin, and the terrors of the wrath of God for sin, whensoever, in this estate, thou camest to God, and prayed for mercy, and said, I am a miserable sinner—Lord give me mercy, hast thou not felt that the Lord hath answered thee comfortably, and hath filled thine heart with joy, even when, in thy prayer, thou sighest and sobbest unspeakably? What meaneth that joy? Even that as soon as thou openest thy mouth with liberty to seek that water of life, the Lord convoyeth some portion of it into thine heart to quench thy thirst.

Now, after he hath cried twice, he subjoineth in the next words, 'If thou, O Lord, straitly markest iniquities, O Lord, who shall stand?' This, no question, followeth by way of preoccupation. It might have been objected to him in his prayer, (for many are the temptations of the godly,) by his conscience pleading for God against him, or God himself might have said, Thou prayest to me, and yet thou art a sinner, how should I hear thee? How darest thou stand before me? it is a wonder that, in my fierce wrath, I destroy thee not. To this he answereth, first, by way of confession, It is true, O Lord, that if thou wilt straitly mark iniquity that no flesh can stand in thy presence, but they must be consumed, through the rage of thy displeasure. Then he answereth, by way of correction, 'But mercy is with thee.' The meaning is, Thou takest no heed to our iniquities, but, of thy free mercy and grace, thou pardonest them all in thy Son Jesus Christ; for none of the saints, none of the fathers, none of the prophets ever got mercy, but through that blood of Jesus Christ, who was slain from the beginning of the world; through his blood only was the wrath of God pacified. Except God's justice be first satisfied, there is no place left to mercy; therefore, saith he, my refuge is to thy mercy. Indeed, our estate, who live now, is far better than the estate of them who lived before Christ came into the world; for they saw the death and satisfaction of Christ, and remission of sin in his blood, but afar off; but we see them now already past, and we may say, that now God in Christ is merciful to us, is become our Father, and hath forgiven all our sins.

Now, out of these words, and by this example of the prophet, ye may see what is the estate of God's children in prayer, to wit, when, in affliction, they seek to repair to God by prayer, they will not so soon begin to pray, but as soon their guilty consciences will begin to knock and challenge them, as unworthy to be heard. The conscience will stand up, and, if it be not cleansed, it will present thy sins before thee, and set them in order in all their circumstances. Albeit thou forget thy sins after thou hast got thy pleasure, yet thou shalt see that thy conscience hath marked them all; and as a man cannot read when the book is closed, yet being opened, they may read therein; even so, albeit when our consciences are benumbed, we see not the ugliness and guiltiness of sin, yet when God wakeneth them, we will see sin in the own colour, and find the ugliness and guiltiness thereof. Our sins will come in, and stand up as mountains, and will hide the blessed face and presence of God from thee. Sin goeth betwixt us and God, and separateth us from God.

The saints find in experience, that it is not an easy thing to find a familiar access to God in prayer. Except our consciences first be purged, we can have no access to God; therefore, whosoever would draw near to God, let him seek to follow the counsel of the Apostle in the 10th chapter of the Epistle to the Hebrews, and the 22d verse, where he saith, 'Let us draw near with a true heart in an assurance of faith, sprinkled in our hearts from an evil conscience.' No flesh can have a favourable access to God, except his conscience be first purged from guiltiness; yea, that which we speak of the guiltiness of sin, we speak also of sin itself, that except it be quite taken away out of his sight, that he will not look favourably upon us. And this is that which the prophet saith here, 'If thou, O Lord, straitly markest iniquities, O Lord, who shall stand?' For, as guiltiness of sin stayeth us to behold God, so sin itself stayeth God from beholding us, miserable wretches, with the eyes of his compassion. So long, therefore, as thy conscience is not purged, when thou goest to present thyself before his majesty, if thy conscience be wakened, thou wilt find God marking thy sins,—laying them to thy charge,—and wilt find him as a terrible judge, compassed about with burning wrath, ready to destroy thee: and if he mark thee, thou hast no standing, and if thou appear not clothed with the righteousness and perfect satisfaction that Jesus, through his blood, hath purchased for thee, thou darest not presume to approach, for then his fierce wrath shall be poured out upon thee.

Further, we learn hereof, that whenever we would have our prayers accepted, we should begin with an humble confession, of our sins and unworthiness, and with an earnest prayer to forgive the same. Yea, we must aggreadge [aggravate] our sins by all circumstances, as the prophet doeth here. No, none; not the holiest saints, fathers, nor prophets, could be able to stand, if he marked their iniquity, let be himself, who was such an unworthy wretch, who was laden with so many and great sins. Thou must not extenuate thy sins before God, if thou wouldest find favour with God, as many men commonly do, saying, We are all sinners; yea, many men have sinned more, and have done worse deeds than I have done.

That is not the way to find God's favour. Thou must be very abject, vile, and contemptible in thine own account, if thou wouldest have the Lord to account of thee. Then where shall we get a remedy to help an evil conscience? For sin taketh away all joy and confidence in prayer.

The next words furnish a fair remedy—'But mercy is with thee.' Lord, it is not thy justice I look to, but thy mercy; thy justice holdeth me aback, but thy mercy allureth me. I flee from thy justice, and I claim to thy mercy. So when a man desireth his prayers to be heard, he must first have a sight of his own misery, guiltiness, and unworthiness, and of the fierceness of the Lord's wrath for the same; and in all humility he must confess the same. Next, he must have a sight of the Lord's mercy, and hope that it is possible that God be reconciled with him; except that these two be joined together he cometh not duly prepared. The one without the other will not serve; both are necessary. For without the knowledge, sight, and feeling of our misery, of sin, and of the wrath of God for the same, we will never be earnest in prayer. Who will ask, except he find his want? And without an humble confession there is no coming before God. Thou must not do as the Pharisee did. Read that parable of the Pharisee and of the Publican, (Luke xviii). The Pharisee was so blinded with self-love, that he could not see the filthiness and corruption of his own heart; and, therefore, not only in the presence of man, whom he might deceive, would he justify himself, but also in the very presence of God, who cannot be deceived, and who searcheth the hearts, he would boast of his righteousness, and condemn the poor Publican. But what found he? It is said he went home not justified, that all men might fear thereafter to come before God with a conceit of their worthiness. Thou must follow the example of the poor Publican, who, being ashamed of himself, would not look up to heaven, but looked down and smote his breast, and said, 'O God be merciful to me a sinner.' Next, if thou have no more but a sight, sense, and confession of thy misery, will that be sufficient? No, for albeit thou sawest all thy sins, and foundest the burden thereof, and foundest the Lord as a judge in a judgment pursuing thee, and heaping daily judgment upon judgment, and wrath upon wrath, that will never make thee to draw near to the Lord, but by the contrary, will make thee to turn thy back upon the Lord; for, as a malefactor hath no pleasure to behold the face of a judge, because his countenance is terrible, no more can the sinner abide the countenance of God. His judgments and his wrath may make us astonished and stupefied, but, if there be no more, they will never make us to come to God. Then if this be not sufficient, what more is requisite? Even a sight of the Lord's mercy, for that is most forcible to allure, as the prophet saith here, and as the Church of God sayeth, (Can. i. 2), 'Because of the savour of thy good ointments, therefore the virgins love thee.' This only is forcible to allure the sinner; for all the judgments of God, and curses of the law, will never allure him. What was the chief thing that moved the Prodigal son to return home to his father? Was it chiefly the distress, the disgrace, and poverty wherewith he was burdened, or the famine that almost caused him to starve? No, but the chief thing was this, he remembered that he had a loving father. That maketh him to resolve with an humble confession to go home. (Luke xv.) Even so is it with a sinner; it is not terrors and threatenings that chiefly will move him to come to God, but the consideration of his manifold and great mercies. Therefore, if the Lord waken thy conscience, present thy sins before thee, threaten thee, and heap judgments on thee, then say, Lord, I deserve to be threatened, and always to be plagued; but, Lord, thou knowest my nature, these things will not make me to come to thee, but will put me away from thee. Therefore, let me see thy manifold mercies towards sinners, to allure me, and then I shall come unto thee.

So we see the remedy against an evil conscience, to wit, an humble confession of sin and unworthiness, and a fleeing from the justice of God, to his mercy. The fairest and sweetest thing in the world is to feel the mercy of God. But herein there is great hardness and difficulty. It is not so easily attained unto, as men commonly think; for his mercy is compassed about with his justice, and with his wrath against sinners, as with a wall of fire; and he who will come to grace, he must come through a consuming fire; and, when he presseth to come near, the fire of God's wrath will hold him off, and will strike out and burn up the impenitent sinner, as fire doeth the stubble; so it is a harder thing than many think it to be, to win God's mercy. And how shall this be remedied? By what means shall we get through this wall of fire? Truly, he who would mean to pass through fire had need to be well armed; the man who presseth to approach near to that inviolable majesty, who can abide no sort of uncleanness, and would draw near to the throne of his grace, must be well armed against the justice and wrath of God, which debarreth sinners. Surely there is none armour in the world, that can preserve us from that raging and consuming fire, of the justice and wrath of God, but only the righteousness and satisfaction of Jesus Christ. Let a man use all the means in the world, and he be not found in Christ, he shall have none access to come through the justice and wrath of God, to the throne of grace; yea, his soul and his conscience must be sprinkled and purged from dead works, with that blood which was offered up to God to that end, by his eternal Spirit, (Heb. ix). Without he be dipped in that blood, he will find God a terrible judge. And after that, through faith in the death and blood of Jesus, thou comest to that throne of grace, thou shalt hear the sweetest and most comfortable voice that ever was, that is. All thy sins are forgiven thee in that blood. And if a man were condemned to die for some heinous crime, if the king would say, I absolve thee, I forgive thee, thou shalt live: what joy and comfort would that voice bring to the heart of him who was condemned. The Apostle saith, (Heb. x. 22) 'Let us go to the throne of grace with a true heart, and purged from an evil conscience through the blood of Jesus Christ,' that is, think not to come to that throne of grace, except first thou be purged with that blood. Therefore, as ever thou wouldest be in heaven, or see the face of God to thy comfort, seek to have faith in Christ Jesus; look what necessity is laid upon a sinner; either must he be banished from the presence and face of God for ever, and be casten into the society of the damned, or else if he would be saved, he must be imped and engrafted by a true and lively faith in Jesus Christ. Make thee for it with all thy main, to get a gripe of Christ as ever thou wouldest be saved.

Now after he hath met this objection, which God, or his own conscience in God's cause, might have casten in, he was so unworthy to be heard, by an humble confession of unworthiness, and by fleeing from his justice, and claiming to his great mercies, he setteth down the end of this mercy and free forgiveness of sins when he saith, 'But mercy is with thee, that thou mayest be feared.' The end wherefore the Lord granteth mercy and forgiveness of sins to sinners, is that they may obey, serve and worship God with pleasure and alacrity. No man can ever be able to glorify God, and to serve him cheerfully, but the man who hath assurance that his sins are freely forgiven him in that eternal love of God, through the blood of Jesus; for none can glorify God, except first he be glorified of God. Albeit the natural man got never so many and great benefits, yet because he hath none assurance of the forgiveness of his sins he can never glorify God nor be thankful to him. On the other part, it is impossible, and if thou have a sure persuasion that thy sins are forgiven thee, but thou wilt be careful in some measure to meet the Lord God in love, to pleasure him, and to thank him. For the first effect that floweth from the remission of sins, is sanctification or glorification: And it is not possible but if thou be glorified, thou must glorify the Lord again. But the question may be here proponed, wherein standeth our glorifying of God? Hath he need of our glorification? Can our service be profitable to him? Can our well-doing extend to him? Hath he need of any thing that we can do? I answer; Indeed it is true, our well-doing cannot extend to him, as David confesseth of himself in the 16th Psalm and the 2d verse. All the kings and monarchs in the world cannot do any thing that is profitable and steadable [available] to God. We are not able to add anything to the glory of God, for his glory is infinite, and to an infinite thing, nothing can be added, for if anything could be added it were not infinite. The Father, the Son and the Holy Spirit perfectly glorified one another from all eternity. 'Glorify me,' saith Christ, 'with that glory which I had with thee before the foundation of the world was laid.' That blessed Trinity was as perfect in glory before the creation of the world as it hath been ever since. Our glorifying of God standeth only in this, when the Lord illuminateth our minds that we may see his glory in all his properties, that we in our hearts, with pleasure and cheerfulness consent thereunto, allow of it, and with our mouths proclaim that glory which we see to be in him. And it lieth not in man nor angel to impair his glory. The good and the evil, the weal and the wo, the commodity and incommodity of all, cometh to our own selves; and happy is that man that glorifieth God, and miserable is he that glorifieth him not, for our felicity standeth not in that that we ourselves be glorified, but in this, that we glorify our Lord eternally, for that end were we created, and to that end were we redeemed with that precious ransom, even that we should glorify the Lord; and happy is that creature that hath some purpose, thirst and desire to glorify God in this life, for he may be assured that one day the Lord shall glorify him eternally in heaven. That soul, I say, shall be perfected in the life to come, and without all impediment shall cry with the blessed angels, 'Holy, holy, holy, is the God of heaven, the whole world is full of his glory.' There shall it find 'in his countenance satiety of joy, and at his right hand pleasures for ever.'

Mark here last, (and I shall end with it,) that the feeling of the mercy of God in Jesus Christ bringeth out obedience and cheerful service of God; yea, of all arguments to move a man to abstain from sin, and to serve the Lord with pleasure, that is the most pithy and forcible. The shame of the world, the fear of temporal judgment, the horror of conscience, and the fear of the pains of hell, will not be so steadable; it may be that they repress raging lusts and furious affections for a time, but they will not mortify sin and slay corruption, and will never cause a man with pleasure to serve and obey God. But if a man hath found that God hath loved him so well that he hath given his only son to die, that he might live, it is not possible but that man, in some measure, will set himself with alacrity and cheerfulness to serve God. Therefore, the Apostle, when he would persuade Christians to abstain from sin, and to serve God, what argument useth he chiefly? Read Rom. xii. 1, he proponeth the mercy of God offering Jesus to die for them, for there he saith, 'I beseech you, brethren, through the mercies of God, that ye offer up yourselves a living sacrifice.' Therefore, if thou wouldest covet to do the Lord's will cheerfully, pray the Lord, that he would not so much threaten thee, and propone terrors to thee as that he would make thee sensible of his mercies in Jesus Christ. The vain Papist speaks little, or nothing almost, to the people of this mercy of God in Jesus Christ, but propones to the people the pains of Hell and fire of Purgatory, to stay them from sin and to make them serve God, and do good works; but if there be no more, it will never make them to bring forth such obedience, as either is acceptable to God, or yet profitable to themselves. The Lord, therefore, make us to be sensible of his unspeakable love in Jesus, that we may set ourselves with pleasure to serve and glorify him here, that so we may be assured that he shall glorify us, in the kingdom of heaven, which Jesus hath purchased to us by his precious blood. To this Jesus, with the Father, and the Holy Spirit, be all praise, honour and glory, for now and ever. So be it.

# Henry Smith

HENRY SMITH was born in Leicestershire in 1550. He entered Queen's College, Cambridge (1573), but transferred to Lincoln College, Oxford, in 1575. His parents were wealthy, but he chose, after taking his B. A. in 1578, to enter the ministry. He later (from 1587) became a famous preacher at St Clement Danes, London, where he was lecturer. Thomas Fuller tells us that he was known as 'silver-tongued Smith', and that 'he was peaceable in Israel' and 'disdained railing and invectives, the symptom of a sick wit': 'if he chanced to fall on a sharp reproof, he wrapped it up in such pleasing expressions that the persons concerned therein had their souls divided betwixt love and anger at the hearing thereof'. Antony a Wood wrote that he was 'esteemed the miracle and wonder of his age, for his prodigious memory, and for his fluent, eloquent and practical way of preaching'. He was relieved of his holy office ('suspended') by Aylmer, the Bishop of London, but soon reinstated through the powerful influence of Lord Burghley. The information laid against him was that he was a Puritan; in fact he merely leant, theologically, towards certain Puritan concepts. He collected his sermons at the end of his life, and they were published—dedicated to Burghley—in 1592, the year following his death.

# The Poor Man's Tears
Matt. 10:42.
*He that shall give to one of the least of these a cup of cold water in my name, he shall not lose his reward.*

THIS ELOQUENT sermon, one of Smith's most famous, is on a social theme: poverty. The emphasis, in the late 1580s when it must have been preached, on everlasting hell-fire suggests that Smith had Puritan inclinations, but only mild ones. It is instructive to compare the matter of the paragraph following his remarks on hell with Cranmer's emphasis, in his homilies included in this selection, on 'quick and lively faith': this is a consistent theme in the history and development of Church of England thinking.

When he attacks men who rob under threat of violence 'upon Gad's Hill . . . and such like places' he equates them with the Anabaptists. This was a separatist, radical sect which arose in Switzerland in the early 1520s. They were originally pacifists who believed in adult baptism (infant baptism being meaningless to them), who wished to have nothing whatever to do with the state, but to band together, as 'saints', and keep their own laws, based on primitive Christianity. They regarded themselves as elected. They were burnt by Catholics and mock-'baptized' (i.e. drowned) by the Protestants. There were in the early sixteenth century some six sects who had anabaptism (re-baptism) in common; but the name was given to them by their opponents and is not accurate, since they rejected infant baptism altogether. When a group under Jan Mattys, and then John of Leyden, took over Münster for a while they ran wild, thus discrediting their cause. However, Anabaptism (doubtless owing to the cruel intolerance with which it was treated) has had a powerful influence. The Quaker doctrine of 'inner light' is taken over from an Anabaptist, and many modern low-church practices have their root in the movement. Smith's use of the term is doubtless merely abusive (cf. our own use of 'communist' or 'fascist', as the case may be, to describe phenomena we dislike), though the Anabaptists did believe in the common holding of goods, and there were Anabaptists in England from about 1534; further, they exercised a strong influence on some of Smith's ferociously Puritan contemporaries, such as the probably half-mad separatist Robert Browne (also protected by Burghley), who submitted to episcopalianism but, it seems, did not change his views. Smith's position is more central than that of Browne and his followers, in whose 'Brownist' views Congregationalism originated.

In general this plain though finely written sermon is an excellent example of Elizabethan charitable thinking: of Christian exhortation to an aspect of good works. It is affecting and effective because it is not extravagant.

THE ARGUMENT I have to entreat of is only of giving alms to the poor, and when and in what sort we ought to relieve the poor. Herein, for your better instruction, I will shew what alms is, how and to whom alms must be given, and wherefore we are to give alms. I know in these days, and in this iron age, it is as hard a thing to persuade men to part with money, as to pull out their eyes, and cast them away; or to cut off their hands, and give them away; or to cut off their legs, and throw them away. Nevertheless, I cannot but wonder that men are so slow in giving of alms, and so hard-hearted towards the relief of the poor, when the promises of God warrant them not to lose their reward. St. John saith, 'He that hath the substance of this world, and seeth his brother want, how can the love of God be in him?' (1 John iii. 17.) This is a question which can hardly be answered of a great number; no, it will not be considered of a number, nor regarded of a number. And yet the evangelist hereby layeth open unto all persons, that he which hath wealth, seeing his brother in want, and will not relieve him, he loseth the love of God: which love is so great as is the love of a natural mother unto her own child; nay, more than that, it is a love so firmly settled, that it is impossible to be removed.

There are many rich persons that think scorn to relieve the poor, of whose hard dealing we have precedent in Luke xvi. The rich man in his lifetime would not relieve Lazarus, but despised him; yea, he forgot God, and thought there was no God (but his gold) that could in justice punish him for despising the poor. Lazarus died for want, and so did Dives for all his wealth, who soon after, being in hell, beheld Lazarus in heaven, triumphing in Abraham's bosom, while he was tormented in hell-fire. This fire burneth, scaldeth, scorcheth, and tormenteth; of which, when the rich man felt the smart, though all too late, he sorrowed and repented, and would fain have sent word thereof unto his friends. But he could have no messenger for all his lordly livings, nor no releasement of his torments for all his bags of gold. Now, to whom would he have sent word? Forsooth, to a number of his friends, that indeed think there is no God nor devil, no heaven, no hell, nor torments in hell-fire after this life. This example of Dives may admonish such hard-hearted persons to be mollified with the tears of the poor, that they may, when Dives hath dined, let Lazarus have the crumbs.

We read in Matthew, that when Christ cometh to judgment, he 'will say to them on the left hand, Go from me, ye cursed, into hell-fire, which was prepared from the beginning,' &c.; by which appeareth, that hell-fire is not only hot, but it is everlastingly hot, and never hath end. Let therefore hell-fire, and the eternal torments thereof, admonish you to be merciful to the poor. To this also may be added, what he will say to the righteous, 'Go ye into everlasting joys,' which never shall have end. 'When I came among you as a stranger, you received me; when I was naked, you clothed me; and when I was hungry, you fed and refreshed me.' Which proveth that the kingdom of heaven belongs unto him that harboureth strangers, clotheth the naked, feedeth the hungry, comforteth the sick, and doth perform such charitable acts of compassion. Yet we are not, as the papists, to account it meritorious, but to do it as a faithful Christian, in faith and true zeal of a Christian life; for 'every tree that bringeth not forth good fruit is hewn down, and cast into the fire.' It is not enough for us only to bear fair leaves, but we must also bring forth good fruit, otherwise let us be sure our Saviour Christ will forsake us.

The prophet Isaiah saith, 'If thou break thy bread unto the poor, and pour forth thy heart unto them, thy light shall rise in darkness, thy dimness shall be as the noontide, and God shall still guide thee' (Isa. lviii. 7, 10, 11). Whereby appeareth, that those deeds of charity are commonly performed by the righteous that still seek to enjoy the pleasures of heaven, which are so far beyond the common imagination of men, that no heart can think, no ear can hear, no tongue can speak, no pen can write the unspeakable pleasures thereof.

Christ saith, 'It is a deed more blessed to give to them than to take from them' (Acts xx. 35); for the excellency of Christians consisteth in leading a godly life, and giving of alms, as the excellency of all things is shewed in their giving. The sun giveth his light, the moon her light, the stars their light, the clouds their water, the trees their fruit, the earth her herbs, the herbs their flowers, the flowers their seeds, and the seeds their increase; yea, beasts and birds, fowls and fishes, give naturally in their kind, and are more careful and loving one to another than we, which made Job say, 'Go to the beasts of the field, and they will teach thee' (Job xxxv. 11). For man is most unnatural to man, and so far digressing from nature in his kind, that let some ungodly rich cormorants see a poor person beg, this is their present sentence of him, Whip the rogues! To Bridewell with these rogues! It is pity these rogues be suffered to live! Then if they fall sick, let them famish, starve, and die; all is one to them, for of them they shall receive no comfort.

Augustus Caesar, a heathenish emperor, thought that day to be lost wherein he did not benefit some poor person, and with money relieve him from penury. And I doubt not but some godly men there be that take delight in relieving the poor with their continual alms, not superstitiously to be seen of men, but secretly to be seen of God. The Lord increase the number of them, and make their example redound to the relief of thousands!

Alms is a charitable relief given by the godly to the sick, to the lame, the blind, the impotent, the needy, the hungry, and poorest persons, even such as are daily vexed with continual want; to whom, even of duty, and not of compulsion, we ought to impart some part of that which God hath mercifully bestowed upon us. For as we daily seek for benefits at God's hand, which he doth continually give us, so ought we therewith to relieve the poor, sith God hath so commanded us. The performance whereof we ought not to drive off from time to time, but to do it when they desire to have it done. For the true obedience of God doth forbid us to prolong or drive off the doing of good things, as appeareth in Noah, who, when he was commanded, did enter the ark; Abraham, when he was commanded, did forthwith offer up his son Isaac, and did circumcise his house upon the same day he was appointed. A learned writer, called Nazianzen, saith of himself, that when in his youth he had once lost the tenor of good life, grey hairs were got about his head ere he recovered it again. Whereby I gather, that when we are young, if we harden our hearts against the poor, if we do not willingly impart our bread to them, but drive their hungry stomachs stubbornly from our doors, that doubtless grey hairs will come upon our heads, before we can find the right way to pity and compassion. O let us take heed that our hearts be not hardened against the poor, nor that we give our alms to get glory of the world; but so let us give our alms that the one hand may not know what the other doth. Yea, we ought to give with such equality, that our poor neighbours may be relieved, to whom indeed we ought to become contributors, as Job was. All people have not one belly; for as one chimney may be hot, so another may be cold; one pot moist with liquor, when another may be dry; one's purse empty, when another's is full; so one poor man's belly full, and another's empty. That is a good commonwealth that looketh to every member in the commonwealth, and those men are worthy of riches that look daily to the feeding of their poor neighbours.

Let therefore the tears of the poor admonish you to charity, that when Dives hath dined, Lazarus may have the crumbs.

Now let us proceed, and consider what we must give, and to whom we must give. In the text we are willed to give, though it be but a cup of cold water, or a piece of bread. This containeth matter both for the taker and the giver. Bread will serve beggars, and they must be no choosers; yet bread will not serve some beggars, that boldly upon Gad's Hill, Shooter's Hill, and such like places, take men's horses by the head, and bid them deliver their purses. For these fellows are of the opinion of the Anabaptists, that every man's goods must be common to them, or else they will force them to part them; but these are saucy beggars, which ought to be suppressed by godly policy. As for the other sort of beggars, and other poor persons, they must be content to take up their cross, endeavour themselves patiently to suffer their ordinary grievances, and remember that man's nature may be satisfied with a little.

As touching how much we should give, we are taught, that if we have much, we should give accordingly; if we have but little, give what we can spare. Saint Luke counselleth us, 'if we have two coats, we must give one to him that hath none; and of meat likewise' (Luke iii. 11). But as touching this question, little need to be spoken, when our own covetous hearts are ready enough to frame excuses.

Some will make a question of their alms, and say, they know not what the party is that demandeth relief, or beggeth alms of them. Oh, say some, I suspect he is an idle person, dishonest, or perhaps an unthrift; and therefore refuse to give any relief at all. To this I answer, They are needless doubts; for we ought to relieve them, if we know them not for such persons, and let their bad deeds fall on their own necks; for if they perish for want, we are in danger of God's wrath for them; but to give unto such as we know of lewd behaviour, thereby to continue them in their wickedness, were very offensive. We are not still tied to one place for giving our charity, but it stretcheth far; for we are commanded not only to relieve our own countrymen, but also strangers, and such as dwell in foreign nations.

Again, here the giver may learn to give freely; for the thing he giveth is but bread or water. Bread is the fruit of the earth; and for that the earth gives it us, we may the better give it again. But bread in this place signifieth all things necessary; for the fare and cheer in old time was contained under the title of *bread*, and all manner of drink under the title of *water*. But in this, as in all other things, the simplicity of the old world is quite gone out, and new and corrupt things are lately crept in. In the old time Jacob desired he might have bread in his journey; but now the case is altered, for we must have sundry dishes of contrary devices, framed for the taste of the mouth, and pleasantness of the stomach, which is used with great superfluity, and far more cost than needeth. Better now to fill the belly than the eye; although to content the common multitude, the eye is the only thing which must be pleased. Yet, when you are in the midst of all your jollity and costly fare, let the tears of the poor admonish you to relieve them, that when Dives hath dined, Lazarus may have the crumbs.

The tears of men, women, and children are grievous and pitiful; and tears give cause of great compassion, especially the tears of such as therewith are constrained to beg for their relief. But if the tears of the rich are for the loss of their goods, or the tears of parents for the death of their children, or the tears of kind-natured persons for the loss of friends, or other wrongs sustained, ought generally to be regarded and pitied; then much more should the tears of those breed great compassion in the hearts of Christians, whom beggary, want, and extremity of miserable hunger, constraineth to shed tears in most grievous and lamentable sort. Oh, what shall a man say unto those pitiful faces which are made moist through the extremity of hunger, wherein are most bitter and sharp effects, a thing above all extremes?

To a hungry body every bitter thing is sweet, and every foul thing seems clean. Hunger made the apostles glad to eat the ears of corn, David glad to eat the shew-bread, Lazarus desirous to eat crumbs, and Elias content with meal. In the destruction of Jerusalem, it made the mother eat her own child; and in the wailings of Jeremiah, people to eat their own ordure. It made people cry to Pharaoh for bread; it made an ass's head and the dung of pigeons to be eaten in Samaria, and others to swoon and lie dead in the streets. The affliction of hunger causes bitter tears, and brought all these things to pass. David saith that God 'numbered all his tears in a bottle' (Ps. lvi. 8). David's tears were worthy to be preserved; but if ever tears were worthy to be numbered, the tears that are shed for famine, howsoever men neglect to regard them, they are undoubtedly gathered together into God's bottle, and thence they rain as waters out of vials, in way of revengement of those that take no compassion of such a woful spectacle.

Tears are the last thing that man, woman, or child can move by; and where tears move not, nothing will move. I therefore exhort you, by the lamentable tears which the poor do daily shed through hunger and extreme misery, to be good unto them, to be charitable and merciful unto them, and to relieve those whom you see with misery distressed.

The Scripture saith, 'Give to every one that asketh' (Luke vi. 30). God gave herbs and other food unto every living thing. Every commonwealth that letteth any member in it to perish for hunger, is an unnatural and uncharitable commonwealth. But men are now-a-days so full of doubts, through a covetous desire to themselves, that they cannot abide to part with anything to the poor, notwithstanding that God hath promised he will not forget the work and love which you have shewed in his name to the poor and distressed.

Some will say for their excuse, that they are overcharged by giving to a number of persons, and therefore they cannot give to so many beggars; for by so doing they might soon become beggars themselves. David answered this objection very well, and saith thus, 'I never saw the just man forsaken, nor his seed beg his bread' (Ps. xxxvii. 25); whereby he meant, that in all the time that he had lived (and the like for any man living the years of David), he scarcely ever saw that upon an upright heart in giving, a man was brought to beggary.

There are a number that will deny a poor body a penny, and plead poverty to them, though they seem to stand in never so great extremes; when, in a far worser sort, they will not stick immediately to spend ten or twenty shillings. The rich worldling makes no conscience to have ten or twenty dishes of meat at his table, when in truth the one half might sufficiently satisfy nature, the rest run to the relief of the poor; and yet in the end he might depart better refreshed with one dish than commonly he is with twenty. Some will not stick to have twenty coats, twenty houses, twenty farms, yea, twenty lordships, and yet go by a poor person whom they see in great distress, and never relieve him with one penny, but say, God help you; I have not for you. There are lawyers that will not stick to undo twenty poor men, and merchants that make no conscience to eat out twenty others, that have their hundreds out at usury, their chests crammed full of crowns, and their coffers full of golden gods, or glistering angels, that will go by twenty poor, miserable, hungry, impotent, and distressed persons, and yet not bestow one penny on them; and though they do most shamefully ask it, yet can they most shamefully deny it, and refuse to perform it.

The people of this world can very easily find a staff to beat a dog; they are never without excuses, but ready to find delays, and very pregnant to devise new shifts to keep in their alms. Now will I shew you reasons why we should give. God saith, 'Whoso giveth to the poor, lendeth to the Lord, and shall be sure to find it again' (Prov. xix. 17), and receive for the same an hundred fold. And again, 'Blessed is he that considereth of the poor and needy; the Lord shall deliver him in the day of trouble' (Ps. xli. 1). Hereby appeareth, that we shall receive our alms again, except we doubt whether God's word be true or no. For confirmation whereof the prophet David saith, 'The testimonies of God are true and righteous' (Ps. xix. 9). And God speaks by the mouth of the prophet Isaiah, saying, 'The word is gone out of my mouth, and it shall not return' (Isa. xiv. 23; lv. 11). The promise which God made to Sarah was found true; his promise made to the children of Israel was found true; his promise to Joshua in the overthrowing of his enemies was found true. God promiseth David his kingdom, to Solomon he promised wisdom, to Pharaoh he threatened destruction by water, to Saul the loss of his kingdom, and to Solomon the dividing of his kingdom; all which, and far more, proved true. Then let us not doubt of God's promises, but fear his judgments; for from time to time they have been found true and just. Let us consider that we must die, and leave our goods we know not to whom; then, while we are here, let us distribute thereof unto the poor, that we may receive our reward in the kingdom of heaven. God saith by St. Luke, 'O fool, this night will I fetch away thy soul, and then that which thou hast got, who shall possess it?' Here is a question worth the noting, and meet for rich men to consider, especially such as hoard up wealth, and have no regard to the relief of the poor. Do they think that the wealth which they have gathered together will come to good after their decease? No; it will melt and consume away like butter in the sun. The reason is, because they would not do as God hath commanded them, in distributing part of that to the poor which was lent them by the Lord.

The children of God, in the 6th of the Apocalypse, cry out, 'How long, O Lord, thou that art holy and true, dost thou not judge and revenge our blood upon those that dwell on the earth?' (Rev. vi. 10.) Whereby appeareth that God exerciseth good men, and those whom he loveth, in the troubles of this world, which we account long; yet is their time but short, although their trouble makes it seem long. But these, I say, ought to be content; and all those that do trust in God must be content to relieve one another for a time, since after a short time we shall doubtless find the fruits of our alms again. Short is man's life while we are in this world; David compareth it to a vapour, to a bubble, to wind, to grass, to a shadow, to smoke, and every fading thing that consumeth in a moment. Isaiah compareth it to the removing of a tabernacle, and Job to an eagle's wing or a weaver's shuttle. So that our life is but short; and after a few days, though you think them many, whatsoever you mercifully bestow upon the poor here on earth, you shall certainly find the same again both in heaven and on earth. Solomon, in the 21st of the Proverbs, saith, 'He that stoppeth his ear at the cry of the poor, shall cry himself, and not be heard' (Prov. xxi. 13). 'The bread of the needy is the life of the poor: he that keepeth it from them is a man of blood' (Ecclus. xxxiv. 21). St. Paul saith, No man giveth but he that hath received (1 Cor. xv. 3); and an ancient father of the church doth charge the rich with waste, for which they shall surely answer. Art thou not, saith he, a robber, in keeping another man's substance, and to reckon it as thine own? It is the bread of the hungry which thou dost retain, the coat due to the naked thou lockest in thy house, the shoes that appertain to the barefoot lie drying in thy house, and the gold which should relieve the poor lies cankering in thy coffers. Which saying, as it teacheth the liberality due unto the poor, so it blameth the careless rich, that account all to be their own, and will part with nothing, keeping to themselves more than is sufficient. But to such St. James saith, that at the latter day the mite in the crumbs, the moths in the garments, and the rust in the gold, shall fret them like cankers (James v. 2, 3). Ambrose saith, It is no greater sin to take from him that rightly possesseth, than, being able, not to give him that wanteth.

The right rich man, that duly deserveth that name, is not known by his possession, by his costly fare, and costly building; by his sumptuous palace, by his plate, jewels, and substance; but by considering the poor and needy. Whereof Austin saith thus, The rich are proved by the poverty of others. So that still the Scriptures and fathers prescribe not an indifferency, but a necessity, not at pleasure, but upon duty, that the poor and needy should be considered and relieved.

Where is the large liberality become that in times past was rooted in our forefathers? They were content to be liberal, though they applied it to evil purposes. The successors of those which in times past gave liberally to maintain abbots, friars, monks, nuns, masses, dirges, trentals, and all idolatry, seeing the abuses thereof, may now bestow it to a better use, namely, to foster and feed the poor members of Christ.

The world is as great as it hath been, the people now are more rich than they have been, and more covetous than they have been, yea, they have more knowledge than ever they had; yet they want the desire they have had to become liberal, and seem therein most wilfully ignorant.

The extortioner can spare nought unto the poor, for joining house to house, and land to land, though he have the poor man's curse for it. The prophet Isaiah saith, The extortioner doeth no good to the poor, but daily seeketh to root them forth of doors. The pride of apparel maketh us forget the patches of the poor; our costly fare, their extreme hunger; and our soft lodging, their miserable lying.

Oh how liberal were people in times past to maintain superstition! and now how hard-hearted are they grown, not to keep the poor from famishing! Will ye make a scorn of the poor and needy? The poor now perisheth by the rich men, and no man considereth it. This is not the right duty of faithful Christians; this ought not to be the fruits of our profession; neither is this the mercy which we learn by the word.

Therefore, towards the relief of the poor, I say, Give, and give gladly; for the bread that is given with a stony heart is called stony bread, though necessary to be taken by the poor to slake hunger; yea, it is but sour bread. Such a giver, in my opinion, is next kinsman unto Satan, for he gave Christ stones instead of bread; but this man giveth Christians stony bread. The wise man saith, Lay up thy alms in the hands of the poor, and know that in the end what thou keepest thou shalt lose; but that thou givest to the poor shall be as a purse about thy neck. For as this life waxeth old, and our days pass away, so shall this vain pelf pass away from us, neither shall riches help in the day of vengeance; but the corruption abideth, which fretteth like a canker. Then what shall it profit to get all the world? And when the world forsaketh us, that shall be most against us that best we loved while we were in the world. Let every man therefore persuade himself that his soul is better than those subtle riches, the possession whereof is variable and uncertain, for they pass from us much more swiftly than they came unto us; and albeit we have the use of them even till the last day, yet at length we must leave them to others. Then, ere you die, lay them forth for the profit of your poor brethren. Learn to forsake the covetous world before it forsake you, and learn counsel of our Saviour Christ, who adviseth you to 'make friends of the wicked mammon' (Luke xvi. 9).

We see daily that every one is good to the poor (as we commonly say), but they will give them nought but words. Then, I say, great boast and small roast makes unsavoury mouths. Yet if words will do any good, the poor shall not want them; for it doth cost nothing to say, Alas! good soul, God help thee, God comfort thee, I would I were able to help thee; and such commonly will say so that have store of wealth lying by them. Such still wish well unto themselves in wishing themselves able; but of such wishing and such wishers I say, as a beggar said to a bishop who made the like answer, that if such wishes were worth but one halfpenny to the poor, I doubt they would not be so liberal. I wish you, good brethren, leave wishing, and fall to some doing. You lock up, and will not lose; you gather together even the devil and all; and why? Because you would fain hatch the cockatrice's egg; you nurse up a canker for yourselves; you keep the pack that shall trouble your voyage unto God, as Christ saith, 'Oh how hard shall it be for a rich man to be saved. It shall be easier for a camel to go through a needle's eye' (Matt. xix. 23, 24). This he saith not, because no rich man shall be preserved; but because the merciless rich man shall be damned. We are admonished to liberality by sundry natural examples. The clouds, if they be full, do yield forth their rain; much rain is a burden to clouds, and much riches are burdens to men. It is said of Abraham (Gen. xiii. 12), that he was burdened with gold; yet Abraham was a good man, but it burdened his head to be busied with the cares of gold. Again, to eat much, to drink much, and to rest much, is a burden to the soul, though it be pleasant to the body; and in Luke xii. 19, it appeareth, that abundance of riches maketh one to eat much, drink much, and rest much; then, were it not for the covetous minds of those that have much, they might impart to the poor one part of that which they daily spend in superfluity. If this be not amended, I let you to understand, that the poor must cry, and their voice shall be heard, their distress considered, and your vengeance shall be wrought. I tell you troth, even in Jesus Christ, that the poor have cried unto the Lord, and he hath heard them. With speed, therefore, open your ears; if not to man, yet to Christ, who continually commandeth us to give and bestow upon the poor and needy. 'Give, and it shall be given you,' saith he by Luke, chap. vi. 38; and setteth before our eyes the example of the poor widow's mite; as also the example of a covetous rich man, who, demanding how he might obtain eternal life, was answered thus by him, 'Go, sell all thou hast, and give to the poor' (Matt. xix. 21); not that it is necessary for every man so to do, or that a man cannot be saved without he do so; but thereby teaching him particularly to loathe the world, and generally seek means for the daily cherishing and the refreshing of the poor. Do not continually feed your equals, for that is offensive; but when you may spare to spend and banquet yourselves, then call the poor and impotent, and refresh your poor distressed neighbours and brethren; and when Dives hath dined, let Lazarus have the crumbs. And still remember the saying of St. Matthew, 'Blessed are the merciful, for they shall obtain mercy' (Matt. v. 7).

To conclude. Beloved in the Lord, let me entreat you rich men to consider it is your duty to remember the poor, and their continual want; you that eat till you blow, and feed till your eyes swell with fatness; that taste first your coarse meats, and then fall to finer fare; that have your several drinks for your stomach, and your sorts of wine for your appetite; impart some of your superfluity unto the poorer, who, being comforted by you, will doubtless pray for you, that God will bless you and yours, and increase your store a thousand-fold; which if they shall forget, yet the promises of God remain inviolable towards you for the same.

If the proud would leave their superfluity in apparel, their excess in embroidery, their vanity in cuts, guards, and pounces, their excess in spangling, their fantastical feathers, and needless bravery, the greater part would suffice towards the relief of the poor, and yet they have sufficient to suffice nature.

Let the glutton seek only to suffice nature, and leave his daily surfeiting in belly cheer; then might the poor be fed with that which he oftentimes either loathsomely vomits forth, or which worketh as an instrument to shorten his own life.

Let the whoremonger leave off his dalliance, and his inordinate expenses for maintaining of his wickedness; and it shall be good for his body, and better for his soul, yea, his purse shall be the heavier, and he thereby better able to relieve the poor.

Let every artificer and tradesman live orderly, avoiding superfluous expenses, not spending his money vainly at dice, tables, cards, bowling, betting, and such like, but live, as becometh civil Christians, in the fear of God; they may have sufficient for the maintenance of themselves and their family, and yet the poor may be by them sufficiently relieved.

Let us consider that we, who have our beginning from God, ought generally to bend our actions towards the pleasing of God; and doing as he commandeth us, we please him; for if we help the poor, we help him; and doing all charitable actions to the poor, he accounteth it as done unto himself.

Let us generally learn not to contemn or despise the poor, but according to our abilities help them, and consider of their extremes, and at any hand not disdain and upbraid them with the titles of base rogues, or such like; but in all godly Christian means cherish and comfort them with such charitable relief as we may in reason afford unto them, yea, and consider of their case as if it were our own.

Let us take example of good Cornelius the captain, of whom mention is made in the Acts of the Apostles, to whom the angel of God appearing in a vision, said thus, 'Cornelius, thy prayer and thine alms are come up before God' (Acts x. 4). Lo, here the reward, and also of whom thou shalt be rewarded.

Let us consider of their misery, that with hungry chops and lank bellies would willingly feed on that which you wastefully consume; the poor, I say, would find good comfort of that which commonly you fling to your dogs and on your dunghills; and let us have regard to their coldness, their nakedness, their misery and grievous necessity; think of this, and comfort them. And let us be mindful that poverty and want compelleth many an honest person to take in hand the performance of much vile and slavish business; and that therefore they deserve to be succoured with mercy and pity, rather than to be despised for their poor estate. Oh think, if some hard-hearted persons were in their miserable estate, how gladly would they be refreshed, that now scarcely yield one penny to their relief!

Lastly, let us call to mind the example of the widow of Sarepta, whose provision and store was little, and when the prophet of the Lord came to her to ask her bread, she answered, 'I have nothing but a little flour in a barrel, and a little oil in a cruse' (1 Kings xvii), which notwithstanding she willingly bestowed upon him; for which a thing worthy memory followed; for her barrel was again filled with flour, and her pot with oil. This was the Lord's doing, for fostering the poor prophet of the Lord. Sure the plenty that cometh by the poor is much; for the field of the poor is fruitful, it surrendereth again the fruit to them that give aught; yea, if it be but a cup of cold water, as saith our Saviour Christ (Mark x). To whom be all honour, power and dominion, now and for ever. Amen!

## Richard Hooker

HOOKER IS perhaps the greatest theologian that the Church of England has had; consequently, despite his learning, intelligence —and a temperament as naturally eirenic as that of Hales (a sermon by whom is contained in this book), who must have been influenced by him—and mastery of English prose, he is not always consistent or easy to follow. His views have inevitably been the subject of much controversy. His gift was for writing; as a preacher his delivery was often monotonous. But he must be read with attention. He is a seminal figure. And unlike Hales he is explicit in all his views.

Richard Hooker—the 'judicious', 'a Knight of Romance among caitiff brawlers'—was born near Exeter, and showed prodigious intelligence and grasp of learning in his youth. His father, whose family had used the name Vowell interchangeably with Hooker for some time, was of good family but was now poor. Under the auspices of the (theologically) Calvinistically inclined Jewel, Bishop of Salisbury, he was sent to Corpus Christi, Oxford (Hales was to follow him, and to feel his influence there). He took orders in 1581, preached in London, and made a miserable marriage with the shrewish daughter of his landlady, a draper's wife. The short-sighted and guileless Hooker, a man of 'mean stature' who fixed his eyes upon one spot while he preached, may well have been absent-minded; but the judgement that he therefore probably did not 'notice' the unpleasantness of his wife (by whom he had four children) is possibly an unsound one.

In 1584 he became rector of a Hertfordshire parish. In the following year he gained the Mastership of the Temple, Whitgift having supported him against the strongly urged claims of William Travers (*c*. 1548-1635), who was the afternoon lecturer there. Travers was a Puritan (Presbyterian) who refused to join the Church of England, and he immediately began a series of attacks on Hooker, whose important reply—the most eloquent of his sermons, for sermon in effect it is—is printed below. Hooker disliked public controversy, and asked Whitgift for a quiet living, where he could set forth his position in the way most suited to him. Accordingly he was sent to Boscombe in Wiltshire (1591), and then to a Kentish parish (1595-1600), where he died in 1600. In this decade he produced his *Treatise of the Laws of Ecclesiastical Polity* (1594-7: the last three books, of which the penultimate seventh is not wholly authentic, were published posthumously: VI and VIII in 1648, VII in 1662).

Whitgift had agreed to Hooker's request to 'eat [his] own bread in privacy' and 'see God's blessing spring out of [his] mother earth' because he, above all, wished the work on *Ecclesiastical Polity* completed. He had himself been engaged in a controversy with the Puritan, Thomas Cartwright, between 1572 and 1577; but he could not find time to conclude it. Now Whitgift himself, though a staunch supporter of the 1559 Settlement, was *theologically* not only a Puritan but an extreme Calvinist. In 1595 he helped to draw up, and approved, as Archbishop of Canterbury, the Lambeth Articles. (The Queen disliked them, and they were never authorized.) These were Supralapsarian (i.e. advocated that God had decided on the election and the non-election of individuals before the Fall), and it may even be argued that they were to the left of Calvin's own theology. Only 'the will and good pleasure of God' determined 'predestination to life'; 'Of the predestinated there is a fore-limited...number which can be neither diminished nor increased'; 'It is not placed in the ...power of every man to be saved....' It is instructive, then, that Whitgift was so ardent a defender of the 1559 Settlement—and that he regarded Hooker so highly, for it will soon become apparent what Hooker's attitude to these Articles must have been.

Hooker was claimed by the nineteenth-century Anglo-Catholics as one of their true spiritual fathers; he has been claimed as one whose views are central to the Church of England; he has also been called Latitudinarian. Since his writings as a whole are dense and complex (some were destroyed by his wife's detestable Puritan relatives), though they have their grand simplicities, justifications for all of these opinions—and others, such as that he was a 'Calvinist predestinarian, rejecting reprobation'—may be found. But the claim that he was essentially middle-of-the-road Church of England is the most convincing, since little that Hooker wrote on doctrine or on the relationship between Church and State conflicts with the Anglican settlement, which he in any case regarded as a continuously changing one. He did grant that the Roman Catholic Church was a true Church, and he was praised by Pope Clement VIII; but his message was one of tolerance, and his acknowledgement of the truth of Roman Catholicism was qualified by his percipient recognition that *certain forms of true churches might be more suitable at certain times and in certain places than others*. This was not the view of the nineteenth-century Anglo-Catholics, who, though they would not acknowledge the Pope, were un-Englishly nostalgic for Rome's excessive ritual—a ritual that suits the Latin temperament, but is too ornate for what may be called the English temperament (cf. the grand prose of Cranmer, the preaching of Latimer, the free and mind-dizzying rhetoric of Donne: these spontaneous splendours are not to be responded to, by most Englishmen, in a context of fixed and rigorously extreme gorgeousness).

Hooker was extremely learned; he tried, usually with success, to curb his ingeniousness with pragmatism. He was above all the apologist of the 1559 Settlement (which the nineteenth-century High Churchmen, like their non-jurist predecessors of the late seventeenth century, fundamentally resented); but, writing over thirty years after it, he was aware of the organic, changing nature of the Church which it had rediscovered after the hysterical Marian interlude. There are inconsistencies in Hooker; but some of these reflect upon the Church of England's own ambiguities. He was unclear about the exact nature of the Eucharist; he wrote to justify episcopacy—in which he certainly believed—but refused to condemn the continental Protestant Churches just as he refused to condemn Rome.

The broad outlines of Hooker's position, however, are clear. There are three main points. He was Erastian; he was convinced of the necessity of a Protestant Church *of England*; and he resisted Puritan extremism. Hooker's elaborations of the Erastian position are his most important contribution to political thought, for they influenced mainstream political theorists (most importantly, Locke) as well as ecclesiastics. Hooker's Erastianism and his Anglicanism are aptly covered by a quotation from *Ecclesiastical Polity*:

> Unto me it seemeth almost out of doubt and controversy, that every independent multitude, before any certain form of regiment established, hath, under God's supreme authority, full dominion over itself...God creating mankind did endue it naturally with full power to guide itself, in what kind of societies soever it should choose to live...and that power which naturally whole societies have, may be derived into many, few, or one, under whom the rest shall then live in subjection.

The third point becomes clear in the 'Answer' to Travers's supplication against him printed below.

I have chosen two sermons from Hooker. The first is, for

him, an unusually fine piece of preaching (although he may himself have delivered it poorly). The second, the answer to Travers, is a fine summary of his position.

## A Remedy against Sorrow and Fear: Delivered in a Funeral Sermon
John 14:27.
*Let not your hearts be troubled, nor fear.*

HOOKER HAS been called a 'Christian existentialist', and, as this sermon demonstrates, not entirely without reason. For while he sticks carefully to the teachings of the Church, he keeps his congregation's mind on them by means of his psychological knowledge. For 'fear' the modern reader may, if he so prefers, read 'dread', *'Angst'*, 'anxiety'. He understands the fear that has been bred by the reformers' insistence upon the existence of elect and non-elect, and he seeks to reassure (he had said, to Travers's horror, 'I doubt not but God was merciful to save thousands of our fathers living in popish superstitions, inasmuch as they sinned ignorantly'), but he will not do so by cheap means. He sees that people cannot easily be comforted by Christ's exhortation to his followers 'let not your hearts be troubled, nor fear': for the kinds of fear of which Hooker speaks trouble all men. He discusses different kinds of fear, and leads up to this justification of Christ's exhortation: 'All which do show, that we are to stand in fear of nothing more than the extremity of not fearing'.

THE HOLY Apostles having gathered themselves together by the special appointment of Christ, and being in expectation to receive from him such instructions as they had been accustomed with, were told that which they least looked for, namely, that the time of his departure out of the world was now come. Whereupon they fell into consideration, first, of the manifold benefits which his absence should bereave them of; and secondly, of the sundry evils which themselves should be subject unto, being once bereaved of so gracious a Master and Patron. The one consideration overwhelmed their souls with heaviness, the other with fear. Their Lord and Saviour, whose words had cast down their hearts, raiseth them presently again with chosen sentences of sweet encouragement. 'My dear, it is for your own sakes that I leave the world. I know the affections of your hearts are tender, but if your love were directed with that advised and staid judgment which should be in you, my speech of leaving the world, and going unto my Father, would not a little augment your joy. Desolate and comfortless I will not leave you; in spirit I am with you to the world's end: whether I be present or absent, nothing shall ever take you out of these hands; my going is to take possession of that, in your names, which is not only for me but also for you prepared; where I am, you shall be. In the mean while, "My peace I give; not as the world giveth, give I unto you: let not your hearts be troubled, nor fear." ' The former part of which sentence having otherwise already been spoken of, this unacceptable occasion to open the latter part thereof here I did not look for. But so God disposeth the ways of men. Him I heartily beseech, that the thing which he hath thus ordered by his providence, may through his gracious goodness turn unto your comfort.

Our nature coveteth preservation from things hurtful. Hurtful things being present do breed heaviness, being future do cause fear. Our Saviour to abate the one speaketh thus unto his disciples, 'Let not your hearts be troubled;' and to moderate the other, addeth, 'Fear not.' Grief and heaviness in the presence of sensible evils cannot but trouble the minds of men. It may therefore seem that Christ required a thing impossible. Be not troubled. Why, how could they choose? But we must note, this being natural and therefore simply not reprovable, is in us good or bad according to the causes for which we are grieved, or the measure of our grief. It is not my meaning to speak so largely of this affection, as to go over all particulars whereby men do one way or other offend in it; but to teach it so far only as it may cause the very Apostles' equals to swerve. Our grief and heaviness therefore is reprovable sometime in respect of the cause from whence, sometime in regard of the measure whereunto it groweth.

When Christ the life of the world was led unto cruel death, there followed a number of people and women, which women bewailed much his heavy case. It was natural compassion which caused them, where they saw undeserved miseries, there to pour forth unrestrained tears. Nor was this reproved. But in such readiness to lament where they less needed, their blindness in not discerning that for which they ought much rather to have mourned, this our Saviour a little toucheth, putting them in mind that the tears which were wasted for him might better have been spent upon themselves; 'Daughters of Jerusalem, weep not for me, weep for yourselves and for your children.' It is not, as the Stoics have imagined, a thing unseemly for a wise man to be touched with grief of mind; but to be sorrowful when we least should, and where we should lament there to laugh, this argueth our small wisdom. Again, when the Prophet David confesseth thus of himself, 'I grieved to see the great prosperity of godless men, how they flourish and go untouched;' he himself hereby openeth both our common and his peculiar imperfection, whom this cause should not have made so pensive. To grieve at this is to grieve where we should not, because this grief doth rise from error. We err when we grieve at wicked men's impunity and prosperity, because their estate being rightly discerned they neither prosper nor go unpunished. It may seem a paradox, it is a truth, that no wicked man's estate is prosperous, fortunate, or happy. For what though they bless themselves and think their happiness great? Have not frantic persons many times a great opinion of their own wisdom? It may be that such as they think themselves, others also do account them. But what others? Surely such as themselves are. Truth and reason discerneth far otherwise of them. Unto whom the Jews wish all prosperity, unto them the phrase of their speech is to wish peace. Seeing then the name of peace containeth in it all parts of true happiness, when the Prophet saith plainly, that the wicked have no peace, how can we think them to have any part of other than vainly imagined felicity? What wise man did ever account fools happy? If wicked men were wise they would cease to be wicked. Their iniquity therefore proving their folly, how can we stand in doubt of their misery? They abound in those things which all men desire. A poor happiness to have good things in possession. 'A man to whom God hath given riches and treasures and honour, so that he wanteth nothing for his soul of all that it desireth, but yet God giveth him not the power to eat thereof;' such a felicity Solomon esteemeth but as a vanity, a thing of nothing. If such things add nothing to men's happiness where they are not used, surely wicked men that use them ill, the more they have, the more wretched. Of their prosperity therefore we see what we are to think. Touching their impunity, the same is likewise but supposed. They are oftener plagued than we are aware of. The pangs they feel are not always written in their foreheads. Though wickedness be sugar in their mouths, and wantonness as oil to make them look with cheerful countenance; nevertheless if their hearts were disclosed, perhaps their glittering estate would not greatly be envied. The voices that have broken out from some of them, 'O that God had given me a heart senseless, like the flint in the rocks of stone,' which as it can taste no pleasure so it feeleth no woe; these and the like speeches are surely tokens of the curse which Zophar in the Book of Job poureth upon the head of the impious man, 'He shall suck the gall of asps, and the viper's tongue shall slay him.' If this seem light because it is secret, shall we think they go unpunished because no apparent plague is presently seen upon them? The judgments of God do not always follow crimes as thunder doth lightning, but sometimes the space of many ages coming between. When the sun hath shined fair the space of six days upon their tabernacle, we know not what clouds the seventh may bring. And when their punishment doth come, let them make their account in the greatness of their sufferings to pay the interest of that respect which hath been given them. Or if they chance to escape clearly in this world, which they seldom do; in the day when the heavens shall shrivel as a scroll and the mountains move as frighted men out of their places, what cave shall receive them? what mountain or rock shall they get by entreaty to fall upon them? what covert to hide them from that wrath, which they shall be neither able to abide nor to avoid? No man's misery therefore being greater than theirs whose impiety is most fortunate; much more cause there is for them to bewail their own infelicity, than for others to be troubled with their prosperous and happy estate, as if the hand of the Almighty did not or would not touch them. For these causes and the like unto these therefore be not troubled.

Now though the cause of our heaviness be just, yet may not our affections herein be yielded unto with too much indulgency and favour. The grief of compassion whereby we are touched with the feeling of other men's woes is of all other least dangerous. Yet this is a let unto sundry duties; by this we are apt to spare sometimes where we ought to strike. The grief which our own sufferings do bring, what temptations have not risen from it? What great advantage Satan hath taken even by the godly grief of hearty contrition for sins committed against God, the near approaching of so many afflicted souls, whom the conscience of sin hath brought unto the very brink of extreme despair, doth but too abundantly shew. These things wheresoever they fall cannot but trouble and molest the mind. Whether we be therefore moved vainly with that which seemeth hurtful and is not; or have just cause of grief, being pressed indeed with those things which are grievous, our Saviour's lesson is, touching the one, Be not troubled, nor over-troubled for the other. For, though to have no feeling of that which merely concerneth us were stupidity, nevertheless, seeing that as the Author of our salvation was himself consecrated by affliction, so the way which we are to follow him by is not strewed with rushes, but set with thorns, be it never so hard to learn, we must learn to suffer with patience even that which seemeth almost impossible to be suffered; that in the hour when God shall call us unto our trial, and turn this honey of peace and pleasure wherewith we swell into that gall and bitterness which flesh doth shrink to taste of, nothing may cause us in the troubles of our souls to storm and grudge and repine at God, but every heart be enabled with divinely inspired courage to inculcate unto itself, Be not troubled; and in those last and greatest conflicts to remember it, that nothing may be so sharp and bitter to be suffered, but that still we ourselves may give ourselves this encouragement, Even learn also patience, O my soul.

Naming patience I name that virtue which only hath power to stay our souls from being over-excessively troubled: a virtue, wherein if ever any, surely that soul had good experience, which extremity of pains having chased out of the tabernacle of this flesh, angels, I nothing doubt, have carried into the bosom of her father Abraham. The death of the saints of God is precious in his sight. And shall it seem unto us superfluous at such times as these are to hear in what manner they have ended their lives? The Lord himself hath not disdained so exactly to register in the book of life after what sort his servants have closed up their days on earth, that he descendeth even to their very meanest actions, what meat they have longed for in their sickness, what they have spoken unto their children, kinsfolk, and friends, where they have willed their dead carcasses to be laid, how they have framed their wills and testaments, yea the very turning of their faces to this side or that, the setting of their eyes, the degrees whereby their natural heat hath departed from them, their cries, their groans, their pantings, breathings, and last gaspings, he hath most solemnly commended unto the memory of all generations. The care of the living both to live and to die well must needs be somewhat increased, when they know that their departure shall not be folded up in silence, but the ears of many be made acquainted with it. Again when they hear how mercifully God hath dealt with others in the hour of their last need, besides the praise which they give to God, and the joy which they have or should have by reason of their fellowship and communion of saints, is not their hope also much confirmed against the day of their own dissolution? Finally, the sound of these things doth not so pass the ears of them that are most loose and dissolute of life, but it causeth them sometime or other to wish in their hearts, 'Oh that we might die the death of the righteous, and that our end might be like his!' Howbeit because to spend herein many words would be to strike even as many wounds into their minds whom I rather wish to comfort: therefore concerning this virtuous gentlewoman only this little I speak, and that of knowledge, 'She lived a dove, and died a lamb.' And if amongst so many virtues, hearty devotion towards God, towards poverty tender compassion, motherly affection towards servants, towards friends even serviceable kindness, mild behaviour and harmless meaning towards all; if, where so many virtues were eminent, any be worthy of special mention, I wish her dearest friends of that sex to be her nearest followers in two things: Silence, saving only where duty did exact speech; and Patience even then when extremity of pains did enforce grief. 'Blessed are they which die in the Lord.' And concerning the dead which are blessed let not the hearts of any living be overcharged, with grief over-troubled.

Touching the latter affection of fear which respecteth evils to come, as the other which we have spoken of doth present evils; first in the nature thereof it is plain that we are not of every future evil afraid. Perceive we not how they whose tenderness shrinketh at the least rase of a needle's point, do kiss the sword that pierceth their souls quite through? If every evil did cause fear, sin, because it is sin, would be feared; whereas properly sin is not feared as sin, but only as having some kind of harm annexed. To teach men to avoid sin, it had been sufficient for the Apostle to say, 'Fly it.' But to make them afraid of committing sin, because the naming of sin sufficed not, therefore he addeth further, that it is as a 'serpent which stingeth the soul.' Again, be it that some nocive [harmful] or hurtful thing be towards us, must fear of necessity follow hereupon? Not except that hurtful things do threaten us either with destruction or vexation, and that such as we have neither a conceit of ability to resist, nor of utter impossibility to avoid. That which we know ourselves able to withstand we fear not; and that which we know we are unable to defer or diminish, or any way avoid, we cease to fear, we give ourselves over to bear and sustain it. The evil therefore which is feared must be in our persuasion unable to be resisted when it cometh, yet not utterly impossible for a time in whole or in part to be shunned. Neither do we much fear such evils, except they be imminent and near at hand; nor if they be near, except we have an opinion that they be so. When we have once conceived an opinion or apprehended an imagination of such evils prest and ready to invade us; because they are hurtful unto our nature, we feel in ourselves a kind of abhorring; because they are, though near yet not present, our nature seeketh forthwith how to shift and provide for itself; because they are evils which cannot be resisted, therefore she doth not provide to withstand but to shun and avoid. Hence it is that in extreme fear the mother of life contracting herself, avoiding as much as may be the reach of evil, and drawing the heat together with the spirits of the body to her, leaveth the outward parts cold, pale, weak, feeble, unapt to perform the functions of life; as we see in the fear of Belthasar king of Babel. By this it appeareth that fear is nothing else but a perturbation of the mind through an opinion of some imminent evil threatening the destruction or great annoyance of our nature, which to shun it doth contract and deject itself.

Now because not in this place only but otherwhere often we hear it repeated, 'Fear not,' it is by some made a long question, Whether a man may fear destruction or vexation without sinning? First, the reproof wherewith Christ checketh his disciples more than once, 'O men of little faith, wherefore are ye afraid?'

Secondly, the punishment threatened in the 21. of Revelations, to wit, the lake, and fire, and brimstone, not only to murderers, unclean persons, sorcerers, idolaters, liars, but also to the fearful and faint-hearted: this seemeth to argue that fearfulness cannot but be sin. On the contrary side we see that he which never felt motion unto sin had of this affection more than a slight feeling. How clear is the evidence of the Spirit that 'in the days of his flesh he offered up prayers and supplications with strong cries and tears unto him that was able to save him from death, and was also heard in that which he feared!' Whereupon it followeth that fear in itself is a thing not sinful. For is not fear a thing natural and for men's preservation necessary, implanted in us by the provident and most gracious Giver of all good things, to the end that we might not run headlong upon those mischiefs wherewith we are not able to encounter, but use the remedy of shunning those evils which we have not ability to withstand? Let that people therefore which receive a benefit by the length of their prince's days, that father or mother that rejoiceth to see the offspring of their flesh grow like green and pleasant plants, let those children that would have their parents, those men that would gladly have their friends and brethren's days prolonged on earth, (as there is no natural-hearted man but gladly would,) let them bless the Father of lights, as in other things, so even in this, that he hath given man a fearful heart, and settled naturally that affection in him which is a preservation against so many ways of death. Fear then in itself being mere nature cannot in itself be sin, which sin is not nature, but thereof an accessary deprivation.

But in the matter of fear we may sin, and do, two ways. If any man's danger be great, theirs greatest that have put the fear of danger farthest from them. Is there any estate more fearful than that Babylonian strumpet's, that sitteth upon the tops of the seven hills glorifying and vaunting, 'I am a queen' &c.? How much better and happier they whose estate hath been always as his who speaketh after this sort of himself, 'Lord, from my youth have I borne thy yoke!' They which sit at continual ease, and are settled in the lees of their security, look upon them, view their countenance, their speech, their gesture, their deeds: 'Put them in fear, O God,' saith the Prophet, 'that so they may know themselves to be but men,' worms of the earth, dust and ashes, frail, corruptible, feeble things. To shake off security therefore, and to breed fear in the hearts of mortal men, so many admonitions are used concerning the power of evils which beset them, so many threatenings of calamities, so many descriptions of things threatened, and those so lively, to the end they may leave behind them a deep impression of such as have force to keep the heart continually waking. All which do show, that we are to stand in fear of nothing more than the extremity of not fearing.

When fear hath delivered us from that pit wherein they are sunk that have put far from them the evil day, that have made a league with death and have said, 'Tush, we shall feel no harm;' it standeth us upon to take heed it cast us not into that wherein souls destitute of all hope are plunged. For our direction, to avoid as much as may be both extremities, that we may know as a ship-master by his card, how far we are wide, either on the one side or on the other, we must note that in a Christian man there is, first, Nature; secondly, Corruption, perverting Nature; thirdly, Grace correcting, and amending Corruption. In fear all these have their several operations. Nature teacheth simply, to wish preservation and avoidance of things dreadful; for which cause our Saviour himself prayeth, and that often, 'Father, if it be possible.' In which cases corrupt nature's suggestions are, for the safety of temporal life not to stick at things excluding from eternal; wherein how far even the best may be led, the chiefest Apostle's frailty teacheth. Were it not therefore for such cogitations as on the contrary side grace and faith ministereth, such as that of Job, 'Though God kill me;' that of Paul, '*Scio cui credidi*, I know him on whom I do rely;' small evils would soon be able to overwhelm even the best of us. 'A wise man,' saith Solomon, 'doth see a plague coming, and hideth himself.' It is nature which teacheth a wise man in fear to hide himself, but grace and faith doth teach him where. Fools care not where they hide their heads. But where shall a wise man hide himself when he feareth a plague coming? Where should the frighted child hide his head, but in the bosom of his loving father? Where a Christian, but under the shadow of the wings of Christ his Saviour? 'Come, my people,' saith God in the Prophet, 'enter into thy chamber, hide thyself,' &c. But because we are in danger like chased birds, like doves that seek and cannot see the resting holes that are right before them, therefore our Saviour giveth his disciples these encouragements beforehand, that fear might never so amaze them, but that always they might remember, that whatsoever evils at any time did beset them, to him they should still repair, for comfort, counsel, and succour. For their assurance whereof his 'peace he gave them, his peace he left unto them, not such peace as the world offereth,' by whom his name is never so much pretended as when deepest treachery is meant; but 'peace which passeth all understanding,' peace that bringeth with it all happiness, peace that continueth for ever and ever with them that have it.

This peace God the Father grant, for his Son's sake; unto whom, with the Holy Ghost, three Persons, one eternal and everliving God, be all honour, glory, and praise, now and for ever. Amen.

## Mr Hooker's Answer to the Supplication that Mr Travers Made to the Council
*To My Lord of Canterbury His Grace*

FOR SOME years before 1585 the Temple had been managed by largely Presbyterian methods: the Master was Richard Alvey, and he was as pronounced a Puritan as his afternoon lecturer (Reader), Walter Travers, who should have had his place if Burghley—tolerant but sympathetic, like Leicester, to Puritanism—had had his way. Whitgift, however, though doctrinally an extreme left Puritan, was anti-Presbyterian; the Queen, however, rejected his episcopalian nominee, though she also rejected Travers. Whitgift was then able to insinuate the reluctant Hooker into the position.

Now in 1581 Hooker, in a sermon preached at Paul's Cross, had developed an anti-Calvinist line of argument, to the effect that, for human beings, God must be conceived as possessing two wills: the one antecedent, the other consequent. The Puritans misunderstood him, for he was a subtle man, who, as a writer has put it, 'touched the nerve-centre of the Calvinist providentialism'. A remarkably consistent strand running through his thought, and one that is relevant today, is his anxiety to avoid the dangerous practice of investing the texture of history with an over-confident and hubristic providentialism. Hooker was keenly aware of the fear and the envy that motivated the supralapsarianism of the Calvinists (Calvin himself, it may be argued, was not a Supralapsarian: some claim that he was, some that he was not—the truth is that his gift was for vindictive administration, and not at all for theology), he discerned its dangers earlier than most of his contemporaries, and he wished to persuade people of the fact that—though there be an inscrutable God, though there truly be justification by faith—they did live in history, and that, as human beings, they must accept the extreme limitations this put upon them. Hooker's thought rests upon a paradox; but what great man's does not?

Travers, described by a historian as the 'paragon of Elizabethan Puritanism', was an honest and courteous man, but as a Puritan and Presbyterian—and determined to be unparadoxical— he felt he must attack Hooker, and he seized at once on Hooker's 'double-willed' God. The controversy continued until Whitgift decided, after a year, to order Travers to be silent. Immediately Travers, never lacking in courage, addressed the Privy Council (to which the Queen, to counter the Puritan sympathies of some of the others, had appointed Whitgift) a 'Supplication'. This accused Hooker of teaching that the scriptures are not the sole guide to the truth, and of daring to point out that the 'light of nature will not suffer a man not to doubt of ... the light of grace'. The gist of Hooker's thinking is contained in the 'Learned Discourse of Justification', but this is too long to print here. I have therefore chosen to print his 'Answer to the Supplication' (which was addressed not to the Privy Council but simply to the Archbishop). (It should be remembered that the congregations would have been, at least at the outset, pro-Presbyterian—if only on account of Alvey's and Travers's continual indoctrination.) Hooker's personally mild disposition, which felt Calvinism to 'torment weak consciences with infinite perplexities', is one of the indispensable keys to his work; here it is admirably conveyed.

The whole casts light on the manner in which Presbyterian ministers attempted to undermine the Act of Uniformity in this period, and on the extent to which they could go—this was obviously considerable. They were, of course, in hard case; but when, some half-century later, they tried to impose their will on the English people, they failed, first at the hands of Cromwell and then, again, at the Restoration (which their lay followers had brought about). That they had good reasons is undoubtedly true; but these reasons were not to prove acceptable to the will of the English people. One important factor in this refusal of the people to conform to their desired arrangements was undoubtedly Cranmer's use of the English language, for this, enshrined mainly in the Book of Common Prayer, caused the majority to form an inalienable attachment to the established Church.

My commentary occasionally draws on the (very long) 'Discourse of justification' (which, as I have indicated, contains much of the essence of Hooker's thinking) and on the 'Sermon of the Certainty and Perpetuity of Faith in the Elect': both were preached at the Temple during the year 1585-6. I have also drawn, where appropriate, on *Ecclesiastical Polity*.

MY DUTY in most humble wise remembered, may it please your Grace to understand, that whereas there hath been a late controversy raised in the Temple, and pursued by Mr. Travers, upon conceit taken at some words by me uttered with a most simple and harmless meaning; in the heat of which pursuit, after three public invectives, silence being enjoined him by authority, he hath hereupon for defence of his proceedings, both presented the right honourable Lords and other of her Majesty's privy council with a writing, and also caused or suffered the same to be copied out and spread through the hands of so many, that well nigh all sorts of men have it now in their bosoms; the matters wherewith I am therein charged being of such quality as they are, and myself being better known to your Grace than to any other of their Honours besides, I have chosen to offer to your Grace's hands a plain declaration of my innocency, in all those things wherewith I am so hardly and heavily charged, lest if I still remain silent, that which I do for quietness' sake, be taken as an argument that I lack what to speak truly and justly in mine own defence.

2. First, because Mr. Travers thinketh it expedient to breed an opinion in men's minds, that the root of all inconvenient events which are now sprung out, is the surly and unpeaceable disposition of the man with whom he hath to do; therefore the first in the rank of accusations laid against me, is my inconformity, which have so little inclined to so many and so earnest exhortations and conferences, as myself, he saith, can witness to have been spent upon me, for my better fashioning unto good correspondence and agreement.

3. Indeed when at the first, by means of special wellwillers, without any suit of mine, as they very well know, (although I do not think it had been a mortal sin, in a reasonable sort to have showed a moderate desire that way,) yet when by their endeavour without instigation of mine, some reverend and honourable, favourably affecting me, had procured her Majesty's grant of the place; at the very point of my entering thereinto, the evening before I was first to preach, he came, and two other gentlemen joined with him in the charge of this church, (for so he gave me to understand,) though not in the same kind of charge with him: the effect of his conference then was, that he thought it his duty to advise me not to enter with a strong hand, but to change my purpose of preaching there the next day, and to stay till he had given notice of me to the congregation, that

so their allowance might seal my calling. The effect of mine answer was, that as in place where such order is, I would not break it; so here where it never was, I might not of mine own head take upon me to begin it: but liking very well the motion, for the opinion which I had of his good meaning who made it, requested him not to mislike my answer, though it were not correspondent to his mind.

4. When this had so displeased some, that whatsoever was afterwards done or spoken by me, it offended their taste, angry informations were daily sent out, intelligence given far and wide, what a dangerous enemy was crept in; the worst that jealousy could imagine was spoken and written to so many, that at the length some knowing me well, and perceiving how injurious the reports were, which grew daily more and more unto my discredit, wrought means to bring Mr. Travers and me to a second conference. Wherein when a common friend unto us both had quietly requested him to utter those things wherewith he found himself any way aggrieved, he first renewed the memory of my entering into this charge by virtue only of a human creature (for so the want of that formality of popular allowance was then censured); and unto this was annexed a catalogue, partly of causeless surmises, as that I had conspired against him, and that I sought superiority over him; and partly of faults, which to note, I should have thought it a greater offence than to commit, if I did account them faults, and had heard them so curiously observed in any other than myself, they are such silly things; as praying in the entrance of my sermons only, and not in the end, naming bishops in my prayer, kneeling when I pray, and kneeling when I receive the Communion, with such like, which I would be as loth to recite, as I was sorry to hear them objected, if the rehearsal thereof were not by him thus wrested from me. These are the conferences wherewith I have been wooed to entertain peace and good agreement.

5. As for the vehement exhortations he speaketh of, I would gladly know some reason wherefore he thought them needful to be used. Was there any thing found in my speeches or dealings, which gave them occasion, who are studious of peace, to think that I disposed myself to some unquiet kind of proceedings? Surely the special providence of God I do now see it was, that the first words I spake in this place should make the first thing whereof I am accused to appear not only untrue, but improbable, to as many as then heard me with indifferent ears, and do I

doubt not in their consciences clear me of this suspicion. Howbeit, I grant this were nothing, if it might be showed, that my deeds following were not suitable to my words. If I had spoken of peace at the first, and afterwards sought to molest and grieve him, by crossing him in his function, by storming if my pleasure were not asked and my will obeyed in the least occurences, by carping needlessly sometimes at the manner of his teaching, sometimes at this, sometimes at that point of his doctrine; I might then with some likelihood have been blamed, as one disdaining a peaceable hand when it hath been offered. But if I be able (as I am) to prove that myself have now a full year together borne the continuance of such dealings, not only without any manner of resistance, but also without any such complaint as might let or hinder him in his course; I see no cause in the world, why of this I should be accused, unless it be, lest I should accuse, which I meant not. If therefore I have given him occasion to use conferences and exhortations unto peace, if when they were bestowed upon me I have despised them, it will not be hard to show some one word or deed wherewith I have gone about to work disturbance: one is not much, I require but one. Only I require if any thing be showed, it may be proved, and not objected only, as this is, 'That I have joined with such as have always opposed to any good order in this church, and made themselves to be thought indisposed to the present estate and proceedings.' The words have reference, as it seemeth, unto some such things, as being attempted before my coming to the Temple, went not so effectually perhaps forward as he which devised them would have wished. An order, as I learn, there was tendered,* that communicants should neither kneel, as in the most places of the realm; nor sit, as in this place the custom is; but walk to the one side of the table, and there standing till they had received, pass afterward away round about by the other. Which being on a sudden begun to be practised in the church, some sat wondering what it should mean, others deliberating what to do: till such time as at length by name one of them being openly called thereunto, requested that they might do as they had been accustomed; which was granted, and as Mr. Travers had ministered his way to the rest, so a curate was sent to minister to them after their way. Which unprosperous beginning of a thing (saving only for the inconvenience of needless alterations, otherwise harmless) did so disgrace that order in their conceit who had to allow or disallow it, that it took no place. For neither they could ever induce themselves to think it good, and it so much offended Mr. Travers, who supposed it to be the best, that he since that time, although contented himself to receive it as they do at the hands of others, yet hath not thought it meet they should ever receive it out of his, which would not admit that order of receiving it, and therefore in my time hath been always present not to minister but only to be ministered unto.

6. Another order there was likewise devised, an order of much more weight and importance. This soil, in respect of certain immunities and other specialities belonging unto it, seemed likely to bear that which in other places of the realm of England doth not take. For which cause request was made to some of her majesty's privy council, that whereas it is provided by a statute there should be collectors and sidemen in churches, which thing, or somewhat correspondent unto it, this place did greatly want, it would please their Honours to motion such a matter to the Ancients of the Temple. And, according to their honourable manner of helping forward all motions so grounded, they wrote their letters, as I am informed, to that effect. Whereupon, although these Houses never had use of such collectors and sidemen as are appointed in other places, yet they both erected a box to receive men's devotion for the poor, appointing the treasurer of both Houses to take care for bestowing it where need is; and granted further, that if any could be intreated (as in the end some were) to undertake the labour of observing men's slackness in divine duties, they should be allowed, their complaints heard at all times, and the faults they complained of, if Mr. Travers' private admonition did not serve, then by some other means redressed, but according to the old received orders of both Houses. Whereby the substance of their Honours' letters was indeed fully satisfied. Yet because Mr. Travers intended not this, but as it seemeth, another thing; therefore notwithstanding the orders which have been taken, and for any thing I know, do stand still in as much force in this church now as at any time heretofore, he complaineth much that the good orders which he doth mean have been withstood. Now it were hard, if as many as any where oppose unto these and the like orders, in his persuasion good, do thereby make themselves to be thought dislikers of the present state and proceedings. If they whom he aimeth at have any otherwise made themselves to be thought such, it is likely he doth know wherein, and will I hope disclose to whom it appertaineth, both the persons whom he thinketh and the

causes why he thinketh them so ill-affected. But whatsoever the men be, do their faults make me faulty? They do, if I join myself with them. I beseech him therefore to declare wherein I have joined with them. Other joining than this with any man here, I cannot imagine: it may be I have talked, or walked, or eaten, or interchangeably used the duties of common humanity, with some such as he is hardly persuaded of. For I know no law of God or man, by force whereof they should be as heathens and publicans unto me, that are not gracious in the eyes of another man, perhaps without cause, or if with cause, yet such cause as he is privy unto, and not I. Could he or any reasonable man think it a charitable course in me, to observe them that show by external courtesies a favourable inclination towards him, and if I spy out any one amongst them of whom I think not well, hereupon to draw such an accusation as this against him, and to offer it where he hath given up his against me? which notwithstanding I will acknowledge to be just and reasonable, if he or any man living shall show, that I use as much as the bare familiar company but of one, who by word or deed hath ever given me cause to suspect or conjecture him such as here they are termed, with whom complaint is made that I join myself. This being spoken therefore and written without all possibility of proof, doth not Mr. Travers give me over-great cause to stand in some fear lest he make too little conscience how he useth his tongue or pen? These things are not laid against me for nothing; they are to some purpose if they take place. For in a mind persuaded that I am as he deciphereth me, one which refuse to be at peace with such as embrace the truth, and side myself with men sinisterly affected thereunto, any thing that shall be spoken concerning the unsoundness of my doctrine cannot choose but be favourably entertained. This presupposed, it will have likelihood enough which afterwards followeth, that 'many of my sermons have tasted of some sour leaven or other,' that in them he hath 'discovered sundry unsound matters.' A thing greatly to be lamented, that such a place as this, which might have been so well provided for, hath fallen into the hands of one no better instructed in the truth. But what if in the end it be found that he judgeth my words, as they do colours, which look upon them with green spectacles, and think that which they see is green, when indeed that is green whereby they see.

7.* Touching the first point of his discovery, which is about the matter of predestination, to set down that I spake, (for I have it written,) to declare and confirm the several branches thereof, would be tedious now in this writing, where I have so many things to touch that I can but touch them only. Neither is it herein so needful for me to justify my speech, when the very place and presence where I spake, doth itself speak sufficiently for my clearing. This matter was not broached in a blind alley, or uttered where none was to hear it, that had skill with authority to control, or covertly insinuated by some gliding sentence.

8.* That which I taught was at Paul's Cross; it was not huddled in amongst other matters, in such sort that it could pass without noting; it was opened, it was proved, it was some reasonable time stood upon. I see not which way my Lord of London, who was present and heard it, can excuse so great a fault, as patiently, without rebuke or controlment afterwards, to hear any man there teach otherwise than 'the word of God doth,' not as it is understood by the private interpretation of some one or two men, or by a special construction received in some few books, but as it is understood 'by all the churches professing the gospel;' by them all, and therefore even by our own also amongst others. A man that did mean to prove that he speaketh, would surely take the measure of his words shorter.

9.* The next thing discovered, is an opinion about the assurance of men's persuasion in matters of faith. I have taught, he saith, 'That the assurance of things which we believe by the word, is not so certain as of that we perceive by sense.' And is it as certain? Yea, I taught, as he himself I trust will not deny, that the things which God doth promise in his word are surer unto us than any thing we touch, handle, or see; but are we so sure and certain of them? if we be, why doth God so often prove his promises unto us, as he doth, by arguments taken from our sensible experience? We must be surer of the proof than of the thing proved, otherwise it is no proof. How is it, that if ten men do all look upon the moon, every one of them knoweth it as certainly to be the moon as another; but many believing one and the same promises, all have not one and the same fulness of persuasion? How falleth it out, that men being assured of any thing by sense, can be no surer of it than they are; whereas the strongest in faith that liveth upon the earth, hath always need to labour, and strive, and pray, that his assurance concerning heavenly and spiritual things may grow, increase, and be augmented?

10. The sermon wherein I have spoken somewhat largely of

this point, was, long before this late controversy rose between him and me, upon request of some of my friends seen and read by many, and amongst many, some who are thought able to discern; and I never heard that any one of them hitherto hath condemned it as containing unsound matter. My case were very hard, if as oft as any thing I speak displeaseth one man's taste my doctrine upon his only word should be taken for sour leaven.

11. The rest of this discovery is all about the matter now in question, wherein he hath two faults predominant, which would tire out any that should answer unto every point severally: unapt speaking of school-controversies; and of my words sometimes so untoward a reciting, that he which should promise to draw a man's countenance, and did indeed express the parts, at leastwise the most of them, truly, but perversely place them, could not represent a more offensive visage, than unto me mine own speech seemeth in some places, as he hath ordered it. For answer whereunto, that writing is sufficient, wherein I have set down both my words and meaning in such sort, that where this accusation doth deprave the one, and either misinterpret, or without just cause mislike the other, it will appear so plainly, that I may spare very well to take upon me a new and a needless labour here.

12.\* Only at one thing which is there to be found, because Mr. Travers doth here seem to take such a special advantage, as if the matter were unanswerable, he constraineth me either to detect his oversight, or to confess mine own in it. In setting the question between the church of Rome and us about grace and justification, lest I should give them an occasion to say, as commonly they do, that when we cannot refute their opinions, we propose to ourselves such instead of theirs, as we can refute; I took it for the best and most perspicuous way of teaching, to declare first, how far we do agree, and then to show our disagreement; not generally (as Mr. Travers his words would carry it, for the easier fastening of that upon me, wherewith, saving only by him, I was never in my life touched); but about the matter of justification only; for farther I had no cause to meddle at that time. What was then mine offence in this case? I did, as he saith, so set it out as if we had consented in the greatest and weightiest points, and differed only in smaller matters. It will not be found, when it cometh to the balance, a light difference when we disagree, as I did acknowledge that we do, about the very essence of the medicine, whereby Christ cureth our disease. Did I go about to make a shew of agreement in the weightiest points, and was I so fond as not to conceal our disagreement about this? I do wish that some indifferency were used by them that have taken the weighing of my words.

13. Yea, but our agreement is not such in two of the chiefest points, as I would have men believe it is: and what are they? The one is, I said, 'They acknowledge all men sinners, even the Blessed Virgin, though some of them free her from sin.' Put the case I had affirmed, that only some of them free her from sin, and had delivered it as the most current opinion amongst them, that she was conceived in sin: doth not Bonaventure\* say plainly, 'omnes fere,' in a manner all men do hold this? doth he not bring many reasons wherefore all men should hold it? were their voices since that time ever counted, and their number found smaller which hold it, than theirs that hold the contrary? Let the question then be, whether I might say, the most of them 'acknowledge all men sinners, even the Blessed Virgin herself.' To show that their general received opinion is the contrary, the Tridentine\* council is alleged, peradventure not altogether so considerately. For if that council have by resolute determination freed her, if it hold, as Mr. Travers saith it doth, that she was free from sin, then must the church of Rome needs condemn them that hold the contrary. For what that council holdeth, the same they all do and must hold. But in the church of Rome, who knoweth not, that it is a thing indifferent to think and defend the one or the other? So that this argument, the council of Trent holdeth the Virgin free from sin, *ergo*, it is plain that none of them may, and therefore untrue that most of them do, acknowledge her a sinner, were forcible to overthrow my supposed assertion, if it were true that the council did hold this. But to the end it may clearly appear, how it neither holdeth this nor the contrary, I will open what many do conceive of the canon that concerneth this matter. The fathers of Trent perceived, that if they should define of this matter, it would be dangerous howsoever it were determined. If they freed her from original sin, the reasons against them are unanswerable, which Bonaventure and others do allege, but especially Thomas,\* whose line as much as may be they follow. Again if they did resolve the other way, they should control themselves in another thing, which in no case might be altered. For they profess to keep no day holy in the honour of an unholy thing; and the Virgin's conception they honour with a feast, which they could not abrogate without cancelling a constitution of Xystus Quartus.\*

And that which is worse, the world might perhaps hereupon suspect, that if the church of Rome did amiss before in this, it is not impossible for her to fail in other things. In the end, they did wisely cut out their canon by a middle thread, establishing the feast of the Virgin's conception, and leaving the other question doubtful as they found it; giving only a caveat, that no man should take the decree which pronounceth all mankind originally sinful, for a definitive sentence concerning the Blessed Virgin. This in my sight is plain by their own words, 'Declarat haec ipsa sancta Synodus,' &c. Wherefore our countrymen at Rheims, mentioning this point, are marvellous wary, how they speak; they touch it as though it were a hot coal: 'Many godly devout men judge that our blessed lady was neither born nor conceived in sin.' It is not their wont to speak so nicely of things definitively set down in that council.

In like sort we find that the rest which have since the time of the Tridentine synod written of original sin, are in this point for the most part either silent or very sparing in their speech; and when they speak, either doubtful what to think, or whatsoever they think themselves, fearful to set down any certain determination. If I be thought to take the canon of that council otherwise than they themselves do, let him expound it whose sentence was neither last asked nor his pen least occupied in setting it down; I mean Andradius, whom Gregory the Thirteenth hath allowed plainly to confess, that it is a matter which neither express evidence of Scripture, nor the tradition of the Fathers, nor the sentence of the Church hath determined; that they are too surly and self-willed, which, defending either opinion, are displeased with them by whom the other is maintained; finally that the Fathers of Trent have not set down any certainty about this question, but left it doubtful and indifferent.

Now whereas my words, which I had set down in writing before I uttered them, were indeed these, 'Although they imagine that the Mother of our Lord Jesus Christ were for his honour and by his special protection preserved clean from all sin, yet concerning the rest they teach as we do, that all have sinned:' against my words they might with more pretence take exception, because so many of them think she had sin, which exception notwithstanding, the proposition being indefinite and the matter contingent, they cannot take, because they grant that many whom they count grave and devout amongst them think that she was clear from all sin. But whether Mr. Travers did note my words himself, or take them upon the credit of some other man's noting, the tables were faulty wherein it was noted, 'All men sinners, even the Blessed Virgin;' when my speech was rather, 'All men except the Blessed Virgin.'

To leave this; another fault he findeth, that I said, 'They teach Christ's righteousness to be the only meritorious cause of taking away sin, and differ from us only in the applying of it.' I did say and do, 'They teach as we do, that although Christ be the only meritorious cause of our justice, yet as a medicine, which is made for health, doth not heal by being made, but by being applied; so, by the merits of Christ, there can be no life nor justification, without the application of his merits: but about the manner of applying Christ, about the number and power of means whereby he is applied, we dissent from them.' This of our dissenting from them is acknowledged.

14. Our agreement in the former is denied to be such as I pretend. Let their own words therefore and mine concerning them be compared. Doth not Andradius plainly confess; 'Our sins doth shut, and only the merits of Christ open the entering into blessedness?' And Soto, 'It is put for a ground, that all, since the fall of Adam, obtain salvation only by the Passion of Christ: howbeit as no cause can be effectual without applying, so neither can any man be saved, to whom the suffering of Christ is not applied.' In a word, who not? when the council of Trent reckoning up the causes of our first justification, doth name no end but God's glory and our felicity; no efficient but his mercy; no instrumental but baptism; no meritorious but Christ; whom to have merited the taking away of no sin but original is not their opinion: which himself will find, when he hath well examined his witnesses, Catharinus and Thomas. Their Jesuits are marvellous angry with the men out of whose gleanings Mr. Travers seemeth to have taken this; they openly disclaim it, they say plainly, 'Of all the catholics there is no one that did ever so teach,' they make solemn protestation, 'We believe and profess that Christ upon the cross hath altogether satisfied for all sins, as well original as actual.' Indeed they teach, that the merit of Christ doth not take away actual sin in such sort as it doth original; wherein if their doctrine had been understood, I for my speech had never been accused. As for the council of Trent concerning inherent righteousness, what doth it here? No man doubteth but they make another formal cause of justification than we do. In respect whereof, I have showed already that we

disagree about the very essence of that which cureth our spiritual disease. Most true it is which the grand philosopher hath, 'Every man judgeth well of that which he knoweth;' and therefore, till we know the things throughly whereof we judge, it is a point of judgment to stay our judgment.

15. Thus much labour being spent in discovering the unsoundness of my doctrine, some pains he taketh further to open faults in the manner of my teaching, as that 'I bestowed my whole hour and more, my time and more than my time, in discourses utterly impertinent to my text.' Which if I had done, it might have past without complaining of to the privy-council.

16. But I did worse, as he saith; 'I left the expounding of the Scriptures, and my ordinary calling, and discoursed upon school-points and questions, neither of edification, nor of truth.' I read no lecture in the law or in physic. And except the bounds of ordinary calling may be drawn like a purse, how are they so much wider unto him than to me, that he within the limits of his ordinary calling should reprove that in me which he understood not, and I labouring that both he and others might understand, could not do this without forsaking my calling? The matter whereof I spake was such, as being at the first by me but lightly touched, he had in that place openly contradicted, and solemnly taken upon him to disapprove. If therefore it were a school-question, and unfit to be discoursed of there, that which was in me but a proposition only at the first, wherefore made he a problem of it? Why took he first upon him to maintain the negative of that which I had affirmatively spoken, only to show mine own opinion, little thinking that ever it would have made a question? Of what nature soever the question were, I could do no less than there explain myself to them, unto whom I was accused of unsound doctrine; wherein if to show what had been through ambiguity mistaken in my words, or misapplied by him in this cause against me, I used the distinctions and helps of schools, I trust that herein I have committed no unlawful thing. These school-implements\* are acknowledged by grave and wise men not unprofitable to have been invented. The most approved for learning and judgment do use them without blame; the use of them hath been well liked in some that have taught even in this very place before me; the quality of my hearers is such, that I could not but think them of capacity very sufficient for the most part to conceive harder than I used any; the cause I had in hand did in my judgment necessarily require them which were

then used; when my words spoken generally without distinctions had been perverted, what other way was there for me, but by distinctions to lay them open in their right meaning, that it might appear to all men whether they were consonant to truth or no? And although Mr. Travers be so inured with the city, that he thinketh it unmeet to use any speech which savoureth of the school, yet his opinion is no canon. Though unto him, his mind being troubled, my speech did seem like fetters and manacles, yet there might be some more calmly affected which thought otherwise; his private judgment will hardly warrant his bold words, that the things which I spake 'were neither of edification nor truth.' They might edify some other, for any thing he knoweth, and be true for any thing he proveth to the contrary. For it is no proof to cry, 'Absurdities, the like whereunto have not been heard in public places within this land since Queen Mary's days.' If this came in earnest from him, I am sorry to see him so much offended without cause; more sorry, that his fit should be so extreme, to make him speak he knoweth not what. That I neither 'affected the truth of God, nor the peace of the Church,' *mihi pro minimo est*. It doth not much move me when Mr. Travers doth say that, which I trust a greater than Mr. Travers will gainsay.

17. Now let all this which hitherto he hath said be granted him, let it be as he would have it, let my doctrine and manner of teaching be as much disallowed by all men's judgments as by his, what is all this to his purpose? He himself allegeth this to be the cause why he bringeth it in; the High Commissioners 'charge him with an indiscretion and want of duty in that he inveighed against certain points of doctrine taught by me as erroneous, not conferring first with me, nor complaining of it to them.' Which faults, a sea of such matter as he hath hitherto waded in will never be able to scour from him. For the avoiding of schism and disturbance in the Church, which must needs grow if all men might think what they list and speak openly what they think; therefore by a decree agreed upon by the Bishops* and confirmed by her Majesty's authority, it was ordered that erroneous doctrine, if it were taught publicly, should not be publicly refuted; but that notice thereof should be given unto such as are by her Highness appointed to hear and to determine such causes. For breach of which order, when he is charged with lack of duty, all the faults that can be heaped upon me will make but a weak defence for him: as surely his defence is not much

stronger, when he allegeth for himself, that 'he was in some hope his speech in proving the truth, and clearing those scruples which I had in myself, might cause me either to embrace sound doctrine, or suffer it to be embraced of others, which if I did he should not need to complain;' that 'it was meet he should first discover what I had sown, and make it manifest to be tares, and then desire their scythe to cut it down;' that 'conscience did bind him to do otherwise than the foresaid order requireth;' that 'he was unwilling to deal in that public manner, and wished a more convenient way were taken for it;' that 'he had resolved to have protested the next sabbath-day, that he would some other way satisfy such as should require it, and not deal more in that place.' Be it imagined, (let me not be taken as if I did compare the offenders, when I do not, but their answers only,) be it imagined that a libeller did make this apology for himself; 'I am not ignorant that if I have just matter against any man the law is open, there are judges to hear it, and courts where it ought to be complained of; I have taken another course against such or such a man, yet without breach of duty, forasmuch as I am able to yield a reason of my doing; I conceived some hope that a little discredit amongst men would make him ashamed of himself, and that his shame would work his amendment; which if it did, other accusation there should not need:' could his answer be thought sufficient, could it in the judgment of discreet men free him from all blame? No more can the hope which Mr. Travers conceived to reclaim me by public speech, justify his fault against the established order of the church.

18. His thinking it meet 'he should first openly discover to the people the tares that had been sown amongst them, and then require the hand of authority to mow them down,' doth only make it a question whether his opinion that this was meet, may be a privilege or protection against that lawful constitution which had before determined of it as of a thing unmeet. Which question I leave for them to discuss whom it most concerneth. If the order be such that it cannot be kept without hazarding a thing so precious as a good conscience, the peril whereof could be no greater to him than it needs must be to all others whom it toucheth in like causes; when this is evident, it will be a most effectual motive not only for England, but also for other reformed churches, even Geneva itself, (for they have the like,) to change or take that away which cannot but with great inconvenience be observed. In the meanwhile, the breach of it may in

such consideration be pardoned, (which truly I wish, howsoever it be), yet hardly defended as long as it standeth in force uncancelled.

19. Now whereas he confesseth another way had 'been more convenient,' and that he found in himself secret unwillingness to do that which he did, doth he not plainly say in effect that the light of his own understanding proved the way he took perverse and crooked; reason was so plain and pregnant against it, that his mind was alienated, his will averted to another course? yet somewhat there was which so far overruled, that it must needs be done even against the very stream: what doth this bewray? Finally, his purposed protestation, whereby he meant openly to make it known, that he did not allow this kind of proceeding, and therefore would satisfy men otherwise, 'and deal no more in this place,' showeth his good mind in this, that he meant to stay himself from further offending; but it serveth not his turn. He is blamed because the thing he had done was amiss, and his answer is, That which I would have done afterward had been well, if so be I had done it.

20. But as in this he standeth persuaded that he hath done nothing besides duty, so he taketh it hardly that the High Commissioners should charge him with indiscretion. Whereof as if he could so wash his hands, he maketh a long and a large declaration concerning the carriage of himself; how he waded in matters 'of smaller weight,' and how in things of greater 'moment;' how warily he dealt; how 'naturally he took his things rising from the text;' how closely he kept himself 'to the Scripture he took in hand;' how much pains he 'took to confirm the necessity of believing justification by Christ only,' and to show how 'the church of Rome denieth that a man is saved by faith alone without works of the law;' what 'the Sons of Thunder would have done' if they had been in his case; that his 'answer was very temperate, without *immodest* or reproachful speech;' that when he might 'before all have reproved me,' he did not, 'but contented himself with exhorting me' before all 'to follow Nathan's example and revisit my doctrine;' when he might have followed St. Paul's example in 'reproving' Peter, he did not, but exhorted me with Peter to 'endure to be withstood.' This testimony of his discreet carrying himself in the handling of his matter, being more agreeably framed and given him by another than by himself, might make somewhat for the praise of his person; but for defence of his action unto them by whom he is thought undiscreet for not

conferring privately before he spake, will it serve to answer that when he spake he did it considerately? He perceiveth it will not, and therefore addeth reasons such as they are. As namely how he purposed at the first to take another course, and that was this, 'publicly to deliver the truth of such doctrine as I had otherwise taught, and at convenient opportunity to confer with me upon such points.' Is this the rule of Christ, If thy brother offend openly in his speech, control it first with contrary speech openly, and confer with him afterwards upon it, when convenient opportunity serveth? Is there any law of God or of man whereupon to ground such a resolution, any Church extant in the world where teachers are allowed thus to do or to be done unto? He cannot but see how weak an allegation it is, when he bringeth in his following this course, first in one matter and so afterwards in another, to approve himself now following it again. For if the very purpose of doing a thing so uncharitable be a fault, the deed is a greater fault; and doth the doing of it twice make it the third time fit and allowable to be done? The weight of the cause, which is his third defence, relieveth him as little. The weightier it was the more it required conference, advice, and consultation, the more it stood him upon to take good heed that nothing were rashly done or spoken in it. But he meaneth 'weighty' in regard of the wonderful danger, except he had presently withstood me, without expecting a time of conference. 'This cause being of such moment that might prejudice the faith of Christ, encourage the ill-affected to continue still in their damnable ways, and other weak in faith to suffer themselves to be seduced to the destruction of their souls, he thought it his bounden duty to speak before he talked with me.' A man that should read this and not know what I had spoken might imagine that I had at the least denied the divinity of Christ. But they which were present at my speech, and can testify that nothing passed my lips more than is contained in their writings, whom for soundness of doctrine, learning, and judgment, Mr. Travers himself doth, I dare say, not only allow, but honour; they which heard and do know, that the doctrine here signified in so fearful manner, the doctrine that was so dangerous to the faith of Christ, that was so likely to 'encourage ill-affected men to continue still in damnable ways,' that gave so great cause to tremble for fear of the present 'destruction of souls,' was only this; 'I doubt not but God was merciful to save thousands of our fathers living heretofore in popish superstitions, inasmuch as they sinned ignorantly;' and this spoken in a sermon, the greatest part whereof was against popery; they will hardly be able to discern how Christianity should herewith be so grievously shaken.

21. Whereby his fourth excuse is also taken from him. For what doth it boot him to say, 'The time was short wherein he was to preach after me,' when his preaching of this matter perhaps ought, surely might have been either very well omitted, or at the least more conveniently for a while deferred, even by their judgments that cast the most favourable aspect towards these his hasty proceedings. The poison which men had taken at my hands was not so quick and strong in operation as in eight days to make them past cure; by eight days' delay there was no likelihood that the force and power of his speech could die; longer meditation might bring better and stronger proofs to mind than extemporal dexterity could furnish him with; and who doth know whether time, the only mother of sound judgment and discreet dealing, might have given that action of his some better ripeness, which by so great festination hath, as a thing born out of time, brought small joy unto him that begat it? Doth he think it had not been better that neither my speech had seemed in his eyes as an arrow sticking in a thigh of flesh, nor his own of a child whereof he must needs be delivered by an hour? His last way of disburdening himself is, by casting his load upon my back, as if I had brought him by former conferences out of hope that any fruit would ever come of conferring with me. Loth I am to rip up those conferences, whereof he maketh but a slippery and loose relation. In one of them the question between us was, whether the persuasion of faith concerning remission of sins, eternal life, and whatsoever God doth promise unto man, be as free from doubting as the persuasion which we have by sense concerning things tasted, felt, and seen. For the negative I mentioned their example, whose faith in Scripture is most commended, and the experience, which all faithful men have continually had of themselves. For proof of the affirmative which he held I desiring to have some reason, heard nothing but 'all good writers' oftentimes inculcated. At the length, upon request to see some one of them, Peter Martyr's Common Places were brought, where the leaves were turned down at a place sounding to this effect, 'That the Gospel doth make true Christians more virtuous than moral philosophy did make heathens:' which came not near the question by many miles.

22.\* In the other conference he questioned about the matter of reprobation, misliking first that I had termed God a permissive, and no positive cause of the evil, which the schoolmen do call *malum culpae*; secondly that to their objection who say, 'If I be elected, do what I will, I shall be saved,' I had answered, that the will of God in this thing is not absolute but conditional, to save his elect believing, fearing, and obediently serving him; thirdly that to stop the mouths of such as grudge and repine against God for rejecting castaways, I had taught that they are not rejected no not in the purpose and counsel of God, without a foreseen worthiness of rejection going though not in time yet in order before. For if God's electing do in order (as needs it must) presuppose the foresight of their being that are elected, though they be elected before they be; nor only the positive foresight of their being, but also the permissive of their being miserable, because election is through mercy, and mercy doth always presuppose misery: it followeth, that the very chosen of God acknowledge to the praise of the riches of his exceeding free compassion, that when he in his secret determination set it down, 'Those shall live and not die,' they lay as ugly spectacles before him, as lepers covered with dung and mire, as ulcers putrefied in their fathers' loins, miserable, worthy to be had in detestation; and shall any forsaken creature be able to say unto God, Thou didst plunge me into the depth and assign me unto endless torments only to satisfy thine own will, finding nothing in me for which I could seem in thy sight so well worthy to feel everlasting flames?

23. When I saw that Mr. Travers carped at these things, only because they lay not open, I promised at some convenient time to make them clear as light both to him and to all others. Which if they that reprove me will not grant me leave to do, they must think that they are for some cause or other more desirous to have me reputed an unsound man, than willing that my sincere meaning should appear and be approved. When I was farther asked what my grounds were, I answered that St. Paul's words concerning this cause were my grounds. His next demand, what author I did follow in expounding St. Paul and gathering the doctrine out of his words, against the judgment, he saith, 'of all churches and all good writers.' I was well assured that to control this overreaching speech, the sentences which I might have cited out of Church Confessions, together with the best learned monuments of former times, and not the meanest of our own, were mo in number than perhaps he would willingly have heard

of; but what had this booted me? For although he himself in generality do much use those formal speeches, 'all churches,' and 'all good writers:' yet as he holdeth it in the pulpit lawful to say in general, the Paynims think this, or the Heathen that, but utterly unlawful to cite any sentence of theirs that say it; so he gave me at that time great cause to think, that my particular alleging of other men's words to show their agreement with mine, would as much have displeased his mind, as the thing itself for which they had been alleged. For he knoweth how often he hath in public place bitten me for this, although I did never in any sermon use many of the sentences of other writers, and do make most without any; having always thought it meetest neither to affect nor to contemn the use of them.

24.\* He is not ignorant, that in the very entrance to the talk which we had privately at that time, to prove it unlawful altogether in preaching, either for confirmation, declaration, or otherwise, to cite any thing but mere canonical scripture, he brought in, 'The Scripture is given by inspiration, and is profitable to teach, to improve,' &c. urging much the vigour of these two clauses, 'the man of God,' and 'every good work.' If therefore the work were good which he required at my hands, if privately to show why I thought the doctrine I had delivered to be according to St. Paul's meaning were a good work, can they which take the place before alleged for a law condemning every man of God who in doing the work of preaching any way useth human authority, like it in me, if in the work of strengthening that which I had preached, I should bring forth the testimonies and the sayings of mortal men? I alleged therefore that which might under no pretence in the world be disallowed, namely reason; not meaning thereby mine own reason as now it is reported, but true, sound, divine reason; reason whereby those conclusions might be out of St. Paul demonstrated, and not probably discoursed of only; reason proper to that science whereby the things of God are known; theological reason, which out of principles in Scripture that are plain, soundly deduceth more doubtful inferences, in such sort that being heard they neither can be denied, nor any thing repugnant unto them received, but whatsoever was before otherwise by miscollecting gathered out of darker places, is thereby forced to yield itself, and the true consonant meaning of sentences not understood is brought to light. This is the reason which I intended. If it were possible for me to escape the ferula in any thing I do or speak, I had undoubtedly escaped it in this. In this I did that which by some is enjoined as the only allowable, but granted by all as the most sure and safe way whereby to resolve things doubted of, in matters appertaining to faith and Christian religion. So that Mr. Travers had here small cause given him to be weary of conferring, unless it were in other respects than that poor one which is here pretended, that is to say, the little hope he had of doing me any good by conference.

25. Yet behold his first reason of not complaining to the High Commission is, that sith I offended only through an overcharitable inclination, he conceived good hope, when I should see the truth cleared and some scruples which were in my mind removed by his diligence, I would yield. But what experience soever he had of former conferences, how small soever his hope was that fruit would come of it if he should have conferred, will any man judge this a cause sufficient why to open his mouth in public without any one word privately spoken? He might have considered that men do sometimes reap where they sow but with small hope; he might have considered that although unto me (whereof he was not certain neither) but if to me his labour should be as water spilt or poured into a torn dish, yet to him it could not be fruitless to do that which order in Christian churches, that which charity among Christian men, that which at any man's hands even common humanity itself, at his many other things besides did require. What fruit could there come of his open contradicting in so great haste with so small advice, but such as must needs be unpleasant and mingled with much acerbity? Surely he which will take upon him to defend that in this there was no oversight, must beware lest by such defences he leave an opinion dwelling in the minds of men that he is more stiff to maintain what he hath done, than careful to do nothing but that which may justly be maintained.

26. Thus have I, as near as I could, seriously answered things of weight: with smaller I have dealt as I thought their quality did require. I take no joy in striving, I have not been nuzzled [trained] or trained up in it. I would to Christ they which have at this present enforced me hereunto, had so ruled their hands in any reasonable time, that I might never have been constrained to strike so much as in mine own defence. Wherefore to prosecute this long and tedious contention no further, shall I wish that your Grace and their Honours (unto whose intelligence the dutiful regard which I have of their judgments

maketh me desirous that as accusations have been brought against me, so this my answer thereunto may likewise come) did both with the one and the other, as Constantine with the books containing querulous matter. Whether this be convenient to be wished or no, I cannot tell. But sith there can come nothing of contention but the mutual waste of the parties contending, till a common enemy dance in the ashes of them both, I do wish heartily that the grave advice which Constantine gave for re-uniting of his clergy, so many times upon so small occasions in so lamentable sort divided, or rather the strict commandment of Christ unto his that they should not be divided at all, may at length if it be his blessed will, prevail so far at the least in this corner of the Christian world, to the burying and quite forgetting of strife, together with the causes which have either bred it or brought it up; that things of small moment never disjoin them, whom one God, one Lord, one Faith, one Spirit, one Baptism, bands of great force, have linked; that a respective eye towards things wherewith we should not be disquieted make us not, as through infirmity the very patriarchs themselves sometimes were, full gorged, unable to speak peaceably to their own brother; finally that no strife may ever be heard of again but this, who shall hate strife most, who shall pursue peace and unity with swiftest paces.

## NOTES

p. 182. *An order, as I learn, there was tendered...*: 'Item, that all communicants do receive kneeling....': from Archbishop Parker's *Advertisements*, 1566, which attempted to enforce common observance, but which tried to give as little offence as possible to both sides. Alvey and Travers may have been breaking the law, though it is a matter of dispute whether the *Advertisements* were 'covered' by the 1559 Act of Uniformity or not. Hooker does not seem to think they were; none the less, as the Victorian editor has it, 'Eldership [was] covertly tried in the Temple'.

p. 184. 7: 'In praying for deliverance from all adversity... by entreating for mercy towards all, we declare that affection wherewith Christian charity thirsteth after the good of the whole world, we discharge that duty which the Apostle himself doth impose on the Church of Christ, as a *commendable* office, a sacrifice *acceptable* in God's sight, a service according to his heart whose *desire* is "to have all men saved"...' (*Ecclesiastical Polity*). The italics are Hooker's. The whole of the first part of the 'Justification' sermon deals (at too great a length, perhaps, to hold its audience's complete attention) with this matter.

p. 185. *8*: he refers to the 1581 sermon already mentioned. *9*: 'Now the minds of all men being so darkened as they are with the foggy damp of original corruption, it cannot be that any man's heart living should be either so enlightened ... as to be perfect, neither doubting nor shrinking at all' ('The Certainty and Perpetuity ...').

p. 186. *12*: 'As for such as hold with the Church of Rome, that we cannot be saved by Christ alone without works; they do not only by a circle of consequence, but directly, deny the foundation of faith; they hold it not, no not so much as by a slender thread' ('Justification').

p. 187. *Bonaventure*: St Bonaventure, Giovanni di Fidanza, a Franciscan theologian of the thirteenth century. Hooker would never reject, as the left-wing Protestants did, medieval scholasticism. But St Francis was the first great underminer of the Catholic orthodoxy, and Bonaventure was an Augustinian who was extremely, though constructively, critical of Aristotelian metaphysics as applied to theology.   *Tridentine*: relating to the Council of Trent.   *Thomas*: Aquinas, who is part of a tradition challenged by Bonaventure.   *Xystus Quartus*: Sixtus IV, nepotic Pope from 1471 to 1484.

p. 190. *These school-implements* ...: Hooker could have quoted Calvin himself to support this: *Institutes*, 1, i, c. 16, section 9.

p. 191. ... *a decree agreed upon by the Bishops* ...: the *Advertisements* mentioned above: Hooker refers to the item that admonishes preachers to 'use sobriety and discretion' and to avoid creating dissension. The Queen had probably approved, but Leicester had used his influence to get the text altered, and the question of the exact standing of the *Advertisements* has given rise to controversy.

p. 195. *22*: this is an important brief summary of Hooker's thinking. A distinction is made between an omnipotent God's necessary *foresight* and his *will and mercy*; it follows that, God being inscrutable, no man need count himself damned. Hooker was only a 'Calvinist predestinarian' in the sense that he accepted God's inevitable foresight: he could not go so far as to assert that all men would be saved, but he would not make Calvin's error of confusing an omnipotent foresight with a frightful decree. The inscrutability of God leaves the question of election wholly open. In an age when all but a very few believed in the existence, at the end of mortality or of the world, of heaven, purgatory (rejected by Hooker) or hell, no one could dare state that all would be saved. There are innumerable ways, not comprehensible to human beings, in which God might save all men—innumerable ways in which he might damn them all. This is the point of *justification by faith*: do not attempt to be a saint upon earth or become a mystical transcendentalist—accept the mystery, but as an inscrutability, and trust in the love and goodness of God. From such unfeigned trust some virtue, albeit flawed, must necessarily flow.

p. 197. *24*: Hooker has been called a rationalist, but he was not. He merely acknowledged that men will use reason (just as they will live as though they possess free will, whether they do so or not), and he therefore would not, as he eloquently here argues, reject post-scriptural conjecture out of hand.

# Robert Sanderson

SANDERSON, SUBJECT (like Hooker and Donne) of one of Walton's famous *Lives*, was born in 1587 at Rotherham in Yorkshire, and educated at its grammar school. He went on to Lincoln College, Oxford, of which he became a Fellow in 1606. He was ordained in 1611, and held a number of livings thereafter. He early gained the attention of Laud, and in 1631 was made a chaplain to King Charles I. In 1642 he was appointed to the important post of Regius Professor of Divinity at (Royalist) Oxford; he was ejected in 1648, and spent some time in prison. At the Restoration he was reinstated; from 1660 until his death three years later he was Bishop of Lincoln.

Sanderson was one of the most orthodox Church of England priests of the seventeenth century; but he was not—as he has been called—a 'casuist'. He was rather a moderate. He denounced monopolies and lawyers—from the pulpit; his sermons as a whole do not give the impression of a bigoted or opportunistic man. Walton's *Life* confirms his general honesty of purpose and his generally reconciliatory and privately pious nature. Sanderson is most famous for his *Nine Cases of Conscience Occasionally Determined* (1678), which displays his real distinction: that of moral theologian. This is evident in the characteristc sermon given below.

[IN ST PAUL'S CHURCH, LONDON — *AD POPULUM*]
1 Cor. 7:24.
*Brethren, let every man, wherein he is called, therein abide with God.*

THIS SERMON was preached in St Paul's Church on 4 November 1621. It is not given here as a particularly lively example of early seventeenth-century preaching—for it begins ponderously—but as one too typical, as given by a sensible orthodox Anglican, to ignore. Moreover, as Sanderson rises to his occasion, so he becomes more eloquent. It is in effect a moral sermon, suggesting ways in which the people, many of whom had become seditious, should behave. Sanderson's main interest lay in reconciling a moderate Anglicanism with good behaviour—and he saw that social and other abuses were not conducive to good behaviour. This sermon, though some of its points—especially at the beginning—are too heavily laboured, is essentially one of good sense. Nor is he without wit—as when he remarks that 'whereas the devil's greatest business is to tempt the devil'. Occasionally, too, he has real satirical power, as in the passages on 'Monkery'.

The first part of the sermon (Sections 1-22) is an attack on the corruption of the rich, though its framework is one of general admonition to everyone to exercise their function and attend to their proper 'calling': to work rather than to be idle. That it is an attack on abuses becomes increasingly clear as it proceeds. Thus, by Section 18, he is openly attacking those 'whose either birth, breeding . . . it sorteth not, as they think, to be tied to labour in any vocation'. Section 19 attacks gallants who gamble and dress well (but they are not criticized for going to the theatre). Section 20 tells the wealthy to look in their pedigrees for those ancestors who performed humble tasks. In the following section he tactfully turns to 'sturdy beggars', who presented a serious social problem in Elizabethan and Jacobean times. But this is only done to push home the message that charity to those in real want is a necessity and a duty. The importance of the distinction between the idle and the needy is given some emphasis. Sanderson's psychology is here effective: by criticizing idleness in harsh terms, he appeals to his congregation's imagination—who are then unlikely to ignore his plea for the needy.

The second part of the sermon analyses the nature of 'callings', and displays some sympathy with Puritan disapproval of gambling and sports (though Sanderson was later to recommend Sunday sports for the 'lower orders'). Characteristically, Sanderson distinguishes between the law and morality. By Section 29 he has reached his chief point: 'The public good is one of those main respects which enforce the necessity of a calling . . .'; in the course of it he is able to renew his attack on abuses (as the notes after the sermon make clear). Section 30 denounces usurers, who are compared with drunkards.

The rest of the sermon requires less comment: it offers sensible and moderate moral advice to those in search of a vocation, and only returns to the attack on abuses at the end.

This (revised by the author in his lifetime: the attack on usurers is softened in the final version) is not a great sermon. But it has many moments of fine language; and it is illustrative of both the attitude of a non-Puritan moralist and of the fact that highly orthodox churchmen, supporters of the King, were perfectly capable of denouncing many of those abuses of which Parliament—increasingly becoming the enemy of the King—complained. The Anglican clergy were not entirely the King's creatures, as they are too often represented to have been.

IF FLESH and blood be suffered to make the gloss, it is able to corrupt a right good Text. It easily turneth the doctrine of God's grace into wantonness, and as easily the doctrine of Christian liberty into licentiousness. These Corinthians, being yet but carnal, for the point of liberty consulted, it seemeth, but too much with this cursed gloss, which taught them to interpret their calling to the Christian Faith as an exemption from the duties of all other callings, as if their spiritual freedom in Christ had cancelled *ipso facto* all former obligations, whether of nature or civility. The husband would put away his wife, the servant disrespect his master, every other man break the bonds of relation to every other man; and all under this pretence, and upon this ground, that Christ hath made them free. In this passage of the chapter the Apostle occasionally correcteth this error. Principally, indeed, as the present argument led him, in the particular of Marriage; but with a further and more universal extent to all outward states and conditions of life. The sum of his doctrine this. He that is yoked with a wife must not put her away, but count her worthy of all love; he that is bound to a master must not despise him, but count him worthy of all honour; every other man that is tied in any relation to any other man must not neglect him, but count him worthy of all good offices and civil respects suitable to his place and person, though she, or he, or that other, be infidels and unbelievers. The Christian Calling doth not at all prejudice, much less overthrow, it rather establisheth and strengtheneth, those interests, that arise from natural relations, or from voluntary contracts, either domestical or civil, betwixt man and man. The general rule to this effect he conceiveth in the form of an exhortation, that every man, notwithstanding his calling unto liberty in Christ, abide in that station wherein God hath placed him, contain himself within the bounds thereof, and cheerfully and contentedly undergo the duties that belong thereto, verse 17. *As God hath distributed to every man, as the Lord hath called every one, so let him walk*. And lest this exhortation, as it fareth with most other, especially such as come in but upon the by, as this doth, should be slenderly regarded, the more fully to commend it to their consideration and practice, he repeateth it once again, verse 20. *Let every man abide in the same calling wherein he was called*. And now again once more, in the words of this verse, concluding therewith the whole discourse into which he had digressed, *Brethren, let every man, wherein he is called, therein abide with God.*

2. From which words, I desire it may be no prejudice to my present discourse, if I take occasion to entreat at this time of a very needful argument, viz. concerning the Necessity, Choice, and Use of particular Callings. Which whilst I do, if any shall blame me for shaking hands with my Text, let such know, First, that it will not be very charitably done, to pass a hard censure upon another's labour, no, nor yet very providently for their own good, to slight a profitable truth for some little seeming impertinency. Secondly, that the points proposed are indeed not impertinent: the last of them, which supposeth also the other two, being the very substance of this exhortation, and all of them such as may without much violence be drawn from the very words themselves, at leastwise if we may be allowed the liberty, which is but reasonable, to take in also the other two verses, the seventeenth and the twentieth, in sense and for substance all one with this, as anon in the several handling of them will in part appear. But howsoever, Thirdly, which St. Bernard deemed a sufficient apology for himself in a case of like nature, *Noverint me non tam intendisse, &c.* let them know that, in my choice of this Scripture, my purpose was not so much to bind myself to the strict exposition of the Apostolical Text, as to take occasion therefrom to deliver what I desired to speak, and judged expedient for you to hear: concerning, first, the Necessity, secondly, the Choice, and thirdly, the Use of particular Callings.

3. Points, if ever needful to be taught and known, certainly, in these days most. Wherein some, habituated in idleness, will not betake themselves to any Calling, like a heavy jade [horse], that is good at bit, and nought else. These would be soundly spurred up, and whipped on end [endlessly]. Other some, through weakness, do not make a good choice of a fit Calling, like a young unbroken thing that hath mettle and is free, but is ever wrying the wrong way. These would be fairly checked, turned into the right way, and guided with a steady and skilful hand. A third sort, and I think the greatest, through unsettledness, or discontentedness, or other untoward humour, walk not soberly, and uprightly, and orderly in their Calling, like an unruly colt, that will over hedge and ditch: no ground will hold him, no fence turn him. These would be well fettered and side-hanckled\* for leaping. The first sort are to be taught the Necessity of a Calling; the second, to be directed for the Choice of their Calling; the third, to be bounded and limited in the Exercise of their Calling. Of which three in their order: and of the First, first; the

Necessity of a Calling.

4. The Scriptures speak of two kinds of Vocations or Callings; the one, *ad Foedus*, the other, *ad Munus*. The usual known terms are, the general and the particular Calling. *Vocatio ad Foedus*, or the general Calling, is that wherewith God calleth us, either outwardly in the ministry of His Word, or inwardly by the efficacy of His Spirit, or jointly by both, to the faith and obedience of the Gospel, and to the embracing of the Covenant of grace and of mercy and salvation by Jesus Christ. Which is therefore termed the general Calling: not for that it is of larger extent than the other, but because the thing whereunto we are thus called is one and the same, and common to all that are called. The same duties, and the same promises, and every way the same conditions. Here is no difference in regard of persons: but *one Lord, one Faith, one Baptism, one body, and one Spirit, even as* we *are* all *called in one hope of* our *Calling*. That's the general Calling. *Vocatio ad Munus*, our particular Calling, is that wherewith God enableth us, and directeth us, and putteth us on to some special course and condition of life, wherein to employ ourselves, and to exercise the gifts He hath bestowed upon us, to His glory, and the benefit of ourselves and others. And it is therefore termed a particular Calling, not as if it concerned not all in general, (for we shall prove the contrary anon,) but because the thing whereunto men are thus called is not one and the same to all, but differenced with much variety according to the quality of particular persons. *Alius sic, alius vero sic: Every man hath his proper gift of God; one man on this manner, another on that*. Here is ἴδιον χάρισμα : some called to be Magistrates, some Ministers, some Merchants, some Artificers, some one thing, some another, as to their particular Callings. But as to the general Calling, there is κοινὴ σωτηρία, *the common Salvation*: all called to the same state of being the servants and children of God; all called to the performance of the same duties of servants, and to the expectation of the same inheritance of children; all called to be Christians. Of both which Callings, the general and particular, there is not, I take it, any where in Scripture mention made so expressly and together as in this passage of our Apostle, especially at the twentieth verse. *Let every man abide in the same calling wherein he was called*. Where, besides the matter, the Apostle's elegancy is observable in using the same word in both significations: the Noun signifying the particular, and the Verb the general Calling. *Let every one abide in*

*the same calling wherein he was called*, bearing sense, as if the Apostle had said, Let every man abide in the same particular Calling, wherein he stood at the time of his general Calling. And the same, and no other, is the meaning of the words of my Text.

5. Whence it appeareth that the Calling my Text implieth, and wherein every man is here exhorted to abide, is to be understood of the particular, and not of the general Calling. And of this particular Calling it is we now intend to speak. And that in the more proper and restrained signification of it, as it importeth some settled course of life with reference to business, office, and employment: accordingly as we say a man is called to be a Minister, called to be a Lawyer, called to be a Tradesman, and the like. Although I cannot be ignorant that our Apostle, as the stream of his argument carried him, here taketh the word in a much wider extent, as including not only such special courses of life as refer to employment, but even all outward personal states and conditions of men whatsoever, whether they have such reference, or no: as we may say, a man is called to marriage or to single life, called to riches or poverty, and the like.

6. But omitting this larger signification, we will hold ourselves, either only or principally, to the former, and by Calling understand a special, settled course of life, wherein mainly to employ a man's gifts and time for his own and the common good. The necessity whereof whilst we mention, you are to imagine not an absolute and positive, but a conditional and suppositive necessity. Not as if no man could be without one *de facto*: daily experience in these dissolute times manifesteth the contrary, but because *de jure* no man should be without one. This kind of Calling is indeed necessary for all men. But how? Not as a necessary thing *ratione termini*, so as the want thereof would be an absolute impossibility, but *virtute praecepti*, as a necessary duty, the neglect whereof would be a grievous and sinful enormity. He that will do that which he ought, and is in conscience bound to do, must of necessity live in some Calling or other. That is it we mean by the Necessity of a Calling. And this Necessity we are now to prove.

7. And that, first, from the obedience we owe to every of God's Ordinances, and the account we must render for every of God's Gifts. Amongst those Ordinances this is one, and one of the first, that in the sweat of our faces every man of us should eat our bread. The force of which precept let none think to avoid by a quirk, that forsooth it was laid upon Adam after his

transgression, rather as a curse which he must endure, than as a duty which he should perform. For, first, as some of God's curses, such is His goodness, are promises as well as curses, as is that of the enmity between the Woman's seed and the Serpent's, so some of God's curses, such is His Justice, are precepts as well as curses, as is that of the Woman's subjection to the Man. This, of eating our bread in the sweat of our face, is all the three: it is a curse: it is a promise: it is a precept. It is a curse, in that God will not suffer the earth to afford us bread without our sweat. It is a promise, in that God assureth us we shall have bread for our sweat. And it is a precept too, in that God enjoineth us, if we will have bread, to sweat for it. Secondly, although it may not be gainsaid, but that that injunction to Adam was given as a curse, yet the substance of the injunction was not the thing wherein the curse did formally consist. Herein was the curse, that whereas, before the Fall, the task which God appointed man was with pleasure of body and content of mind, without sweat of brow or brain, now, after the Fall, he was to toil and forecast for his living, with care of mind and travail of body, with weariness of flesh and vexation of spirit. But as for the substance of the injunction, which is that every man should have somewhat to do, wherein to bestow himself and his time and his gifts, and whereby to earn his bread, in this it appeareth not to have been a curse, but a precept of Divine institution, that Adam, in the time and state of innocency, before he had deserved a curse, was yet enjoined his task, to dress and to keep the garden. And as Adam lived himself, so he bred up his children. His two firstborn, though heirs apparent of all the world, had yet their peculiar employments, the one in tillage, the other in pasturage. And as many since as have walked orderly, have observed God's Ordinance herein, working with their hands the thing that is good in some kind or other: those that have set themselves in no such good way, our Apostle elsewhere justly blaming as inordinate or disorderly walkers. And how can such disorderly ones hope to find approvance in the sight of our God, who is a God of Order? He commandeth us to live in a Calling, and woe to us if we neglect it.

8. But say there were no such express command for it: the very distribution of God's gifts were enough to lay upon us this necessity. Where God bestoweth, He bindeth; and to whom any thing is given, of him something shall be required. The inference is stronger than most are aware of, from the ability to the duty,

from the gift to the work, from the fitting to the Calling. Observe how this Apostle knitteth them together at the seventeenth verse, *As God hath distributed to every man, as the Lord hath called every one, so let him walk*. God hath distributed to every man some proper gift or other; and therefore every man must glorify God in some peculiar Calling or other. And in Eph. iv, having alleged that of the Psalm, *He gave gifts unto men*, immediately he inferreth, *He gave some Apostles, some Prophets, &c.* as giving us to understand that for no other end God did bestow upon some Apostolical, upon others Prophetical, upon others gifts in other kinds, but that men should employ them, some in the Apostolical, some in the Prophetical, some in Offices and Callings of other kinds. And if we confess that Nature doth not, we may not think the God of Nature doth bestow abilities whereof He intendeth not use; for that were to bestow them in vain. Sith then he bestoweth gifts and graces, upon every man some or other, and none in vain, let every man take heed that he receive them not in vain: let every man beware of napkening up the talent which was delivered him to trade withal. Let all, *as every one hath received the gift*, even so *minister the same one to another, as good stewards of the manifold graces of God. The manifestation of the Spirit* being *given to every man to profit withal*, he that liveth unprofitably with it, and without a Calling, abuseth the intent of the Giver, and must answer for his abuse.

9. Secondly, the Necessity of a Calling is great in regard of a man's self; and that more ways than one. For man being by nature active, so as he cannot be long but he must be doing, he that hath no honest vocation to busy himself in, that hath nothing of his own to do, must needs, from doing nothing, proceed to doing naught. That saying of Cato was subscribed by the wiser Heathens as an oracle, *Nihil agendo male agere disces. Idleness teacheth much evil*, saith the wise son of Sirach, nay, *all kind of evil*, as some Copies have it. It hath an ear open to every extravagant motion, it giveth entertainment to a thousand sinful fancies, it exposeth the soul to all the assaults of her ghostly enemies; and, whereas the devil's greatest business is to tempt other men, the idle man's only business is to tempt the devil. Experience of all histories and times showeth us what advantages the devil hath won upon godly and industrious men otherwise, as upon David, in the matter of Uriah, and many others, only by watching the opportunity of their idle hours, and plying them with suggestions of noisome lusts at such times as they

had given themselves but some little intermission more than ordinary from their ordinary employments. How will he not then lead captive at his pleasure those, whose whole lives are nothing else but a long vacation, and their whole care nothing but to make up a number, and to waste the good creatures of God? There is no readier sanctuary for thee then, good Christian, when the devil pursueth thee, than to betake thyself at once to prayer, and to the works of thy Calling. Fly thither, and thou art safe, as in a castle. *Non licet* is a very good, and proper, and direct answer, when the devil would tempt thee to sin: it is evil, and I may not do it; but yet *Non vacat* is the stronger answer and surer: I am busy, and I cannot do it. That giveth him scope to reply; and it is not safe to hold argument with the devil upon any terms. He is a cunning sophister; and thou mayest be circumvented by a subtilty before thou art aware. But this stubborn and blunt answer cutteth off all reply, and dishearteneth the tempter for that time. It was St. Hierom's advice to his friend, *Semper boni aliquid operis facito, ut diabolus te semper inveniat occupatum*, Be always doing something, that the devil may never find thee at leisure. There is no cross, no holy water, no exorcism so powerful to drive away and to conjure down the fiend, as employment is, and faithful labour in some honest Calling.

10. Thirdly, Life must be preserved, families maintained, the poor relieved: this cannot be done without bread, for that is *the staff of life*; and bread cannot be gotten, or not honestly, but in a lawful vocation or calling. Which whoever neglecteth, is in very deed no better than a very thief: the bread he eateth he cannot call his own. *We hear*, saith St. Paul, writing to the Thessalonians, *that there are some among you that walk inordinately, and work not at all, but are busy-bodies. Them therefore that are such we command and exhort by our Lord Jesus Christ, that they work with quietness, and eat their own bread*. As if it were not their own bread, if not gotten with the work of their own hands, and in the sweat of their own faces. And again, writing to the Ephesians, *Let him that stole steal no more: but rather let him labour, &c*. If he will not steal, he must labour; and if he do not labour, he doth steal: steal from himself, steal from his family, steal from the poor.

11. He stealeth from himself, and so is a kind of *Felo de se*. Spend he must; and if there be no gettings to repair what is spent, the stock will shrink and waste, and beggary will be the

end. God hath ordained labour as a proper means whereby to obtain the good things of this life: without which, as there is no promise, so ordinarily there is no performance of those blessings of plenty and sufficiency. God hath a bountiful hand: *He openeth it, and filleth all things living with plenteousness*; but, unless we have a diligent hand wherewith to receive it, we may starve. 'No mill,' we say, 'no meal.' And he that by the sloth of his hands disfurnisheth himself of the means of getting, he is as near of kin to a waster as may be,—they may call brothers,—and it is but just if God's curse light upon him and that he hath, and bring him to want, it to nothing.

12. He stealeth also from his family, which should eat the fruit of his labours. The painful housewife,—see in what a happy case her husband is, and her children, and her servants, and all that belong to her. They are not afraid of hunger, or cold, or any such thing: they are well fed, and well clad, and carefully looked unto. *Her husband praiseth her*, and her servants; and her children, when they have kneeled down and asked her blessing, *arise up, and call her blessed*. But the idle man that, for want of a course to live in, impoverisheth himself, and his family whom he is bound to maintain, is a burden to his friends, an eye-sore to his kindred, the shame of his name, the ruin of his house, and the bane of his posterity. He bequeatheth misery to his offspring instead of plenty: they that should fare the better for him, are undone by him; and he that should give his children God's blessing and his, pulleth upon himself God's curse and theirs. *If any provide not for his own, and specially for those of his own house, he hath denied the faith, and is* in that respect even *worse than an infidel*. The very infidels take themselves bound to this care. Let not him that professeth the faith of Christ, by his supine carelessness this way, justify the infidel and deny the Faith.

13. He stealeth also, which is the basest theft of all, from the poor, in robbing them of that relief which he should minister unto them out of his honest gettings, the overplus whereof is their proper revenue. The good housewife, of whom we heard something already out of the thirty-first chapter of the Proverbs, *seeketh wool and flax, layeth her hands to the spindle, and her hands hold the distaff*. But *cui bono*, and to what end, and for whose sake, all this? Not only for herself, *to make her coverings of tapestry*, though that also; nor yet only for her household, *to clothe them in scarlet*, though that also; but withal that she might have somewhat in her hands, *to reach out to the poor and*

*needy;* like another Dorcas, to make *coats and garments* for them, that their loins might bless her. So every man should be painful and careful to get some of the things of this earth by his faithful labour, not as a foolish worldling, to make a Mammon of it, but, as a wise steward, to make him friends with it. So *distributing* it *to the necessities of* the poor *Saints,* that it may redound also upon the by to his own advantage: whilst sowing to them temporal things, the comfort of his alms, he reapeth in recompence of it their spiritual things, the benefit of their prayers. St. Paul exhorteth the Ephesians by word of mouth, and it was the very close of his solemn farewell, when he took his last leave of them, and should see their face no more, that *by their labour they ought to support the weak, and minister to the necessities of others; remembering the words of the Lord Jesus, how He said, It is more blessed to give than to receive.* And, after his departure, he thought it needful for him to put them in mind of the same duty once again by letter: *Let him that stole steal no more, but rather let him labour, working with his hands the thing that is good, that he may have to give him that needeth.* Lay all this that I have now last said together, and say if you know a verier thief than the idle person, that stealeth from himself, and so is a foolish thief; stealeth from his family and friends, and so is an unnatural thief; stealeth from the poor, and so is a base thief.

14. Fourthly, and lastly, a Calling is necessary in regard of the Public. God hath made us sociable creatures, contrived us into policies, and societies, and commonwealths; made us fellow-members of one body, and *every one another's members.* As therefore we are not born, so neither must we live, to and for ourselves alone; but our parents, and friends, and acquaintance, nay, every man of us hath a kind of right and interest in every other man of us, and our Country and the Commonwealth in us all. And as in the artificial body of a clock one wheel moveth another, and each part giveth and receiveth help to and from other, and as in the natural body of a man, consisting of many members, all the members *have not the same office,* for that would make a confusion, yet there is no member in the body so mean or small, but hath its proper faculty, function, and use, whereby it becometh useful to the whole body, and helpful to its fellow-members in the body, so should it be in the civil body of the State, and in the mystical body of the Church. Every man should *conferre aliquid in publicum,* put to his helping

hand to advance the common good, employ himself some way or other, in such sort, as he may be serviceable to the whole body, and profitable to his fellow-members in the body. For which reason the ancient renowned Commonwealths were so careful to ordain, that no man should live but in some profession, and to take district examination who did otherwise; and to punish them, some with fasting, some with infamy, some with banishment, yea, and some with death. The care of the Indians, Egyptians, Athenians, and other herein, Historians relate, and I omit. It were to be wished that Christian Commonwealths would take some greater care, if but from their example, to rid themselves of such unnecessary burdens as are good for nothing but to devour the fruits of the land; and either force these drones to take pains for their living, or else thrust them out of the hives for their idleness.

15. Which course if it were taken, what would become of many thousands in the world, *quibus anima pro sale*? who like swine live in such sensual and unprofitable sort, as we might well doubt whether they had any living souls in their bodies at all or no, were it not barely for this one argument, that their bodies are a degree sweeter than carrion. I mean all such, of what rank and condition soever they be, as for want of a calling misspend their precious time, bury their Master's talent, waste God's good creatures, and wear away themselves in idleness, without doing good to themselves, to their friends, to human society. Infinite is the number of such unprofitable burdens of the earth; but there are, amongst other, three sorts of them especially, whereof the world ringeth, and such as a man that hath to speak of this argument can scarce balk without some guilt of unfaithfulness. It is no matter how you rank them, for there is never a better of the three. And therefore take them hand over head as they come: they are Monks, Gallants, and Rogues.

16. First those, κακὰ θηρία, *evil beasts, slow bellies*, stall-fed Monks and Friars, who live mued up [cooped up] in their cells and cloisters, like boars in a frank,\* pining themselves into lard, and beating down their bodies till their girdles crack. I quarrel not the first institution and original of these kind of men, which was then excusably good, the condition of those times considered, and might yet be tolerably followed even in these times, if those gross superstitions and foul abuses, which in process of time have adhered, and are by long and universal custom grown almost essential thereunto, could be fairly removed. But Monkery

was not then that thing which it is now. There was not then that opinion of sanctity and perfection, in the choice; that imposition of unlawful, unnatural, and, to some men, impossible Vows, in the entrance; that clog of ridiculous habits and ceremonies, and regular irregular observances, in the use; that heavy note of apostasy upon such as altered their course, in the loose: all which now there are. Those, by their fastings, and watchings, and devotions, and charity, and learning, and industry, and temperance, and unaffected austerity, and strictness of life, won from many of the ancient Fathers, as appeareth in their writings, ample and large testimonies of their virtue and piety. And that most deservedly: although their willingness, out of a zealous desire to excite others to the imitation of their virtues, to set forth their praises in the highest panegyric strains they could, drew from their pens now and then such hyperbolical excesses, *in modo loquendi*, as gave occasion to those superstitions in after ages, which they then never dreamed of. But such were those Monks of old: so good, so godly. Whereas these of later times, by their affected, absurd habits, and gestures, and rules; by their gross and dull ignorance; by their insufferable pride, though pretending humility; and their more than Pharisaical overlooking of others; by their insatiable avarice, and palpable arts of getting into their hands the fattest of the earth, and that under colour of Religion, and pretences of poverty; by their sensual wallowing in all ease and idleness and fulness of bread, and (the fruits of these) in abominable and prodigious filthiness and luxury; became as proverbs and as by-words in the mouths and pens of men of all sorts. No sober writer almost of any note, even in those darker times, but noted and bewailed the corrupt estate of the Church and Clergy in that behalf; for by this time, you must know, these drones had thrust themselves, against all reason and common sense, into the rank of Churchmen, and shrouded themselves under the title of the Clergy. Divers godly and learned men wrote against the abuses, desired a reformation, laboured to have Monkery reduced, if not to the first institution, (there seemed to be little hope of that, things were so far out of course,) yet at leastwise to some tolerable expression of it. The Poets wanted no sport the while; who made themselves bitterly merry with descanting upon the lean skulls, and the fat paunches of these lazy gutlings: there was fleshhold enough for the rhyming Satirists and the Wits of those times, whereon to fasten the sorest and the strongest teeth they had.

17. Not to insist upon other differences, that which concerneth the point we have in hand argueth a manifest and wide declination in these kind of men from their primitive purity. The ancient Monks lived upon the labour of their hands, and thereby not only maintained themselves, which they might do with a very little in that course of abstinence and austerity wherein they lived, but relieved many others, and did many pious and charitable works, out of that they had earned with their fingers. And when, about St. Augustin's and St. Hierome's times, Monks began to relish ease, and, under pretence of reading and prayer, to leave off working, and to live upon the sweat of other men's brows, both those good Fathers misliked it: St. Hierome to Rusticus alleging the laudable custom of the Monasteries in Egypt, which admitted none to be Monks but with express condition of labour; and St. Augustine, in a just Treatise, opposing it not without some bitterness, rebuking them as contumacious and peevishly perverse who, reading in the Scriptures, that he that will not labour should not eat, do yet resist the Apostle's admonition, and under pretence that they may have leisure to read, refuse to obey what they do read. But ease is pleasing to flesh and blood, and will not be easily wrung from those that have any while given themselves to it, especially when it can pretend the face and colour of Religion. So that for all this the humour still increased and spread, till at length there grew whole Orders of disorderly Mendicants, begging, runagate Friars, who, by their affected poverty, diverting the charity of well-minded people from those that were truly poor, enriched themselves with the spoils of the poor; and, under colour of long prayers, made a prey, not now, as those craving Pharisees of old whose simplicity they pity, of widows' houses, but of goodly lordships and whole countries before them. It is well known in this our land, how both Church and Commonwealth groaned under the burden of these heavy lubbers: the Commonwealth, whilst they became lords of very little less, by their computation who have travailed in the search, than the one half of the temporalties of the Kingdom; and the Church, whilst they ingrossed into their hands the fruits of most of the best benefices in the Realm, allowing scarce so much as the chaff towards the maintenance of those that trod out the corn. Their profession is, God be thanked, now long since suppressed, and their habitations demolished, by the violent and Jehu-like reformation of a mighty King [Henry VIII]; and the land by that means well purged of

these over-spreading locusts. There is nothing of them now remaineth, but the rubbish of their nests and the stink of their memory, unless it be the sting of their devilish sacrilege in robbing the Church by damnable impropriations.*

18. But let them go. The next we meet withal are those, with whose either birth, or breeding, or estate it sorteth not, as they think, to be tied to labour in any vocation. It is the sin of many of the gentry, whom God hath furnished with means and abilities to do much good, to spend their whole days and lives in an unprofitable course of doing either nothing, or as good as nothing, or worse than nothing. I cannot be so either stupid, as not to apprehend, or rigorous, as not to allow, a difference in the manner of employment, and in other circumstances thereto belonging, between those that are nobly or generously born and bred, and those of the meaner and ordinary rank. Manual and servile and mechanic trades and arts are for men of a lower condition. But yet no man is born, no man should be bred, unto idleness. There are generous and ingenuous and liberal employments, sortable to the greatest births and educations. For some man whom God hath blessed with power and authority in his country, with fair livings and large revenues, with a numerous family of servants, retainers, and tenants, and the like, it may be a sufficient Calling, and enough to take up his whole time, even to keep hospitality, and to order and overlook his family, and to dispose of his lands and rents, and to make peace, and preserve love and neighbourhood among them that live near or under him. He that doth but this as he ought to do, or is otherwise industrious for the common good, must be acknowledged a worthy member of the Commonwealth; and his course of life, a Calling, although perhaps not so toilsome, yet *in suo genere* as necessary and profitable, as that of the Husbandman, Merchant, Lawyer, Minister, or any other.

19. But for our mere or parcel [part-time] Gallants, who live in no settled course of life, but spend half the day in sleeping, half the night in gaming, and the rest of their time in other pleasures and vanities, to as little purpose as they can devise, as if they were born for nothing else but to eat and drink, and snort and sport, who are spruce and trim as the lilies,—Solomon in all his royalty was not clothed like one of these,—yet they neither sow, nor reap, nor carry into the barn, they neither labour nor spin, nor do any thing else for the good of human society: let them know, there is not the poorest contemptible creature, that

crieth oysters and kitchen-stuff in the streets, but deserveth his bread better than they; and his course of life is of better esteem with God and every sober wise man, than their's. A horse that is neither good for the way, nor the cart, nor the race, nor the wars, nor any other service, let him be of never so good a breed, never so well marked and shaped, yet he is but a jade: his Master setteth no store by him, thinketh his meat ill-bestowed on him: every man will say, better knock him on the head than keep him: his skin, though not much worth, is yet better worth than the whole beast besides.

20. Consider this, you that are of noble or generous birth. *Look unto the rock, whence you were hewn*; and to the pit, whence you were digged. Search your pedigrees, collect the scattered monuments and histories of your ancestors, and observe by what steps your worthy progenitors raised their houses to the height of gentry or nobility. Scarce shall you find a man of them that gave any accession, or brought any noted eminency, to his house, but either serving in the Camp, or sweating at the Bar, or waiting at the Court, or adventuring on the Seas, or trucking [bartering] in his Shop, or some other way industriously bestirring himself in some settled Calling and course of life. You usurp their arms, if you inherit not their virtues; and those ensigns of honour and gentry which they by industry achieved, sit no otherwise upon their shoulders than as rich trappings upon asses' backs, which serve but to render the poor beast more ridiculous. If you, by brutish sensuality, and spending your time in swinish luxury, stain the colours and embase the metals of those badges of your gentry and nobility which you claim by descent, think, when we worship or honour you, we do but flout you; and know, the titles we in courtesy give you, we bestow upon their memories whose degenerate offspring you are, and whose arms you unworthily bear; and they do no more belong to you, than the reverence the good man did to Isis belonged to the ass that carried her image.

21. The third sort of those that live unprofitably and without a Calling, are our idle sturdy Rogues and vagrant town's-end beggars, the very scabs, and filth, and vermin of the Commonwealth. I mean such as have health, and strength, and limbs, and are in some measure able to work and take pains for their living, yet rather choose to wander abroad the country, and to spend their days in a most base and ungodly course of life; and, which is yet more lamentable, by I know not what connivance, contrary

to all Conscience, Equity, and Law, are suffered. All Christian Commonwealths should be the Israels of God; and in His Israel, God, as He promised there should be some always poor, on whom to exercise charity (Matt. xxvi. 11), so He ordained there should be no beggar, to make a trade and profession of begging. Plato, than whom never any laid down a more exact idea of an happy Commonwealth, alloweth not any beggar therein, alleging, that where such were tolerated, it was impossible but the State must abound with pilfering and whoring and all kind of base villany. The Civil Laws have flat constitutions against them, in the titles *De mendicantibus non invalidis*. But I think never Kingdom had more wholesome Laws in both kinds, I mean both for the competent relief of the orderly poor, and for sharp restraint of disorderly vagabonds, than those provisions which in many of our own memories have been made in this land. But *Quid leges sine moribus...?* Those Laws are now no Laws, for want of due execution; but beggars are beggars still, for want of due correction. *Et vetabitur semper, et retinebitur*: the saying is truer of rogues and gypsies in England, than ever it was of mathematicians in Rome. You, to whose care the preservation of the Justice, and thereby also of the Peace of the land, is committed, as you tender the Peace and Justice of the land, as you tender your own quiet and the safety of your neighbours, as you tender the weal of your country and the honour of God, breathe fresh life into the languishing Laws by severe execution; be rather cruel to these vipers than to the State. So shall you free us from the plague, and yourselves from the guilt, and them from the opportunities, of infinite sinful abominations.

22. But we are unreasonable to press you thus far, or to seek to you or any others for Justice in this matter, having power enough in our own hands to do ourselves justice upon these men, if we would but use it. Even by making a strait covenant with our ears, not to heed them; and with our eyes, not to pity them; and with our hands, not to relieve them. Say I this altogether of myself? or saith not the Apostle even the same? (2 Thess. iii. 10) He that will not labour, let him not eat: relieve him not. But hath not Christ required us to feed the hungry, and to clothe the naked, and to be free and charitable to the poor? Nothing surer. God forbid any man should preach against charity and almsdeeds. But remember, that as God approveth not alms or any other work, if without charity, so nor charity itself, if without discretion. (1 Cor. xiii. 3; 1 Tim. v. 5, 6.) *Honour*

*widows*, saith St. Paul, but those *that are widows indeed*: so relieve the poor, but relieve those that are poor indeed. Not every one that asketh, not every one that wanteth, nay more, not every one that is poor, is poor indeed; and he that in his indiscreet and misguided charity should give to every one that asketh, or wanteth, or is poor, meat, or clothing, or alms, would soon make himself more hungry, and naked, and poor, than he that is most hungry, or naked, or poor. The poor, whom Christ commendeth to thee as a fit object for thy charity, the poor indeed, are those that want not only the things they ask, but want also means to get without asking. A man that is blind, or aged, and past his work; a man that is sick, or weak, or lame, and cannot work; a man that desireth it, and seeketh it, and cannot get work; a man that hath a greater charge upon him than his honest pains can maintain; such a man as one of these, he is poor indeed. Let thine ears be open, and thine eyes open, and thy bowels open, and thy hands open, to such a one: it is a charitable deed, and a *sacrifice of sweet smelling. With such sacrifices God is well pleased*. (Phil. iv. 18; Heb. xiii. 16.) Forget not thou to offer such sacrifices upon every good opportunity; and be well assured God will not forget in due time to reward thee. But for a lusty, able, upright man, as they style him in their own dialect, that had rather beg, or steal, or both, than dig, he is no more to be relieved as a poor man than a woman that hath poisoned her husband is to be honoured as a widow. Such a woman is a widow, for she hath no more an husband than any other widow hath; but such a woman is not a widow indeed, as St. Paul would be understood, not such a widow as he would have honoured: it is alms to hang up such a widow, rather than to honour her. And I dare say, he that helpeth one of these sturdy beggars to the stocks, and the whip, and the house of correction, not only deserveth better of the Commonwealth, but doth a work of greater charity in the sight of God, than he that helpeth him with meat, and money, and lodging. For he that doth this, corrupteth his charity by a double error. First, he maintaineth, and so encourageth, the other in idleness, who, if none would relieve him, would be glad to do any work rather than starve. And secondly, he disableth his charity, by misplacing it, and unawares robbeth the poor, whilst he thinketh he relieveth them. As he that giveth any honour to an idol robbeth the true God, to whom alone all religious honour is due, so he that giveth any alms to an idle beggar robbeth the truly poor, to whom properly all the fruits of our alms are due. And so it cometh to pass oftentimes, as St. Ambrose sometimes complained, that the maintenance of the poor is made the spoil of the loiterer.

23. But I forget myself, and you, and the time, whilst I give way to my just indignation against these base excrements of the Commonwealth. You have seen the Necessity of a Calling: without it, we despise God's ordinance, and smother His gifts, we expose ourselves to sinful temptations, we deprive ourselves, our families, and the poor of due maintenance, we withdraw our bounden service from the Commonwealth. It is not the pretence of devotion that can exempt the lazy Monk, nor of birth, the riotous Gallant, nor of want, the able Beggar, nor of any other thing, any other man, from this common Necessity. And that is the sum of our first point, viz. the Necessity of a Calling. Proceed we now to the second, the Choice of a Calling.

24. A point indeed, I must confess, not directly intended in the words of my Text; yet being after a sort implied therein, (for the Apostle's wish, that every particular man would abide in his own proper station and particular Calling, cannot but imply that there is a difference and choice of such Callings,) and being withal a matter of such great consequence to be taught and known, I thought it would be more expedient for the present discharge of my duty in this place to take it in, though with some hazard of the imputation of impertinency to myself, than, by passing it over, to defraud them (and it is likely there are many such here present) whom it may concern in point of conscience, of such instructions as may give them profitable directions in a business so material. Concerning which, it behoveth every man the rather to have an especial care, because much of a man's comfort and content in this life dependeth thereupon. It being scarce possible, that that man's life should be comfortable to him, or he go on with any cheerfulness in his course, that liveth in a Calling for which neither he is fit, nor the Calling fit for him. Neither will the consideration hereof be useful only for such as are yet free to choose, but even for those also who have already made their choice. For, since the very same rules which are to direct us in the Choice of our Calling are to help us also for the Trial of our Callings, it can be no loss to the best of us all to give heed to those Rules, thereby either to rectify our choice, or to quicken our alacrity in what we have chosen, by warranting our courses to our own souls, and silencing many unnecessary scruples, which are wont frequently to arise concerning this

matter in the consciences of men.

25. And first, we are to lay this as a firm ground, that that is every man's proper and right Calling whereunto God calleth him. For He is the Author, as of our general, so of our particular Callings too: *As the Lord hath called every one*, verse 20. When, therefore, we speak of the choice of a Calling, you are not so to understand it, as if it were left free for us ever to make our choice where, and as we list. The choice that is left to us, is nothing but a conscionable inquiry which way God calleth us, and a conscionable care to take that way. So that if it shall once appear that God calleth us this way or that way, there is no more place for choice: all that we have to do is to obey. *Obsequium sufficit esse meum*. The inquiries we are to make, ordinarily, are, as you shall hear anon, what lawfulness there is in the thing, what abilities there are in us, what warrant we have from without. But all these must cease, when God once expresseth Himself, and calleth us with an audible voice. No more inquiry then into the thing, how lawful it is. If God bid Peter *kill and eat*, and send him to preach unto the Gentiles, there is no answering Μηδαμῶς, Κύριε, *Not so, Lord*, nor alleging the uncleanness of the meat, or the unlawfulness of going into the way of the Gentiles. *Injusta justa habenda*: what God will have clean, he must not account common. His very call to any thing maketh it lawful. No more inquiry into ourselves, how able we are. If God call Moses, one of a slow speech, and not eloquent, from the sheepfold, to plead for his people before a tyrant; or Gideon, a mean stripling, of a small family and tribe, from the threshing-floor, to deliver Israel out of the hands of the oppressors; or Jeremy, a very child, and one that could not speak, from his cottage in Anathoth, to set him over nations and kingdoms, to root out and to plant; or Amos, a plain country fruit-gatherer, from the herd in Tekoah, to prophesy at Bethel, and in the King's court, it is fruitless and unseasonable modesty to allege unsufficiency or unworthiness. (Exod. iv. 10, &c; Judges vi. 14, 15; Jer. i. 6, &c; Amos vii. 13-15.) *Juvat idem Qui jubet*. Where He setteth on work, He giveth strength to go through with it. His very calling of any man maketh him able. No more inquiry into outward means, what warrant we have. If God call Paul to be an Apostle, and to bear His name before the Gentiles, and Kings, and the children of Israel, it is needless to confer with flesh and blood, or to seek confirmation at Jerusalem from them which were Apostles before him, by the imposition of

their hands. (Rom. i. 1; Acts ix. 15; Gal. i. 16, 17.) God's work in him supplieth abundantly the want of those solemnities; and Paul is as good an Apostle as the best of them, although he be *an Apostle, not of men, neither by man* (Gal. i. 1). God's calling any man to any office sealeth his warrant. *Non tutum renuisse Deo*. Away with all excuses and pretences and delays. When God calleth, submit thy will, subdue thy reason, answer His call, as Samuel was taught to do (1 Sam. iii. 9, 10): *Speak, Lord, for thy servant heareth*.

26. If it were expedient for us, that God should still deal with us as He did long with the Jewish, and a while with the infant Christian Church, by immediate inspirations, and call us either by secret enthusiasms or sensible insinuations, as He did many of them, into the way wherein He would have us walk, the rule for our choice would be easy: or rather there would need no rule at all, because indeed there would be left no choice at all, but this only, even to get up and be doing, to put ourselves speedily into that way whereunto He did point us. But since the wisdom of God hath thought it better for us to take counsel from His written Word, which He hath left us for our ordinary direction in this and all other difficulties, rather than to depend upon immediate and extraordinary inspirations, it will be very profitable for us to draw thence some few Rules, whereby to make reasonable judgments concerning any course of life, whether that it be whereunto God hath called us, or no. The Rules, as I have partly intimated already, may be reduced to three heads, according as the inquiries we are to make in this business are of three sorts. For they either concern the course itself, or else ourselves that should use it, or else, thirdly, those that have right and power over us in it. If there be a fail in any of these, as, if either the course itself be not lawful, or we not competently fit for it, or our Superiors will not allow of us, or it, we may well think God hath not called us thither. God is just, and will not call any man to that which is not honest and good. God is all-sufficient, and will not call any man to that which is above the proportion of his strength. God is wonderful in His Providence, and will not call any man to that whereto He will not open him a fair and orderly passage. Somewhat, by your patience, of each of these.

27. And first, of the Course we intend. Wherein let these be our inquiries. First, whether the thing be simply and in itself lawful, or no. Secondly, whether it be lawful so as to be made a

Calling, or no. Thirdly, whether it will be profitable, or rather hurtful, to the Commonwealth. Now observe the Rules. The first Rule this, Adventure not on any course without good assurance that it be in itself lawful. The ground of this Rule is plain and evident. For it cannot be, that God, who hateth, and forbiddeth, and punisheth every sin in every man, should call any man to the practice of any sin. *Let him that stole steal no more*, saith St. Paul, *but rather let him labour with his hands the thing that is good* (Eph. iv. 28). If it be not something that is good, it is good for him to hold his hands off. Let him be sure, God never called him to labour in that; and he were as good hold to his old trade, and steal still, as labour with his hand the thing that is not good. If Diana of Ephesus be an idol, Demetrius his occupation must down (Acts xix. 25-27): he must make no more silver shrines for Diana, though by that craft he have his wealth. Tertullian excellently enlargeth himself in this argument in his book *De Idolatria*, strongly disapproving their practice, who, being Christians, yet got their living by making statues, and images, and other ornaments to sell to heathen idolaters. Offenders against this Rule are not only such as live by stealing, and robbing, and piracy, and persecuting, and witchcraft, and other such like ungodly practices as are made capital even by the Laws of men, and punishable by death; but all such also, as maintain themselves by, or get their living in, any course absolutely condemned by the Law of God, howsoever they may find amongst men either express allowance, as whores and bawds do in the holy Mother Church of Rome; or at least some kind of toleration by connivance, as charmers, and fortune-tellers, and wisards,* do amongst us. Which sort of people it is scarce credible how generally and miserably our common ignorants are besotted with the opinion of their skill; and how pitifully they are gulled by their damnable impostures, through their own foolish credulity. These superstitions helped to root out the Amorites out of the land of Canaan (Deut. xviii. 10-12); and it may pass among Saul's best acts, that he rooted out these superstitions out of the land of Israel (1 Sam. xxviii. 9). And great pity it is, that such as make a trade of these superstitions are not by some severe provisions rooted out of this and every other Christian Land. Let this first rule be remembered of us in every choice and trial of our Callings. No unlawful thing can be a lawful calling.

28. No, nor yet every lawful thing neither. For many things

may be lawful in the private use, which yet may not lawfully be made a Calling, or trade of life. Who can reasonably deny the lawfulness of many disports and recreations, as bowling, or shooting, or even cards and dice? And yet who can reasonably think it to be a commendable Calling, for any man to be a professed bowler, or archer, or gamester, and nothing else? Therefore take a second Rule. Make not a Calling of that, which was not made to be a Calling. If you shall ask, how you shall know a thing to be such? I answer, generally, all such things are of this nature, as are indifferent for men of all sorts and Callings to use with due caution and circumstances; and, more especially, matters of delight and recreations are such. And the reasons are good. The ground of particular Callings is some particular gift of God, according to the differences that are to be found in particular men in regard either of the soul or of the body, or of outward things: whereas such things as these, whereof we now speak, become of lawful and commendable use, not so much from any special ability received from God, which should be exercised therein, as from the common necessity of our weak nature, which is to be refreshed thereby. And the end also, for which God permitteth us these things, is not to employ our strength and time in them, but to give us some refreshing when we are wearied with former labour, and so to fit us for fresh and future employment. The works of our Callings, they are as our meats and drinks; these of delight, as sauces or as physic; and as sauces or physic they are to be used, and not otherwise. As absurd then as it would be for a man to accustom himself to no other diet but slabber-sauces* and drugs, so absurd a thing it is for a man to have no other Calling but dicing, and carding, and gaming. Amongst offenders against this Rule, that I reckon not jugglers, and fiddlers, and tumblers, and bear-wards, and rope-dancers, and rhymers, and the rest of that rabble, they may thank the baseness of their condition rather than the lawfulness of their course. I strike rather, at those that are both eminent and pernicious; especially those bawds of unthriftiness and almost every other vice: (for where Unthriftiness is, there is almost every other vice,) I mean those parcel-gallants that have nothing to live on but their wits, and no other use of their wits, but to distill a kind of maintenance from juicy heirs and flush novices by play. I would our pantomimes also and stage-players would examine themselves and their Callings by this Rule. If they should have been tried by the Bench of Fathers and Councils of old, or would have put it to most voices among later Divines both Popish and Reformed, they had been utterly cast and condemned by the first Rule, and not have been reprieved till now; most holding, not the Calling only, but the very practice and thing itself unlawful and damnable. For my own part, I dare not at all say the practice is, neither will I now say the Calling is, unlawful. Only let them that make a Calling of it consider themselves and their Calling well, and examine whether God hath bestowed upon them some gifts which they might have employed a better way; and what inducements they have, and of what weight those inducements are, to give their consciences security, that they have done well in embracing this as their Calling. And when they have done thus, freely and faithfully, as in the sight of God, if their own hearts condemn them not, neither do I. In the mean time, I would but be their remembrancer of thus much only, that there are some things lawful to do, which are not lawful to live by; some things lawful as delights, which are not lawful as Callings. And so much for that second Rule.

29. There is yet a third Rule behind, and that is this. Resolve not upon that course for thy Calling, what pretences soever, or what reasons thou mayest have for the lawfulness of it otherwise, which is rather hurtful than profitable for the Commonwealth. The public good is one of those main respects which enforce the necessity of a calling: the same respect then must of necessity enforce such a calling as may at least stand with the public good. *The manifestation of the Spirit is given to every man*, saith our Apostle after, at the twelfth chapter (Cor. xii. 7), *to profit withal*. Yea, perhaps to profit himself withal. If it were but so, yet that were enough to infer more, sith the private good is included in the public, *tanquam trigonum in tetragono*. But the Apostle meant to speak home; and therefore he made choice of a word that will not admit that gloss of private profit: πρὸς τὸ συμφερόν. That very word impliedly preferreth the public good before the private, and scarce alloweth the private, other than as it is interwoven in the public. Now things in themselves lawful, and at some times useful, may, in regard of the end, or of the matter, or by some accident otherwise, happen at some other times to be hurtful to the Commonwealth; and hereof such due consideration would be had in the choice and exercise of our Callings, as ever to have one eye upon the common good, and not wholly to look after our own private gain. Offenders against this Rule are most of our engrossers,* and forestallers,* and sundry kinds of

hucksters* and regraters;* as also those that export money, corn, or other needful commodities out of the land in times of want or scarceness, or bring in unnecessary commodities when there is plenty at home; and all those that project new devices, and unjust monopolies, to fill their own coffers, perhaps not without pretension of some small benefit to the Commonwealth, but certainly not without sensible and grievous pressures of those that are a great part of the Commonwealth.

30. Thus have we delivered three Rules concerning the quality of a right Calling, and pointed out some special offenders against each of them. And now methinks I see the usurer hugging himself, and clapping his sides, that he hath come off so fairly: surely his Calling is absolute good, whereon none of these Rules could fasten. But it is indeed with the usurer, in this case, as with the drunkard. If the drunkard should ask me against which of the Ten Commandments he offended, I confess, I could not readily give him a direct, punctual answer. Not that he sinneth not against any; but because he sinneth against so many of them that it is hard to say against which most. He sinneth against the sixth Commandment, by distempering his body; he sinneth against the seventh, by inflaming his lust; he sinneth against the eighth, by making waste of the good creatures of God. Right so is it with our usurer in this case. He would pose me, that should ask me the question, which of these three Rules fetcheth in the usurer and his Calling. Verily I cannot well tell which most: I think every one of the three may: howsoever, among the three I am sure I have him. If Usury be simply unlawful, as most of the learned have concluded, then the first Rule hath him. I should be very tender to condemn any thing as simply unlawful, which any even imaginary conjuncture of circumstances would render lawful; and would choose rather, by an over-liberal charity to cover *a multitude of sins* (1 Pet. iv. 8), if I may abuse the Apostle's phrase to that sense, than by a too superstitious restraint make one. Yet the Texts of Scripture are so express, and the grounds of Reason, brought by learned men, seem so strong against all usury, that I have much ado to find so much charity in myself as to absolve any kind of usury, properly so called, with what cautions or circumstances soever qualified, from being a sin. But I will suspect mine own and the common judgment herein, and admit for this once, *dato non concesso*, that usury be in some case lawful, and so our usurer escape the first Rule; which yet cannot be, till his teeth be knocked out for

biting. But you must knock out his brains too, before he escape our second Rule. I dare say, the most learned usurer that liveth, (and they say some learned ones are usurers,) will never be able to prove that usury, if it be at all lawful, is so lawful as to be made a Calling. Here all his Doctors and his Proctors and his Advocates leave him. For, can it possibly enter into any reasonable man's head to think, that a man should be born for nothing else, but to tell out money, and take in paper? which, if a man had many millions of gold and silver, could take up but a small portion of that precious time which God would have spent in some honest and fruitful employment. But what do I speak of the judgment of reasonable men in so plain a matter? wherein I dare appeal to the conscience, even of the usurer himself; and it had need be a very plain matter that a man would refer to the conscience of an usurer. No honest man need be ashamed of an honest Calling: if then the usurer's Calling be such, what need he care who knoweth, or why should he shame with it? If that be his trade, why doth he not in his bills and bonds and *Noverints*, make it known to all men by those presents that he is an usurer, rather than write himself gentleman, or yeoman, or by some other style? But say yet our usurer should escape, at least in the judgment of his own hardened conscience, from both these Rules, as from the sword of Jehu and Hazael: there is yet a third Rule, like the sword of Elisha, to strike him stone-dead, and he shall never be able to escape that. Let him show wherein his Calling is profitable to human society. He keepeth no hospitality: if he have but a barr'd chest, and a strong lock to keep his God and his Scriptures, his Mammon and his Parchments, in it, he hath houseroom enough. He fleeceth many, but clotheth none. He biteth and devoureth, but eateth all his morsels alone. He giveth not so much as a crumb, no, not to his dearest broker or scrivener: only, where he biteth, he alloweth them to scratch what they can for themselves. The King, the Church, the Poor, are all wronged by him, and so are all that live near him: in every common charge, he slippeth the collar, and leaveth the burden upon those that are less able. It were not possible usurers should be so bitterly inveighed against by sober Heathen Writers, so severely censured by the Civil and Canon Laws, so uniformly condemned by godly Fathers and Councils (Jer. xv. 10), so universally hated by all men of all sorts, and in all ages and countries, as histories and experience manifest they ever have been and are, if their practice and Calling had been any way profitable, and not indeed every way hurtful and incommodious both to private men and public societies. If any thing can make a Calling unlawful, certainly the usurer's Calling cannot be lawful.

31. Our first care past, which concerneth the Calling itself, our next care in our choice must be, to inquire into ourselves, what Calling is most fit for us, and we for it. Wherein our inquiry must rest especially upon three things, our Inclination, our Gifts, and our Education. Concerning which, let this be the first Rule. Where these three concur upon one and the same Calling, our consciences may rest assured that that Calling is fit for us; and we ought, so far as it lieth in our power, to resolve to follow that. This Rule, if well observed, is of singular use for the settling of their consciences, who are scrupulous and doubtful concerning their inward Calling to any office or employment. Divines teach it commonly, and that truly, that every man should have an inward Calling from God for his particular course of life; and this in the Calling of the Ministry is by so much more requisite than in most other Callings, by how much the business of it is more weighty than theirs, as of things more immediately belonging unto God. Whence it is, that in our Church none are admitted into Holy Orders, until they have personally and expressly made profession before the Bishop, that they find themselves 'inwardly called and moved thereunto.' But because, what that inward Calling is, and how it should be discerned, is a thing not so distinctly declared and understood, generally, as it should be, it often falleth out, that men are distressed in conscience with doubts and scruples in this case, whilst they desire to be assured of their inward Calling, and know not how. We are to know, therefore, that to this inward Calling there is not of necessity required any inward, secret, sensible testimony of God's blessed, sanctifying Spirit to a man's soul, (for then an unsanctified man could not be rightly called,) neither yet any strong working of the Spirit of illumination, (for then a mere heathen man could not be rightly called,) both which consequents are false. For Saul and Judas were called, the one to the Kingdom, the other to the Apostleship (1 Sam. x. 24; John vi. 70); of whom it is certain the one was not, and it is not likely the other was, endued with the Holy Spirit of sanctification. And many Heathen men have been called to several employments, wherein they have also laboured with much profit to their own and succeeding times, who in all probability never had any other inward motion, than what might arise from some or all of these three things

now specified, viz. the Inclination of their nature, their personal Abilities, and the care of Education. If it shall please God to afford any of us any further gracious assurance than these can give us, by some extraordinary work of His Spirit within us, we are to embrace it with joy and thankfulness, as a special favour; but we are not to suspend our resolutions for the choice of a course, in expectation of that extraordinary assurance; since we may receive comfortable satisfaction to our souls without it, by these ordinary means now mentioned. For, who need be scrupulous where all these concur? Thy Parents have from thy childhood destinated thee to some special course, admit the Ministry, and been at the care and charge to breed thee up in learning, to make thee in some measure fit for it: when thou art grown to some maturity of years and discretion, thou findest in thyself a kind of desire to be doing something that way in thy private study by way of trial; and withal some measure of knowledge, discretion, and utterance, though perhaps not in such an eminent degree as thou couldst wish, yet in such a competency, as thou mayest reasonably persuade thyself thou mightest thereby be able, with His blessing, to do some good to God's people, and not be altogether unprofitable in the Ministry. In this so happy concurrence of Propension, Abilities, and Education, make no further inquiry, doubt not of thine inward Calling, tender thyself to those that have the power of admission for thy outward Calling; which once obtained, thou art certainly in thine own proper course. Up and be doing, for the Lord hath called thee, and, no doubt, the Lord will be with thee.

32. But say, these three do not concur, as oftentimes they do not. A man may be destinated by his friends, and accordingly bred, out of some covetous, or ambitious, or other corrupt respect, to some Calling, wherefrom he may be altogether averse, and whereto altogether unfit: as we see some parents, that have the donations or advocations of Church Livings in their hands, must needs have some of their children (and for the most part they set by the most untoward and misshapen chip of the whole block, to make timber for the pulpit,) but some of their children they will have thrust into the Ministry, though they have neither a head nor a heart for it. Again, a man may have a good sufficiency in him for a Calling, and yet out of a slothful desire of ease and liberty, if it seem painful or austere; or an ambitious desire of eminency and reputation, if it seem base and contemptible; or some other secret corruption, cannot set his mind that

way; as Solomon saith, there may be *a price in the hand of a fool, to buy wisdom, and* yet the fool *have no heart to it* (Pro. xvii. 16). And divers other occurrents there may be, and are, to hinder this happy conjuncture of Nature, Skill, and Education. Now in such cases as these, where our Education bendeth us one way, our inclination swayeth us another way, and, it may be, our gifts and abilities lead us a third, in this distraction, what are we to do? which way to take? what Calling to pitch upon? In point of Conscience, there can no more be given general rules, to meet with all cases, and regulate all difficulties, than in point of Law, there can be general resolutions given to set an end to all suits, or provisions made to prevent all inconveniences. Particulars are infinite, and various; but rules are not, must not, cannot be so. He whose case it is, if he be not able to direct himself, should do well to take advice of his learned Counsel. This we can readily do in matters of Law, for the quieting of our estates: why should we not do it at least as readily in matter of Conscience, for the quieting of our souls? But yet for some light, at least in the generality, what if thou shouldst proceed thus?

33. First, have an eye to thy Education; and if it be possible to bring the rest that way, do so rather than forsake it. For besides that it would be some grief to thy parents, to whom thou shouldest be a comfort, to have cast away so much charge as they have been at for thy education; and some dishonour to them withal whom thou art bound by the law of God and Nature to honour, to have their judgments so much slighted, and their choice so little regarded by their child (Exod. xx. 12): the very consideration of so much precious time as hath been spent in fitting thee to that course, which would be almost all lost upon thy change, should prevail with thee to try all possible means, rather than forgo it. It were a thing indeed much to be wished, that parents, and friends, and guardians, and all those other whatsoever, that have the education of young ones committed unto them, (all greedy desires to make their children great, all base, penurious niggardness in saving their own purses, all fond cherishing of their children in their humours, all doting opinion of their forwardness and wit and towardliness, all other corrupt partial affections whatsoever, laid aside,) would, out of the observation of their natural propensions and inclinations, and of their particular abilities and defects, frame them from the beginning to such courses, as wherein they were likeliest to go on with cheerfulness and profit. This indeed were to be wished; but

this is not always done. If it have not been so done to thee, the fault is theirs that should have done it, and not thine; and thou art not able now to remedy that which is past and gone. But as for thee, and for the future, if thy parents have not done their part, yet do not thou forget thy duty: if they have done one fault, in making a bad choice, do not thou add another, in making a worse change: disparage not their judgments by misliking, neither gainsay their wills by forsaking their choice, upon every small incongruity with thine own judgment or will. If thine inclination draw thee another way, labour throughly to subdue thy nature therein: suspect thine own corruption: think this backwardness proceedeth not from true judgment in thee, but issueth rather from the root of some carnal affection: consider thy years are green, affections strong, judgment unsettled: hope that this backwardness will grow off, as years and staidness grow on: pray and endeavour that thou mayest daily more and more wean thy affections from thine own bent, and take liking to that course whereunto thou hast been so long in framing. Thus possibly thou mayest in time make that cheerful and delightful unto thee, which now is grievous and irksome. And as for thy insufficiency, if that dishearten thee, which is indeed a main rub, do thus. Impute thy former non-proficiency to thine own sloth and negligence: think, if after so long time spent in this course, thou hast attained to no greater perfection in it, how long it would be ere thou shouldest come to a tolerable mediocrity in another: resolve not to lose all that precious time forepast by beginning the world anew, but rather save as much of it as is redeemable, by adding to thy diligence: suspect that it cometh from thy pride, that thou canst not content thyself with a Calling wherein thou mayest not be excellent; and imagine that God, of purpose to humble thee, might divert thy education to another, for which thou art less apt: observe what strange things past belief, and such as have seemed insuperable, have been conquered and subdued by the obstinacy and improbity of unwearied labour, and of assiduity: doubt not, but by God's blessing upon thy faithful industry, to attain in time, if not to such perfection as thou desirest, and mightest perhaps have attained in some other course, if thou hadst been bred up to it, yet to such a competent sufficiency, as may render thy endeavours acceptable to God, comfortable to thyself, and serviceable to community. If by these and the like considerations, and the use of other good means, thou canst bring thy affections to some indifferent liking of, and thy abilities to some indifferent mediocrity for, that course which Education hath opened unto thee, thou hast no more to do: there's thy course, that's thy Calling, that's the work whereunto God hath appointed thee.

34. But if, after long striving, and pains, and trial, thou canst neither bring thy mind to it, nor do any good upon it, having faithfully desired and endeavoured it, so that thou must needs leave the course of thy Education; or, which is another case, if thy Education have left thee free, as many Parents, God knoweth, are but too careless that way, then, Secondly, thou art in the next place to consider of thy Gifts and Abilities, and to take direction from them rather than from thine Inclination. And this Rule I take to be very sound: not only from the Apostle's intimation, verse 17, *As God hath distributed to every man, as the Lord hath called every one*, where he seemeth to make the choice of men's Callings to depend much upon the distribution of God's gifts; but withal for two good reasons. One is because our gifts and abilities, whether of body or mind, being in the brain or hand, are at a better certainty than our propensions and inclinations are, which are seated in the heart. The heart is *deceitful above all things* (Jer. xvii. 9); and there are so many rotten corruptions in it, that it is a very hard thing for a man to discern his own inclinations and propensions, whether they spring from a sound or from a corrupt root. Whereas in the discerning of our Gifts and Abilities, we are less subject to gross errors and mistakings: I mean for the truth and reality of them; howsoever we are apt to overvalue them for the measure and degree. Now it is meet, in the choice of our Callings, we should follow the surer guide, and therefore rather be led by our Gifts than by our Inclinations. The other reason is, because our Inclinations cannot so well produce Abilities, as these can draw on them. We say indeed, there is nothing hard to a willing mind; and, in some sense, it is true. Not as if a willing mind could make us do more than we are able: a man can do no more than he can do, be he never so willing; but because a willing mind will make us *exserere vires*, stir up ourselves to do as much as we are able, which we use not to do in those things we go unwillingly about. Willingness then may quicken the strength we have; but it doth not put any new strength into us. But Abilities can produce Inclinations *de novo*, and make them where they find them not. As we see every other natural thing is inclinable to the exercise of those natural faculties that are in it, so

certainly would every man have strongest inclination to those things whereto he hath strongest Abilities, if wicked and untoward affections did not often corrupt our Inclinations, and hinder them from moving their own proper and natural way. It is best then, to begin the choice of our Callings from our Abilities, which will fetch on Inclinations; and not from our Inclinations, which, without Abilities, will not serve the turn.

35. Concerning which Gifts or Abilities, what they are, and how to make true judgment of them, and how to frame the choice of our Callings from them, to speak punctually and fully would require a large discourse. I can but touch at some few points therein, such as are of daily use, and proceed. First, by Gifts and Abilities we are to understand not only those of the mind, judgment, wit, invention, memory, fancy, eloquence, &c, and those of the body, health, strength, beauty, activity, &c, but also those which are without, birth, wealth, honour, authority, reputation, kindred, alliance, &c. generally any thing that may be of use or advantage unto us for any employment. Secondly, as our Abilities on the one side, so, on the other side, all our wants and defects, which might disable us more or less for any employment, are to be duly weighed and considered of, and the one laid against the other, that we may know how to make, as near as we can, a just estimate of our strength and sufficiency. Thirdly, it is the safer way to undervalue than to overprise ourselves, lest, ignorantly confident, we affect a Calling above our strength, which were to fly with waxen wings, and to owe the world a laughter. Be we sure of this: if God have not gifted us for it, He hath not called us to it. Fourthly, in the judging of our Abilities, we should have a regard to the outward circumstances of times and places, and the rest. Those Gifts which would have made a sufficient Priest in the beginning of the Reformation, in that dearth of learning and penury of the Gospel, now the times are full of knowledge and learning would be all little enough for a Parish Clerk. Fifthly, something would be yielded to the judgments of other men concerning our Abilities. It is either secret pride, or base faintness of heart, or dull sloth, or some other thing, and not true modesty in us, if, being excellently gifted for some weighty employment in every other man's judgment, we yet withdraw ourselves from it with pretensions of unsufficiency. Sixthly, and lastly, let us resolve on that course, *caeteris paribus*, not only for which we are competently fit, but for which we are absolutely fittest. A good actor, it may

be, could very sufficiently act any part in the play, represent the majesty of a King, or the humour of a swaggerer, or the pranks of a bedlam, or any thing; but yet if he be notedly excellent at some part rather than another, he would not willingly be put from that, to act another. *Ergo histrio hoc videbit in scena, quod non videbit [vir] sapiens in vita?* Shame we to let these men be wiser in their generations, than we in our's. And thus much for abilities.

36. There is yet a doubt remaineth concerning a man's Inclination. In case we have examined our Gifts, and find them in a good measure of competency for such or such a course, and yet remain still averse from it, and cannot by any possible means work over our affections to any tolerable liking of it, in such a case, what is to be done, or how shall we judge what Calling is fittest for us to take? whether that whereto our Abilities lead us, or that whereto our Inclinations draw us? As I conceive it, in such a case we are to hold this order. First, if our Inclinations cannot be won over to that course for which our Abilities lie fittest, we are to take a second surview of our Abilities, to see if they be competently fit for that whereto our Inclination swayeth us; and if upon due unpartial examination we find they are, we may then follow the sway of our Inclination. The reason this. A man's Inclination cannot be forced. If it can be fairly won over, well and good; but violence it cannot endure at any hand. And therefore, if we cannot make it yield to us in reason, there is no remedy, we must in wisdom yield to it, provided ever it be honest; or else all is lost. Whatever our sufficiencies be, things will not fadge that are undertaken without an heart: there is no good to be done against the hair.

37. But then, secondly, if upon search we find ourselves altogether unsufficient and unfit for that Calling whereunto our inclination is strong and violently carried, we are to oppose that Inclination with a greater violence, and to set upon some other Calling, for which we are in some mediocrity gifted, speedily and resolvedly, and leave the success to Almighty God. The reason this. It being certain that God never calleth any man but to that, for which He hath in some competent measure enabled him, we are to hold that for a pernicious and unnatural inclination at the least, if not rather for a wicked and diabolical suggestion, which so stiffly exciteth us to a function whereto we may be assured God never called us.

38. But yet, thirdly, (and I would commend it unto you as

a principal good rule, and the fairest outlet of all other from amid these difficulties,) we should do well to deal with these mutinous and distracting thoughts within us, as wise Statists do when they have to deal with men divided in opinions and factions and ends. How is that? They use to bethink themselves of a middle course, to reduce all the several opinions to a kind of temper, so as no side be satisfied fully in the proposals they have tendered, and yet every side in part: as we commonly hold those to be the justest arbitrators, and to make the best and the fairest end of differences between the parties for whom they arbitrate, that, by pleasing neither, please both. So here, if our Educations, Abilities, and Inclinations look several ways, and the Inclination be peremptory and stiff, and will not condescend to either of the other two, it will be a point of good wisdom in us, if we can bethink ourselves of some such meet temper as may in part give satisfaction to our Inclinations, and yet not leave our Gifts and Educations wholly unsatisfied. And that is easily done by proposing the full latitude of our Educations and Abilities, as the utmost bounds of our choice, and then leaving it to our Inclinations to determine our particular choice within those bounds. For no man's Education or Gifts run so mathematically and by the line to that point whereto they direct him, but that there is a kind of latitude in them; and that for the most part, by reason of the great variety and affinity of offices and employments, very large and spacious. One instance shall serve both to exemplify and illustrate this Rule. A man designed by his parents to the Ministry, and for that end brought up in the University, studieth there philosophy, and history, and the arts, and the tongues, and furnisheth himself with general knowledge which may enable him, as for the work of the Ministry, so for the exercise of any other profession that hath to do with Learning: so as not only the Calling of the Ministry, but that of the Lawyer too, and of the Physician, and of the Tutor, and Schoolmaster, and sundry other besides these, do come within the latitude of his education and abilities. Certainly, if his mind would stand thereunto, no course would be so proper for such a man as that which he was intended for, of the Ministry. But he proveth obstinately averse from it, and cannot be drawn by any persuasion of friends or reason to embrace it. It is not meet to force his Inclination quite against the bent of it; and yet it is pity his Abilities and Education should be cast away. This middle course therefore is to be held: even to leave it free for him to make his choice of Law, or Physic, or Teaching, or any other profession that belongeth to a Scholar, and cometh within his latitude, which of them soever he shall find himself to have the strongest inclination or propension unto. And the like course we are to hold in other cases of like nature: by which means our Inclinations, which cannot be driven to the centre, may yet be drawn within the circumference of our Educations and Abilities. He that observeth these Rules I have hitherto delivered, with due respect to his Education, Abilities, and Inclination, and dealeth therein faithfully and unpartially and in the fear of God, may rest secure in his conscience of his inward Calling.

39. But there must be an outward Calling too: else yet all is not right. The general Rule, Πάντα εὐσχημόνως, *Let all things be done honestly, and in order*, enforceth it. There are some Callings, which, conscionably discharged, require great pains and care; but yet the profits will come in, whether the duties be conscionably performed, or no. Our Calling of the Ministry is such; and such are all those offices as have annexed unto them a certain standing revenue, or annual fee. Now into such Callings as these every unworthy fellow that wanteth maintenance and loveth ease would be intruding, as we of the Clergy find it but too true; and there would be no order kept herein, if there were not left in some others a power to keep back unsufficient men. There are again divers Callings necessary for the public, which yet bring in either no profits at all, if not rather a charge, or at least profits improportionable to the pains and dangers men must undergo in them: such as are the Callings of a Justice of Peace, the High Sheriff of a County, a Constable, Churchwarden, Soldier, &c. Now from these Callings men of sufficiency, to avoid trouble and charge, would withdraw themselves; and so the King and Country should be served either not at all, or by unworthy ones. Here likewise would be no order, if there were not left in some others a power to impose those offices upon sufficient men. It may be, those in whom either power resideth, may sometimes, yea, often abuse it, for they are but men; keeping back sufficient men, and admitting unsufficient, into callings of the former; sparing sufficient men, and imposing upon unsufficient, offices of the latter kind. This is not well. But yet what wise man knoweth not that there could not be avoided a necessity of general inconveniences, if there should not be left a possibility of particular mischiefs? And therefore it is needful there should be this power of admitting and refusing, of sparing and

imposing, in Church and Commonwealth, though it may happen to be thus mischievously abused, rather than, for want of this power, a multitude of unsufferable inconveniences, as needs there must, should ensue. And from this power must every man have his warrant for his outward Calling to any office or employment in Church or Commonwealth.

40. Now then to frame a case to either of these two sorts of Calling. A man desireth a lawful Calling, suppose the Ministry: not only his Inclination bendeth him, but his Education also leadeth him, and his Gifts encourage him that way: hitherto all things concur, to seal unto his conscience God's Calling him to this function. But for so much as he hath not, as it is not fit any man should have, power to give himself either Orders to be a Priest, or institution into a pastoral charge, he must, for his admission into that holy function, depend upon those to whom the power of admitting or refusing in either kind is committed. He may tender himself and his gifts to examination, and modestly crave admission, which once obtained, he hath no more to do: his Calling is warranted, and his choice at an end. But if that be peremptorily denied him, whether reasonably, or no, it now mattereth not, he is to rest himself content a while, to employ himself at his study, or in some other good course for the time, and to wait God's leisure and a further opportunity. And if, after some reasonable expectation, upon further tender with modest importunity, he cannot yet hope to prevail, he must begin to resolve of another course, submit himself to authority and order, acknowledge God's Providence in it, possess his soul in patience, and think, that for some secret corruption in himself, or for some other just cause, God is pleased that he should not, or not yet, enter into that Calling.

41. On the other side, a gentleman liveth in his country in good credit and account, known to be a sufficient man both for estate and understanding, thought every way fit to do the King and his Country service in the Commission of the Peace; yet himself, either out of a desire to live at ease and avoid trouble, or because he thinketh he hath as much business of his own as he can well turn him to, without charging himself with the cares of the public, or possibly out of a privy consciousness to himself of some defect, as, it may be, an irresolution in judgment, or in courage, or too great a propension to foolish pity, or for some other reason which appeareth to him just, thinketh not that a fit Calling for him, and rather desireth to be spared. But for so

much as it is not fit a man should be altogether his own judge, especially in things that concern the public, he must herein depend upon those to whom the power of sparing or imposing in this kind is committed. He may excuse himself by his other many occasions, allege his own wants and insufficiencies, and what he can else for himself, and modestly crave to be spared. But if he cannot by fair and honest suit get off, he must submit himself to authority and order, yield somewhat to the judgment of others, think that God hath His secret work in it, and rest upon the warrant of this outward Calling.

42. The outward Calling then is not a thing of small moment, or to be lightly regarded. Sometimes, as in the case last proposed, it may have the chief and the casting voice; but where it hath least, it hath always a negative, in every regular choice of any calling or course of life. And it is this outward Calling, which, I say not principally, but even alone, must rule every ordinary Christian in the judging of other men's Callings. We cannot see their hearts: we know not how God might move them: we are not able to judge of their inward Callings. If we see them too neglectful of the duties of their Calling, if we find their gifts hold very short and unequal proportion with the weight of their Calling, or the like, we have but little comfortable assurance, to make us confident that all is right within. But yet, unless it be such as are in place of authority and office to examine men's sufficiencies, and accordingly to allow or disallow them, what hath any of us to do to judge the heart, or the conscience, or the inward Calling of our brother? So long as he hath the warrant of an orderly outward Calling, we must take him for such as he goeth for, and leave the trial of his heart to God and to his own heart. And of this second general point, the choice of a Calling, thus far.

43. Remaineth now the third and last point proposed, the Use of a man's Calling. Let him walk in it. Let him abide in it. Let him *abide therein with God*, here in my Text. At this I aimed most, in my choice of this Text; and yet of this I must say least. Preachers ofttimes do with their proposals, as parents sometimes do with their children: though they love the later as well, yet the first go away with the largest portions. But I do not well, to trifle out that little sand I have left in apologies. Let us rather on to the matter, and see what duties our Apostle here requireth of us, under these phrases of abiding in our callings, and abiding therein with God.

44. It may seem he would have us stick to a course, and when we are in a Calling, not to forsake it, nor change it, no, not for a better, no, not upon any terms. Perhaps some have taken it so; but certainly the Apostle never meant it so. For taking the word Calling in that extent wherein he treateth of it in this chapter, if that were his meaning, he should consequently teach that no single man might marry, nor any servant become free: which are apparently contrary, both unto common reason, and unto the very purpose of the chapter. But taking the word as we have hitherto specially intended it and spoken of it, for some settled station and course of life, whereby a man is to maintain himself, or wherein to do profitable service to human society, or both, is it yet lawful for a man to change it, or is he bound to abide in it perpetually without any possibility or liberty to alter his course upon any terms? I answer, it is lawful to change it, so it be done with due caution. It is lawful, first, in subordinate Callings. For where a man cannot warrantably climb unto an higher, but by the steps of an inferior Calling, there must needs be supposed a lawfulness of relinquishing the inferior. How should we do for generals for the wars, if colonels and lieutenants and captains and common soldiers might not relinquish their charges? and how for Bishops in the Church, if beneficed men and college-governors were clenched and riveted to their cures, like *a nail in a sure place*, not to be removed? Nay, we should have no Priests in the Church of England, since a Priest must be a Deacon first, if a Deacon might not leave his station, and become a Priest. But St. Paul saith, *They that have used the office of a Deacon well, purchase to themselves a good degree* (1 Tim. iii. 13). And so in lower Callings it is, that men should give proof of their worthiness for higher. It is lawful, secondly, yea, necessary, when the very Calling itself, though in itself good and useful, doth yet by some accident become unlawful or unuseful. As when some manufacture is prohibited by the State; or when some more exact device of later invention hath made the old unprofitable. It is lawful, thirdly, when a man by some accident becometh unable for the duties of his Calling, as by age, blindness, maim, decay of estate, and sundry other impediments which daily occur. It is lawful, fourthly, where there is a want of sufficient men, or not a sufficient number of them in some Callings, for the necessities of the State and Country. In such cases, Authority may interpose, and cull out men from other Callings, such as are fit, and may be spared, to serve in those.

Not to branch out too many particulars, it is lawful generally, where either absolute necessity enforceth it, or lawful authority enjoineth it, or a concurrence of weighty circumstances, faithfully and soberly and discreetly laid together, seemeth to require it.

45. But then it must be done with due cautions. As, first, not out of a desultory lightness. Some men are ever restless, as if they had windmills in their heads: every new crotchet putteth them into a new course. But these rolling stones carry their curse with them: they seldom gather moss; and who prove many conclusions, it is a wonder, if their last conclusion prove not beggary. If thou art well, keep thyself well: lest, thinking to meet with better, thou find worse. Nor, secondly, out of the greediness of a covetous or ambitious lust. Profit and credit are things, respectively amongst other things, to be considered both in the choice and change; but not principally, and above all other things, certainly not wholly, and without, or against all other things. Thirdly, nor out of sullenness, or a discontentedness at thy present condition. Content groweth from the mind, not from the condition; and therefore change of the Calling, the mind unchanged, will either not afford content, or not long. Thy new broom, that now sweepeth clean all discontents from thee, will soon grow stubbed, and leave as much filth behind to annoy thee, as the old one thou flungest away. Either learn with St. Paul in whatsoever state thou art, to be therewithal content (Phil. iv. 11), or never hope to find content in whatsoever state thou shalt be. Much less, fourthly, out of an evil eye against thy neighbour that liveth by thee. There is not a baser sin than envy, nor a fouler mark of envy than to forsake thine own trading to justle thy neighbour out of his. Nor, fifthly, out of degenerous false-heartedness. That man would soon dare to be evil, that dareth not long be good. And he that flincheth from his Calling, at the first frown, who can say he will not flinch from his conscience, at the next? In an upright course, fear not the face of man, neither *leave thy place, though the spirit of a Ruler rise up against thee* (Eccl. x. 4). Patience will conjure down again that spirit in time: only, if thou keep thyself within thy circle. But, sixthly, be sure thou change not, if thy Calling be of that nature that it may not be changed. Some degrees of Magistracy seem to be of that nature; and therefore some have noted it rather as an act of impotency in Charles the fifth, than a fruit either of humility, or wisdom, or

devotion, that he resigned his crown, to betake himself to a cloister. But our Calling of the Ministry is certainly such. There may be a change of the station or degree in the Ministry, upon good cause, and with due circumstances; but yet still so as that the main Calling itself remain unchanged. This Calling hath in it something that is sacred, and singular, and different from other Callings. As therefore things once dedicated and hallowed to religious services were no more to return to common uses, for that were to profane them *ipso facto*, and to make them unclean, so persons once set apart for the holy work of the Ministry,—*Separate me Paul and Barnabas*,— and invested into their Calling with solemn collation of the Holy Ghost in a special manner, if any more they return to be of that lump from which they are separated, they do, as it were, puff the blessed breath of Christ back into His own face, and renounce their part in the Holy Ghost. Bethink thyself well therefore beforehand, and consider what thou art in doing, when thou beginnest to reach forth thine hand towards this spiritual plough: know, when it is once there, it may not be pulled back again, no, not for a Dictatorship. That man can be no less than disorderly at the least, that forsaketh his Orders. You see I do but point at things as I go, which would require further enlarging; because I desire to have done.

46. This then, that we should persevere in our Callings until death, and not leave or change them upon any consideration whatsoever, is not the thing our Apostle meaneth by abiding in our Callings. The word importeth divers other Christian duties concerning the use of our Callings. I will but touch at them, and conclude. The first is Contentedness: that we neither repine at the meanness of our own, nor envy at the eminence of another's Calling. *Art thou called being a servant? care not for it*, saith this Apostle, but a little before my Text (1 Cor. vii. 21). All men cannot have rich, or easy, or honourable Callings: the necessity of the whole requireth that some should drudge in baser and meaner offices. *If all the body were eye, where were the hearing?* (1 Cor. xii. 17.) And if there were none to grind at the mill, there would soon be none to sit upon the throne. Solomon's temple had not been reared to this hour, if there had not been burden-bearers and labourers, as well as curious workers in stone, and brass, and gold. There should be no shame in that whereof there can be no want: nay, *much more those members of the body, which seem to be more feeble, are necessary*.

(1 Kings v. 15; 1 Cor. xii. 22.) Grudge not then at thine own lot, for not the meanest Calling but hath a promise of God's blessing, neither envy another's lot; for not the greatest Calling but is attended with worldly vexations. Whatsoever thy Calling is, *therein abide*, be content with it.

47. The second is Faithfulness, and Industry, and Diligence. What is here called abiding in it, is, at verse 17, called walking in it; and, in Rom. xii [7], *waiting on it: Let him that hath an office, wait on his office. It is required in stewards that a man be found faithful* (1 Cor. iv. 2; 1 Pet. iv. 10); and every man, in his Calling, is a steward. He that professeth a Calling and doth nothing in it, doth no more abide in it than he that leaveth it, or he that never had it. *Spartam quam nactus es, orna*. Whatsoever Calling thou hast undertaken, therein abide: be painful in it.

48. The third is, Sobriety; that we keep ourselves within the proper bounds and limits of our Callings. For how doth he abide in his Calling that is ever and anon flying out of it, or starting beyond it, like an extravagant soldier that is always breaking rank? Uzzah had better have ventured the falling than the fingering of the Ark, though it tottered. It is never well, when the cobbler looketh above the ankle; nor when laymen teach us what, and how, we should teach them. The Pope should have done well to have thrown away his keys, as they say one of them once did, before he had taken the sword into his hands; and midwives well, to go teach all nations, before they baptize them in the Name of the Father, and of the Son, and of the Holy Ghost. Let it be the singular absurdity of the Church of Rome, to allow Vicars to dispose of Crowns, and women of Sacraments. As for thee, whatsoever thy Calling be, therein abide: keep within the bounds of it.

49. But yet *abide with God*. That clause was not added for nothing: it teacheth thee also some duties. First, so to demean thyself in thy particular Calling, as that thou do nothing but what may stand with thy general Calling. Magistrate, or Minister, or Lawyer, or Merchant, or Artificer, or whatsoever other thou art, remember thou art withal a Christian. Pretend not the necessities of thy particular Calling to any breach of the least of those Laws of God, which must rule thy general Calling. God is the author of both Callings, of thy general Calling, and of thy particular Calling too. Do not think He hath called thee to service in the one, and to liberty in the other; to justice in the one, and to cousenage in the other; to simplicity in the one, and to

dissimulation in the other; to holiness in the one, and to profaneness in the other; in a word, to an entire and universal obedience in the one, and to any kind or degree of disobedience in the other.

50. It teacheth thee, secondly, not to ingulf thyself so wholly into the business of thy particular Calling, as to abridge thyself of convenient opportunities for the exercise of those religious duties, which thou art bound to perform by virtue of thy general Calling, as prayer, confession, thanksgiving, meditation, &c. God alloweth thee to serve thyself; but He commandeth thee to serve Him too. Be not thou so all for thyself, as to forget Him; but as thou art ready to embrace that liberty which He hath given thee, to serve thyself, so make a conscience to perform those duties which He hath required of thee for His service. Work, and spare not; but yet pray too, or else work not. Prayer is the means to procure a blessing upon thy labours, from His hands, who never faileth to serve them that never fail to serve Him. Did ever any man *serve God for nought?* A man cannot have so comfortable assurance that he shall prosper in the affairs he taketh in hand, by any other means, as by making God the Alpha and Omega of his endeavours; by beginning them in His Name, and directing them to His glory. Neither is this a point of duty only, in regard of God's command, or a point of Wisdom only, to make our labours successful; but it is a point of justice too, as due by way of restitution. We make bold with His Day, and dispense with some of that time which He hath sanctified unto His service, for our own necessities. It is equal we should allow Him at least as much of ours, as we borrow of His, though it be for our necessities or lawful comforts. But if we rob Him of some of His time, as too often we do, employing it in our own businesses, without the warrant of a just necessity, we are to know that it is theft, yea, theft in the highest degree, sacrilege; and that therefore we are bound, at least as far as petty thieves were in the Law (Exod. xxii. 1; 2 Sam. xii. 6), to a fourfold restitution. Abide in thy Calling, by doing thine own part, and labouring faithfully; but yet so, as God's part be not forgotten, in serving Him daily.

51. It teacheth thee, thirdly, to watch over the special sins of thy particular Calling. Sins, I mean, not that cleave necessarily to the Calling, for then the very Calling itself should be unlawful; but sins, unto the temptations whereof the condition of thy Calling layeth thee open, more than it doth unto other sins, or

more than some other Callings would do unto the same sins; and wherewith, whilst thou art stirring about the businesses of thy Calling, thou mayest be soonest overtaken, if thou dost not heedfully watch over thyself and them. The Magistrate's sins, partiality and injustice; the Minister's sins, sloth and flattery; the Lawyer's sins, maintenance and collusion; the Merchant's sins, lying and deceitfulness; the Courtier's sins, ambition and dissimulation; the Great Man's sins, pride and oppression; the Gentleman's sins, riot and prodigality; the Officer's sins, bribery and extortion; the Countryman's sins, envy and discontentedness; the Servant's sins, talebearing and purloining. In every state and condition of life there is a kind of opportunity to some special sin, wherein if our watchfulness be not the greater, mainly to oppose it and keep it out, we cannot *abide therein with God*.

All that I have done all this while, in my passage over this Scripture, is but this. I have proved the necessity of having a Calling, laid down directions for the choice and trial of our Callings, and showed what is required of us in the use of our Callings for the abiding therein with God. And having thus dispatched my message, it is now time I should spare both your ears and my own sides. God grant that every one of us may remember so much of what hath been taught as is needful for each of us, and faithfully apply it unto our own souls and consciences, and make a profitable and seasonable use of it in the whole course of our lives, even for Jesus Christ's sake, His Blessed Son, and our alone Saviour. To whom, &c.

NOTES

p. 205. *side-banckled*: so tightly reined as to be unable to jump.

p. 213. *frank*: sty where boars are fattened.

p. 216. *impropriations*: the annexation of a benefice to a lay person. Sanderson is attacking certain 'lay rectors' who enjoyed the tithes of a church but who often failed in their duties of repairing the chancel—and were not brought to book for it.

p. 223. *wisards*: mountebanks; quacks at fairs.

p. 224. *slabber-sauces*: foul, viscous gravies.

p. 225. *engrossers*: hoarders of corn who intend to sell when the price is high. *forestallers*: those who buy up produce as it is being delivered to the market with the intention of selling it at a higher price at the same market.

p. 226. *bucksters*: farmers who ask exorbitant prices for grain when it is scarce so that the poor have to 'make bread of fern roots'. *regraters*: those who put up the price of corn and vegetables by buying and re-selling.

# Thomas Adams

THOMAS ADAMS was one of the most fascinating and gifted preachers of his time. Southey foolishly compared him to Shakespeare; but his prose was (and still is) neglected. It is not known when he was born. He was a preacher in Willington, Bedfordshire, in 1612, vicar of Wingrave in Buckinghamshire in 1614, and later chaplain to Sir Henry Montagu, the Lord Chief Justice. Although usually classed as a Puritan, and certainly regarded as such by his nineteenth-century rediscoverers and by his (too few) modern admirers, he is a somewhat more ambiguous figure than this simple label suggests—as what little is known of his history bears out. He was much in demand as a preacher at St Paul's Cross (the sermon below was delivered there), and was so friendly with John Donne as to feel able to dedicate a printed sermon to him in 1623: in this dedication he mentions Donne and the Prebend-Residentaries of St Paul's (of which Donne was of course Dean) as 'my very good patrons'. Further, though clearly a Puritan in important aspects of his theology, which is unorthodox and original, and though against the theatres, there is evidence to suggest that in 1653 he was sequestered from St Bennet's (at Paul's Wharf), of which he had been rector since 1630.

He supported the Puritan clergy, but criticized Puritanism for its 'schismatic spirit': the horn of the Puritans is 'the secret of their strength ... precious enough, if only it were out of the unicorn's head', for the unicorn 'wounds the church'.

Adams is a literary genius whose poetic vigour of language competes with his fascinated Calvinistic inclinations. His preaching departs in many ways from the standard forms of his contemporary Puritans: his sermons are dramatic in a poetic sense, recollecting the very plays whose performance the Puritans abhorred; he draws examples from 'wanton' field sports; he is as fascinated as Webster (whose play *The White Devil* has been shown to have been first performed in February 1612) with human depravity, and he forms some distinctly curious and interesting views on this. Attempts to categorize him are fruitless: a new study of his work is needed. One must not mistake frenzied condemnation of lust (and other human manifestations) for pure Puritan theology when one is confronted by inspired language. And one must give Southey at least this credit: in calling Adams 'the prose Shakespeare of Puritan theologians' he did draw attention to writing which at its best rises to the level of

Donne's, Andrewes's and Jeremy Taylor's. I should, admittedly contentiously, describe him as a fascinating Church of England man. A man who remained in Anglican orders and who never displayed separatist tendencies, and who was moreover (most probably) sequestered under the Commonwealth, can hardly be called Puritan. He bitterly attacked despoilers of the Church. His attacks on 'profanities' are not more bitter than those of the acknowledgedly Anglican clergy—only better expressed. He defended learning, not something of which the Puritans approved. But let him speak for himself.

THE WHITE DEVIL: OR, THE HYPOCRITE UNCASED
John 12:6.
*This he said, not that he cared for the poor; but because he was a thief, and had the bag, and bare what was put therein.*

THIS SERMON was preached at St Paul's Cross on 7 March 1612. The text quotes John's comment on Judas's motives in asking why Mary, instead of anointing the feet of Jesus with costly ointment, should not have sold it for 'three hundred pence' and given this to the poor. Jesus answered: 'Let her alone: against the day of my burying hath she kept this. For the poor always ye have with you; but me ye have not always.' Judas was of course entrusted with money: hence his 'bag'.

The dramatic vividness of Adams's language in this sermon needs no comment. But it is hard to discover any especially Calvinist theology in it. He is not saying much more than Sanderson—no Puritan—said in the sermon of his given here (though he does glancingly condemn the theatres). His 'white devil' is Judas, to whom he compares those who profess faith and charity but have none in their hearts. It has been suggested that in the passage 'For the second table, you have read ... complains of wrong' Adams implies that 'all things are permissible which are authorised by God, and that this instruction should be communicated direct to the heart of the elect'. This is surely to ignore the message of the sermon, which, although it contains one of the most wholesale (and therefore instructive) condemnations of the abuses which troubled people in James's reign, does not ever state explicitly that even Judas and his like have been selected by God—for damnation.

The matter is less simple. Certainly Adams states that God gave Judas the bag and that he knew what he was doing. But he also remarks that 'A hypocrite is in greatest difficulty to be cured' (implying that cure is possible); and, on the question of usury, says that 'hell-fire shall decide the question'. He also continually exhorts his city-listeners to practise charity not only in the world but also in their hearts. He preached elsewhere: 'If [hell] be metaphorical, as Austin [Augustine] seems elsewhere to intimate, and some modern divines are of mind: and as the gold, pearls and precious stones of the walls streets and gates of the heavenly Jerusalem ... were metaphorical; so likewise it should seem that the fire of hell should also be figurative: And if it be so, it is yet something else, that is much more terrible and intolerable.'

Adams was no Calvinist vulgarian. He was rather in the tradition of the Elizabethan playwrights: fascinated by a reprobate humanity, just as the 'atheist' Marlowe was in his *Dr. Faustus*. Faustus says to Mephistophilis, 'Come, I think hell's a fable'; the reply is, 'Aye, think so still, till experience change thy mind.' Earlier, before making his pact, Faustus has asked Mephistophilis: 'Where are you damned?', to which the latter replies tersely, 'In hell'. 'How comes it then that thou art out of hell?' 'Why,' Mephistophilis blandly answers, 'this is hell, nor am I out of it.'

This was the kind of poetic thinking which interested Adams. There is no evidence that Marlowe believed in Christ's redeeming power (and no evidence that he did not). Adams did. But this belief did not crush the curiosity within his mind—and indeed, why should it have done so? Thus his monopolists, layabouts, crooked lawyers and other rascals are presented as if they were characters from some contemporary play. He is almost as fascinated by their villainy as he is anxious to guide them to know Christ in their hearts as Judas pretended to and did not. But he will not be God's proxy and damn them. He is puzzled when he speaks of two kinds of thieves, of the law broken and 'all this without wrong, for the earth is his . . .' But this God is not the terrible God of Calvin; rather he is inscrutable. In Adams we have faith grafted on to morality—but all swept forward by a spate of inspired prose. 'The world', he said in his dedication of this sermon when he published it in 1615, 'would think I had brought forth a strange child.'

I AM to speak of Judas, a devil by the testimony of our Saviour, —'Have I not chosen you twelve, and one of you is a devil?' John vi. 7,—yet so transformed into a show of sanctimony, that he who was a devil in the knowledge of Christ seemed an angel in the deceived judgment of his fellow-apostles. A devil he was, black within and full of rancour, but white without, and skinned over with hypocrisy; therefore, to use Luther's word, we will call him the 'white devil.' Even here he discovers himself, and makes good this title. Consider the occasion thus:—

Christ was now at supper among his friends, where every one showed him several kindness; among the rest, Mary pours on him a box of ointment. Take a short view of her affection:—(1.) She gave a precious unction, spikenard; Judas valued it at three hundred pence, which (after the best computation) is with us above eight pounds; as if she could not be too prodigal in her love. (2.) She gave him a whole pound, ver. 3: she did not cut him out devotion by piecemeal or remnant, nor serve God by the ounce, but she gave all: for quality, precious; for quantity, the whole pound. Oh that our service to God were answerable! We rather give one ounce to lust, a second to pride, a third to malice, &c., so dividing the whole pound to the devil: she gave all to Christ. (3.) To omit her anointing his feet, and wiping them with the hairs of her head; wherein her humility and zeal met: his feet, as unworthy to touch his head; with her hairs, as if her chief ornament was but good enough to honour Christ withal, the beauty of her head to serve Christ's feet. 'She brake the box,' *tanquam ebria amore*, and this of no worse than alabaster, that Christ might have the last remaining drop: and the whole house was filled with the odour;' at this repines Judas, pretending the poor, for he was 'white;' intending his profit, for he was a 'devil.'

The words contain in them a double censure:—I. Judas's censure of Mary; this repeatingly folded up: εἶπε δὲ τοῦτο, ' he said thus,' with reference to his former words, ver. 5, 'Why was not this,' &c. II. God's censure of Judas: this partly, 1. Negative, 'he cared not for the poor;' to convince his hypocrisy, that roved at the poor, but levelled at his profit; like a ferryman, looking toward charity with his face, rowing toward covetousness with his arms. 2. Affirmative, demonstrating, (1.) His meaning, 'he was a thief;' (2.) His means, 'he had the bag;' (3.) His maintenance, 'he bare what was given, or put therein.'

I. In Judas's censure of Mary, many things are observable, to his shame, our instruction; and these, 1. Some more general; 2. Some more special and personal; all worthy your attention, if there wanted nothing in the deliverance.

1. Observe that St John lays this fault on Judas only; but St Matthew, chap. xxvi. 8, and Mark, chap. xiv. 4, charge the disciples with it, and find them guilty of this repining; and that (in both, ἀγανακτοῦντες) not without indignation. This knot is easily untied: Judas was the ringleader, and his voice was the voice of Jacob, all charitable; but his hands were the hands of Esau, rough and injurious. Judas pleads for the poor; the whole synod likes the motion well, they second it with their verdicts, their words agree; but their spirits differ. Judas hath a further reach: to distil this ointment through the lembic of hypocrisy into his own purse; the apostles mean plainly: Judas was malicious against his Master; they simply thought the poor had more need. So sensible and ample a difference do circumstances put into one and the same action: presumption or weakness, knowledge or ignorance, simplicity or craft, do much aggravate or mitigate an offence. The apostles consent to the circumstance, not to the substance, setting, as it were, their hands to a blank paper: it was in them pity rather than piety; in Judas neither pity nor piety, but plain perfidy, an exorbitant and transcendent sin, that would have brought innocence itself into the same condemnation; thus the aggregation of circumstances is the aggravation of offences. Consider his covetise, fraud, malice, hypocrisy, and you will say his sin was monstrous; *sine modo*, like a mathematical line, *divisibilis in semper divisibilia*,—infinitely divisible. The other apostles receive the infection, but not into so corrupted stomachs, therefore it may make them sick, not kill them: sin they do, but not unto death. It is a true rule even in good works: *Finibus, non officiis, discernendae sunt virtutes a vitiis*,—Virtues are discerned from vices, not by their offices, but by their ends or intents: neither the outward form, no, nor often the event, is a sure rule to measure the action by. The eleven tribes went twice, by God's special word and warrant, against the Benjamites, yet in both assaults received the overthrow. *Cum Pater Filium, Christus corpus, Judas Dominum, res eadem, non causa, non intentio operantis*,—When God gave his Son, Christ gave himself, Judas gave his Master; here was the work, not the same cause nor intention in the workers (Augustine). The same rule holds proportion in offences: here they all sin, the apostles in the imprudence of their censure, Judas in the impudence of his rancour.

I might here, first, lead you into the distinction of sins; secondly, or traverse the indictment with Judas, whereby he accuseth Mary, justifying her action, convincing his slander; thirdly, or discover to you the foulness of rash judgment, which often sets a rankling tooth into virtue's side; often calls charity herself a harlot, and a guilty hand throws the first stone at innocence, John viii. 7.

But that which I fasten on is the power and force of example. Judas, with a false weight, set all the wheels of their tongues agoing: the steward hath begun a health to the poor, and they begin to pledge him round. Authority shows itself in this, to beget a likeness of manners: *Tutum est peccare autoribus illis,*—It is safe sinning after such authors; if the steward say the word, the *fiat* of consent goes round. *Imperio maximus, exemplo major,*—He that is greatest in his government is yet greater in his precedent. A great man's livery is countenance enough to keep drunkenness from the stocks, whoredom from the post, murder and stealth from the gallows: such double sinners shall not escape with single judgments; such leprous and contagious spirits shall answer to the justice of God, not only for their own sins, but for all theirs whom the pattern of their precedency hath induced to the like. To the like, said I? nay, to worse; for if the master drink *ad plenitudinem*, to fulness, the servant will *ad ebrietatem*, to madness; the imitation of good comes, for the most part, short of the pattern, but the imitation of ill exceeds the example. A great man's warrant is like a charm or spell, to keep quick and stirring spirits within the circle of combined mischief, a superior's example is like strong or strange physic, that ever works the servile patients to a likeness of humours, of affections: thus when the mother is a Hittite, and the father an Amorite, the daughter seldom proves an Israelite, Ezek. xvi. 45. *Regis ad exemplum totus componitur orbis,*—Greatness is a copy, which every action, every affection strives to write after. The son of Nebat is never without his commendation following him, 'he made Israel to sin,' 1 Kings xv. 30, and xvi. 15. The imitation of our governors' manners, fashion, vices, is styled obedience: if Augustus Caesar loves poetry, he is nobody that cannot versify; now, saith Horace, 'Scribimus indocti, doctique poemata passim.' When Leo lived, because he loved merry fellows, and stood well-affected to the stage, all Rome swarmed with jugglers, singers, players. To this, I think, was the proverb squared: *Confessor Papa, confessor populus,*—If the Pope be an honest man, so will the people be.

*In vulgus manant exempla regentum* (Cyprian). The common people are like tempered wax, whereon the vicious seal of greatness makes easy impression. It was a custom for young gentlemen in Athens to play on recorders; at length Alcibiades, seeing his blown cheeks in a glass, threw away his pipe, and they all followed him. Our gallants, instead of recorders, embrace scorching lust, staring pride, staggering drunkenness, till their souls are more blown than those Athenians' cheeks. I would some Alcibiades would begin to throw away these vanities, and all the rest would follow him. Thus spreads example, like a stone thrown into a pond, that makes circle to beget circle, till it spread to the banks. Judas's train soon took fire in the suspectless disciples; and Satan's infections shoot through some great star the influence of damnation into the ear of the commonalty. Let the experience hereof make us fearful of examples.

Observe, that no society hath the privilege to be free from a Judas; no, not Christ's college itself: 'I have chosen you twelve, and behold one of you is a devil;' and this no worse man than the steward, put in trust with the bread of the prophets. The synod of the Pharisees, the convent of monks, the consistory of Jesuits, the holy chair at Rome, the sanctified parlour at Amsterdam, is not free from a Judas. Some tares will show that 'the envious man' is not asleep. They hear him preach that 'had the words of eternal life,' John vi. 68; they attend him that could 'feed them with miraculous bread,' ver. 51; they followed him that could 'quiet the seas and control the winds,' Matt. xxvi.: they saw a precedent in whom there was no defect, no default, no sin, no guile; yet, behold, one of them is a hypocrite, an Iscariot, a devil. What! among saints? 'Is Saul among the prophets?' 1 Sam. x. 12. Among the Jews, a wicked publican, a dissolute soldier, was not worth the wondering at: for the publicans, you may judge of their honesty when you always find them coupled with harlots in the Scripture; for the soldiers, (that robbed Christ in jest, and robbed him in earnest,) they were irreligious ethnics; but amongst the sober, chaste, pure, precise Pharisees, to find a man of sin was held uncouth, monstrous. They run from their wits, then, that run from the church because there are Judases. Thus it will be till the great Judge with his fan shall 'purge his floor,' Matt. iii. 12; till the 'angels shall carry the wheat into the barn of glory,' Matt. xiii. 30. Until that day comes, some rubbish will be in the net, some goats amongst the sheep, some with the mark of the beast in the congregation of saints; an Ishmael in the family of Abraham; one without his wedding garment at the marriage-feast; among the disciples a Demas, among the apostles a Judas.—Thus generally.

2.—(1.) Observe: Judas is bold to reprove a lawful, laudable, allowable work: 'he said thus.' I do not read him so peremptory in a just opportunity. He could swallow a gudgeon, though he kecks [vomits] at a fly; he could observe, obey, flatter the compounding Pharisees, and thought he should get more by licking than by biting; but here, because his mouth waters at the money, his teeth rankle the woman's credit, for so I find malignant reprovers styled: *corrodunt, non corrigunt; correptores, immo corruptores*,—they do not mend, but make worse; they bite, they gnaw. Thus was Diogenes surnamed Cynic for his snarling: *conviciorum canis*, the dog of reproaches. Such forget that *monendo plus, quam minando possumus*,—mercies are above menaces. Many of the Jews, whom the thunders of Sinai, terrors of the law, *humanas motura tonitrua mentes*, moved not, John Baptist wins with the songs of Zion. Judas could feign and fawn, and fan the cool wind of flattery on the burning malice of the consulting scribes. Here he is hot, sweats and swells without cause; either he must be unmerciful or over-merciful; either wholly for the reins, or all upon the spur. He hath soft and silken words for his Master's enemies, coarse and rough for his friends; there he is a dumb dog and finds no fault, here he is a barking cur and a true man instead of a thief; he was before an ill mute, and now he is a worse consonant: but as Pierius's ambitious daughters were turned to magpies for correcting the Muses (Ovid. Metam., lib. ii.), so God justly reproves Judas for unjustly reproving Mary. *Qui mittit in altum lapidem, recidit in caput ejus* (Ierom. ad. Rust. Monach.),—A stone thrown up in a rash humour falls on the thrower's head, to teach him more wisdom. He that could come to the Pharisees, (like Martial's parrot, χαίρε, or like Jupiter's priests to Alexander with a *Jove sate*,) commending their piety, which was without mercy, here condemns mercy, which was true piety and pity.

I could here find cause to praise reprehension: if it be reasonable, seasonable, well-grounded for the reprover, well-conditioned for the reproved. I would have no profession more wisely bold than a minister's, for sin is bold, yea, saucy and presumptuous. It is miserable for both, when a bold sinner and a cold priest shall meet; when he that should lift up his voice like a trumpet doth but whisper through a trunk. Many men are dull beasts without a goad, blind Sodomites without a guide, deaf adders and idols without ears, forgetful, like Pharaoh's butler, without memories: our connivance is sinful, our silence baneful, our allowance damnable. Of sin, neither the fathers, factors, nor fautors [patrons] are excusable; nay, the last may be worst, whiles they may, and will not help it, Rom. xiii. 2. Let Rome have the praise without our envy or rivality: *Peccatis Roma patrocinium est*. Sodomy is licensed, sins to come pardoned, drunkenness defended, the stews maintained, perjury commended, treason commanded. As sinful as they think us, and we know ourselves, we would blush at these. *Nihil interest, sceleri an faveas, an illud facias,*—There is little difference between permission and commission, between the toleration and perpetration of the sin: he is an abettor of the evil that may and will not better the evil. *Amici vitia, si feras, facis tua*. Thy unchristian sufferance adopts thy brother's sins for thine own, as children of thy fatherhood. Of so great a progeny is many a sin-favouring magistrate; he begets more bastards in an hour than Hercules did in a night; and, except Christ be his friend, God's sessions will charge him with the keeping of them all. No private man can plead exemption from this duty, for *amicus* is *animi custos*, —he is thy friend that brings thee to a fair and free end. Doth human charity bind thee to reduce thy neighbour's straying beast, and shall not Christianity double thy care to his erring soul? *Cadit asina, et est qui sublevet; perit anima, non est qui recogitet,*—The fallen beast is lifted up, the burdened soul is let sink under her load.

(2.) Observe his devilish disposition, bent and intended to stifle goodness in others, that had utterly choked it in himself. Is the apostle Judas a hinderer of godliness? Surely man hath not a worse neighbour, nor God a worse servant, nor the devil a better factor, than such a one: an Aesop's dog, that because he can eat no hay himself, lies in the manger and will not suffer the horse. He would be an ill porter of heaven-gates, that having no lust to enter himself, will not admit others; as Christ reproved the lawyers, Luke xi. 52. They are fruitless trees that cumber the ground, chap. xiii. 7; cockle and darnel, that hinder the good corn's growth; malicious devils, that plot to bring more partners to their own damnation, as if it were *aliquid socios habuisse doloris,*—some ease to them to have fellows in their misery.

Let me pant out a short complaint against this sin: *dolendum a medico, quod non delendum a medicina,*—we may bewail where we cannot prevail. The good old man must weep, though he cannot drive away the disease of his child with tears. Thou that hinderest others from good works, makest their sins thine, which, I think, thou needest not do, for any scarcity of thine own; whiles thou temptest a man to villany, or withstandest his piety, thou at once pullest his sins and God's curse on thee. For the author sins more than the actor, as appears by God's judgment in paradise, Gen. iii. 14, &c., where three punishments were inflicted on the serpent, as the original plotter; two on the woman, as the immediate procurer; and but one on Adam, as the party seduced. Is it not enough for thee, O Judas, to be a villain thyself, but thou must also cross the piety of others? Hast thou spoiled thyself, and wouldst thou also mar Mary?

(3.) Nay, observe: he would hinder the works of piety through colour of the works of charity, diverting Mary's bounty from Christ to the poor, as if respect to man should take the wall of God's service. Thus he strives to set the two tables of the law at war, one against the other; both which look to God's obedience, as the two cherubims to the mercy-seat, Exod. xxv. 20; and the catholic Christian hath a catholic care. I prefer not the laws of God one to the other: 'one star here differs not from another star in glory.' Yet I know the best distinguisher's caution to the lawyer: 'This is the commandment, and the other is (but) like unto it,' Matt. xxii. 38, 39. Indeed I would not have sacrifice turn mercy out of doors, as Sarah did Hagar; nor the fire of zeal drink up the dew and moisture of charity, as the fire from heaven dried up the water at Elijah's sacrifice, 1 Kings xviii. 38; neither would I that the precise observation of the second table should gild over the monstrous breaches of the first. Yet I have heard divines (reasoning this point) attribute this privilege to the first table above the second: that God never did (I will not say, never could) dispense with these commandments which have himself for their proper and immediate object. For then (say they) he should dispense against himself, or make himself no God, or more. He never gave allowance to any to have another god; another form of worship; the honour of his name he will not give to another; nor suffer the profaner of his holy day to escape unpunished. For the second table, you have read him commanding the brother 'to raise up seed to his brother,' Deut. xxv. 5, notwithstanding the law, 'Thou shalt not commit adultery,' Matt. xii. 24; commanding the Israelites to rob the Egyptians, Exod. xi. 2. without infringing the law of stealth; all this without wrong, for 'the earth is his, and the fulness thereof!' Thou art a father of many children: thou sayest to the younger, 'Sirrah, wear you the coat to-day which your other brother wore yesterday;' who complains of wrong? We are all (or, at least, say we are all) the children of God: have earthly parents a greater privilege than our heavenly? If God then have given dispensation to the second table, not to the first, the observation of which (think you) best pleaseth him?

Let not then, O Judas, charity shoulder out piety; nay, charity will not, cannot; for 'faith worketh by love,' Gal. v. 6. And love never dined in a conscience where faith had not first broken her fast. Faith and love are like a pair of compasses; whilst faith stands perfectly fixed in the centre, which is God, love walks the round, and puts a girdle of mercy about the loins. There may indeed be a show of charity without faith, but there can be no show of faith without charity. Man judgeth by the hand, God by the heart.

Hence our policies in their positive laws lay severe punishments on the actual breaches of the second table, leaving most sins against the first to the hand of the almighty justice. Let man's name be slandered, *currat lex*, 'the law is open,' Acts xix. 38; be God's name dishonoured, blasphemed, there is no punishment but from God's immediate hand. Carnal fornication speeds, though not ever bad enough, yet sometimes worse than spiritual, which is idolatry. Yet this last is *majus adulterium*, the greater adultery; because *non ad alteram mulierem*, 1 Cor. vi. 15, *sed ad alterum Deum*, Hos. ii. 2.—it is not the knitting of the body to another woman, but of the soul to another God. The poor slave is convented to the spiritual court, and meets with a shrewd penance for his incontinence; the rich nobleman, knight, or gentleman, (for Papists are no beggars,) breaks the commissary's cords as easily as Samson the Philistine's withs, and puts an excommunication in his pocket. All is answered: 'Who knows the spirit of man, but the spirit of man?' and, 'He stands or falls to his own master,' Rom. xiv. 4. Yet again, who knows whether bodily stripes may not procure spiritual health, and a seasonable blow to the estate may not save the soul 'in the day of the Lord Jesus?' 1 Cor. v. 5. Often *detrimentum pecuniae et sanitatis; propter bonum animae* (Aquinas), a loss to the purse, or a cross to the corpse, is for the good of the conscience. Let me then complain, are there no laws for atheists, that would scrape out the deep engraven characters of the soul's eternity out of their consciences, and think their souls as vanishing as the spirits of dogs; not contenting themselves to lock up this damned persuasion in their own bowels, but belching out this unsavoury breath to the contagion of others? Witness many an ordinary that this is an ordinary custom; that in despite of the oracles of heaven, the prophets, and the secretaries of nature, the philosophers, would enforce that either there is no God, or such a one as had as good be none: nominal protestants, verbal neuters, real atheists. Are there no laws for image-worshippers, secret friends to Baal, that eat with us, sit with us, play with us, not pray with us, nor for us, unless for our ruins? Yes, the sword of the law is shaken against them: alas, that but only shaken! But either their breasts are invulnerable, or the sword is obtuse, or the strikers troubled with the palsy and numbness in the arms. Are there no laws for blasphemers, common swearers, whose constitutions are so illtempered of the four elements, that they take and possess several seats in them: all earth in their hearts, all water in their stomachs, all air in their brains, and (saith St James) all fire in their tongues, James iii. 6; they have heavy earthen hearts, watery and surfeited stomachs, light, airy, mad brains, fiery and flaming tongues. Are there no laws to compel them on these days, that 'God's house may be filled?' Luke xiv. 23; no power to bring them from the 'puddles to the springs?' Jer. ii. 13; from walking the streets, sporting in the fields, quaffing in taverns, slugging*, wantonising on couches, to watch with Christ 'one hour in his house of prayer?' Matt. xxvi. 40. Why should not such blisters be lanced by the knife of authority, which will else make the whole body of the commonwealth, though not incurable, yet dangerously sick? I may not seem to prescribe, give leave to exhort: *non est meae humilitatis dictare vobis,* &c. (Bernard) It suits not with my mean knowledge to direct you the means, but with my conscience to rub your memories. Oh, let not the pretended equity to men countenance out our neglect of piety to God!

(4.) Lastly, observe his unkindness to Christ. What, Judas, grudge thy Master a little unction! And, which is yet viler, from another's purse! With what detraction, derision, exclamation, wouldest thou have permitted this to thy fellow-servant, that repinest it to thy Master! How hardly had this been derived from thy own estate, that didst not tolerate it from Mary's! What! Thy Master, that honoured thee with Christianity, graced thee with apostleship, trusted thee with stewardship, wilt thou deny him this courtesy, and without thine own cost? Thy Master, Judas, thy Friend, thy God, and yet in a sweeter note, thy Saviour, and canst not endure another's gratuital kindness towards him? Shall he pour forth the best unction of his blood, to bathe and comfort thy body and soul, and thou not allow him a little refection? Hath Christ hungered, thirsted, fainted, sweated, and must he instantly bleed and die, and is he denied a little unction? and dost thou, Judas, grudge it? It had come more tolerably from any mouth: his friend, his follower, his professor, his apostle, his steward! Unkind, unnatural, unjust, unmerciful Judas.

Nay, he terms it no better than waste and a loss: Εἰς τί ἡ ὑτωλεια αὕτη; *Ad quid perditio haec?*—'Why is this waste?' Matt. xxvi. 8. What, lost and given to Jesus! Can there be any waste in the creature's due service to the Creator? No; *pietas est proprietate sumptus facere* (Tertullian)—this is godliness, to be at cost with God: therefore our fathers left behind them *deposita pietatis*, pledges, evidences, sure testimonies of their religion, in honouring Christ with their riches; I mean not those in the days of Popery, but before ever the locusts of the Papal sea made our nation drunk with that enchanted cup. They thought it no waste either *nova construere, aut vetera conservare,*—to build new monuments to Christ's honour, or to better the old ones. We may say of them, as Rome bragged of Augustus Caesar: *Quae invenerunt lateritia, reliquerunt marmorea,*—What they found of brick, they left of marble; in imitation of that precedent in Isaiah, though with honester hearts: 'The bricks are fallen down, but we will build with hewn stones. The sycamores are cut down, but we will change them into cedars,' chap. ix. 10. In those days charity to the church was not counted waste. The people of England, devout like those of Israel, cried one to another, *Afferte*, Bring ye into God's house; till they were stayed with a statute of mortmain, like Moses's prohibition, 'The people bring too much,' Exod. xxxvi. 6. But now they change a letter, and cry, *Auferte*, take away as fast as they gave; and no inhibition of God or Moses, gospel or statute, can restrain their violence, till the alabaster-box be as empty of oil as their own consciences are of grace. We need not stint your devotion, but your devoration; every contribution to God's service is held waste: *Ad quid perditio haec?* Now any required ornament to the church is held waste; but the swallowing down, I say not of ornaments, as things better spared, but of necessary maintenance, tithes, fruits, offerings, are all too little. Gentlemen in these cold countries have very good stomachs; they can devour, and digest too, three or four plump parsonages. In Italy, Spain, and those hot countries, or else nature and experience too lies, a temporal man cannot swallow a morsel or bit of spiritual preferment, but it is reluctant in his stomach, up it comes again. Surely these northern countries, coldly situate, and farther from the tropic, have greater appetites. The Africans think the Spaniards gluttons; the Spaniards think so of the Frenchmen; Frenchmen, and all, think and say so of Englishmen, for they can devour whole churches; and they have fed so liberally, that the poor servitors, (ashamed I am to call them so,) the vicars, have scarce enough left to keep life and soul together: not so much as *sitis et fames et frigora poscunt* (Juvenal, Sat. 14),—the defence of hunger, and thirst, and cold, requires. Your fathers thought many acres of ground well bestowed, you think the tithe of those acres a waste. Oppression hath played the Judas with the church, and because he would prevent the sins incurable by our fulness of bread, hath scarce left us bread to feed upon, Daniel's diet among the lions, or Elias's in the wilderness. I will not censure you in this, ye citizens; let it be your praise, that though you 'dwell in ceiled houses' yourselves, 'you let not God's house lie waste,' Hag. i. 4; yet sometimes it is found that some of you, so careful in the city, are as negligent in the country, where your lands lie; and there the temples are often the ruins of your oppression, *monumenta rapinae*; your poor, undone, blood-sucked tenants, not being able to repair the windows or the leads, to keep out rain or birds. If a levy or taxation would force your benevolence, it comes malevolently from you, with a 'Why is this waste?' Raise a contribution to a lecture, a collection for a fire, an alms to a poor destitute soul, and lightly there is one Judas in the congregation to cry, *Ad quid perditio haec?*—'Why is this waste?' Yet you will say, if Christ stood in need of an unction, though as costly as Mary's, you would not grudge it, nor think it lost. Cozen not yourselves, ye hypocrites; if ye will not do it to his church, to his poor ministers, to his poor members, neither would you to Christ, Matt. xxv. 40; if you clothe not them, neither would you clothe Christ if he stood naked at your doors. Whiles you count that money lost which God's service receiveth of you, you cannot shake away Judas from your shoulders. What would you do, if Christ should charge you, as he did the young man in the gospel, 'Sell all, and give to the poor,' Matt. xix. 21, that think superfluities a waste? *Oh, durus sermo!*—a hard sentence! Indeed, 'a cup of cold water,' Matt. x. 42, is bounty praised and rewarded, but in them that are not able to give more; 'the widow's two mites' are accepted, because all her estate, Luke xxi. 4. If God thought it no waste to give you plenty, even all you have, think it no waste to return him some of his own. Think not the oil waste which you pour into the lamp of the sanctuary, Exod. xxv. 6; think not the bread waste which you cast on the waters of adversity, Eccles. xi. 1; think nothing lost whereof you have feoffed God in trust. But let me teach you soberly to apply this, and tell you what indeed is waste:—

(1.) Our immoderate diet,—indeed not diet, for that contents nature, but surfeit, that overthrows nature,—this is waste. Plain Mr Nabal, 1 Sam. xxv. 36, made a feast like a prince. Dives, Luke xvi., hath no other arms to prove himself a gentleman, but a scutcheon of these three colours: first, he had money in his purse, he was rich; secondly, he had good rags on his back, clothed in purple; thirdly, dainties on his table, he fared deliciously, and that every day: this was a gentleman without heraldry. It was the rule, *ad alimenta, ut ad medicamenta,*—to our meat as to our medicine: man hath the least mouth of all creatures, *malum non imitari, quod sumus*. Therefore it is ill for us not to imitate that which we are; not to be like ourselves. There are many shrewd contentions between the appetite and the purse: the wise man is either a neuter or takes part with his purse. To consume that at one banquet which would keep a poor man with convenient sustenance all his life, this is waste. But, alas! our slavery to epicurism is great in these days: *mancipia serviunt dominis, domini cupiditatibus,*—servants are not more slaves to their masters, than their masters are slaves to lusts. Timocreon's epitaph fits many:—'Multa bibens, et multa vorans, mala plurima dicens,' &c.,—He ate much and drank much, and spake much evil. We sacrifice to our palates as to gods: the rich feast, the poor fast, the dogs dine, the poor pine? *Ad quid perditio haec?*—'Why is this waste?'

(2.) Our unreasonable ebrieties:—'Tenentque / Pocula saepe homines, et inumbrant ora coronis.' They take their fill of wine here, as if they were resolved, with Dives, they should not get a drop of water in hell. Eat, drink, play; *quid aliud sepulchro bovis inscribi poterat?*—what other epitaph could be written on the sepulchre of an ox? *Epulonum crateres, sunt epulonum carceres,* —their bowls are their bolts; there is no bondage like to that of the vintage. The furnace beguiles the oven, the cellar deceives the buttery; we drink away our bread, as if we would put a new petition into the Lord's prayer, and abrogate the old: saying no more, with Christ, 'Give us this day our daily bread,' but, Give us this day our daily drink; *quod non in diem, sed in mensem sufficit,*—which is more than enough for a day, nay, would serve a month. Temperance, the just steward, is put out of office: what place is free from these alehouse recusants, that think better of their drinking-room than Peter thought of Mount Tabor? *Bonum est esse hic,*—'It is good being here,' Matt. xvii. 4, *ubi nec Deus, nec daemon,*—where both God and the devil are fast asleep. It is a question whether it be worse to turn the image of a beast to a god, or the image of God to a beast; if the first be idolatry, the last is impiety. A voluptuous man is a murderer to himself, a covetous man a thief, a malicious a witch, a drunkard a devil; thus to drink away the poor's relief, our own estate: *Ad quid perditio haec?*—'Why is this waste?'

(3.) Our monstrous pride, that turns hospitality into a dumb show: that which fed the belly of hunger now feeds the eye of lust; acres of land are metamorphosed into trunks of apparel; and the soul of charity is transmigrated into the body of bravery: this is waste. We make ourselves the compounds of all nations: we borrow of Spain, Italy, Germany, France, Turkey and all; that death, when he robs an Englishman, robs all countries. Where lies the wealth of England? In three places: on citizens' tables, in usurers' coffers, and upon courtiers' backs. God made all simple, therefore, woe to these compounded fashions! God will one day say, *Hoc non opus meum, nec imago mea est,*—This is none of my workmanship, none of my image. One man wears enough on his back at once to clothe two naked wretches all their lives: *Ad quid*, &c.—'Why is this waste?'

(4.) Our vainglorious buildings, to emulate the skies, which the wise man calls 'the lifting up of our gates too high,' Prov. xvii. 19. Houses built like palaces; tabernacles that, in the master's thought, equal the mansion of heaven; structures to whom is promised eternity, as if the ground they stood on should not be shaken, Heb. xii. 16. Whole towns depopulate to rear up one man's walls; chimneys built in proportion, not one of them so happy as to smoke; brave gates, but never open; sumptuous parlours, for owls and bats to fly in: pride began them, riches finished them, beggary keeps them; for most of them moulder away, as if they were in the dead builder's case, a consumption. Would not a less house, Jeconiah, have served thee for better hospitality?

Jer. xxii. Our fathers lived well under lower roofs; this is waste, and waste indeed, and these worse than the devil. The devil had once some charity in him, to turn stones into bread, Matt. iv. 3; but these men turn bread into stones, a trick beyond the devil: *Ad quid perditio haec?*—'Why is this waste?'

(5.) Our ambitious seeking after great alliance: the 'son of the thistle must match with the cedar's daughter,' 2 Kings xiv. 9. The father tears dear years out of the earth's bowels, and raiseth a bank of usury to set his son upon, and thus mounted, he must not enter save under the noble roof; no cost is spared to ambitious advancement: *Ad quid*, &c.—'Why is this waste?'

Shall I say our upholding of theatres, to the contempt of religion; our maintaining ordinaries, to play away our patrimonies; our four-wheeled porters; our antic fashions; our smoky consumptions; our perfumed putrefaction: *Ad quid perditio haec?* —Why are these wastes? Experience will testify at last that these are wastes indeed; for they waste the body, the blood, the estate, the freedom, the soul itself, and all is lost thus laid out; but what is given (with Mary) to Christ is lost like sown grain, that shall be found again at the harvest of joy.

II. We have heard Judas censuring Mary, let us now hear God censuring Judas:—

1. And that, first, negatively: 'he cared not for the poor.' For the poor he pleads, but himself is the poor he means well to; but let his pretence be what it will, God's witness is true against him: 'he cared not for the poor.'

(1.) Observe: Doth Christ condemn Judas for condemning Mary? Then it appears he doth justify her action; he doth, and that after in express terms: 'Let her alone,' &c., ver. 7. Happy Mary, that hast Jesus to plead for thee! blessed Christians, for whom 'Jesus Christ is an advocate!' 1 John ii. 1. 'He is near me that justifies me; who will contend with me? Behold, the Lord will help me; who is he that can condemn me?' Isa. l. 8, 9. Hence David resigns his protection into the hands of God: 'Judge me, O God, and defend my cause against the unmerciful people,' Ps. xliii. 1. And Paul yet with greater boldness sends a frank defiance and challenge to all the actors and pleaders that ever condemnation had, that they should never have power to condemn him, since Jesus Christ justifies him, Rom. viii. 33. Happy man whose cause God takes in hand to plead! Here is a Judas to accuse us, a Jesus to acquit us; Judas slanders, Jesus clears; wicked men censure, the just God approves; earth judgeth evil what is pronounced good in heaven! Oh, then, do well, though, *fremunt gentes*, great men rage, though perverseness censures, impudence slanders, malice hinders, tyranny persecutes; there is a Jesus that approves: his approbation shall outweigh all their censures; let his Spirit testify within me, though the whole world oppose me.

(2.) Observe: It is the nature of the wicked to have no care of the poor. *Sibi nati, sibi vivunt, sibi moriuntur, sibi damnantur,*— They are all for themselves, they are born to themselves, live to themselves; so let them die for themselves, and go to hell for themselves. The fat bulls of Bashan love 'the lambs from the flock, and the calves from the stall,' &c., 'but think not on the affliction of Joseph,' Amos vi. 4. Your gallant thinks not the distressed, the blind, the lame to be part of his care; it concerns him not. True; and therefore heaven concerns him not. It is infallible truth, if they have no feeling of others' miseries they are no members of Christ, Heb. xiii. 3. Go on now in thy scorn, thou proud royster; admire the fashion and stuff thou wearest, whiles the poor mourn for nakedness; feast royal Dives, while Lazarus can get no crumbs. Apply, Absalom, thy sound, healthful limbs to lust and lewdness, whiles the same blind, maimed, cannot derive a penny from thy purse, though he move his suit in the name of Jesus; thou givest testimony to the world, to thy own conscience, that thou art but a Judas. Why, the poorest and the proudest have, though not *vestem communem*, yet *cutem communem*,—there may be difference in the fleece, there is none in the flesh; yea, perhaps, as the gallant's perfumed body is often the sepulchre to a putrefied soul, so a white, pure, innocent spirit may be shadowed under the broken roof of a maimed corpse. Nay, let me terrify them: 'Not many rich, not many mighty, not many noble are called,' 1 Cor. i. 26. It is Paul's thunder against the flashes of greatness: he says not, 'not any,' but 'not many;' for *servatur Lazarus pauper, sed in sinu Abrahami Divitis* (Aug. in Ps. v),—Lazarus the poor man is saved, but in the bosom of Abraham the rich. It is a good saying of the son of Sirach, 'The affliction of one hour will make the proudest stoop,' Ecclus. xi. 27, sit upon the ground, and forget his former pleasure; a piercing misery will soften your bowels, and let your soul see through the breaches of her prison, in what need distress stands of succour. Then you will be charitable or never, as physicians say of their patients, 'Take whiles they be in pain;' for in health nothing will be wrung out of them. So long as health and prosperity clothe you, you reck not the poor. Nabal looks to his sheep, what cares he for David? If the truth were known, there are many Nabals now, that love their own sheep better than Christ's sheep. Christ's sheep are fain to take coats, their own sheep give coats. Say some that cavil, If we must care for the poor, then for the covetous; for they want what they possess, and are indeed poorest. No; pity not them that pity not themselves, who in despite of God's bounty will be miserable; but pity those whom a fatal distress hath made wretched.

Oh how unfit is it among Christians, that some should surfeit whiles other hunger! 1 Cor. xi. 21; that one should have two coats, and another be naked, yet both one man's servants! Luke iii. 11. Remember that God hath made many his stewards, none his treasurer; he did not mean thou shouldst hoard his blessings, but extend them to his glory. He that is infinitely rich, yet keeps nothing in his own hands, but gives all to his creatures. At his own cost and charges he hath maintained the world almost six thousand years. He will most certainly admit no hoarder into his kingdom; yet, if you will needs love laying up, God hath provided you a coffer: the poor man's hand is Christ's treasury. The besotted worldling hath a greedy mind, to gather goods and keep them; and, lo, his keeping loseth them: for they must have either *finem tuum*, or *finem suum*,—thy end, or their end. Job tarried and his goods went, chap. i.; but the rich man went, and his goods tarried, Luke xii. *Si vestra sunt, tollite vobiscum*,—If they be yours, why do you not take them with you? No, *hic acquiruntur, hic amittuntur*,—here they are gotten, here lost. But, God himself being witness, (nay, he hath passed his word,) what we for his sake give away here, we shall find again hereafter; and the charitable man, dead and buried, is richer under the ground than he was above it. It is a usual song, which the saints now sing in heaven—'That we gave, / That we have.' This riddle poseth the worldling, as the fishermen's did Homer: *Quae cepimus, reliquimus; quae non cepimus, nobiscum portamus*,— What we caught, we left behind us; what we could not catch, we carried with us. So, what we lose, we keep; what we will keep, we shall lose: he that loseth his goods, his lands, his freedom, his life for Christ's sake, shall find it, Matt. x. 39. This is the charitable man's case: all his alms, mercies, relievings are, wisely and without executorship, sown in his lifetime; and the harvest will be so great by that time he gets to heaven, that he shall receive a thousand for one: God is made his debtor, and he is a sure paymaster. Earth hath not riches enough in it to pay him;

his requital shall be in heaven, and there with no less degree of honour than a kingdom.

Judas cares not for the poor. Judas is dead, but this fault of his lives still: the poor had never more need to be cared for; but how? There are two sorts of poor, and our care must be proportionable to their conditions: there are some poor of God's making, some of their own making. Let me say, there are God's poor, and the devil's poor: those the hand of God hath crossed; these have forced necessity on themselves by a dissolute life. The former must be cared for by the compassion of the heart, and charity of the purse: God's poor must have God's alms, a seasonable relief according to thy power; or else the Apostle fearfully and peremptorily concludes against thee, 'The love of God is not in thee,' 1 John iii. 17. If thou canst not find in thy heart to diminish a grain from thy heap, a penny from thy purse, a cut from thy loaf, when Jesus Christ stands at thy door and calls for it; profess what thou wilt, the love of earth hath thrust the love of heaven out of thy conscience. Even Judas himself will pretend charity to these.

For the other poor, who have pulled necessity on themselves with the cords of idleness, riot, or such disordered courses, there is another care to be taken: not to cherish the lazy blood in their veins by abusive mercy; but rather chafe the stunted sinews by correction, relieve them with punishment, and so recover them to the life of obedience. 'The sluggard lusteth,' and hath an empty stomach; he loves sustenance well, but is loath to set his foot on the cold ground for it. The laws' sanction, the good man's function saith, 'If he will not labour, let him not eat,' 2 Thess. iii. 10. For experience telleth that where sloth refuseth the ordinary pains of getting, there lust hunts for it in the unwarranted paths of wickedness; and you shall find, that if ever occasion should put as much power into their hands as idleness hath put villany into their hearts, they will be ready to pilfer your goods, fire your house, cut your throats. I have read of the king of Macedon, descrying two such in his dominions, that *alterum e Macedonia fugere, alterum fugare fecit*,—he made one fly out of his kingdom, and the other drive him. I would our magistrates would follow no worse a precedent; indeed, our laws have taken order for their restraint. Wheresoever the fault is, they are rather multiplied; as if they had been sown at the making of the statute, and now, as from a harvest, they arise ten for one. Surely our laws make good wills, but they have bad luck for executors; their wills are not performed, nor their legacies distributed; I mean the legacies of correction to such children of sloth: *impunitas delicti invitat homines ad malignandum*. Sin's chief encouragement is the want of punishment; favour one, hearten many. It is fit, therefore, that *poena ad paucos, metus ad omnes perveniat,*—penalty be inflicted on some, to strike terror into the rest.

It was St Augustine's censure: *Illicita non prohibere, consensus erroris est* (Epist. 182, ad Bonif.),—Not to restrain evil is to maintain evil. The commonwealth is an instrument, the people are the strings, the magistrate is the musician; let the musician look that the instrument be in tune, the jarring strings ordered, and not play on it to make himself sport, but to please the ears of God. *Doctores*, the ministers of mercy, now can do no good, except *ductores*, the ministers of justice, put to their hands. We can but forbid the corruption of the heart; they must prohibit the wickedness of the hand. Let these poor be cared for that have no care for themselves; runagates, renegades, that will not be ranged (like wandering planets) within the sphere of obedience. 'Yet a little more sleep,' says the sluggard; but *modicum non habet bonum,*—their bunch will swell to a mountain, if it be not prevented and pared down. Care for these, ye magistrates, lest you answer for the subordination of their sins: for the other let all care, that care to be received into the arms of Jesus Christ.

(3.) Observe: Judas cares not for the poor. What! and yet would he for their sakes have drawn comfort from the Son of God? What a hypocrite is this! Could there be so deep dissimulation in an apostle? Yes, in that apostle that was a devil. Lo, still I am haunted with this white devil, hypocrisy; I cannot sail two leagues, but I rush upon this rock: nay, it will encounter, encumber me quite through the voyage of this verse. Judas said, and meant not, there is hypocrisy; he spake for the poor, and hates them, there is hypocrisy; he was a privy thief, a false steward, &c., all this not without hypocrisy. Shall I be rid of this devil at once, and conjure him out of my speech? God give me assistance, and add you patience, and I will spend a little time to uncase this white devil, and strip him of all his borrowed colours.

Of all bodily creatures, man (as he is God's image) is the best; but basely dejected, degenerated, debauched, simply the worst. Of all earthly creatures a wicked man is the worst, of all men a wicked Christian, of all Christians a wicked professor, of all professors a wicked hypocrite, of all hypocrites a wicked, warped, wretched Judas. Take the extraction or quintessence of all corrupted men, and you have a Judas. This then is a Judas: a man degenerate, a Christian corrupted, a professor putrefied, a gilded hypocrite, a white-skinned devil. I profess I am sparingly affected to this point, and would fain shift my hands of this monster, and not encounter him; for it is not to fight with the unicorns of Assyria, nor the bulls of Samaria, nor the beasts of Ephesus,—neither absolute atheists, nor dissolute Christians, nor resolute ruffians, the horns of whose rapine and malice are no less manifest than malignant, but at once imminent in their threats, and eminent in their appearance,—but to set upon a beast, that hath with the heart of a leopard, the face of a man, of a good man, of the best man; a star placed high in the orb of the church, though swooped down with the dragon's tail, because not fixed; a darling in the mother's lap, blessed with the church's indulgence, yet a bastard; a brother of the fraternity, trusted sometimes with the church's stock, yet no brother, but a broker of treacheries, a broacher of falsehoods. I would willingly save this labour, but that the necessity of my text overrules my disposition.

I know these times are so shameless and impudent, that many strip off the white, and keep the devil; wicked they are, and without show of the contrary. Men are so far from giving house-room to the substance of religion, that they admit not an out-room for the show; so backward to put on Christ, that they will not accept of his livery; who are short of Agrippa, Acts xxvi. 28, scarce persuaded to seem Christians, not at all to be. These will not drink hearty draughts of the waters of life, nay, scarce vouchsafe, like the dogs that run by Nilus, to give a lap at Jacob's well; unless it be some, as they report, that frequent the sign of it, to be drunk. They salute not Christ at the cross, nor bid him good-morrow in the temple, but go blustering by, as if some serious business had put haste into their feet, and God was not worthy to be stayed and spoken withal. If this be a riddle, shew me the day shall not expound it by a demonstrative experience. For these I may say, I would to God they might seem holy, and frequent the places where sanctimony is taught; but the devil is a nimble, running, cunning fencer, that strikes on both hands, *duplici ictu*, and would have men either *non sanctos, aut non parum sanctos*,—not holy, or not a little holy, in their own opinion, and outward ostentation: either no fire of devotion on the earth, or that that is, in the top of the chimney. That subtle 'winnower' persuades men that they are all chaff and no wheat, or all wheat and no chaff; and would keep the soul either lank with ignorance, or rank with insolence: let me therefore woo you, win you to reject both these extremes, between which your hearts lie, as the grain betwixt both the millstones.

Shall I speak plainly? You are sick at London of one disease (I speak to you settled citizens, not extravagants,) and we in the country of another. A sermon against hypocrisy in most places of the country is like phlebotomy to a consumption, the spilling of innocent blood. Our sicknesses are cold palsies and shaking agues; yours in the city are hotter diseases, the burning fevers of fiery zeal, the inflammations and imposthumes of hypocrisy. We have the frosts, and you have the lightnings; most of us profess too little, and some of you profess too much, unless your courses were more answerable. I would willingly be in none of your bosoms; only I must speak of Judas. His hypocrisy was vile in three respects:—

*First*, He might have been sound. I make no question but he heard his Master preach, and preached himself, that God's request is the heart: so Christ schools the Samaritan woman, John iv.; so prescribed the scribe, 'Thou shalt love the Lord with all thy heart,' &c., Mark xii. 30. *Corde*, Judas, with the heart, which thou reservest like an equivocating Jesuit; nay, *toto corde*, for it is not *tutum*, except it be *totum*, with the whole heart, which thou never stoodest to divide, but gavest it wholly to him that wholly killed it, thy Master's enemy, and none of thy friend, the devil. Thou heardest thy Master, thy friend, thy God, denounce many a fearful, fatal, final woe against the Pharisees: *hac appellatione, et ob hanc causam*,—under this title, and for this cause; hypocrites, and because hypocrites. As if his woes were but words, and his words wind, empty and airy menaces, without intention of hurt, or extension of a revengeful arm, behold thou art a hypocrite; thou art therefore the worse because thou mightest be better.

*Secondly*, He seemed sound. *Spem vultu simulat, premit altum corde dolorem*, nay, *dolum* rather; craft rather than grief, unless he grieved that out of his cunning there was so little coming, so small prize or booty; yet, like a subtle gamester, he keeps his countenance, though the dice do not favour him. And as Fabius Maximus told Scipio, preparing for Africa, concerning

Syphax, *Fraus fidem in parvis sibi perstruit, ut cum operae pretium sit, cum magna mercede fallat* (Liv. Annal., lib. xiii); Judas creeps into trust by his justice in trifles, that he might more securely cheat for a fit advantage. Without pretence of fidelity, how got he the stewardship? Perhaps if need required, he spared not his own purse in Christ's service; but he meant to put it to usury: he carried not the purse, but to pay himself for his pains, thus *jactura in loco, res quaestuosissima*,—a seasonable damage is a reasonable vantage; in this then his vileness is more execrable, that he seemed good.

If it were possible, the devil was then worse than himself, when he came into Samuel's mantle. Jezebel's paint made her more ugly. If ever you take a fox in a lamb's skin, hang him up, for he is the worst of the generation. A Gibeonite in his old shoes, a Seminary in his haircloth, a ruffian in the robes of a Jacobine, fly like the plague. These are so much the worse devils, as they would be holy devils; true traitors, that would fight against God with his own weapons; and by being out-of-cry religious, run themselves out of breath to do the church a mischief.

*Thirdly*, he would seem thus to his Master, yet knew in his heart that his Master knew his heart; therefore his hypocrisy is the worst. Had he been an alien to the commonwealth of Israel, and never seen more of God than the eye of nature had discovered, (yet, says even the heathen, ἔχει Θεὸς ἔκδικον ὄμμα (Homer), —God hath a revenging eye,) then no marvel if his eyes had been so blind as to think Christ blind also, and that he, which made the eye, had not an eye to see withal; but he saw that Son of David give sight to so many sons of Adam, casually blind, to one naturally and born blind, John ix. 32,—*miraculum inauditum*, a wonder of wonders,—and shall Judas think to put out his eye that gave them all eyes? Oh, incredible, insensible, invincible ignorance!

You see his hypocrisy: methinks even the sight of it is disuasion forcible enough, and it should be needless to give any other reason than the discovery; yet whiles many censure it in Judas, they condemn it not in themselves, and either think they have it not, or not in such measure. Surely, we may be no Judases, yet hypocrites; and who will totally clear himself? Let me tell thee, if thou doest, thou art the worst hypocrite, and but for thee we had not such need to complain. He that clears himself from all sin is the most sinner, and he that says he hath not sinned in hypocrisy is the rankest hypocrite; but I do admit a distinction. All the sons of Adam are infected with this contamination, some more, some less. Here is the difference, all have hypocrisy, but hypocrisy hath some: *aliud habere peccatum, aliud haberi a peccato,*—it is one thing for thee to possess sin, another thing for sin to possess thee. All have the same corruption, not the same eruption; in a word, all are not hypocrites, yet who hath not sinned in hypocrisy? Do not then send your eyes, like Dinah's, gadding abroad, forgetting your own business at home; strain not courtesy with these banquets, having good meat carved thee, to lay it liberally upon another man's trencher; be not sick of this plague and conceal it, or call it by another name. Hypocrisy is hypocrisy, whatsoever you call it; and as it hath learned to leave no sins naked, so I hope it hath not forgot to clothe itself. It hath as many names as Garnet had, and more Protean shapes than the Seminaries: the white devil is in this a true devil; *multorum nominum, non boni nominis,*—of many names, but never a good one. The vileness of this white devil appears in six respects:—

First, It is the worst of sins, because it keeps all sins: they are made sure and secure by hypocrisy. Indeed some vices are quartermasters with it, and some sovereigns over it, for hypocrisy is but another sin's pander; except to content some affected guest, we could never yield to this filthy Herodias, Matt. xiv. 9. It is made a stalking-horse for covetousness. Under long prayers many a Pharisee devours the poor, houses, goods, and all. It is a complexion for lust, who, were she not painted over with a religious show, would appear as loathsome to the world as she is indeed. It is a sepulchre of rotten impostures, which would stink like a putrefied corpse, if hypocrisy were not their cover. It is a mask for treason, whose shopful of poisons, pistols, daggers, gunpowder-trains, would easily be spied out, had hypocrisy left them barefaced. Treachery under this vizard thrusts into court revels, nay, court counsels, and holds the torch to the sports, nay, the books to serious consultations; deviseth, adviseth, plots with those that provide best for the commonwealth. Thus are all sins beholden to hypocrisy; she maintains them at her own proper cost and charges.

Secondly, It is the worst of sins, because it counterfeits all virtues. He that counterfeits the king's coin is liable to death; if hypocrisy find not death, and *mortem sine morte*, death without death, for counterfeiting the King of heaven's seal-manual of grace, it speeds better than it merits. Vice is made virtue's ape in a hypocrite's practice. If he see Chusi run, this Ahimaaz will outrun him; he mends his pace, but not his path; the good man goes slower, but will be at heaven before him. Thus thriftiness in a saint is counterfeited by niggardliness in a hypocrite; be thou charitable, behold he is bountiful, but not except thou may behold him; his vainglorious pride shall emulate thy liberality; thou art good to the poor, he will be better to the rich; he follows the religious man afar off, as Peter did Christ, but when he comes to the cross he will deny him. Thus hypocrisy can put blood into your cheeks, (like the *Aliptae*,) and better your colours, but you may be sick in your consciences, and almost dead at the heart, and *non est medicamen in hortis*,—there is no medicine in this drugster's shop can cure you.

Thirdly, A hypocrite is a kind of honest atheist; for his own good is his god, his heaven is upon earth, and that not the peace of his conscience, Phil. iv. 7, or that kingdom of heaven which may be in a soul living on earth, Rom. xiv. 17, but the secure peace of a worldly estate. He stands in awe of no judge but man's eye; that he observes with as great respect as David did the eyes of God. If man takes notice, he cares not, yet laughs at him for that notice, and kills his soul by that laughter: so Pygmalion-like, he dotes on his own carved and painted piece; and perhaps dies Zeuxis's death, who, painting an old woman, and looking merrily on her, brake out into a laughter that killed him. If the world do not praise his doings, he is ready to challenge it, as the Jews God, 'Wherefore have we fasted, and thou seest it not?' Isa. lviii. 3. He crosseth Christ's precept, Matt. vi. 3, the left hand must not be privy to the right hand's charity. He dares not trust God with a penny, except before a whole congregation of witnesses, lest perhaps God should deny the receipt.

Fourthly, A hypocrite is hated of all, both God and man: the world hates thee, Judas, because thou retainest to Christ; Christ hates the more, because thou but only retainest, and doest no faithful service. The world cannot abide thee, thou hypocrite, because thou professest godliness; God can worse abide thee, because thou doest no more than profess it. It had been yet some policy, on the loss of the world's favour, to keep God's; or if lost God's, to have yet kept in with the world. Thou art not thy own friend, to make them both thy enemies. Miserable man, destitute of both refuges, shut out both from God's and the world's doors! Neither God nor the devil loves thee; thou hast been true to none of them both, and yet most false of all to thyself. So this white devil, Judas, that for the Pharisees' sake betrayed his Master, and for the devil's sake betrayed himself, was in the end rejected of Pharisees and Master; and like a ball, tossed by the rackets of contempt and shame, bandied from the Pharisees to Christ, from Christ to the Pharisees, from wall to wall, till he fell into the devil's hazard, not resting like a stone, till he came to his centre, εἰς τὸν τόπον τὸν ἴδιον, 'into his own place,' Acts i.25. Purposeth he to go to Christ? His own conscience gives him a repulsive answer: No, 'thou hast betrayed the innocent blood,' Matt. xxvii.4. Goes he to the chief priests and elders? Cold comfort: 'What is that to us? see thou to that.' Thus your ambo-dexter proves at last ambo-sinister; he that plays so long on both hands hath no hand to help himself withal. This is the hypocrite's misery; because he wears God's livery, the world will not be his mother; because his heart, habit, service, is sin-wedded, God will not be his father. He hath lost earth, for heaven's sake, and heaven for earth's sake, and may complain, with Rebekah's fear of her two sons, 'Why should I be deprived of you both in one day?' Gen. xxvii.45; or as sorrowful Jacob expostulated for his, 'Me have you robbed of my children: Joseph is not, and Simeon is not, and will you take Benjamin also? all these things are against me,' Gen. xlii.36. This may be the hypocrite's mournful dirge: 'My hypocrisy hath robbed me of all my comforts: my Creator is lost, my Redeemer will not own me; and will ye take away (my beloved Benjamin) the world also? all these things are against me.' Thus an open sinner is in better case than a dissembling saint. There are few that seem worse to others than they are in themselves; yet I have both read and heard of some that have, with broken hearts and mourning bowels, sorrowed for themselves as if they had been reprobates, and not spared so to proclaim themselves, when yet their estate was good to Godward, though they knew it not. Perhaps their wickedness and ill-life hath been grievous, but their repentance is gracious: I may call these black saints. The hypocrite is neat and curious in his religious outside, but the linings of his conscience are as 'filthy and polluted rags,' Isa. lxiv. 6: then I say still, a black saint is better than a white devil.

Fifthly, Hypocrisy is like the devil, for he is a perfect hypocrite; so he began, with our first parents, to put out his apparent horns in paradise: *Non moriemini,*—'Ye shall not die,' Gen. iii.4; yet he knew this would kill them. A hypocrite then is the child of the devil, and (quoth Time, the midwife) as like the father as it may possibly look. He is 'the father of lies,' John viii. 44; and there is no liar like the hypocrite, for, as Peter said to Ananias, 'Thou hast not lied to men, but to God,' Acts v. 4. Nay, the hypocrite is his eldest son. Now, the privilege of primogeniture\* by the law was to have 'a double portion,' Deut. xxi. 17; wretched hypocrite in this eldership! Matt. xxiv. 51. Satan is called a prince, and thus stands his monarchy, or rather anarchy: the devil is king; the hypocrite his eldest son. 2 Chron. xxi. 3, Job xvi. 11, Eph. ii. 2; the usurer his younger; atheists are his viceroys in his several provinces, for his dominion is beyond the Turk's for limits; epicures are his nobles; persecutors his magistrates; heretics his ministers; traitors his executors; sin his law; the wicked his subjects; tyranny his government; hell his court; and damnation his wages. Of all these the hypocrite is his eldest son.

Lastly, A hypocrite is in greatest difficulty to be cured. Why should the minister administer physic to him that is perfectly sound? Matt. ix. 12, 13; or why should Christ give his blood to the righteous? Well may he be hurt and swell, swell and rankle, rankle and fester, fester and die, that will not bewray his disease, lest he betray his credit. 'Stultorum incurata pudor malus ulcera celat' (Horace). A man of great profession, little devotion, is like a body so repugnantly composed, that he hath a hot liver and a cold stomach: that which heats the stomach, overheats the liver; that which cools the liver, overcools the stomach: so, exhortations that warm his conscience, inflame his outward zeal; dissuasives to cool his hypocrisy, freeze his devotion. He hath a flushing in his face, as if he had eaten fire; zeal burns in his tongue, but come near this glowworm, and he is cold, dark, squalid. Summer sweats in his face, winter freezeth in his conscience. March, many forwards in his words, December in his actions; pepper is not more hot in the tongue's end, nor more cold at heart; and, to borrow the words of our worthy divine and best characterer, we think him a saint, he thinks himself an angel, flatterers make him a god, God knows him a devil.

This is the white devil: you will not think how glad I am that I am rid of him. Let him go; yet I must not let you go till I have persuaded you to hate this monster, to abhor this devil. Alas! how forget we, in these days, to build up the cedar work of piety, and learn only to paint it over with vermilion! We white and parget the walls of our profession, but the rubbish and cobwebs of sin hang in the corners of our consciences. Take heed; a Bible under your arms will not excuse a false conscience in your bosoms; think not you fathom the substance when you embrace the shadow: so the fox seeing sweetmeats in the vial, licked the glass, and thought he had the thing; the ignorant sick man eats up the physicians' bill, instead of the receipt contained in it. It is not a day of seven, nay, any hour of seven days, the grudged parting with an alms to a fire, the conjuring of a *Paternoster*, (for the heart only prays,) or once a-year renewing thy acquaintance with God in the sacrament, can privilege or keep impune thy injuries, usuries, perjuries, frauds, slanders, oppressions, lusts, blasphemies. Beware of this white devil, lest your portion be with them in hell whose society you would defy on earth. 'God shall smite thee, thou painted wall,' Acts xxiii. 3, and wash off thy vermilion dye with the rivers of brimstone. You have read of some that heard Christ preach in their pulpits, feasted at his communion-table, cast out devils in his name, yet not admitted: whiles they wrought miracles, not good works, cast out devils from others, not sins from themselves, Luke xiii. 26, &c., they miss of entrance. Go then and solace thyself in thy bodily devotion: thou hearest, readest, receivest, relievest; where is thy conscience, thy heart, thy spirit? God asks not for thy livery, but thy service; he knows none by their confession, but by their conversation. Your looks are the objects of strangers' eyes, your lives of your neighbours', your consciences of your own, all of God's. Do not Ixion-like take a cloud for Juno, a mist for presumption of a sound and solid faith: more can say the creed than understand it, than practise it. Go into your grounds in the dead of winter, and of two naked and destitute trees you know not which is the sound, which the doted; the summer will give Christ's mark: 'By their fruits ye shall know them,' Matt. vii. 20.

I speak not to discourage your zeal, but to hearten it, but to better it. Your zeal goes through the world, ye worthy citizens. Who builds hospitals? the city. Who is liberal to the distressed gospel? the city. Who is ever faithful to the crown? the city. Beloved, your works are good; oh, do not lose their reward through hypocrisy! I am not bitter, but charitable; I would fain put you into the chariot of grace with Elias, and only wish you to put off this mantle, 2 Kings ii. 13. Oh that it lay in my power to prevail with your affections as well as your judgments! You lose all your goodness, if your hearts be not right; the ostentation of man shall meet with the detestation of God. You lose your attention now, if your zeal be in your eye, more than heart. You lose your prayers, if when the ground hath your knee, the world hath your conscience: as if you had two gods—one for Sundays, another for work-days; one for the church, another for the change. You lose your charity, whiles you give glozingly, illiberally, too late: not a window you have erected but must bear your names. But some of you rob Peter to pay Paul: take tenths from the church, and give not the poor the twentieths of them. It is not seasonable, nor reasonable charity, to undo whole towns by your usuries, enclosures, oppressions, impropriations; and for a kind of expiation, to give three or four the yearly pension of twenty marks: an almshouse is not so big as a village, nor thy superfluity whereout thou givest, like their necessity whereout thou extortest; he is but poorly charitable that, having made a hundred beggars, relieves two. You lose all your credit of piety, whiles you lose your integrity; your solemn censuring, mourning for the time's evil, whiles yourselves are the evil cause thereof; your counterfeit sorrow for the sins of your youth, whiles the sins of your age are worse; your casting salt and brine of reproof at others' faults, whiles your own hearts are most unseasoned: all these artificial whitings are but thrifty leasings, sick healths, bitter sweets, and more pleasing deaths. Cast then away this bane of religion, hypocrisy; this candle with a great wick and no tallow, that often goes out quickly, never without stench; this fair, flattering, white devil. How well have we bestowed this pains, I in speaking, you in hearing, if this devil be cast out of your consciences, out of your conversations! It will leave some prints behind it in the best, but bless not yourselves in it, and God shall bless you from it. Amen.

2. The affirmative part of God's censure stands next to our speech: describing, (1.) His meaning; (2.) His means; (3.) His maintenance:—

(1.) His meaning was to be a thief, and shark [swindle] for himself, though his pretence pleaded *forma pauperis*, in the behalf of the poor. He might, perhaps, stand upon his honesty, and rather than lose his credit, strive to purge himself from his suspectless neighbours; but there need no further jury pass upon him, God hath given testimony, and his witness is beyond exception: 'Judas is a thief.' A thief! who saw him steal? He that hath now condemned him for his pains. Indeed the world did not so take him, his reputation was good enough, John xiii.29; yet he was a thief, a crafty, cunning, cheating thief.

There are two sorts of thieves: public ones, that either with a violent hand take away the passengers' money, or rob the house at midnight; whose church is the highway: there they pray, not to God, but on men;* their dwelling, like Cain's, very unsure; they stand upon thorns, whiles they stand upon certainties. Their refuge is a wood; the instrument of their vocation, a sword: of these some are land-thieves, some sea-thieves; all rove on the sea of this world, and most commonly suffer shipwreck, some in the deep, some on a hill. I will say little of these, as not pertinent to my text, but leave them to the jury; and speak of thieves like Judas, secret robbers, that do more mischief, with less present danger to themselves. These ride in the open streets, whiles the other lurk in close woods. And to reason, for these private thieves are in greater hazard of damnation: the grave exhortations of the judge, the serious counsel of the assistant minister, together with the sight of present death, and the necessity of an instant account with God, work strongly on a public thief's conscience; all which the private thief neither hath, nor hath need of in the general thought. The public thief wants but apprehension, but this private thief needs discovery; for they lie close as treason, dig low like pioneers, and though they be as familiar with us as familiars, they seem stranger than the Indians.

To define this manner of thieves: A private thief is he that without danger of law robs his neighbour; that sets a good face on the matter, and hath some profession to countenance it: a fair cloak hides a damnable fraud; a trade, a profession, a mystery, like a Rome-hearted Protestant, hides this devilish Seminary under his roof without suspicion. To say truth, most of our professions (thanks to ill professors) are so confounded with sins, as if there went but a pair of shears between them; nay, they can scarce be distinguished: you shall not easily discern between a hot, furious professor and a hypocrite, between a covetous man and a thief, between a courtier and an aspirer, between a gallant and a swearer, between an officer and a bribe-taker, between a servitor and a parasite, between farmers and poor-grinders, between gentlemen and pleasure-lovers, between great men and madmen, between a tradesman and a fraudsman, between a moneyed man and a usurer, between a usurer and the devil. In many arts, the more skilful the more ill-full; for now-a-days *armis potentior astus*, fraud goes beyond force: this makes lawyers richer than soldiers, usurers than lawyers, the devil than all. The old lion, saith the fable, when his nimble days were over, and he could no longer prey by violence, kept his den with a feigned sickness; the suspectless beasts, drawn thither to a dutiful visitation, thus became his prey: *cunning* served his turn when his *canning* failed. The world, whiles it was young, was simple, honest, plain-dealing: gentlemen then delved in the ground, now the soles of their feet must not touch it; then they drank water, now wine will not serve, except to drunkenness; then they kept sheep, now they scorn to wear the wool; then Jacob returned the money in the sack's mouth, Gen. xliii. 12, now we are ready to steal it, and put it in. Plain-dealing is dead, and, what we most lament, it died without issue. Virtue had but a short reign, and was soon deposed; all the examples of sin in the Bible are newly acted over again, and the interest exceeds the principal, the counterpart the original. The apostasy now holds us in our manner: we leave God for man, for Mammon. Once, *orbis ingemuit factum se videns Arianum,*—the world groaned, seeing itself made an Arian; it may now groan worse, *factum se videns Machiavellum,*—seeing itself made a Machiavel: *nisi Deus opem praestat, deperire mundum restat.* Grieved Devotion had never more cause to sing—

'Mundum dolens circumivi:
Fidem undique quaesivi,' &c.;—

'The world I compassed about,
Faith and honesty to find out;
But country, city, court, and all,
Thrust poor devotion to the wall:
The lawyer, courtier, merchant, clown,
Have beaten poor Devotion down;
All wound her, till, for lack of breath,
Fainting Devotion bleeds to death.'

But I am to deal with none but thieves, and those private ones; and because Judas is the precedent, I will begin with him that is most like him, according to the proverb which the Grecians had of Philo Judaeus: Ἢ Πλάτων Φιλονίζει, ἢ Φίλων Πλατωνίζει, *Aut Plato Philonem sequitur, aut Platonem Philo,*—Either Plato followed Philo, or Philo imitated Plato. Let me only change the names: Either Judas played the Pope, or the Pope plays the Judas. This is the most subtle thief in the world, and robs all Christendom under a good colour. Who can say he hath a black eye or a light finger? for experience hath taught him, that *cui pellis leonina non sufficit, vulpina est assuenda,*—

> 'When the lion's skin cannot threat,
> The fox's skin can cheat.'

Pope Alexander was a beast, that having entered like a fox, he must needs reign like a lion; worthy he was to die like a dog: for *vis consilii expers, mole ruit sua,*—power without policy is like a piece without powder. Many a Pope sings that common ballad of hell, *Ingenio perii, qui miser ipse meo* (Ovid),—

> 'Wit, whither wilt thou? Woe is me;
> My wit hath wrought my misery.'

To say truth, their religion is nothing in the circumstance but craft; and policy maintains their hierarchy, as Judas's subtlety made him rich. Judas was put in trust with a great deal of the devil's business; yet not more than the Pope. Judas pretended the poor, and robbed them; and doth not the Pope, think you? Are there no alms-boxes rifled and emptied into the Pope's treasury? Our fathers say that the poor gave Peter-pence to the Pope, but our grandfathers cannot tell us that the Pope gave Caesar-pence to the poor. Did not he sit in the holy chair, as Augustus Caesar in his imperial throne, and cause the whole Christian world to be taxed? Luke ii. 1. And what! Did they freely give it? No; a taxation forced it. What right, then, had the Pope to it? Just as much as Judas had to his Master's money. Was he not then a thief? Yet what need a rich man be a thief? The Pope is rich, and needs must, for his comings-in be great: he hath rent out of heaven, rent out of hell, rent out of purgatory; but more sacks come to his mill out of purgatory than out of hell and heaven too; and for his tolling let the world judge: therefore saith Bishop Jewel, 'He would be content to lose hell and heaven too, to save his purgatory.' Some by pardons he prevents from hell; some by indulgences he lifts up to heaven; and infinite by ransoms from purgatory: not a jot without money. *Cruces, altaria, Christum,*—He sells Christ's cross, Christ's blood, Christ's self, all for money. Nay, he hath rent from the very stews, a hell above-ground, and swells his coffers by the sins of the people; he suffers a price to be set on damnation, and maintains lust to go to law for her own: gives whoredom a toleration under his seal, that lust, the son of idleness, hath free access to liberty, the daughter of pride.

Judas was a great statesman in the devil's commonwealth, for he bore four main offices;—either he begged them shamefully, or he bought them bribingly, or else Beelzebub saw desert in him, and gave him them gratis for his good parts, for Judas was his white boy;—he was a hypocrite, a thief, a traitor, a murderer. Yet the Pope shall vie offices with him, and win the game too for plurality. The Pope sits in the holy chair, yet a devil: perjury, sodomy, sorcery, homicide, parricide, patricide, treason, murder, &c., are essential things to the new Papacy. He is not content to be steward, but he must be vicar, nay, indeed, Lord himself; for what can Christ do, and the Pope cannot do? Judas was nobody to him. He hath stolen Truth's garment, and put it on Error's back, turning poor Truth naked out of doors; he hath altered the primitive institutions, and adulterated God's sacred laws, maintaining *vagas libidines*; he steals the hearts of subjects from their sovereigns, by stealing fidelity from the hearts of subjects, and would steal the crown from the king's head;—and all under the shadow of religion. This is a thief, a notable, a notorious thief; but let him go: I hope he is known well enough, and every true man will bless himself out of his way.

I come to ourselves: there are many kinds of private thieves in both the houses of Israel and Aaron; *in foro et choro*,—in change and chancel, commonwealth and church. I can tax no man's person; if I could, I would abhor it, or were worthy to be abhorred: the sins of our times are the thieves I would arraign, testify against, condemn, have executed; the persons I would have 'saved in the day of the Lord.'

[1.] If there be any magistrates (into whose mouths God hath put the determination of doubts, and the distribution of right into their hands) that suffer popularity, partiality, passion, to rule, overrule their judgments, these are private thieves; they rob the poor man of his just cause and equity's relief, and no law can touch them for it. Thus may causes go, not according to right, but friendship; as Themistocles's boy could say, 'As I will, the whole senate will: for as I will, my mother wills; as my mother wills, my father wills; as my father wills, the whole senate will.' Thus as a groom of a chamber, a secretary of the closet, or a porter of the gate will, the cause must go. This is horrible theft, though not arraignable: hence a knot is found in a bulrush; delay shifts off the day of hearing; a good paint is set on a foul pasteboard; circumstances are shuffled from the bar; the sun of truth is clouded; the poor confident plaintiff goes home undone; his moans, his groans are vented up to heaven; the just

God sees and suffers it, but he will one day judge that judge. Who can indict this thief? What law may pass on him? What jury can find him? What judge can fine him? None on earth; there is a bar he shall not escape. If there be any such, as I trust there is not, they are thieves.

[2.] If there be any lawyer that takes fees on both hands, one to speak, another to hold his peace, (as Demosthenes answered his bragging fellow-lawyer,) this is a thief, though the law doth not call him so. A mercenary tongue, and a money-spelled conscience, that undertakes the defence of things known to his own heart to be unjust, is only proper to a thief. He robs both sides: the adverse part in pleading against the truth, his own client in drawing him on to his further damage. If this be not, as the Roman complained, *latrocinium in foro*, thievery in the hall, there is none. Happy Westminster-hall, if thou wert freed from this kind of cutpurses! If no plummets, except of unreasonable weight, can set the wheels of their tongues agoing, and then if a golden addition can make the hammer strike to our pleasure; if they keep their ears and mouths shut, till their purses be full, and will not understand a cause till they feel it; if they shuffle difficulties into plainness, and trip up the law's heels with tricks; if they, surgeon-like, keep the client's disease from healing till he hath no more money for salve: then, to speak in their own language, *Noverint universi*, 'Be it known to all men by these presents,' that these are thieves; though I could wish rather, that *noverint ipsi*, they would know it themselves, and reform it.

[3.] If there be any officer that walks with unwashen hands, —I mean, with the foul fingers of bribery,—he is a thief: be the matter penal or capital, if a bribe can pick justice's lock, and plead innocent, or for itself, being nocent, and prevail, this is theft. Theft? Who is robbed? The giver? Doth not the freedom of his will transfer a right of the gift to the receiver? No; for it is not a voluntary or willing will; but as a man gives his purse to the over-mastering thief, rather than venture his life, so this his bribe, rather than endanger his cause. Shall I say, the thief hath as much right to the purse as the officer to the bribe; and they are both, though not equally palpable, yet equally culpable thieves. Is the giver innocent, or nocent? Innocent, and shall not innocence have her right without a bribe? Nocent, and shall gold conceal his fault or cancel his punishment? Dost thou not know whether, and wilt thou blind thyself beforehand with a bribe? for bribes are like dust thrown in the eyes of justice, that she cannot without pain look on the sunshine of truth. Though a second to thyself receive them, wife or friend, by thy allowance, they are but stolen goods, coals of fire put in the roof of thy house: 'for fire shall devour the houses of bribes,' Job xv. 34. And there have been many houses built, (by report,) the first stone of whose foundation was hewn out of the quarry of bribery. These are thieves.

[4.] There is thievery too among tradesmen: and who would think it? Many, they say, rob us, but we rob none; yes, but they think that *verba lactis* will countenance *fraudem in factis,—* smooth words will smother rough deeds. This web of theft is many ways woven in a shop or warehouse, but three especially:—

*First*, By a false weight, and no true measure, whose content or extent is not justifiable by law, Deut. xxv. 13; or the cunning conveyances in weighing or meting, such as cheat the buyer. Are not these pretty tricks to pick men's purses? The French word hath well expressed them; they are legerdemains. Now had I not as good lose my purse on Salisbury plain as in London Exchange? Is my loss the less, because violence forbears, and craft picks my purse? The highway thief is not greater abomination to God than the shop-thief, Prov. xi. 1; and for man, the last is more dangerous: the other we knowingly fly, but this laughs us in the face whiles he robs us.

*Secondly*, By insufficient wares, which yet, with a dark window and an impudent tongue, will appear good to the buyer's eye and ear too. Sophistry is now fled from the schools into shops; from disputation to merchandising. He is a silly tradesman that cannot sophisticate his wares, as well as he hath done his conscience; and wear his tongue with protestations barer than trees in autumn, the head of old age, or the livings of churchmen. Oaths indeed smell too rank of infidelity; marry, we are Protestants, and protest away our souls: there is no other way to put off bad wares, and put up good moneys. Are not these thieves?

*Thirdly*, By playing, or rather preying, upon men's necessities: they must have the commodity, therefore set the dice on them; *vox latronis*, the advantage taken of a man's necessity is a trick beyond Judas. Thou shouldest rather be like Job, 'a foot to lame necessity,' chap. xxix. 15, and not take away his crutch. Or perhaps God hath put more wit into thy brains than his, thou seest further into the bargain, and therefore takest opportunity to abuse his plainness: thou servest thyself in gain, not him in love; thou mayest, and laugh at the law, but there is a law thou hast transgressed, that, without Jesus Christ, shall condemn thee to hell.

Go now, applaud yourselves, ye sons of fraud, that eagle-eyed scrupulosity cannot find you faulty, nor the lion-handed law touch you; please yourselves in your security. You practise belike behind the hangings, and come not on the public stage of injury; yet you are not free from spectators: *testante Numine, homine, daemone*,—God, men, angels, devils, shall witness against you. *Ex cordibus, ex codicibus*,—By your hearts, by your books God shall judge you. Injury is often in the one, perjury in the other; the great Justice will not put it up: they shall be convicted thieves.

[5.] There are thieves crept into the church too; or rather they encroach on the church: for ministers cannot now play the thieves with their livings, they have nothing left to steal; but there are secret Judases can make shift to do it. *Difficilis magni custodia census*. The eagles flock to a carcase, and thieves hanker about rich doors; at the dispersion of church livings, they cried as the Babylonians, 'To the spoil, to the spoil.' The church was once rich, but it was *diebus illis*, in the golden time, when honesty went in good clothes, and ostentation durst not give religion the checkmate; now they plead prescription, and prove them their own by long possession. I do not tax all those for private thieves that hold in their hands lands and possessions that were once the church's, but those that withhold such as are due to churchmen. Their estates were once taken away by more than God's mere sufferance, for a just punishment for their idleness, idolatry, and lusts: sure there is some Achanism in the camp of the Levites, that makes this plague-sore run still; there are some disobedient and fugitive Jonahs that thus totter our ship. I complain not that *claustra* are turned into *castra*; abbeys into gentlemen's houses; places of monition, to places of munition; but that men rob *aram Dominicam*, God's house, to furnish *haram domesticam*, their own houses. This is theft, and sacrilegious theft; a succession of theft: for the fingers of the sons are now heavier than the loins of their fathers; those were *improbi Papistae*, wicked Papists, and these are *improbi rapistae*, ungodly robbers.

This is a monstrous theft, and so exceeding all thefts, as *non nisi in Deum fieri potest* (Augustine),—it can be committed against none but God. When Scipio robbed the temple of Tholossa, there was not a man that carried away any of the gold who ever prospered after it; and, I pray you, tell me how many have thrived with the goods of the church? They go from man to man without rest, like the ark among the Philistines, 1 Sam.v., which was removed from Ashdod to Gath, from Gath to Ekron, as if it could find no place to rest in, but vexed the people that kept it, till it returned to its old seat in Israel. Oftentimes these goods, left by gentlemen to their heirs, prove gangrenes to their whole estates; and 'house is joined to house,' Isa.v.8, so fast, God's house to their own, that the fire which begins at the one consumes the other: as the eagle, that stole a piece of meat from the altar, carried a coal with it that set her nest on fire. I am persuaded many a house of blood in England had stood at this hour, had not the forced springs of impropriations turned their foundation to a quagmire. In all your knowledge, think but on a church-robber's heir that ever thrived to the third generation. Yet, alas! horror to my bones, and shame to my speech! there are not wanting among ourselves that give encouragement to these thieves: and without question, many a man, so well otherwise disposed, would have been reclaimed from this sin but for their distinctions of competencies. I appeal to their consciences, there is not a humorist living that in heart thinks so, or would forbear their reproof, were he not well provided for. These are the foxes, that content not themselves to steal the grapes, but they must forage the vine, Cant.ii.25: thus yet still is 'God's house made a den of thieves,' Matt.xxi.13. Without envy or partiality they are thieves.

[6.] There is more store of thieves yet: covetous landlords, that stretch their rents on the tenter-hooks of an evil conscience, and swell their coffers by undoing their poor tenants. These sit close, and stare the law in the face, yet, by their leave, they are thieves. I do not deny the improvement of old rents, so it be done with old minds,—I mean, our forefather's charity,—but with the devil, to set right upon the pinnacles, and pitch so high a price of our lands that it strains the tenants' heart-blood to reach it, is theft, and killing theft. What all their immoderate toil, broken sleeps, sore labours can get, with a miserable diet to themselves, not being able to spare a morsel of bread to others, is a prey to the landlords' rapine: this is to rob their estates, grind their faces, suck their bloods. These are thieves.

[7.] Engrossers; that hoard up commodities, and by stopping their community raise the price: these are thieves. Many blockhouses in the city, monopolies in the court, garners in the country, can testify there are now such thieves abroad. We complain of a dearth; sure the heavens are too merciful to us that are so unmerciful one towards another. Scarcity comes without God's sending: who brings it then? Even the devil and his brokers, engrossing misers. The commonwealth may often blow her nails, unless she sit by an engrosser's fire: her limbs may be faint with hunger, unless she buy grain at an engrosser's price. I confess this is a sin which the law takes notice of, but not in the full nature, as theft. The pick-purse, in my opinion, doth not so much hurt as this general robber; for they rob millions. These do not, with Joseph, buy up the superfluity of plenty to prevent a dearth, but hoard up the store of plenty to procure a dearth: rebels to God, trespassers to nature, thieves to the commonwealth. If these were apprehended and punished, neither city nor country should complain as they do. Meantime the people's curse is upon them, and I doubt not but God's plague will follow it, if repentance turn it not away: till when, they are private thieves.

[8.] Enclosers; that pretend a distinction of possessions, a preservation of woods, indeed to make better and broader their own territories, and to steal from the poor commons: these are horrible thieves. The poor man's beast is his maintenance, his substance, his life; to take food from his beast, is to take the beast's food from his belly: so he that encloseth commons is a monstrous thief, for he steals away the poor man's living and life; hence many a cottager, nay, perhaps farmer, is fain (as the Indians do to devils) to sacrifice to the lord of the soil a yearly bribe for a *ne noceat*. For though the law forbids such enclosures, yet *quod fieri non debet, factum valet*,—when they are once ditched in, say the law what it will, I see no throwing out. Force bears out what fraud hath borne in. Let them never open their mouths to plead the commonwealth's benefit; they intend it as much as Judas did when he spake for the poor. No, they are thieves, the bane of the common good, the surfeit of the land, the scourge of the poor; good only to themselves, and that in opinion only, for they do it 'to dwell alone,' Isa.v.8: and they dwell alone indeed, for neither God nor good angel keeps them company; and for a good conscience, it cannot get through their quicksets. These are the thieves, though they have enclosed their theft, to keep the law out and their wickedness in: yet the day shall come their lands shall be thrown out, their lives thrown out, and their souls thrown out; their lands out of their possessions, their lives out of their bodies, their souls out of heaven, except repentance and restitution prevail with the great Judge for their pardon. Meantime they are thieves.

[9.] Many taphouse-keepers, taverners, victuallers, which the provident care of our worthy magistrates hath now done well to restrain; if at least this Hydra's heads do not multiply. I do not speak to annihilate the profession: they may be honest men, and doubtless some are, which live in this rank; but if many of them should not chop away a good conscience for money, drunkenness should never be so welcome to their doors. The dissolute wretch sits there securely, and buys his own sickness with a great expense, which would preserve the health of his poor wife and children at home, that lamentably moan for bread whiles he lavisheth all in drink. Thus the pot robs him of his wits, he robs himself of grace, and the victualler robs him of his money. This theft might yet be borne, but the commonwealth is here robbed too. Drunkenness makes so quick riddance of the ale that this raiseth the price of malt, and the good sale of malt raiseth the price of barley: thus is the land distressed, the poor's bread is dissolved into the drunkard's cup, the markets are hoisted up. If the poor cannot reach the price, the maltmaster will; he can utter it to the taphouse, and the taphouse is sure of her old friend, drunkenness. Thus theft sits close in a drinking-room, and robs all that sail into that coast. I confess they are (most of them) bound to suffer no drunkenness in their houses, yet they secretly acknowledge that if it were not for drunkenness, they might shut up their doors, as utterly unable to pay their rents. These are thieves.

[10.] Flatterers, that eat like moths into liberal men's coats, —the bane of greatness,—are thieves, not to be forgotten in this catalogue. These rob many a great man of his goodness, and make him rob the commonwealth of her happiness. Doth his lord want money? He puts into his head such fines to be levied, such grounds enclosed, such rents improved. Be his maintainer's courses never so foul, either he furthers them or he smothers them: sin hath not a more impudent bawd, nor his master a more impious thief, nor the commonwealth a more sucking horse-leech. He would raise himself by his great one, and cannot contrive it but by the ruin of others. He robs the flattered of his goods, of his grace, of his time, of his freedom, of his soul: is not this a thief? *Beneficia, veneficia,*—All their good is poison. They are *dominis arrisores, reipublicae arrosores,*—their masters' spaniels, the commonwealth's wolves. Put them in your *Paternoster*, let them never come in your creed: pray for them, but trust them no more than thieves.

[11.] There is another nest of thieves more in this city, brokers and breakers. I conjoin them in my description for the likeness of their condition: brokers, that will upon a good pawn lend money to a devil, whose extortion, by report, is monstrous, and such as to find in men is improbable, in Christians impossible; the very vermin of the earth. Indeed man had a poor beginning; we are the sons of Adam, Adam of dust, dust of deformity, deformity of nothing, yet made by God; but these are bred, like monsters, of the corruption of nature and wicked manners, and carry the devil's cognisance. For breakers, such as necessity compels to it I censure not; if they desire with all their hearts to satisfy the utmost farthing, and cannot, God will then accept votal restitution for total restitution, that which is affected for that which is effected, the will for the deed: and in those, debt is not (as the vulgar speech is) deadly sin; a sore it may be, no sin. But they that with a purpose of deceit get goods into their hands in trust, and then without need hide their heads, are thieves; for the intent to steal in their minds directed their injurious hands. The law arraigns them not, the judgment-seat of God shall not acquit them. These steal more quickly and with more security than a highway robber, who all his lifetime is in perpetual danger. It is but passing their words, allowing a good price, conveying home the wares, and on a sudden dive under the waters; a close concealment shall save them five hundred pound in a thousand. They live upon others' sweat, fare richly upon others' meat; and the debtor is often made a gentleman, when the creditor is made a beggar.

Such false Gibeonites enrich scriveners: their unfaithfulness hath banished all trust and fidelity. Time was, that *Noverint universi* was unborn, the lawyer himself knew not what an obligation meant. Security stood on no other legs but promises, and those were so sound that they never failed their burden; but Time, adulterating with the harlot Fraud, begot a brood of *Noverints*: and but for these shackles, debt would often show credit a light pair of heels. Therefore, now, *plus creditur annulis quam animis* (Seneca),—there is more faith given to men's seals than to their souls. 'Owe nothing but love,' saith the Apostle, Rom. xiii. 8; all owe this, but few pay it: or if they do, it is cracked money, not current in God's exchequer; for our love is dissimulation, and our charity is not cold, but dead. But these bankrupts, of both wealth and honesty, owe all things but love, and more than ever they mean to pay, though you give them time till doomsday. These are thieves.

[12.] The twelfth and last sort of thieves (to make up the just dozen) are the usurers. This is a private thief like Judas, and for the bag like Judas, which he steals from Christ like Judas, or rather from Christians, that have more need, and therefore worse than Judas. This is a man made out of wax: his *Paternoster* is a pawn; his creed is the condition of this obligation; his religion is all religation, a binding of others to himself, of himself to the devil: for look how far any of the former thieves have ventured to hell, the usurer goes a foot further by the standard. The poet exclaims against this sin—'Hinc usura vorax, avidumque, in tempore foenus,' &c.; describing in that one line the names and nature of usury. *Foenus, quasi foetus*. It is a teeming thing, ever with child, pregnant, and multiplying. Money is an unfruitful thing by nature, made only for commutation; it is a preternatural thing it should engender money; this is *monstrosus partus*, a prodigious birth. *Usura, quasi propter usum rei*. The nature of it is wholly devouring: their money to necessity is like cold water to a hot ague, that for a time refresheth, but prolongs the disease. The usurer is like the worm we call the timber-worm, (*Teredo*,) which is wonderful soft to touch, but hath teeth so hard that it eats timber; but the usurer eats timber and stones too. The prophet hedgeth it in between bribery and extortion: 'In thee have they taken gifts to shed blood: thou hast taken usury and increase, and thou hast greedily gained of thy neighbours by extortion, and hast forgotten me, saith the Lord. Therefore I have smitten my hands at thy dishonest gain,' &c., Ezek. xxii. 12, 13. You hear God's opinion of it. Beware this dishonest gain; take heed lest this casting your money into a bank cast not up a bank against you; when you have found out the fairest pretexts for it, God's justice shall strike off all: 'Let no man deceive you with vain words: for such things God's wrath will fall on the children of disobedience,' Eph. v. 6. Infinite colours, mitigations, evasions, distinctions are invented, to countenance on earth heaven-exploded usury: God shall then frustrate all, when he pours his wrath on the naked conscience. God saith, 'Thou shalt not take usury:' go now study paintings, excuses, apologies, dispute the matter with God; hell-fire shall decide the question. 'I have no other trade to live on but usury.' Only the devil first made usury a trade. But can this plea in a thief, 'I have no other trade to live on but stealing,' protect and secure him from the gallows?

The usurer then is a thief; nay, a double thief, as the old Roman law censured them, that charged the thief with restitution double, the usurer with fourfold; concluding him a double thief. Thieves steal sometimes, usurers always. Thieves steal for necessity, usurers without need. The usurer wounds deeper with a piece of paper than the robber with a sword. Many a young gentleman, newly broke out of the cage of wardship, or blessed with the first sunshine of his one-and-twenty, goes from the vigilance of a restraining governor into the tempting hand of a merciless usurer, as if he came out of God's blessing into the warm sun. Many a man, that comes to his lands ere he comes to his wits, or experience of their villany, is so let blood in his estate by usury, that he never proves his own man again.

Either prodigality, or penury, or dissembled riches, borrow on usury. To rack the poor with overpulls, all but devils hold monstrous. To lend the prodigal is wicked enough, for it feeds his issue with ill-humours, and puts *stibium* into his broth, who was erst sick of the vomiting disease, and could not digest his father's ill-gotten patrimony. For the rich that dissemble poverty, to borrow on usury,—'For there is that maketh himself poor, and hath great riches,'Prov.xiii.7,—they do it either to defeat creditors or to avoid taxation and subsidies, or some such sinister respects. The gentleman that borroweth on usury, by racking his rents makes his tenants pay his usury. The farmer so borrowing, by enhancing his corn makes the poor pay his usury. The tradesman raiseth his wares, that the buyer must pay his usury. I will not tax every borrower: it is lawful to suffer injury, though not to offer it; and it is no sin for the true man to give his purse to the thief, when he cannot choose. To redeem his lands, liberty, life, he may (I suppose) give interest; but not for mere gain only which he may get by that wicked money, lest he encourage the usurer, for a receiver upholds a thief. This is the cutpurse, whose death is the more grievous because he is reprieved till the last sessions: a gibbet is built in hell for him, and all the gold in the world cannot purchase a pardon. I know there is mercy in Christ's blood to any repentant and believing sinner, but, excepted Zaccheus, show me the usurer that repents; for as humility is the repentance of pride, and abstinence the repentance of surfeit, so is restitution the repentance of usury. He that restores not repents not his usury; and then *non remittitur peccatum, nisi restituatur ablatum* (Augustine),—the sin is retained, till the gains of usury be restored. This is *durus sermo, sed verus sermo*,—a hard saying, but true. 'Then we may give all.' Do, if they be so gotten: *Dabit Deus meliora, majora, plura*,— God will give better things, God will give greater things, God will give more things; as the prophet to Amaziah, 2 Chron. xxv. 9, 'The Lord is able to give thee more than this.'

Thus I have discovered by occasion of Judas some privy thieves: if without thanks, yet not without conscience; if without profit, yet not without purpose of profit. Indeed these are the sins which I vowed with myself to reprove; not that others have not done it, or not done it better than I, from this place. I acknowledge both freely; yet could I not pass this secret thief, Judas, without discovering his companions, or, as it were, breaking open the knot of thieves, which under allowed pretences are arrant cutpurses to the commonwealth. How to punish, how to restrain, I meddle not: it is enough to discharge my conscience, that I have endeavoured to make the sins hateful to the trespassers, to the trespassed: *Deus tam faciat commodum, quam fecit accommodum*,—God make it as prevalent as I am sure it is pertinent!

(2.) and (3.) Give me leave, yet ere I leave, to speak a word of the bag: first, his means; and, secondly, his maintenance. I will join them together; a fit and a fat booty makes a thief. Judas hath got the bag, and the bag hath got Judas; he could not carry it, but he must make it light enough for his carriage: he empties it into his own coffer, as many stewards rise by their good lord and master's fall. Judas means to be a thief, and Satan means to fit him with a booty; for after he had once wrought journey-work with the devil, he shall not want work, and a subject to work on. I will limit my remaining speech to these three heads: —First, The difficulty, to bear the bag, and not to be covetous. Secondly, The usual incidency of the bag to the worst men. Thirdly, The progress of sin; only faint not in this last act.

[1.] It is hard to bear the bag, and not to be covetous. Judas is bursar, and he shuts himself into his pouch: the more he hath, the more he covets. The apostles, that wanted money, are not so having: Judas hath the bag, and yet he must have more, or he will filch it. So impossible is it that these outward things should satisfy the heart of man. *Soli habent omnia, qui habent habentem omnia*,—They alone possess all things that possess the possessor of all things. The nature of true content is to fill all the chinks of our desires, as the wax doth the seal. None can do this but God, for (as it is well observed) the world is round, man's heart three-cornered: a globe can never fill a triangle, but one part will be still empty; only the blessed Trinity can fill these three corners of man's heart. I confess the bag is a thing much reckoned of, and makes men much reckoned of; for *pecuniae obediunt omnia*,—all things make obeisance to money. *Et qui ex divitiis tam magni fiunt, non miror si divitias tam magni faciant*, —they may admire money whom money makes admired. Such is the plague and dropsy the bag brings to the mind, that the more covetousness drinks down, the thirstier it is. This is a true drunkard: *dum absorbet vinum, absorbetur a vino*,—he drinks down his wealth, and his wealth drinks down him. *Qui tenet marsupium, tenetur a marsupio* (Ambrose),—He holds his purse fast, but not so fast as his purse holds him: the strings of his bag tie his heart faster than he ties the strings of his bag. He is a jailer to his jailer, a prisoner to his prisoner, he jails up his gold in the prison of his coffer, his gold jails up him in the prison of covetousness; thus *dum vult esse praedo, fit praeda* (Augustine), —whiles he would come to a prey, he becomes a prey. The devil gets his heart, as the crab the oyster: the oyster lies gaping for air on the sands, the crab chops in her claw, and so devoureth it; whiles the covetous gapes for money, the devil thrusts in his hairy and cloven foot, I mean his baits of temptation, and chokes the conscience.

Thus the bag never comes alone, but brings with it cares, saith Christ, Matt. xiii. 22; snares, saith Paul, 1 Tim. vi. 9. It is better to be without riches than, like Judas, conjured into the circle of his bag: his heaven is among his bags; in the sight of them he applauds himself against all censures, revilings, curses. It had profited some to have wanted the bag; and this the wicked (waked) consciences confess dying: wishing to be without riches, so they were without sins; yea, even those their riches have procured. It is none of God's least favours, that wealth comes not trolling in upon us; for many of us, if our estate were better to the world, would be worse to God. The poor labourer hath not time to luxuriate: he trusts to God to bless his endeavours, and so rests content; but the bag commonly makes a man either *prodigum* or *avarum*, a prodigal man or a prodigious man; for *avarus monstrum*, the covetous man is a monster. How many wretches hath this bag drowned, as they swam over the sea of this world, and kept them from the shore of bliss! Be proud then of your bag, ye Judases: when God's bailiff, Death, shall come with a *habeas corpus*, what shall become of your bag? or rather of yourselves for your bag? Your bag will be found, but yourselves lost. It will be one day said of you, as great as the bag hath made you, as the poet sung of Achilles (Ovid):—

'Iam cinis est, et de tam magno restat Achille,
Nescio quid, parvam quod non bene compleat urnam;'—

'A great man living holds much ground: the brim
Of his days fill'd, how little ground holds him!
Great in command, large in land, in gold richer:
His quiet ashes, now, scarce fill a pitcher.'

Can your bag commute any penance in hell? or can you by a fine answer your faults in the star-chamber of heaven? No; Judas and his bag too are perished, Acts viii. 20. As he gave religion the bag for the world, so the world gave him the bag, and turned him a-begging in that miserable country where all the bags in the world cannot purchase 'a drop of water to cool his tongue,' Luke xvi. 24. Thus are the covetous Judas and his bag well met.

[2.] The bag is most usually given to the worst men: of the apostles, he that was to betray Christ is made his steward. Goods are in themselves good: *Ne putentur mala, dantur et bonis; ne putentur summa bona, dantur et malis* (Augustine),—Lest they should be thought not good, they are given to good men; lest they should be thought too good, they are given to evil men. Doubtless some rich men are in heaven, and some poor out; because some rich in the purse are poor in the spirit, and some poor in purse are proud in spirit: and it is not the bag, but the mind, which condemns a man; for the bag is more easily contemned than the mind conquered. Therefore foolish Crates, to throw away his money into the sea,—*Ego mergam te, ne mergar a te*, I will drown thee, lest thou drown me,—since wealth well-employed comforts ourselves, relieves others, and brings us, as it were, the speedier way to heaven, and perhaps to a greater portion of glory; but for the most part, the rich are enemies to goodness, and the poor friends. Lazarus, the poor man, was in Abraham's bosom, and it was Dives that went to hell: the rich, and not the poor.

Search the Scriptures, consult all authors, and who are they that have sailed through the world in the tallest vessels: and you shall meet loaden with the bag, Cains, Nimrods, Hams, Ishmaels,

Esaus, Sauls, Ahabs, Labans, Nabals, Demases, Judases, devils, the slime of nature, the worst of men, and as bad as the best of devils. What do men cast to swine and dogs, but draff and carrion? What else are the riches that God gives to the wicked men? Himself is pleased to call them by these names. If they were excellent things, they should never be cast on those God hates ('I have hated Esau') and means to condemn. There is no privilege, then, in the bag to keep thee from being a Judas; nay, therefore thou art most likely, and thereby made most likely, to be a Judas. Who hath so much beauty as Absalom? who so much honour as Nebuchadnezzar? who so much wealth as Nabal? who the bag but Judas?

Surely God is wise in all his ways; he knows what he does: Judas shall hence bag up for himself the greater damnation. It is then no argument of God's favour to be his purse-bearer; no more than it was a sign that Christ loved Judas above the other apostles because he made him his steward: he gave the rest grace, and him the bag; which sped best? The outward things are the scatterings of his mercies, like the gleaning after the vintage: the full crop goes to his children. Ishmael shall have wealth, but Isaac the inheritance; Esau his pleasures, but Jacob goes away with blessing. God bestows favours upon some, but they are angry favours; they are in themselves *bona*, goods, and from God, *dona*, gifts,—for he is not only a living God, Heb. ix. 14, but a giving God, James i. 17,—but to the receivers, banes. The Israelites had better have wanted their quails, than eaten them with such sauce. Judas had better been without the bag, than have had the bag, and the devil with it.

I would have no man make his riches an argument of God's disfavour and his own dereliction; no, but rather of comfort, if he can find his affections ready to part with them at Christ's calling. I never was in your bosoms: how many of you lay up this resolution in your closet among your bags? how many resolve, said I, nay, perform this? You cannot want opportunity in these days. I would wish you to try your hearts, that you may secure your consciences of freedom from this Judasm: oh, how few Good-riches there be in these days! But one apostle goes to hell, and he is the richest. Make then your riches a means to help you to heaven; whither you can have no direct and ready way, till you have gotten the moon beneath your feet (Rev. xii. 1; I mean the world. Lay up your bag in the bosom of charity, and your treasure in the lap of Christ, and then the bag shall not hinder, but further your flight to heaven.

[3.] Observe how Judas runs through sin, from one wickedness to another, without stay: from covetousness to hypocrisy, from hypocrisy to theft, from theft to treason, from treason to murder; for since he could not get the ointment bestowed on Christ, he means to get Christ himself, Matt. xxvi. 14, 15; and to this purpose goes instantly to the elders and priests with a *Quid dabitis*, &c. He values the ointment at three hundred pence, and Christ at but thirty; as if he was worth no more than the interest-money, ten in the hundred: and herein he makes his own price, for they gave him his asking. He betrays Jesus Christ a man, Jesus Christ his Master, Jesus Christ his Maker; as if he would destroy his Saviour, and mar his Maker.

Thus he runs from sin to sin, and needs he must, for he that the devil drives feels no lead at his heels. Godliness creeps to heaven, but wickedness runs to hell. Many Parliament-Protestants go but a statute pace, yet look to come to heaven; but, without more haste, it is like to be when the Pharisees come out of hell. But *facilis descensus Averni*; were you blinder than superstition, you may find the way to hell. It is but slipping down a hill, and hell stands at the bottom; this is the cause that Judas runs so fast.

I have read of one Ruffus, that upon his shield painted God on the one side, and the devil on the other, with this motto: *Si tu me nolis, iste rogitat,*—If thou, O God, wilt none of me, here is one will. Either God must take him suddenly, or he will run quick to the devil. The gallant gallops in riot; the epicure reels a drunken pace; the lustful scorns to be behind, he runs from the fire of lust to the fire of hell, as the fondly impatient fish leaps out of the boiling pan into the burning flame. The swearer is there ere he be aware, for he goes by his tongue; the covetous rides post, for he is carried on the back of Mammon; the usurer sits still in his chair or the chimney-corner, lame of the gout, and can but halt, yet he will be at hell as soon as the best runner of them all.

Usury is a coach, and the devil is driver; needs must he go whom the devil drives. He is drawn to hell in pomp, by two coach-horses, wild spirits, with wings on their heels, swifter than Pegasus or Mercury—Covetousness and Infidelity. What makes him put money to use but covetousness. What makes him so wretchedly covetous but want of faith? Thus he is hurried to hell in ease, state, triumph. If any be worthy to bear the usurer company, let it be the rioter; though they be of contrary dispositions, yet in this journey fitly and accordantly met: for the usurer commonly hath money, but no coach, and the prodigal gallant hath a coach, but no money. If they want more company, let them take in the cheater; for he waits upon both these, and may perhaps fail of the like opportunity.

Thus because the ways to hell are full of green, smooth, soft, and tempting pleasures, infinite run apace with Judas, till they come to 'their own place.' But heaven's way is harsh and ascending, and the 'gate narrow.' Indeed, the city of glory is capacious and roomy: 'In my Father's house there are many mansions,' saith Christ, John xiv.2. It is *domus speciosa, et domus spatiosa*, —not either scant of beauty, or pent of room. But the gate hath two properties: it is low, strait, and requires of the enterers a stooping, a stripping.

*Low.* Pride is so stiff that many a gallant cannot enter: you have few women with the topgallant headtires get here, they cannot stoop low enough; few proud in and of their offices, that have eaten a stake and cannot stoop; few sons of pride, so starched and laced up that they cannot without pain salute a friend; a wonderful scarcity of over-precise, over-dissolute, factious humorists, for they are so high in their own conceits that they cannot stoop to this low gate. The insolent, haughty, well-opinioned of themselves cannot be admitted, for 'not humbled to this day,' Jer.xliv.10. This low gate and a high state do not accord. Wretched fools, that rather refuse the glory within, than stoop for entrance! as if a soldier should refuse the honour of knighthood because he must kneel to receive it.

*Strait*, or narrow. As they must stoop that enter this low gate, so they must strip that enter this strait gate. No make-bates\* get in, they are too full of tales and lies. God, by word of mouth, excludes them: 'Into it shall enter no unclean thing, or that worketh abomination or lies,' Rev.xxi.27. Few litigious neighbours, they have so many suits, contentions, *nisi-priuses* on their backs, that they cannot get in. Some lawyers may enter, if they be not overladen with fees. You have few courtiers taken into this court, by reason there is no coach-way to it, the gate is too narrow. No officers, that are big with bribes. Not an encloser; he hath too much of the poor commons in his belly. The usurer hath no hope; for, besides his bags, he hath too much wax and paper about him. The citizen hopes well; but a false measure sticks so cross in his mouth that he cannot thrust in his head. The gentleman makes no question, and there is great possibility, if two things do not cross him—a bundle of racked rents, or a kennel of lusts and sports. The plain man is likely, if his ignorance can but find the gate. Husbandmen were in great possibility, but for the hoarding of corn and hoising of markets. Tradesmen, if they would not swear good credit into their bad wares, might be admitted. Ministers may enter without doubt or hindrance, if they be as poor in their spirits as they are in their purses. But impropriators have such huge barns full of church grains in their bellies, that they are too great. Let all these take the physic of repentance, to abate their swollen souls, or there will be no entrance.

You hear how difficult the way is to heaven, how easy to hell; how fast sin runs, how slowly godliness creeps; what should you then do, but 'strive to enter in at the narrow gate?' which you shall the better do if you lighten yourselves of your bags. Oh, do not, Judas-like, for the bag, sell your honesty, conscience, heaven! The bag is a continent to money, and the world is a continent to the bag; and they shall all perish, 'Meat for the belly, and the belly for meat,'—gold for the purse, and the purse for gold,—'but God shall destroy them both,' 1 Cor. vi. 13. Trust not then a wealthy bag, nor a wealthy man, nor the wealthy world; all will fail: but trust in God, whose 'mercy endureth for ever.' The time shall come that

> 'Deus erit pro numine,
> Cum mundus sit pro nomine,
> Cum homo pro nemine;'—

God shall be God when the world shall be no world, man no man; or at least no man, no world of our expectation, or of ability to help us. To God, then, our only help, be all praise, power, and glory, now and for ever! Amen.

NOTES

p. 257. *slugging*: loitering, idling.

p. 273. *primogeniture*: the legal procedure by which the inheritance passes to the eldest son.

p. 276. *there they pray, not to God, but on men*: there is a concealed pun in 'pray': *prey*.

p. 294. *make-bates*: people who cause quarrelling: trouble-makers.

## Lancelot Andrewes

LANCELOT ANDREWES was born in London in 1555. In 1565 he was admitted to Merchant Taylors' School, where he was recognized as a brilliant pupil by the distinguished pioneer educationalist Richard Mulcaster, then headmaster. He later went to Pembroke College, Cambridge, of which he was elected Fellow in 1576; he took orders in 1580. He acquired, it is said largely by private study, a prodigious learning: fifteen languages and a knowledge of Christianity probably unequalled in his time. His lectures were well known in and around Cambridge even before he was ordained: 'he was scarce reputed a pretender to learning and pietry then in Cambridge, who made not himself a disciple of Mr. Andrewes . . .', it was later observed. Andrewes became Master of Pembroke in 1589. It is important, in view of Andrewes's controversial role in the history of the Church of England, that he was regarded by at least one intelligent observer as one whose opinions were compounded of 'a certain mixture of all sides of religions', which, he however added, were pleasing to some Catholics. But there is no doubt that at this time he had strong Puritan connections. And in the late 1580s he had success in dissuading recusants from their position. He opposed the Calvinistic 1595 Lambeth Articles of Archbishop Whitgift (whose chaplain he had been from 1586). Characteristically, he believed them to be too rigid. As vicar of St Giles, Cripplegate and prebendary of St Paul's his sermons had become famous by the early 1590s. Yet already his greatest interest lay in pastoral duties and in attempts to settle the doubts of various kinds of dissidents; even in those difficult times, this was his chief intention. When he was hasty with a certain imprisoned Puritan, who complained of it, he acknowledged that he had behaved in an unchristian manner.

Despite his great reputation, Andrewes, a gentle man, was singularly unambitious. He refused two bishoprics offered him by Elizabeth, and his dislike of controversy (although he was obliged to enter into it) was very well known. Under James I he became Bishop of Chichester (1605-9), Bishop of Ely (1609-19), and finally Bishop of Winchester until his death in 1626. That he did not become Archbishop of Canterbury in 1616 was possibly as much owing to his personal reluctance as to any other factor. He was as distinguished for his tact as for his learning; natural tact often goes along with a dislike of occupying positions in which it is frequently impossible to exercise it.

Andrewes is often regarded as the link between Hooker and Laud. This is justified in so far as he certainly built upon the theological foundations laid by Hooker; he also believed in the doctrine of the Divine Right of Kings. But this doctrine may be interpreted in different ways by different temperaments. For Andrewes it provided not perhaps the most conservative but rather the least unconservative means of producing a reasonable settlement. Though High Church in his own preferences, he was unlike Laud inasmuch as he preferred to leave certain vital matters open to individual conscience. Thus, while he himself believed in the Real Presence, he did not claim that this belief rested in Scripture: it was not, he insisted, necessary. Although subservient to James (as in the matter of the Essex divorce), he disliked 'action' and politics. Forced into the position of famous preacher, and thus forced to some extent into the political arena, some of his best sermons (the least good are over-recondite) incidentally reflect the conflict in him between public responsibility and private contemplation.

Lancelot Andrewes took part in the Hampton Court Conference and made important contributions to the Authorized Version of the Bible. He was deeply involved in the controversy over the Oath of Allegiance, which after the Gunpowder Plot required the English Catholics to deny papal authority even more than heretofore: of his writings on the subject, the reply to Cardinal Bellarmin of 1610 is the most important, since in it he took the opportunity to fully define the nature of the differences between the Church of England and Rome. For him Anglicanism rested on the Gospels and on 'the centuries ... before Constantine, and [the] two after'—and, one must add, on the 'reason' upon which his predecessor Hooker had placed so much emphasis.

Andrewes as preacher is as important in the history of English prose as in that of sermon-style. He was the initiator (in the pulpit) of the 'witty', or 'metaphysical' style: ornate, punning, learnedly allusive, full of ingenious figures of speech (conceits), acutely analytical of the text—and yet frequently poetic. Both Lyly and, more to the point, Thomas Nashe, admired him and went to listen to him. Lyly's euphuistic prose (see Drant's euphuistic sermon given here), for all its historical importance, is to our taste almost intolerably convoluted; but Nashe absorbed the 'metaphysicality' to produce some of the most vigorous and vital prose of the Elizabethan period.

Andrewes's prose, as we read it in the sermons, is undoubtedly an acquired taste. It is not widely read. But, despite the over-all complexity of structure, he could be both brief and laconic. And it needs reading aloud: for it was constructed to be delivered orally. He appealed to T. S. Eliot, who is largely responsible for his twentieth-century reputation, on the grounds that his sermons are inaccessible except to those who can 'elevate' themselves to his subject: believers possessed of great learning. But this is not wholly true. Andrewes, unlike Lyly, has a great mind; he is profoundly serious in his desire to unite those of the Christian faith; he is powerful. His treatment of his subject is worth some study—even if we cannot easily follow him all the time, his best sermons are all of a piece. His abstruseness has been somewhat exaggerated. Many of his metaphors are 'homely' as well as beautiful—some even anticipating the pastoral metaphysicality of Marvell. If he is eruditely elegant then he is also immediately graceful—and the near-poetic rhythms of his prose rival those of Donne.

## Sermon of the Passion, Good Friday, 1604
Lamentations 1:12.
*Have ye no regard, O all ye that pass by the way? Consider, and behold, if ever there were sorrow like My sorrow, which was done unto Me, wherewith the Lord did afflict Me in the day of the fierceness of his wrath.*

ANDREWES'S FINEST sermons were preached at the great Church Festivals. This one was preached before James I at the Chapel at Whitehall on 6 April 1604. It has been assessed as the greatest of all sermons on this subject of Christ's Passion, obviously enough central to Christianity. There is certainly nothing recondite about its opening. It draws attention to the lonely anguish of Christ, as distinct from the relative consolations of even the most desperate of 'our sufferings' in the most forceful manner: 'In all our sufferings ... was'. (By the first *sicut* Andrewes, as he makes clear, means 'just as'—and is it not a psychological commonplace that suffering men are consoled by the fact that others have been in their case?) No more vivid way of demonstrating the unique nature of Christ's loneliness and forsakenness in this ordeal could be devised. Andrewes brings the picture of the crucified Christ to the eyes of the congregation. The message of the sermon is the nature and significance of the extremities which Christ suffered so that man could be saved; despite its weight of learning and the (then obligatory) parallels drawn between Old and New Testament, it is not overly 'theological'. Rather it seeks to 'ripen us to regard', quicken our sense of Christ's extreme and unique example. Consequently Andrewes is at pains to emphasize (and here his powers of tact are very apparent: for example, 'In this one peradventure some *sicut* may be found ...') the differences between our suffering, however acute, and that of Christ: 'wounded, melted, and bereft leaf and fruit, that is, all manner of comfort'. It is typical that Andrewes should find it 'dangerous to define' Christ's state of mind in his agony: he prefers to arouse wonder and 'regard'. Having succeeded in this, he continues to point out the reason for this unique suffering: 'God was a doer in it'. But why, when there was no sin in Christ? And the answer is: 'He took upon Him the person of others'. Therefore 'we ... are ... the principals in this act'.

It is curious that this sermon, preached by one even now notorious amongst some for his 'Romanism', and renowned for his 'overworked analysis of [his] text', should be so lucid and theologically unoriginal that it presents few difficulties. True, Andrewes could 'overwork' his analyses, could be over-recondite. But this example shows no more than an inspired *presentation*: a piece of prose, less rhetorical than most of Donne, which is entirely pertinent and always to the point. Even the matter of Justification by Faith is but faintly implied; and one would not guess from it that Andrewes's own practice, as priest, leaned markedly to the ritualistic. Since the allusions are explained in the text, it might be preached—and to effect—today.

AT THE very reading or hearing of which verse, there is none but will presently conceive, it is the voice of a party in great extremity. In great extremity two ways: 1. First, in such distress as never was any, 'If ever there were sorrow like My sorrow;' 2. And then in that distress, having none to regard Him; 'Have ye no regard, all ye?'

To be afflicted, and so afflicted as none ever was, is very much. In that affliction, to find none to respect him or care for him, what can be more? In all our sufferings, it is a comfort to us that we have a *sicut*; that nothing has befallen us, but such as others have felt the like (1 Cor. 10. 13). But here, *si fuerit sicut*; 'If ever the like were'—that is, never the like was.

Again, in our greatest pains it is a kind of ease, even to find some regard. Naturally we desire it, if we cannot be delivered, if we cannot be relieved, yet to be pitied. It showeth there be yet some that are touched with the sense of our misery, that wish us well, and would give us ease if they could. But this Afflicted here findeth not so much, neither the one nor the other; but is even as He were an out-cast both of Heaven and earth. Now verily an heavy case, and worthy to be put in this book of Lamentations.

I demand then, 'Of whom speaketh the Prophet this? of himself, or of some other?' This I find; there is not any of the ancient writers but do apply, yea in a manner appropriate, this speech to our Saviour Christ. And that this very day, the day of His Passion, truly termed here the day of God's wrath, and wheresoever they treat of the Passion, ever this verse cometh in. And to say the truth, to take the words strictly as they lie, they cannot agree, or be verified of any but of Him, and Him only. For though some other, not unfitly, may be allowed to say the same words, it must be in a qualified sense; for in full and perfect propriety of speech, He and none but He. None can say, neither Jeremy, nor any other, *si fuerit dolor Meus*, as Christ can; no day of wrath like to His day, no sorrow to be compared to His, all are short of it, nor His to any, it exceedeth them all.

And yet, according to the letter, it cannot be denied but they be set down by Jeremy in the person of his own people, being then come to great misery; and of the holy city, then laid waste and desolate by the Chaldees (Hos. II. 1). What then? *Ex Aegypto vocavi Filium Meum*, 'out of Egypt have I called My Son,' was literally spoken of this people too, yet is by the Evangelist applied to our Saviour Christ (Matt. 2.15). 'My God, my God, why hast Thou forsaken me?' at the first uttered by David (Ps. 22. 1); yet the same words our Saviour taketh Himself (Mat. 27. 46), and that more truly and properly, than ever David could; and of those of David's, and of these of Jeremy's, there is one and the same reason.

Of all which the ground is that correspondence which is between Christ, and the Patriarchs, Prophets, and people before Christ, of whom the Apostle's rule is, *omnia in figura contingebant illis*; 'that they were themselves types' (1 Cor. 10. 11), and their sufferings forerunning figures of the great suffering of the Son of God. Which maketh Isaac's offering, and Joseph's selling, and Israel's calling from Egypt, and that complaint of David's, and this of Jeremy's, appliable to Him; that He may take them to Himself, and the Church ascribe them to Him, and that in more fitness of terms, and more fulness of truth, than they were at the first spoken by David, or Jeremy, or any of them all.

And this rule, and the steps of the Fathers proceeding by this rule, are to me a warrant to expound and apply this verse, as they have done before, to the present occasion of this time; which requireth some such Scripture to be considered by us as doth belong to His Passion, Who this day poured out His most precious Blood, as the only sufficient price of the dear purchase of all our redemptions.

Be it then to us, as to them it was, and as most properly it is, the speech of the Son of God, as this day hanging on the cross, to a sort of careless people, that go up and down without any manner of regard of these His sorrows and sufferings, so worthy of all regard. 'Have ye no regard? O all ye that pass by the way, consider and behold, if ever there were sorrow like to my sorrow, which was done unto me, wherewith the Lord afflicted me in the day of the fierceness of His wrath.'

Here is a complaint, and here is a request. A complaint that we have not, a request that we would have the pains and Passions of our Saviour Christ in some regard. For first He complaineth, and not without cause, 'Have ye no regard?' And then, as willing to forget their former neglect, so they will yet do it, He falleth to entreat, 'O consider and behold!'

And what is that we should consider? The sorrow which He suffereth, and in it two things; the quality, and the cause. 1. The quality, *Si fuerit sicut*; 'if ever the like were;' and that either in respect of *Dolor*, or *Dolor Meus*, 'the sorrow suffered,' or 'the Person suffering.' 2. The cause: that is God That in His wrath, in His fierce wrath, doth all this to Him. Which cause will not leave us, till it have led us to another cause in ourselves, and to another yet in Him; all which serve to ripen us to regard.

These two then specially we are moved to regard. 1. Regard is the main point. But because therefore we regard but faintly, because either we consider not, or not aright, we are called to consider seriously of them. As if He should say, Regard you not? If you did consider, you would; if you consider as you should, you would regard as you ought. Certainly the Passion, if it were throughly considered, would be duly regarded. Consider then.

So the points are two: 1. The quality, and 2. the cause of His suffering. And the duties are two: 1. To consider, and regard; 2. So to consider that we regard them, and Him for them.

'Have ye no regard,' &c.? To ease this complaint, and to grant this request, we are to regard; and that we may regard, we are to consider the pains of His Passion. Which, that we may reckon no easy common matter of light moment, to do or not to do as we list; first, a general stay is made of all passengers, this day. For, as it were from His cross, doth our Saviour address this His speech to them that go to and fro, the day of His Passion, without so much as entertaining a thought, or vouchsafing a look that way. *O vos qui transitis!* 'O you that pass by the way,' stay and consider. To them frameth He His speech, that pass by; to them, and to them all, *O vos omnes, qui transitis,* 'O all ye that pass by the way, stay and consider.'

Which very stay of His showeth it to be some important matter, in that it is of all. For, as for some to be stayed, and those the greater some, there may be reason; the most part of those that go thus to and fro, may well intend it, they have little else to do. But to except none, not some special person, is hard. What know we their haste? their occasions may be such, and so urgent, as they cannot stay. Well, what haste, what business soever, pass not by, stay though. As much to say as, Be they never so great, your occasions; they are not, they cannot be so great as this. How urgent soever, this is more, and more to be intended. The regard of this is worthy the staying of a journey. It is worth the considering of those, that have never so great affairs in hand. So material is this sight in His account. Which serveth to shew the exigence of this duty. But as for this point, it needeth not be stood upon to us here at this time; we are not going by, we need not be stayed, we have stayed all other our affairs to come hither, and here we are all present before God, to have it set before us, that we may consider it. Thither then let us come.

That which we are called to behold and consider, is His sorrow. And sorrow is a thing which of itself nature inclineth us to behold, 'as being ourselves in the body' (Heb. 13.3), which may be one day in the like sorrowful case. Therefore will every good eye turn itself, and look upon them that lie in distress. Those two in the Gospel that passed by the wounded man (Lu. 10.32), before they passed by him, though they helped him not as the Samaritan did, yet they looked upon him as he lay. But, this party here lieth not, He is lift up as the serpent in the wilderness (Joh. 3.14), that unless we turn our eyes away purposely, we can neither will nor choose but behold Him.

But because, to behold and not to consider is but to gaze, and gazing the Angel blameth in the Apostles themselves (Acts 1.11), we must do both—both 'behold' and 'consider;' look upon with the eye of the body, that is 'behold;' and look into with the eye of the mind, that is 'consider.' So saith the Prophet here. And the very same doth the Apostle advise us to do. First, ἀφορᾶν, to look upon Him, that is, to 'behold,' and then ἀναλογίζεσθαι, to think upon Him (Heb. 12.2), that is, to 'consider' His sorrow. Sorrow sure would be considered.

Now then, because as the quality of the sorrow is, accordingly it would be considered—for if it be but a common sorrow the less will serve, but if it be some special, some very heavy case, the more would be allowed it; for proportionably with the suffering, the consideration is to arise;—to raise our consideration to the full, and to elevate it to the highest point, there is upon His sorrow set a *si fuerit sicut*, a note of highest eminency; for *si fuerit sicut*, are words that have life in them, and are able to quicken our consideration, if it be not quite dead; for by them we are provoked, as it were, to 'consider,' and considering to see whether ever any *sicut* may be found to set by it, whether ever any like it.

For if never any, our nature is to regard things exceeding rare and strange; and such as the like whereof is not else to be seen. Upon this point then, there is a case made, as if He should say, 'if ever the like, regard not this;' but if never any, be like yourselves in other things, and vouchsafe this, if not your chiefest, yet some regard.

To enter this comparison, and to show it for such. That are we to do, three sundry ways; for three sundry ways, in three sundry words, are these sufferings of His here expressed, all three within the compass of the verse.

The first is *Mac-ob* [Heb.], which we read 'sorrow,' taken from a wound or stripe, as all do agree.

The second is *Gholel* [Heb.]; we read 'Done to me,' taken from a word that signifieth melting in a furnace, as St. Hierome noteth out of the Chaldee, who so translateth it.

The third is *Hoga* [Heb.], where we read afflicted, from a word which importeth renting off, or bereaving. The old Latin turneth it *Vindemiavit me*, as a vine whose fruit is all plucked off. The Greek, with Theodoret, ἀπεφύλλισέ με, as a vine or tree whose leaves are all beaten off, and is left naked and bare.*

In these three are comprised His sufferings—wounded, melted, and bereft leaf and fruit, that is, all manner of comfort.

Of all that is penal, or can be suffered, the common division is, *sensus et damni*, grief for that we feel, or for that we forego. For that we feel in the two former, wounded in body, melted in soul; for that we forego in the last, bereft all, left neither fruit nor so much as a leaf to hang on Him.

According to these three, to consider His sufferings, and to begin first with the first. The pains of His body, His wounds and His stripes.

Our very eye will soon tell us no place was left in His body, where He might be smitten and was not. His skin and flesh rent with the whips and scourges, His hands and feet wounded with the nails, His head with the thorns, His very heart with the spear-point; all His senses, all His parts laden with whatsoever wit or malice could invent. His blessed body given as an anvil to be beaten upon with the violent hands of those barbarous miscreants, till they brought Him into this case of *si fuerit sicut*. For Pilate's *Ecce Homo!* (Joh. 19. 5) his shewing Him with an *Ecce*, as if he should say, Behold, look if ever you saw the like rueful spectacle; this very showing of his showeth plainly, He was then come into woeful plight—so woeful as Pilate verily believed His very sight so pitiful, as it would have moved the hardest heart of them all to have relented and said, This is enough, we desire no more. And this for the wounds of His body, for on this we stand not.

In this one peradventure some *sicut* may be found, in the pains of the body; but in the second, the sorrow of the soul, I am sure, none. And indeed, the pain of the body is but the body of pain; the very soul of sorrow and pain is the soul's sorrow and pain. Give me any grief, save the grief of the mind, saith the

Wise Man; for, saith Solomon, 'The spirit of a man will sustain all his other infirmities, but a wounded spirit, who can bear?' (Prov.18.14.) And of this, this of His soul, I dare make a case, *Si fuerit sicut*.

'He began to be troubled in soul,' saith St. John (12.27); 'to be in an agony,' saith St. Luke (22.44); 'to be in anguish of mind and deep distress,' saith St. Mark (14. 33). To have His soul round about on every side environed with sorrow, and that sorrow to the death. Here is trouble, anguish, agony, sorrow, and deadly sorrow; but it must be such, as never the like: so it was too.

The estimate whereof we may take from the second word of melting, that is, from His sweat in the garden (Lu. 22.44); strange, and the like whereof was never heard or seen.

No manner violence offered him in body, no man touching Him or being near Him; in a cold night, for they were fain to have a fire within doors, lying abroad in the air and upon the cold earth, to be all of a sweat, and that sweat to be blood; and not as they call it *diaphoreticus*, 'a thin faint sweat,' but *grumosus*, 'of great drops;' and those so many, so plenteous, as they went through His apparel and all; and through all streamed to the ground, and that in great abundance;—read, enquire, and consider, *si fuerit sudor sicut sudor iste*; 'if ever there were sweat like this sweat of His.' Never the like sweat certainly, and therefore never the like sorrow. Our translation is, 'Done unto Me;' but we said the word properly signifieth, and so S. Hierome and the Chaldee paraphrast read it, 'melted Me.' And truly it should seem by this fearful sweat of His He was near some furnace, the feeling whereof was able to cast Him into that sweat, and to turn His sweat into drops of blood. And sure it was so; for see, even in the very next words of all to this verse, He complaineth of it; *Ignem misit in ossibus meis*, 'that a fire was sent into His bones' (Lam. 1.13) which melted Him, and made that bloody sweat to distil from Him. That hour, what His feelings were, it is dangerous to define; we know them not, we may be too bold to determine of them. To very good purpose it was, that the ancient Fathers of the Greek Church in their Liturgy, after they have recounted all the particular pains, as they are set down in His Passion, and by all, and by every one of them, called for mercy, do after all shut up all with this, Δι' ἀγνωστῶν κόπων καὶ βασάνων ἐλέησον καὶ σῶσον ἡμᾶς, 'By Thine unknown sorrows and sufferings, felt by Thee, but not distinctly known by us, Have mercy upon us, and save us!'

Now, though this suffice not, nothing near, yet let it suffice, the time being short, for His pains of body and soul. For those of the body, it may be some may have endured the like; but the sorrows of His soul are unknown sorrows, and for them none ever have, ever have or ever shall suffer the like, the like, or near the like in any degree.

And now to the third. It was said before, to be in distress, such distress as this was, and to find none to comfort, nay not so much as to regard Him, is all that can be said to make His sorrow a *non sicut*. Comfort is it by which, in the midst of all our sorrows, we are *confortati*, that is strengthened and made the better able to bear them all out. And who is there, even the poorest creature among us, but in some degree findeth some comfort, or some regard at some body's hands? For if that be not left, the state of that party is here in the third word said to be like the tree, whose leaves and whose fruit are all beaten off quite, and itself left bare and naked both of the one and of the other.

And such was our Saviour's case in these His sorrows this day, and that so as what is left the meanest of the sons of men, was not left Him, not a leaf. Not a leaf! Leaves I may well call all human comforts and regards, whereof He was then left clean desolate. 1. 'His own' (Joh. 1. 11), they among whom He had gone about all His life long, healing them, teaching them, feeding them, doing them all the good He could, it is they that cry, 'Not Him, no, but Barabbas rather' (Joh. 18. 40); 'away with Him' (Joh. 19. 15), "His blood be upon us and our children' (Mat. 27. 25). It is they that in the midst of His sorrows shake their head at Him, and cry, 'Ah, thou wretch' (Mar. 15. 29. 36); they that in His most disconsolate estate cry Eli, Eli, in most barbarous manner, deride Him and say, 'Stay, and you shall see Elias come presently and take Him down.' And this was their regard.

But these were but withered leaves. They then that on earth were nearest Him of all, the greenest leaves and likest to hang on, and to give Him some shade; even of them some bought and sold Him, others denied and forswore Him, but all fell away, and forsook Him. Ἀπεφύλλισέ με, saith Theodoret, not a leaf left.

But leaves are but leaves, and so are all earthly stays. The fruit then, the true fruit of the Vine indeed, the true comfort in all heaviness, is *desuper*, 'from above,' is divine consolation. But *Vindemiavit Me*, saith the Latin text;—even that was, in this His sorrow, this day bereft Him too. And that was His most sorrowful complaint of all others; not that His friends upon earth, but that His Father from Heaven had forsaken Him; that neither Heaven nor earth yielded Him any regard, but that between the passioned powers of His soul, and whatsoever might any ways refresh Him, there was a traverse drawn, and He left in the state of a weather-beaten tree, all desolate and forlorn. Evident, too evident, by that His most dreadful cry, which at once moved all the powers in Heaven and earth, 'My God, My God, why hast Thou forsaken Me?' (Mat. 27.46.) Weigh well that cry, consider it well, and tell me, *si fuerit clamor sicut clamor iste*, 'if ever there were cry like that of His:' never the like cry, and therefore never the like sorrow.

It is strange, very strange, that of none of the martyrs the like can be read, who yet endured most exquisite pains in their martyrdoms; yet we see with what courage, with what cheerfulness, how even singing, they are reported to have passed through their torments. Will ye know the reason? St. Augustine setteth it down: *martyres non eripuit, sed nunquid deseruit?* 'He delivered not His martyrs, but did He forsake them?' He delivered not their bodies, but He forsook not their souls, but distilled into them the dew of His heavenly comfort, an abundant supply for all they could endure. Not so here. *Vindemiavit Me*, saith the Prophet; *Dereliquisti Me*, saith He Himself;—no comfort, no supply at all.

Leo it is that first said it, and all antiquity allow of it, *Non solvit unionem, sed subtraxit visionem*. 'The union was not dissolved: true, but the beams, the influence was restrained,' and for any comfort from thence His soul was even as a scorched heath-ground, without so much as any drop of dew of divine comfort; as a naked tree—no fruit to refresh Him within, no leaf to give Him shadow without; the power of darkness let loose to afflict Him, the influence of comfort restrained to relieve Him. It is a *non sicut* this, it cannot be expressed as it should, and as other things may; in silence we may admire it, but all our words will not reach it. And though to draw it so far as some do, is little better than blasphemy, yet on the other side to shrink it so short as other some do, cannot be but with derogation to His love, Who, to kindle our love and loving regard, would come to a *non sicut* in His suffering; for so it was, and so we must allow it to be. This, in respect of His passion, *Dolor*.

Now in respect of His Person, *Dolor Meus*. Whereof, if it please you to take a view even of the Person thus wounded, thus afflicted and forsaken, you shall then have a perfect *non sicut*. And indeed the Person is here a weighty circumstance, it is thrice repeated—*Meus, Mihi, Me*, and we may not leave it out. For as is the Person, so is the Passion; and any one, even the very least degree of wrong or disgrace, offered to a person of excellency, is more than a hundred times more to one of mean condition; so weighty is the circumstance of the person. Consider then how great the Person was; and I rest fully assured here we boldly challenge and say, *si fuerit sicut*.

*Ecce Homo!* saith Pilate first: a Man He is as we are, and were He but a Man, nay, were He not a Man, but some poor dumb creature, it were great ruth to see Him so handled as He was.

'A Man,' saith Pilate, and a 'just Man,' saith Pilate's wife. 'Have thou nothing to do with that just Man.' And that is one degree farther. For though we pity the punishment even of malefactors themselves, yet ever most compassion we have of them that suffer and be innocent. And He was innocent; Pilate and Herod, and 'the prince of this world,' His very enemies, being his judges (Lu. 23.14, 15; Joh. 14. 30).

Now among the innocent, the more noble the person, the more heavy the spectacle. And never do our bowels yearn so much as over such. 'Alas, alas for that noble Prince' (Jer.22.18), saith this Prophet;—the style of mourning for the death of a great personage. And He that suffered here is such, even a principal Person among the sons of men, of the race royal, descended from Kings. Pilate styled Him so in his title (John 19.22), and he would not alter it.

Three degrees. But yet we are not at our true *quantus*. For He is yet more, more than the highest of the sons of men, for He is the Son of the Most High God. Pilate saw no farther but *Ecce Homo!* the centurion did, *vere Filius Dei erat Hic*,' 'now truly This was the Son of God' (Mar.15.39). And here all words forsake us, and every tongue becometh speechless.

We have no way to express it but *a minore ad majus;*—thus. Of this book, the book of Lamentations, one special occasion was the death of King Josias; but behold a greater than Josias is here.

Of King Josias, as a special reason of mourning, the Prophet saith, *Spiritus oris nostri, christus Domini* (Lam.4.20), 'the very breath of our nostrils, the Lord's anointed,' for so are all good Kings in their subjects' accounts, he is gone. But behold, here is not *christus Domini*, but *Christus Dominus*, 'the Lord's christ,' but the 'Lord Christ Himself' (Lu. 2. 11); and that not coming to an honourable death in battle as Josias did, but to a most vile reproachful death, the death of malefactors in the highest degree. And not slain outright as Josias was, but mangled and massacred in most pitiful strange manner; wounded in Body, wounded in Spirit, left utterly desolate. O consider this well, and confess the case is truly put, *si fuerit Dolor sicut Dolor meus!* Never, never the like person; and if as the person is, the passion be, never the like Passion to His.

It is truly affirmed, that any one, even the least drop of blood, even the least pain, yea of the body only, of this so great a Person, any *Dolor* with this *Meus*, had been enough to make a *non sicut* of it. That is enough, but that is not all; for add now the three other degrees; add to this Person those wounds, that sweat and that cry, and put all together, and I make no manner question the like was not, shall not, cannot ever be. It is far above all that ever was or can be, *abyssus est*. Men may drowsily hear it and coldly affect it, but principalities and powers stand abashed at it. And for the quality both of the Passion and of the Person, that never the like, thus much.

Now to proceed to the cause and to consider it, for without it we shall have but half a regard, and scarce that. Indeed, set the cause aside, and the passion, as rare as it is, is yet but a dull and heavy sight, we list not much look upon spectacles of that kind, though never so strange, they fill us full of pensive thoughts and make us melancholic. And so doth this, till upon examination of the cause we find it toucheth us near; and so near, so many ways, as we cannot choose but have some regard of it.

What was done to Him we see. Let there now be a quest of enquiry to find who was doer of it. Who? who but the 'power of darkness,' wicked Pilate, bloody Caiaphas, the envious Priests, the barbarous soldiers (Lu. 22. 53)? None of these are returned here. We are too low by a great deal, if we think to find it among men. *Quae fecit Mihi Deus*, 'it was God That did it.' An hour of that day was the hour of the 'power of darkness;' but the whole day itself, is said here plainly, was the day of the wrath of God. God was a doer in it; 'wherewith God hath afflicted Me.'

God afflicteth some in mercy, and others in wrath. This was in His wrath. In His wrath God is not alike to all; some he afflicteth in His more gentle and mild, others in His fierce wrath. This was in the very fierceness of His wrath. His sufferings, His sweat, and cry, show as much; they could not come but from a wrath *si fuerit sicut*, for we are not past *non sicut*, no not here,—in this part it followeth us still, and will not leave us in any point, not to the end.

The cause then in God was wrath. What caused this wrath? God is not wroth but with sin, nor grievously wroth but with grievous sin. And in Christ there was no grievous sin; nay, no sin at all. God did it, the text is plain. And in His fierce wrath he did it. For what cause? For, God forbid, God should do as did Annas the high-priest, cause Him to be smitten without cause (Joh. 18. 22)! God forbid, saith Abraham (Gen. 18.25), 'the Judge of the world should do wrong' to any! To any, but specially to His own Son, that His Son, of Whom with thundering voice from Heaven He testifieth, all His joy and delight were in Him, 'in Him only He was well-pleased' (Mat. 3.17). And how then could His wrath wax hot to do all this unto Him?

There is no way to preserve God's justice, and Christ's innocency both, but to say as the Angel said of Him to the Prophet Daniel (9.26), 'The Messias shall be slain,' *ve-en-lo* [Heb.], 'shall be slain but not for Himself.' 'Not for Himself?' For whom then? For some others. He took upon Him the person of others, and so doing, justice may have her course and proceed.

Pity it is to see a man pay that he never took; but if he will become a surety, if he will take on him the person of the debtor, so he must. Pity to see a silly poor lamb lie bleeding to death; but if it must be a sacrifice, such is the nature of a sacrifice, so it must. And so Christ, though without sin in Himself, yet as a surety, as a sacrifice, may justly suffer for others, if He will take upon Him their persons; and so God may justly give way to His wrath against Him.

And who be those others? The Prophet Esay telleth us (Isa. 53.4-6), and telleth it us seven times over for failing, 'He took upon Him our infirmities, and bare our maladies. He was wounded for our iniquities, and broken for our transgressions: the chastisement of our peace was upon Him, and with His stripes were we healed. All we as sheep were gone astray, and turned every man to his own way; and the Lord hath laid upon Him the iniquity of us all.' 'All,' 'all,' even those that pass to and fro, and for all this regard neither Him nor His Passion.

The short is, it was we that for our sins, our many great and grievous sins,—*Si fuerit sicut*, the like whereof never were,—should have sweated this sweat and have cried this cry; should have been smitten with these sorrows by the fierce wrath of

God, had not He stepped between the blow and us, and latched it in His own body and soul, even the dint of the fierceness of the wrath of God. O the *non sicut* of our sins, that could not otherwise be answered!

To return then a true verdict. It is we—we, wretched sinners that we are—that are to be found the principals in this act, and those on whom we seek to shift it, to drive it from ourselves, Pilate and Caiaphas and the rest, but instrumental causes only. And it is not the executioner that killeth the man properly, that is, they; no, nor the judge, which is God in this case; only sin, *solum peccatum homicida est*, 'sin only is the murderer,' to say the truth, and our sins the murderers of the Son of God; and the *non sicut* of them the true cause of the *non sicut* both of God's wrath, and of His sorrowful sufferings.

Which bringeth home this our text to us, even into our own bosoms, and applieth it most effectually to me that speak and to you that hear, to every one of us, and that with the Prophet Nathan's application; *Tu es homo*, 'Thou art the man,' even thou, for whom God in 'His fierce wrath' (2 Sam. 12.7) thus afflicted Him. Sin then was the cause on our part why we, or some other for us.

But yet what was the cause, why He on His part? what was that that moved Him thus to become our surety, and to take upon Him our debt and danger? that moved Him thus to lay upon His soul a sacrifice for our sin? Sure, *oblatus est quia voluit*, saith Esay again (Isa. 53.7), 'Offered He was for no other cause, but because He would.' For unless He would, He needed not. Needed not for any necessity of justice, for no lamb was ever more innocent; nor for any necessity of constraint, for twelve legions of Angels were ready at His command, but because He would.

And why would He? No reason can be given but because He regarded us:—Mark that reason. And what were we? Verily, utterly unworthy even His least regard, not worth the taking up, not worth the looking after. *Cum inimici essemus*, saith the Apostle (Rom. 5.8); 'we were His enemies,' when He did it, without all desert before, and without all regard after He had done and suffered all this for us; and yet He would regard us that so little regard Him. For when he saw us a sort of forlorn sinners, *non prius natos quam damnatos*, 'damned as fast as born,' as being 'by nature children of wrath' (Eph. 2.3), and yet still 'heaping up wrath against the day of wrath,' by the errors of our life, till the time of our passing hence; and then the 'fierce wrath of God' ready to overwhelm us (Rom. 2.5), and to make us endure the terror and torments of a never dying death, another *non sicut* yet: when, I say, He was in this case, He was moved with compassion over us and undertook all this for us. Even then in His love He regarded us, and so regarded us that He regarded not Himself, to regard us.

Bernard saith most truly, *Dilexisti me Domine magis quam Te, quando mori voluisti pro me*: 'In suffering all this for us Thou showedst, Lord, that we were more dear to Thee, that Thou regardest us more than Thine ownself;' and shall this regard find no regard at our hands?

It was sin then, and the heinousness of sin in us, that provoked wrath and the fierceness of His wrath in God; it was love, and the greatness of His love in Christ, that caused Him to suffer the sorrows, and the grievousness of these sorrows, and all for our sakes.

And indeed, but only to testify the *non sicut* of this His love, all this needed not that was done to Him. One, any one, even the very least of all the pains He endured, had been enough; enough in respect of the *Meus*, enough in respect of the *non sicut* of His person. For that which setteth the high price on this sacrifice, is this; that He which offereth it unto God, is God. But if little had been suffered, little would the love have been thought that suffered so little, and as little regard would have been had of it. To awake our regard then, or to leave us excuseless, if we continue regardless, all this He bare for us; that he might as truly make a case of *Si fuerit amor sicut amor Meus*, as He did before of *Si fuerit dolor sicut dolor Meus*. We say we will regard love; if we will, here it is to regard.

So have we the causes, all three: 1. Wrath in God; 2. Sin in ourselves; 3. Love in Him.

Yet have we not all we should. For what of all this? What good? *Cui bono?* That, that, is it indeed that we will regard if any thing, as being matter of benefit, the only thing in a manner the world regardeth, which bringeth us about to the very first words again. For the very first words which we read, 'Have ye no regard?' are in the original, *lo alechem* [Heb.], which the Seventy turn, word for word, οὐ πρὸς ὑμᾶς ; and the Latin likewise, *nonne ad vos pertinet?* Pertains it not to you, that you regard it no better? for these two, pertaining and regarding, are folded one in another, and go together so commonly as one is taken often for the other. Then to be sure to bring us to regard, he urgeth this: 'Pertains not all this to you?' Is it not for your good? Is not the benefit yours? Matters of benefit, they pertain to you, and without them love and all the rest may pertain to whom they will.

Consider then the inestimable benefit that groweth unto you from this incomparable love. It is not impertinent this, even this, that to us hereby all is turned about clean contrary; that 'by His stripes we are healed,' by His sweat we refreshed, by His forsaking we received to grace. That this day, to Him the day of the fierceness of God's wrath, is to us the day of the fulness of God's favour, as the Apostle calleth it, 'a day of salvation' (2 Cor. 6.2). In respect of that He suffered, I deny not, an evil day, a day of heaviness; but in respect of that which He by it hath obtained for us, it is as we truly call it a good day, a day of joy and jubilee. For it doth not only rid us of that wrath which pertaineth to us for our sins; but farther, it maketh that pertain to us whereto we had no manner of right at all.

For not only by His death as by the death of our sacrifice, by the blood of His cross as by the blood of the paschal lamb, the destroyer passeth over us, and we shall not perish (Ex. 12.13); but also by His death, as by the death of our High Priest (Nu. 35.25)—for He is Priest and Sacrifice both—we are restored from our exile, even to our former forfeited estate in the land of Promise. Or rather, as the Apostle saith (Rom. 5.15), *non sicut delictum sic donum*; not to the same estate, but to one nothing like it, that is, one far better than the estate our sins bereft us. For they deprived us of Paradise, a place on earth; but by the purchase of His blood we are entitled to a far higher, even the Kingdom of Heaven; and His blood, not only the blood of 'remission,' to acquit us of our sins, but 'the blood of the Testament too,' to bequeath us and give us estate in that Heavenly inheritance (Mat. 26.28).

Now whatsoever else, this I am sure is a *non sicut*, as that which the eye by all it can see, the ear by all it can hear, the heart by all it can conceive, cannot pattern it, or set the like by it. 'Pertains not this unto us' neither? Is not this worth the regard? Sure if any thing be worthy the regard, this is most worthy of our very worthiest and best regard.

Thus have we considered and seen, not so much as in this sight we might or should, but as much as the time will give us leave. And now lay all these before you, every one of them a *non sicut* of itself; the pains of His body esteemed by Pilate's

*Ecce*; the sorrows of His soul, by His sweat in the garden; the comfortless estate of His sorrows, by His cry on the cross; and with these, His Person, as being the Son of the Great and Eternal God. Then join to these the cause: in God, 'His fierce wrath;' in us, our heinous sins deserving it; in Him, His exceeding great love, both suffering that for us which we had deserved, and procuring for us that we could never deserve; making that to appertain to Himself which of right pertained to us, and making that pertain to us which pertained to Him only, and not to us at all but by His means alone. And after their view in several, lay them all together, so many *non sicuts* into one, and tell me if His complaint be not just and His request most reasonable.

Yes sure, His complaint is just, 'Have ye no regard?' None? and yet never the like? None? and it pertains unto you? 'No regard?' As if it were some common ordinary matter, and the like never was? 'No regard?' As if it concerned you not a whit, and it toucheth you so near? As if He should say, Rare things you regard, yea, though they no ways pertain to you: this is exceeding rare, and will you not regard it? Again, things that nearly touch you you regard, though they be not rare at all: this toucheth you exceeding near, even as near as your soul toucheth you, and will you not yet regard it? Will neither of these by itself move you? Will not both these together move you? What will move you? Will pity? Here is distress never the like. Will duty? Here is a Person never the like. Will fear? Here is wrath never the like. Will remorse? Here are sins never the like. Will kindness? Here is love never the like. Will bounty? Here are benefits never the like. Will all these? Here they be all, all above any *sicut*, all in the highest degree.

Truly the complaint is just, it may move us; it wanteth no reason, it may move; and it wanteth no affection in the delivery of it to us, on His part to move us. Sure it moved Him exceeding much; for among all the deadly sorrows of His most bitter Passion, this, even this, seemeth to be His greatest of all, and that which did most affect Him, even the grief of the slender reckoning most men have it in; as little respecting Him, as if He had done or suffered nothing at all for them. For lo, of all the sharp pains He endureth He complaineth not, but of this He complaineth, of no regard; that which grieveth Him most, that which most He moaneth is this. It is strange He should be in pains, such pains as never any was, and not complain Himself of them, but of want of regard only. Strange, He should not make request, O deliver Me, or relieve Me! But only, O consider and regard Me! In effect as if He said, None, no deliverance, no relief do I seek; regard I seek. And all that I suffer, I am content with it, I regard it not, I suffer most willingly, if this I may find at your hands, regard.

Truly, this so passionate a complaint may move us, it moved all but us; for most strange of all it is, that all the creatures in Heaven and earth seemed to hear this His mournful complaint, and in their kind to show their regard of it. The sun in Heaven shrinking in his light, the earth trembling under it, the very stones cleaving in sunder, as if they had sense and sympathy of it, and sinful men only not moved with it. And yet it was not for the creatures this was done to Him, to them it pertaineth not; but for us it was, and to us it doth. And shall we not yet regard it? shall the creature, and not we? shall we not?

If we do not, it may appertain to us, but we pertain not to it; it pertains to all but all pertain not to it. None pertain to it but they that take benefit by it; and none take benefit by it no more than by the brazen serpent, but they that fix their eye on it. Behold, consider, and regard it; the profit, the benefit is lost without regard.

If we do not, as this was a day of God's 'fierce wrath' against Him, only for regarding us; so there is another day coming, and it will quickly be here, a day of like 'fierce wrath' against us (Ps. 90.11), for not regarding Him. 'And who regardeth the power of His wrath?' He that doth, will surely regard this.

In that day, there is not the most careless of us all but shall cry as they did in the Gospel (Mark 4.38), *Domine, non ad Te pertinet, si perimus?* 'Pertains it not to Thee, carest Thou not that we perish?' Then would we be glad to pertain to Him and His Passion. Pertains it to us then, and pertains it not now? Sure now it must, if then it shall.

Then to give end to this complaint, let us grant Him His request, and regard His Passion. Let the rareness of it, the nearness to us, let pity or duty, fear or remorse, love or bounty; any of them or all of them; let the justness of His complaint, let His affectionate manner of complaining of this and only this, let the shame of the creatures' regard, let our profit or our peril, let something prevail with us to have it in some regard.

Some regard! Verily, as His sufferings, His love, our good by them are, so should our regard be a *non sicut* too; that is, a regard of these, and of nothing in comparison of these. It should be so, for with the benefit ever the regard should arise.

But God help us poor sinners, and be merciful unto us! Our regard is a *non sicut* indeed, but it is backward, and in a contrary sense; that is, no where so shallow, so short, or so soon done. It should be otherwise, it should have our deepest consideration this, and our highest regard.

But if that cannot be had, our nature is so heavy, and flesh and blood so dull of apprehension in spiritual things, yet at leastwise some regard. Some I say; the more the better, but in any wise some, and not as here no regard, none at all. Some ways to show we make account of it, to withdraw ourselves, to void our minds of other matters, to set this before us, to think upon it, to thank Him for it, to regard Him, and stay and see whether He will regard us or no. Sure He will, and we shall feel our 'hearts pricked' (Acts 2. 37) with sorrow, by consideration of the cause in us—our sin; and again, 'warm within us' (Lu. 24. 32), by consideration of the cause in Him—His love; till by some motion of grace He answer us, and show that our regard is accepted of Him.

And this, as at all other times, for no day is amiss but at all times some time to be taken for this duty, so specially on this day; this day, which we hold holy to the memory of His Passion, this day to do it; to make this day, the day of God's wrath and Christ's suffering, a day to us of serious consideration and regard of them both.

It is kindly to consider *opus diei in die suo*, 'the work of the day in the day it was wrought;' and this day it was wrought. This day therefore, whatsoever business be, to lay them aside a little; whatsoever our haste, yet to stay a little, and to spend a few thoughts in calling to mind and taking to regard what this day the Son of God did and suffered for us; and all for this end, that what He was then we might not be, and what He is now we might be for ever.

Which Almighty God grant we may do, more or less, even every one of us, according to the several measures of His grace in us!

## SERMON OF THE NATIVITY, CHRISTMAS, 1622
Matt. 2:1-2.
*Behold there came wise men from the East to Jerusalem,*
*Saying, Where is the King of the Jews That is born? For we have*
*seen His star in the East, and are come to worship Him.*

THIS, ANDREWES'S most famous sermon (because Eliot admired, and used a passage in it, notably the phrase 'a cold coming they had of it . . .', for his poem 'The Journey of the Magi'), was preached before the King at Whitehall on the Christmas Day of 1622. Andrewes's Nativity sermons had been a regular feature at the Court since 1605.

This sermon presents, in the main, no more serious difficulties than the preceding example from Andrewes. The making 'all run on a star' is characteristic, and the effective and touching metaphor, though it becomes involved, is no harder to follow than it is mellowly appropriate to the occasion. Once again, the emphasis is on faith and on the psychology of faith. Andrewes is very sensible of the fact that faith must not be an abstraction, but something 'quick and lively'. The paradoxically simple faith of the Wise Men is compared with the kind of faith we should hold. This faith he bases on prophecy and reason rather than on scholastic discourse (for Andrewes, though involute, was not scholastically inclined). Andrewes's 'reason' is contained in his beautiful description of the 'cold' and the hard coming of the Magi, and their cheerfulness in the face of it. The remark that 'Christ is no wild-cat' is a rebuke to Puritan zealousness. But, like that of the Passion sermon given above, the prose of this speaks for itself.

THERE BE in these two verses two principal points, as was observed when time was; 1. The persons that arrived at Jerusalem, 2. and their errand. The persons in the former verse, whereof hath been treated heretofore. Their errand in the latter, whereof we are now to deal.

Their errand we may best learn from themselves out of their *dicentes*, &c. Which, in a word, is to worship Him. Their errand our errand, and the errand of this day.

This text may seem to come a little too soon, before the time; and should have stayed till the day it was spoken on, rather than on this day. But if you mark them well, there are in the verse four words that be *verba diei hujus*, 'proper and peculiar to this very day.' 1. For first, *natus est* is most proper to this day of all days, the day of His Nativity. 2. Secondly, *vidimus stellam*; for on this day it was first seen, appeared first. 3. Thirdly, *venimus;* for this day they set forth, began their journey. 4. And last, *adorare Eum;* for 'when He brought His only-begotten Son into the world, He gave in charge, Let all the Angels of God worship Him' (Heb.1.6). And when the Angels to do it, no time more proper for us to do it as then. So these four appropriate it to this day, and none but this.

The main heads of their errand are 1. *Vidimus stellam*, the occasion; 2. and *Venimus adorare*, the end of their coming. But for the better conceiving it I will take another course, to set forth these points to be handled.

Their faith first: faith—in that they never ask, 'Whether He be.' but 'Where He is born;' for that born He is, that they steadfastly believe.

Then 'the work or service' of this faith, as St. Paul calleth it (Phil.2.17); 'the touch or trial,' as St. Peter (1 Pet.1.7.); the *ostende mihi*, as St. James (Jam.2.18); of this their faith in these five. 1. Their confessing of it in *venerunt dicentes*. *Venerunt*, they were no sooner come, but *dicentes*, they tell it out; confess Him and His birth to be the cause of their coming. 2. Secondly, as confess their faith, so the ground of their faith; *vidimus enim*, for they had 'seen' His star; and His star being risen, by it they knew He must be risen too. 3. Thirdly, as St. Paul calls them in Abraham's, *vestigia fidei*, 'the steps of their faith' (Rom.4.12), in *venimus*, 'their coming'—coming such a journey, at such a time, with such speed. 4. Fourthly, when they were come, their diligent enquiring Him out by *ubi est?* for here is the place of it, asking after Him to find where He was. 5. And last, when they had found Him, the end of their seeing, coming, seeking; and all for no other end but to worship Him. Here they say it, at the 11th verse they do it in these two acts; 1. *procidentes*, their 'falling down,' 2. and *obtulerunt*, their 'offering' to Him. Worship Him with their bodies, worship Him with their goods; their worship and ours the true worship of Christ.

The text is of a star, and we may make all run on a star, that so the text and day may be suitable, and Heaven and earth hold a correspondence. St. Peter calls faith 'the day-star rising in our hearts' (2 Pet. 1. 19), which sorts well with the star in the text rising in the sky. That in the sky manifesting itself from above to them; this in their hearts manifesting itself from below to Him, to Christ. Manifesting itself by these five: 1. by *ore fit confessio*, 'the confessing of it' (Rom. 10. 10.); 2. by *fides est substantia*, 'the ground of it' (Heb. 11. 1); 3. by *vestigia fidei*, 'the steps of it' in their painful coming (Rom. 4. 12); 4. by their *ubi est?* 'careful enquiring;' 5. and last, by *adorare Eum*, 'their devout worshipping.' These five, as so many beams of faith, the day-star risen in their hearts. To take notice of them. For every one of them is of the nature of a condition, so as if we fail in them, *non lucet nobis stella haec*, 'we have no part in the light, or conduct of this star.' Neither in *stellam*, 'the star itself,' nor in *Ejus*, 'in Him Whose the star is;' that is, not in Christ neither.

We have now got us a star on earth for that in Heaven, and these both lead us to a third. So as upon the matter three stars we have, and each his proper manifestation. 1. The first in the firmament; that appeared unto them, and in them to us—a figure of St. Paul's Ἐπεφάνη χάρις, ' the grace of God appearing, and bringing salvation to all men,' Jews and Gentiles and all (Tit. 2. 11). 2. The second here on earth is St. Peter's *Lucifer in cordibus;* and this appeared in them, and so must in us (2 Pet. 1. 19). Appeared 1. in their eyes—*vidimus;* 2. in their feet—*venimus;* 3. in their lips—*dicentes ubi est;* 4. in their knees—*procidentes*, 'falling down;' 5. in their hands—*obtulerunt*, 'by offering.' These five every one a beam of this star. 3. The third in Christ Himself, St. John's star. 'The generation and root of David, the bright morning Star, Christ' (Rev. 22. 16). And He, His double appearing. 1. One at this time now, when He appeared in great humility; and we see and come to Him by faith. 2. The other, which we wait for, even 'the blessed hope, and appearing of the great God and our Saviour' in the majesty of His glory (Tit. 2. 13).

These three: 1. The first that manifested Christ to them;

2. The second that manifested them to Christ; 3. The third Christ Himself, in Whom both these were as it were in conjunction. Christ 'the bright morning Star' of that day which shall have no night; the *beatifica visio*, 'the blessed sight' of which day is the *consummatum est* of our hope and happiness for ever.

Of these three stars the first is gone, the third yet to come, the second only is present. We to look to that, and to the five beams of it. That is it must do us all the good, and bring us to the third.

St. Luke calleth faith the 'door of faith.' At this door let us enter. Here is a coming, and 'he that cometh to God,' and so he that to Christ, 'must believe, that Christ is' (Acts 14.27): so do these. They never ask *an sit*, but *ubi sit?* Not 'whether,' but 'where He is born.' They that ask *ubi Qui natus?* take *natus* for granted, presuppose that born He is. Herein is faith—faith of Christ's being born, the third article of the Christian Creed.

And what believe they of Him? Out of their own words here; 1. first that *natus*, that 'born' He is, and so Man He is—His human nature. 1. And as His nature, so His office in *natus est Rex*, 'born a King.' They believe that too. 3. But *Judaeorum* may seem to be a bar; for then, what have they to do with 'the King of the Jews?' They be Gentiles, none of His lieges, no relation to Him at all: what do they seeking or worshipping Him? But weigh it well, and it is no bar. For this they seem to believe: He is so *Rex Judaeorum*, 'King of the Jews,' as He is *adorandus a Gentibus*, 'the Gentiles to adore Him.' And though born in Jewry, yet Whose birth concerned them though Gentiles, though born far off in the 'mountains of the East.' They to have some benefit by Him and His birth, and for that to do Him worship, seeing *officium fundatur in beneficio* ever. 4. As thus born in earth, so a star He hath in Heaven of His own—*stellam Ejus*, 'His star;' He the owner of it. Now we know the stars are the stars of Heaven, and He that Lord of them Lord of Heaven too; and so to be adored of them, of us, and of all. St. John puts them together (Rev.22.16); 'the root and generation of David,' His earthly; and 'the bright morning star,' His Heavenly or Divine generation. *Haec est fides Magorum*, this is the mystery of their faith. In *natus est*, man; in *stellam Ejus*, God. In *Rex*, 'a King,' though of the Jews, yet the good of Whose Kingdom should extend and stretch itself far and wide to Gentiles and all; and He of all to be adored. This, for *corde creditur*, the day-star itself in their hearts. Now to the beams of this star.

Next to *corde creditur* is *ore fit confessio*, 'the confession' of this faith. It is in *venerunt dicentes*, they came with it in their mouths. *Venerunt*, they were no sooner come, but they spake of it so freely, to so many, as it came to Herod's ear and troubled him not a little that any King of the Jews should be worshipped beside himself. So then their faith is no bosom-faith, kept to themselves without ever a *dicentes*, without saying any thing of it to any body. No; *credidi, propter quod locutus sum*, 'they believed and therefore they spake' (Ps. 116.10). The star in their hearts cast one beam out at their mouths. And though Herod who was but *Rex factus* could evil brook to hear of *Rex natus*,— must needs be offended at it, yet they were not afraid to say it. And though they came from the East, those parts to whom and their King the Jews had long time been captives and their underlings, they were not ashamed neither to tell, that One of the Jews' race they came to seek; and to seek Him to the end 'to worship Him.' So neither afraid of Herod, nor ashamed of Christ; but professed their errand, and cared not who knew it. This for their confessing Him boldly.

But faith is said by the Apostle (Heb. 11.1) to be ὑπόστασις, and so there is a good 'ground;' and ἔλεγχος, and so hath a good 'reason' for it. This puts the difference between *fidelis* and *credulus*, or as Solomon terms him (Pro. 14.15) *fatuus, qui credit omni verbo;* between faith and lightness of belief. Faith hath ever a ground; *vidimus enim*,—an *enim*, a reason for it, and is ready to render it. How came you to believe? *Audivimus enim*, 'for we have heard an Angel,' say the shepherds (Lu. 2.20). *Vidimus enim*, 'for we have seen a star' say the Magi, and this is a well-grounded faith. We came not of our own heads, we came not before we saw some reason for it—saw that which set us on coming; *Vidimus enim stellam Ejus.*

*Vidimus stellam*—we can well conceive that; any that will but look up, may see a star. But how could they see the *Ejus* of it, that it was His? Either that it belonged to any, or that He it was it belonged to. This passeth all perspective; no astronomy could show them this. What by course of nature the stars can produce, that they by course of art or observation may discover. But this birth was above nature. No trigon, triplicity, exaltation could bring it forth. They are but idle that set figures for it. The star should not have been His, but He the star's, if it had gone that way. Some other light then, they saw this *Ejus* by.

Now with us in Divinity there be but two in all; 1. *Vespertina*, and 2. *Matutina lux. Vespertina*, 'the owl-light' of our reason or skill is too dim to see it by. No remedy then but it must be as Esay calls it, *matutina lux*, 'the morning light' (Isa.58.8), the light of God's law must certify them of the *Ejus* of it. There, or not at all to be had whom this star did portend.

And in the Law, there we find it in the twenty-fourth of Numbers. One of their own Prophets that came from whence they came, 'from the mountains of the East,' was ravished in spirit, 'fell in a trance, had his eyes opened,' and saw the *Ejus* of it many an hundred years before it rose. Saw *orietur in Jacob*, that there it should 'rise,' which is as much as *natus est* here. Saw *stella*, that He should be 'the bright morning-Star,' and so might well have a star to represent Him. Saw *sceptrum in Israel*, which is just as much as *Rex Judaeorum*, that it should portend a King there—such a King as should not only 'smite the corners of Moab,' that is Balak their enemy for the present; but 'should reduce and bring under Him all the sons of Seth,' that is all the world; for all are now Seth's sons, Cain's were all drowned in the flood. Here now is the *Ejus* of it clear. A Prophet's eye might discern this; never a Chaldean of them all could take it with his astrolabe. Balaam's eyes were opened to see it, and he helped to open their eyes by leaving behind him this prophecy to direct them how to apply it, when it should arise to the right *Ejus* of it.

But these had not the law. It is hard to say that the Chaldee paraphrase was extant long before this. They might have had it. Say, they had it not: if Moses were so careful to record this prophecy in his book, it may well be thought that some memory of this so memorable a prediction was left remaining among them of the East, his own country where he was born and brought up. And some help they might have from Daniel too, who lived all his time in Chaldea and Persia, and prophesied among them of such a King, and set the just time of it.

And this, as it is conceived, put the difference between the East and the West. For I ask, was it *vidimus in Oriente* with them? Was it not *vidimus in Occidente?* In the West such a star —it or the fellow of it was seen nigh about that time, or the Roman stories deceive us. Toward the end of Augustus' reign such a star was seen, and much scanning there was about it. Pliny saith it was generally holden, that star to be *faustum sydus*, 'a lucky comet,' and portended good to the world, which few or no comets do. And Virgil, who then lived, would needs take upon him to set down the *ejus* of it, ... *Ecce Dionaei*, &c. (Ecl. 9.47)—entitled Caesar to it. And verily there is no man that can without admiration read his sixth Eclogue, of a birth that time expected, that should be the offspring of the gods, and that should take away their sins. Whereupon it hath gone for current —the East and West, *Vidimus* both.

But by the light of their prophecy, the East they went straight to the right *Ejus*. And for want of this light the West wandered, and gave it a wrong *ejus;* as Virgil, applying it to little Salonine: and as evil hap was, while he was making his verses, the poor child died; and so his star shot, vanished, and came to nothing. Their *vidimus* never came to a *venimus;* they neither went, nor worshipped Him as these here did.

But by this we see, when all is done, hither we must come for our morning-light; to this book, to the word of prophecy. All our *vidimus stellam* is as good as nothing without it. That star is past and gone, long since; 'Heaven and earth shall pass, but this word shall not pass' (Lu. 21.33). Here on this, we to fix our eye and to ground our faith. Having this, though we neither hear Angel nor see star, we may by the grace of God do full well. For even they that have had both those, have been fain to resolve into this as their last, best, and chiefest point of all. Witness St. Peter (2 Pet. 1.17-19): he, saith he, and they with him, 'saw Christ's glory, and heard the voice from Heaven in the Holy Mount.' What then? After both these, *audivimus* and *vidimus*, both senses, he comes to this, *Habemus autem firmiorem*, &c. 'We have a more sure word of prophecy' than both these; *firmiorem*, a 'more sure,' a more clear, than them both. And *si hic legimus*—for *legimus* is *vidimus*, 'if here we read it written,' it is enough to ground our faith, and let the star go.

And yet, to end this point; both these, the star and the prophecy, they are but *circumfusa lux*—without both. Besides these there must be a light within in the eye; else, we know, for all them nothing will be seen. And that must come from Him, and the enlightening of His Spirit. Take this for a rule; no knowing of *Ejus absque Eo*, 'of His without Him,' Whose it is. Neither of the star, without Him That created it; nor of the prophecy, without Him That inspired it. But this third coming too; He sending the light of His Spirit within into their minds, they then saw clearly, this the star, now the time, He the Child That this day was born.

He That sent these two without, sent also this third within, and then it was *vidimus* indeed. The light of the star in their eyes, the 'word of prophecy' in their ears, the beam of His Spirit in their hearts; these three made up a full *vidimus*. And so much for *vidimus stellam Ejus*, the occasion of their coming.

Now to *venimus*, their coming itself. And it follows well. For it is not a star only, but a load-star; and whither should *stella Ejus ducere*, but *ad Eum?* 'Whither lead us, but to Him Whose the star is?' The star to the star's Master.

All this while we have been at *dicentes*, 'saying' and seeing; now we shall come to *facientes*, see them do somewhat upon it. It is not saying nor seeing will serve St. James (2.18); he will call, and be still calling for *ostende mihi*, 'show me thy faith by some work.' And well may he be allowed to call for it this day; it is the day of *vidimus*, appearing, being seen. You have seen His star, let Him now see your star another while. And so they do. Make your faith to be seen; so it is—their faith in the steps of their faith. And so was Abraham's first by coming forth of his country; as these here do, and so 'walk in the steps of the faith of Abraham' (Rom. 4.12), do his first work.

It is not commended to stand 'gazing up into Heaven' (Acts 1.11) too long; not on Christ Himself ascending, much less on His star. For they sat not still gazing on the star. Their *vidimus* begat *venimus;* their seeing made them come, come a great journey. *Venimus* is soon said, but a short word; but many a wide and weary step they made before they could come to say *Venimus*, Lo, here 'we are come;' come, and at our journey's end. To look a little on it. In this their coming we consider, 1. First, the distance of the place they came from. It was not hard by as the shepherds—but a step to Bethlehem over the fields; this was riding many a hundred miles, and cost them many a day's journey. 2. Secondly, we consider the way that they came, if it be pleasant, or plain and easy; for if it be, it is so much the better. 1. This was nothing pleasant, for through deserts, all the way waste and desolate. 2. Nor secondly, easy neither; for over the rocks and crags of both Arabias, specially Petraea, their journey lay. 3. Yet if safe—but it was not, but exceeding dangerous, as lying through the midst of the 'black tents of Kedar' (Cant.1.4), a nation of thieves and cut-throats; to pass over the hills of robbers, infamous then, and infamous to this day. No passing without great troop or convoy. 4. Last we consider the time of their coming, the season of the year. It was no summer progress. A cold coming they had of it at this time of the year, just the worst time of the year to take a journey, and specially a long journey in. The ways deep, the weather sharp, the days short, the sun farthest off, *in solstitio brumali*, 'the very dead of winter.' *Venimus*, 'we are come,' if that be one, *venimus*, 'we are now come,' come at this time, that sure is another.

And these difficulties they overcame, of a wearisome, irksome, troublesome, dangerous, unseasonable journey; and for all this they came. And came it cheerfully and quickly, as appeareth by the speed they made. It was but *vidimus, venimus*, with them; 'they saw,' and 'they came;' no sooner saw, but they set out presently. So as upon the first appearing of the star, as it might be last night, they knew it was Balaam's star; it called them away, they made ready straight to begin their journey this morning. A sign they were highly conceited of His birth, believed some great matter of it, that they took all these pains, made all this haste that they might be there to worship Him with all the possible speed they could. Sorry for nothing so much as that they could not be there soon enough, with the very first, to do it even this day, the day of His birth. All considered, there is more in *venimus* than shows at the first sight. It was not for nothing it was said in the first verse, *ecce venerunt;* their coming hath an *ecce* on it, it well deserves it.

And we, what should we have done? Sure these men of the East shall rise in judgment against the men of the West, that is us, and their faith against ours in this point. With them it was but *vidimus, venimus;* with us it would have been but *veniemus* at most. Our fashion is to see and see again before we stir a foot, specially if it be to the worship of Christ. Come such a journey at such a time? No; but fairly have put it off to the spring of the year, till the days longer, and the ways fairer, and the weather warmer, till better travelling to Christ. Our Epiphany would sure have fallen in Easterweek at the soonest.

But then for the distance, desolateness, tediousness, and the rest, any of them were enough to mar our *venimus* quite. It must be no great way, first, we must come; we love not that. Well fare the shepherds, yet they came but hard by; rather like them than the Magi. Nay, not like them neither. For with us the nearer, lightly the farther off; our proverb is you know, 'The nearer the Church, the farther from God.'

Nor it must not be through no desert, over no Petraea. If rugged or uneven the way, if the weather ill-disposed, if any never so little danger, it is enough to stay us. To Christ we cannot travel, but weather and way and all must be fair. If not, no journey, but sit still and see farther. As indeed, all our religion is rather *vidimus*, a contemplation, than *venimus*, a motion, or stirring to do ought.

But when we do it, we must be allowed leisure. Ever *veniemus*, never *venimus*; ever coming, never come. We love to make no very great haste. To other things perhaps; not to *adorare*, the place of the worship of God. Why should we? Christ is no wild-cat. What talk ye of twelve days? And if it be forty days hence, ye shall be sure to find His Mother and Him; she cannot be churched till then. What needs such haste? The truth is, we conceit Him and His birth but slenderly, and our haste is even thereafter. But if we be at that point, we must be out of this *venimus;* they like enough to leave us behind. Best get us a new Christmas in September; we are not like to come to Christ at this feast. Enough for *venimus*.

But what is *venimus* without *invenimus*? And when they come, they hit not on Him at first. No more must we think, as soon as ever we be come, to find Him straight. They are fain to come to their *ubi est?* We must now look back to that. For though it stand before in the verse, here is the right place of it. They saw before they came, and came before they asked; asked before they found, and found before they worshipped. Between *venimus*, 'their coming,' and *adorare*, 'their worshipping,' there is the true place of *dicentes, ubi est?*

Where, first, we note a double use of their *dicentes*, these wise men had. 1. As to manifest that they knew, *natus est*, 'that He is born,' so to confess and ask what they knew not, the place where. We to have the like.

2. Secondly, set down this; that to find where He is, we must learn of these to ask where He is, which we full little set ourselves to do. If we stumble on Him, so it is; but for any asking we trouble not ourselves, but sit still as we say, and let nature work; and so let grace too, and so for us it shall. I wot well, it is said in a place of Esay (Isa.65.1), 'He was found,' *a non quaerentibus*, 'of some that sought Him not,' never asked *ubi est?* But it is no good holding by that place. It was their good hap that so did. But trust not to it, it is not every body's case, that. It is better advice you shall read in the Psalm (24.6), *haec est generatio quaerentium*, 'there is a generation of them that seek Him.' Of which these were, and of that generation let us be. Regularly there is no promise of *invenietis* but to *quaerite*, of

finding but to such as 'seek.' It is not safe to presume to find Him otherwise.

I thought there had been small use now of *ubi est?* Yet there is except we hold the ubiquity, that Christ is *ubi non*, 'any where.' But He is not so. Christ hath His *ubi*, His proper place where He is to be found; and if you miss of that, you miss of Him. And well may we miss, saith Christ Himself, there are so many will take upon them to tell us where, and tell us of so many *ubis. Ecce hic*, 'Look you, here He is;' *Ecce illic*, nay then, 'there.' *In deserto*, 'in the desert' (Mat. 24.23). Nay, *in penetralibus*, 'in such a privy conventicle' you shall be sure of Him. And yet He, saith He Himself, in none of them all. There is then yet place for *ubi est?* I speak not of His natural body, but of His mystical—that is Christ too.

How shall we then do? Where shall we get this 'where' resolved? Where these did. They said it to many, and oft, but gat no answer, till they had got together a convocation of Scribes, and they resolved them of Christ's *ubi*. For they in the East were nothing so wise, or well seen, as we in the West are now grown. We need call no Scribes together, and get them tell us, 'where.' Every artisan hath a whole Synod of Scribes in his brain, and can tell where Christ is better than any learned man of them all. Yet these were wise men; best learn where they did.

And how did the Scribes resolve it them? Out of Micah. As before to the star they join Balaam's prophecy, so now again to His *orietur*, that such a one should be born, they had put Micah's *et tu Bethlehem*, the place of His birth. Still helping, and giving light as it were to the light of Heaven, by a more clear light, the light of the Sanctuary.

Thus then to do. And to do it ourselves, and not seek Christ *per alium;* set others about it as Herod did these, and sit still ourselves. For so, we may hap never find Him no more than he did.

And now we have found 'where,' what then? It is neither in seeking nor finding, *venimus* nor *invenimus:* the end of all, the cause of all is in the last words, *adorare Eum*, 'to worship Him.' That is all in all, and without it all our seeing, coming, seeking, and finding is to no purpose. The Scribes they could tell, and did tell where He was, but were never the nearer for it, for they worshipped Him not. For this end to seek Him.

This is acknowledged: Herod, in effect, said as much. He would know where He were fain, and if they will bring him word where, he will come too and worship Him, that he will. None of that worship. If he find Him, his worshipping will prove worrying; as did appear by a sort of silly poor lambs that he worried, when he could not have his will on Christ. Thus he at His birth (Mat. 2. 16).

And at His death, the other Herod, he sought Him too; but it was that he and his soldiers might make themselves sport with Him. Such seeking there is otherwhile. And such worshipping; as they in the judgment-hall worshipped Him with *Ave Rex* (Lu. 23. 11), and then gave Him a bob blindfold (John 19. 3). The world's worship of Him for the most part.

But we may be bold to say, Herod was 'a fox' (Lu. 13. 32). These mean as they say; to worship Him they come, and worship Him they will. Will they so? Be they well advised what they promise, before they know whether they shall find Him in a worshipful taking or no? For full little know they, where and in what case they shall find Him. What, if in a stable, laid there in a manger, and the rest suitable to it; in as poor and pitiful a plight as ever was any, more like to be abhorred than adored of such persons? Will they be as good as their word, trow? Will they not step back at the sight, repent themselves of their journey, and wish themselves at home again? But so find Him, and so finding Him, worship Him for all that? If they will, verily then great is their faith. This, the clearest beam of all.

'The Queen of the South,' who was a figure of these Kings of the East (Mat. 12. 42), she came as great a journey as these. But when she came, she found a King indeed, King Solomon in all his royalty. Saw a glorious king, and a glorious court about him. Saw him, and heard him; tried him with many hard questions, received satisfaction of them all. This was worth her coming. Weigh what she found, and what these here—as poor and unlikely a birth as could be, ever to prove a King, or any great matter. No sight to comfort them, nor a word for which they any whit the wiser; nothing worth their travel. Weigh these together, and great odds will be found between her faith and theirs. Theirs the greater far.

Well, they will take Him as they find Him, and all this notwithstanding, worship Him for all that. The Star shall make amends for the manger, and for *stella Ejus* they will dispense with *Eum*.

And what is it to worship? Some great matter sure it is, that Heaven and earth, the stars and Prophets, thus do but serve to lead them and conduct us to. For all we see ends in *adorare*.

*Scriptura et mundus ad hoc sunt, ut colatur Qui creavit, et adoretur Qui inspiravit;* 'the Scripture and world are but to this end, that He That created the one and inspired the other might be but worshipped.' Such reckoning did these seem to make of it here. And such the greater treasurer of the Queen Candace. These came from the mountains in the East; he from the uttermost part of Aethiopia came, and came for no other end but only this—to worship; and when they had done that, home again. *Tanti est adorare.* Worth the while, worth our coming, if coming we do but that, but worship and nothing else. And so I would have men account of it.

To tell you what it is in particular, I must put you over to the eleventh verse, where it is set down what they did when they worshipped. It is set down in two acts προσκυνεῖν, and προσφέρειν, 'falling down,' and 'offering.' Thus did they, thus we to do; we to do the like when we will worship. These two are all, and more than these we find not.

We can worship God but three ways, we have but three things to worship Him withal. 1. The soul He hath inspired; 2. the body He hath ordained us; 3. and the worldly goods He hath vouchsafed to bless us withal. We to worship Him with all, seeing there is but one reason for all.

If He breathed into us our soul, but framed not our body, but some other did that, neither bow your knee nor uncover your head, but keep on your hats, and sit even as you do hardly. But if He hath framed that body of yours and every member of it, let Him have the honour both of head and knee, and every member else.

Again, if it be not He That gave us our worldly goods but somebody else, what He gave not, that withhold from Him and spare not. But if all come from Him, all to return to Him. If He send all, to be worshipped with all. And this in good sooth is but *rationabile obsequium,* as the Apostle calleth it (Rom. 12. 1). No more than reason would, we should worship Him with all.

Else if all our worship be inward only, with our hearts and not our hats as some fondly imagine, we give Him but one of three; we put Him to His thirds, bid Him be content with that, He gets no more but inward worship. That is out of the text quite. For though I doubt not but these here performed that also, yet here it is not. St. Matthew mentions it not, it is not to be seen, no *vidimus* on it. And the text is a *vidimus,* and of a star; that is, of an outward visible worship to be seen of all.

There is a *vidimus* upon the worship of the body, it may be seen —*procidentes*. Let us see you fall down. So is there upon the worship with our worldly goods, that may be seen and felt—*offerentes*. Let us see whether, and what you offer. With both which, no less than with the soul, God is to be worshipped. 'Glorify God with your bodies, for they are God's,' saith the Apostle (1 Cor.6.20). 'Honour God with your substance, for He hath blessed your store,' saith Solomon (Pro.3.9). It is the precept of a wise King, of one there; it is the practice of more than one, of these three here. Specially now; for Christ hath now a body, for which to do Him worship with our bodies. And now He was made poor to make us rich, and so *offerentes* will do well, comes very fit.

To enter farther into these two would be too long, and indeed they be not in our verse here, and so for some other treatise at some other time.

There now remains nothing but to include ourselves, and bear our part with them, and with the Angels, and all who this day adored Him.

This was the load-star of the Magi, and what were they? Gentiles. So are we. But if it must be ours, then we are to go with them; *vade, et fac similiter*, 'go, and do likewise' (Lu.10.37). It is *stella gentium*, but *idem agentium* 'the Gentiles' star,' but 'such Gentiles as overtake these and keep company with them.' In their *dicentes*, 'confessing their faith freely;' in their *vidimus*, 'grounding it thoroughly;' in their *venimus*, 'hasting to come to Him speedily;' in their *ubi est?* 'enquiring Him out diligently;' and in their *adorare Eum*, 'worshipping Him devoutly.' *Per omnia* doing as these did; worshipping and thus worshipping, celebrating and thus celebrating the feast of His birth.

We cannot say *vidimus stellam;* the star is gone long since, not now to be seen. Yet I hope for all that, that *venimus adorare*, 'we be come thither to worship.' It will be the more acceptable, if not seeing it we worship though. It is enough we read of it in the text; we see it there. And indeed as I said, it skills not for the star in the firmament, if the same Day-Star be risen in our hearts that was in theirs, and the same beams of it to be seen, all five. For then we have our part in it no less, nay full out as much as they. And it will bring us whither it brought them, to Christ. Who at His second appearing in glory shall call forth these wise men, and all that have ensued the steps of their faith, and that upon the reason specified in the text; for I have seen their star shining and showing forth itself by the like beams; and as they came to worship Me, so am I come to do them worship. A *venite* then, for a *venimus* now. Their star I have seen, and give them a place above among the stars. They fell down: I will lift them up, and exalt them. And as they offered to Me, so am I come to bestow on them, and to reward them with the endless joy and bliss of My Heavenly Kingdom.

To which, &c.

# JOHN DONNE

JOHN DONNE, one of the first 'modern' men in the sense of his awareness of the break-up of established values brought about by the discoveries of the Renaissance, is as famous for his poetry as for his preaching. He wrote some of the greatest love poetry, and some of the greatest religious poetry (in particular the 'Divine Poems') in any language. He was famous, too, for his amatory exploits in his youth, and for his capacity for getting through money. Here the emphasis must, of necessity, be laid on his relationship to the Church of England, and on his religious position. For a lively, if not always accurate, introduction to the life of Donne the reader can do no better than turn to Isaac Walton's famous *Life*; the standard biography is by R. C. Bald (1970).

Donne, of distinguished ancestry on at least his mother's side, was born in London in 1572. He spoke of himself as 'being derived from such a stock and race as, I believe, no family ... hath endured more ... for obeying the Teachers of Roman Doctrine, than it hath done'. His own upbringing was Catholic (though not Jesuit). He acquired an excellent education, though his knowledge of Greek seems to have been small (he knew Hebrew well). He went to Oxford at twelve, to Hart Hall, which was suspected of harbouring Catholics. He could not take a degree because he had no intention of subscribing to the Oath of Supremacy and to the Thirty-Nine Articles, which was required of all students when they reached sixteen years of age. He probably then went on to Cambridge. In the early 1590s he was a law student at Thavies and, subsequently, Lincoln's Inn (1591-4 or later). Here he was at first under the influence of active Catholics and Jesuits. His reaction against Catholicism began, however, in this same period. At first it took the form of an antagonism towards the Jesuits that was shared by many of Donne's fellow-Catholics, although this was not to come to a head until 1594 when the so-called archpriest controversy was precipitated by the death of Cardinal William Allen, trainer of Roman Catholic mission priests, at the English College in Rome. One faction wished to destroy Elizabeth's government; the other—of which Donne was one—wished to remain loyal. On the question of leaving the Roman Catholic Church, however, Donne later wrote that the disadvantages of his adherence did not 'transport me to any violent and sudden determination, till I had, to the measure of my poor wit and judgment, surveyed and digested the whole body of Divinity, controverted between ours and the Roman Church'. Throughout the mid-nineties, influenced by scepticism and Renaissance new thinking, he hovered between Catholicism and Protestantism—dissatisfied with both. By 1598, however, Donne had decided to renounce his official Catholicism, and to conform to the Church of England: had he not done so, then he could not have become a secretary to the recently appointed Lord Keeper of the Great Seal, Sir Thomas Egerton (himself an ex-recusant who later helped prosecute such Catholics as Campion, Mary Queen of Scots and the Earl of Arundel). Donne lost this job in 1602 because of his secret marriage to Ann More, whose choleric father objected to it and who had too much influence over Egerton (who was reluctant to dismiss Donne) for him to resist his will.

Then followed the most difficult years of his life. He tried to obtain secular employment in Ireland, but James I felt that his behaviour over his marriage disqualified him. He suffered from nervous illness, studied assiduously, and wrote much, including *Biathanatos* (not published until 1646), which is, significantly, a study of suicide ('I have often such a sickly inclination', he wrote in it) and is not unsympathetic to that act. When he gave his friend Sir Robert Ker a manuscript of it in 1619 he remarked that 'it is a Book written by *Jack Donne*, and not by D[octor] *Donne*.'

At this time Donne came under the influence of Thomas Morton, a noted anti-Romanist and then Dean of Gloucester (he was to be ejected from his bishopric of Durham in 1646 at the age of eighty-two; he lived on until the age of ninety-five). Morton evidently tried, but without success, to persuade Donne to enter the Church; but, despite his poverty, he refused to do so. In 1610 he published *Pseudo-Martyr*, dedicated to King James (who by now was taking a personal interest in him): the gist of this book is that Catholics ought to take the Oath of Allegiance —and that those who refused were not entitled to the status of martyrs. Yet its tone towards Catholics (but not the Jesuits, whom he attacks bitterly) is remarkably sympathetic. At this same time Donne was racked by doubts and was probably on the edge of mental breakdown: he was haunted by his behaviour as a young man, terrified of death and perhaps of hell ('death before doth cast / Such terror'). Suffering from what would now be diagnosed as an acute depression, Donne regarded such 'melancholy'—as it was then called, though the term had a very wide range of application—as a serious sin. He equated 'melancholy in the soul' with 'distrust of salvation'. This theme was to be a most persistent and vivid one in his sermons (he had thought himself a toad, and that God too thought him a toad, he later preached).

After a period abroad with Sir Robert Drury (1611-12), which seems to have relieved his morbidity of spirit, Donne came to live in Drury Lane. Now his hopes of finding employment began to build up again. He began (1613) seriously to think of the Church (Morton had by then tried to persuade him to take orders yet again—and James I himself urged this course: the pressure was therefore extreme). Through a former benefactor he approached Viscount Rochester (formerly Robert Ker)—and it so happened that at the very time he did so, Rochester needed an able man to serve him: to break up the marriage of his lover, the Countess of Essex, to the Earl. Whatever part Donne had to play in this unpleasant business, he certainly supported his new patron, whom the King made Earl of Somerset so that his wife should maintain her rank. Not insignificantly, Donne now fell seriously ill. His financial situation was desperate, his wife was also ill—and they lost a child. Yet he was busy studying Hebrew (and, says Walton, Greek) and the history of Christianity and its more esoteric theologians. He had originally written to Rochester of his intention to 'make my profession Divinity'; yet he seemed unable to make up his mind. He became M. P. for Taunton in the Addled Parliament of April-June 1614, in which (however privately critical) he discreetly took the side of the King in committee (he avoided debates). After this abortive parliament had been dissolved he desperately, and perhaps surprisingly, tried to obtain secular employment (for example, as ambassador to Venice). But, despite the efforts of Somerset, King James refused: he was determined to have Donne as a priest. By November 1614 he made the decision: he was ordained in the following January. He became a royal Chaplain, and was soon a favourite preacher at Court. In 1621 he became Dean of St Paul's, and from then until his death ten years later was the most famous preacher in the country.

The reason Donne gave for holding back from the Church was that he disliked the notion of attaining financial security from such a source; and this was undoubtedly one of his motives. However, his own conscience—a quite remarkably sensitive one—was another important factor. Critics have pointed out, too, that it is precisely at the time of his ordination that he appears most cynically self-seeking and ready to manipulate others for his purposes. They ignore the fact not only that it was then hardly possible to achieve financial security (and Donne especially needed this because of his wife's very delicate health: she died in 1617) without having influential friends but also that Donne was a most unusual, complex, eclectic and introspective man. As has been rightly said, his dramatic sermons—in terms of language the greatest ever preached—were simply an extension of the private spiritual exercises (of which we have abundant evidence) in which he had been indulging during the years of his poverty and despair. Whether or not we believe, as he certainly did, in the redemptive power of Jesus Christ as Son of God, we are incapable of not responding to the force of his message that sin (or a sense of guilt) is terrible, and yet that God is none the less merciful. Donne's approach is that of a poet, and its psychological acuteness (heightened by his intensely histrionic and rhetorical presentation) anticipates the climate of thought which is today usually described, not always helpfully, as 'existentialist'. This approach characterizes all the 160 extant sermons by Donne (145 appeared in 1640, though some had been printed in his lifetime; the rest have been collected gradually).

Donne, being a many-sided man, and one of strong physical appetites and equally strong spiritual aspirations, was sensitive and sympathetic to most currents of thought. If he seems to have 'played safe' in his life (not a few have called him an opportunist), this must be put down not to lack of courage but, mainly, to the unfortunate fate of so many of his Catholic ancestors (and his own brother had died as a result of harbouring a priest), and to the fact that his inner life was the main theatre of his activity. Although ultimately not a sceptic, he had absorbed enough of the scepticism then current (as evidenced in the works of Montaigne, Marlowe—notorious at Cambridge while Donne himself was there—and many others) to be suspicious of the 'enthusiasm' that led to martyrdom. He is peculiarly 'modern' in this attitude, too.

The distinction between 'Jack Donne' and 'Dr Donne' (made by himself) has of course been taken too far. When Donne became a priest it was to be a preacher, and undoubtedly his sermons—classics of our prose—are the culmination of his greatest religious poems, the 'Divine Poems' (mostly though not all composed 1609-11, and certainly before he became a priest); these, too, follow on, logically enough, from the love poetry, the satires and the elegies (mostly of the 1590s). The whole *oeuvre* develops quite naturally.

Donne's sermons should be allowed, so far as is possible, to speak for themselves. Their theology is orthodox Church of England; but their presentation is anything but orthodox. Their main theme may perhaps be most aptly illustrated by a short reference, in *Biathanatos*, to the 'presumed suicide' of Judas—the most terrible example of a sinner to a Christian. Matthew (27.5) says that he repented and then hanged himself as one who had 'betrayed the innocent blood'. But Acts (1. 18) quotes Peter as saying that he bought a field with his thirty pieces of silver, and then 'falling headlong . . . burst asunder in the midst, and all his bowels gushed out'. Donne quotes Origen, the third-century Biblical exegete, regarded as of great authority: 'For it may be . . . that Satan which had entered into him, stayed with him till Christ was betrayed, and then left him, and thereupon repentance followed'. He adds: 'And perchance, says he [Origen], he went to prevent, and go before his Master, who was to die, and so to meet him with his naked soul, that he might gain Mercy by his confession and prayers.'

A Sermon of Valediction at My Going into
Germany, at Lincoln's Inn, April 18, 1619
Eccles. 12:1.
*Remember now thy Creator in the days of thy youth.*

THE IMMEDIATE occasion for this sermon was Donne's imminent departure for Germany, as he had been appointed chaplain to Lord Doncaster (May 1619-January 1620), who had been sent there as mediator to the German princes. As a Spanish diplomat of the time truthfully wrote, 'the vanity of the present King of England is so great he will always think it is of great importance that peace shall be made by his means, so that his authority may be increased'. Donne was himself deeply concerned with the problem of the European Protestants; but he was unwell, and reluctant to leave. It was now that he sent Sir Robert Ker (not to be confused with his namesake, the notorious Earl of Somerset, who was tried for murder and spent years in prison; this Ker, an old personal friend, became Earl of Ancrum in 1633) the treatise on suicide, *Biathanatos*: 'publish it not, but yet burn it not . . .' He was in an unhappy and consequently a dramatic frame of mind: he thought he might die, and more than once alluded to this possibility in letters. His state is best illustrated not only by this sermon, but also by his poem 'A Hymn to Christ at the Author's Last Going into Germany'. Readers will note the specific echo of this in the final passage of the sermon beginning 'Remember me thus'; but the sermon is, as a whole, a generalization of the mood the poem more personally evokes:

> In what torn ship soever I embark,
> That ship shall be my emblem of thy ark;
> What sea soever swallow me, that flood
> Shall be to me an emblem of thy blood;
> Though thou with clouds of anger do disguise
> Thy face; yet through that mask I know those eyes,
>     Which, though they turn away sometimes,
>         They never will despise.
>
> I sacrifice this Island unto thee,
> And all whom I loved there, and who loved me;
> When I have put our seas 'twixt them and me,
> Put thou thy sea betwixt my sins and thee.
> As the tree's sap doth seek the root below

In winter, in my winter now I go,
    Where none but thee, th'eternal root
        Of true love I may know.

Nor thou nor thy religion dost control,
The amorousness of an harmonious soul,
But thou wouldst have that love thyself: as thou
Art jealous, Lord, so I am jealous now,
Thou lov'st not, till from loving more, thou free
My soul; who ever gives, takes liberty:
    O, if thou car'st not whom I love
        Alas, thou lov'st not me.

Seal then this bill of my divorce to all,
On whom those fainter beams of love did fall;
Marry those loves, which in youth scattered be
On fame, wit, hopes (false mistresses) to thee.
Churches are best for prayer, that have least light:
To see God only, I go out of sight:
    And to 'scape stormy days, I choose
        An everlasting night.

However, Donne was never one to withdraw altogether his personality. He was a strange mixture of exhibitionist and contemplative—and from the tensions and paradoxes generated by these opposing poles of his personality is derived much of the power of his sermons. It is typical of the man that he should take so little trouble to disguise the state of his own mind, which was haunted by death. The famous text he chose more than likely refers to his extreme sense of guilt about his own early years (for while we must not exaggerate the legend of the 'two Donnes', there is no doubt that he did). It is a sermon preached in expectation of imminent death.

WE MAY consider two great virtues, one for the society of this life, thankfulness, and the other for attaining the next life, repentance; as the two precious metals, silver and gold: of silver (of the virtue of thankfulness) there are whole mines, books written by philosophers, and a man may grow rich in that metal, in that virtue, by digging in that mine, in the precepts of moral men; of this gold (this virtue of repentance) there is no mine in the earth; in the book of philiosophers, no doctrine of repentance; this gold is for the most part in the washes; this repentance in matters of tribulation; but God directs thee to it in this text, before thou come to those waters of tribulation, remember now thy Creator before those evil days come, and then thou wilt repent the not remembering him till now. Here then the Holy Ghost takes the nearest way to bring a man to God, by awaking his memory; for, for the understanding, that requires long and clear instruction; and the will requires an instructed understanding before, and is in itself the blindest and boldest faculty; but if the memory do but fasten upon any of those things which God hath done for us, it is the nearest way to him. Remember therefore, and remember now, though the memory be placed in the hindermost part of the brain, defer not thou thy remembering to the hindermost part of thy life, but do that now *in die*, in the day, whilst thou hast light, now *in diebus*, in the days, whilst God presents thee many lights, many means; and *in diebus juventutis*, in the days of thy youth, of strength, whilst thou art able to do that which thou purposest to thyself; and as the word imports, *bechurotheica,* in diebus electionem tuarum*, in the days of thy choice, whilst thou art able to make thy choice, whilst the grace of God shines so brightly upon thee, as thou mayest choose the way, and so powerfully upon thee, as that thou mayest walk in that way. Now, in this day, and in these days remember first the Creator, that all these things which thou labourest for, and delightest in, were created, made of nothing; and therefore thy memory looks not far enough back, if it stick only upon the creature, and reach not to the Creator, remember thy Creator, and remember thy Creator; and in that, first that he made thee, and then what he made thee; he made thee of nothing, but of that nothing he hath made thee such a thing as cannot return to nothing, but must remain for ever; whether happy or miserable, that depends upon thy *remembering thy Creator now in the days of thy youth*.

First remember; which word is often used in the Scripture

for considering and taking care: for, God remembered Noah and every beast with him in the ark; as the word which is contrary to that, forgetting is also for the affection contrary to it, it is neglecting, *Can a woman forget her child, and not have compassion on the son of her womb?* (Isa. xlviii. 15.) But here we take not remembering so largely, but restrain it to the exercise of that one faculty, the memory; for it is *stomachus animae* [the stomach of the soul]. The memory, says St. Bernard, is the stomach of the soul, it receives and digests, and turns into good blood, all the benefits formerly exhibited to us in particular, and exhibited to the whole church of God: present that which belongs to the understanding, to that faculty, and the understanding is not presently settled in it; present any of the prophecies made in the captivity, and a Jew's understanding takes them for deliverances from Babylon, and a Christian's understanding takes them for deliverances from sin and death, by the Messias Christ Jesus; present any of the prophecies of the Revelation concerning antichrist,* and a papist will understand it of a single, and momentane [momentary], and transitory man, that must last but three years and a half; and a protestant may understand it of a succession of men, that have lasted so one thousand years already: present but the name of bishop or of elder, out of the Acts of the Apostles, or their epistles, and other men will take it for a name of equality, and parity, and we for a name and office of distinction in the hierarchy of God's church. Thus it is in the understanding that is often perplexed; consider the other faculty, the will of man, by those bitternesses which have passed between the Jesuits and the Dominicans, (amongst other things belonging to the will) whether the same proportion of grace, offered to men alike disposed, must necessarily work alike upon both their wills? And amongst persons nearer to us, whether that proportion of grace, which doth convert a man, might not have been resisted by perverseness of his will? By all these difficulties we may see, how untractable, and untameable a faculty the will of man is. But come not with matter of law, but matter of fact, *Let God make his wonderful works to be had in remembrance* (Ps. cxi. 4): present the history of God's protection of his children, from the beginning, in the ark, in both captivities, in infinite dangers; present this to the memory, and howsoever the understanding be beclouded, or the will perverted, yet both Jew and Christian, Papist and Protestant, Puritan and Protestant, are affected with a thankful acknowledgment of his former mercies and benefits, this issue of that faculty of their memory is alike in them all: and therefore God in giving the law, works upon no other faculty but this, *I am the Lord thy God which brought thee out of the land of Egypt*; he only presents to their memory what he had done for them. And so in delivering the Gospel in one principal seal thereof, the sacrament of his body, he recommended it only to their memory, *Do this in remembrance of me*. This is the faculty that God desires to work upon; and therefore if thine understanding cannot reconcile differences in all churches, if thy will cannot submit itself to the ordinances of thine own church, go to thine own memory; for as St. Bernard calls that the stomach of the soul, we may be bold to call it the gallery of the soul, hanged with so many, and so lively pictures of the goodness and mercies of thy God to thee, as that every one of them shall be a catechism to thee, to instruct thee in all thy duties to him for those mercies: and as a well-made, and well-placed picture, looks always upon him that looks upon it; so shall thy God look upon thee, whose memory is thus contemplating him, and shine upon thine understanding, and rectify thy will too. If thy memory cannot comprehend his mercy at large showed to his whole church, (as it is almost an incomprehensible thing, that in so few years he made us of the Reformation, equal even in number to our adversaries of the Roman church,) if thy memory have not held that picture of our general deliverance from the navy; (if that mercy be written in the water and in the sands, where it was performed, and not in thy heart) if thou rememberest not our deliverance from that artificial hell, the vault, (in which, though his instruments failed of their plot, they did not blow us up; yet the devil goes forward with his plot, if ever he can blow out; if he can get that deliverance to be forgotten.) If these be too large pictures for thy gallery, for thy memory, yet every man hath a pocket-picture about him, Emanuel, a bosom book, and if he will turn over but one leaf, and remember what God hath done for him even since yesterday, he shall find even by that little branch a navigable river, to sail into that great and endless sea of God's mercies towards him, from the beginning of his being.

Do but remember, but remember now: Of his own will begat he us with the word of truth, that we should be as the first fruits of his creatures (Jas.i.18): that as we consecrate all his creatures to him, in a sober, and religious use of them, so as the first fruits of all, we should principally consecrate ourselves to his service betimes. Now there were three payments of first fruits appointed by God to the Jews: the first was, *primitiae spicarum*, of their ears of corn, and this was early about Easter; the second was *primitiae panum*, of loaves of bread, after their corn was converted to that use; and this, though it were not so soon, yet it was early too, about Whitsuntide; the third was *primitiae frugum*, of all their fruits and revenues; but this was very late in Autumn, at the fall of the leaf, in the end of the year. The two first of these, which were offered early, were offered partly to God, and partly to man, to the priest; but in the last, which came late, God had no part: he had his part in the corn, and in the loaves, but none in the latter fruits. Offer thyself to God; first, as *primitias spicarum*, (whether thou glean in the world, or bind up whole sheaves, whether thy increase be by little and little, or apace;) and offer thyself, as *primitias panum*, when thou hast kneaded up riches, and honour, and favour in a settled and established fortune, offer at thy Easter, whensoever thou hast any resurrection, any sense of raising thy soul from the shadow of death; offer at thy Pentecost,* when the Holy Ghost visits thee, and descends upon thee in a fiery tongue, and melts thy bowels by the power of his word; for if thou defer thy offering till thy fall, till thy winter, till thy death, howsoever they may be thy first fruits, because they be the first that ever thou gavest, yet they are such, as are not acceptable to God; God hath no portion in them, if they be not offered till then; offer thyself now; for that is an easy request; yea offer to thyself now, that is more easy; *Viximus mundo; vivamus reliquum nobis ipsis* (Basil); Thus long we have served the world; let us serve ourselves the rest of our time, that is, the best part of ourselves, our souls, *Expectas ut febris te vocet ad poenitentiam?* Hadst thou rather a sickness should bring thee to God, than a sermon? Hadst thou rather be beholden to a physician for thy salvation, than to a preacher? Thy business is to remember; stay not for thy last sickness, which may be a lethargy in which thou mayest forget thine own name, and his that gave thee the name of a Christian, Christ Jesus himself: thy business is to remember, and thy time is now, stay not till that angel come which shall say and swear, that time shall be no more (Rev.x.6).

Remember then, and remember now; *In die*, In the day; the Lord will hear us *In die qua invocaverimus*, In the day that we shall call upon him (Ps.xx.9); and in *quacunque die*, In what day soever we call (Ps.cxxxviii.3), and in *Quacunque die velociter exaudiet* (Ps.cii.2), As soon as we call in any day. But all this is *opus diei*, a work for the day; for in the night, in our last night, those thoughts that fall upon us, they are rather dreams, than true rememberings; we do rather dream that we repent, than repent indeed, upon our death-bed. To him that travels by night a bush seems a tree, and a tree seems a man, and a man a spirit; nothing hath the true shape to him; to him that repents by night, on his deathbed, neither his own sins, nor the mercies of God have their true proportion. Fool, says Christ, this night they will fetch away thy soul; but he neither tells him, who they be that shall fetch it, nor whither they shall carry it; he hath no light but lightnings: a sudden flash of horror, first, and then he goes into fire without light, *Numquid Deus nobis ignem pacavit? Non, sed diabolo, et angelis* (Chrysostom): Did God ordain hell-fire for us? no, but for the devil, and his angels. And yet we that are vessels so broken, as that there is not a sherd left, to fetch water at the pit, that is, no means in ourselves, to derive one drop of Christ's blood upon us, nor to wring out one tear of true repentance from us, have plunged ourselves into this everlasting, and this dark fire, which was not prepared for us; a wretched covetousness, to be intruders upon the devil; a wretched ambition, to be usurpers upon damnation. God did not make the fire for us; but much less did he make us for that fire; that is, make us to damn us. But now the judgment is given, *Ite maledicti*, Go ye accursed; but yet this is the way of God's justice, and his proceeding, that his judgments are not always executed, though they be given. The judgments and sentences of Medes and Persians are irrevocable, but the judgments and sentences of God, if they be given, if they be published, they are not executed. The Ninevites had perished, if the sentence of their destruction had not been given; and the sentence preserved them; so even in this cloud of *Ite maledicti*, Go ye accursed, we may see the daybreak, and discern beams of saving light, even in this judgment of eternal darkness; if the contemplation of his judgment brings us to remember him in that day, in the light and apprehension of his anger and correction.

For this circumstance is enlarged; it is not *in die*, but *in diebus*, not in one, but in many days; for God affords us many days, many lights to see and remember him by. This remembrance of God is our regeneration, by which we are new creatures; and therefore we may consider as many days in it, as in the first creation. The first day was the making of light; and our first day is the knowledge of him, who says of himself, *Ego sum lux mundi*, I am the light of the world, and of whom St. John testifies, *Erat lux vera*, He was the true light, that lighteth every man into the world. This is then our first day the true passion of Christ Jesus. God made light first, that the other creatures might be seen; *Frustra essent si non viderentur* (Ambrose), It had been to no purpose to have made creatures, if there had been no light to manifest them. Our first day is the light and love of the Gospel; for the noblest creatures of princes, (that is, the noblest actions of princes, war, and peace, and treaties) *frustra sunt*, they are good for nothing, they are nothing, if they be not showed and tried by this light, by the love and preservation of the Gospel of Christ Jesus: God made light first, that his other works might appear, and he made light first, that himself (for our example) might do all his other works in the light: that we also, as we had that light shed upon us in our baptism, so we might make all our future actions justifiable by that light, and not *erubescere evangelium*, not be ashamed of being too jealous in this profession of his truth. Then God saw that the light was good: the seeing implies a consideration; that so a religion be not accepted blindly, nor implicitly; and the seeing it to be good implies an election of that religion, which is simply good in itself, and not good by reason of advantage, or conveniency, or other collateral and by-respects. And when God had seen the light, and seen that it was good, then he severed light from darkness; and he severed them, *non tanquam duo positiva*, not as two essential, and positive, and equal things, not so, as that a brighter and a darker religion, (a good and a bad) should both have a being together, but *tanquam positivum et primitivum*, light and darkness are primitive, and positive, and figure this rather, that a true religion should be established, and continue, and darkness utterly removed; and then and not till then, (till this was done, light severed from darkness) there was a day; and since God hath given us this day, the brightness of his Gospel, that this light is first presented, that is, all great actions begun with this consideration of the Gospel; since all other things are made by this light, that is, all have relation to the continuance of the Gospel, since God hath given us such a head, as is sharp-sighted in seeing the several lights, wise in discerning the true light, powerful in resisting foreign darkness; since God hath given us this day, *Qui non humiliabit animam suam in die hac*, as Moses speaks of the days of God's institution (Levit. xxiii), he that will not remember God now, in this day, is impious to him, and unthankful to that great instrument of his, by whom this day-spring from on high hath visited us.

To make shorter days of the rest, (for we must pass through all the six days in a few minutes) God in the second day made the firmament to divide between the waters above, and the waters below; and this firmament in us, is *terminus cognoscibilium*, the limits of those things which God hath given man means and faculties to conceive, and understand: he hath limited our eyes with a firmament beset with stars, our eyes can see no farther: he hath limited our understanding in matters of religion with a starry firmament too; that is, with the knowledge of those things, *quae ubique, quae semper*, which those stars which he hath kindled in his church, the fathers and doctors, have ever from the beginning proposed as things necessary to be explicitly believed, for the salvation of our souls; for the eternal decrees of God, and his unrevealed mysteries, and the inextricable perplexities of the school, they are waters above the firmament: here Paul plants, and here Apollos waters; here God raises up men to convey to us the dew of his grace, by waters under the firmament; by visible sacraments, and by the word so preached, and so interpreted, as it hath been constantly, and unanimously from the beginning of the church. And therefore this second day is perfected in the third, in the *congregentur aquae*, let the waters be gathered together; God hath gathered all the waters, all the waters of life in one place; that is, all the doctrine necessary for the life to come, into his church: and then *producet terra*, here in this world are produced to us all herbs and fruits, all that is necessary for the soul to feed upon. And in this third day's work God repeats here that testimony, *videt quod bonum*, he saw that it was good; good, that here should be a gathering of waters in one place, that is, no doctrine received that had not been taught in the church; and *videt quod bonum*, he saw it was good, that all herbs and trees should be produced that bore seed; all doctrines that were to be proseminated and propagated, and to be continued to the end, should be taught in the church: but for doctrines which were but to vent the passion of vehement men, or to serve the turns of great men for a time, which were not seminal doctrines, doctrines that bore seed, and were to last from the beginning to the end; for these interlineary doctrines, and marginal, which were no part of the first text, here is no testimony that God sees that they are good. And, *In diebus istis*, If in these two days, the day when God makes thee a firmament, shows thee what thou art, to limit thine understanding and thy faith upon, and the day where God makes thee a sea, a collection of the waters, (shows thee where these necessary things must be taught in the church) if in those days thou wilt not remember thy Creator, it is an irrecoverable lethargy.

In the fourth day's work, let the making of the sun to rule the day be the testimony of God's love to thee, in the sunshine of temporal prosperity, and the making of the moon to shine by night, be the refreshing of his comfortable promises in the darkness of adversity; and then remember that he can make thy sun to set at noon, he can blow out thy taper of prosperity when it burns brightest, and he can turn the moon into blood, he can make all the promises of the Gospel, which should comfort thee in adversity, turn into despair and obduration. Let the first day's work, which was the creation of *Omnium reptibilium*, and *Omnium volatilium*, Of all creeping things, and of all flying things, produced out of water, signify and denote to thee, either thy humble devotion, in which thou sayest of thyself to God, *Vermis ego et non homo*, I am a worm and no man; or let it be the raising of thy soul in that, *pennas columbae dedisti*, that God hath given thee the wings of a dove to fly to the wilderness, in a retiring from, or a resisting of temptations of this world; remember still that God can suffer even thy humility to stray, and degenerate into an uncomely dejection and stupidity, and senselessness of the true dignity and true liberty of a Christian: and he can suffer this retiring thyself from the world, to degenerate into a contempt and despising of others, and an overvaluing of thine own perfections. Let the last day in which both man and beasts were made out of the earth, but yet a living soul breathed into man, remember thee that this earth which treads upon thee, must return to that earth which thou treadest upon, thy body, that loads thee, and oppresses thee to the grave, and thy spirit to him that gave it. And when the Sabbath-day hath also remembered thee, that God hath given thee a temporal sabbath, placed thee in a land of peace, and an ecclesiastical sabbath, placed in a church of peace, perfect all in a spiritual sabbath, a conscience of peace, by remembering now thy Creator, at least in one of these days of the week of thy regeneration, either as thou hast light created in thee, in the first day, that is, thy knowledge of Christ; or as thou hast a firmament created in thee the second day, that is, thy knowledge what to seek concerning Christ, things appertaining to faith and salvation; or as thou hast a sea created in thee; the third day, that is, a church where all the knowledge is reserved and presented to thee; or as thou hast a sun and moon in the fourth day, thankfulness in prosperity, comfort in adversity, or as thou hast *reptilem humilitatem*, or *volatilem fiduciam*, a humiliation in thyself, or an exaltation in Christ, in thy fifth day, or as thou hast a contemplation of thy mortality and immortality in the sixth day, or a desire of a spiritual sabbath in the seventh, in those days remember thou thy Creator.

Now all these days are contracted into less room in this text, *in diebus bechurotheica*, is either, *in the days of thy youth*, or *electionem tuarum*, in the days of thy heart's desire, when thou enjoyest all that thou couldest wish. First, therefore if thou wouldest be heard in David's prayer; *Delicta juventutis*; O Lord remember not the sins of my youth (Ps. xxv. 7); remember to come to this prayer, *In diebus juventutis*, In the days of thy youth. Job remembers with much sorrow (xxix. 4), how he was in the days of his youth, when God's providence was upon his tabernacle: and it is a late, but a sad consideration, to remember with what tenderness of conscience, what scruples, what remorses we entered into sins in our youth, how much we were afraid of all degrees and circumstances of sin for a little while, and how indifferent things they are grown to us, and how obdurate we are grown in them now. This was Job's sorrow, and this was Tobias's comfort (Tobit i. 4), when I was but young, all my tribes fell away; but I alone went after to Jerusalem. Though he lacked the counsel, and the example in his elders, yet he served God; for it is good for a man, that he bear his yoke in his youth (Lam. iii. 27): for even when God had delivered over his people purposely to be afflicted, yet himself complains in their behalf, *That the persecutor laid the very heaviest yoke upon the ancient* (Isa. xlvii. 6): it is a lamentable thing to fall under a necessity of suffering in our age, *Labore fracta instrumenta, ad Deum ducis, quorum nullus usus?* (Basil) Wouldest thou consecrate a chalice to God that is broken? no man would present a lame horse, a disordered clock, a torn book to the king; *Caro jumentum* (Aug.), Thy body is thy beast; and wilt thou present that to God, when it is lamed and tired with excess of wantonness? When thy clock, (the whole course of thy time) is disordered with passions, and perturbations; when thy book (the history of thy life,) is torn, a thousand sins of thine own torn out of thy memory, wilt thou then present thyself thus defaced and mangled to Almighty

God? *Temperantia non est temperantia in senectute, sed impotentia incontinentiae* (Basil), Chastity is not chastity in an old man, but a disability to be unchaste; and therefore thou dost not give God that which thou pretendest to give, for thou hast no chastity to give him. *Senex bis puer;* but it is not *bis juvenis*, an old man comes to the infirmities of childhood again; but he comes not to the strength of youth again.

Do this then *in diebus juventutis*, in thy best strength, and when thy natural faculties are best able to concur with grace; but do it; *in diebus electionum*, in the days when thou hast thy heart's desire; for if thou have worn out this word, in one sense, that it be too late now, to remember him in the days of youth, that is, spent forgetfully, yet as long as thou art able to make a new choice, to choose a new sin, that when thy heats of youth are not overcome, but burnt out, then thy middle age chooses ambition, and thy old age chooses covetousness; as long as thou art able to make thy choice thou art able to make a better than this; God testifies that power, that he hath given thee; *I call heaven and earth to record this day, that I have set before you life and death; choose life* (Deut. xxx. 19): if this choice like you not, *If it seem evil unto you to serve the Lord*, saith Joshua (xxiv. 15), then *choose ye this day whom ye will serve*. Here is the election day; bring that which ye would have, into comparison with that which ye should have; that is, all that this world keeps from you, with that which God offers to you; and what will ye choose to prefer before him? for honour, and favour, and health, and riches, perchance you cannot have them though you choose them; but can you have more of them than they have had, to whom those very things have been occasions of ruin? The market is open till the bell ring; till thy last bell ring the church is open, grace is to be had there: but trust not upon that rule, that men buy cheapest at the end of the market, that heaven may be had for a breath at last, when they that hear it cannot tell whether it be a sigh or a gasp, a religious breathing and anhelation after the next life, or natural breathing out, and exhalation of this; but find a spiritual good husbandry in that other rule, that the prime of the market is to be had at first: for howsoever, in thine age, there may be by God's strong working, *dies juventutis*, a day of youth, in making thee then a new creature; (for as God is *antiquissimus dierum*, so in his school no man is superannuated,) yet when age hath made a man impotent to sin, that is not *dies electionum*, it is not a day of choice; but remember God now, when thou hast a choice, that is, a power to advance thyself, or to oppress others by evil means; now *in die electionum*, in those thy happy and sunshine days, remember him.

This is then the faculty that is excited, the memory; and this is the time, now, now whilst we have power of election: the object is, the Creator, remember the Creator: first, because the memory can go no farther than the creation; and therefore we have no means to conceive, or apprehend anything of God before that. When men therefore speak of decrees of reprobation, decrees of condemnation, before decrees of creation; this is beyond the counsel of the Holy Ghost here, *Memento Creatoris*, Remember the Creator, for this is to remember God a condemner before he was a Creator: this is to put a preface to Moses' Genesis, not to be content with his *in principio*, to know that *in the beginning God created heaven and earth*, but we must remember what he did *ante principium*, before any such beginning was. Moses' *in principio*, that beginning, the creation we can remember; but St. John's *in principio*, that beginning, eternity, we cannot; we can remember God's *fiat* in Moses, but not God's *erat* in St. John: what God hath done for us, is the object of our memory, not what he did before we were: and thou hast a good and perfect memory, if it remember all that the Holy Ghost proposes in the Bible; and it determines in the *memento Creatoris*: there begins the Bible, and there begins the creed, *I believe in God the Father, maker of heaven and earth*; for when it is said, *The Holy Ghost was not given, because Jesus was not glorified* (John vii.39), it is not truly *non erat datus*, but *non erat*; for, *non erat nobis antequam operaretur*; it is not said there, the Holy Ghost was not given, but it is the Holy Ghost was not: for he is not, that is, he hath no being to us-ward, till he works in us which was first in the creation: remember the Creator then, because thou canst remember nothing backward beyond him, and remember him so too, that thou mayest stick upon nothing on this side of him, that so neither *height, nor depth, nor any other creature may separate thee from God* (Rom.viii.ult.); not only not separate thee finally, but not separate so, as to stop upon the creature, but to make the best of them, thy way to the Creator; we see ships in the river; but all their use is gone, if they go not to sea; we see men freighted with honour, and riches, but all their use is gone, if their respect be not upon the honour and glory of the Creator; and therefore says the apostle, *Let them that suffer, commit their souls to God, as to a faithful Creator*

(1 Pet. iv. ult.); that is, be made them, and therefore will have care of them. This is the true contracting, and the true extending of the memory, to remember the Creator, and stay there, because there is no prospect farther, and to remember the Creator, and get thither, because there is no safe footing upon the creature, till we come so far.

Remember then the Creator, and remember thy Creator, for, *Quis magis fidelis Deo?* (Basil) Who is so faithful a counsellor as God? *Quis prudentior sapiente?* Who can be wiser than wisdom? *Quis utilior bono?* or better than goodness? *Quis conjunctior Creatore?* or nearer than our Maker? and therefore remember him. What purposes soever thy parents or thy prince have to make thee great, how had all those purposes been frustrated, and evacuated, if God had not made thee before: this very being is thy greatest degree; as in arithmetic how great a number soever a man express in many figures, yet when we come to number all, the very first figure is the greatest and most of all; so what degrees or titles soever a man have in this world, the greatest and the foundation of all, is, that he had a being by creation: for the distance from nothing to a little, is ten thousand times more than from it to the highest degree in this life: and therefore remember thy Creator, as by being so, he hath done more for thee than all the world besides; and remember him also, with this consideration, that whatsoever thou art now, yet once thou wast nothing.

He created thee, *ex nihilo*, he gave thee a being, there is matter of exaltation, and yet all this from nothing; thou wast worse than a worm, there is matter of humiliation; but he did not create thee *ad nihilum*, to return to nothing again, and there is matter for thy consideration, and study, how to make thine immortality profitable unto thee; for it is a deadly immortality, if thy immortality must serve thee for nothing but to hold thee in immortal torment. To end all, that being which we have from God shall not return to nothing, nor the being which we have from men neither. As St. Bernard says of the image of God in man's soul, *Uri potest in gehenna, non exuri*, That soul that descends to hell, carries the image of God in the faculties of that soul thither, but there that image can never be burnt out, so those images and those impressions, which we have received from men, from nature, from the world, the image of a lord, the image of a councillor, the image of a bishop, shall all burn in hell, and never burn out; not only these men, but these offices are not to return to nothing; but as their being from God, so their being from man, shall have an everlasting being, to the aggravating of their condemnation. And therefore remember thy Creator, who, as he is so, by making thee of nothing, so he will ever be so, by holding thee to his glory, though to thy confusion, from returning to nothing; for the court of heaven is not like other courts, that after a surfeit of pleasure or greatness, a man may retire; after a surfeit of sin there is no such retiring, as a dissolving of the soul into nothing; but God is from the beginning the Creator, he gave all things their being, and he is still thy Creator, thou shalt evermore have that being, to be capable of his judgments.

Now to make up a circle, by returning to our first word, remember: as we remember God, so for his sake, let us remember one another. In my long absence, and far distance from hence, remember me, as I shall do you in the ears of that God, to whom the farthest east, and the farthest west are but as the right and left ear in one of us; we hear with both at once, and he hears in both at once; remember me, not my abilities; for when I consider my apostleship that I was sent to you, I am in St. Paul's *quorum, quorum ego sum minimus* (1 Cor. xv. 9), the least of them that have been sent; and when I consider my infirmities, I am in his *quorum*, in another commission, another way, *quorum ego maximus* (1 Tim. i. 15); the greatest of them; but remember my labours, and endeavours, at least my desire, to make sure your salvation. And I shall remember your religious cheerfulness in hearing the word, and your christianly respect towards all them that bring that word unto you, and towards myself in particular far above my merit. And so as your eyes that stay here, and mine that must be far off, for all that distance shall meet every morning, in looking upon that same sun, and meet every night, in looking upon the same moon; so our hearts may meet morning and evening in that God, which sees and hears everywhere; that you may come thither to him with your prayers, that I, (if I may be of use for his glory, and your edification in this place) may be restored to you again; and may come to him with my prayer, that what Paul soever plant amongst you, or what Apollos soever water, God himself will give the increase: that if I never meet you again till we have all passed the gate of death, yet in the gates of heaven, I may meet you all, and there say to my Saviour and your Saviour, that which he said to his Father and our Father, *Of those whom thou hast given me, have*

*I not lost one.* Remember me thus, you that stay in this kingdom of peace, where no sword is drawn, but the sword of justice, as I shall remember you in those kingdoms, where ambition on one side, and a necessary defence from unjust persecution on the other side hath drawn many swords; and Christ Jesus remember us all in his kingdom, to which, though we must sail through a sea, it is the sea of his blood, where no soul suffers shipwreck; though we must be blown with strange winds, with sighs and groans for our sins, yet it is the Spirit of God that blows all this wind, and shall blow away all contrary winds of diffidence, or distrust in God's mercy; where we shall be all soldiers of one army, the Lord of hosts, and children of one choir, the God of harmony and consent: where all clients shall retain but one counsellor, our advocate Christ Jesus, not present him any other fee but his own blood, and yet every client have a judgment on his side, not only in a not guilty, in the remission of his sins, but in a *venite benedicti*, in being called to the participation of an immortal crown of glory: where there shall be no difference in affection, nor in mind, but we shall agree as fully and perfectly in our hallelujah, and *gloria in excelsis*, as God the Father, Son, and Holy Ghost agreed in the *faciamus hominem* at first: where we shall end, and yet begin but then; where we shall have continual rest, and yet never grow lazy; where we shall be stronger to resist, and yet have no enemy; where we shall live and never die, where we shall meet and never part.

NOTES

    p. 340. *bechurotheica*: from the Hebrew: 'he chose'.
    p. 341. *antichrist*: this word is actually used only in the Epistles of John; but here Donne is alluding to the strange beasts of Revelations with whom Antichrist was usually identified. Naturally the 'papists' to whom Donne refers took a different view.
    p. 343. *Pentecost*: Whitsun: the feast falling on the fiftieth day after Passover, when first fruits were presented. The Holy Ghost descended on the Apostles on this day: Donne's implications are obvious.

## A Lent Sermon Preached to the King, at Whitehall
Matt. 6:21.
*For, where your treasure is, there will your heart be also.*

THIS SERMON was probably preached at Court at the beginning of Lent. Though Donne was nearing the beginning of his last year, there are no signs here of weakness or lack of vigour such as has been discerned in some of his sermons of a year or two earlier. This, and particularly in its magnificent opening passage, is one of Donne's most poetic sermons. In the analysis of the 'trinity against our unity'—the lack of heart, the doubtful heart, the irresolute heart—he once again demonstrates his powers of psychological penetration (and, undoubtedly, draws upon his own past and present experience). The first state is equated with a sort of *ennui*, and is carefully distinguished from the heart emptied by a 'pouring out' into the hands of God; the second with that scepticism from which Donne himself had suffered—'content to be racked every day, in hope to be an inch or two taller at last'; the third with a more universal state, that of *inattention*. Donne is careful, as almost always, to bring home his message to his congregation by appealing to their own self-knowledge—and he quickens them into this task by his dramatic language. The Pythagorean Y symbol was not one which this congregation would have found difficult to grasp. The passage about corruption in the country, in Westminster, in the city and in the Church, though mostly supported by scriptural references, shows Donne's non-partisan outspokenness on matters of social injustice. It is claimed that he had not eyes to see the troubles that were to come within a few years of his death. But had he not? 'God will enable enemies (though he loves not those enemies) to afflict that people that love not him. And these, war...' And a little further on, 'Do all in the fear of God: in all warlike preparations, remember the Lord of Hosts...'

I HAVE seen minute-glasses;* glasses so short-lived. If I were to preach upon this text, to such a glass, it were enough for half the sermon; enough to show the worldly man his treasure, and the object of his heart (*for, where your treasure is, there will your heart be also*) to call his eye to that minute-glass, and to tell him, there flows, there flies your treasure, and your heart with it. But if I had a secular* glass, a glass that would run an age; if the two hemispheres of the world were composed in the form of such a glass, and all the world calcined and burnt to ashes, and all the ashes, and sands, and atoms of the world put into that glass, it would not be enough to tell the godly man what his treasure, and the object of his heart is. A parrot, or a stare, docile birds, and of pregnant imitation, will sooner be brought to relate to us the wisdom of a council-table, than any Ambrose, or any Chrysostom, men that have gold and honey in their names, shall tell us what the sweetness, what the treasure of heaven is, and what that man's peace, that hath set his heart upon that treasure. As nature hath given us certain elements, and all bodies are composed of them; and art hath given us a certain alphabet of letters, and all words are composed of them: so, our blessed Saviour, in these three chapters of this Gospel, hath given us a sermon of texts, of which, all our sermons may be composed. All the articles of our religion, all the canons of our church, all the injunctions of our princes, all the homilies of our fathers, all the body of divinity, is in these three chapters, in this one sermon in the Mount: where, as the preacher concludes his sermon with exhortations to practice, (*whosoever heareth these sayings of mine, and doth them*—Matt. vii. 24) so he fortifies his sermon, with his own practice, (which is a blessed and a powerful method) for, as soon as he came out of the pulpit, as soon as he came down from the Mount, he cured the first leper he saw (Matt. viii. 1), and that, without all vain glory: for he forbade him to tell any man of it.

Of this noble body of divinity, one fair limb is in this text, *Where your treasure is, there will your heart be also*. Immediately before, our blessed Saviour had forbidding us the laying up of treasure in this world, upon this reason, that *here moths and rust corrupt, and thieves break in, and steal*. There, the reason is, because the money may be lost; but here, in our text it is, because the man may be lost: *for where your treasure is, there your heart will be also*: so that this is equivalent to that, *What profit to gain the whole world, and lose a man's whole soul?* (Matt. xvi. 26.) Our text, therefore, stands as that proverbial, that hieroglyphical letter, Pythagoras's Y; that hath first a stalk, a stem to fix itself, and then spreads into two beams. The stem, the stalk of this letter, this Y, is in the first word of the text, that particle of argumentation, *for*: Take heed where you place your treasure: for it concerns you much, where your heart be placed; and, *where your treasure is, there will your heart be also*. And then opens this symbolical, this catechistical letter, this Y, into two horns, two beams, two branches; one broader, but on the left-hand, denoting the treasures of this world; the other narrower, but on the right-hand, treasure laid up for the world to come. Be sure ye turn the right way: for, *where your treasure is, there will your heart be also*.

First then, we bind ourselves to the stake, to the stalk, to the staff, the stem of this symbolical letter, and consider in it, that firmness and fixation of the heart, which God requires. God requires no unnatural things at man's hand: whatsoever God requires of man, man may find imprinted in his own nature, written in his own heart. This firmness then, this fixation of the heart, is natural to man: every man does set his heart upon something: and Christ in this place does not so much call upon him, that he would do so, set his heart upon something; as to be sure that he set it upon the right object. And yet truly, even this first work, to recollect ourselves, to recapitulate ourselves, to assemble and muster ourselves, and to bend our hearts entirely and intensely, directly, earnestly, emphatically, energetically, upon something, is, by reason of the various fluctuation of our corrupt nature, and the infinite multiplicity of objects, such a work as man needs to be called upon, and excited to do it. Therefore is there no word in the Scriptures so often added to the heart, as that of entireness; *Toto corde, omni corde, pleno corde*: Do this with all thine heart, with a whole heart, with a full heart: for whatsoever is indivisible, is immoveable; a point, because it cannot be divided, cannot be moved: the centre, the poles, God himself, because he is indivisible, is therefore immoveable. And when the heart of man is knit up in such an entireness upon one object, as that it does not scatter, nor subdivide itself; then, and then only is it fixed. And that is the happiness in which David fixes himself; not in his *Cor paratum, My heart is prepared, O God, my heart is prepared*; (for so it may be, prepared even by God himself, and yet scattered and subdivided by us:) but, in his *Cor fixum, My heart is fixed, O God, my heart is fixed; awake my glory, awake my psaltery and harp*:

*I myself will awake early, and praise thee, O Lord, among the people* (Ps. lvii. 7). A triumph that David returned to more than once: for he repeats the same words, with the same pathetical earnestness again (Ps. cviii. 1). So that his glory, his victory, his triumph, his peace, his acquiescence, his all-sufficiency in himself, consisted in this, that his heart was fixed: for this fixation of the heart, argued and testified an entireness in it. When God says, *Fili, da mihi cor; My son, give me thy heart*; God means, the whole man. Though the apostle say (1 Cor. xii. 17), *The eye is not the man, nor the ear is not the man*; he does not say, the heart is not the man: the heart is the man; the heart is all: and, as Moses was not satisfied with that commission that Pharaoh offered him, that all the men might go to offer sacrifice (Exod. x.viii); but Moses would have all their young, and all their old; all their sons, and all their daughters; all their flocks, and all their herds; he would have all; so, when God says, *Fili, da mihi cor, My son, give me thy heart*, God will not be satisfied with the eye, if I contemplate him in his works: (for that is but the godliness of the natural man) nor satisfied with the ear, with hearing many sermons: (for that is but a new invention, a new way of making beads, if, as the papist thinks all done, if he have said so many *aves*, I think all done, if I have heard so many sermons.) But God requires the heart, the whole man, all the faculties of that man: for only that that is entire, and indivisible, is immoveable: and that that God calls for, and we seek for, in this stem of Pythagoras's symbolical letter, is this immoveableness, this fixation of the heart. And yet, even against this, though it be natural, there are many impediments: we shall reduce them to a few; to three: these three. First, there is *cor nullum*, a mere heartlessness, no heart at all, incogitancy [thoughlessness], inconsideration: and then there is, *cor et cor, cor duplex*, a double heart, a doubtful, a distracted heart; which is not incogitancy, nor inconsideration, but perplexity and irresolution: and lastly, *cor vagum*, a wandering, a wayfaring, a weary heart; which is neither inconsideration, nor irresolution, but inconstancy. And this is a trinity against our unity; three enemies to that fixation and entireness of the heart, which God loves: inconsideration, when we do not debate; irresolution, when we do not determine; inconstancy, when we do not persevere: and upon each of these, be pleased to stop your devotion, a few minutes.

The first is, *cor nullum*, no heart at all, incogitancy, thoughtlessness. An idle body, is a disease in a state; an idle soul, is a monster in a man. *That body that will not work, must not eat* (2 Thess. iii. 10), but starve: that soul that does not think, not consider, cannot be said to actuate, (which is the proper operation of the soul) but to evaporate; not to work in the body, but to breathe, and smoke through the body. We have seen estates of private men wasted by inconsideration, as well as by riot; and a soul may perish by a thoughtlessness, as well as by ill thoughts: God takes it as ill to be slighted, as to be injured: and God is as much slighted *in corde nullo*, in our thoughtlessness and inconsideration, as he is opposed and provoked *in corde maligno*, in a rebellious heart. There is a good nullification of the heart, a good bringing of the heart to nothing. For the fire of God's Spirit may take hold of me, and (as the disciples that went with Christ to Emmaus, were affected) my heart may burn within me, when the Scriptures are opened, that is, when God's judgments are denounced against my sin; and this heat may overcome my former frigidity and coldness, and overcome my succeeding tepidity and lukewarmness, and may bring my heart to a mollification, to a tenderness, as Job found it (xxiii. 16); *The Almighty hath troubled me, and made my heart soft* : for there are hearts of clay, as well as hearts of wax; hearts, whom these fires of God, his corrections, harden. But if these fires of his, these denunciations of his judgments, have overcome first my coldness, and then my lukewarmness, and made my heart soft for better impressions; the work is well advanced, but it is not all done: for metal may be soft, and yet not fusile; iron may be red-hot, and yet not apt to run into another mould. Therefore there is a liquefaction, a melting, a pouring out of the heart, such as Rahab speaks of, to Joshua's spies (Josh. ii. 11; v. 1); (*As soon as we heard how miraculously God had proceeded in your behalf, in drying up Jordan, all our hearts melted within us, and no man had any spirit left in him.*) And when upon the consideration of God's miraculous judgments or mercies, I come to such a melting and pouring out of my heart, that there be no spirit, that is, none of mine own spirit left in me; when I have so exhausted, so evacuated myself, that is, all confidence in myself, that I come into the hands of my God, as pliably, as ductilely, as that first clod of earth, of which he made me in Adam, was in his hands, in which clod of earth, there was no kind of reluctation against God's purpose; this is a blessed nullification of the heart. When I say to myself, as the apostle professed of himself, *I am nothing* (2 Cor. xii. 11); and then say to God, Lord, though

I be nothing, yet behold, I present thee as much as thou hadst to make the whole world of; O thou that madest the whole world of nothing, make me, that am nothing in mine own eyes, a new creature in Christ Jesus: this is a blessed nullification, a glorious annihilation of the heart. So is there also a blessed nullification thereof, in the contrition of heart, in the sense of my sins; when, as a sharp wind may have worn out a marble statue, or a continual spout worn out a marble pavement, so, my holy tears, made holy in his blood that gives them a tincture, and my holy sighs, made holy in that Spirit that breathes them in me, have worn out my marble heart, that is, the marbleness of my heart, and emptied the room of that former heart, and so given God a vacuity, a new place to create a new heart in. But when God hath thus created a new heart, that is, re-enabled me, by his ordinance, to some holy function, then, to put this heart to nothing, to think nothing, to consider nothing; not to know our age, but by the church-book, and not by any action done in the course of our lives, for our God, for our prince, for our country, for our neighbour, for ourselves, (ourselves are our souls;) not to know the seasons of the year, but by the fruits which we eat, and not by observation of the public and national blessings, which he hath successively given us; not to know religion, but by the conveniency, and the preferments to be had in this, or in the other side; to sit here, and not to know if we be asked upon a surprise, whether it were a prayer, or a sermon, or an anthem that we heard last; this is such a nullification of the heart, such an annihilation, such an exinanition thereof, as reflects upon God himself; for, *Respuit datorem, qui datum deserit* (Tertullian), He that makes no use of a benefit, despises the benefactor. And therefore, *A rod for his back, qui indiget corde, that is without a heart* (Prov. x. 13), Without consideration what he should do; nay, what he does. For this is the first enemy of this firmness and fixation of the heart, without which, we have no treasure; and we have done with that, *cor nullum*, and pass to the second, *cor et cor, cor duplex*, the double, the divided, the distracted heart, which is not inconsideration, but irresolution.

This irresolution, this perplexity is intended in that commination from God, *The Lord shall give them a trembling heart* (Deut. xxviii. 65): this is not that *cor nullum*, that melted heart, in which *there was no spirit left in them*, as in Joshua's time; but *cor pavidum*, a heart that should not know where to settle, nor what to wish; but, as it follows there *In the morning he shall* say, *Would God it were evening; and in the evening, Would God it were morning.* And this is that which Solomon may have intended in his prayer, *Give thy servant an understanding heart* (1 Kings iii. 9): *Cor docile*, so St. Hierome reads it, a heart able to conceive counsel: for that is a good disposition, but it is not all: for, the original is, *Leb shemmeany* [Heb.], that is, *Cor audiens*, A heart willing to hearken to counsel. But all that, is not all that is asked; Solomon asks there a heart to discern between good and evil; so that it is a prayer for the spirit of discretion, of conclusion, of resolution; that God would give him a heart willing to receive counsel, and a heart capable to conceive and digest counsel, and a heart able to discern between counsel and counsel, and to resolve, conclude, determine. It were a strange ambitious patience in any man, to be content to be racked every day, in hope to be an inch or two taller at last: so is it for me, to think to be a dram or two wiser, by hearkening to all jealousies, and doubts, and distractions, and perplexities, that arise in my bosom, or in my family; which is the rack and torture of the soul. A spirit of contradiction may be of use in the greatest councils; because thereby matters may be brought into farther debatement. But a spirit of contradiction in mine own bosom, to be able to conclude nothing, resolve nothing, determine nothing, not in my religion, not in my manners, but occasionally, and upon emergencies; this is a sickly complexion of the soul, a dangerous impotency, and a shrewd and ill-presaging crisis. If Joshua had suspended his assent of serving the Lord, till all his neighbours, and their families, all the kings and kingdoms about him, had declared theirs the same way, when would Joshua have come to that protestation, *I and my house will serve the Lord?* If Esther had forborne to press for an audience to the king, in the behalf, and for the life of her nation, till nothing could have been said against it, when would Esther have come to that protestation, *I will go; and if I perish, I perish?* If one mill-stone fell from the north pole, and another from the south, they would meet, and they would rest in the centre; nature would concentre them. Not to be able to concentre those doubts, which arise in myself, in a resolution at last, whether in moral or in religious actions, is rather a vertiginous giddiness, than a wise circumspection, or wariness. When God prepared great armies, it is expressed always so, *Tanquam unis vir, Israel went out as one man* (1 Sam. xi. 7). When God established his beloved David to be king, it is expressed so; *Uno corde*, he sent them out, with *one heart to make David king* (1 Chron. xii. 38). When God accelerated the propagation of his church, it is expressed so; *Una anima, The multitude of them that believed, were of one heart, and one soul* (Acts iv. 32). Since God makes nations, and armies, and churches one heart, let not us make one heart two, in ourselves; a divided, a distracted, a perplexed, an irresolved heart: but in all cases, let us be able to say to ourselves, This we should do. God asks the heart, a single heart, an entire heart; for, whilst it is so, God may have some hope of it. But when it is a heart and a heart, a heart for God, and a heart for Mammon, howsoever it may seem to be even, the odds will be on Mammon's side against God; because he presents possessions, and God but reversions; he the present and possessory things of this world, God but the future and speratory* things of the next. So then, the *cor nullum*, no heart, thoughtlessness, incogitancy, inconsideration; and the *cor duplex*, the perplexed, and irresolved, and inconclusive heart, do equally oppose this firmness and fixation of the heart which God loves, and which we consider in this stem and stalk of Pythagoras's symbolical letter: and so does that which we proposed for the third, the *cor vagum*, the wandering, the wayfaring, the inconstant heart.

Many times, in our private actions, and in the cribration [sifting] and sifting of our consciences, (for that is the sphere I move in, and no higher) we do overcome the first difficulty, inconsideration; we consider seriously: and sometimes the second, irresolution; we resolve confidently: but never the third, inconstancy: if so far, as to bring holy resolutions into actions; yet never so far, as to bring holy actions into habits. That word which we read deceitful, (*The heart is deceitful above all things; who can know it?*—Jer. xvii. 9) is in the original *gnacob*; and that is not only *fraudulentum*, but *versipelle*, deceitful because it varies itself into divers forms; so that it does not only deceive others (others find not our heart the same towards them to-day, that it was yesterday) but it deceives ourselves: we know not what, nor where our heart will be hereafter. Upon those words of Esay (Isa. xlvi. 8), *Redite prevaricatores ad cor; Return, O sinner, to thy heart: Longe eos mittit*, says St. Gregory, God knows whither that sinner is sent, that is sent to his own heart: for, where is thy heart? Thou mayest remember where it was yesterday; at such an office, at such a chamber: but yesterday's affections are changed to day, as to-day's will be, to-morrow. *They have despised my judgments*; so God complains in Ezekiel (xx. 16); that is, They are not moved with my punishments; they call all, natural accidents: and then it follows, *They have polluted my sabbaths*; they have come to a more faint, and dilute, and indifferent way, in their religion. Now what hath occasioned this neglecting of God's judgments, and this diluteness and indifferency in the ways of religion? That that follows there, *Their hearts went after their idols*: Went? Whither? Everywhither: for, *Quot vitia tot recentes deos* (Hierome): so many habitual sins, so many idols: and so, every man hath some idol, some such sin; and then, that idol sends him to a further idol, that sin to another: for every sin needs the assistance, and countenance of another sin, for disguise and palliation. We are not constant in our sins, much less in our more holy purposes. We complain, and justly, of the church of Rome, that she would not have us receive *in utraque*, in both kinds: but, alas! who amongst us, does receive *in utraque*, so, as that when he receives bread and wine, he receives with a true sorrow for former, and a true resolution against future sins? Except the Lord of heaven create new hearts in us, of ourselves, we have *cor nullum*, no heart; all vanishes into incogitancy. Except the Lord of heaven concentre our affections, of ourselves, we have *cor et cor*, a cloven, a divided heart, a heart of irresolution. Except the Lord of heaven fix our resolutions, of ourselves, we have *cor vagum*, a various, a wandering heart; all smokes into inconstancy. And all these three are enemies to that firmness, and fixation of the heart, which God loves, and we seek after. But yet how variously soever the heart do wander, and how little awhile soever it stay upon one object; yet, that that thy heart does stay upon, Christ in this place calls thy treasure: for, the words admit well that inversion; *Where your treasure is, there will your heart be also*, implies this; where your heart is, that is your treasure. And so we pass from this stem and stalk of Pythagoras's symbolical letter, the firmness and fixation of the heart, to the horns and beams thereof: a broader, (but on the left hand) and in that, the corruptible treasures of this world; and a narrower, (but on the right hand) and in that, the everlasting treasures of the next. On both sides, that that you fix your heart upon, is your treasure; *For, where your heart is, there is your treasure also*.

Literally, primarily, radically, *thesaurus*, treasure, is no more but *Depositum in crastinum*, Provision for to-morrow; to show how little a proportion, a regulated mind, and a contented heart may make a treasure. But we have enlarged the signification of these words, provision, and, to-morrow: for, provision must signify as long as there shall be a to-morrow, till time shall be no more: but waiving these infinite extensions, and perpetuities, is there any thing of that nature, as, (taking the word treasure in the narrowest signification, to be but provision for to-morrow) we are sure shall last till to-morrow? Sits any man here in an assurance, that he shall be the same to-morrow, that he is now? You have your honours, your offices, your possessions, perchance under seal; a seal of wax; wax, that hath a tenacity, an adhering, a cleaving nature, to show the royal constancy of his heart, that gives them, and would have them continue with you, and stick to you. But then, wax, if it be heat, hath a melting, a fluid, a running nature too: so have these honours, and offices, and possessions, to them that grow too hot, too confident in them, or too imperious by them. For these honours, and offices, and possessions, you have a seal, a fair and just evidence of assurance; but have they any seal upon you, any assurance of you till to-morrow? Did our blessed Saviour give day, or any hope of a to-morrow, to that man, to whom he said, *Fool, this night they fetch away thy soul?* Or is there any of us, that can say, Christ sayed not that to him?

But yet, a treasure every man hath: *An evil man, out of the evil treasure of his heart, bringeth forth that which is evil*, says our Saviour (Luke vi.45): every man hath some sin upon which his heart is set; and, *Where your heart is, there is your treasure also. The treasures of wickedness profit nothing*, says Job (x.2); it is true: but yet, treasures of wickedness there are. *Are there not yet treasures of wickedness in the house of the wicked?* (Mic. vi.10.) Consider the force of that word, yet; yet, though you have the power of a vigilant prince executed by just magistrates; yet, though you have the piety of a religious prince, seconded by the assiduity of a laborious clergy; yet, though you have many helps, which your fathers did, and your neighbours do want, and have (by God's grace) some fruits of those many helps; yet, for all this, *Are there not yet treasures of wickedness in the house of the wicked?* No? *Are there not scant measures, which are an abomination to God*, says the prophet there; which are not only false measures of merchandise, but false measures of men: for, when God says that, he intends all this; Is there not yet supplantation in court, and misrepresentations of men? When Solomon, who understood subordination of places which flowed from him, as well as the highest, which himself possessed, says, and says experimentally for his own, and prophetically for future times, *If a ruler* (a man in great place) *hearken to lies, all his servants are wicked* (Prov.xxix.22): are there not yet misrepresentations of men in courts? Is there not yet oppression in the country? A starving of men, and pampering of dogs? *A swallowing of the needy? A buying of the poor for a pair of shoes, and a selling to the hungry refuse corn?* (Amos viii.5) Is there not yet oppression in the country? Is there not yet extortion in Westminster? *A justifying of the wicked for a reward, and a taking away of the righteousness of the righteous from him?* (Isa. v.23) Is there not yet extortion in Westminster? Is there not yet collusion and circumvention in the city? Would they not seem richer than they are, when they deal in private bargains with one another? And would they not seem poorer than they are, when they are called to contribute for the public? Have they not increased their riches by trade, and lifted up their hearts upon the increase of their riches? (Ezek.xxviii.5.) Have they not slackened their trade, and lain down upon clothes laid to pledge (Amos ii 8), and ennobled themselves by an ignoble and lazy way of gain? Is there not yet collusion and circumvention in the city? Is there not yet hypocrisy in the church? In all parts thereof? Half-preachings, and half-hearings? Hearings and preachings without practice? Have we not national sins of our own, and yet exercise the nature of islanders, in importing the sins of foreign parts? And though we better no foreign commodity, not manufacture that we bring in, we improve the sins of other nations; and, as a weaker grape growing upon the Rhine, contracts a stronger nature in the Canaries; so do the sins of other nations transplanted amongst us. Have we not secular sins, sins of our own age, our own time, and yet sin by precedent of former, as well as create precedents for future? And, not only silver and gold, but vessels of iron and brass, were brought into the treasury of the Lord; not only the glorious sins of high places, and national sins, and secular sins; but the wretchedest beggar in the street, contributes to this treasure, the treasure of sin; and to this mischievous use, to increase this treasure, the treasure of sin, is a subsidy man. He begs in Jesus's name, and for God's sake; and in the same name, curses him that does not give. He counterfeits a lameness, or he loves his lameness, and would not be cured; for his lameness is his stock, it is his demesne, it is (as they call their occupations in the city) his mystery. *Are there not yet treasures of wickedness in the house of the wicked*, when even they, who have no houses, but lie in the streets, have these treasures?

There are: and then, as the nature of treasure is to multiply, so does this treasure, this treasure of sin; it produces another treasure, *Thesaurizamus iram*, We treasure up unto ourselves *wrath against the day of wrath* (Rom. ii. 5): for it is of the sins of the people that God speaks, when he says, *Is not this laid up in store with me, and sealed up amongst my treasures?* (Deut. xxxii. 34.) He treasures up the sins of the disobedient: but where? In the treasury of his judgments. And then, that treasury he opens against us in this world, his treasures of snow, and treasures of hail (Job xxxviii. 22), that is, unseasonableness of weather, barrenness and famine; and he bringeth his winds out of his treasury (Ps. cxxxv. 7), contrary winds, or storms and tempests, to disappoint our purposes; and, as he says to Cyrus, *I will give thee (even thee Cyrus*, though God cared not for Cyrus, otherwise than as he had made Cyrus his scourge) *I will give thee the treasures of darkness, and the hidden treasures of secret places* (Isa. xlv. 3). God will enable enemies (though he loves not those enemies) to afflict that people that love not him. And these, war, and dearth, and sickness, are the weapons of God's displeasure; and these he pours out of his treasury, in this world. But then, for the world to come, he shall open his treasury, (for, whatsoever moved our translators to render that word, armoury, and not treasury, in that place (Jer. l. 25), yet evidently it is treasury, and in that very word, *otzar* [Heb.], which they translate treasury, in all those places of Job, and David, and Isaiah, which we mentioned before, and in all other places) he shall open that treasury, (says that prophet) and bring forth the weapons, not as before, of displeasure, but in a far heavier word, the weapons of his indignation. And, in the bowels and treasury of his mercy, let me beseech you, not to call the denouncing of God's indignation, a satire of a poet, or an invective of an orator: as Solomon says, *There is a time for all things*: there is a time for consternation of presumptuous hearts, as well as for redintegration of broken hearts; and the time for that, is this time of mortification, which we enter into, now. Now therefore, let me have leave to say, that the indignation of God is such a thing, as a man would be afraid to think he can express it, afraid to think he does know it; for the knowledge of the indignation of God, implies the sense and feeling thereof: all knowledge of that, is experimental; and that is a woeful way, and a miserable acquisition, and purchase of knowledge. To recollect, treasure is provision for the future: no worldly thing is so; there is no certain future: for the things of this world pass from us; we pass from them; the world itself passes away to nothing. Yet a way we have found to make a treasure, a treasure of sin; and we teach God thrift and providence: for, when we arm, God arms too; when we make a treasure, God makes a treasure too; a treasure furnished with weapons of displeasure for this world, and weapons of indignation for the world to come. But then, *As an evil man, out of the evil treasure of his heart, bringeth forth that which is evil; so,* (says our Saviour) *the good man, out of the good treasure of his heart, bringeth forth that which is good* (Lu.vi.45): which is the last stroke that makes up Pythagoras's symbolical letter, that horn, that beam thereof, which lies on the right hand; a narrower way, but to a better land; through straits; it is true; but to the Pacific Sea, the consideration of the treasure of the godly man in this world, and God's treasure towards him, both in this, and the next.

Things dedicated to God, are called often, *The treasures of God; Thesauri Dei,* and *thesauri sanctorum Dei*: the treasures of God, and the treasures of the servants of God, are, in the Scriptures, the same thing (Lu.vi.45); and so a man may rob God's treasury, in robbing an hospital. Now, though to give a talent, or to give a jewel, or to give a considerable proportion of plate, be an addition to a treasury; yet to give a treasury to a treasury, is a more precious, and a more acceptable present; as to give a library to a library, is more than to give the works of any one author. A godly man is a library in himself, a treasury in himself, and therefore fittest to be dedicated and appropriated to God. Invest thyself therefore with this treasure of godliness: What godliness? Take it in the whole compass thereof, and godliness is nothing but the fear of God: for, he that says in his first chapter, *Initium sapientiae, The fear of God is the beginning of wisdom* (Pro.i.7); says also, in the twenty-second, *Finis modestiae, The fear of God is the end of modesty;* the end of humility: no man is bound to direct himself to any lower humiliation, than to the fear of God. When God promised good Hezekias all those blessings, wisdom, and knowledge, and stability, and strength of salvation; that that was to defray him, and carry him through all, was this, *The fear of the Lord shall be his treasure* (Isa.xxxiii.6). And therefore, *Thesaurizate vobis fundamentum, Lay up in store for yourselves a good foundation against the time to come* (1 Tim.vi.19). Do all in the fear of God: in all warlike preparations, remember the Lord of hosts, and fear him; in all treaties of peace, remember the Prince of peace, and fear him; in all consultations, remember the Angel of the great council, and fear him: fear God as much at noon, as at midnight; as much in the glory and splendour of his sunshine, as in his darkest eclipses: fear God as much in thy prosperity, as in thine adversity; as much in thy preferment, as in thy disgrace. Lay up a thousand pound to-day in comforting that oppressed soul that sues; and lay up ten thousand pound to-morrow, in paring his nails that oppresses: lay up a million one day, in taking God's cause to heart; and lay up ten millions next day, in taking God's cause in hand. Let every soul lay up a penny now, in resisting a small temptation; and a shilling anon, in resisting a greater; and it will grow to be a treasure, a treasure of talents, of so many talents, as that the poorest soul in the congregation, would not change treasure with any *plate* fleet, nor *terra-firma* fleet, nor with those three thousand millions, which (though it be perchance a greater sum than is upon the face of Europe at this day, after a hundred years embowelling of the earth for treasure) David is said to have left for the treasure of the temple, only to be laid up in the treasury thereof, when it was built: for the charge of the building thereof, was otherwise defrayed. *Let your conversation be in heaven* (Phil.iii.20): Cannot you get thither? You may see, as St. John did (Rev.xxi.2), heaven come down to you: heaven is here; here in God's church, in his word, in his sacraments, in his ordinances; set thy heart upon them, the promises of the Gospel, the seals of reconciliation, and thou hast that treasure, which is thy *viaticum*, for thy transmigration out of this world, and thy bill of exchange for the world thou goest to. For, as the wicked make themselves a treasure of sin and vanity, and then God opens upon them a treasure of his displeasure here, and his indignation hereafter: so the godly make themselves a treasure of the fear of God, and he opens unto them a treasure of grace and peace here, and a treasure of joy and glory hereafter. And when of each of these treasures, here, and hereafter, I shall have said one word, I have done.

*We have treasure*, though *in earthen vessels*, says the apostle (2 Cor.iv.7). We have; that is, we have already the treasure of grace, and peace, and faith, and justification, and sanctification: but yet, in earthen vessels, in vessels that may be broken; peace that may be interrupted, grace that may be resisted, faith that may be enfeebled, justification that may be suspected, and sanctification that may be blemished. But we look for more; for joy, and glory; for such a justification, and such a sanctification, as shall be sealed, and riveted in a glorification. Manna putrefied if it were kept by any man, but a day; but in the ark, it never putrefied. That treasure, which is as manna from heaven, grace, and peace, yet, here, hath a brackish taste: when grace, and peace, shall become joy and glory in heaven, there it will be sincere. *Sordescit quod inferiori miscetur naturae, etsi in suo genere non sordidetur* (Aug.): Though in the nature thereof, that with which a purer metal is mixed, be not base; yet, it abases the purer metal. He puts his example in silver and gold; though silver be a precious metal, yet it abases gold. Grace, and peace, and faith, are precious parts of our treasure here; yet, if we mingle them, that is, compare them with the joys, and glory of heaven; if we come to think, that our grace, and peace, and faith here, can no more be lost, than our joy and glory there; we abase, and over-alloy those joys, and that glory. *The kingdom of heaven is like a treasure*, says our Saviour (Matt.xiii.44). But is that all? Is any treasure like unto it? None: for, (to end where we begun) treasure is *Depositum in crastinum*, Provision for to-morrow. The treasure of the worldly man is not so; he is not sure of any thing to-morrow. Nay, the treasure of the godly man is not so in this world; he is not sure, that this day's grace, and peace, and faith, shall be his to-morrow. When I have joy and glory in heaven, I shall be sure of that, to-morrow. And that is a term long enough: for, before a to-morrow, there must be a night; and shall there ever be a night in heaven? No more than day in hell. *There shall be no sun in heaven* (Rev.xxi.23); therefore no danger of a sun-set. And for the treasure itself, when the Holy Ghost hath told us, that the walls and streets of the city are pure gold, that the foundations thereof are all precious stones, and every gate of an entire pearl; what hath the Holy Ghost himself left to denote unto us, what the treasure itself within is? The treasure itself, is the Holy Ghost himself, and joy in him. As the Holy Ghost proceeds from Father and Son, but I know not how; so there shall something proceed from Father, Son, and Holy Ghost, and fall upon me, but I know not what. Nay, not fall upon me neither; but enwrap me, embrace me: for, I shall not be below them, so as that I shall not be upon the same seat with the Son, at the right hand of the Father, in the union of the Holy Ghost: rectified by the power of the Father, and feel no weakness; enlightened by the wisdom of the Son, and feel no scruple; established by the joy of the Holy Ghost, and feel no jealousy. Where I shall find the fathers of the first age, dead five thousand years before me; and they shall not be able to say they were there a minute before me. Where I shall find the blessed and glorious martyrs, who went not *per viam lactèam*, but *per viam sanguineam*; not by the milky way of an innocent life, but by the bloody way of a violent death; and they shall not contend with me for precedency in their own right, or say, We came in by purchase, and you but by pardon. Where I shall find the virgins, and not be despised by them, for not being so; but hear that redintegration, which I shall receive in Christ Jesus, called virginity, and entireness. Where all tears shall be wiped from mine eyes; not only tears of compunction for myself, and tears of compassion for others; but even tears of joy, too: for, there shall be no sudden joy, no joy unexperienced there; there I shall have all joys, altogether, always. There Abraham shall not be gladder of his own salvation, than of mine; nor I surer of the everlastingness of my God, than of my everlastingness in him. This is that treasure, of which the God of this treasure, gives us those spangles; and that single money, which this mint can coin, this world can receive, that is, prosperity, and a good use thereof, in worldly things; and grace, and peace, and faith, in spiritual. And then reserve for us the exaltation of this treasure, in the joy and glory of heaven, in the mediation of his Son Christ Jesus, and by the operation of his blessed Spirit. Amen.

NOTES

p. 355. *minute-glasses:* sand-glasses that take one minute to run.   *secular:* used here in the special sense of a whole age: a secular glass would take a whole age, even all history, to run.

p. 361. *speratory:* hopeful; not desperate.

DEATH'S DUEL, OR, A CONSOLATION TO THE SOUL, AGAINST THE DYING LIFE, AND LIVING DEATH OF THE BODY. DELIVERED IN A SERMON AT WHITEHALL, BEFORE THE KING'S MAJESTY, AT THE BEGINNING OF LENT, 1631.
Psalm 68:20.
*And unto God the Lord, belong the issues of [i.e. from] death.*

THIS IS Donne's last and most famous sermon. It was preached on 25 February; Donne died on 31 March. He had been taken ill during the previous Autumn, and had been unable to preach (as he usually did) his sermon on 5 November, the anniversary of Gunpowder Plot. In the December he made his will, certain at last that he was really dying; his mother died in the January. He said that he would preach on Candlemas Day (2 February), but was unable to do so. Walton (whose account of the last weeks is substantially correct) writes:

> At his coming thither [to London], many of his friends (who with much sorrow saw his sickness had left him but so much flesh as did only cover his bones), doubted his strength to perform that task, and did therefore dissuade him from it, assuring him, however, it was likely to shorten his life; but he passionately denied their requests, saying, 'He would not doubt that that God, who in so many weaknesses has assisted him with an unexpected strength, would now withdraw it in his last employment, professing a holy ambition to perform that sacred work.' And when, to the amazement of some beholders, he appeared in the pulpit, many of them thought he presented himself, not to preach mortification by a living voice, but mortality by a decayed body and a dying face. And doubtless many did secretly ask that question in Ezekiel (xxxviii.3), 'Do these bones live? or, can that soul organize that tongue to speak so long time as the sand in that glass will move towards its centre, and measure out an hour of this dying man's unspent life? Doubtless it cannot.' And yet, after some faint pauses in his zealous prayer, his strong desires enabled his weak body to discharge his memory of his preconceived meditations, which were of dying; the text being, 'To God the Lord belong the issues of death.' Many that then saw his tears, and heard his faint and hollow voice, professing they thought the text prophetically chosen, and that

Dr. Donne *had preached his own funeral sermon.*

This sermon was published, prefaced by a picture of Donne in his shroud, shortly after his death. It is obvious that he took the event—and the text—with the utmost seriousness. Death had always fascinated and terrified him, and on the day after he delivered it he told a friend (Walton relates) that he was 'in a serious contemplation of the providence and goodness of God to me: *who am less than the least of his mercies.* . . . I am to be judged by a merciful God, *who is not willing to see what I have done amiss. . . . I am therefore full of inexpressible joy, and shall die in peace.'* The title 'Death's Duel' was not Donne's. Although Shakespeare's sonnet beginning 'Poor soul, the centre of my sinful earth' cannot be shown to be specifically Christian, it is very much in the spirit of the main argument of this sermon: its last line is 'And death once dead, there's no more dying then'.

The sermon is preached not only in the expectation of his own, but also in the knowledge of his mother's recent death; furthermore, Donne remembers the death of his wife in 1617. He had once called semen an 'excremental jelly', and Ann Donne had had dangerous miscarriages as well as many children; a stillborn child was the immediate cause of her death. Hence the bitterness and savagery of the passage about the womb, where 'we are taught cruelty, by being fed with blood'. Now he welcomes death. Life is itself a death, and we are delivered into it 'wound up in that winding-sheet' (i. e. a caul—though not everyone, of course, is actually born in a caul). Redemption from absolute death is achieved only because Christ rose 'without seeing corruption'. But this, Donne asserts—without theology—is a mystery: *'we shall all be changed'.* His vision proceeds to contrast the vileness of death—in its physical sense of putrefaction—and the miraculous resurrection of the dead. He confronts the 'most inglorious and contemptible vilification, the most deadly and peremptory nullification of man, that we can consider': the facts of putrefaction and dispersion. At least Ezekiel saw bones when he asked, 'Can these bones live?'; but 'If we say, Can this dust live? perchance it cannot'. Yet God can recompact 'this dust into the same body' and give an issue from such an utter dispersal. This is inexplicable; yet 'Our critical day is not the very day of our death, but the whole course of our life . . .' Still, we shall die. What redeems us is the 'super-miraculous' fact that God, as Christ, 'could die'. Christ suffered, but not all his torments could quench his love: he died voluntarily, spontaneously. Only this can point towards an explanation of God's mercy, and of his intention to re-animate what was become dust.

The sermon, which is remarkable not only for the conventionality and, indeed, relative absence of its theology but also for its simplicity and eloquence, shows how far Donne was from either the Roman Catholicism of his youth or Puritanism. At the back of it lies the doctrine of Justification by Faith; it is a highly dramatic and convincing demonstration of how doctrine can be the very opposite of abstract.

BUILDINGS STAND by the benefit of their foundations that sustain them, support them; and of their buttresses that comprehend them, embrace them; and of their contignations (jointing) that knit and unite them. The foundation suffers them not to sink; the buttresses suffer them not to swerve; the contignation and knitting, suffer them not to cleave. The body of our building is in the former part of this verse; it is this; *He that is our God, is the God of salvation; ad salutes*, of salvations in the plural, so it is in the original; the God that gives us spiritual and temporal salvation too. But of this building, the foundation, the buttresses, the contignation are in this part of the verse, which constitutes our text, and in the three diverse acceptations of the words amongst our expositors, *Unto God the Lord belong the issues of death*. For, first the foundation of this building, (that our God is the God of all salvation) is laid in this, *That unto this God the Lord belong the issues of death*; that is, it is his power to give us an issue and deliverance, even then when we are brought to the jaws and teeth of death, and to the lips of that whirlpool, the grave; and so in this acceptation, this *exitus mortis*, this issue of death is *liberatio a morte*, a deliverance from death; and this is the most obvious, and most ordinary acceptation of these words, and that upon which our translation lays hold, *the issues from death*. And then, secondly, the buttresses, that comprehend and settle this building; that *He that is our God is the God of salvation*, are thus raised; *Unto God the Lord belong the issues of death*, that is, the disposition and manner of our death, what kind of issue, and transmigration we shall have out of this world, whether prepared or sudden, whether violent or natural, whether in our perfect senses, or shaked and disordered by sickness; there is no condemnation to be argued out of that, no judgment to be made upon that, for howsoever they die, *precious in his sight, is the death of his saints*, and with him are the issues of death, the ways of our departing out of this life, are in his hands; and so, in this sense of the words, this *exitus mortis*, the issue of death, is *liberatio in morte*, a deliverance in death; not that God will deliver us from dying, but that he will have a care of us in the hour of death, of what kind soever our passage be; and this sense, and acceptation of the words, the natural frame and contexture doth well and pregnantly administer unto us. And then lastly, the contignation and knitting of this building, that *He that is our God, is the God of all salvation*, consists in this, *Unto this God the Lord belong the issues of death*, that is, that this God the Lord, having united and knit both natures in one, and being God, having also come into this world, in our flesh, he could have no other means to save us, he could have no other issue out of this world, nor return to his former glory, but by death. And so in this sense, this *exitus mortis*, the issue of death, is *liberatio per mortem*, a deliverance by death, by the death of this God our Lord, Christ Jesus; and this is St. Augustine's acceptation of the words, and those many and great persons, that have adhered to him. In all these three lines then, we shall look upon these words; first, as the God of power, the Almighty Father, rescues his servants from the jaws of death; and then, as the God of mercy, the glorious Son, rescued us, by taking upon himself the issue of death; and then, (between these two,) as the God of comfort, the Holy Ghost, rescues us from all discomfort by his blessed impressions beforehand, that what manner of death soever be ordained for us, yet this *exitus mortis*, shall be *introitus in vitam*, our issue in death, shall be an entrance into everlasting life. And these three considerations, our deliverance *a morte, in morte, per mortem*, from death, in death, and by death, will abundantly do all the offices of the foundation, of the buttresses, of the contignation of this our building, that *He that is our God, is the God of all salvation*, because *Unto this God the Lord belong the issues of death*.

First then, we consider this *exitus mortis*, to be a *liberatio a morte*; that with *God the Lord are the issues of death*, and therefore in all our deaths, and deadly calamities of this life, we may justly hope of a good issue from him; and all our periods and transitions in this life, are so many passages from death to death. Our very birth, and entrance into this life, is *exitus a morte*, an issue from death; for in our mother's womb, we are dead so, as that we do not know we live; not so much as we do in our sleep; neither is there any grave so close, or so putrid a prison, as the womb would be to us, if we stayed in it beyond our time, or died there, before our time. In the grave the worms do not kill us: we breed and feed, and then kill those worms, which we ourselves produced. In the womb the dead child kills the mother that conceived it, and is a murderer, nay a parricide, even after it is dead. And if we be not dead so in the womb, so, as that being dead, we kill her that gave us our first life, our life of vegetation, yet we are dead so as David's idols are dead; in the womb, we have eyes and see not, ears and hear not (Ps. cxv. 6). There in the womb we are fitted for works of darkness, all the while deprived of light; and there, in the womb, we are taught cruelty, by being fed with blood; and may be damned though we be never born. Of our very making in the womb, David says, *I am wonderfully and fearfully made* (Ps. cxxxix. 14), and *Such knowledge is too excellent for me* (Ps. cxxxix. 6); for, *Even that is the Lord's doing, and it is wonderful in our eyes* (Ps. cxviii. 23), *Ipse fecit nos, It is he that hath made us, and not we ourselves* (Ps. c. 3), no, nor our parents neither. *Thy hands have made me, and fashioned me round about*, says Job (x. 8); and, (as the original word is) *Thou hast taken pains about me*; and yet says he, *Thou dost destroy me*: though I be the master-piece of the great Master, (man is so) yet if thou do no more for me, if thou leave me where thou madest me, destruction will follow. The womb, which should be the house of life, becomes death itself, if God leave us there. That which God threatens so often, the shutting of the womb, is not so heavy nor so discomfortable a curse, in the first as in the latter shutting; nor in the shutting of barrenness, as in the shutting of weakness, when children are come to the birth, and there is not strength to bring forth (Isa. xxxvii. 3). It is the exaltation of misery, to fall from a near hope of happiness. And in that vehement imprecation the prophet expresses the height of God's anger, *Give them, O Lord, what wilt thou give them? Give them a miscarrying womb* (Hos. ix. 14). Therefore as soon as we are men, (that is, inanimated, quickened in the womb) though we cannot ourselves, our parents have reason to say in our behalf, *Wretched man that he is, who shall deliver him from this body of death?* (Rom. vii. 24.) For, even the womb is the body of death, if there be no deliverer. It must be he that said to Jeremy (i. v), *Before I formed thee I knew thee, and before thou camest out of the womb I sanctified thee.* We are not sure that there was no kind of ship nor boat to fish in, nor to pass by, till God prescribed Noah that absolute form of the ark; that word which the Holy Ghost by Moses, uses for the ark, is common to all kinds of boats, *thebah*; and is the same word that Moses uses for the boat that he was exposed in (Ex. ii. 3), that his mother laid him in an ark of bulrushes. But we are sure that Eve had no midwife when she was delivered of Cain; therefore she might well say, *Possedi virum a Domino* (Gen. iv. 1), I have gotten a man from the Lord; wholly, entirely from the Lord: it is the Lord that hath enabled me to conceive, the Lord hath infused a quickening soul into that conception, the Lord hath brought into the world that which himself had quickened; without all this might Eve say, my body had been but the house of death, and *Domini Domini sunt exitus mortis*, To God the Lord belong the issues of death.

But then this *exitus a morte*, is but *introitus in mortem*; this issue, this deliverance from that death, the death of the womb, is an entrance, a delivering over to another death, the manifold deaths of this world. We have a winding-sheet in our mother's womb, that grows with us from our conception, and we come into the world wound up in that winding-sheet; for we come to seek a grave. And, as prisoners, discharged of actions, may lie for fees, so when the womb hath discharged us, yet we are bound to it by cords of flesh, by such a string, as that we cannot go thence, nor stay there. We celebrate our own funeral with cries, even at our birth, as though our threescore and ten years of life were spent in our mother's labour, and our circle made up in the first point thereof. We beg one baptism with another, a sacrament of tears; and we come into a world that lasts many ages, but we last not. *In domo Patris*, (says our blessed Saviour, speaking of heaven) *multae mansiones* (John xiv. 2), There are many, and mansions, divers and durable; so that if a man cannot possess a martyr's house, (he hath shed no blood for Christ) yet he may have a confessor's; he hath been ready to glorify God, in the shedding of his blood. And if a woman cannot possess a virgin's house, (she hath embraced the holy state of marriage) yet she may have a matron's house; she hath brought forth, and brought up children in the fear of God. *In domo Patris*, In my Father's house, in heaven, there are many mansions, but here upon earth, *The Son of man hath not where to lay his head* (Matt. viii. 20), says he himself. No? *terram dedit filiis hominum*. How then hath God given this earth to the sons of men? He hath given them earth for their materials, to be made of earth; and he hath given them earth for their grave and sepulture, to return and resolve to earth; but not for their possession. *Here we have no continuing city* (Heb. xiii. 14); nay, no cottage that continues; nay, no we, no persons, no bodies that continue. Whatsoever moved St. Hierome to call the journeys of the Israelites in the wilderness, mansions, the word (Ex. xvii. 1), (the word is *nasang*) signifies but a journey, but a peregrination: even the Israel of God hath no mansions, but journeys, pilgrimages in this life. By that measure did Jacob measure his life to Pharaoh, *The days of the years of my pilgrimage* (Gen. xlvii. 9). And though the apostle would not say, *Morimur*, That whilst we are in the body, we are dead, yet he says, *Peregrinamur*, Whilst we are in the body, we are but in a pilgrimage, and we are absent from the Lord (2 Cor.v.6). He might have said dead; for this whole world is but an universal churchyard, but one common grave; and the life and motion, that the greatest persons have in it, is but as the shaking of buried bodies in their graves by an earthquake. That which we call life, is but *hebdomada mortium*, a week of deaths, seven days, seven periods of our life spent in dying; a dying seven times over, and there is an end. Our birth dies in infancy, and our infancy dies in youth, and youth, and the rest die in age; and age also dies, and determines all. Nor do all these, youth out of infancy, or age out of youth, arise so, as a phoenix out of the ashes of another phoenix formerly dead, but as a wasp, or a serpent out of carrion, or as a snake out of dung; our youth is worse than our infancy, and our age worse than our youth; our youth is hungry and thirsty after those sins which our infancy knew not, and our age is sorry and angry that it cannot pursue those sins which our youth did. And besides, all the way so many deaths, that is, so many deadly calamities accompany every condition, and every period of this life, as that death itself would be an ease to them that suffer them. Upon this sense does Job wish that God had not given him an issue from the first death, from the womb; *Wherefore hast thou brought me forth out of the womb? O that I had given up the ghost, and no eye had seen me; I should have been, as though I had not been* (x.18,19).

And not only the impatient Israelites in their murmuring, (*Would to God we had died by the hand of the Lord, in the land of Egypt*—Ex. xvi.3,) but Elijah himself, when he fled from Jezebel, and went for his life, as that text says, under the juniper-tree, requested that he might die, and said, *It is enough, now O Lord take away my life* (1 Kings xix.4). So Jonah (iv.3) justifies his impatience, nay his anger towards God himself; *Now O Lord take I beseech thee my life from me, for it is better for me to die, than to live.* And when God asked him, *Dost thou well to be angry for this?* and after, (about the gourd) *Dost thou well to be angry for that?* he replies, *I do well to be angry even unto death.* How much worse a death, than death, is this life, which so good men would so often change for death. But if my case be St. Paul's case, *Quotidie morior* (1 Cor.xv.3), That I die daily, that something heavier than death fall upon me every day; if my case be David's case, *Tota die mortificamur* (Ps.xliv.22), All the day long we are killed, that not only every day, but every hour of the day, something heavier than death falls upon me: though that be true of me, *Conceptus in peccatis*, I was shapen in iniquity, and in sin did my mother conceive me (Ps.li.5), (there I died one death) though that be true of me, *Natus filus irae*, I was born, not only the child of sin, but the child of the wrath of God for sin, which is a heavier death, yet *Domini Domini sunt exitus mortis*, With God the Lord are the issues of death; and after a Job, and a Joseph, and a Jeremy, and a Daniel, I cannot doubt of a deliverance; and if no other deliverance conduce more to his glory, and my good, yet, *He hath the keys of death* (Rev. 1.18), and he can let me out at that door, that is, deliver me from the manifold deaths of this world, the *omni die*, and the *tota die*, the every day's death, and every hour's death, by that one death, the final dissolution of body and soul, the end of all.

But then, is that the end of all? Is that dissolution of body and soul, the last death that the body shall suffer? (for of spiritual deaths we speak not now;) it is not. Though this be *exitus a morte*, it is *introitus in mortem*; though it be an issue from the manifold deaths of this world, yet it is an entrance into the death of corruption, and putrefaction, and vermiculation\*, and incineration, and dispersion, in, and from the grave, in which every dead man dies over again. It was a prerogative peculiar to Christ, not to die this death, not to see corruption. What gave him this privilege? Not Joseph's great proportions of gums and spices, that might have preserved his body from corruption and incineration, longer than he needed it, longer than three days; but yet would not have done it for ever. What preserved him then? Did his exemption, and freedom from original sin, preserve him from this corruption and incineration? It is true, that original sin hath induced this corruption and incineration upon us. If we had not sinned in Adam, mortality had not put on immortality, (as the apostle speaks—1 Cor.xv.53) nor corruption had not put on incorruption, but we had had our transmigration from this to the other world, without any mortality, any corruption at all. But yet since Christ took sin upon him, so far as made him mortal, he had it so far too, as might have made him see this corruption and incineration, though he had no original sin in himself. What preserved him then? Did the hypostatical union of both natures, God and man, preserve his flesh from this corruption, this incineration? it is true, that this was a most powerful embalming: to be embalmed with the divine nature itself, to be embalmed with eternity, was able to preserve him from corruption and incineration for ever: and he was embalmed so, embalmed with the divine nature, even in his body, as well as in his soul; for the Godhead, the divine nature, did not depart, but remain still united to his dead body in the grave. But yet for all this powerful embalming, this hypostatical union of both natures, we see, Christ did die; and for all this union which made him God and man, he became no man, for the union of body and soul makes the man, and he, whose soul and body are separated by death, (as long as that state lasts) is, (properly) no man. And therefore as in him, the dissolution of body and soul was no dissolution of the hypostatical union, so is there nothing that constrains us to say, that though the flesh of Christ had seen corruption and incineration in the grave, this had been any dissolving of the hypostatical union; for the divine nature, the Godhead, might have remained with all the elements and principles of Christ's body, as well as it did with the two constitutive parts of his person, his body and soul. This incorruption then was not in Joseph's gums and spices; nor was it in Christ's innocency and exemption from original sin; nor was it, (that is, it is not necessary to say it was) in the hypostatical union. But this incorruptibleness of his flesh, is most conveniently placed in that, *Non dabis, Thou wilt not suffer thy Holy One to see corruption* (Ps. xvi. 10). We look no further for causes or reasons in the mysteries of our religion, but to the will and pleasure of God. Christ himself limited his inquisition in that; *Ita est*, Even so, Father, for so it seemed good in thy sight (Matt. xi. 26). Christ's body did not see corruption, therefore, because God had decreed that it should not. The humble soul, (and only the humble soul is the religious soul) rests himself upon God's purposes, and his decrees; but then, it is upon those purposes, and decrees of God, which he hath declared and manifested; not such as are conceived and imagined in ourselves, though upon some probability, some verisimilitude. So, in our present case, Peter proceeded in his sermon at Jerusalem (Acts ii. 31; xiii. 35), and so Paul in his at Antioch; they preached Christ to be risen without having seen corruption, not only because God had decreed it, but because he had manifested that decree in his prophet. Therefore does St. Paul cite by special number the second Psalm for that decree, and therefore both St. Peter and St. Paul cite that place in the sixteenth Psalm; for, when God declares his decree and purpose in the express word of his prophet, or when he declares it in the real execution of the decree, then he makes it ours, then he manifests it to us. And therefore as the mysteries of our religion are not the objects of our reason, but by faith we rest in God's decree and purpose, (it is so, O God, because it is thy will it should be so) so God's decrees are ever to be considered in the manifestation thereof. All manifestation is either in the Word of God, or in the execution of the decree; and when these two concur and meet, it is the strongest demonstration that can be: when therefore I find those marks of adoption, and spiritual filiation, which are delivered in the Word of God, to be upon me; when I find that real execution of his good purpose upon me, as that actually I do live under the obedience, and under the conditions which are evidences of adoption and spiritual filiation, then, and so long as I see these marks, and live so, I may safely comfort myself in a holy certitude, and a modest infallibility of my adoption. Christ determines himself in that, the purpose of God; because the purpose of God was manifest to him: St. Peter and St. Paul determine themselves in those two ways of knowing the purpose of God, the Word of God before the execution of the decree in the fulness of time. It was prophesied before, said they, and it is performed now; Christ is risen without seeing corruption.

Now this which is so singularly peculiar to him, that his flesh should not see corruption, at his second coming, his coming to judgment, shall be extended to all that are then alive, their flesh shall not see corruption; because (as the apostle says, and says as a secret, as a mystery, (*Behold I show you a mystery; we shall not all sleep,*) that is, not continue in the state of the dead in the grave) *but we shall all be changed* (1 Cor.xv.51). In an instant we shall have a dissolution, and in the same instant a redintegration, a recompacting of body and soul; and that shall be truly a death, and truly a resurrection, but no sleeping, no corruption. But for us, who die now, and sleep in the state of the dead, we must all pass this posthume death, this death after death, nay this death after burial, this dissolution after dissolution, this death of corruption and putrefaction, of vermiculation and incineration, of dissolution and dispersion, in, and from the grave. When those bodies which have been the children of royal parents, and the parents of royal children, must say with Job (xvii.14), *To corruption, Thou art my father, and to the worm, Thou art my mother and my sister.* Miserable riddle, when the same worm must be my mother, and my sister, and myself. Miserable incest, when I must be married to mine own mother and sister, and be both father and mother, to mine own mother and sister, beget and bear that worm, which is all that miserable penury, when my mouth shall be filled with dust, and the worm shall feed, and feed sweetly upon me (Job xxiv.20). When the ambitious man shall have no satisfaction if the poorest alive tread upon him, nor the poorest receive any contentment, in being made equal to princes, for they shall be equal but in dust (Job xxiii.24). One dieth at his full strength, being wholly at ease, and in quiet, and another dies in the bitterness of his soul, and never eats with pleasure; but they lie down alike in the dust, and the worm covers them (Job xxiv.11). The worm covers them in Job, and in Esay (Isa.xli.14), it covers them, and is spread under them, (the worm is spread under thee, and the worm covers thee). There is the mats and the carpet that lie under; and there is the state and the canopy that hangs over the greatest of the sons of men. Even those bodies that were the temples of the Holy Ghost, come to this dilapidation, to ruin, to rubbish, to dust: even the Israel of the Lord, and Jacob himself had no other specification, no other denomination but that, *Vermis Jacob*, Thou worm Jacob. Truly, the consideration of this posthume death, this death after burial, that after God, with whom are the issues of death, hath delivered me from the death of the womb, by bringing me into the world, and from the manifold deaths of the world, by laying me in the grave, I must die again, in an incineration of this flesh, and in a dispersion of that dust; that all that monarch that spread over many nations alive, must in his dust lie in a corner of that sheet of lead, and there but so long as the lead will last: and that private and retired man, that thought himself his own for ever, and never came forth, must in his dust of the grave be published, and, (such are the revolutions of graves) be mingled in his dust, with the dust of every highway, and of every dunghill, and swallowed in every puddle and pond; this is the most inglorious and contemptible vilification, the most deadly and peremptory nullification of man, that we can consider. God seems to have carried the declaration of his power to a great height, when he sets the prophet Ezekiel, in the valley of dry bones, and says, *Son of man can these bones live?* (Ezek.xxxvii.3) as though it had been impossible; and yet they did; the Lord laid sinews upon them, and flesh, and breathed into them, and they did live. But in that case there were bones to be seen; something visible, of which it might be said, Can this, this live? but in this death of incineration and dispersion of dust, we see nothing that we can call that man's. If we say, Can this dust live? perchance it cannot. It may be the mere dust of the earth which never did live, nor shall; it may be the dust of that man's worms which did live, but shall no more; it may be the dust of another man that concerns not him of whom it is asked. This death of incineration and dispersion is to natural reason the most irrecoverable death of all; and yet *Domini Domini sunt exitus mortis, Unto God the Lord belong the issues of death*, and by recompacting this dust into the same body, and re-inanimating the same body with the same soul, he shall in a blessed and glorious resurrection, give me such an issue from this death, as shall never pass into any other death, but establish me in a life, that shall last as long as the Lord of life himself. And so have you that that belongs to the first acceptation of these words, (*Unto God the Lord belong the issues of death*) that though from the womb to the grave, and in the grave itself, we pass from death to death, yet, as Daniel speaks, The Lord our God is able to deliver us, and he will deliver us. And so we pass to our second accommodation of these words (*Unto God the Lord belong the issues of death*) that it belongs to God, and not to man, to pass a judgment upon us at our death, or to conclude a dereliction on God's part, upon the manner thereof.

Those indications which physicians receive, and those presagitions* which they give for death or recovery in the patient, they receive, and they give, out of the grounds and rules of their art: but we have no such rule or art to ground a presagition of spiritual death, and damnation upon any such indication as we see in any dying man: we see often enough to be sorry, but not to despair; for the mercies of God work momentanely, in minutes; and many times insensibly to by-standers, or any other than the party departing, and we may be deceived both ways: we use to comfort ourselves in the death of a friend, if it be testified that he went away like a lamb, that is, but with any reluctation; but God knows, that may have been accompanied with a dangerous damp and stupefaction, and insensibility of his present state. Our blessed Saviour admitted colluctations [wrestlings] with death, and a sadness even in his soul to death, and an agony even to a bloody sweat in his body, and expostulations with God, and exclamations upon the cross. He was a devout man, who upon his death-bed, or death-turf (for he was a hermit) said, *Septuaginta annis Domino servivisti, et mori times?* (Hilarion) Hast thou served a good master threescore and ten years, and now art thou loth to go into his presence? yet Hilarion was loth. He was a devout man (a hermit) that said that day that he died, *Cogitate hodie coepisse servire Domino, et hodie finiturum*, Consider this to be the first day's service that ever thou didst thy Master, to glorify him in a Christian and constant death; and, if thy first day be thy last day too, how soon dost thou come to receive thy wages; yet Barlaam could have been content to have stayed longer for it; make no ill conclusion upon any man's lothness to die. And then, upon violent deaths inflicted, as upon malefactors, Christ himself hath forbidden us by his own death to make any ill conclusion; for his own death had those impressions in it; he was reputed, he was executed as a malefactor, and no doubt many of them who concurred to his death, did believe him to be so. Of sudden deaths there are scarce examples, to be found in the Scriptures, upon good men; for death in battle cannot be called sudden death: but God governs not by examples, but by rules; and therefore make no ill conclusions upon sudden death; nor upon distempers neither, though perchance accompanied with some words of diffidence and distrust in the mercies of God. The tree lies as it falls; it is true; but yet it is not the last stroke that fells the tree; nor the last word, nor last gasp that qualifies the soul. Still pray we for a peaceable life, against violent deaths, and for time of repentance against sudden deaths, and for sober and modest assurance against distempered and diffident deaths, but never make ill conclusion upon persons overtaken with such deaths. *Domini, Domini sunt exitus mortis*, To God the Lord belong the issues of death, and he received Samson, who went out of this world in such a manner (consider it actively, consider it passively; in his own death, and in those whom he slew with himself) as was subject to interpretation hard enough; yet the Holy Ghost hath moved St. Paul to celebrate Samson, in his great catalogue (Heb. xi), and so doth all the church. Our critical day is not the very day of our death, but the whole course of our life: I thank him, that prays for me when my bell tolls; but I thank him much more, that catechises me, or preaches to me, or instructs me how to live, *fac hoc et vives*, there is my security; the mouth of the Lord hath spoken it, *Do this and thou shalt live*. But though I do it yet I shall die too, die a bodily, a natural death; but God never mentions, never seems to consider that death, the bodily, the natural death. God doth not say, Live well, and thou shalt die well; well, that is an easy, a quiet death; but live well here, and thou shalt live well for ever. As the first part of a sentence pieces well with the last, and never respects, never hearkens after the parenthesis that comes between, so doth a good life here, flow into an eternal life, without any consideration what manner of death we die. But whether the gate of my prison be opened with an oiled key (by a gentle and preparing sickness) or the gate be hewed down, by a violent death, or the gate be burnt down by a raging and frantic fever; a gate into heaven I shall have; for, from the Lord is the course of my life, and with God the Lord are the issues of death; and farther we carry not this second acceptation of the words, as this issue of death is *liberatio in morte*, God's care that the soul be safe, what agony soever the body suffer in the hour of death; but pass to our third and last part; as this issue of death is *liberatio per mortem*, a deliverance by the death of another, by the death of Christ.

*Sufferentiam Job audiistis et vidistis finem Domini*, says St. James (v.11). You have heard of the patience of Job, says he; all this while you have done that: for in every man, calamitous, miserable man, a Job speaks. *Now see the end of the Lord*, saith that apostle, which is not that end which the Lord proposed to himself (salvation to us) nor the end which he proposes to us (conformity to him) but, *See the end of the Lord*, says he, the end that the Lord himself came to, death, and a painful, and a shameful death. But why did he die? and why die so? *Quia Domini Domini sunt exitus mortis* (as St. Augustine interpreting this text, answers that question—De Civit. Dei i. 17; c. xviii) because to this God our Lord belonged these issues of death; *Quid apertius diceretur?* says he there; What can be more obvious, more manifest, than this sense of these words? In the former part of the verse it is said, *He that is our God is the God of salvation; Deus salvos faciendi*, so he reads it, The God that must save us; Who can that be, saith he, but Jesus? For therefore that name was given him, because he was to save us (Matt. i.21): And to this Jesus, saith he, this Saviour, belongs the issues of death, *Nec oportuit cum de hac vita alios exitus habere, quam mortis*, Being come into this life in our mortal nature, he could not go out of it any other way than by death. *Ideo dictum* (saith he) therefore it is said, *To God the Lord belong the issues of death; Ut ostenderetur moriendo nos salvos facturum*, to show that his way to save us, was to die. And from this text doth St. Isidore prove, that Christ was truly man (which as many sects of heretics denied, as that he was truly God) because to him, though he were *Dominus Dominus* (as the text doubles it) God the Lord, yet to him, to God the Lord belonged the issues of death. *Oportuit cum pati*, more cannot be said, than Christ himself saith of himself, *These things Christ ought to suffer* (Lu. xxiv.26); he had no other way but by death. So then, this part of our sermon must necessarily be a passion sermon, since all his life was a continual passion, all our Lent may well be a continual good-Friday; Christ's painful life took off none of the pains of his death; he felt not the less then, for having felt so much before; nor will anything that shall be said before, lessen, but rather enlarge your devotion to that which shall be said of his passion, at the time of the due solemnization thereof. Christ bled not a drop the less at last, for having bled at his circumcision before, nor will you shed a tear the less then, if you shed some now. And therefore be now content to consider with me, how to this *God the Lord belonged the issues of death.*

*That God the Lord*, the Lord of life could die, is a strange contemplation; that the Red Sea could be dry (Ex.xiv.21); that the sun could stand still (Josh.x.12); that an oven could be seven times heat and not burn; that lions could be hungry and not bite, is strange, miraculously strange; but super-miraculous, that God could die: but that God would die, is an exaltation of that; but, even of that also, it is a super-exaltation, that God should die, must die; and *non exitus* (saith St. Augustine) God the Lord had no issue but by death, and *oportuit pati* (saith Christ himself) all this Christ ought to suffer, was bound to suffer. *Deus ultionum Deus*, saith David, God is the God of revenges; he would not pass over the sin of man unrevenged, unpunished. But then, *Deus ultionum libere egit* (says that place) The God of revenges works freely; he punishes, he spares whom he will; and would he not spare himself? He would not. *Dilectio fortis ut mors* (Cant.viii.6), Love is as strong as death; stronger; it drew in death, that naturally was not welcome. *Si possibile* (saith Christ) *If it be possible let this cup pass*, when his love, expressed in a former decree with his Father, had made it impossible. Many waters quench not love; Christ tried many; he was baptized out of his love, and his love determined not there; he wept over Jerusalem out of his love, and his love determined not there; he mingled blood with water in his agony, and that determined not his love; he wept pure blood, all his blood, at all his eyes, at all his pores; in his flagellations, and thorns; to the Lord our God belonged the issues of blood; and these expressed, but these did not quench his love.

He would not spare, nay, he would not spare himself; there was nothing more free, more voluntary, more spontaneous than the death of Christ; it is true, *libere egit*, he died voluntarily; but yet, when we consider the contract that had passed between his Father and him, there was an *oportuit*, a kind of necessity upon him: all this Christ ought to suffer. And when shall we date this obligation, this *oportuit*, this necessity, when shall we say it began? Certainly this decree by which Christ was to suffer all this, was an eternal decree; and was there anything before that that was eternal? Infinite love, eternal love; be pleased to follow this home, and to consider it seriously, that what liberty soever we can conceive in Christ to die, or not to die, this necessity of dying, this decree is as eternal as that liberty; and yet how small a matter made he of this necessity, and this dying? His Father calls it but a bruise, and but a bruising of his heel (*The serpent shall bruise his heel*—Gen.iii.15) and yet that was, that the serpent should practise and compass his death. Himself calls it but a baptism, as though he were to be the better for it; *I have a baptism to be baptized with* (Lu.xii.50); and he was in pain till it was accomplished; and yet this baptism was his death. The Holy Ghost calls it joy; (*For the joy which was set before him he endured the cross*—Heb.xii.2) which was not a joy of his reward after his passion, but a joy that filled him even in the midst of those torments, and arose from them. When Christ calls his passion *calicem*, a cup, and no worse, (*Can ye drink of my cup* —Matt.xx.22,) he speaks not odiously, not with detestation of it; indeed it was a cup; *salus mundo*, a health to all the world; and *quid retribuem*, says David, *What shall I render unto the Lord?* (Ps.cxvi.12.) Answer you with David, *Accipiam calicem*, I will take the cup of salvation. Take that, that cup of salvation his passion, if not into your present imitation, yet into your present contemplation, and behold how that Lord who was God yet could die, would die, must die for your salvation.

That Moses and Elias talked with Christ in the transfiguration both St. Matthew (xvii.3) and St. Mark (ix.4) tell us; but what they talked of, only St. Luke (ix.31); *Dicebant excessum ejus*, says he; they talked of his decease, of his death, which was to be accomplished at Jerusalem. The word is of his Exodus, the very word of our text, *Exitus*, his issue by death. Moses, who in his Exodus had prefigured this issue of our Lord, and in passing Israel out of Egypt through the Red Sea, had foretold in that actual prophecy Christ's passing of mankind through the sea of his blood, and Elias, whose Exodus, and issue out of this world, was a figure of Christ's ascension, had no doubt a great satisfaction, in talking with our blessed Lord, *De excessu ejus*, of the full consummation of all this in his death, which was to be accomplished at Jerusalem. Our meditation of his death should be more visceral, and affect us more, because it is of a thing already done. The ancient Romans had a certain tenderness, and detestation of the name of death; they would not name death, no not in their wills; there they would not say, *Si mori contingat*, but *Si quid humanitus contingat*, not if or when I die, but when the course of nature is accomplished upon me. To us, that speak daily of the death of Christ, (he was crucified, dead and buried) can the memory or the mention of our death be irksome or bitter? There are in these latter times amongst us, that name death freely enough, and the death of God, but in blasphemous oaths and execrations. Miserable men, who shall therefore be said never to have named Jesus, because they have named him too often; and therefore hear Jesus say, *Nescivi vos*, I never knew you; because they made themselves too familiar with him. Moses and Elias talked with Christ of his death only in a holy and joyful sense of the benefit which they and all the world were to receive by it. Discourses of religion should not be out of curiosity, but edification. And then they talked with Christ of his death, at that time when he was at the greatest height of glory, that ever he admitted in this world; that is, his transfiguration. And we are afraid to speak to the great men of this world of their death, but nourish in them a vain imagination of immortality and immutability. But *Bonum est nobis esse hic*, (as St. Peter said there) It is good to dwell here, in this consideration of his death, and therefore transfer we our tabernacle, (our devotion) through some of these steps, which God the Lord made to his issue of death, that day.

Take in his whole day, from the hour that Christ ate the passover upon Thursday, to the hour in which he died the next day. Make this present day, that day in thy devotion, and consider what he did, and remember what you have done. Before he instituted and celebrated the sacrament, (which was after the eating of the passover) he proceeded to the act of humility, to wash his disciples' feet; even Peter's, who for a while resisted him. In thy preparation to the holy and blessed sacrament, hast thou with a sincere humility sought a reconciliation with all the world, even with those who have been averse from it, and refused that reconciliation from thee? If so, (and not else) thou hast spent that first part, of this his last day, in a conformity with him. After the sacrament, he spent the time till night in prayer, in preaching, in psalms. Hast thou considered that a worthy receiving of the sacrament consists in a continuation of holiness after, as well as in a preparation before? If so, thou hast therein also conformed thyself to him: so Christ spent his time till night. At night he went into the garden to pray, and he prayed *prolixius*; he spent much time in prayer (Lu.xxii.44). How much? because it is literally expressed that he prayed there three several times, and that returning to his disciples after his first prayer, and finding them asleep, said, *Could ye not watch with me one hour?* (Matt.xxvi.40.) It is collected that he spent three hours in prayer. I dare scarce ask thee whither thou wentest, or how thou disposedst of thyself, when it grew dark and after, last night. If that time were spent in a holy recommendation of thyself to God, and a submission of thy will to his; then it was spent in a conformity to him. In that time, and in those prayers were his agony and bloody sweat. I will hope that thou didst pray; but not every ordinary and customary prayer, but prayer actually accompanied with shedding of tears, and dispositively, in a readiness to shed blood for his glory in necessary cases, puts thee into a conformity with him. About midnight he was taken and bound with a kiss. Art thou not too conformable to him in that? Is not that too literally, too exactly thy case? At midnight to have been taken, and bound with a kiss? From thence he was carried back to Jerusalem; first to Annas, then to Caiaphas, and (as late as it was) there he was examined, and buffeted, and delivered over to the custody of those officers, from whom he received all those irrisions, and violences, the covering of his face, the spitting upon his face, the blasphemies of words, and the smartness of blows which that gospel mentions. In which compass fell that *gallicinium*, that crowing of the cock, which called up Peter to his repentance. How thou passedst all that time last night, thou knowest. If thou didst anything then that needed Peter's tears, and hast not shed them, let me be thy cock: do it now; now thy Master (in the unworthiest of his servants) looks back upon thee, do it now. Betimes in the morning, as soon as it was day, the Jews held a council in the high priest's house, and agreed upon their evidence against him, and then carried him to Pilate, who was to be his judge. Didst thou accuse thyself when thou wakedst this morning, and wast thou content to admit even false accusations, that is, rather to suspect actions to have been sin which were not, than to smother and justify such as were truly sins? Then thou spentest that hour in conformity to him. Pilate found no evidence against him; and therefore to ease himself, and to pass a compliment upon Herod, tetrarch of Galilee, who was at that time at Jerusalem, (because Christ being a Galilean, was of Herod's jurisdiction) Pilate sent him to Herod; and rather as a madman than a malefactor, Herod remanded him with scorns to Pilate to proceed against him; and this was about eight of the clock. Hast thou been content to come to this inquisition, this examination, this agitation, this cribration, this pursuit of thy conscience, to sift it, to follow it from the sins of thy youth to thy present sins, from the sins of thy bed to the sins of thy board, and from the substance to the circumstance of thy sins? That is time spent like thy Saviour's. Pilate would have saved Christ by using the privilege of the day in his behalf, because that day one prisoner was to be delivered; but they chose Barabbas. He would have saved him from death, by satisfying their fury, with inflicting other torments upon him, scourging, and crowning with thorns, and loading him with many scornful and ignominious contumelies; but this redeemed him not; they pressed a crucifying. Hast thou gone about to redeem thy sin, by fasting, by alms, by disciplines, and mortifications, in the way of satisfaction to the justice of God? That will not serve, that is not the right way. We press an utter crucifying of that sin that governs thee, and that conforms thee to Christ. Towards noon Pilate gave judgment; and they made such haste to execution, as that by noon he was upon the cross. There now hangs that sacred body upon the cross, re-baptized in his own tears and sweat, and embalmed in his own blood alive. There are those bowels of compassion, which are so conspicuous, so manifested, as that you may see them through his wounds. There those glorious eyes grew faint in their light, so as the sun, ashamed to survive them, departed with his light too. And there that Son of God, who was never from us, and yet had now come a new way unto us, in assuming our nature, delivers that soul which was never out of his Father's hands, into his Father's hands, by a new way, a voluntary emission thereof; for though to this God our Lord belong these issues of death, so that, considered in his own contract, he must necessarily die; yet at no breach, nor battery which they had made upon his sacred body, issues his soul, but *emisit*, he gave up the ghost: and as God breathed a soul into the first Adam, so this second Adam breathed his soul into God, into the hands of God. There we leave you, in that blessed dependency, to hang upon him, that hangs upon the cross. There bathe in his tears, there suck at his wounds, and lie down in peace in his grave, till he vouchsafe you a resurrection, and an ascension into that kingdom which he hath purchased for you, with the inestimable price of his incorruptible blood. Amen.

NOTES

p. 378. *vermiculation*: the condition of being infested with and consumed by worms.

p. 382. *presagitions*: prognostications; prognoses.

# JOHN HALES

HALES, THE 'ever memorable', could be so only for his great comment on the various Puritan notions of election: 'Nobody would conclude another man to be damned if he did not wish him to be so.' Hence his resolute Anglicanism, which is in the direct tradition of Cranmer, Jewel and Hooker.

He was born in 1584 in Bath, and was educated at Bath Grammar School and Corpus Christi, Oxford (B.A. 1603). He became a fellow of Merton in 1605, and a lecturer in Greek at Oxford in 1612. From 1613 to 1649 he was a fellow of Eton. He attended the Synod of Dort (1618-19), where he reported (as chaplain to Sir Dudley Carleton, who was at that time English ambassador to the Hague) in favour of the Arminians. It was then that he 'bid John Calvin good night'. He became chaplain to Laud in 1639, and accepted the canonry of Windsor, though with much reluctance. The Puritans threw him out of his canonry (1642) and deprived him of his fellowship (1649). He managed to survive, and even to dispense charity, by selling his library and other possessions, and by acting as tutor to the Bishop of Salisbury's nephew. Until his death in 1656 he lived quietly at Eton in the house of a former servant.

Hales was a man of learning, acute subtlety and wit, a member of the 'metaphysical' generation, Ben Jonson's intimate, and a member of Lucius Cary, Lord Falkland's famous circle (which used to gather at Falkland's estate at Tew). But he was essentially a 'private' man, who enjoyed discourses only with civilized and gentle minds (such as those of Falkland and his circle). 'He had', wrote his friend Clarendon, also a member of the Falkland group, 'whether from his natural temper ... or from his long retirement ... or from his profound judgment and discerning spirit, contracted some opinions which were not received, nor by him published, except in private discourses ... he would often say his opinions, he was sure, did him no harm, but he was far from confident that he might not do others harm....'

As a consequence of this attitude he was not much given to publishing, and was doubtless not a party to the issue of some of his sermons in 1613. His *Schism and Schismatics* (written 1636, published anonymously 1642) perfectly reflects his own and the moderate Church of England's position. It annoyed Laud by its liberal attitude, which is perhaps why it was not published until later; but Hales was in the event able to satisfy the Archbishop, in whose trust he remained.

Latitudinarianism is not perhaps any more satisfactory a term than others that were originally used opprobiously. But it does point to an attitude quite commonly held in the seventeenth-century Church of England; Hales has been called a representative of it. The danger is to identify him (and others called Latitudinarians) over-closely with it. The Latitudinarians stood between the High Anglicanism of such as Laud and the conservative Puritans, and they tended to combine mysticism with reason, although one or two were rationalists. The seventeenth century was a questioning one, and therefore an ingenious and metaphysical one. The Cambridge Platonists (Cudworth, More, John Smith, Whichcote and others) flourished from the early 1630s onwards. These men were conformist, but they wanted, in this at least like Hales, freedom to speculate. They therefore had Arminian sympathies, and tended to ignore public doctrine as irrelevant. Some were of a more mystical temper than others, and some regarded the institution of the Church of England as important while others were hardly interested in it; but, though they all opposed Hobbes's materialism, the results of their thinking were ultimately against their Church's interests, for it contributed to the semi-rationalism of the eighteenth century (and, more indirectly, to the Broad Church outlook of nineteenth-century English Christians). As a whole one might fairly say that most of the seventeenth-century Latitudinarians would not have objected to these results. (Most of them, incidentally, were Aristotelians.)

Hales was an Oxford man, whereas Latitudinarianism originated in and at first flourished mainly in Cambridge. The following sermon provides an opportunity to judge his position, since its subject is the question of how nonconformsists of either extreme should be dealt with.

## OF DEALING WITH ERRING CHRISTIANS
Rom. 14.1.
*Him that is weak in the faith receive, but not to doubtful disputations.*

HALES MAKES his own temperamental position clear in the opening paragraph. The implication is that he (personally) is happier in 'a small, a private, a retired auditory', and he appeals to the authority of St James. He is careful, however, to distinguish between what he considers to be his own method of fulfilling his vocation and that of others: 'At my hands is only required truth in sincerely discharging a common care, *at others*, care of profitably delivering a *common truth*' (my italics). The temper of the sermon as a whole is genial and obviously anti-Puritan: the passage on God's goodness beginning at 'The Heathen, speaking of God . . .' would have been anathema to any Puritan, but well accords with the remarks on *love* in Cranmer's homilies, and may indeed be taken as a development of them made at a later time and in different—and increasingly dangerous—circumstances. Yet there is nothing here that might be styled 'proto-Cambridge Platonist'; and if we assert that Hales tends to a Latitudinarian position, may we not mistake a tolerant disposition for an innovatory one? Are those contemporary members of the Church of England who do not think of dealing with 'imbecilities' by persecution necessarily sympathetic with Latitudinarianism? Hales's text from St Paul 'set[s] the bounds how far our love must reach': the language of his plea for tolerance of weakness of judgment in interpretation of the Scriptures makes it clear that his own position conforms with that of the Church: these ideas 'have taken root in the hearts of men of shallow capacity'. We must here, again, distinguish between true Latitudinarianism, and mere realism: 'many [i. e. not all] of these things of themselves are harmless and indifferent...' Hales is not against all disputation ('an excellent help to bring the truth to light'), but only against the hysterical or pettifogging sort that was then dividing the nation and threatening the Church. He certainly recommends the exercise of charity to all and sundry, heathen and Christian; but one can by no means infer from his language that he is not convinced of the propriety of the Thirty-Nine Articles—which themselves, indeed, realistically gloss over *some* points as being 'harmless and indifferent', since they are stated with a deliberate elasticity.

However, there is in Hales a trace of semi-Pelagianism, and it is this which relates him to the development of Latitudinarianism. He quotes Julian of Eclanum (a Pelagian, deprived of his bishopric in 417, who disputed with Augustine). What is now called semi-Pelagianism, however, was a reaction against the extremes of both Augustine and Pelagius (who disputed), and it laid (and lays?) an equal emphasis on divine grace and human free will; it is not necessarily outlawed by Article 17 of the Thirty-Nine Articles, which deals (quite properly) with predestination by not defining it but leaving it, in effect, as an open question. We might, if we employ the sort of over-subtlety in public debate against which Hales is here preaching (in acknowledgement, doubtless, of the dangers presented by his own subtle mind), accuse Hales of being tainted with Arianism, or Socinianism, or of being a proto-Unitarian; but his discourse is lucid, public, and he is here exercising the caution (his perhaps a shade ironic lack of confidence in the harmlessness of his own opinions) attributed to him by Clarendon.... This public practice may, it is true, be interpreted as 'Latitudinarian'; but it may, too, be interpreted as pleading for the preservation of such an institution as the Church of which Hales was a member.... For, as has been noted, he does speak quite forcefully of the views of the 'weak' as erroneous. He goes on to remind us that we are all weak, but carefully does not recommend any throwing away of such body of truth as reposes in his Church. He speaks, rather, of what *attitude* to take to *erring* (the word is itself significant) Christians.

The passage beginning 'But I am all this while in a generality only ...' is a clear recommendation not only to cut down doubtful disputation' in written form, but also to *continue with* established practice. 'The teaching the people by voice' is, he says, necessary, 'should all of us everywhere speak but the same things'. Of what is he thinking? Teaching of what? Nothing but the *Book of Homilies*, and what they teach, can answer this question—these against, of course, the background of the established liturgy and accompanying ritual. What, again, can be the drift of the passage beginning 'Justinian the Emperor...' but that the Church of England should look to its affairs? There can otherwise be nothing in his recipe, for he does not tell us to throw out the Book of Common Prayer. The 'first in [the] order of weak persons' can be no other than the man of upright life who is outside the Church of England: he should be 'wooed by us'. What can he mean by a *'true* faith' (my italics) but an

Anglican one? However, he does immediately advance the view that 'honest conversation' is 'surer' than 'true faith'—and here again he may fairly be related to the development of the Latitudinarian attitude. ('Conversation' may here be equated with 'good works': 'the action of living or having one's being *in* or *among*'.) But he stops short of heresy: 'it [good works] brings us not to heaven'.

Hales certainly seems somewhat to lessen the all-important emphasis on faith as trust; but his intentions were none the less to preserve the authority of this Church rather than to overbroaden its basis (as Latitudinarianism did). There must be, he states, 'bare belief' as well as accomplishment of God's will. The emphases are reversed, but the argument is still essentially Cranmer's. His remarks on the wicked man who is a true professor of the faith are unexceptionable, despite their continuation of his emphases. He then comes to the 'greatest sort of men . . . in a mediocrity . . . every one of us': the man who does not have the sufficiency of faith he ought to have, the man who is misinformed ('not so catechized in the mysteries of faith'), or the man who is informed but is troubled by some persistent failure in his behaviour. In each of these cases Hales counsels charity, gentleness and avoidance of self-glorification; but his intention is to inspire to good behaviour rather than to broaden the actual faith. He himself did not waver, but remained in his posts until he was ejected from them.

The passage discussing the English Roman Catholics (beginning 'And here I may not pass by that singular moderation . . .') clears Hales of Roman tendencies as surely as the general tenor of the sermon clears him from Puritanism. He ends by refusing, after all, to advise the authorities on methods of dealing with 'doubtful disputation'; but his two messages have been clear: toleration and the preservation of the middle way. It is perhaps interesting to speculate on what might have happened if Laud and his allies, who had charge of things, had listened to Hales. Could a softening of their High Church rigidity have prevailed over the spiritual aroogance and fanaticism of the other side? Even if not, we can hardly blame Hales for advocating tolerance. He was an ingenious and idiosyncratic man, and—like Donne and a few others of his time—a peculiarly 'modern' one; but he confined his ideas to a small, safe circle. In defending tolerance he was in no way abandoning the modern Anglican position.

MIGHT IT so have pleased God, that I had in my power the choice of my ways, and the free management of my own actions, I had not this day been *seen*, (for so I think I may better speak: *seen* may I be of many, but to be *heard* with any latitude and compass, my natural imperfection doth quite cut off:) I had not, I say, in this place this day been seen; ambition of great and famous auditories I leave to those whose better gifts and inward endowments are admonitioners unto them of the great good they can do, or otherwise thirst after popular applause. Unto myself have I evermore applied that of St. Jerome, a small, a private, a retired auditory, better accords both with my will and my abilities. Those unto whose discretion the furniture of this place is committed, ought especially to be careful, since you come hither to hear, to provide you those who can be heard; for the neglect of this one circumstance, how poor soever it may seem to be, is no less than to offend against that 'faith which cometh by hearing;' and to frustrate, as much as in them is, that end for which alone these meetings were ordained. We that come to this place, as God came to Elias in the mount, in a soft and still voice, to those which are near us, are that which the grace of God doth make us, unto the rest we are but statues: such therefore as my imperfection in this kind shall offend, such as this day are my spectators only, know, I trust, whom they are to blame. At my hands is only required truth in sincerely discharging a common care, at others, care of profitably delivering a common truth. As for me, the end of whose coming is to exhort you to a gracious interpreting of each other's imperfections, having first premised this apology for myself, it is now time to descend to the exposition of that scripture, which I have proposed, 'Him that is weak in the faith receive, but not to doubtful disputations.'

Goodness, of all the attributes by which a man may be styled, hath chief place and sovereignty; goodness, I say, not that metaphysical conceit which we dispute of in our schools, and is nothing else but that perfection which is inwardly due unto the being of every creature, and without which, either it is not at all, or but in part, that whose name it bears: but that which the common sort of men do usually understand, when they call a man good; by which is meant nothing else, but 'a soft, and sweet, and flexible disposition.' For all other excellencies and eminent qualities which raise in the minds of men some opinion and conceit of us, may occasion, peradventure, some strong respect in another kind; but impression of love and true respect, nothing can give but this: greatness of place and authority may make us feared, depth of learning admired, abundance of wealth may make men outwardly obsequious unto us; but that which makes one man a god unto another, that which doth tie the souls of men unto us, that which like the eye of the bridegroom, in the book of Canticles, iv.9, 'ravishes the heart of him that looks upon it,' is goodness: without this, mankind were but (as one speaks) 'Stones heapt together without mortar, or pieces of boards without any cement to combine and tie them together:' For this it hath singular in it, above all other properties of which our nature is capable, that it is the most available to human society, incorporating, and, as it were, kneading us together by softness of disposition, by being compassionate, by gladly communicating to the necessity of others, by transfusing ourselves into others, and receiving from others into ourselves. All other qualities, how excellent soever they are, seem to be somewhat of a melancholic and solitary disposition; they shine then brightest, when they are in some one alone, or attained unto by few; once make them common, and they lose their lustre: but goodness is more sociable; and rejoiceth in equalling others unto itself, and loses its nature, when it ceases to be communicable. The Heathen, speaking of God, usually style him by two attributes, *Optimus* and *Maximus*, the one importing his goodness, the other his power. In the first place they called him *Optimus*, a name signifying his goodness, giving the precedency unto it; and in the second place *Maximus*, a name betokening his power: yea, goodness is that wherein God himself doth most delight himself; and therefore all the acts of our Saviour, while he conversed on earth among men, were purely the issues of his tenderness, without any aspersion of severity, two only excepted: I mean his chasing the profaners out of the temple, and the curse laid upon the innocent fig-tree: and yet, in both these, mercy rejoiced against judgment, and his goodness had the preeminence. For the first brought some smart with it indeed, but no harm at all, as fathers use to chastise their children by means that fear them, more than hurt them. The second of itself was nothing, as being practised on a creature dull and senseless of all smart and punishment; but was merely exemplary for us. Christ whips our fruitlessness in the innocent fig-tree; like as the manner was among the Persians, when their great men had offended, to take their garments and beat them. Now that gracious way of goodness, which it pleased our Saviour thus to tread himself before us, the same hath he left behind him to be gone by us, and hath ordained us a course of religious and Christian service unto him, known by nothing more than goodness and compassion. The very Heathen themselves, though utter enemies unto it, have candidly afforded us this testimony. Ammianus Marcellinus taxing Georgius, a factious and proud bishop of Alexandria, for abusing the weakness of Constantius the Emperor, by base talebearing, and privy informations, notes precisely that he did it, 'quite besides the meaning of his profession, whose especial notes were gentleness and equity.' And Tertullian tells us, that anciently among the Heathen, the professors of Christianity were called, not *Christiani*, but *Chrestiani*, from a word signifying benignity and sweetness of disposition. The learned of our times, who for our instruction have written *de Notis Ecclesiae*, by what notes and signs we may know the church of Christ, may seem to have but ill forgotten this, which the Heathen man had so clearly discovered. For what reason is there, why that should not be one of the chiefest notes of the church of Christ, which did so especially characterize a Christian man, except it were the decay of it at this day in the church: of this thing therefore, so excellent in itself, so useful, so principally commended by the precept and example of our blessed Saviour, one especial part is, if not the whole, which here by our Apostle is commended unto us, when he speaks unto us of kindly intreating, and making much of such, who are, as he calls them, 'weak in the faith.' 'Him that is weak in the faith receive, but not to doubtful disputations.'

To know the natural ground and occasion of which words, it shall be very pertinent to note unto you, that with the church of Christ, as it signifies a company of men on earth, it fares no otherwise than it doth with other societies, and civil corporations. One thing there is unavoidable, and natural to all societies, which is the greatest occasioner, yea, the very ground of disunion and dissent; I mean, inequality of persons and degrees. All are not of the same worth, and therefore all cannot carry the same esteem and countenance: yet all, even the meanest, are alike impatient of discountenance and contempt, be the persons never so great from whence it proceeds. Wherefore we find that in states governed by the people, nothing did more exasperate the common sort, than the conceit of being contemned by men of greater place. For the taking away therefore of tumult and combustion, which through this inequality might arise, it was anciently counted an excellent policy in the Roman state, that men of greater account and place did, as it were, share the inferior sort amongst themselves, and every one, according to his ability, entertained some part of them as clients, to whom they yielded all lawful favour and protection. Even thus it fares with the church of God, it cannot be that all in it should be of equal worth, it is likewise distinguished into *people* and *nobles*. Some there are, and those that either through abundance of spiritual graces, or else of natural gifts, do far outstrip a great part of other Christians; these are the nobles of the church, whom our Apostle somewhere calls 'strong men in Christ.' Others there are, and those most in number, who either because God hath not so liberally blest them with gifts of understanding and capacity, or by reason of some other imperfections, are either not so deeply skilled in the mysteries of Christ, and of godliness, or otherwise weak in manners and behaviour; and these are the many of the church, whom our Apostle sometimes calls 'brethren of low degree,' sometime 'babes in Christ,' 1 Cor. iii. 1. and here in my text 'the weak and sick in faith.' Men by nature querulous, and apt to take exception; 'A sick man,' saith Electra in the tragedy, 'is a pettish and wayward creature, hard to be pleased;' as therefore with the sick, so are we now to deal with a neighbour, weak and sick of his spiritual constitution, and much we are to bear with his frowardness, where we cannot remedy it. For, as Varro sometimes spake of the laws of wedlock, 'Either a man must amend, or endure the faults of his wife; he that amends them makes his wife the better, but he that patiently endures them makes himself the better:' so is it much more true in dealing with our weak brethren, if we can by our behaviour remedy their imbecilities, we make them the better; if not, by enduring them we shall make ourselves the better; for so shall we increase the virtue of our patience, and purchase to ourselves, at God's hand, a more abundant reward. A great part of the lustre of a Christian man's virtue were utterly obscure, should it want this mean of showing itself. For were all men strong, were all of sufficient discretion, to see and judge of conveniency, where were the glory of our forbearance? As well therefore to increase the reward of the strong man in Christ, as to stop the whining and murmuring of the weaker sort, and to give content at all hands, our Apostle, like a good Tribune, in this text gives a rule of Christian popularity, advising the man of worthier parts, to avoid all slighting behaviour, to open the arms of tenderness and compassion, and to demerit by all courtesy the men of meaner rank, so to prevent all inconvenience that might arise out of disdainful and respectless carriage. For God is not like unto mortal princes, jealous of the man whom the people love; in the world, nothing is more dangerous for great men than the extraordinary favour and applause of the people; many excellent men have miscarried by it. For princes stand much in fear when any of their subjects hath the heart of the people. It is one of the commonest grounds upon which treason is raised; Absalom had the art of it, who by being plausible, by commiserating the people's wrongs, and wishing their redress; 'O that I were a judge to do this people good!' 2 Sam. xv. 4. by putting out his hand, and embracing, and kissing every one that came nigh him; so stole away the hearts of the people, that he had well-nigh put his father besides his kingdom. But what alters and undoes the kingdoms of this world, *that* strengthens and increases the kingdom of God; Absalom, the popular Christian, that hath the art of winning men's souls and making himself beloved of the people, is the best subject in the kingdom of grace, for this is that which our Apostle expresses in the phrase of 'receiving the weak.'

Now it falls out oftentimes, that men offend through intempestive compassion and tenderness, as much as by over much rigidness and severity; as much by familiarity, as by superciliousness and contempt: wherefore even our love and courtesy must be managed by discretion. St. Paul saw this well, and therefore he prescribes limits to our affections; and having in the former part of my text counselled us, as Christ did St. Peter, to let loose our nets to make a draught; to do as Joseph did in Egypt, open our garners and store-houses, that all may come to buy, to admit of all, to exclude none from our indulgence and courtesy: in this second part, 'But not to doubtful disputations;' he set the bounds how far our love must reach. As Moses, in the xix. of Exodus, sets bounds about Mount Sinai, forbidding the people, that they go not up to the hill, or come within the borders of it; so hath the Apostle appointed certain limits to our love and favour, within which it shall not be lawful for the people to come. Enlarge we the phylacteries of our goodness as broad as we list, give we all countenance unto the meaner sort, admit we them into all inwardness and familiarity; yet unto disputations and controversies, concerning profounder points of faith and religious mysteries, the meaner sort may be by no means admitted. For give me leave now to take this for the meaning of the words; I know they are very capable of another sense: as if the Apostle's counsel had been unto us, to entertain with all courtesy our weaker brethren, and not over-busily to enquire into, or censure their secret thoughts and doubtings, but here to leave them to themselves, and to God who is the judge of thoughts: for many there are, otherwise right good men, yet weak in judgment, who have fallen upon sundry private conceits, such as are unnecessary differencing of meats and drinks, distinction of days, or (to exemplify myself in some conceit of our times) some singular opinions concerning the state of souls departed, private interpretations of obscure texts of scripture, and others of the same nature: of these or the like thoughts, which have taken root in the hearts of men of shallow capacity, those who are more surely grounded may not presume themselves to be judges; many of these things of themselves are harmless and indifferent, only to him that hath some prejudicate opinion of them, they are not so; and of these things, they who are thus or thus conceited, shall be accountable to God, and not to man, to him alone shall they stand or fall; wherefore, bear (saith the Apostle) with these infirmities, and take not on you to be lords of their thoughts, but gently tolerate these their unnecessary conceits and scrupulosities. This though I take to be the more natural meaning of the words, (for indeed it is the main drift of our Apostle's discourse in this chapter) yet choose I rather to follow the former interpretation. First, because of the authority of sundry learned interpreters; and, secondly, because it is very requisite that our age should have something said unto it concerning this over-bold intrusion of all sorts of men into the discussing of doubtful disputations. For disputation, though it be an excellent help to bring the truth to light, yet many times, by too much troubling the waters, it suffers it to slip away unseen, especially with the meaner sort, who cannot so easily espy when it is mixed with sophistry and deceit. 'Him that is weak in the faith receive, but not to doubtful disputations.'

This my text therefore is a spiritual regimen and diet for these who are of a weak and sickly constitution of mind, and it contains a recipe for a man of crazy and diseased faith. In which, by that which I have delivered, you may plainly see there are two general parts. *First*, An admonition of courteous entertainment to be given to the weaker sort, in the first words, 'Him that is weak in the faith receive.' *Secondly*, The restraint and bound of this admonition, how far it is to extend, even unto all Christian offices, excepting only the hearing of 'doubtful disputations.'

In the *first* part we will consider; *First*, who these weak ones are of whom the Apostle speaks, and how many kinds of them there be, and how each of them may be the subject of a Christian man's goodness and courtesy. *Secondly*, Who these persons are, to whom this precept of entertaining is given, and they are two; either the private man, or the public magistrate. In the second general part we will see what reasons we may frame to ourselves, why these weak ones should not be admitted to questions and doubtful disputations. Which points severally, and by themselves, we will not handle, but we will so order them, that still as we shall have in order discovered some kind of weak man, whom our Apostle would have received, we will immediately seek how far forth he hath a right to be an hearer of sacred disputation, and this as far only as it concerns a private man: and for an upshot in the end, we will briefly consider by itself, whether, and how far this precept of bearing with the weak pertains to the man of public place, whether in the church, or in the commonwealth.

And *first*, Concerning the weak, as he may be a subject of Christian courtesy in private. And here, because that in comparison of him that is strong in Christ, every man, of what estate soever, may be said to be weak, that strong man only excepted, we will in the number of the weak contain all persons whatsoever. For I confess, because I wish well to all, I am willing that all should reap some benefit by my text. As therefore the woman in the gospel, who in touching only the hem of Christ's garment, did receive virtue to cure her disease; so all weak persons whatsoever, though they seem to come behind, and only touch the hem of my text, may peradventure receive some virtue from it to redress their weakness; nay, as the king in the gospel, that made a feast, and willed his servants to go out to the highway's side, to the blind, and the lame, and force them in, that his house might be full: so what lame or weak person soever he be, if I find him not in my text, I will go out and force him in, that the doctrine of my text may be full, and that the goodness of a Christian man may be like the widow's oil, in the book of Kings, that never ceased running so long as there was a vessel to receive it. Wherefore to speak in general, there is no kind of man, of what life, of what profession, of what estate and calling soever, though he be an Heathen, and idolater, unto whom the skirts of Christian compassion do not reach. St. Paul is my author, 'Now whilst you have time' (saith he) 'do good unto all men, but especially to the household of faith.' Galat. ii. 4. The household of faith indeed hath the preeminence; it must be chiefly, but not alone respected. The distinction that is to be made, is not by excluding any, but not participating alike unto all. God did sometime indeed tie his love to the Jewish nation only, and gave his laws to them alone: but afterward he enlarged himself, and instituted an order of serving him promiscuously, capable of all the world. As therefore our religion is, so must our compassion be, catholic. To tie it either to persons, or to place, is but a kind of moral Judaism. Did not St. Paul teach us thus much, common reason would. There must of necessity be some free intercourse with all men, otherwise the passages of public commerce were quite cut off, and the common law of nations must needs fall. In some things we agree, as we are men, and thus far the very Heathen themselves are to be received. For the goodness of a man, which, in Solomon's judgment, extendeth even to a beast, much more must stretch itself to a man of the same nature with him, be his condition what it will. St. Paul loved the Jews, because they were 'his brethren according to the flesh;' Rom. ix. 3. We that are of the Heathen, by the same analogy, ought to be as tenderly affected to the rest of our brethren, who though they be not as we are now, yet now are that which we sometimes were. 'It is an easy thing,' saith St. Austin, 'to hate evil men, because they are evil; but to love them as they are men, this is a rare and a pious thing.' The offices of common hospitality, of helping distressed persons, feeding the hungry, and the like, are due not only betwixt Christian and Christian, but between a Christian and all the world. Lot, when the angels came to Sodom, and sat in the streets; Abraham, when he saw three men coming toward him, stood not to enquire who they were, but out of the sense of common humanity, ran forth and met them, and gladly entertained them, not knowing whom they should receive. St. Chrysostom considering the circumstances of Abraham's fact, that he sat at his tent door, and *that* in the heat of the day, that he came to meet them, thinks, he therefore sat in public, and endured the inconvenience of the heat, even for this purpose, that he might not let slip any occasion of being hospital. The writings of the fathers run much in commendation of the ancient monks, and were they such as they report, well did they deserve to be commended; for their manner was to sit in the fields, and by the highway sides, for this end, that they might direct wandering passengers into the way, that they might relieve all that were distressed by want, or bruising or breaking of any member, and carry them home into their cells, and perform unto them all duties of humanity. This serves well to tax us, who affect a kind of intempestive prudence, and unseasonable discretion, in performing that little good we do, from whom so hardly, after long enquiry and entreaty, drops some small benevolence, like the sun in winter, long ere it rise, and quickly gone. How many occasions of Christian charity do we let slip, when we refuse to give our alms, unless we first cast doubts, and examine the persons, their lives, their necessities, though it be only to reach out some small thing, which is due unto him, whatsoever he be. It was anciently a complaint against the church, that the liberality of the Christians made many idle persons. Be it that it was so, yet no other thing befell them than what befalls their Lord, who knows and sees that his sun-shine and his rain is every day abused, and yet the sun becomes not like sackcloth, nor the heavens as brass; unto him must we, by his own command, be like: and whom then can we exclude, that have a pattern of such courtesy proposed to us to follow? We read in our books of a nice Athenian being entertained in a place by one given to hospitality, finding anon that another was received with the like courtesy, and then a third, growing very angry; I looked, said he, for a friend's house, but I am fallen into an inn to entertain all comers, rather than a lodging for some private and especial friends. Let it not offend any that I have made Christianity rather an inn to receive all, than a private house to receive some few. For so both the precepts and examples I have brought, teach us to extend our good, not to this or that man, but to mankind; like the sun that ariseth not on this or that nation, but on the whole world. Julian observes of the fig-tree, 'That above all trees it is most capable of grafts and scions of other kinds, so far, as that all variety will be brought to take nourishment from one stock.' Beloved, a Christian must be like unto Julian's fig-tree, so universally compassionate, that so all sorts of grafts, by a kind of Christian inoculation, may be brought to draw life and nourishment from his root.

But I am all this while in a generality only, and I must not forget, that I have many particular sick patients, in my text, of whom every one must have his recipe, and I must visit them all ere I go. But withal, I must remember my method, which was, still as I spake of receiving the weak, to speak likewise of excluding them from disputation. So must I needs, ere I pass away, tax this our age, for giving so general permission unto all, to busy themselves in doubtful cases of religion. For nothing is there that hath more prejudiced the cause of religion, than this promiscuous and careless admission of all sorts to the hearing and handling of controversies, whether we consider the private case of every man, or the public state of the church. I will touch but one inconvenience which much annoys the church, by opening this gate so wide to all comers; for by the great press of people that come, the work of the Lord is much hindered. Not to speak of those, who out of weakness of understanding fall into many errors, and by reason of liberty of bequeathing their errors to the world by writing, easily find heirs for them. There is a sort that do harm by being unnecessary, and though they sow not tares in the field, yet fill the Lord's floor with chaff: for what need this great breed of writers, with which in this age the world doth swarm? how many of us might spare the pains in committing our meditations to writing, contenting ourselves to teach the people *viva voce*, and suffering our conceits quietly to die in their birth? The teaching the people by voice is perpetually necessary, should all of us every where speak but the same things. For all cannot use books, and all that can, have not the leisure. To remedy therefore the want of skill in the one, and of time in the other, are we set in this ministry of preaching. Our voices are confined to a certain compass, and tied to the individuating properties of *here* and *now*: our writings are unlimited. Necessity therefore requires a multitude of speakers, a multitude of writers not so. G. Agricola, writing *de animantibus subterraneis*, reports of a certain kind of spirits that converse in minerals, and much infest those that work in them; and the manner of them when they come, is, to seem to busy themselves according to all the customs of workmen; they will dig, and cleanse, and melt, and sever metals; yet when they are gone, the workmen do not find that there is any thing done: so fares it with a great part of the multitude, who thrust themselves into the controversies of the times; they write books, move questions, frame distinctions, give solutions, and seem sedulously to do whatsoever the nature of the business requires; yet if any skilful workman in the Lord's mines shall come and examine their work, he shall find them to be but spirits in minerals, and that with all this labour and stir there is nothing done. I acknowledge it to be very true, which St. Austin spake; 'It is a thing very profitable, that divers tracts be written by divers men, after divers fashions, but according to the same analogy of faith, even of the same questions, that some might come into the hands of all, to some on this manner, to another after that.' For this may we think to have been the counsel of the Holy Ghost himself, who may seem even for this purpose, to have registered the selfsame things of Christ, by three of the Evangelists, with little difference. Yet notwithstanding, if this speech of St. Austin admit of being qualified, then was there no time which more than this age required should be moderated, which I note, because of a noxious conceit spread in our universities, to the great hindering of true proficiency in study, springing out from this root. For many of the learned themselves are fallen upon this preposterous conceit, That learning consisteth rather in variety of turning and quoting of sundry authors, than in soundly discovering and laying down the truth of things. Out of which arises a greater charge unto the poor student, who now goes by number rather than weight, and the books of the learned themselves, by ambitiously heaping up the conceits and authorities of other men, increase much in the bulk, but do as much imbase in true value. Wherefore as Gideon's army of two and thirty thousand, by prescript from God, was brought unto three hundred; so this huge army of disputes might, without any hazard of the Lord's battles, be well contracted into a smaller number. Justinian the Emperor, when he found that the study of the civil law was surcharged, and much confused, by reason of the great heaps of unnecessary writings, he calls an assembly of learned men, caused them to search the books, to cut off what was superfluous, to gather into order and method the sum and substance of the whole law: Were it possible that some religious Justinian might, after the same manner, employ the wits of some of the best learned in examining the controversies, and selecting out of the best writers what is necessary, defaulting unnecessary and partial discourses, and so digest into order and method, and leave for the direction of posterity, as it were, Theological Pandects, infinite store of our books might well lie by, and peaceably be buried, and after-ages reap greater profit with smaller cost and pains. But that which was possible in the world, united under Justinian, in this great division of kingdoms, is peradventure impossible. Wherefore having contented myself to show what a great and irremediable inconvenience this free, and uncontrollable venturing upon theological disputes hath brought upon us, I will leave this project as a speculation, and pass from this general doctrine unto some particulars. For this generality, and heap of sick persons, I must divide into their kinds, and give every one his proper recipe.

The first in this order of weak persons, so to be received and cherished by us, is one of whom question may be made, whether he may be called weak or no; he may seem to be rather dead: for no pulse of infused grace beats in him. I mean, such a one who hath but small, or peradventure no knowledge at all in the mystery of Christ, yet is, otherwise, a man of upright life and conversation, such a one as we usually name a moral man. Account you of such a one as dead, or how you please, yet methinks I find a recipe for him in my text. For this man is even to be wooed by us; as sometimes one Heathen man wished of another, 'Being what thou art, would that thou wert ours.' This man may speak unto a Christian, as Ruth does unto Boaz, 'Spread the skirt of thy garment over me, for thou art a near kinsman.' Ruth.iii.9. Two parts there are that do completely make up a Christian man, a true faith, and an honest conversation. The first, though it seem the worthier, and therefore gives unto us the name of Christians, yet the second, in the end, will prove the surer. For true profession, without honest conversation, not only saves not, but increases our weight of punishment: but a good life, without true profession, though it brings us not to heaven, yet it lessens the measure of our judgment: so that a moral man, so called, is a Christian by the surer side. As our Saviour saith of one in the gospel, that had wisely and discreetly answered him, 'Thou art not far from the kingdom of heaven;' Matt. xii.3,4. so may we say of these men, Suppose that as yet they be not of, yet certainly far from the kingdom of heaven they cannot be. Yea, this sincerity of life, though severed from true profession, did seem such a jewel in the eyes of some of the ancient fathers, that their opinion was, and so have they in their writings (erroneously doubtless) testified it. That God hath in store for such men not only this mitigating mercy, of which but now I spake, but even saving grace, so far forth as to make them possessors of his kingdom. Let it not trouble you, that I intitle them to some part of our Christian faith, and therefore without scruple to be received as weak, and not to be cast forth as dead. Salvianus disputing what faith is, 'What might this faith be?' (saith he) 'I suppose it is nothing else, but faithfully to believe Christ, and this is to be faithful unto God, which is nothing else but faithfully to keep the commandments of God.' Not therefore only a bare belief, but the fidelity and trustiness of God's servants, faithfully accomplishing the will of our Master, is required as a part of our Christian faith. Now all those good things which moral men by the light of nature do, are a part of God's will written in their hearts; wherefore so far as they were conscientious in performing them (if Salvianus his reason be good) so far have they title and interest in our faith. And therefore Regulus, that famous Roman, when he endured infinite torments, rather than he would break his oath, may thus far be counted a martyr, and witness for the truth. For the crown of martyrdom fits not only on the heads of those who have lost their lives, rather than they would cease to profess the name of Christ, but on the head of every one that suffers for the testimony of a good conscience, and for righteousness sake. And here I cannot pass by one very general gross mistaking of our age. For in our discourses concerning the notes of a Christian man, by what signs we may know a man to be one of the visible company of Christ, we have so tied ourselves to this outward profession, that if we know no other virtue in a man, but that he hath conned his creed by heart, let his life be never so profane, we think it argument enough for us to account him within the pale and circuit of the church: on the contrary side, let his life be never so upright, if either he be little seen in, or peradventure quite ignorant of the mystery of Christ, we esteem of him but as dead; and those who conceive well of those moral good things, as of some tokens giving hope of life, we account but as a kind of Manichees, who thought the very earth had life in it. I must confess that I have not yet made that proficiency in the schools of our age, as that I could see, why the second table, and the acts of it, are not as properly the parts of religion and Christianity, as the acts and observations of the first. If I mistake, then it is St. James that hath abused me; for he describing religion by its proper acts, tells us, that 'True religion, and undefiled before God and the Father, is, to visit the fatherless and the widow in their affliction, and to keep himself unspotted of the world.' Jas. i.27. So that the thing which in an especial refined dialect of the new Christian language signifies nothing but morality and civility, *that* in the language of the Holy Ghost imports true religion. Wherefore any difference that the Holy Ghost makes notwithstanding, the man of virtuous dispositions, though ignorant of the mystery of Christ, be it Fabricius, or Regulus, or any ancient Heathen man, famous for sincerity and uprightness of carriage, hath as sure a claim and interest in the church of Christ, as the man deepest skilled in, most certainly believing, and openly professing all that is written in the holy books of God, if he endeavour not to 'show his faith by his works.' Jam. 11.18. The ancients therefore, where they found this kind of men, gladly received them, and conversed familiarly with them, as appears by the friendly intercourse of epistles of St. Basil with Libanius, of Nazianzen and Austin, with sundry others; and antiquity hath either left us true, or forged us false epistles betwixt St. Paul himself and Seneca. Now as for the admitting of any of these men to the discussing of the doubts in our religious mysteries, who either know not, or peradventure contemn them, there needs not much be said: by a canon of one of the councils of Carthage it appears, it had sometimes been the erroneous practice of some Christians to baptize the dead, and to put the sacrament of Christ's body into their mouths. Since we have confessed these men to be in a sort dead, as having no supernatural quickening grace from above, to put into their hands the handling of the word of life at all, much more of discussing of the doubtful things in it, were nothing else, but to baptize a carcase, and put the communion bread into the mouth of the dead. Wherefore leaving this kind of weak person to your courteous acceptance, let us consider of another, one quite contrary to the former; a true professor, but a man of profane and wicked life, one more dangerously ill than the former: have we any recipe for this man? May seem for him there is no balm in Gilead, he seems like unto the leper in the law, unto whom no man might draw near. And by so much the more dangerous is his case, because the condition of conversing with Heathen men, be they never so wicked, is permitted unto Christians by our Apostle himself, whereas with this man, all commerce seems, by the same Apostle, to be quite cut off. For in the 1 Cor. v. St. Paul having forbidden them formerly all manner of conversing with fornicators, infamous persons, and men subject to grievous crimes; and considering at length how impossible this was, because of the Gentiles with whom they lived, and amongst whom necessarily they were to converse and trade, he distinguishes between the fornicators of this world, and the fornicators which were brethren. I meant not (saith the blessed Apostle, expounding himself) 'that ye should not admit of the fornicators of this world;' 1 Cor. v. 10. that is, such as were Gentiles, for then must ye have sought a new world. So great and general a liberty at that time had the world assumed for the practice of that sin of fornication, that strictly to have forbidden them the company of fornicators, had almost been to have excluded them the society of mankind. But, saith he, 'If a brother be a fornicator, or a thief, or a railer; with such a one partake not, no not so much as to eat.' 1 Cor. v. 11. Wherefore the case of this person seems to be desperate; for he is not only mortally sick, but is bereft of all help of the physician. Yet notwithstanding all this, we may not give him over for gone; for when we have well searched our boxes, we shall find a recipe even for him too. Think we that our Apostle's meaning was, that we should acquaint ourselves only with the good, and not the bad; as physicians in the time of pestilence look only to the sound, and shun the diseased? Our Saviour Christ familiarly conversed, ate, and drank with publicans and sinners, and gives the reason of it, because he 'came not to call the righteous, but sinners to repentance.' Matth. ix. 13. Is Christ contrary to Paul? This reason of our Saviour concerns every one on whom the duty of saving of souls doth rest. It is the main drift of his message, and unavoidably he is to converse, yea, eat and drink with all sorts of sinners, even because he is to call, not the righteous, but sinners to repentance. Necessary it is that some means be left to reclaim notorious offenders, let their disease be never so dangerous. 'I know not whether ought that can be tried, in the extremity of danger, will prove salutary; certainly to try nothing, must be destructive.' Who can tell whether in this extremity, were it at the last cast, it may some way profit to receive him; but this we all know, that altogether to cast him out of the society of good men, is to cut him off from all outward means of health. The leper in the law, though he were excluded the multitude, yet had he access unto the priest. Beloved, the priest in the new law hath much greater privilege than the ancient had; he was only a judge, and could not cure; but this is both a judge and a physician, and can both discern and cure the leprosy of our souls; wherefore he is not to be excluded from the most desperately sick person. Neither doth this duty concern the priest alone; for, as Tertullian sometimes spake in another case, 'Against traitors and public enemies every man is a soldier;' so is it true in this. Every one who is of strength to pull a soul out of the fire, is for this business, by counsel, by advice, by rebuking, a priest, neither must he let him lie there to expect better help. Again, no man so ill, but hath some good thing in him, though it breaks not out, as being clouded and darkened with much corruption. We must take heed, that we do not mistake in thinking there is nothing else but evil, where we often see it. We must therefore entertain even near friendship with such a one to discover him. 'No man is perfectly discovered,' saith St. Austin, 'but by his inward acquaintance.' As therefore they who seek for treasure, give not over by reason of clay and mire, so long as there is any hope to speed; so may we not cast off our industry, though it labour in the most polluted soul; 'that so at length, through charitable patience and long-suffering, we may discover in him some good things which may content us for the present, and give hope of better things to come.' For as they that work in gold and costly matter, diligently save every little piece that falls away; so goodness, wheresoever it be, is a thing so precious, that every little spark of it deserves our care in cherishing. Many miscarry through the want of this patience in those who undertake them, whilst they despair of them too soon: Whilst they rebuke us, as if they hated, and upbraid rather then reprehend. As unskilful physicians, who suffer their patients to die under their hands, to hide their error, blame their patients' intemperance: so let us take heed, lest it be not so much the strength of the disease, as the want of skill in us, which we strive to cover and veil over with the names of contumacy, intemperance, or the like. David received an express message from the prophet, that the child conceived in adultery should surely die; yet he ceased not his prayers, and tears, and fasting, as long as there was life in it. We receive no such certain message concerning any man's miscarriage, and why then should we intermit any office which Christian patience can afford? Wherefore, what Maecenas sometime spake loosely in another sense, that we may apply more properly to our purpose, Let our weak person here be lame, hand and foot, hip and thigh, sick in head and heart; yet so long as there is life in him, there is no cause we should despair. How knowest thou how potent the word of God may be through thy ministry, 'out of these stones to raise up children unto Abraham?' Luke iii. 8. I cannot therefore persuade myself, that this prohibition of St. Paul, of which we but now spake, so far extended, as that it quite interdicted good men the company of the sinners, be they never so gross. For when he delivered men unto Satan, (the greatest thing that ever he did in this kind) it was, 'to the mortifying of the flesh, that so the spirit might be safe in the day of the Lord.' 1 Cor. v. 5. But this is worse, for by this peremptory excluding the gross sinner from the good, a greater gap is opened to the liberty of the flesh, and a more immediate way could not be found to bring final destruction on him at that day. The extent therefore of St. Paul's precept, though given in shew to all, I take to reach no farther than the weak, and such as are in danger of infection; for the weaker sort of men are always evermore the most, and a charge given unto the most, is commonly given under the style of all. Our Apostle therefore jealous of the tenderer sort, whom every unwholesome blast doth easily taint, seems, what he intended for the most, to make general to all. The reason which the Apostle gives does warrant this restraint; 'See ye not,' saith he, 'that a little leaven sours the whole lump?' 1 Cor. v.6. If therefore there be any part of the lump out of shot and danger of souring and contagion, on it this precept can have no extent: and surely some wrong it were to the church of Christ, to suppose that all were necessarily subject to souring and infection, upon supposal of some admission of leaven. Evil indeed is infectious, but neither necessarily, nor yet so, that it need fright us from those who are diseased with it. Contagious diseases which seize on our bodies, infect by natural force and means, which we cannot prevent: but no man drinks down this poison, whose will is not the hand that takes the cup: so that to converse with men of diseased minds, infects us not, except we will. Again, Aristotle, in his problems, makes a question, 'Why health doth not infect as well as sickness.' For we grow sick many times by incautiously conversing with the diseased, but no man grows well by accompanying the healthy. Thus indeed it is with the healthiness of the body; it hath no transient force on others. But the strength and healthiness of the mind carries with it a gracious kind of infection: and common experience tells us, that nothing profits evil men more than the company of the good. So that strength of mind, accompanied with the preservative of the grace of God, may not only, without fear of contagion, safely converse with ungracious sinners, but by so doing, as it were infect them, and make them such as himself is. No cause therefore hitherto, why the true professors, though notorious sinners, should not be partakers of our Christian courtesies. And therefore as of the former, so of this my conclusion is, we must receive him. Only let me add St. Paul's words in another place, 'Ye that are strong receive such a one.'

Having thus far spoken of his admission, let us now a little consider of his restraint, and see whether he may have any part in hearing and handling religious controversies; where plainly to speak my mind, as his admission before was, so his exclusion here is much more necessary: the way to these schools should be open to none, but to men of upright life and conversation: and *that* as well in regard of the profane and wicked men themselves, as of the cause which they presume to handle: for as for themselves, this is but the field wherein they sow and reap their own infamy and disgrace. Our own experience tells us, how hard a thing it is for men of behaviour known to be spotless, to avoid the lash of those men's tongues, who make it their chief fence to disgrace the persons, when they cannot touch the cause. For what else are the writings of many men but mutual pasquils and satires against each other's lives, wherein digladiating like Eschines and Demosthenes, they reciprocally lay open each other's filthiness to the view and scorn of the world. The fear therefore of being stained, and publicly disgraced, might be reason enough to keep them back from entering these contentions. And as for the cause itself, into which this kind of men do put themselves, needs must it go but ill with it: for is it possible that those respects, which sway and govern their ordinary actions, should have no influence upon their pens? It cannot be, that they who speak, and plot, and act wickedness, should ever write uprightly. Doubtless, as in their lives, so in the causes they undertake, they nourish hopes full of improbity. Besides all this, the opinion of the common sort is not to be contemned, whom no kind of reason so much abuses, and carries away, as when the discredit of the person is retorted on the cause; which thing our adversaries here at home amongst us know very well, a master-piece of whose policy it is, to put into the hands of the people such pamphlets which hurt not our cause at all, but only discredit our persons. St. Chrysostom observes out of the ancient customs of the Olympic Games, that whensoever any man offered himself to contend in them, he was not to be admitted till public proclamation had been made throughout the multitude to this purpose. Whether any man knew him to be either a servant, or a thief, or otherwise of infamous life. And if any imputation in this kind were proved against him, it was sufficient to keep him back. Had the Heathen this care that their vanities should not be discredited? how great then must our care be, that they which enter into these exercises be of pure and upright condition? Let men's skill and judgment therefore be never so good, yet if their lives be notoriously subject to exception, let them know, that there is no place for them in these Olympics. Men indeed, in civil business, have found out a distinction, between an honest man, and a good commonwealthsman: and therefore Fabricius, in the Roman story, is much commended, for nominating to the consulship Ruffinus, a wicked man, and his utter enemy, because he knew him to be serviceable to the commonwealth, for those wars which were then depending. But in the business of the Lord, and commonwealth of God, we can admit of no such distinction. For God himself, in the book of Psalms, staves them off with a 'What hast thou to do to take my words into thy mouth, since thou hatest to be reformed?' Ps. 1. 17. The world, for the managing of her matters, may employ such as herself hath fitted: 'But let every one who names the name of God, depart from iniquity.' 2 Tim. ii. 19. For these reasons therefore it is very expedient, that none but right good men should undertake the Lord's quarrels, the rather, because there is some truth in that which Quintilian spake, 'As impossible it is that good and bad thoughts should harbour in the same heart, as it is for the same man to be jointly good and bad.' And so, from the consideration of this sick person, let us proceed to visit the next.

The weak persons, I have hitherto treated of, are the fewest, as consisting in a kind of extreme. For the greatest sort of men are in a mediocrity; of men, eminently good, or extremely ill, the number is smallest; but this rank of sick persons, that now we are to view, is an whole army, and may be, every one of us, if we do well examine ourselves, shall find ourselves in it: for the weak, whom we now are to speak of, is he that hath not that degree and perfection of faith, and strength of spiritual constitution, that he ought to have. Wherefore our recipe here must be like the tree of life in the book of Revelation, it must be medicine to heal whole nations. For who is he amongst men that can free himself from this weakness? Yea, we ourselves, that are set over others for their cure, may speak of ourselves and our charge, as Iolaus, in Euripides, doth of himself and Hercules's children, 'We take care of these, ourselves standing in need of others care for us.' Hippocrates counsels his physician, to look especially that himself be healthy, 'fair of colour, and full of flesh.' For otherwise, saith he, how can he give comfort and hope of success to a sick patient, who, by his ill colour and meagreness, bewrays some imperfection of his own. But what physician of soul and manners is capable of this counsel? or who is it, that, taking the cure of others, doth not in most of his actions bewray his own disease? Even thus hath it pleased God to tie us together with a mutual sense of each other's weakness; and as ourselves receive and bear with others; so for ourselves interchangeably must we request the same courtesy at others' hands. Notwithstanding, as it is with the health of our bodies, no man at any time is perfectly well, only he goes for an healthy man, who is least sick: so fares it with our souls. God hath included all under the name of weak, some peradventure are less weak than others, but no man is strong. It is but a miserable comfort to judge our own perfections only by others' defects, yet this is all the comfort we have.

Let us leave therefore those, who, by reason of being less crazy, pass for healthy, and consider of those whom some sensible and eminent imperfection above others hath ranked in the number of the weak. And of those there are sundry kinds, especially two. One is weak, because he is not yet fully informed, not so sufficiently catechized in the mysteries of faith, whom farther institution may bring to better maturity: The other peradventure is sufficiently grounded for principles of faith, yet is weak, by reason either of some passion, or of some irritatory and troublesome humour in his behaviour. There is no man so perfect, but hath somewhat in his behaviour that requireth pardon.

As for the imperfection of the former of these, it is the weakness of infancy and childhood in faith, rather than a disease: and with this weak man we are especially to bear above all others. For as for him that is weak through gross and wilful ignorance, or contumacy, or the like, it is pardonable, if sometimes we yield him not that measure of courtesy which were meet; but to be cruel against infancy and childhood were inhumanity. The manner of our recipe for these men, our Apostle somewhere expresses, where he tells us of some that must 'be fed with milk, and not strong meat:' 1 Cor. iii. 2. unto these we must rather be as nurses than physicians; by gently submitting ourselves to the capacity of the learner, by lending our hand, by lessening our steps to keep them in equi-pace with us, till they come up to their full growth. As Christ, being God, emptied himself, and became man like to us, so must we lay down our gifts of wit, in which we flatter ourselves, and take ourselves to be as gods, and in shew and fashion become like one of them. Grave men have thought it no disparagement to have been seen with their little sons, toying and practising with them their childish sports: and if any take offence at it, they are such as know not what it is to be fathers. Those therefore who bear the office of fathers amongst other men, to bring up the infancy of babes in Christ, must not blush to practise this part of a father, and out of St. Paul's lesson of 'becoming all to all,' 1 Cor. iv.22. learn to become a child to children; do it he may very well, without any impeachment to himself. He that helps one up that is fallen, throws not himself down to lie by him, but gently stoops to lift him up again; but of this weak person I have little need, I trust, to speak. For no man in these days can be long weak, but by his own default, so long and careful teaching as hath been, and every day is, must needs take from men all pretence of weakness in this kind: for what is the end of all this labour and pains in teaching, but that ye might at length not need a teacher. Wherefore from this I come unto that other weak person, strong in faith, but weak in carriage and behaviour.

Having before proved, that Christian courtesy spreads itself to all sorts of men, to the infidel, to the gross notorious sinner, then will it, without any straining at all, come home to all the infirmities of our weaker brethren: for that which can endure so great a tempest, how can it be offended with some small drops. Is Christian patience like unto St. Peter's resolution, that durst manfully encounter the high priest's servant, yet was daunted at the voice of a silly maiden; whatsoever it is that is irksome unto us in the common behaviour of our brethren, it were strange we should not be able to brook. Epictetus considering with himself the weakness which is usual in men, still to make the worst of what befalls us, wittily tells us, that every thing in the world hath two handles, one turned toward us, which we may easily take, the other turned from us, harder to be laid hold of; the first makes all things easy, the second not so; the instance that he brings is my very purpose; 'Be it,' saith he, 'thy brother hath offended thee, here are two hand-fasts, one of the offence, the other of thy brother. If thou take hold of that of the offence, it will be too hot for thee, thou wilt not easily endure the touch of it: but if thou lay hold of that of thy brother, this will make all behaviour tolerable. There is no part of our brother's carriage towards us, but if we search it, we shall find, some hand-fast, some circumstance, that will make it easy to be born.' If we can find no other, the circumstance of our Saviour Christ's example will never fail: an example which will not only make us to endure the importunity of his ordinary behaviour, but all his outrageous dealing whatsoever. For, saith St. Chrysostom, 'Didst thou know that thy brother intended particular mischief against thee, that he would embrue his hand in thy blood, yet kiss that hand; for thy Lord did not refuse to kiss that mouth that made the bargain for his blood.' It is storied of Protagoras, that being a poor youth, and carrying a burthen of sticks, he so piled them, and laid them together with such art and order, that he made them much more light and easy to be born. Beloved, there is an art among Christians, like unto that of Protagoras, of so making up and ordering our burthens, that they may lie with much less weight upon our shoulders; this art, if we could learn it, would make us take all in good part at our brother's hand, were he as bad as Nabal was, of whom his own servant complained, that he was 'such a man of Belial, that no man could speak unto him.' 1 Sam. xxv. 17.

Wherefore, leaving you to the study and learning of this most Christian art, I will a little consider for what reasons we may not admit of these two sorts of weak men to controversy. For first, as for the unlearned, in private, nothing more usual with them than to take offence at our dissentions, and to become more uncertain and unjointed upon the hearing of any question discussed: it is their usual voice and question to us, Is it possible that we should be at one in these points in which yourselves do disagree? thus cast they off on our backs the burthen of their back-sliding and neutrality; wherefore to acquaint them with disputation in religion, were, as it were, to blast them in their infancy, and bring upon them some improsperous disease to hinder their growth in Christ.

Secondly, What one said of other contentions, 'In civil wars no man is too weak to do a mischief,' we have found too true in these our holy wars; no man is too weak (I say not) to do mischief, but to be a principal agent and captain in them. Simple and unlearned souls, trained up by men of contentious spirits, have had strength enough to be authors of dangerous heresies; Priscilla and Maximilla, silly women laden with iniquity, were the chief ring-leaders in the errors of the Montanists; and as it is commonly said, 'Weaklings are able to begin a quarrel, but the prosecution and finishing is a work for stronger men;' so hath it fared here. For that quarrel which these poor souls had raised, Tertullian, a man of great wit and learning, is drawn to undertake: so that for a Barnabas to be drawn away to error, there needs not always the example and authority of a Peter.

A third reason is the marvellous violence of the weaker sort in maintaining their conceits, if once they begin to be opinionative. For one thing there is that wonderfully prevails against the reclaiming of them, and that is, The natural jealousy they have of all that is said unto them by men of better wits, stand it with reason never so good, if it sound not as they would have it. A jealousy founded in the sense of their weakness, arising out of this, that they suspect all to be done for no other end, but to circumvent and abuse them. And therefore when they see themselves to be too weak in reasoning, they easily turn them to violence. The monks of Egypt, otherwise devout and religious men, anciently were for the most part unlearned, and generally given over to the error of the Anthropomorphitae, who held, that God had hands and feet, and all the parts that a man hath, and was in outward shape and proportion like to one of us. Theophilus, a learned bishop of Alexandria, having fallen into their hands, was so roughly used by them, that ere he could get out of their fingers, he was fain to use his wits, and to crave aid of his equivocating sophistry, and soothly to tell them, 'I have seen your face as the face of God.' Now when Christian and religious doubts must thus be managed with wilfulness and violence, what mischief may come of it is already so plain, that it needs not my finger to point it out. Wherefore let every such weak person say unto himself, as St. Austin doth, 'Let others reason, I will marvel; let others dispute, I will believe.'

As for the man strong in passion, or rather weak, for the strength of passion is the weakness of the passionate; great reason hath the church to except against him. For first of all, from him it comes, that our books are so stuffed with contumelious malediction, no Heathen writers having left the like example of choler and gross impatience. An hard thing I know it is, to write without affection and passion in those things which we love, and therefore it is free so to do, to those who are lords over themselves. It seems our Saviour gave some way to it himself. For somewhat certainly his kinsmen saw in his behaviour, when, as St. Mark reports, they went forth to lay hold upon him, 'thinking he was beside himself.' Mark iii. 21. But for those who have not the command of themselves, better it were they laid it by; St. Chrysostom excellently observeth, that the prophets of God, and Satan, were by this notoriously differenced, that they which gave oracles by motion from the devil, did it with much impatience and confusion, with a kind of fury and madness; but they which gave oracles from God by divine inspiration, gave them with all mildness and temper; if it be the cause of God which we handle in our writings, then let us handle it like the prophets of God, with quietness and moderation, and not in the violence of passion, as if we were possessed, rather than inspired. Again, what equity or indifferency can we look for in the carriage of that cause, that falls into the handling of these men: What man, overtaken with passion, remembers impartially to compare cause with cause, and right with right; on what cause he happens, that is he resolute to maintain; as a fencer to the stage, so comes he to write, not upon conscience of quarrel, but because he proposes to contend; yea, so potently hath this rumour prevailed with men that have undertaken to maintain a faction, that it hath broken out to the tempting of God, and the dishonour of martyrdom. Two friars in Florence, in the action of Savonarola, voluntarily, in the open view of the city, offered to enter the fire: so to put an end to the controversy, that he might be judged to have the right, who, like one of the three children in Babylon, should pass untouched through the fire. But I hasten to visit one weak person more, and so an end.

He whom we now are to visit, is a man weak through heretical an erring faith; now whether or no we have any receipt for him, it may be doubtful: for St. Paul advises us to avoid the man that is a maker of sects, knowing him to be damned. Yet, if as we spake of not admitting to us the notorious sinner, no not to eat, so we teach of this, that it is delivered respectively to the weaker sort, as justly for the same reasons we may do: we shall have a recipe here for the man that errs in faith, and rejoiceth in making of sects: which we shall the better do, if we can but gently draw him on to a moderation to think of his conceits only as of opinions; for it is not the variety of opinions, but our own perverse wills, who think it meet, that all should be conceited as ourselves are, which hath so inconvenienced the church. Were we not so ready to anathematize each other, where we concur not in opinion, we might in hearts be united, though in our tongues we were divided, and that with singular profit to all sides. It is 'the unity of the Spirit in the bond of peace,' Ephes. iv. 3. and not identity of conceit, which the Holy Ghost requires at the hands of Christians. I will give you one instance, in which, at this day, our churches are at variance; the will of God, and his manner of proceeding in predestination, is undiscernible, and shall so remain until that day, wherein all knowledge shall be made perfect; yet some there are, who, with probability of scripture, teach, that the true cause of the final miscarriage of them that perish, is that original corruption that befell them at the beginning, increased though the neglect or refusal of grace offered. Others, with no less favourable countenance of scripture, make the cause of reprobation only the will of God, determining freely of his own work, as himself pleases, without respect to any second cause whatsoever. Were we not ambitiously minded, every one to be lord of a sect, each of these tenets might be profitably taught and heard, and matter of singular exhortation drawn from either; for on the one part, doubtless it is a pious and religious intent, to endeavour to free God from all imputation of unnecessary rigour, and his justice from seeming injustice and incongruity: and on the other side, it is a noble resolution, so to humble ourselves under the hand of Almighty God, as that we can with patience hear, yea, think it an honour, that so base creatures as ourselves should become the instruments of the glory of so great a Majesty, whether it be by eternal life, or by eternal death, though for no other reason but for God's good will and pleasure's sake. The authors of these conceits might both freely (if peaceably) speak their minds, and both singularly profit the church: for since it is impossible, where scripture is ambiguous, that all conceits should run alike, it remains, that we seek out a way, not so much to establish an unity of opinion in the minds of all, which I take to be a thing likewise impossible, as to provide, that multiplicity of conceit trouble not the church's peace. A better way my conceit cannot reach unto, than that we would be willing to think, that these things, which with some shew of probability we deduce from scripture, are at the best but our opinions: for this peremptory manner of setting down our own conclusions, under this high commanding form of necessary truths, is generally one of the greatest causes, which keeps the churches this day so far asunder; when as a gracious receiving of each other, by mutual forbearance in this kind, might peradventure, in time, bring them nearer together.

This peradventure, may some man say, may content us in

case of opinion indifferent, out of which no great inconvenience, by necessary and evident proof, is concluded: but what recipe have we for him that is fallen into some known and desperate heresy? Even the same with the former. And therefore anciently, heretical and orthodox Christians, many times, even in public holy exercise, conversed together without offence. It is noted in the ecclesiastic stories, that the Arrians and right believers so communicated together in holy prayers, that you could not distinguish them till they came to the Doxology, which the Arrians used with some difference from other Christians. But those were times of which we read in our books, but we have lost the practice of their patience. Some prejudice was done unto the church by those, who first began to intermingle with public ecclesiastical duties, things respective unto private conceits. For those Christian offices in the church ought, as much as possibly they may, be common unto all, and not to descend to the differences of particular opinions. Severity against, and separation from heretical companies, took its beginning from the heretics themselves: and if we search the stories, we shall find, that the church did not, at their first arising, thrust them from her, themselves went out: and as for severity, that which the Donatists sometimes spake in their own defence; 'She was the true church, not which raised, but which suffered persecution,' was *de facto* true for a great space. For when heresies and schisms first arose in the church, all kinds of violence were used by the erring factions; but the church seemed not for a long time to have known any use of a sword, but only of a buckler, and when she began to use the sword, some of her best and chiefest captains much misliked it. The first law in this kind that ever was made, was enacted by Theodosius against the Donatists, but with this restraint, that it should extend against none, but only such as were tumultuous, and till that time they were not so much as touched with any mulct, though but pecuniary, till that shameful outrage committed against Bishop Maximian, whom they beat down with bats and clubs, even as he stood at the altar: so that not so much the error of the Donatists, as their riots and mutinies were by imperial laws restrained. That the church had afterward good reason to think, that she ought to be rather salutary than pleasing; that sometimes there was more mercy in punishing than forbearing, there can no doubt be made. St. Austin (a man of as mild and gentle spirit as ever bare rule in the church) having, according to his natural sweetness of disposition, earnestly written against violent and sharp dealing with heretics, being taught by experience, did afterward retract, and confess an excellent use of wholesome severity in the church. Yet could I wish that it might be said of the church, which was sometimes observed of Augustus, 'He had been angry with, and severely punished many of his kin, but he could never endure to cut any of them off by death.' But this I must request you to take only as my private wish, and not as a censure, if any thing have been done to the contrary. When Absalom was up in arms against his father, it was necessary for David to take order to curb him, and pull him on his knees; yet we see how careful he was he should not die, and how lamentably he bewailed him in his death: what cause was it that drove David into this extreme passion? Was it doubt of heir to the kingdom? that could not be; for Solomon was now born, to whom the promise of the kingdom was made: Was it the strength of natural affection? I somewhat doubt of it; three years together was Absalom in banishment, and David did not very eagerly desire to see him: the scripture indeed notes, that the king longed for him; yet in this longing was there not any such fierceness of passion, for Absalom saw not the king's face for two years more after his return from banishment to Jerusalem: What then might be the cause of his strength of passion, and commiseration in the king? I persuade myself it was the fear of his son's final miscarriage, and reprobation, which made the king (secure of the mercies of God unto himself) to wish he had died in his stead, that so he might have gained for his ungracious child some time of repentance. The church, who is the common mother of us all, when her Absaloms, her unnatural sons, do lift up their hands and pens against her, must so use means to repress them, that she forget not that they are the sons of her womb, and be compassionate over them, as David was over Absalom, loth to unsheath either sword, but most of all the temporal; for this were to send them quick dispatch to hell.

And here I may not pass by that singular moderation of this church of ours, which she hath most Christianly expressed towards her adversaries of Rome, here at home in her bosom, above all the reformed churches I have read of. For out of desire to make the breach seem no greater than indeed it is, and to hold communion and Christian fellowship with her, so far as we possibly can, we have done nothing to cut off the favourers of that church. The reasons of their love and respect to the church of Rome we wish, but we do not command, them to lay down: their lay-brethren have all means of instruction offered them. Our edicts and statutes, made for their restraint, are such as serve only to awaken them, and cause them to consider the innocency of that cause, for the refusal of communion in which they endure (as they suppose) so great losses. Those who are sent over by them, either for the retaining of the already perverted, or perverting others, are either returned by us back again to them, who dispatched them to us; or, without any wrong unto their persons, or danger to their lives, suffer an easy restraint; which only hinders them from dispersing the poison they brought. And had they not been stickling in our state business, and meddling with our prince's crown, there had not a drop of their blood fallen to the ground; unto our sermons, in which the swervings of that church are necessarily to be taxed by us, we do not bind their presence; only our desire is, they would join with us in those prayers and holy ceremonies, which are common to them and us. And so accordingly, by singular discretion was our Service-book compiled by our fore-fathers, as containing nothing that might offend them, as being almost merely a compendium of their own Breviary and Missal; so that they shall see nothing in our meetings, but that they shall see done in their own; though many things which are in theirs, here, I grant, they shall not find. And here indeed is the great and main difference betwixt us. As it is in the controversy concerning the canonical books of scripture: whatsoever we hold for scripture, that even by that church is maintained, only she takes upon her to add much, which we cannot think safe to admit: so fares it in other points of faith and ceremony; whatsoever it is we hold for faith, she holds it as far forth as we: our ceremonies are taken from her; only she, over and above, urges some things for faith, which we take to be error, or at the best but opinion; and for ceremony, which we think to be superstition: so that to participate with us, is, though not throughout, yet in some good measure, to participate with that church; and certainly were that spirit of charity stirring in them, which ought to be, they would love and honour us, even for the resemblance of that church, the beauty of which themselves so much admire. The glory of these our proceedings, even our adversaries themselves do much envy; so that from hence it is, that in their writings they traduce our judiciary proceedings against them, for sanguinary and violent; striving to persuade other nations, that such as have suffered by course of public justice for religion only, and not for treason have died, and pretend we what we list, our actions are as bloody and cruel as their own: wherefore if a perfect pattern of dealing with erring Christians were to be sought, there were not any like unto this of ours; which, as it takes not to itself liberty of cruelty, so it leaves not unto any the liberty of destroying their own souls in the error of their lives. And now that we may at once conclude this point concerning heretics, for prohibiting these men access to religious disputations, it is now too late to dispute of that; for from this, that they have already unadvisedly entered into these battles, are they become that which they are: let us leave them therefore as a sufficient example and instance of the danger of intempestive and immodest meddling in sacred disputes.

I see it may be well expected, that I should, according to my promise, add instruction for the public magistrate, and show how far this precept in receiving the weak concerns him.

I must confess I intended, and promised so to do, but I cannot conceive of it, as a thing befitting me to step out of my study, and give rules for government to commonwealths, a thing befitting men of greater experience to do. Wherefore I hope you will pardon me if I keep not that promise, which I shall with less offence break than observe: and this I rather do, because I suppose this precept to concern us especially, if not only, as private men, and that in case of public proceeding, there is scarce room for it. Private men may pass over offences at their pleasure, and may be, in not doing it, they do worse; but thus to do, lies not in the power of the magistrate, who goes by laws, prescribing him what he is to do. Princes and men in authority do many times much abuse themselves, by affecting a reputation of clemency, in pardoning wrongs done to other men, and giving protection to sundry offenders, against those who have just cause to proceed against them. It is mercy to pardon wrong done against ourselves, but to deny the course of justice to him that calls for it, and to protect offenders, may peradventure be some inconsiderate pity, but mercy it cannot be. All therefore that I will presume to advise the magistrate is, a general inclinableness to merciful proceedings.

And so I conclude, wishing unto them who plentifully sow mercy, plentifully to reap it at the hand of God, with an hundred-fold increase, and that the blessing from God, the father of mercies, may be upon them all, as on the sons of mercy, as many as are the sands on the sea-shore in multitude. The same God grant, that the words which we have heard this day, &c.

# William Laud

WILLIAM LAUD, son of a Reading taylor, was born in 1573. He was educated at Reading Free School and then at St John's, Oxford, of which he became President in 1611. He was ordained in 1601. From this time he made himself unrelenting enemies—by his lack of sympathy to all shades of Puritanism— and staunch friends, by his evident sincerity, learning and ability. He married Lady Rick (a *divorcée*) in 1605. In 1615 he became Archdeacon of Huntingdon, and in the following year Dean of Gloucester. When he became Bishop of St Davids in 1621 he resigned the presidency of his college. It was at Charles I's accession that he became really prominent and influential, since the King rightly had confidence in him as an administrator, and knew of his qualities from his friend Buckingham, whose confessor Laud had been since 1621. He was transferred to Bath and Wells (1626), and became a Privy Councillor in 1627. In 1629 he was appointed Chancellor of his old university, where he introduced reforms. In 1633, having refused the offers of a cardinal's hat, he became Archbishop of Canterbury. He proceeded to enforce Church of England uniformity with the utmost severity, and then, in 1637, made the most serious error of his life: he ordered the Scottish clergy to use the Book of Common Prayer. This was the chief, if indirect, cause of the war that brought both Laud and Charles to the block. In 1640, as obstinate and courageous as ever, he imposed an oath (the so-called '*etcetera* oath') on all the learned professions: 'Never to consent to alter the government of this Church . . . as it stands now established'; the King was forced to abrogate this, and in 1641 Laud was arrested. Later, after an unconstitutional trial, he was beheaded (1645). He could have escaped, and the Dutchman Hugo Grotius (decidedly more inclined to Rome than Laud) urged him to do so; but he refused.

It was Laud's gift for administration that led him (even if in old age) to the block. He was a disciple of Richard Hooker who eventually carried Hooker's views further than Hooker would have wished or thought wise. Accusations of popery against Laud are as absurd as accusations of puritanism are against some others; but then in these turbulent and confused times such epithets were hurled about much as 'fascist', 'moderate', or 'communist' are today. In Laud they found a vulnerable target. He was by persuasion what we should now call High Church, or Anglo-Catholic. In a disputation with 'Fisher the Jesuit' (1622) he maintained that both the Church of England and the Church of Rome are branches of the Church Catholic. Hooker would have supported this, but out of tolerance; in Laud there was undoubtedly a trace of nostalgia for the pre-Reformation days of nominal unity—but such a nostalgia does not constitute popery, and he never, like his friend Grotius, advocated reunion.

Laud had his own (anti-Calvinistic) doctrinal views, but was never a bigot in this matter. What he was interested in was *uniformity of observance*. In this he was undoubtedly over-dogmatic, over-rigorous, pedantic. In his early days he irritated the authorities at Oxford University by his anti-Calvinist zeal over observance. As Dean of Gloucester he had every right to move the communion table to the east end of the choir, but he was not tactful in the argument with his bishop that ensued. Tact was never in Laud's nature, and it has to be added that what fairly might be called a 'Hookerian' tact is characteristic of the spirit of the Church of England.

Laud became one of the triumvirate that ruled England from 1625 until 1640: Charles, its head, used Wentworth (later Strafford) as his secular arm and Laud as his religious. The times were intolerable for all three men: they inherited a social, political and religious situation which the well-intentioned but inept —indeed, ridiculous and arrogant—James I had made worse. But of the three only Strafford was really at all competent, in pragmatic terms, to cope. Charles was a noble man who died a martyr's death, but he lacked flexibility, and he was badly compromised by his marriage to a sturdy Roman Catholic, to whose advice he far too readily listened. He was guilty of duplicity and insensitivity to constitutional issues; and then he was kept short of money, he was the king, and his fiercest opponents were equally insensitive—some were fanatics. Laud's lack of tact and passion for exact outward observance turned him into an authoritarian. His actions in regard to Scotland were, in the circumstances, almost lunatic. He was unduly severe in the punishments (including mutilation) which he served out to the dissenters, and he never tried to understand their point of view, or properly recognized the uses to which he could put its diversity (many Presbyterians, who were monarchists, fought alongside Charles). To claim that he missed an opportunity is to claim too much; but he was obviously the wrong man for his job, whose impossibility drove him into an undue rigidity.

Hooker had viewed the two Church of England Sacraments

(drastically reduced from the seven of the Roman Catholic Church) as mysteries, not mere signs; Laud developed this into a Sacramentalism full-blooded enough to cause him to be regarded as guilty of popery. But Laud himself preached sermons, and recognized that not only Luther, Calvin and other continental Protestants, but also the Church of England itself, held preaching to be a mark of true worship. He did not object to variations in doctrine if the dissenters would conform, so that preaching frightened him mainly because it encouraged people not to conform. He consequently tried to suppress the Puritan lecturers—holders of 'lectureships' (not benefices) who preached frequently—and to make the communion table and not the pulpit the centre of the church. His intentions cannot be criticized, but his methods were, as always, tactless, over-severe and largely ineffectual.

Laud was not, as one might expect, an outstanding preacher. His most interesting (and effective) writing is to be found in his *Diary* (1694). I have chosen a sermon preached before he gained power: it reveals the man himself as clearly as any of the sermons.

[PREACHED AT WHITEHALL]
Ps. 21: 6-7.
*For Thou hast* set him *as blessings for ever: Thou hast made him glad with the joy of Thy countenance.*
*Because the King trusteth in the Lord: and in the mercy of the most High he shall* not miscarry.

THIS SERMON was preached at Court on 24 March 1622 (new style), this being the last day of the year (old style), to commemorate 'the beginning of [James I's] most gracious reign'. Laud was by now Bishop of St Davids and confessor to the King's favourite, Buckingham. The Archbishop of Canterbury at this time was George Abbot, who had (theologically) Calvinist leanings, and who, though basically a 'King's man', had done all he could to further the cause of the left wing within the Church of England. His views had early offended Laud; and he himself did so again when in 1616 he refused, on principles of justice, to uphold the King's wishes in the matter of the Essex divorce suit. This provides a part of the general context of the sermon, the occasion of which, of course, was an important one. Laud records it in his *Diary*, but adds no remarks upon it except that he was commanded to print it.

This sermon is in essence an elaboration of the doctrine known as the 'Divine Right of Kings'. This, in modified form, is still central to Church of England philosophy (it is expounded in one of the homilies of 1559, 'against wilful rebellion'), but in Stuart times, and by Laud in particular, it was pushed—if defensively—too far, as the means by which the Roman Catholic James II was later (1688) got rid of aptly demonstrate. Laud pushes it too far here because James was not a good king, and his proper function should have been to criticize him in so far as he was able to do so. The doctrine held that if a king was bad, then he was bad because his kingdom had merited punishment; rebellion was a sin against God, and the unjustly treated subject must meekly submit as if to God. Now this view is logical, and it tries to relate the situation of a people to God's morality. But it may, to put it mildly, become offensive, and when it does so it is the duty of the clergy to exercise their influence, which has its own authority. Even in the context of the reign of James I (that of his son is a different one) Laud failed to exercise such influence, and exposed the public authoritarianism that is so at odds with the privately humble one.

However, Laud is (characteristically) exceedingly scrupulous in his definitions. He reminds the court that a king must have 'religion and holiness', and he should turn 'the graces which God hath given him to the benefit of them which are committed to him'. Indeed, he is in effect a boring (alas) pedant preaching to a boring pedant (as James was). He most scrupulously reminds him of his duties. But he does not, as he should, obliquely admonish him. He thanks God for him personally—'for no prince hath ever kept more firm to religion'—and he does not in any way modify, as he might, his remarks that a 'blessed Government is a great joy'.

The sermon as a whole displays Laud's pedantry, his scholastically inclined integrity and his tactlessness (for example, it was unnecessary to quote from Aquinas).

MY TEXT begins where every good man should end: that is, in 'blessing.' Not an Esau, but he 'cries' when the 'blessing' is gone. This psalm is a thanksgiving for David, for the King (Gen. xxvii. 34). In thanksgiving, two 'blessings': (1.) One, in which God blesseth us; and for that we give thanks: (2.) The other, by which we bless God; for he that praiseth Him, and gives Him thanks, is said to 'bless' Him (Exod. xviii. 10).

Now we can no sooner meet 'blessing' in the text, but we presently find two authors of it, God and the King: for there is 'God blessing' the King, and the 'King blessing' the people. And a King is every way in the text: for David the King set the psalm for the people; and the people they sing the psalm rejoicing for the King. And all this is, 'that the King may rejoice in Thy strength, O Lord.' And when this psalm is sung in harmony, between the King and the people, then there is 'blessing'.

This psalm is sung in Jerusalem; but the music of it is as good in the Church of Christ as in their Temple. Nor did the spirit of prophecy in David so fit this psalm to him, as that it should honour none but himself. No; for in this the learned agree, that the letter of the psalm reads David; that the spirit of the psalm eyes Christ; that the analogy in the psalm is for every good King that makes David his example, and Christ his God.

The psalm in general is a thanksgiving for the happy estate of the King. In particular, it is thought a fit psalm to be recited when the King hath recovered health; or when a gracious King begins his reign; because these times are times of blessing from the King: and these are, or ought to be, times of thanksgiving from the people. My text then is in part for the day: for I hoped well it would have been *tempus restaurationis*, a time of perfect restoring for the King's health;\* and thanks were due for that; and it is *dies creationis*, the anniversary day of his crown; and thanks is due for that. And there is great reason, if you will receive the 'blessing', that you give the 'thanks'.

The text itself is a reason of that which is found, verse 5. There it is said, that 'God hath laid great dignity and honour upon the King,' and here is the 'means' by which, and the 'reason' why, He hath laid it there. So three parts will divide the text, and give us order in proceeding. The first is the 'means' by which God lays honour upon the King. Not honour only, which they all have as kings: but that great honour in His salvation which attends good and gracious kings. And the 'means' are two-fold in the text; *dando et laetificando*, by giving and by joying. By giving the King as a 'blessing' to the people: 'Thou hast given him, or set him, as blessings for ever.' And by joying the King for 'blessing' the people: 'Thou hast made him glad with the joy of Thy countenance.' The second is the 'reason' both of the honour and of the means of laying it upon the King: and that is *quia sperat*, because the King puts his trust in the Lord. The third is the 'success' which his honour shall have by his hope 'that in the mercy of the most High he shall not be moved, he shall not miscarry.'

(I.) I begin at the first. The 'means' by which God adds honour even to the majesty of princes. And because that doubles in the text, I will take the first in order, which is *dando*; Thou layest great honour upon the King, 'by giving, or setting, him as blessings for ever.' In which means of laying honour the circumstances are three.

(1.) And the first of the three tells us what a King is: and that is worth the knowing. And mark the Holy Ghost, how He begins. He describes not a King by any of his human infirmities, such as all men have; and no mean ones are registered of David, the particular King spoken of; no, that had been the way to dishonour the King, which is no part of God's intention. But He begins at that which crowns the crown itself. He is *benedictio*, a 'blessing,' and no less, to the people. And therefore in all things, and by all men, is to be spoken of, and used, as a 'blessing.'

Now it is one thing for a King to be 'blessed' in himself, and another thing to be 'given,' or 'set up,' as a 'public blessing' to other men. David was both, and he speaks of both. A King then is a 'blessing' to, or in, himself, as the Septuagint and Tremellius give the words, *dedisti illi benedictiones*, 'Thou hast given blessings' to him, when by God's grace he is *particeps sanctificationis*, partaker of God's hallowing Spirit. For no man, King or subject, can be 'blessed' in his soul without religion and holiness. And if these be counterfeits, such also is his 'blessedness.'

But a King is given as a 'blessing' to others, when in the riches of God's grace upon him, he is made *Divinae Bonitatis fons medius*, a mediate fountain of God's goodness and bounty streaming to the people: when he turns the graces which God hath given him to the benefit of them which are committed to him. For mark the heavens, and the earth will learn. God did not place the sun in the heavens only for height, but that it might have power to 'bless' the inferior world, with beams, and light, and warmth, and motion. David was thus, and thus was Christ, and such is every King, in his proportion, that sets up these for his example. It is not easy to match David: but a better example than Christ cannot be found; and therefore when Clem[ens] Alex[andrinus] had described a King indeed, one that is *beatus et benedicens*, a blessed and a blessing King; or, if you will, as it is here in the abstract, *ipsa benedictio*, 'blessing' itself; he is at *cujusmodi est Dominus*, such as is Christ. There, the perfect example of 'blessing.'

Now while the King is said to be a 'blessing,' let me put you in mind that there is a double 'benediction'; *descendens una, altera ascendens*, one descending, and another ascending. That which descends, is the 'blessing of benefit'; that is the King's 'blessing.' He above, and this drops from him. In this like God, whose immediate Vicegerent he is; for 'God's blessings' also are said to 'come down' and descend (Jas. i. 17). The 'blessing' which ascends is that of praise, and thanks, and fair interpretation of princes' actions; and this is the people's 'blessing.' And they are both in Scripture together. For there, 'Solomon's blessing' comes down upon the people; and the people's 'blessing' goes up back again to 'Solomon' (1 Kings viii. 55, 66).

Between these two is the happy commerce that a Prince hath with his people, when they strive to out-bless one another. When the King labours the people's good, that is his 'blessing' descending upon them: and the people labour his honour, that is their 'blessing' reaching up to him. And in this sense also, as well as the former, a King is said, *poni in benedictionem*, to be set up as a 'blessing,' that is, for one whom the people ought to bless. For God's ordinance (1 Pet. ii. 17), 'honour the King,' doth as much, if not more require the people to 'bless,' that is, to 'honour,' the King, than it doth the King to 'bless,' that is, to 'do good to,' his people. And there is no good division between a King and his people, but this one;—that in parting of this 'great good' of a gracious government, the King's part be the 'honour,' the people's part may be the 'benefit,' and both meet again in the 'blessing.' And it is so in my text:—for Ar[ias] Mont[anus] renders the original by *pones eum*; there the King blesses the people: and the Septuagint and Tremel[lius] by *posuisti ei*; there God promises that He will, or rather saith He already hath; and ties the people that they do 'bless' the King.

And you may observe too, that while a King keeps to the two great examples of the text, David and Christ, he is not only a 'blessing,' but he comes as he writes, plural; and so it is in the text, *benedictiones*, not one, but many 'blessings.' And indeed the blessings which descend from a King upon a people seldom come single and alone: and in this, Kings keep their honour, that they 'bless' by 'number.' Esau could not believe that his father Isaac, who was far less than a King to 'bless,' 'had but one blessing in his store' (Gen. xxvii. 38).

But be the 'blessings' never so many, never so great; be the assistants which a King hath, never so deserving;—and David had his 'worthies' you know;—yet none of them may share with him in his 'honour of blessing the people,' nor none ought to steal away the hearts of his people upon any popular pretences whatsoever. For these 'wheels,' of what compass soever they be, move all in his strength, and therefore ought to move to the conservation of his 'honour.'

And this is in the text too: for David, no question, had a wise and provident council, nobles of great worth; and these wanted not their deserved honours:—God forbid they should:—and yet when it came to 'blessing the people,' that great means of specialty of honour to a King, there David stands alone without a sharer. *Dedisti*, yea but whom? not *eos*, but *eum*: not 'them,' but 'him,' as 'blessings' to the people. The vision which Ezekiel saw (i. 15), seems to me an expression of this: it was a vision of 'wheels;' the 'wheels' were many; the 'motion' uniform; one wheel within another, the less within the greater; yet in the apparition, these under wheels have no name, but only the 'great compassing wheel,' *rota ecce una*, one wheel appeared. And in this case, every man is bound to be in the service, but the best may not look to share in the 'honour.'

And seldom mean they well to Princes, that against the praise of the Holy Ghost in this place, *dedisti eum*, Thou hast given 'him' as 'blessings,' will needs be thought 'blessers of the people:' for such men do but fish and bait in troubled waters to their own advantage. Yet these men speaking oftentimes with more freedom, than either truth or temper, so long as they find fault with the present government, never want, saith Hooker, 'attentive and favourable hearers.' Never. For my part I will keep to the words of my text: and if there be a 'blessing'—as who sees not but there is?—under God, I will go to *dedisti eum*, him whom God hath given.

If you think I have stayed too long in this circumstance, I hope you will pardon me. You should be as loth as I to go from amidst the 'blessings:' but I must proceed.

(2.) Secondly, then, a King, a 'blessing;' yea, but how long continues he so? My text answers, it is 'for ever.' 'For ever:' and so Christ and David are both in the letter. 'Christ a blessing for ever;' and that simply, for 'of His Kingdom no end' (Lu.i.33). 'David a blessing for ever:' but that not in himself, but as Christ was to descend from him, as he was *Radix Jesse* (Isa.xi.1-11), from whence did spring Christ the 'blessing for ever.' And Christian Kings in their generations, 'a blessing for ever' too: but that limited; as they profess Christ, and as they imitate David.

Now David is observed to have 'blessed' the people under him three ways; and to these three generals, all the 'blessings' of a King are reducible. These three are, The true worship of the true God, that is the first; the second is, Preservation from foreign enemies; and the third is, Life and vigour of justice and judgment among the people. The closer a King keeps to these three, the larger his 'blessings:' but if he fall short in any of these, so much doth he lessen his 'blessings' upon the people.

For if he maintain not true 'religion' among them, then his 'blessings' are not 'for ever,' but end in the 'peace and plenty' of this life. If he preserve them not from 'foreign violence,' then his 'blessings' reach not so far as to the 'ever' of this life, but are hewn down by the sword of the 'enemy.' If he do keep out foreign force, yet if 'justice and judgment' be not in life and in blood at home, his best 'blessings' will be abused, even by them which are trusted with dispensing them, and that for 'ever.'

Now this *in perpetuum*, 'for ever,' was absolute in Christ: but in David, and in other Kings, be they never so eminent in their times, it is but respectively for ever; that is, not for the 'ever' of eternity: no, nor for the 'ever' of time; but only for the 'ever' of perpetuity of their own reign, in their allotted time. And this is a large 'for ever.' For you can have no longer blessings from the best King, than God gives him time to bless in: for he is constant in 'blessing,' that gives it not over but with life, and this was Josias's honour (2 Kings xxiii. 25).

And yet I may not forget, that sometimes this 'for ever' extends the blessings of Kings beyond their life, namely, when they bless their people with a 'blessing successor'; for the Septuagint read it here εἰς αἰῶνα αἰῶνος, and that implies 'succession;' so it is a 'present' and an 'after blessing.' A blessing in 'himself,' and a blessing in his 'seed.' In his 'person' and in his 'posterity' a 'blessing.' And the text fitted David home. In 'himself,' all his life; and in Solomon after his life, a 'blessing for ever.' And in this the text applies itself, and so will do, I hope, 'for ever:' and

I will ever pray, that the King may be a 'blessing' long, and 'his Solomon' after him, to his people, even *in seculum seculi*, age after age, in an 'ever of succession,' and so proceed.

(3.) Thirdly, then, the King is a 'blessing' to his people, and that 'for ever;' but who makes him so? yea, now we are come to the great Father of blessings, God Himself; for if you mark, the text begins at *Tu dedisti*, or *Tu posuisti*; 'Thou Lord hast given him,' 'Thou hast set him for blessings.' And God as in other, so in this particular, very gracious; for no people can merit this at God's hand, that their King should be a 'blessing' to them, and continue so. No, you see *Tu dedisti*, 'Thou hast given him,' makes him *donum*, a mere gift, no purchase.

Again, no King can promise and perform this out of his own strength, that he will be a 'blessing' to his people, and that 'for ever.' No, you see *Tu posuisti*, 'Thou hast set him,' keeps him at His disposing, leaves him not to his own. And indeed in this, a King's felicity is born as Christ's was, by an overshadowing power. And you cannot, no not with a curious eye, search all the reasons how he is set for blessings; because God, in disposing it, hath hid *lumen intra umbram*, and thickened the veil that is drawn over it.

There is much, I confess, in the King, to compass the affections of his people; and there is much in the people, not to distaste the heart of their King for trifles, not to urge him with indignities. But when all is done, and the 'blessing' stands between the King and the people, ready to 'descend' from the one to the other; yet you must go to *Tu dabis*, 'Thou, Lord, shalt give it.' For if He give it not, it will not be had. There will be a rub where it is not looked for, and a stop in the blessing. For is there conquest over enemies, or rest from them? why that is *Tua gratia*, God's favour: so Saint Basil. Is a King, or a State, famous for the ordering of it? why there is *auxilium a Te*, all help from God: so Theodor[et]. And God sells neither His help nor His favour. It is all at *Tu dedisti*, His gift, His free gift, wherever it is.

There is a great error in the world, I pray God it be not as common as great; and it is, to think that this 'blessing' can be brought about by policy only. 'Policy' is necessary; and I deny nothing but the 'only.' And they which maintain that, leave no room for *Tu dabis*, 'Thou shalt give the blessing;' but will carry the world before them whether God will or no. Whereas, there is more in *Tu dabis*, in God's gift, than in all the policies of the world. And it must needs be so; for all 'policy' is but a piece of

God's gift, a branch of God's wisdom; therefore not so great as the whole. And no policy can promise itself success; there it must needs wait and stay for *Tu dabis*; therefore not so great as that upon which it attends. And when miserable events dog the wisest projects, then Ahithophel himself will confess this; though perhaps not till he 'go home to hang himself' (2 Kings xvii. 2-3).

With this 'politic' error, went another of 'destiny.' The former leaves God's altar, and the 'sacrifice is to their own net' (Hab. i.16). This other hampers God in the 'net,' and makes both His blessings upon Kings, and His blessings from Kings to the people, to be all 'fatal.' And this was too common among the Heathen. So Flav[ius] Vopiscus, *fato remp[ublicam] regi satis constat*; it is evident enough that Kingdoms are governed by 'fate.' And then, where is *Tu dedisti?* 'Thou hast given him,' if he and his blessings must be whether God will or not?

But these blind men had 'blessings,' and knew not whence they came, unless, perhaps, they understood 'providence' by 'fate:'—and Minut[ius] Fel[ix] is not much against it. And if they did, then 'providence,' and *Tu dabis*, are all one; for God never gives a 'blessing' to a King and his people, but He gives it, and orders it by 'providence.' Yet here the wisest of the Heathen are inexcusable, in that they enjoyed the gift, and would not serve the giver. Look right, therefore, upon the author of 'blessings;' and where it is, *Tu dedisti*, 'Thou hast given him' as 'blessings,' as it is with us, there know, it is worth 'thanks,' both from Prince and people: and where it is *Tu dabis*, 'Thou shalt give,'— and my text is read both ways,—there know it is worth the asking, both for Prince and people; that God will give their King unto them as 'blessings for ever.'

And as it is, *Tu dedisti*, 'Thou hast given,' so that is not all, but, *Tu dedisti prius*, 'Thou hast given first.' God is first in the work, wherever a gracious King is a blessing to his people. For that which is simply a gift in the text, is a 'prevention.' And, *praevenis eum*, prevents the King with blessings first, that he after may bless the people; so that, in this common blessing, God is the prime mover, as well as in grace given to particular men. And it is true of both, which Saint Augustine delivers but of one, *avertat Deus hanc amentiam*, God turn away this frenzy from us, that in His own gifts—and here it is, *Tu dedisti*—we should place ourselves first, and set Him after. No; wherever comes *Tu dedisti*, 'Thou hast given,' God is evermore first in the work to begin it, yea, and last in the work to perfect it, or else no 'blessing'.

And therefore mark the text, and you shall find, that wheresoever there is *Tu dedisti*, 'Thou hast given,' there is still *posuisti*, and *disposuisti*, 'Thou hast set him,' and 'disposed him' to be so. And these two perfect the gift:—for *Tu pones*, that sets and settles the King to be 'blessings;'—and there is his constancy; not a 'blessing' to-day, and none to-morrow. And, *dispones eum*, for so Tremellius will have it, that disposes and orders the King in his 'blessings;'—and there is his wisdom, to sit and steer his passengers; that he may make all things suit with the opportunities, and fit the varieties of the people: for they, do the Governor never so worthily, will not think themselves 'blessed,' if they be not fitted. And a Commonwealth, when the humours of the people feel a spring, and are swelling, as it was once said of that of Rome, suffers almost all those various motions, *quae patitur in homine uno mortalitas*, which 'mortality itself suffers in a particular man.'

And it should not be passed over neither, for whose mouths David fits this passage. And, first, there is no question but that David speaks it for himself:—and there is the King acknowledging *Tu dedisti*, God's gift in making him all the 'blessings' that he is to his people. Next, I find, *pii loquuntur*; they are the faithful that speak it: not a religious and a good subject, but he is at *Tu dabis*, that God would bless his King, and make him a blessing for ever.

And, therefore, when God gives, and the King 'blesses,' and the people take no notice of it, it is gross ingratitude; when they have a 'blessing,' and know it not, it is a dangerous slumber; when they may have a 'blessing,' and will not, it is a sullen pet, and shows they have no mind to be thankful, either to God or the King, for blessing them.

Against this; say, 'the blessings are not perfect.' Well, suppose that; what then? Are not the best actions of the best men mixed? Shall we refuse degrees of happiness, because they are not Heaven? No sure: for Angels dwell not in bodies of men. And in the very text it is not simply, 'Thou hast given blessings,' but the words are, *dedisti eum*; 'Thou hast given him as blessings.' Therefore, the blessings here spoken of, come not immediately from God to the people, that they should be thought every way perfect; but they are strained *per eum*, through him, through the man, and therefore must relish a little of the strainer, him and his mortality. And there cannot be a greater wrong done unto

Princes, in the midst of their care for the people, than for men to think they are not 'blessed' by them, upon supposal that some things may be imperfect; for 'the secret lets and difficulties in public proceedings,' and in the managing of great State affairs, are both 'innumerable, and inevitable' (Hooker); and this every discreet man should consider.

And now I am come to the second means of God's laying honour upon the King. The first, you see, was by giving him as 'blessings:'—and this second is *laetificando*, by making him glad with the joy of his countenance. The text goes on cheerfully, and so I hope you do in hearing it, from 'blessing' to 'joy;' and here, again, the circumstances are three.

(1.) And first, God lays honour upon the King, *laetificando*, by 'joying' him, while he 'blesses' the people. And the 'joy' which God gives cannot but be great; and, therefore, the Septuagint expresses it by two words, εὐφρανεῖς ἐν χαρᾷ, ' Thou shalt joy him with joy,' that is, 'Thou shalt make him exceeding glad.' And it is requisite a King should have 'joy,' great 'joy,' for he cannot sit at the stern, without a great deal of care; and, therefore, it is fit he should be rewarded with a great deal of 'joy.'

Now, if a King will not fail of this 'joy,' he must go to the right owner of it, God Himself, that both hath and gives abundantly. If he seek it in himself, if in the very 'people which he blesses,' it will not ever there be found. For, when a King 'blesses' his people, if the blessing be as discreetly taken as it is graciously meant, then there is 'joy,' 'great joy,' of all hands: but when a people hath surfeited upon 'peace,' and 'plenty,' it is hard to please them with 'blessing' itself; and every little thing is a burden to them, that in long time have felt the weight of none. And in such times, malcontents are stirring; and there want not in all states those that are *docti in perturbanda reipub[licae] pace*, very learned in disturbing the 'peace' of the commonwealth: and the factious aim of such men, is either to hinder and divert the 'blessings' which are ready, and upon the point of descending from the King upon the people; or else in misinterpreting or extenuating blessings already come down. And these, let the world doat on them while they will, are the hinderers of mutual joy between the Prince and the people.

Therefore, if the King will look to the preservation of his own 'joy,' he must seek it where these cannot hinder it, at *Tu laetificasti*, 'Thou, Lord, hast joyed' him. And the word in my text is χαρά, which signifies a joy that is inward, and referred to the mind. And *Tu laetificasti*, is ever at this joy; let the intentions be right and honourable, and joy will follow them. It was David's case: I will forbear to tell you how scornfully, how unworthily, he was used by the basest of the people; but God kept close to him, *Tu laetificasti*, and made him joyful.

(2.) Secondly, where you find *Tu laetificasti*, God joying David, there the 'joy' is not like lightning, a flash and gone, but a true and permanent joy; true in regard of the author of it, God; for here is another *Tu dedisti*, God gave this also: and true in regard of the object of it upon which it settles, which is God too; God, and 'the light of His countenance.' And how can it be other than true 'joy,' that hath God at both ends of it, as this hath? For it begins at God the author; and it continues, and ends, in God, the object.

'God;' but not simply so expressed in the text, but 'God' and 'His countenance,' expressing after the manner of men:—for a man is joyed at the countenance he loves;—and yet not simply so neither, not his countenance only, but the 'joy' of 'his countenance.' And a man would not see sadness in the face he loves; joy there rejoices him. But no 'countenance' like to God's; an eye upon the beauty of 'His countenance' fills with joy.

Now, *vultus Dei*, God's countenance here, signifies God's presence; so Bellarm[ine]. It is true; yet not His presence only, but His favour and His love too; so Theodor[et]. It is true; yet not empty love only, but succour and protection too: so Euthym[ius]. It is true; yet it is not these alone, but all these and more.

And this considered, it is no great matter how you read my text; *a*, or *cum*, or *juxta*, or *apud vultum*;—for the King needs all, and God gives all;—for when he is once come to *Tu laetificasti*, this joy begins at *a vultu*, 'from His countenance;'—it goes on *cum vultu*, 'in company with His countenance;'—it enlarges itself *juxta vultum*, when it comes 'near His countenance:'—and, at the last, it shall be made perfect *apud vultum*, when it comes 'to His countenance,' to vision.

And as David's cares were great, so God would answer them with degrees of 'joy:' for, had God any more faces than one, as Ar[ias] Mont[anus] renders the original *eum faciebus Ejus*, He would hide none of them from David. If any were more comfortable than other, He shall see that. And, indeed, though the 'countenance of God' be but one and the same, yet it doth not look joy upon all men: but His aspects to the creature are planetary, as it were, and various. And David is happy, that, in the midst of all these various turns of 'God's countenance,' *a*, and *cum*, and *juxta*, and *apud*, we find not, nor I hope never shall, that disastrous aspect of opposition, which is *contra*, against; for then all 'joy' were gone;—for if it should be *Rex contra vultum Dei*, then it were all sin; and if it should be *vultus Dei contra Regem*, both which God forbid, then it were all punishment; in neither 'joy,' in neither 'blessing.' It is far better in my text, if we take care to hold it there, *cum vultu*, 'with,' or in, the favour of 'His countenance.'

(3.) Thirdly, this joy begins at the King; *laetificasti eum*, thou hast made him glad. He must have the greatest care, and therefore the 'joy' must be first or chiefest in him. And if you will take a view of my text, you will find 'him' excellently seated for the purpose; for I find *eum*, that is, David, that is, the King, standing between *laetificasti* and *gaudium*, as if God would have the King's place known by 'joy' on the right hand, and 'joy' on the left; here God places the King; this is His ordinance, to season his cares; therefore, if any attempt to displace him, to plunge him into grief, to make him struggle with difficulties, it is a kind of deposing him. The care of Government should be eased, not discomfited: else, doubtless, God would never have placed David between *laetificasti* and *gaudium*, joy and joy.

And it is fit for the people, especially the greater, in their families, to look to this, that David may keep *inter laetificasti et gaudium*, the place where God hath set him: for, when all is done, and the brain weary of thinking, this will be found true;— they cannot hold their places *in gaudio*, in joy, if David sit not sure in his. And it is an excellent observation made by Cassiodore, a Senator he was, and Secretary of State to Theodoricus, and after a most strict and devoted Christian, 'he makes all sad that endeavours not the King's joy:' *et omnes affligit qui Regi aliquid necessarium subtrahit*; 'and he afflicts all men, that withholds necessaries from the King.' And, certainly, it is the glory of a State, to keep David upright where God sets him: and that you see is *inter laetificasti et gaudium*, between joy and joy, where God ever keep him and his.

(II.) And now I am come to the second general of the text, the reason both of the thing, and the means,—of the honour, and the manner,—of God's laying it upon Kings: and the reason is *quia sperat*, because the King puts his trust in the Lord;—in which may it please you to observe three circumstances.

The first of these is the virtue itself, which God first gave the

Prophet, and for which He after gave him a blessing to the people, and joy in himself. The virtue is hope; that hope 'in the Lord.' Now, hope follows the nature of faith; and such as the 'faith' is, such is the hope. Both must be *in Domino*, 'in the Lord,' or neither can be true.

And it is, in a sort, with the denial of hope in any creature, that the hope which is founded upon God alone, I say 'alone,' as the prime author, may be firm, and not divided. *Nulli hominum fidens*, trusting upon no man, is Theodoret. 'Not in armies, nor in riches, nor in any strength of man,' is Euthymius. 'Not in sword, nor spear, nor shield, but in the name of the Lord of Hosts,' is David himself (1 Kings xvii.45). And David could not lay better hold any where; for since before, all lies upon God, *Tu dedisti*, and, *Tu laetificasti*, 'Thou hast given,' and, 'Thou hast made glad;' where could any man fasten better? And, indeed, the words are a reciprocal proof, either to other:—for because God gives David hopes; and because David hopes, God gives more abundantly, honour, blessing, and joy. It is in the text, *quia sperat*, even because he trusts.

Secondly, is 'trust' then, and relying upon God, a matter of such consequence, that it alone stands as a cause of these? Yes, 'hope' and 'trust' rightly laid upon God, have ever been in his children *loco meriti*, instead of merit. And whatever may be thought of this 'hope,' it is a King's virtue in this place. And Thomas [Aquinas] proves it, that 'hope' is necessary for all men, but especially for princes. And the more trust in God, *honoratior princeps*, the more honour hath the King, as Apollinarius observes it. And therefore 'hope' is not here a naked expectation of somewhat to come; but it is 'hope,' and the ground of hope, 'faith,' as some later divines think not amiss. And 'faith' embraces the verity of God, as well as the promises made upon it: and this was right:—for so God promised, and so David believed He would perform (2 Kings vii. 29).

And since we have found 'faith' and 'hope' in this action of 'trusting God,' as our English well expresses it, let us never seek to shut out 'charity;' and if 'faith,' 'hope,' and 'charity' be together, as they love to go, then you may understand the text, *quia sperat*, because he 'hopes,' *de toto cultu*, of the entire worship of God. For, as St Isidore observes, 'in all inward worship, which is the heart of religion, are these three, faith, hope, and charity.' And in the most usual phrase of Scripture, though not ever, scarce one of these is named, but all are understood to be present; and if so, then, because he trusts, is as much as *quia colit*, because he worships. So at last we are come to the cause indeed, why God set David for such a 'blessing' to his people; why He filled him with such 'joy of His countenance:' and all was, *quia cultor*, because he was such a religious worshipper.

It is in the text, then, that a King's religion is a great cause of his happiness. The greatest politicians that are have confessed thus far, that some religion is necessary to make a King a 'blessing' to his people, and a commonwealth happy: but the matter is not great with them, whether it be a true or a false religion, so it be one. But they are here in a miserable error; for since they suppose a religion necessary, as they must, my text will turn all the rest upon them; that true religion is most apt, and most able, to 'bless' and 'honour' both King and people.

For, first, truth is stronger than falsehood, and will so prove itself, wheresoever it is not prevented or abused; and therefore it is more able. Next, true religion breeds ever true 'faith,' and true 'hope' in God; which no false religion can: therefore it is more apt. Then, true hope and faith have here the promise of God for the King's 'joy,' and the people's 'blessing,' even *quia sperat*, because he trusts, whereas the rest have only His permission:— therefore it is both; both more apt and more able to bless King and Commonwealth than any false religion, or superstition, is or can be.

It was but a scoff of Lucian to describe Christians, simple and easy to be abused; or if any in his time were such, the weakness of the men must not be charged upon their religion: for Christ Himself, the founder of religion, though he did un-sting the serpent in all His charge to His Apostles, yet He left his virtue unchecked; nay, he commanded that, 'Be innocent, but yet as wise as serpents' (Matt. x. 16). And this wisdom and prudence is the most absolute virtue for a commonwealth. So that till Christians forsake Christ's rule, Lucian's scoff takes no hold of them.

Thirdly, since *quia sperat*, the faith and religion of a King, is that which brings God to give him as a 'blessing,' it must not be forgotten, that trust in God is *inter fundamenta Regum*, amidst the very foundations of Kings. And *spes* is *quasi pes*: 'hope,' saith Isidore, 'is the foot and the resting-place.' Now no building can stand, if the foundation be digged from under it. The buildings are the blessings of a state:—a prime foundation of them is the King's trust in God:—take away the truth of this 'hope,' 'faith,' and 'religion,' and I cannot promise the blessings to stand:

for then there is never another *quia*, or cause, in the text, to move God to give. But if the cause stand, as Theodor[et] and Euthym[ius] here make it, all is well.

And here it were sacrilege for me, and no less, to pass by his Majesty, without thanks both to God and him. To him, for *quia sperat*, because he trusteth; for no prince hath ever kept more firm to religion. And it is *sperans* in the present in my text; he continueth it, and will continue it. And to God for *quia dedit*, because in mercy He hath given him this 'blessing' so to trust, and by this trust in Him, to be this and many other blessings to us.

And so I come to the last part of my text, which is the happy success which David shall have for trusting in the Lord. It is a reward, and rewards come last. And it is,—that in this trust he shall not slide, he shall not miscarry. And here, to make all parts even, are three circumstances too.

The first of these is the 'success,' or 'reward' itself; and it is a great one: *non commovebitur*, he shall not be 'moved;' or at least not removed, not 'miscarry.' And this is a great 'success,'— to have to do with the greatest moveables in the world, the people, and not 'miscarry.' So that trust in the Lord makes a King, in the midst of a mighty people, *petram in mari turbido*, 'a rock in a working sea:' ebb, and flow, and swell, yet insolent waves dash themselves in pieces of all sides the rock; and the King is at *non commovebitur*, 'he shall not be moved.'

Secondly, this great 'success' doth not attend on Kings for either their wisdom or their power, or any thing else that is simply theirs:—no, we must fall back to *spes in Domino*, their trust in the Lord: yea, and this trust, too, is not simply upon the Lord, but upon His 'mercy.' And, indeed, to speak properly, man hath no ground of his hope but 'mercy,' no stay upon the slippery but 'mercy:'—for if he look upon God and consider Him in justice; if he look upon himself, and weigh his soul by merit, it is impossible for a man to 'hope,' or in 'hope' not to 'miscarry.' And therefore the prophet here, though he promise *non commovebitur*, that the King shall not miscarry, yet he dares promise it nowhere else than *in misericordia*, in 'mercy.'

Thirdly, I will not omit the expression, Whose 'mercy' it is that gives success to princes; and that is *Altissimi*, 'the mercy of the Most High,' which is one of God's usual names in Scripture. Now *sperat et non commovebitur*; the King's 'hope' and his 'success,' do both meet in the 'highest mercy.' It is true, 'hope' stands below, and out of sight: for 'hope that is seen is no hope'

(Rom. viii. 24), yet as low as it stands, it contemplates God *qua Altissimus*, as He is at highest. And this shows the strength of this virtue of 'hope:' for as 'hope' considered in nature is in men that are warm and spirited, so it is also considered as a virtue. And therefore give it but due footing, which is upon 'mercy,' and in the strength of that, it will climb to God, were it possible. He should be 'higher' than He is.

The footing of 'hope' is low, therefore it seeks 'mercy:' and the King's hope keeps the foot of the hill: *Rex humili corde sperat*: so Saint August[ine]. And the best hope begins lowest; not at merit, but at 'mercy.' But then mark how it soars:—for the same hope that bears the soul of man company upon earth, mounts till it comes *ad Altissimum*, to the Most High in heaven.

Now in this mercy-seat it is observable, three grandees are met together; 'blessing,' 'joy,' and 'hope,' and yet there is no strife for precedency: for 'blessing' goes first; 'joy' comes after, for no man so joyful as he that is 'blessed;' and then 'hope,' to supply the defects of both, because nor 'blessings' nor 'joy' can be perfect in this life.

And they have chosen to themselves an excellent and safe place in the 'mercy of the Most High.' An excellent place, and all receive virtue from it. For that David is able to be a 'blessing' to the people; that he can 'joy' in the blessing; that his 'hope' can support him through the cares in ordering the blessing, ere he can come to the 'joy:' all is from mercy.

And a safe place it is;—for there are in all times, and in all states, *conatus impiorum*, endeavours of wicked men, and the labour of these is, to turn 'blessing' itself into a curse; to overcloud 'joy' with sorrow at least, if not desolation; to crush 'hope,' or rather, *decollare*, to behead it. No place safe from these attempts but that which is high and out of reach; and no place so high as *sinus Altissimi*, the bosom of the Highest, which is 'His mercy.'

The reason, then, why David shall not miscarry; nay, not so much as *nutare*, shake, as Ar[ias] Mont[anus] renders it, why the sceptre in his hand shall not be κάλαμος σαλευόμενος, 'a shaken reed,'—and that is the word here in the Septuagint, σαλευθῇ —is the 'mercy of the Highest' (Matt. xi. 7). And when his feet are got upon this, he shall not slide. And Apollinarius calls the feet of the King, while they rest upon God's 'mercy', bold and confident feet, that dare venture, and can stand firm any where; and so no question they can, that are upheld by 'mercy.'

And now to reach down some of the mercies of the Highest upon ourselves; for when I read David at *Rex sperat*, 'the King trusts in the Lord,' and hear him speaking in the third person, as of another King, methinks the prophecy is worth the bringing home to our most gracious Sovereign. For his constancy in religion is known to the world:—and the freedom of his life argues his trust in the Lord;—and the assurance of his 'hope' shall not vanish. For, let him keep to the 'mercy of the Highest,' and there 'he shall not miscarry.'

And give me leave to speak a little out of my *spes in Domino*, 'my trust in the Lord:' methinks I see, *non commovebitur*, 'he shall not miscarry,' three ways doubling upon him. First, for his 'private' [affairs]; I have two great inducements, among many in another kingdom, to think that he is so firm in the mercies of God that he 'cannot miscarry.' The one is as old as November 5, 1605. The powder was ready then, but the fire could not kindle. The other is as young as January last, the 9th. The water was too ready then, and he fell into it. Neither of these elements have any mercy, but 'the mercy of the Highest' was his acquittance from both. In the first, he learned that when desperate men have sacramented themselves to destroy, God can prevent and deliver (Acts xxiv. 12). In the second, he learned that a 'horse is but a vain thing to save a man' (Ps. xxxiii. 15); but God can take up, take out, and deliver. And in the very psalms for that day, morning prayer, thus I read: 'God is our help and strength, a very present help in trouble' (Ps. xlvi. 1). And I know not what better use he can make of this than that which follows in the next verse; 'I will not fear,' nor distrust God, 'though the earth be moved.'

Next, methinks, I have a *non commovebitur*, he shall not miscarry, for, or in, his 'public affairs.' Prophet I am none, but my heart is full, that the 'mercy of the Highest,' which hath preserved him in great sicknesses, and from great dangers, hath more work for him yet to do; the peace of Christendom is yet to settle. Will God honour this island in him, and by his wisdom, to order the peace, and settle the distracted state, of Christendom, and edge the sword upon the common enemy of Christ? Why should there not be trust in God, that in the 'mercy of the Highest he shall not miscarry?'

Thirdly, for that which is greater than both these to him, the eternal safety of his soul, here is a *non commovebitur*; 'he shall not miscarry' for this neither, for so some read, and some expound, the word of my text, 'Thou shalt give him everlasting felicity.' Therefore let him be strong, and of a good courage, for in 'the mercy of the Most High there is no miscarrying.'

Thus you have seen the 'King's blessing,' the 'King's joy,' the 'King's hope,' and the 'King's assurance.' In the first you have seen, that the King is a 'blessing' to his people; that a gracious king, such as God hath given us, is a blessing 'for ever;' that he is so, *quia Tu dedisti*, because God hath given, and set him to be so. From 'blessing' to 'joy;'—and there you have seen, that the joy which follows a blessed Government is a great joy, a true and a permanent joy, a joy that is either first or chiefest in the King. Now 'blessing' and 'joy' are both grounded upon 'hope;' this 'hope' in the Lord; this 'hope' includes 'faith,' and 'religion,' and so this 'hope' stands amidst the foundations of kings. The 'success' assured unto him, is, *non commovebitur*, 'he shall not miscarry,' not so long as he rests on 'mercy;' that 'mercy of the Highest.'

*Non commovebitur*, drive wind and tide, 'he shall not miscarry.' Shall not? What? is it absolute then for David, or for any King? No, I say not so neither. There is a double condition in the text, if David will not miscarry; the one is *ex parte Davidis*, on David's side, and that is at *sperat*, a religious heart to God, that cannot but trust in Him. The other is *ex parte Dei*, on God's side, and that is at *misericordia*, a merciful providence over the King, which knows not how to forsake, till it be forsaken, if it do then. Let us call in the prophet for witness:—'When I said, My foot hath slipped, Thy mercy, O Lord, held me up' (Ps. xciv. 18). Now the foot of a man slips from the condition, from the trust, as Cassian observes, *mobilitate arbitrii*, 'by the changings of the will,' which is too free to sin, and breach of trust: the holder up in the slip is 'mercy;' therefore it is safest relying upon the condition which is on God's side, that is, 'mercy,' for that holds firm, when men break.

And mark my text; 'hope' goes before, and *non commovebitur*, 'he shall not miscarry.' follows after; but yet it follows not, till the 'mercy of the Highest' be come in between. And indeed to speak properly, all those things which the Scripture attributes to the 'faith' and 'hope' of man, are due only *misericordiae Altissimi*, to the 'mercy of the Highest,' which both gives and rewards them.

And yet for all this, the 'hope' of the believer, and the 'mercy of God,' in whom he trusts, are happily joined in my text;

because the 'hope of faith' can obtain nothing without the 'mercy of the Highest;' and that 'mercy' and 'goodness' will not profit any man, that doth not believe and trust in it. And 'hope' and 'mercy' are not better fitted to secure David, than 'mercy' and the 'Highest' are, to make him apprehensive of his assurance; for 'goodness and mercy' are invalid without 'power;' now that is supplied by *Altissimus*, 'the Highest.' And power is full of terror when it stands apart from goodness; and that is supplied by 'mercy;' when both meet, the 'hope' of man is full. So David cannot but see all firm on God's side; and sure he is not to miscarry, if he look to performance of his own. And though it be safest relying upon God, yet it is never safe to disjoin them whom God hath put together. And therefore as He is merciful, so man must be faithful, he must trust.

And now to end at home. David is gone long since to his 'hope,' the 'mercy of the Highest:' but a King, a gracious King, is living over us in 'peace,' and 'happiness,' as our eyes see this day.

I know he remembers why God set him over this great and numerous people; that is, *in benedictionem*, even to 'bless' them: and that he hath been a 'blessing' unto them, malice itself cannot deny. And I make no question but he will go on with the text, and be 'blessings' to them 'for ever.' 'For ever,' through his whole time; and 'for ever,' in his generous posterity. *Tu dedisti*, God's gift is through all this; and I will ever pray, that it may never fail.

He hath given this people, all his time, the 'blessing of peace;' and the sweet 'peace' of the people is *praeconium regnantium*, 'the glory of kings.' And God's gift is in this too: for though it be the King that 'blesses,' yet it is God that gives 'blessing' to blessing itself. And suppose 'peace' end in war, *Tu dedisti*, God's gift reaches thither too; for 'the battle is the Lord's.' The 'battle,' yes, and the victory (1 Kings xvii.47). For, saith Saint Basil, *dextera victrix*, 'Whosoever be the enemy, the right hand that conquers him is the Lord's.'

Now for his 'blessing,' it is fit he should receive 'joy;' but if he will have that true, and permanent—and no other is worth the having—he must look it *in vultu Dei*, in God's countenance. If he look it anywhere else, especially where the joy of his countenance shines not, there will be but false representations of joy that is not.

This day, the anniversary of his crown, is, to all his loving subjects, *dies gaudii*, and *dies spei*, a day of joy, and a day of hope. 'A day of joy;' for what can be greater, than to see a just and a gracious King multiplying his years? And 'a day of hope;' and what can be fitter, than to put him in mind, even this day, that a King's strength is at *sperat in Domino*, his trust in the Lord, 'the preserver of men' (Job vii. 20)? That as God upon this day did settle his hope, and his right to this kingdom, upon him; so upon this day, which in this year's revolution proves His day too, *dies Domini*, the Lord's day as well as his, he would continue the settling of his hope on Him, by whom 'all the Kings of the earth bear rule' (Prov. viii. 15, 16).

I say, 'settle upon Him,' and His mercy, that is the last. The very feet of Kings stand 'high;' and in high places slips are dangerous. Nothing so fit, so able to stand by them, as *misericordia Altissimi*, 'the mercy of the Highest.' In the goodness and the power of this mercy, he hath stood a King now almost five-and-fifty years; nay, a King he was before he could stand. Through many dangers the 'mercy of the Highest' hath brought him safe. Let him not go from under it, and it follows my text, 'his right hand shall find out all that hate him;' and for himself, *non commovebitur*, 'he shall not be moved,' not miscarry.

And so we offer up our evening sacrifice unto God for him, and for ourselves, that God will ever give, and he may ever be, a 'blessing' to his people:—that his years may multiply, and yet not outlive his 'joy:'—that this day may come about often, and yet never return but *in gaudio vultus Dei*, in the 'joy of God's countenance,' upon the King; and, *in gaudio vultus Regis*, in the 'joy' of the King's countenance, upon the people:—that the 'mercy of the Most High' may give him 'hope' in the Lord, and strengthen it:—that his 'hope' may rest upon the 'mercy' that gave it:—that in all his businesses, as great as his place, his 'success' may be *non commoveri*, not to miscarry:—that he may go on a straight course from 'blessing' others in this life, to be 'blessed' himself in heaven; and that all of us may enjoy temporal 'blessings' under him, and eternal with him for evermore. And this Christ Jesus for His infinite merit and mercy sake grant unto us:—to Whom, with the Father, and the Holy Spirit, Three Persons, and one God, be ascribed all might, majesty, and dominion, this day, and for ever. Amen.

NOTE

p. 430. *perfect restoring for the King's health*: James had trouble, probably gout, with his knee.

## Thomas Hooker

THOMAS HOOKER, born about 1586, is by no means to be confused with his namesake Richard. He was a Fellow of Emmanuel College, Cambridge, and in 1620 became rector of Esher in Surrey. Later, his activities in Essex led to his being cited for nonconformity in 1629; and in 1630 he went to Holland. In 1633 he emigrated to America, where he became a pastor in Massachusetts; in 1636 he was transferred to Hartford, Connecticut, where he remained until his death in 1647. He published a number of theological works.

Hooker was not an extreme Puritan, and it was pressure from Laud and his Commissioners which caused him to leave the country. He had a lectureship at Chelmsford (Essex), and some complained of him. He prudently withdrew from this position. But attacks upon him from some Essex clergy continued, even though he had satisfied the London Bishops (June 1629) of his conformity. Many Essex vicars signed a petition in his favour; but he was again summoned to appear before the Court of Commissioners. He (to express it in modern terms) 'jumped bail' (for in such cases sureties were required) and left for Holland. (Whether his zeal led him to remit the monies due to his friends is not known.) His last sermon delivered in England, an extract from which is given below, is instructive. It is not extreme in its language; but it well illustrates the moderate Puritan position: unlike others Calvinistically inclined (for example, the Archbishops of Canterbury, Whitgift and Abbot), Hooker is clearly a separatist. But he chose to leave rather than to face the terrible music he knew very well was to come .

### The Danger of Desertion

THIS SERMON was preached (we do not know where) in 1630, on the eve of Hooker's departure for Holland. It is a statement of the moderate Puritan position, but is none the less fairly extreme in its claim to represent God's (moderately Puritan?) position. After all, he begins by speaking of God's abandonment of England. (One can hardly forget that his own passage was already booked.) Since Donne's friend Adams is usually called a Puritan without qualification—a rash judgment—it is worth comparing his *The White Devil* to this piece. True, this comes just eighteen years after Adams's sermon; but Adams—even if he was not sequestered, which he almost certainly was—remained not only in England but a functionary of England's church.

BRETHREN, CAST your thoughts afar off. What is become of those famous Churches, Pergamius and Thyatira, and the rest? Who would have thought that Jerusalem should have been made a heap of stones, and a vagabond people? Hos.7.9 *Plead with your mother, and call her Loammi, ye are not my people, and I will not be your God*. Thus as I may say, he sues out a bill of divorcement, as it was in the old Law, those that had anything against their wives, sued out a bill of divorcement, and so doth God, Hos.2.2. she *is not my people, nor my beloved, let her cast away her fornications and idolatry, lest I make her as at the first*, that is, in Egypt poor and miserable: as if he should say to England, plead with England my Ministers, in the way of my truth, and say unto them, let them cast away their rebellions, lest I make her as I found her in captivity in the days of bondage.

But how doth God depart from a people?

1. When he takes away his love from a people, and as his respect, so his means too.

2. When he takes away his protection by taking down the walls, that is, these two great means of safety, Magistrates and Ministers.

3. When instead of counselling, comes in bribing, and instead of teaching, daubing [falsification], when God either takes away the hedges, or the stakes are rotten, then God is going.

4. When God takes away the benefit of both these helps, and they are signs of God's departing.

May God cast off a people, and unchurch a nation? then let it teach us to cast off all security, for miseries are nigh by all probabilities. When we observe what God hath done for us, all things are ripe for ruin, and yet we fear it not, we promise safety to ourselves, and consider not that England is like so to be harrowed, we cannot entertain a thought that England shall be destroyed; when there are so many professors in it, we cannot be persuaded of it, according to the conviction of our judgments, either it must not be, or not yet, as if it were impossible for God to leave England, as if God were a cockering [pampering] father over lewd and stubborn children: God may leave a Nation that is but in outward covenant with him, and why not England?

England's sins have been great, yea and their mercies great. England hath been a mirror of mercy, yet God may leave us, and make us a mirror of his justice. Look how he spake to the people in Jer.7. that *bragged of the Temple of the Lord, Sacrifices and offerings*: And what may not God which destroyed

Shilo, destroy thee O England? Go to Bohemia, from thence to the Palatinate, and so to Denmark. Imagine you were there, what shall you see, nothing else but as Travellers say, Churches made heaps of stones, and those Bethels wherein God's name was called upon, are made defiled Temples for Satan and superstition to reign in? You cannot go two or three steps, but you shall see the heads of dead men, go a little further, and you shall see their hearts picked out by the fowls of the air, whereupon you are ready to conclude that Tilly* hath been there. Those Churches are become desolate, and why not England? Go into the Cities and Towns, and there you shall see many compassed about with the chains of captivity, and every man bemoaning himself. Do but cast your eyes abroad, and there you shall see poor fatherless children sending forth their breaths, with fear, crying to their poor helpless mothers. Step but a little farther, and you shall see the sad wife bemoaning her husband, and that is her misery, that she cannot die soon enough; and withal she makes funeral Sermons of her children within herself, for that the Spaniard may get her little ones, and bring them up in Popery and superstition; and then she weeps and considers with herself: If my husband be dead, it is well, happily he is upon the rack, or put to some cruel tortures, and then she makes funeral Sermons, and dies a hundred times before she can die. Cast your eyes afar off, set your souls in their souls' stead, and imagine it were your own condition, why may not England be thus, who knows but it may be my wife, when he hears of some in torments? Ah! Brethren, be not high minded, but fear, as we have this bounty on the one side, so may we have this severity on the other; therefore prank not up yourselves with foolish imaginations, as who dare come to England, the Spaniards have enough, the French are too weak: Be not deceived, who thought Jerusalem the Lady of Kingdoms, whither the Tribes went to worship, should become a heap of stones, a vagabond people, and why not England? Learn therefore to hear and fear, God can be a God without England, do not say there are many Christians in it, can God be beholding to you for your Religion? No surely, for rather then he will maintain such as profess his Name and hate him, *he will raise up these stones' children unto Abraham*; He will rather go to the Turks, and say you are my people, and I will be your God. But will you let God go, England? Why are you so content to let him go? Oh! lay hold on him, yea hang on him, and say thou shalt not go. Do you think that Rome will part with her religion, and forsake her gods? nay, an hundred would rather lose their lives. Will you let God go? Oh England plead with your God! and let him not depart. You should only part with your rebellions, he will not part with you. *Leave us not.* We see the Church is very importunate to keep God with them still, they lay hold on God with words of argument.

Thou hope of Israel, do not leave us: they beset God with their prayers, and watch him at the Town's end that he might not go away. No thou shalt not go away, thou shalt abide with us still, they are importunate with God not to leave them.

Hence note this Doctrine.

*That it is the importunate desire of Saints to keep God with them* . . . . I deal plainly with you, and tell you what God hath told me: I must tell you on pain of salvation, will you give ear and believe. I poor Ambassador of God am sent to do this message unto you, though I am low, yet my message is from above, he that sent me, grant that it may be believed for his sake. Suppose God hath told me this night that he will destroy England, and lay it waste, what say you brethren to it? It is my message that God bade me do, he expects your answer, what sayest thou oh England, I must return an answer to my Master that sent me tonight, why speak you not an answer? I must have one. Do you like well of it, would you have England destroyed? would you put the old men to trouble, and the young men to the sword? would you have your women widows, and your maids defiled? would you have your children, your dear ones to be thrown upon the pikes, and dashed against the walls? or would you have them brought up in idolatry under the necessity of preaching which is worst of all? would you see those Temples wherein we worship God burnt, and your own houses? will you see England laid waste without inhabitants? are you willing to it? are you content? God bade me ask, why do you not answer me? I must not stir without it, I must have it, I am an importunate Ambassador, send me not away sad, speak comfortably and cheerfully unto me. Are you willing to have God with you still, you are, are you not? I am glad of it; but you must not only say so, but use the means, plead with God: And though his hand be up, and his sword drawn; yet suffer him not to destroy, but to sheath it in the blood of our enemies, God grant it, and I should be glad to see England flourish still, and so are you, are you not? you are. Now if it come to pass that England be not, but destroyed and laid desolate, thank yourselves, and not God, he delights not in it. We may take up the complaint of the Prophet, Isa. 64.7. *No man stirs up himself to lay hold upon God*: For this is our misery, if that we have quietness and commodity we are well enough, thus we play mock-holy-day with God, the Gospel we make it our pack-horse: God is going, his glory is departing, England hath seen her best days, and now evil days are befalling us: God is packing up his Gospel, because nobody will buy his wares, nor come to his price. Oh lay hands on God! and let him not go out of your coasts, he is agoing, stop him, and let not thy God depart, lay siege against him with humble and hearty closing with him, suffer him not to say, as if that he were going, farewell, or fare ill England. God hath said he will do this, and because that he hath said it, he will do it, therefore prepare to meet thy God O England! Amos 4.12. lest God complain of thee as he did of Jerusalem, lest my soul depart from thee, and I make thee a desolate land not inhabited . . . .

NOTE

p. 451. *Tilly*: Count Tilly was one of the Roman Catholic generals in the Thirty Years War (to which Hooker had been alluding); he and his marauding troops had a reputation for cruelty.

## MARK FRANK

MARK FRANK was born in 1613. He was one of the most notable 'middle-of-the-way' men of his time, whose sermons have a quiet and instructive eloquence that is salutary in the violent age in which he lived. By 1634 he had become a Fellow of Pembroke College, Cambridge. Ten years later he was ejected by Puritans ('parliamentary visitors'). But he survived, and was made Master of his old College in 1662. In 1664, the year of his death, he became Archdeacon of St Albans and Canon of St Paul's. His *Course of Sermons* was published in 1642.

## [The First Sermon on Christmas Day]

Isaiah 11:10.

*And in that day there shall be a root of Jesse, which shall stand for an ensign of the people; to it shall the Gentiles seek: and his rest shall be glorious.*

THIS IS the first of Frank's sermons for Christmas Day, and it is not certainly known either when or where it was preached—except that it was before 1642. It is evident, from its beginning onwards, that Frank is exhorting his congregation to regard Charles I as their proper spiritual mentor. But he is aware that Charles has political faults, and is at (tactful) pains to explain that people must, despite these, understand the ineluctable divinity of his position. The first three paragraphs of the sermon might, indeed, be interpreted as an oblique apology for the *temporal* behaviour of Charles (which was seldom wise). There is throughout the sermon an exquisite understanding of the difficulties of his listeners; there is perhaps a hint that the leader of the Church, properly reverenced in that capacity, might himself find it easier to 'reconcile all enmities and difference ... unite all disagreeing spirits'. Frank, in the course of this, as of other, sermons shows himself as a subtle though subdued (and subduing) mind, anxious to promote moderation—but never for one moment swayed from his belief in the Sovereign as Head of the Church.

The choice of text is as significant as the choice of the Old Testament story with which Mark Frank begins his sermon. This needs some explication (in those difficult days the more ingenious preachers, especially ones who desired to achieve compromise without bloodshed, were prepared to forgo strict theology in the interests of putting the message across). Jesse was the father of David, then (as occasionally now) regarded as the 'root' of Jesus. The comparison of Jesse to the later Hezekiah at the beginning of Frank's second paragraph is not without point: one must note the remark 'and perhaps not amiss in a lower sense'. Charles's political behaviour had never been astute; and Frank's choice of Hezekiah may well give us an indication of the date of this sermon.

The Scots, on 20 August 1640, had crossed the Tweed into England—in the Second Bishops' War—and on 30 August had entered Newcastle after defeating the King's forces (28 August) at Newborn-on-Tyne. By October Charles had been forced to pay £860 per day to the Scots until a settlement had been reached. On 11 December the 'Root and Branch' petition, to abolish episcopacy, had been presented. One may therefore fairly confidently date Frank's sermon as having been preached on the Christmas Day of 1640. For Hezekiah took (according to the Old Testament) immediate measures upon his accession to break up the idolatrous customs into which the people of Judah had fallen during the reign of his father, Ahaz; moreover, he was under serious threat of invasion by the Assyrians, who had already occupied the neighbouring kingdom of Israel. When he refused to pay the tribute demanded by the Assyrians, he was consequently invaded by them—with the result most famously recorded by Byron in his poem about the defeat of the Assyrian King Sennacherib. It is not without significance that Hezekiah was thereupon stricken with extreme illness (Charles's notorious pride and obstinacy?), from which only his prayers saved him. The ultimate verdict on Hezekiah (despite lapses) was that (According to Chronicles 2—and it is with this record that we are concerned) 'his acts . . . and his goodness, behold, they are written in the vision of Isaiah the Prophet'. Mark Frank was by no means an unsubtle preacher. He expected (as a preacher of today cannot expect) his congregation to know the scripture—and of Hezekiah's weaknesses as well as his faults. Throughout this sermon, then, for 'Assyrians' we may read 'Scots' and for 'Hezekiah', Charles. It may be taken, as a whole, as a gentle and moderate statement of the doctrine of the Divine Right of Kings (see p. 460: *to kiss . . . how it will*). However, it must be noted that the preacher's immediate subject is the birth of Christ.

'AND IN that day there shall be:' and in this day there was, a root of Jesse that put forth its branch. That day was but the Prophecy; this day is the Gospel of it. Now first, (to speak in the Psalmist's phrase,) 'truth flourished out of the earth:' now first the truth of it appeared.

Some indeed have applied it to Hezekiah, and perhaps not amiss in a lower sense; but the Apostle, who is the best commentator ever upon the Prophets, applies it unto Christ (Rom. xv.10). There we find the text, and him it suits to more exactly every tittle of it, and of the chapter hitherto, than to Hezekiah or any else.

He was properly the Branch that was then to grow out of old Jesse's root. For Hezekiah was born and grown up already some years before, thirteen at least. He (Isa.xi.2) it is whom 'the Spirit of the Lord does rest upon,' upon Hezekiah and all of us; it is the Dove going and returning. Upon Him (xi.3) only it is, that the Spirit in all its fulness, with all its gifts, wisdom and understanding and counsel and might and the rest, is poured out upon. He (xi.4) it is alone, that judges the earth in righteousness, which is said of this root. He (xi.5) it is that shall 'smite the earth with the rod or spirit of his mouth,' as it is so attested. He (xi.6) it is that can make the wolf and lamb, the leopard and the kid, the calf, the young lion and the fatling, lie down and dwell together, as is prophesied of him. He the only Prince and God of peace, that can reconcile all enmities and difference, that can unite all disagreeing spirits. In a word, he is the very only He whom God hath set up 'for an ensign to the people,' to whom all the Gentiles flock in, to whom rest and glory both properly belong; the only 'root' too from whence all good things spring, or ever sprung, either to Jesse, or David, or any other. Nor is it the apostle, or we Christians only that thus expound it of Christ; the learnedest of the Jewish Rabbis do so too. *Tam Christiani, quam tota circumcisio fatetur*, says S. Jerome: all the circumcised expositors confess as much; all understand it of the Messiah, only a temporal Messiah they would have, and err in that, because ours, the true one, they will not acknowledge. But we have enough from what they do, from their own confessing it to be spoken of the Messiah, or the Christ.

Of whom we have here four particulars to consider: the stock from whence he was to come; the design upon which he was to come; the success of his design; and the glory of his success.

1. The stock from whence he was to come, is the 'root of Jesse.'

2. The design upon which he was to come, is, to 'stand for an ensign to the people' to come in unto him.

3. The success of his design, is their coming in, and seeking to him: 'to it shall the Gentiles seek.'

4. The glory of his success: 'And his rest shall be glorious.' Rest he shall have in it, and glorious he shall be by it.

And to bring both ends of the text together, nay all the ends of it together, I shall lastly add the time, when this rest shall spring, when this ensign shall stand up, when the Gentiles shall seek, when this rest and glory, or glorious rest, shall be. 'In that day,' says the text. In this day, says the time. In the birth of Christ. In the times of Christ all this should be, and all this was. Both days are one, and this of his birthday, the very first of all these things here, beginning to be fulfilled.

And the sum of all is no more but this, that notwithstanding the most calamitous times, (such as were threatened to the Jews, by bringing upon them the Assyrian, in the former chapter,) there should a day of deliverance at last appear, a day of rest and glory, when the Messiah or Christ should come to perfect all their deliverances; and not only theirs but the Gentiles' also; and build up a Church out of them both unto himself, and dwell and rest gloriously among them, and bring them also to his eternal rest and glory. I begin at the root of this great design, to show you who he is, and whence he comes, that shall thus stand up for the rest and glory of the people. And the root of Jesse here he is called: 'There shall be a root of Jesse.'

In the first verse his style somewhat differs: he is called, 'a rod out of the stem of Jesse, and a branch out of his roots:' and he is them all; and this root in the text, but a metonymy to express them all.

1. He is a rod; the rod, the staff that so comforted old David (Ps. xxiii. 4); that even raises his dead bones out of the grave, and makes him as it were walk still among the living.

The staff that supported dying Jacob, which he leaned upon (Heb. xi. 21), and worshipped, which we may worship too without any idolatry.* A rod, a staff he is to lean upon, a staff that will not fail us; not like the reeds of Egypt, the supports and succours that the world affords us: they will but run into our hands and hurt us, to be sure never be able to hold us up. This Christ is the only staff for that; a staff that will comfort us when we are ready to die, that we may trust to upon our death-beds, that we may commit our dying spirits to, as St. Stephen did (Acts

vii. 59). No other can do that but this of Christ. Indeed, no rod hath either comfort or strength to hold by but only he.

Yet a rod, 2, he is, to rule and correct us too, as there is need; a rod of iron by which God bruises the rebellious spirits. The rod or sceptre of Judah, the shepherd's rod or hook; one to show his kingly power, the other his priestly power over us. So the word denotes two of his prime offices out to us, and may yet intimate a third; the shepherd's rod being not so much to strike, as to direct and lead the straggling sheep into the way: a part of his prophetic office. So a word well chosen to signify unto us all his three offices. And the rod or wand that is carried before the judge, when he goes to the judgment-seat, may not unfitly be added to the other, and put us in mind that this our King, and Priest, and Prophet, shall also come to be our Judge; and we therefore so to carry it, so to yield our obedience to him, so to submit to his rod, as we intend to answer it when he comes to be our Judge, as we expect or hope to have his favour in the day of judgment.

But he is a rod, 3, new springing out of the root; a kind of pliable tender thing, so styled for his meekness and humility, ready to be wound and turned any way for our service, to become any thing, to become all things, for our good. A rod so pliant, so flexible, so pliable, so tender; never any son of man so pliant to his father's will, so flexible to all good, so pliable to do or suffer, so tender over us; never so meek, and humble, and lowly, never any.

Nor did, 4, ever rod grow out of a more unlikely stem: the word used here imports [in Hebrew] a dead trunk cut close down to the earth, no appearance of life or power in it. The royal family of David was come to that; nothing appeared above ground that could give hope of the least bud or leaf. And then it was, that notwithstanding this rod came forth. So low may things be brought to human eyes, and yet rise again: God's time is often then. When our eyes are ready to fail with expectation, and all hopes have given up the ghost; when the family of David, from whence all the promised and looked for hope, was in a condition near an extinguishment; when Herod had usurped the throne, and the Romans settled him and his successsion in it; when not so much as a sprig, or bud, or string of hope could be seen by the quickest sight, then out starts this rod upon a sudden, and prospers to a wonder. Well might the prophet put 'Wonderful' for one of his names; there was never any like him: and it may teach us, first, to adore this wonder, to kiss this rod,—support or comfort us, rule or correct us how it will; and, 2, thankfully admire God's goodness that thus does so unexpectedly often for us.

And upon this next title we may do as much: for he is not only a bare single rod, but a 'branch' that spreads itself abroad into twigs amd little boughs. Two main ones at the first, his divinity and his humanity; from which infinite little twigs and leaves, infinite graces and blessings, are extended to us. 'My servant the Branch,' God calls him (Zech. iii. 8); and the 'Man whose name is the Branch' (vi. 12). The word in both places descends from [a Hebrew root], which signifies any thing that springs or rises, either from above or from below. His divinity, that springs from above, from heaven; and to that alludes the Latin in both those places, which translates [the Hebrew] by *Oriens*, the east or rising sun; and is alluded to by Zachary\* in his *Benedictus*, when he calls him the 'Dayspring from on high,' *Oriens ex alto* (Lu. i. 78). His humanity, that riseth from beneath, from earth, and is sufficiently signified by the 'root of Jesse.' You have them both together, Jer. xxiii : 'I will raise unto David a righteous branch,' and 'This is his name, The Lord our Righteousness.' And from these two all the leaves and fruits of righteousness whatsoever.

For it is not, 2, a mere sprout, or yet a barren one, but flourishing and flowering too. 'Beautiful' and 'glorious' (Isa. iv. 2, 3) 'excellent' and 'comely,' in the same place. *Flos*, the Vulgar reads it, a fair goodly 'flower.' The 'rose of Sharon, and the lily of the valleys' (Cant. ii. 1); a sweet-smelling flower that sent forth its odour into all the world. *Flos odorem suum [...] &c.*, says S. Ambrose. 'A flower when it is cut off loses not its scent, and being bruised it increaseth it: so our Lord Jesus,' says he, 'lost none of his beauty, or sweetness, by being broken and bruised upon the cross; when he was here taken off from the stock of the living, the blood that issued out of his wounds made his beauty more fresh and orient; and his bruising there extracted from him so sweet an odour, that even still every day raiseth the fainting soul out of its swoon, and revives even the dead, that they flourish out of their graves by a resurrection to life eternal.' The original of the word is from [a Hebrew root] for *servavit*, to reserve or keep; and may therefore not unfitly denote the great sweetness and virtue that is reserved and laid up in Christ to sweeten and adorn the stinking and nasty houses of our sinful souls and bodies.

And from the same Hebrew root, so signifying *servavit*, we have *Servator*, our Saviour and Conservator, pointed to us. This 'branch,' this 'flower,' bears in its name the Saviour; and hath been by some drawn into *Nazareus*, to raise a conjecture that Christ was called a Nazarene from Isaiah's *Netzer*, from the word here translated 'branch,' or 'flower.' But this to be sure can be no mistake, to tell you, either from the word or any way else, that our Saviour is designed by it; and this 'rod,' and 'branch,' and 'root' is none but he.

And 'root,' indeed he is, as well as a rod or branch; a root without a metonymy, as well as by it. The very root of all our happiness. The root in which our very life is hid. 'Our life is hid with Christ in God,' says the Apostle (Col.iii.3). The 'root,' 2, and foundation upon which we all are built; we are all but so many twigs of this great vine-root, so many 'branches' from him (John xv.5). The 'root,' 3, whence all good springs up to us, all flowers of art, of nature, all the staves of comfort and rods of hope, all the branches of grace and glory; no name properer to him in all these respects. Nay, 4, even the very 'root of Jesse' too, from whom Jesse had his original, from whom Jesse's family throve into a kingdom, from whence his youngest son's sheep-hook sprang into a sceptre: the 'root of David' himself too, so says he of himself (Rev.xxii.16). Why, then, say we, or why says the prophet, 'the root of Jesse?' Why? Not without reason neither. Jesse was but a poor man in Israel. My family, what is it? says David himself (1 Sam.xviii.18); yet from Jesse would God raise up Christ, that we might know that God can bring any thing out of any thing. He can raise empires out of sheep-cotes; so he did Cyrus, so he did Romulus: the one the founder of the Persian monarchy, the other of the Roman. He raised the first governor of the Jews out of a bulrush-basket, and the first states of the Christian Church out of a fisher-boat: and 'not many mighty, not many noble,' saith S. Paul (1 Cor.i.26-28); 'but God hath chosen the weak things of the world to confound the things that are mighty; and base things of the world, and things that are despised hath God chosen, yea, and things which are not, to bring to nought things that are.' So little is God taken with our greatness, our great birth or breeding.

And it is, 2, to shame our pride, who undervalue mean things; ready enough to say with the unbelieving Jews, 'Can any good thing come out of Nazareth?' Can any great eminent person spring out of the root of Jesse? Yes it can.

And our great ancestors will but shame us, as well as be ashamed of us, if we have nothing to glory of but our relation to their ashes: our high descent is not worth the speaking of, and perhaps if we but trace it a little higher than our own memories (to be sure if to the first beginning) the best and gloriousest princes will find themselves derived from as mean an original as any poor Jesse whatsoever. And this may serve well to cut our plumes, to stop our rantings of our descent and birth, or anything, and teach humility.

To drive that lesson homer, I may note to you, 3, that it is the root of Jesse here, not David, (though otherwise he is called the 'Root of David,' as Rev. v. 5,) lest he should seem either to receive glory from David, or need his name to cover the obscurity of his beginning. There is no glory to that of humility, nor any so truly honourable as the humble spirit.

And 'of Jesse,' 4, not David, to point out as it were the very time of our Messiah's coming; even then when there was scarce any thing to be seen or heard of the house of David; the royal line as it were extinct, and David's house brought back again to its first beginning, to that private and low condition it was in in the days of Jesse. Thus again would God teach us to be humble in the midst of all our ruff, and glory, by thus showing us what the greatest families of the greatest princes may quickly come to, where they may take up ere they are aware. And, 2, to give us the nearest sign both of Christ's coming, and of himself; that when things were at the lowest, then it would be, and that his coming would be in a low condition too; in poverty and humility: 'Root' and 'Jesse' both intimate as much.

And lastly, if we may with some etymologists derive it from [another Hebrew root], and interpret it a gift, there will be as good a reason as any why it is here said rather of Jesse than of David; even because this root of all this good to us, comes merely of free gift. 'So God loved the world,' says S. John (iii. 16), 'that he gave his only-begotten Son;' and 'not by works of righteousness which we have done, but according to his mercy,' says S. Paul (Tit. iii. 4, 5), this great kindness of God our Saviour appeared toward us, this Lord our Saviour appeared to us, as a root, as a rod, as a branch; a root to settle us, a rod to comfort us, a branch to shelter us; a root to give us life, a rod to rule us in it, a branch to crown us for it; a close stubbed root, a weak slender rod, a tender branch full of loveliness, meekness and humility.

And he appeared as they all do, out of the earth, watered by the dew of heaven; they have no other father than the heavenly showers: so by the descending of the Holy Ghost upon the Blessed Virgin, as rain into a dry ground, this holy 'root' put forth, this 'branch' sprang up, without other father of his humanity; which is the meaning both of *erit* in the text, and *egredietur* in the beginning, both of this 'shall be' here, and that 'shall come forth,' or 'there shall grow up,' in the first verse of the chapter. And thus we have the first part of the text, the descent, and stock, and nature, and condition, and birth of Christ, with other things pertaining to it. And now for his design, to be 'set up,' or 'stand for an ensign to the people.'

II. And indeed, for that he was born, to gather the straggling world into one body, to unite the Jew and Gentile under one head, to bring the straying sheep into one fold, to draw all the armies of the earth together into one heavenly host, that we might all march lovingly under the banner of the Almighty, under the command of heaven.

Men had long marched under the command of flesh, earth, and hell. God had suffered all nations, saith S. Paul (Acts xiv. 16), to do so, to 'walk after their own ways.' But now he commands otherwise, commands to repent, and leave those unhappy standards to come in to his (Acts xvii. 30).

And he exempts none, debars none; all men every where are called to it; 'every nation,' and 'every one,' in every nation, that will come shall be 'accepted' (Acts x. 35). 'Every creature,' says he himself (Mark xvi. 15); 'Jew and Greek, bond and free, male and female,' all one here. Be we never so heavy laden with sins and infirmities, under this banner we shall 'find rest' (Gal. iii. 28). Be we never so hotly pursued by our fiercest enemies, here we shall have shelter and protection (Matt. xi. 28, 29). For he is not only an ensign set up to invite us in, but an ensign to protect us too by the armies it leads out for us.

And as it first is set up to call us, and secondly to bring us into a place of defence and safety, so does it, thirdly, stand to us, and not leave us. An ensign may be set up and quickly taken down, but this stands and stands for ever. It is not idly said, when it is here said particularly, it is to 'stand.' Human forces, devices, and designs may be set up, and not stand at all; but God's and Christ's,—theirs will: the gates of hell itself cannot disappoint them, cannot throw down this banner. 'His counsels shall stand, he will do all his pleasure' (Matt. xvi. 18; Isa. xlvi. 10). They do but 'fight against God' that go about to resist it, says

Gamaliel,* the great doctor of the law (Acts v.39).

And will you know the staff,* the colours, and the flag or streamer of this 'ensign'? Why, the staff is his cross, the colours are blood and water, and the streamer the Gospel, or preaching of them to the world. The staff that carried the colours was of old time fashioned like a cross: a cross bar near the top there was, from which the flag or streamer hung; so as it were prefiguring, that all the hosts and armies of the nations were one day to be gathered under the banner of the cross, to which soldiers should daily flow out of all the nations and kingdoms of the earth. By blood and water, the two sacraments, is the way to him; and the word or Gospel preached is the flag waved out to invite all people in.

Come we then in, first, and let not this flag of reconciliation, of peace and treaty—for to such ends are flags sometimes hung out—be set up in vain; let it not stand like an ensign forsaken, upon a hill: come we in to treat with him at least about our everlasting peace, lest it become a flag of defiance by and by.

Come we in, 2, and submit to the conditions of peace, submit to his orders and commands. The Septuagint reads ὁ ἀρχόμενος ἐθνῶν, here, to intimate this: He that stands for an ensign is to be the great Ruler and Commander of the nations; it is requisite therefore that we come in and obey him.

Come we, 3, to this standard, and remember we are also to fight under it: that is the prime reason of ensigns and banners. We promise to do it when we are baptized, and it must be our business to perform it. It is not for us to be afraid of pains or labour, of danger or trouble, of our lives and fortunes, for Christ's service. A soldier scorns it, even he who fights but for a little pay, and that commonly ill paid. And shall we turn cowards when we fight for a kingdom, and that in heaven, which we may be sure of if we fight well?

Above all, 4, if this ensign stand up for us, let us stand up to it, and stand for it to the last. A soldier will venture all to save his colours; rather wrap himself up in them, and die so, than part with them. For Christ, for his word, for his sacraments, for his cross, for our Gospel and religion we should do as much. But I am ashamed; the age has showed us too many cowards, that have not only run away from this standard, but betrayed it too; the more unworthy certainly that they should ever reap fruit or benefit, twig or branch, from the root of Jesse. The very Gentiles in the next words will sufficiently shame them. For to it, to this ensign, 'do all the Gentiles seek.'

III. 'Shall,'—it is, I confess, in the future tense here, reached no further in the prophet's time, but now it does; the prophecy is fulfilled, it so came to pass. And it quickly came so, after the ensign was set up, the cross reared, and the resurrection had displayed it. 'For I, if I be lifted up from the earth,' says he himself (John xii. 32), 'will draw all men to me.' Parthians and Medes, and Elamites, the dwellers in Mesopotamia and Cappadocia, Pontus and Asia, Phrygia and Pamphylia, Egypt and Libya, Rome and Cyrene, as well as the dwellers in Judea (Acts ii. 9); Cretes and Arabians, as well as Israelites; proselytes, as well as Jews; he will draw all in to him. The vast multitudes that came daily in from all quarters of the world, so many Churches of the Gentiles, so suddenly raised and planted, are a sufficient evidence to this great truth. And the [Hebrew] term the Jews at this day give the Christians, [...], the very word in the text for Gentiles, confirms as much by their own confession. So true was both Isaiah's prophecy here, and father Jacob's so long before, that to him should 'the gathering of the people be' (Gen. xlix. 10). But that which is an evidence as great as any, if not above all, is, S. Paul applies the text as fulfilled then (Rom. xv. 12). And there is this only to be added for our particular, that we still go on and continue seeking him.

IV. But there is rest and glory here added to the success of this great design: 'his rest shall be glorious.'

Now by 'his rest,' we in the first place understand the Church, the place where the Psalmist tells us (xxvi. 8) 'his honour dwells;' the place of which himself says no less than (cxxxii. 14) 'This shall be my rest for ever; here will I dwell, for I have delight therein.' And glorious it is the Apostle tells us (Eph. v. 27), 'a glorious church, not having spot or wrinkle;' so glorious that the Prophet says (Isa. lx. 3), 'The Gentiles shall come to its light, and kings to the brightness of its rising.' They shall 'bring gold and increase from Sheba; the flocks of Kedar, and the rams of Nebaioth shall come with acceptance to his altar;' 'The glory of Lebanon shall come unto it;' 'They shall call the walls of it salvation, and the gates praise;' 'The Lord is an everlasting light unto it, and God is its glory.' (Isa. lx. 7, 13, 18, 19.) So that we may well cry out with David, 'Glorious things are spoken of thee, O thou city of God!' Thy Church, thy congregation, O thou Root of Jesse, thou Son of David, which thou hast gathered, and thy churches or holy temples too, which are raised to thee, exceed in glory; the beauty of holiness, thy holy mysteries, thy blessed self art there!

And, indeed, in the holy mysteries of the blessed sacrament, is his second place of rest. There it is that he 'feeds his flock, and rests at noon' (Cant.i.7). And he is glorious there, glorious in his mercies, illustrious in his benefits, wonderful in his being there. No such wonder in the world as his being under these consecrated elements, his feeding our souls with them, his discovering himself from under them, by the comforts he affords us by them.

His cratch* today was a third place of his rest: glorious it was, because, 1, the God of glory rested there: because, 2, the glorious angels displayed their wings, and gave forth their light and sung about it: because, 3, kings themselves came from far to visit it, and laid all their glories down there at his feet. There his rest was glorious too.

Nay, 4, his sepulchre, the place of his rest in death, was as glorious, is as glorious still, as any of the other: and I must tell you, the Latin reads it, *sepulchrum ejus gloriosum*. From thence it is he rose in glory, and by that it was he gained a glorious victory over death and hell: from thence he came forth a glorious conqueror. Thither have devout Christians flocked in incredible numbers. There have miracles been often wrought, there have kings hung up their crowns, there have millions paid their homage. And thence have we all received both grace and glory; from his sepulchre, where he lay down in death and rose again to life.

There is one rest still behind, and it is not only glorious, but itself is glory. His 'rest' himself calls it, yet a rest into which he would have us enter too (Heb.iii.11;iv.9,11). And in heaven it is; no rest to this, no rest indeed any where but there, and perfect glory nowhere else.

And now to wind up all together. This rest and glory, or glorious rest, which ends the text (and it is the best end we can either make or wish), springs from the 'root' at the beginning. The Church itself, and all the rest and glory the Churches ever had, or have, or shall enjoy, grows all from that. Our holy temples, our holy sacraments, our holy days,—this day, the first of all the rest,—all the benefits of his death, resurrection, and ascension into glory,—nay our greatest glory in heaven itself, comes from this little Branch of Jesse, this humble Root; and the way to all is by him and his humility.

And the time suits well, and the day hits fair for all. In that day, says the text, all this you have heard shall be; and that day now is this. Today the Root sprang forth, the Branch appeared. Today the Ensign was displayed to all the people; from this day the Gentiles began their search. This day he began to call in his Church, and the shepherds were the first. Today he first was laid to mortal rest; today the glory of his star appeared to wait upon his cradle. Today we also may enter into his rest, one or other of them.

One of his places of rest we told you was in the church, or holy place: let us seek him there. Another rest of his we mentioned to be in the blessed sacrament: let us seek him there. His ensign is there set up; let us go in to him, and offer our lives and fortunes at his feet, proffer to fight his battles and obey his commands. Strive we, as the Apostle adviseth us (Heb.iv.11), to 'enter into his rest.' Root we and build ourselves upon him. Root we ourselves upon him by humility; build we upon him by faith: grow we up with him 'rooted and grounded in love,' and sprouting out in all good works. Rest we ourselves upon him, and make him our only stay and glory. So when this Root shall appear the second time, and blow up his trumpet, as he here set up his ensign, and our dead roots spring afresh out of their dust, we also may appear with him, with palms and branches in our hands, to celebrate the praises of this Root and Branch of Jesse, and enter joyfully into his rest, into the rest of everlasting glory.

NOTES

p. 458. *The staff . . . idolatry*: a mild rebuke to Puritans, making use of a source from their own favourite Old Testament.

p. 460. *Zachary*: Frank refers here to the priest of the family of Abia—the father of John the Baptist who praises the Lord at the end of Luke 1.

p. 464. *Gamaliel*: the learned and respected rabbi to whom Paul went for instruction because he was regarded as the highest authority on the law.    *And will you know the staff. . . . 'do all the Gentiles seek'*: Parliament, which had met on 13 April 1640 after an interval of ten years, refused Charles's request for money to furnish an army against the Scottish invaders; there had been riots in London in support of Parliament, and Charles had been forced to sign the humiliating Treaty of Ripon, which conceded virtually all the Scots' demands.

p. 466. *cratch*: cradle or manger.

## Hugh Peters

PETERS, THE son of Thomas Dyckwood (who called himself Peters), was born in 1598. He was a lecturer in London, but in 1629 went to Holland and thence to Salem, Massachusetts. He returned to England in 1641 and took a leading part on the side of the militant Puritan cause. He was particularly unpopular with the Presbyterian faction. He was hanged, drawn and quartered on 16 October 1660, as a regicide.

[THE STORMING OF BASING HOUSE]

THIS IS Peters's own account of his part in the storming of the Royalist stronghold, Basing House, at Basingstoke, in 1645. He had it read from all the pulpits soon afterwards. The sermon—for such in effect it is—speaks for itself.

THE ROOMS before the storm, in both houses, were all completely furnished, provisions for some years rather than months; 400 quarters of wheat, bacon divers rooms full, (containing hundreds of flitches,) cheese proportionable, with oatmeal, beef, pork, beer, divers cellars full, and that very good.

A bed in one room, furnished, that cost 1300*l*., popish books many, with copes, and such utensils, that in truth the house stood in its full pride, and the enemy was persuaded that it would be the last piece of ground that would be taken by the parliament, because they had so often foiled our forces that had formerly appeared before it. In the several rooms, and about the house, there were slain seventy-four, and only one woman, the daughter of doctor Griffith, who by her railing provoked our soldiers (then in heat) into a further passion. There lay dead upon the ground, major Cuffle, (a man of great account amongst them, and a notorious papist,) slain by the hands of major Harrison, (that godly and gallant gentleman,) and Robinson the player, who, a little before the storm, was known to be mocking and scorning the parliament and our army. Eight or nine gentlewomen of rank, running forth together, were entertained by the common soldiers somewhat coarsely, yet not uncivilly, considering the action in hand. The plunder of the soldier continued till Tuesday night. One soldier had 120 pieces in gold for his share, others plate, others jewels; amongst the rest, one got three bags of silver, which (he being not able to keep his own counsel) grew to be common pillage amongst the rest, and the fellow had but one half crown left for himself at last.

Also the soldiers sold the wheat to country people, which they held up at good rates a while, but afterwards the market fell, and there was some abatements for haste. After that they sold the householdstuff, whereof there was good store; and the country loaded away many carts, and continued a great while fetching out all manner of householdstuff, till they had fetched out all the stools, chairs, and other lumber, all which they sold to the country people by piecemeal. In these great houses there was not one iron bar left in all the windows (save only what was in the fire) before night. And the last work of all was the lead, and by Thursday morning they had hardly left one gutter about the house. And what the soldiers left, the fire took hold on; which made more than ordinary haste; leaving nothing but bare walls and chimneys in less than twenty hours, being occasioned by the neglect of the enemy, in quenching a fireball of ours at first.

We know not how to give a just account of the number of persons that were within; for we have not three hundred prisoners, and it may be an hundred slain, whose bodies (some being covered with rubbish) came not to our view; only riding to the house on Tuesday night, we heard divers crying in vaults for quarter, but our men could neither come to them nor they to us. But amongst those that we saw slain, one of their officers lying on the ground, seeming so exceeding tall, was measured, and from his great toe to his crown was nine foot in length.

The marquis being pressed by Mr. Peters arguing with him, broke out, and said, that if the king had no more ground in England but Basing-house, he would adventure as he did, and so maintain it to his uttermost, meaning with these papists: comforting himself in this disaster, that Basing-house was called *loyalty*. But he was soon silenced in the question concerning the king and parliament, only hoping that the king might have a day again. And thus the Lord was pleased in a few hours to show us what mortal seed all earthly glory grows upon, and how just and righteous the ways of God are, who takes sinners in their own snares, and lifteth up the heads of his despised people.

This is now the twentieth garrison that hath been taken in this summer by this army; and I believe most of them, the answer of the prayers and trophies of the faith of some of God's servants, the commander of this brigade having spent much time with God in prayer the night before the storm, and seldom fighting without some text of scripture to support him. This time he rested upon that blessed word of God written in the 115th Psalm, ver. 8, *They that make them are like unto them, so is every one that trusteth in them*; which, with some verses going before, was now accomplished.

Whereas the house had ordered that the country people should carry away those buildings, God Almighty had decreed touching that beforehand, nothing remained but a blast of wind to blow down the tottering walls and chimneys: doubtless this providence of God hath a double voice, the one unto the enemy, and the other unto us; the Lord help us with skill to improve it. I hope by this time the state hath a pennyworth for a penny, and I hope they will have full measure and running over.

I wish that the payment and recruiting of this army may not be slighted: it is an easy matter to grieve God in our neglects towards him; and not hard to weary one another. What if the poor soldier had some remembrance, though small, to leave as the acceptance of this service, which is already begun by a worthy member of this house, who hath appointed some medals to be made of gold to be bestowed upon those that ventured on the greatest difficulties.

## Henry Ferne

HENRY FERNE was born in 1602. He was educated at St Mary Hall, Oxford, and later became a fellow of Trinity College, Cambridge. During the Civil War he became Charles I's chaplain. At the Restoration he was made Master of Trinity; in the year of his death, 1662, he was appointed Bishop of Chester.

### Comfort in Adversity
Habakkuk 2:3.
*For the vision is yet for an appointed time, but at the end it shall speak, and not lie: though it tarry, wait for it; because it will surely come, it will not tarry.*

THIS WAS the last sermon heard by Charles I, at Carisbrooke on 29 November 1648. The text is concerned with the dialogue between Habakkuk (which means 'one who embraces') and the Lord after the successful invasion of Judea by the Babylonians under Nebuchadnezzar. The Lord eventually tells him that he would in time walk again through the land.

HE THAT in the work of creation made all things in due proportion for *number, weight*, and *measure*; doth so, and more, in works of the judgment and correction; weighing out, and measuring the proportion, not only by the scale of wisdom, as in the creation, but by the balance of justice too; apportioneth the weight of affliction, and the length of the time, with respect to our continuance in sin. Punishment, or chastisement for sin, looks first at sins past, the greatness of them, and the years or time spent in them: then at our present condition, whether we are made sensible, and sufficiently humbled. Lastly, at our disposition for the future, whether prepared, and firmly resolved for obedience in time to come. Now see the proportion; He usually appoints the weight of the affliction, according to former provocations and sins past, but the length, and continuance of our sufferings according to the effect they have upon us, for humiliation and obedience.

All the comminations [denunciations] we hear denounced against a sinful people, and all the promises we find made to an afflicted Nation, speak thus much, that repentance and amendment is the condition of removing the judgment, as it is the end for which he afflicts it. And if so, then surely will he not cease till he has his end upon us, *for will a man take up a snare* (saith the Prophet) *having caught nothing?* and will the Lord take off his rod till it has wrought upon us?

For the continuance of the rod, see a reason, Isa.9.12. *they returned not to him that had smitten them, therefore his arm was stretched out still*: And for the removal of the rod, Isa.10.5. *Assur was the rod of his* anger, for the chastising of his people, *but when he had performed his whole work upon Mount Sion,* Verse 12. then he takes off the rod, and lays it upon the *Assyrian*. Upon his and their enemies will it be, *virga non removenda, a grounded rod*, as another Prophet calls it, a rod not to be taken off from rebellious and obstinate sinners. Or take we affliction in that other similitude of a furnace, to purge away our dross and corruption; We see the Lord *sitting as a refiner*, to moderate the fire, both for the heat, and continuance of it, not suffering his precious metal to be longer in the furnace than is meet.

But what then means that *duplum* of punishment? Isa.40.2. *She hath received double for all her sins*: As in receiving of reward, there is no *duplum* or exceeding in the merit, no supererogation on our part: so in the receiving of correction no *duplum* or *doubling* of the punishment above the desert of sin. In the point of reward, man cannot take God with an ὑστερεῖ, that he is behind hand with him in the recompense; and in the business of correction, man shall find that upon his amendment, οὐκ ὑστερήσει, God will not be behind hand with a deliverance. That *double received for all her sins*, if it be not meant of the abundant grace and favour wherewith God embraced his people after he had plagued them (as some will have it) but of the punishment, they had suffered (as I rather conceive) then doth it not imply a proportion to the desert of sins past, but signifies the abundant correction they had received, and that *double*; not to what they had deserved, but to what would have been, had they sooner repented; if they had speedily broken off the course of their sins, the time of their sufferings had been so much shorter.

And let not any of us (how eager soever in our desire of ease and deliverance) think we have received at God's hands after that measure, *double for our sins*, we may thank ourselves if the time of our sufferings has been double, to what it might have been if we had been sooner corrected and amended. *I should soon have put down their enemies*, saith God, Ps. 81. It should not have *tarried* on his part, the failing has been on ours. And therefore, if any will be still asking how *soon?* or (as they that in the Psalmist complained they saw no *come*, and requiring a sign; He tells them, *it comes not with observation*; Not our Saviour did the Pharisees, demanding *when the Kingdom of God would come*, and requiring a sign; He tells them, *it comes not with observation*; Not with the outward show of worldly pomp and glory, *but the kingdom of God is within you*, there you must look for it, and know the coming of it, by those beginnings of grace wrought in you.

So neither doth deliverance *come with observation*; Such observation as is made upon outward means, numerous arms, present success, (from which we have been too ready to conclude of the end) but such as is taken from within; The judgment of it must be taken from your selves. Do you find your hearts humbled within you, cast down in the sense of former provocations? *then lift up your heads, for your redemption draweth nigh*. Are your hearts turned within you? then look for a conversation of things, a change of time. Have you *engaged your hearts* (as the Prophet saith) *to approach to the Lord*, to wait upon him, as in the expectation of his good time, so in a course of after obedience? then know he will engage his holy arm for your deliverance, *it will not tarry* after that time, yea, he will *make bare his holy arm* for it, (as the Prophet speaks) show it from heaven, divested of all outward human helps and assistance, do the work himself.

And now, before we seal up the comforts of this assurance, we must remove a double scruple, that may disquiet it. For if we apply what has been spoken of national calamities and deliverances (upon which the text proceeds) to particular men, we find, that wicked men, who remain unamended, enjoy the benefit of such national deliverance, & many righteous men swept away, or cut off by death, see not the promised redemption. The one may seem to question the necessity of our performing the condition of amendment, the other to weaken the certainty of God's performing the promise.

True it is indeed, that righteous men are often involved in the punishment of a sinful Nation, faring worse for those about them; and men still continuing wicked, meet with a deliverance, faring better for those, that by repentance, and turning from their evil ways, have turned away the wrath of God from a Nation. As to the outward man, it often happens (as Saint *Austin* said) *Malis bene, Bonis male*; yet not that to the true advantage of those, not this to the disadvantage of these.

For first, see you in a national deliverance all partaking of the peace and benefit of it: He that by carnal security has *drawn back* from God, and continues uncorrected, as well as he, that in humiliation and amendment of life has *waited* upon God for the deliverance. Both of them indeed enjoy it, one with another, but not one as well as the other, not with that joy, comfort, and blessing from Him, that sends the deliverance. Alas, their *bed is shorter, than that they can stretch themselves on it, and the covering narrower than that they can wrap themselves in it*. The ease they have by such a deliverance is too short, too narrow to afford a content that may *reach unto the soul*. They may obtain a temporal deliverance promiscuously with others, and that *fide aliena*, but to receive and enjoy it with true content and comfort of the *Vivet* promised to the just man, Verse 4. it must be *ex side sua*. So the Psalmist, *My heart trusted in him, and I am helped, therefore my heart greatly rejoiced, &c.* therefore rejoiced greatly, or danced for joy (as the other translation hath it) because it first trusted in him. A double motion of the heart, the first of faith, which carries it upon God for the help, the other of joy, for the receiving it from him: not this truly and really without the former. Then is there true joy, and great joy upon a deliverance, when it has been prayed for first, and *waited* for by faith and patience. He that would not *wait* any longer, 2 Kings 7.2. saw the promised deliverance, and plenty, but did not taste of it. And they that still *draw back* from God, if live to see the deliverance, and taste of it, shall find it as the flesh of quails in their mouths, but *Leanness withal sent into their soul*; which may pine away under all the affluence and abundance of an outward peace.

Take heed therefore, lest there be in any of you, *an evil heart of unbelief*, in *departing from the living God*, an heart that casteth away all patience and care of well-doing; and yet causeth a man to *bless himself*, saying, *I shall have peace though I walk in the imagination of mine heart, and add drunkenness to thirst*; I shall fare as others do in the common calamity or deliverance. But as God declares, *His soul will have no pleasure in those that draw back*; so shall they find, their soul cannot have true pleasure in the deliverance, he will bestow upon a repenting Nation. They may promiscuously with others, be made partakers of it when it comes; but not enjoy it with that comfort, joy, and blessing, as they shall do, who so *wait* for it, as ye heard above.

For the second: We see in common calamities, righteous and good men overborne among the rest by the violence of the *overflowing scourge*; and *swept away* with that *besom of destruction*, wherewith the Lord sometimes cleanseth a land. As to the outward man indeed, they often bear a part in the common sufferings with that people or community, of which they are a part; but then consider that in these general calamities a special hand of providence is over such for their comfort and preservation. Every particular just man hath his assurance for a *Vivet*, till the deliverance come; the promise of it is not far from this text, the *just shall live by his faith*: Live comfortably, live safely, even during the present distress. Yea, when such are cast out into a foreign land, *I will be to them* (saith the Lord) *a little Sanctuary*; or an hiding place, to which they may still retire for refreshment and protection. *And in the day when he makes up his jewels*, they are remembered, Mal. 3. 17. as out of the sweepings of our house we gather ends of gold or silver, or what is precious, casting out the rest to be trod to mire in the streets: so shall he gather his jewels, or precious ones out of the common filth and dust, which *the besom of destruction* has hurried out. There is a *Vivet* for the just man, a special care and provision for his subsistence and comfort till a general deliverance of the Nation come.

Nay, but if that deliverance *tarry* so long, that he be cut off by death before he sees it, how will this promise of a *Vivet*, or a *non tardabit* be made good unto him?

We must know, that temporal promises are not always made good in the same kind, and he that has not faith to look beyond the very thing assured by them, may miss of his desire and expectation: being like to him that fights a battle without a reserve; if his first strength be defeated, he's utterly broken. But he that *against hope can believe in hope*, when his first hope (which rests upon outward visible means, and expects a temporal deliverance) fails, has a reserve, an hope *sure and steadfast, which entereth into that within the vail*. He knows, and shall find, if the promise of a temporal blessing or deliverance be not made good to him in the same kind, it will in a better, nothing at all to his loss or disadvantage: To them that *left houses and lands, &c.* for Christ's sake, houses and lands, and an hundred fold more were promised in this life, not in the same kind surely. We know they did not, they could not receive them so; for they were to receive them (as it is there added) *with persecutions*, which would drive them from houses and lands. It was therefore further made good unto them, by their receiving that inestimable treasure of the Gospel, which would replenish their hearts with such joy and content, that they would not part with it for an hundred times as much as they had forsaken. This hundred-fold in this life they should enjoy till they were put into possession of that kingdom which infinitely transcends all earthly advantages *Adeo satis idoneus Patientiae sequester Deus* (saith *Tertullian*) so sure a trustee is God, so able to restore what is laid up for the reward of patience and innocency. And thus is it with every righteous man, *that waits*, and is cut off by death before he sees the wish'd-for national deliverance; a *justus Vivet*, made good to him even in death itself, he has then his deliverance though the Nation has not; so far is it from *tarrying*, in regard of his particular, that it comes sooner than was expected, and after a better way, than that of an outward temporal deliverance. For he is taken from the evil present, and to come, as good Josiah cut off in his prime by the enemies' sword, and what is denied him in this life, is made good in a better, and for a temporal outward peace expected, presently enjoys an heavenly, and eternal. So that Majesty itself cannot lose by such a change, when as the next life affords *A crown of glory that cannot fade away, a kingdom that cannot be moved.*

To conclude, thus stands the assurance of this promise, *non tardabit, it will not tarry.* To every just man, though cut off before he see the national deliverance, there is a *Vivet* in death itself, which is not a *tarrying*, but an hastening of his deliverance. And to a whole Nation, upon their remarkable and more general repentance and amendment, there is a deliverance assured: *It will not tarry* after they are so fitted for it. Thus, when he has wrought his work of chastisement upon this land, as he *did upon Mount Sion*, Isa. 70. (oh may he hasten it, by our speedy and more general amendment!) then will he turn his hand against every adversary, *will punish the fruit of the stout heart* of all violent men, will *put them in fear, that they may know themselves to be but men*, and how vain all their thoughts and purposes have been.

Then shall all that wait for the salvation of our God, hear him say, *Turn ye prisoners of hope*, and *comfort ye, comfort ye my people, speak comfortably to Jerusalem, tell her, her warfare is accomplished*. And we shall with comfort say, *Lo, this is our God, we have waited for him, and he hath saved us; this is the Lord, we have waited for him, and will rejoice in his salvation*. Even so, O Lord, *haste thee unto us; thou art our helper and Redeemer, make no long tarrying O our God*: Haste thee to the help of thine Anointed, and of thy people of this church, and of this kingdom; and *lead thy people again like a flock, by the hand of Moses and Aaron*. We beg it for Jesus Christ his sake, who bore the chastisement of our peace, to whom with thee O Father, together with the blessed Spirit, be all honour, dominion, &c.

## John Cosin

JOHN COSIN, born in 1594 of a wealthy Norwich family, is one of the more important representatives of the seventeenth-century Anglican tradition. The target of the Puritans, who were convinced of his Papist leanings (he was once accused of 'enticing a young scholar to Popery'), he was, though High Church and a devotee of ornate and elaborate ritual, a ceaseless critic of Roman Catholicism. He wrote a treatise against it in 1656 (published posthumously in 1675), and when he learned that his son had been converted, he disinherited him. His explanation of Anglicanism, written in Paris in 1652 but not published until 1707, is important.

Cosin's career was fairly eventful, and is instructive. He was educated at Caius College, Cambridge. He became librarian and secretary to Overall, Bishop of Lichfield and Coventry, and later (1626) a rector to the county of Durham. His marriage, in 1625, produced four daughters and one son. He early incurred the hostility of the Puritans because of his friendship with William Laud and with Richard Montague, another ardent defender of the middle way between Puritanism and Popery (he became Bishop of Chichester in 1628 and of Norwich in 1638). Through Montague's influence he was commissioned—a delicate task—to prepare the *Collection of Private Devotions* (1627), prayers for the use of the Roman Catholic Henrietta Maria's English maids-of-honour. In 1635 he became Master of Peterhouse, Cambridge, and chaplain to the King; in 1639 Vice-Chancellor of the University; he was deprived of the deanship of Peterborough by the Long Parliament only three days after it had been conferred upon him, largely on account of his High Church practices in the Peterhouse Chapel; when he lost Peterhouse in 1642 he sent the college plate to Charles I and then fled to Paris, where he was appointed chaplain to the Anglican Royalists. He was the most important of the Anglican priests in exile (Montague had died in 1641). He officiated at French Protestant services, and maintained friendly relations with the Huguenots.

At the Restoration he was rewarded by Charles II with the bishopric of Durham, which he held until his death in 1672. He maintained his High Church leanings—some of his elaborations of ritual suggested at the 1661 Convocation were taken over into the 1662 Book of Common Prayer—but nevertheless worked, vainly, for a reconciliation with the Presbyterians at the Savoy

Conference, called in 1661 to try to devise a formula by which the latter could remain members of the Church of England. As bishop, Cosin was a relentless disciplinarian, harrying—with some ruthlessness, such as use of troops—nonconformists and Papists alike. He had a sharp eye for business, selling offices in his patronage and levying dues to provide money for buildings, the Durham library and other worthy causes. He was one of the only three bishops who advocated divorce in cases of adultery.

Cosin was not perhaps always a likeable man, but he was a reasonable one; he is also a clear and intelligent writer and preacher, who moderates his rigid temperament in the interests of reconciliation. He was nothing like as fierce as his friend Montague, and would have been a more effectual archbishop than his less fortunate other friend, Laud. His meticulous list of fourteen disagreements and fourteen agreements between the Church of England and the Roman Catholics—in 'a Letter to the Countess of Peterborough', published in the fourth volume of his *Works* (1843-55)—is an important document.

[IF THOU BE THE SON OF GOD ...]
Matt. 4.6.
*If Thou be the Son of God, cast Thyself down headlong, for it is written, He shall give His Angels charge over Thee, and with their hands they shall hold Thee up, lest at any time Thou dash Thy foot against a stone.*

THIS SERMON was almost certainly preached in the summer of 1625, when a particularly severe plague was raging in the City of London. This explains the reference at the end of the sermon, which is the first of a pair on the same text. Readers of the famous 'Grand Inquisitor' section of Dostoievsky's *The Brothers Karamazov* will find Cosin's comments on this text, which has perplexed many, revealing. Ivan's Grand Inquisitor tells Christ that 'of course, you acted . . . magnificently like God. But men, the weak . . . are they gods? . . . But are there many like you? And could you assume for a moment that men, too, could be equal to such a temptation?' Cosin anticipates an answer by using the devil's temptation of Christ as a parallel to the temptation of ordinary men. His argument is eloquently stated, but clear, and there is a certain anti-mystical homeliness in the manner of its presentation. This quality is a part of the Anglican tradition. There is an interesting allusion to the Synod of Dort (1618-19): 'a wicked and a pernicious opinion that some of our new masters have brought up of late . . . ' The Synod of Dort was set up by the Dutch Reformed Church to deal with the problem of Arminianism, which maintained, against Calvinism, that Jesus Christ died for all men. The doctrines of Arminius were there condemned, a decision (inevitable from the first) that aroused much interest in England. Cosin makes his own anti-Calvinistic position abundantly clear; indeed, the sermon would make no sense within a Calvinist framework. The devil's 'cunning in the Scriptures' is, in effect, an Anglican warning of the extremes of both Puritanism and Roman Catholicism.

So the devil upon a day tempted Christ, so the devil every day tempts us, whose whole life is little else but a time of temptation from our cradle to our grave; and though many and various the temptations are which we suffer from him, yet most an end he works upon us with such as this was, to make us presume upon God's mercy, make us believe that we are the sons of God, and then that we may cast ourselves headlong into what sins we list, that we should be never a whit the worse for it, but as often as we fell down, He and His Angels would take us up again.

I know we will all confess that this should not be, that presumption is a high sin; yet if any such temptation comes, I know not how it comes about, but for all that, we will presume to die for it, we will be venturing to have our will, come of it what will come: and the mischief is, that we have no sense of the devil's device in it, or that there comes any devil to us for the matter.

In which regard, it may do some good to let you see both how the devil deceives you, and how you deceive yourselves; how his way is like a serpent's way over the stones, that over is come, indeed, but a man cannot tell how; that goes so slyly, and creeps so slow, that a man sees him before he knows what way he gat in:— and how your way is like the downfall of a rock, or the fearful way from the height of a pinnacle, where (for all the devil's fair words) there are no Angels to hold you up, but them that will take you by the feet, and dash your head against the stones.

And a better way to let you see both the subtlety (as I say) of his way, and the danger of your own, I cannot take, than in this place of Scripture, where they are both laid out to the open view of all, that when you have seen them and looked upon them, you may (as you use to do in other ways of danger) decline them, and come there no more. If any of you be so presumptuous that he will keep on his old way still, yet (that which for this time concerns me) I shall have quitted myself of an office; and as the man of God told the king (1 Kings 20.22), I shall let you understand where the trains are laid for you.

And it will be a good commodity, this, for them that will use it, to have notice beforehand of an adversary's forces, and of the manner of his fight; we shall ward off his blows the better, when they come; and though his darts be fiery, yet if we make preparation, they may be quenched, as St. Paul speaks (Eph. 6.16), and Satan shall not circumvent us.

For the text then; it is the temptation of the pinnacle, a temptation that the devil uses to bring men to presumption and wantonness withal.

It hath three general parts. The first is, the colouring and oiling of it over, to make it come on the better, by a pretext of being the son of God: 'If thou be the Son of God.'

The second is the temptation, and the very fiery dart itself: Make no more ado, but cast Thyself down headlong.

And the third is the cost which he bestows upon it, to make it fly and pierce the better, by an allegation of a choice piece of Scripture, (which is a cost that he bestowed upon neither of his other temptations,) 'for it is written,' (I have it here in the Psalms to show you,) 'He shall give His Angels charge over Thee, and with their hands they shall bear Thee up, lest at any time Thou dash Thy foot against a stone.'

These three; and these three to be the heads, from whence all other parts of the text, as they shall come in order, and all the parts of our ensuing discourse, are to flow. Of these then, that we may speak that which shall be honourable to Almighty God, and profitable to ourselves, I shall desire you, &c.

THE BIDDING OF THE COMMON PRAYERS
*Pater Noster*

I. 'If Thou be the Son of God.' For the better understanding of which words, and what the devil meant by them in this place, we must a little reflect upon the former temptation. There he used the same phrase before; and here he is up with it again; 'If Thou be the Son of God.' He was much troubled with it, it seems, and a great mote it was in his eye, that by a voice from heaven, as a little while since at His baptism (Matt. 3.17), Christ should be said and proclaimed to be the Son of God. That voice bred all this mischief; and no sooner was it sent from heaven, but up comes the devil from hell to send it back again; and because it came out of the clouds, ye shall see what ways and turnings the devil has to wrap it up in the clouds again, that it might be no more heard of here on earth.

(1.) He comes first like a desperate and a murmuring devil, with a few stones in his hand, and an 'if' of doubt and desperation in his mouth, and tells Christ that sure the voice from heaven was but a deceitful voice; that it could not be that He should be *Filius dilectus*, the well-beloved Son of God; for the children of God do not use to be so dealt withal as He was, to have nothing but a heap of stones set before Him, when they desire food to eat; for what man is there, who if his son ask him bread, would give Him a stone (Matt. 7.9)? and therefore that He was but some hunger-bitten child, who was cast out of the world, and no such beloved Son of God as the voice from heaven made Him believe He was. This was his first 'if;' 'If Thou be the Son of God;' to bring Him by a doubt to despair of it, and to resolve with Himself that the Son of God He was not. And this way would do no good.

Now seeing that would not prevail, he goes another way to work; and here he comes like a fine white devil, like a pure, smooth-tongued hypocrite, with no more doubting 'ifs,' whether He were the Son of God, or no; but an 'if' of flattery in his mouth; that surely the Son of God He was; 'If Thou be the Son of God;' an 'if' of concession and granting, that he would have Him make no question of it, but that He was the very Son of God indeed. So you see the difference betwixt these two 'ifs,' and the sense of it, as it is to be taken in this place.

That you see; and you may see withal the wonderful device of the devil, who can transform himself with one and the same saying in his mouth, to two several shapes. Before, He was not the Son of God, by these very words; and now He is the Son of God, by these very words again. He makes them serve for two contrary purposes; there, he would make it serve for desperation; and when that would not do, here he would make it serve for presumption; that one way or other, he might prevail. In the former temptation he came out like a malcontent and a murmurer, but here he comes forth like a flattering parasite. Well then, if Thou be the Son of God, as I doubt not but Thou art, as now I grant indeed, I was in some doubt before, but now I confess Thou art, now I am of the Voice's mind, which did pronounce Thee to be so at Thy Baptism,—You are His well-beloved Son, and He will be well pleased with whatsoever You please to do. So now He shall have too much of it, as before He had too little; and when the light will not out by taking away the oil, He shall have too much of it, He shall swim in the oil of ostentation, to see an that would put it out.

A case that happens to us all. When a man will not be presumptuous, then he is a fit subject to be brought unto despair; and when he will not be distrustful, then make him to presume. If he will not superstitiously dote upon the Church, then bring him to that which our people are most an end brought unto, make him not care for it at all; or if not that, send him over sea and make him dote again. There might be many more instances; still he comes in extremes and contraries, that if he be refused and known to be a devil in the one, ye may at least accept him, and think him to be an Angel in the other; for who would think it, that he were the man that should tempt anybody to presumption, that had before laboured for distrust? or that he would make the flame fly out of the chimney, and set the whole house a-fire, that had so lately set his foot on it, and done his endeavour to put it quite out? Marry, he that is acquainted with the devil's devices will think it, and know it too; for though it be not the same temptation, yet it is the same devil in both places; and the sudden alteration from one contrary to another, is but to colour the device over, and make us believe they cannot both be ill.

But seeing that by both the devil seeks our destruction, we are to take a like heed of both; though his two 'ifs' be contrary to themselves, yet are they both also contrary to the Word of God, which will neither have us to distrust Him, nor presume upon Him.

(2.) Secondly, 'If Thou be the Son of God,' may be taken as an outfacing argument; as when we would importune a man to do any thing, we use to press and urge him with that which he must not for shame deny; if you be such and such a man, if there be any spark of a good spirit in you, if there be any honesty in you, you will not refuse to do it. So the devil comes as if he must have no denial at all, unless Christ would confess Himself to be none of God's Son, and then the devil had had his end; just as the Jews by his counsel, I make no question, dealt with Pilate, 'If thou let Him go, thou art no friend to Caesar' (Joh. 19. 12), and, 'if He had not been a malefactor, we would never have brought Him unto thee' (Joh. 18. 30). No, the devil he desires you to do nothing but what you must needs yield to yourselves, that it is very requisite to be done; if it were a matter unfitting, he would never ask it at your hands; and this is the strongest temptation of all; though it would not outface Christ, yet it will outface us. And therefore above all other, heed is to be taken of an outfacing temptation.

(3.) Now, thirdly, if Christ were the Son of God, as the devil confesses Him to be, what had he to do with Him? They cry out ere long, 'What have we to do with Thee, O Thou Son of the living God?' (Matt. 8. 29.) No, nothing to do with Him when He comes to torment him. Do but resist the devil and he will fly from you, he will not come near you. Marry, an ye be willing (as Christ made Himself here for our warning of the danger) to go along with him, then he has to do with you in a hundred different ways; be what sons of God ye will, that one way or other, he may make you, as himself is, the sons of darkness; and for the better bringing of his ends about, he will be still sure in all his talk to make an 'if' of it, and so wind in with an ill consequence at last; and by often bringing it into question, whether we be the sons of God, he may at last make it out of question, that we are not the sons of God; bring his *si sis* into a *ne sis* and make us like himself. And so much for the first part of the devil's device; a wonderful and a strange device, to persuade us that we are the sons of God, and by that very persuasion to make us the sons of the devil.

II. For you shall see what his induction is; 'If Thou be the Son of God cast Thyself down headlong;' and this is the second part, the very fiery dart of the devil's temptation.

And here we have three points to consider.

The first is, the ill consequence of the words, that if He were the Son of God, He should presently give a leap from the pinnacle, and work a miracle.

The second is, the presumption which he persuades Him to, to take no ordinary way to go down, but to make no more ado but cast Himself down, and put Himself upon providence.

The third is, that earnest suit which he makes for it; he would not thrust Him down, but of his own accord He Himself must cast Himself down.

(1.) For the first then, it was no good consequence we say, that if He were the Son of God, He should presently cast Himself down. 'Yes,' says the devil, 'by this, all the world shall see that You are the Son of God, if You can leap down and get no hurt.' So this was his drift, because Christ was the Son of God, to make Him brag of it, and carry it out with an ostentation, that the Son of God He was, and not like other men; a device that he has for us, when we are somewhat nearer to God than other men, persuade us not to be content with that, but to blaze it abroad the world and make a boasting and a show of it, as such do that love to be called the professors of the Gospel, and the dear children of God, dearer and whiter and purer sons, and so bolder sons, than any other men whatsoever. But to see now what a *non sequitur* this is, Christ was the Son of God,—well what of that?—therefore He must needs show Himself to be so, and work a miracle when there was no necessity of having any wrought. What a consequence was this here! At other times, indeed, miracles were done by Him, they were all to good ends; but here it could be for no other end but vainglory and ostentation; no other use could have been made of it; and if Christ had yielded to it, or if any man else in the like case should yield to the devil's temptation, he should shew himself indeed, but he should show himself to be none of the sons of God. So this is no good logic, it is an argument of an ill consequence; let us not be carried away with it, if at any time it happens to be our case, as here it was Christ's.

(2.) Second, 'Cast Thyself down;' this is that he looked for, the very temptation itself, that being now aloft, He would make no more ado but presume upon His Father, and pitch His head upon the ground. So now we are come to know why he brought Him up, that it was for nothing else but to have Him down again the faster; it was the way that he took of old for himself, and ever since his device hath been how to get more after him; he would needs exalt himself above the stars, and down he fell lower than the earth; that if he could have got Christ down with him now, he knew by experience (whatsoever his pretence was) that all the Angels of heaven could not have Him up again. But this is it which we are here to observe; by such dealing as this was, we may see to what end all the devil's exaltings come. If he brings any man to the pinnacle, it is but to send him down headlong, faster than ever he came up; by little and little he lifts a man up, first to this preferment, and then to that, and then to another, and to a higher yet; and so when he has gotten him aloft, he can send him downwards again in an instant; not by degrees, as he came up, but like lightning, as he came down himself, and was undone by it for ever (Lu. 10. 18). Perhaps he may let us alone a while, and let us stand upon a pinnacle, to our thinking as safe as them that walk upon the ground; but as soon as a little wind of trouble and adversity comes, then off we go, and we shall be sure to pay for our high standing. This is the devil's course with them that are at league with him, and will follow his devices. Now God has taken another course with His, for He humbles a man first, and then He exalts him afterwards. 'He hath exalted the humble and meek,' saith the blessed Virgin (Lu. 1. 52); and 'he that humbleth himself shall be exalted,' saith our blessed Saviour (Lu. 14. 11). But the devil, he exalts a man first, and then humbles him after; lifts him up on high, *ut lapsu graviore ruat*, that he may cast him headlong down again. So he lifted up Adam and Eve to *eritis sicut dii*, with a conceit that they should be gods themselves, the very height of perfection (Gen. 3.5); and when all came to all, it was for nothing else but that he might bring them down again a great deal lower than they were before, even to be compared unto the beasts that perish.

The lesson is, that if we would not be cast down by him, we must take heed of being any way, or in any matter whatsoever, lifted up by him; for we must not all think to escape as Christ did; He had power to throw the devil down, and He went not up with him for any other purpose but to show us the danger and the hazard men are in, when they will follow the devil to a pinnacle, or their ambition, and other sins they love, to the height. This one may be sure on, that in all manner of sin and temptation there is a casting down; and the devil never allures us to commit a sin, but he makes us withal to throw ourselves down headlong; headlong from the spirit to the flesh, from the commandments of God to the vanities of the world, from high virtues to base vices, and so from being the sons of God and of light, to become the sons of hell and darkness; and he never allures us upwards the other way but to cast ourselves downwards. And this is the second.

(3.) But now, in the third point, there is a little more comfort yet, that the devil must become a suitor to Christ, that He would cast Himself down. A man may wonder, an the devil had such a mind to have Christ down, why he did not throw Him down himself? But alas! it was beyond his power, that; or if it had not, yet that would not have served his turn; for then Christ should not have been in the fault, and it was not the fall, but the fault that he looked after. It is our case, the devil winds us up, and he would gladly have us down again, but he would have us to cast ourselves down, or else the fall may do us some hurt, perhaps, but it can do him no good. It is our sin that he looks after, and he knows it too well, that there must go two persons to a sin, or else it will never be done. It is the devil and man that make up a sin; it is not the devil alone; and sure it is, he can never throw us down unless we consent on to it ourselves. And therefore, though it be one of St. Chrysostom's paradoxes, yet it is a marvellous good one and a Christianlike, that *nemo laeditur nisi a seipso*, that if we throw not ourselves away, the devil hath no power to do it; which is no more than St. Austin and all the ancient Fathers say, that *omne peccatum est voluntarium*, when we sin the fault is in our own wills, for we should not have consented, and then no sin would follow; and therefore it is a wicked and a most pernicious opinion that some of our new masters have brought up of late, (an opinion fit for devils and not for Christians,) that some men are forced and necessitated to sin, and throw themselves away, whether they will or no. I shall beseech you to take heed that they which teach you such things be not listened after, for they savour of the lake, and your souls will be destroyed with the scent. It is not true; God doth not, and the devil cannot, necessitate anybody to sin; and therefore we see in Genesis that he did not cram the forbidden fruit into their mouths, whether they would or no, but he persuades them to take it, and eat it themselves; for full well he knew their own eating, and their own wilfulness, and neither his subtlety, nor his violence, would get them the fall. And when it is said in the Gospel, that the Evil Spirit enters into a man, it is not said that he breaks open the door, or that he does so much as draw the latch, but that he finds it empty and open already, and all things swept and garnished, ready for his entertainment (Mat. 12.44). So that if we reach not out our hands to welcome him when he comes, and set not our doors open to let him in when he knocks, his temptations can never do us hurt; he can but entreat us, as here he did Christ, and if we fall, the fault is our own, we cast ourselves down headlong into misery and sin. That's for the devil's part.

Then for God's part. We may be sure that He, of all others, will not cast us down, if we will keep ourselves up; for He desires not either the death, or the overthrow of any man. And therefore, as it was His command of old in Deuteronomy (22.8), that when a material house were built, there should be battlements made upon the roof, for fear of falling down when any man went up, and spilling his blood; so in His spiritual buildings, He hath set Himself and His own assistance for our battlement, hath made a hedge about us, as the devil said concerning Job (1.10); that unless we will take our raise ourselves and leap over it, or break it down and throw ourselves headlong through it, we are safe enough. This Christ knew well enough, and therefore He trusted to this, that we might learn of Him, how ill a thing it is to trust to ourselves. And that's the third thing and the last there.

Now you shall see what course the devil takes to get this trust away from Him; and so we come to the third part of the text; the cost which he does bestow upon his temptation, to make it enter the better.

III. He comes with a Psalm-book in his hand and a piece of Scripture in his mouth to tell Him that since He would needs trust, he would set Him a-trusting, He should trust as much as He would; that is, He should trust too much. And as in the former temptation he brought Him to the waters of Meribah, to murmur and distrust; so here he brings Him to the waters of Massah, to be wanton and trust beyond His battlements (Num. 20.13,24; Ex.17.7). By the one he would persuade both Him and us, as St. Augustine saith, *Deum non affuturum ubi promisit*, that God hath no care of us according to His promise; by the other, he would persuade us, *Deum affuturum ubi non promisit*, that God would take any care of us, even against His promise: and so by the first he slandereth the God of heaven, as if He were some step-father, a hard man and a god of iron; and by this he slanders Him, as if He were a father to be commanded at a beck, and a god of clouts to be put to base and contemptible offices. First, that we are none of His children, and that if we do trust in Him, He will fail us at the end; and then that we are such beloved children, such dear darlings, that trust in Him, and presume upon Him as much as we will, throw ourselves down headlong into what sin we list, He will be our good father still, He will have mercy at last, and will never suffer us to come unto any hurt for it. This is the sum and the scope of his tempting speech. Now if the time would serve, we should consider it a little more narrowly; I will but begin it and end it at a more [convenient opportunity].

'For it is written.' With the self-same armour that Christ bare off his other dart, with alleging of Scripture, doth the devil sharpen this dart, and throws it in to maintain his argument that presumption is good divinity: since Christ brought Scripture to resist him, he would make his part good with Scripture too; and therefore here he brings it in. Now it is to be noted he doth not so (as I told you at first) in any of his other temptations, and therefore we are to look for some great matter from him here in this. A great matter indeed, and a great deal to be said of it, so much that it will require one whole sermon for itself; and therefore I dare but name it now, and tell you in brief that the reason why the devil hath bestowed such cost upon this temptation, more than upon the rest, is, because he knows a presumptuous sin is a costly sin indeed to us, and would be gainful to him above any else. Therefore it is that, before all others, David desires God to keep him from presumptuous sins (Ps.29.13); for if it comes to this once, the devil has his end, and we have ours an end, that he had, by the very same sin; which is a fearful downfall from heaven and from the mercies of God withal. The sin of presumption, as divines say, being one, or very near one, of the sins against the Holy Ghost, which shall not easily be forgiven. For a conclusion then, since we see thus much already, that above all other sins which the devil would have us commit, this is that he sets his greatest care upon, and, as we say, spends his wits, his learning, his cunning in the Scriptures, his wet and his dry upon it (Matt. 12.31); in that regard are we also to set our greatest care against his, to set watch and ward about our souls; and above all other things, to keep ourselves from presumptuous sins, that is, from a wilful casting ourselves into sin; and when we stand safe already with God's graces and favours, like battlements round about us, to break them all down, and throw ourselves headlong into mischief, where God knows what will become of us. Let us not deceive ourselves, and hope for Angels to come and take us up again, because the devil hath here alleged Scripture for it; for if you will but look into your Psalter anon (91.11,12), after you are gone, you shall find that he hath both abused us, and the place too, and hath cast out the principal matter that made against him, for that Psalm does not say that the Angels shall have an absolute charge either of Him or us, a charge without any limitation at all; that they must hold us up, come we down which way we will, headlong or any way over God's bounds which He hath set us; but that they should hold us up in all His ways. We must keep us here, and then they will look to us. So that out of God's way, the Angels have no charge over us.

The way then will be to keep us there in His ways, and not to run a wanton course in our own; and then we shall be sure of them; they shall stretch their wings over us, and pitch their tents round about us to defend us. They shall preserve us from the snare which we see not, as it is in that Psalm, From the terror of the night, and from the arrow that flieth by day, (and which at this time we have great need on,) from that *daemon meridianus*, the plague that killeth in the darkness, and the sickness that destroyeth in the noon-day (Ps. 91.5,6). All these comforts, and more than these, even the comforts of heaven, shall be to them that so put their trust in God as that they fear Him withal, and walk in His ways, according to that of the Psalmist (147.11), Blessed are they that fear the Lord and put their trust in His mercy; fear Him first and keep His way, and then trust in Him that He will keep us.

To which fear and to which trust, and from all other fears and trusts but these, He bring us That hath purchased mercy for us, Christ Jesus, &c.